MW00609608

LEFT IN THE MIDWEST

LEFT IN THE MIDWEST

St. Louis Progressive Activism
in the 1960s and 1970s

Edited by Amanda L. Izzo and Benjamin Looker

UNIVERSITY OF MISSOURI PRESS

Columbia

Library of Congress Cataloging-in-Publication Data

Names: Izzo, Amanda L., 1977- editor. | Looker, Benjamin, 1978- editor.
Title: Left in the Midwest : St. Louis progressive activism in the 1960s
    and 1970s / edited by Amanda L. Izzo and Benjamin Looker.
Description: Columbia, Missouri : University of Missouri, [2022] | Includes
    bibliographical references and index.
Identifiers: LCCN 2022013708 (print) | LCCN 2022013709 (ebook) | ISBN
    9780826222688 (hardcover) | ISBN 9780826274809 (ebook)
Subjects: LCSH: Progressivism (United States politics)--History--20th
    century. | Social movements--Missouri--Saint Louis--History--20th
    century. | Civil rights--Missouri--Saint Louis--History--20th century. |
    Saint Louis (Mo.)--History. | Saint Louis (Mo.)--Social conditions.
Classification: LCC F474.S257 L44 2022 (print) | LCC F474.S257 (ebook) |
    DDC 977.8/65043--dc23/eng/20220623
LC record available at https://lccn.loc.gov/2022013708
LC ebook record available at https://lccn.loc.gov/2022013709

∞™ This paper meets the requirements of the
American National Standard for Permanence of Paper
for Printed Library Materials, Z39.48, 1984.

Typeface: Aktiv Grotesque and Minion Pro

Portions of Chapter 2 are reproduced from Luke Ritter, "Mothers against the Bomb: The Baby Tooth Survey and the Nuclear Test Ban Movement in St. Louis, 1954–1969," *Missouri Historical Review* 112, no. 2 (Jan. 2018): 107–38, by permission of the author and the State Historical Society of Missouri.

Material in Chapter 4 from Clarence Lang, "Black Power on the Ground: Continuity and Rupture in St. Louis," in *Neighborhood Rebels: Black Power at the Local Level*, edited by Peniel E. Joseph and published 2010 by Palgrave Macmillan, is reproduced with permission of SNCSC.

Chapter 7 is reproduced, with minor updates and revisions, from Chapter 5 of Thomas M. Spencer, *The St. Louis Veiled Prophet Celebration: Power on Parade, 1877–1995* (Columbia: University of Missouri Press, 2000), by permission of the author and the University of Missouri Press.

Chapter 8 is reproduced, with minor updates and expansions, from Rodney C. Wilson, "'The Seed Time of Gay Rights': Rev Carol Cureton, the Metropolitan Community Church, and Gay St. Louis, 1969–1980," *Gateway Heritage* 15, no. 2 (Fall 1994): 34–47, by permission of the author and the Missouri Historical Society.

Chapter 11 is adapted from *Environmental Activism and the Urban Crisis: Baltimore, St. Louis, Chicago*, by Robert R. Gioielli, pages 38 to 67. Used by permission of Temple University Press. ©2014 by Temple University. All Rights Reserved.

Image captions are by the respective chapter authors, except for captions for the following figures, which are by the volume co-editors: 1.1 to 1.3, 3.1 to 3.3, 3.7, 4.1 to 4.9, 5.1, 5.2, 5.4, 5.6, 6.1, 7.1 to 7.3, 8.2, 8.5, 8.7, 10.1 to 10.6, 11.1, 11.3, 13.1, 13.6, 13.9, 14.1 to 14.4.

Cover images (clockwise from top left):
A pro–Equal Rights Amendment rally inside Christ Church Cathedral, February 26, 1977. From the National Organization for Women, Metro St. Louis Chapter Records, State Historical Society of Missouri.

Protest at Jefferson Bank and Trust in fall 1963. From the Charles and Marian O'Fallon Oldham Papers, State Historical Society of Missouri.

St. Louis's first annual pride march, April 20, 1980. Photo by Wilbur Wegener, from the Challenge Metro Collection, Missouri Historical Society Library and Research Center, St. Louis.

Washington University students and others in St. Louis participate in the October 1969 Moratorium to End the War in Vietnam. Courtesy of Washington University Photographic Services Collection, Julian Edison Department of Special Collections, Washington University Libraries.

Contents

Contents

Contents

Acknowledgments

THE VOLUME THAT FOLLOWS REPRESENTS the combined efforts of more than two dozen individuals, from research assistants to our seventeen chapter authors to University of Missouri Press staff. Our first expression of gratitude goes to the chapter contributors, almost all of whom agreed to participate in late 2019 and early 2020, just before the world and their work lives were upended by the COVID-19 pandemic. Despite lengthy archive closures, immense complications to their teaching work, and myriad other personal and professional pandemic-related obstacles, the contributors included here persevered with their components of the project, and we can't adequately express our admiration of them and appreciation for their participation amid such challenging circumstances.

As editors, we were fortunate to have the support and expertise of a number of outstanding archivists and librarians, especially in our efforts to unearth and license a robust slate of illustrations for the chapters. For their help facilitating the inclusion of images that we added to those separately provided by individual chapter authors, we are grateful to the following professionals: Miranda Rectenwald and Sonya Rooney at the Department of Special Collections of Washington University in St. Louis; Charles E. Brown at the St. Louis Mercantile Library; Zachary Palitzsch at the St. Louis Research Center of the State Historical Society of Missouri; Caitlin Stamm and Katie Mascari at the Saint Louis University Archives; Amanda Claunch at the Missouri Historical Society Library and Research Center in St. Louis; and Loni A. Shibuyama at ONE Archives at the USC Libraries in Los Angeles.

Meanwhile, for much-appreciated reference assistance, we are in debt to library faculty Jamie Emery and Rebecca Hyde of the Saint Louis University

Libraries. And our colleague Matthew J. Mancini, professor emeritus of American Studies at Saint Louis University, provided helpful suggestions across the project's journey, especially related to the introduction.

As we sought to illustrate various chapters, we greatly appreciated the generosity of several local organizers, active in the 1960s and 1970s, who personally lent us visual artifacts or allowed us to reprint images they had created. These include Kayla Vaughan, Portia Hunt, and Barb Goedde. Many other such activists, not named here but referenced in individual chapters, provided visual items or interviews directly to the volume's respective contributors, and their selfless contributions of time, memories, and materials have concretely helped to enhance our understanding of this era's activist histories and their significance.

Undertaking a publication of this complexity and length requires substantial financial resources, for costs ranging from image rights to text licensing to subvention and indexing to map creation and beyond. Such costs were generously offset by three sources at Saint Louis University (SLU): the Scholarship Opportunity Fund, the College of Arts and Sciences, and the Beaumont Scholarship Research Fund. The following individuals at SLU helped us acquire and/or manage these internal grants: research strategist David Borgmeyer and post-award specialist Ann Scales of the Office of the Vice President for Research; interim dean Donna LaVoie and business manager Delia King of the College of Arts and Sciences; and administrative assistants Terri Foster of the Department of American Studies and Jennifer Semsar of the Department of Women's and Gender Studies. Without their assistance with finances, this project would not have appeared in anything approaching its present form. That said, the volume's content has in no respect been shaped, restricted, or guided by any grant funders.

Three graduate research assistants from SLU's Department of American Studies provided integral assistance. In the early phases, master's student Taylor Schleisman and doctoral student Darby Ratliff helped convert existing published material to editable text files, and Darby also spent time at St. Louis–area archives checking and expanding various author citations. Most extensively, doctoral student Zackary Davis spent nearly the entire 2021–2022 academic year digging up image options for many of the chapters. Due to Zackary's expert and diligent work and input, this volume is far more visually compelling than it otherwise would have been.

We count ourselves lucky to have benefited from the prowess, acumen, and professionalism of numerous staff members at the University of

Missouri Press. First and foremost, Mary Conley, our acquisitions editor, was a constant source of helpful guidance and encouragement across the three years that this project occupied between proposal submission and completion. Deanna M. Davis insightfully and energetically led the press's marketing team in packaging and publicizing the work. Drew Griffith helpfully smoothed the path through the production process.

It was our good fortune to have Susan Curtis, professor emerita of history and American Studies at Purdue University, as the project's copyeditor. Susan's sensitivity to the goals of the respective authors, combined with her keen eye for detail and consistency, made this a far better final product. Two anonymous peer reviewers provided useful comments and suggestions, and we especially appreciate their careful engagement with a volume of this length. The indexer, June Sawyers, aided substantially in making this a user-friendly book for readers and other researchers.

We finally wish to thank the various colleagues, friends, family, and St. Louis community members who urged us to persevere, even when it occasionally seemed that the project might fall apart, and who impressed upon us the value, especially in our present moment, of fostering and assembling the kinds of historical narratives that this volume's contributors so powerfully bring to life.

LEFT IN THE MIDWEST

Editors' Introduction

Building Progressive Social Movements in St. Louis: Contexts, Crises, and Coalitions

Amanda L. Izzo and Benjamin Looker

IN 1972, NEAL R. PEIRCE, a nationally syndicated *Washington Post* columnist, made a several-day swing through St. Louis while doing research for a breezy trade book on the politics and power struggles of the states of the midcontinental United States. His assessment of the city's cultural energies and inhabitants' forms of political engagement was emphatically negative: this was "not exactly a swinging town," Peirce archly noted, but rather one mired in a "slough of decay and despair." Most striking to Peirce was the "complacency" of residents and leaders. The business community had "let its interest in the city wane." Meanwhile, white St. Louisans clustered in "aging blue-collar neighborhoods where the young people move out and the old folks stay on to vote against bond issues," and the city's growing African American population, Peirce said, didn't manage to vote at even passable rates "apparently because of apathy among the new black residents." All in all, a reader could conclude, a torpid political life and passive detachment from the major social issues of the day were conspicuous features of the city's social landscape.[1]

Peirce's pronouncements matched those of numerous national and local commentators. In 1970, analyzing corporate dominance over St. Louis municipal policymaking, sociologist Richard Edgar noted dismissively that, "So far there has been relatively feeble resistance" from grassroots organizations, due largely to their inability to perceive "who really governs the urban community."[2] Yet such views, however commonplace, also indicated a failure to survey the diverse forms of social activism then percolating through the city. In a host of arenas, progressive organizers were busy challenging institutional leaders, confronting entrenched elites, and seeking to undo ingrained modes of social organization. In fact, a much different view

3

might be suggested by the following series of "snapshots" of the same city in the mid-1960s through early 1970s:

- Candlelight vigils and songs of solidarity on the sidewalks around downtown's city jail, where civil rights demonstrators sit imprisoned after headline-grabbing demonstrations against racist hiring practices at a prominent local bank.[3]

- Crowds of student protestors surrounding Washington University's Air Force ROTC building night after night following revelations of Richard Nixon's "secret war" in Cambodia, until one evening the building itself erupts into flames.

- The constant bustle of gay-liberation organizing work filling the Central West End home of the city's Metropolitan Community Church, an insurgent 1970s religious institution providing a vibrant hub for nascent local queer activism.

- African American students at Saint Louis University, a Catholic school recently condemned in the region's liberal press for campus political apathy, refusing to end their occupation of a key administration building until their demands for Black Studies courses and anti-harassment measures are met.[4]

- Media-savvy organizers at the city's public housing complexes shipping off "welfare menus" and empty food cans to state and federal political leaders, theatrically dramatizing the plight of tenants engaged in the nation's first-ever rent strike in federally subsidized housing.[5]

- Listeners of KMOX radio tuning in to hear abortion-rights pioneer Judith Widdicombe publicize the grassroots Pregnancy Consultation Service, which helps area women evade Missouri's draconian antiabortion statutes, just two days after Phyllis Schlafly's appearance on the same program to inveigh against US military decline.[6]

Examples such as these could fill many pages. They suggest that a metropolis considered stubbornly resistant to social change or even fiercely reactionary by many contemporaries also served as home to highly visible manifestations of some of the defining liberal and left-wing social movements of the postwar decades. Moreover, it is the very contrast between these two different facets of St. Louis's cultural and political life—the city's youthful insurgencies and its long-entrenched power structures, visions of sweeping change and the tenacious embrace of oppressive social orthodoxies—that helped to define the specific tactics, internal cultures,

Figure Intro.1 Members and allies of Saint Louis University's chapter of the Association of Black Collegians occupy the College of Arts and Sciences dean's office in Ritter Hall on April 28, 1969. *Photo by Jack Fahland for the* St. Louis Globe-Democrat, *from the collections of the St. Louis Mercantile Library at the University of Missouri–St. Louis*

and objectives adopted by liberal and radical St. Louis organizing communities, along with the very real limitations they faced in enacting their agendas for change.

The goal of this volume is to bundle together for contemporary audiences a set of illuminating scholarly contributions—both previously published and freshly written—that together explore the wide range of activist movements that took root in the 1960s and 1970s in this city. The chapters presented here collectively demonstrate that, despite St. Louis's post–World War II reputation as a conservative and sleepy midwestern metropolis, progressive organizing proliferated in the city and its immediate region. Documenting wrenching forces of metropolitan change as well as grassroots resilience, contributors also demonstrate how *place* powerfully shaped the agendas, worldviews, and available opportunities for the period's disparate local groups dedicating themselves to visions of a more just future.

No existing publication puts into conversation examinations of such a broad collection of St. Louis organizing initiatives during these tumultuous two decades. To date, the best-remembered and most thoroughly studied of such efforts are racial-justice campaigns by Black freedom movement groups such as the city's trailblazing chapter of the Congress of Racial Equality (CORE), the Action Committee to Improve Opportunities for Negroes (ACTION), and young activists and artists associated with entities as diverse as the Black Liberators, the Black Artists' Group, the Black River Writers, and the Zulu 1200s. Less well known is that the city in this era also generated a plethora of grassroots social-movement initiatives—oftentimes in ways that shaped regional and national agendas—in areas including reproductive rights, lesbian and gay liberation, neighborhood empowerment, antiwar and antimilitarism efforts, women's liberation, student rights on campus, environmental justice, and anti-carceral politics. While generally imagining themselves on the left of the political spectrum, activists associated with these diverse local organizing thrusts pursued different goals and oftentimes found themselves in conflict. Nonetheless, taken together they constituted a distinctive, if overlooked, element of the social and cultural geography of St. Louis during the 1960s and the decade's aftermath.

With its title *Left in the Midwest*, this volume gestures toward the contrast embedded in the anecdotes that opened this introduction: St. Louis understood as a stifling social-movement backwater versus St. Louis as a bustling site for creative activist interventions. As initially conceived, the title was meant to evoke the locally specific experiences of organizing and imagining the world from progressive and radical locations on the political spectrum: *Left in the Midwest* as "on or of the left." But the phrase has another potential meaning: to be "left behind" in a particular place—forgotten, excluded, or abandoned. This latter connotation captures something about the experiences of marginalization, economic precarity, and disempowerment under which local social-movement participants of the 1960s and 1970s labored, as well as the neglect their efforts have faced in subsequent popular memory. And so, the title's two potential meanings, while seemingly in tension, in fact work together to encapsulate something about the day-to-day experiences of those mobilizing for social justice in this particular time and place: too often left behind, but also locating themselves on the left to create bold visions for local and national transformation.

In this volume, we take a broad and ecumenical view of what it meant to locate oneself on the left. The collection does not impose inclusion criteria based on ideological litmus tests or measures of authenticity. Instead, it suggests that progressive activism in the St. Louis region can be usefully understood as encompassing both appeals for institutional and political reform as well as revolutionary visions for more dramatic re-makings of US social and economic structures. Moreover, even the chapters narrating initiatives more properly understood as liberal rather than leftist offer evidence of significant involvement and influence from organizers and thinkers rooted in more radical places on the political spectrum—suggesting the practical importance to St. Louis activist communities of a coalitional politics that could link participants with markedly different commitments. With this inclusive approach to chapter selection, then, we aim not to erase meaningful distinctions in worldviews and political aspirations among the figures described herein, but rather to signal the enduring local relevance of what political historian Douglas Rossinow dubs the "left-liberal tradition" in the twentieth-century US.[7]

The moment right now is propitious for such a collection. On one hand, library bookshelves over the past fifteen years have become increasingly well populated by innovative scholarship on the era's civil rights and Black Power organizing thrusts in St. Louis, indicating a growing interest among readers in this city's distinctive encounters with the social insurgencies of the postwar decades. On the other hand, a new generation of historical researchers is currently delving into the great diversity of movement-building efforts—many of them virtually unmentioned in existing literature—that unfolded in the city during the 1960s and 1970s. Too often, these experiences are considered in isolation. By collecting samples or distillations of such research and seeking to establish dialogues among them, then, this volume is aimed at opening up new historical perspectives not only on St. Louis's recent past, but also more broadly on how US social movements are shaped by—and strive to adapt to—the different local environments in which they take root.

We will leave it to subsequent researchers to evaluate how these intersecting stories from a single city might reshape or modify broader histories of US social movements. With this introduction we intend instead to offer a few contextual notes that might help readers think about the chapters that follow not as a series of unconnected essays but rather as something approaching a cohesive whole. The first section presents a general sketch of the city during this era of rapid change, a time that saw numerous St. Louis communities left behind. As materials here suggest, the immense metropolitan economic, demographic, and policy shifts of the postwar decades, alongside the intensification of what many contemporary observers dubbed "the urban crisis," directly created the local contexts in which activists of the 1960s and 1970s lived and operated. Turning more fully to the experiences of movement participants—those carving out ideological and geographic spaces "on the left" in this midwestern metropolis—the second section aims to synthesize some of the insights that emerge across multiple chapters by describing several distinctive features of the activist landscape in St. Louis in the 1960s and 1970s. The third section explains the volume's organization, highlights gaps in coverage, and suggests areas for future research on St. Louis social movements of this era that may prove particularly fruitful.

Crisis as Context

Perhaps it was a foregone conclusion in 1972 that Peirce would identify the city that had become synonymous with "the urban crisis" as a "slough of decay and despair." In the decades after World War II, the St. Louis region experienced massive rearrangements of populations, economic dislocations, shifting (though not dissipating) lines of residential racial segregation, and efforts by municipal leaders to remake vast segments of the city through land clearance, redevelopment, and urban renewal. The glistening Gateway Arch, rising segment by segment over the Mississippi River between 1963 and 1965, may have symbolized to national observers an optimistic civic mood. Yet numerous indicators signaled ominous prospects for future urban health. In contrast to an emergent architectural landscape that projected modernist excitement, the activist landscape documented in the chapters that follow took shape in an atmosphere of emergency and besiegement.

The most conspicuous measure of the city's postwar slide was the dramatic population loss that began at midcentury and continues to this day. While St. Louis could credibly position itself as a leading urban center around the time of the 1904 World's Fair, when it trailed only New York, Chicago, and Philadelphia in population, the dynamics of decline were already in evidence as it reached its peak population of around 857,000 in the 1950 census. The city's share of the metropolitan population had dropped precipitously in the face of the growth in St. Louis County, decisively severed from the city by the "home-rule" charter adopted in 1876. The population of the metropolitan area as a whole continued to lose ground in relation to its US counterparts. In 1960, the US census counted St. Louis among the country's ten largest cities for the last time.[8]

The modest growth seen during World War II was quickly offset by accelerating waves of suburbanization and flight that left greater sections of the city vacant. The fixed boundaries established in 1876 and the peculiarities of Missouri laws of community incorporation formed an insurmountable barrier for tapping into the region's broader resources to address the resultant problems. Between 1970 and 1980, the city shed over a quarter of its inhabitants, earning it the distinction of being the decade's biggest population loser among US cities and leaving it around 453,000 residents in a metropolitan area of 2.35 million.[9] At the end of the century, after "fifty years of unrelenting population loss," urban planning scholar Robert Beauregard included St. Louis among a handful of US cities that could be categorized as "'hard core' in the world of urban decline."[10]

These losses accompanied economic shifts that, by the 1980s, had to be likewise understood as cataclysmic. In short, capital moved. The nineteenth-century moorings of the city's infrastructure and production sectors positioned it on the "leading edge" of Rust Belt decline.[11] The manufacturing, processing, and wholesaling base that had made St. Louis a regional economic powerhouse, as well as the heavy industry that gave it a wartime boost, were each doomed in their own ways as urban enterprises in a union-dense locale. From clothing to chemicals, coffee to cars, employers chased cheaper land, facilities, and labor as they moved their enterprises to the suburbs, the Sun Belt, foreign countries, and free trade zones.

Meanwhile, the interstate highways that spirited commuters and commerce away from the historic urban core drained the Gateway City's economic lifeforce as a river and railroad transportation hub. Attempts to offset these losses by building a tourist and convention trade were inadequate when not laughable, perhaps best embodied by the sinking of a replica of Christopher Columbus's *Santa Maria* in a storm just months after its arrival as a waterfront attraction at the behest of Mayor Alfonso Cervantes.[12] While the region managed to hold on to some of its central players in the corporate realm, it often did so with Faustian tax-abatement policies and similar incentives that depressed tax revenue and undercut local public investment.

St. Louis's political establishment was ill-equipped to put together a program for addressing problems of such magnitude. "Ward-based factionalism" and the fragmentation of power across municipal offices, political scientist Lana Stein asserts, continued to characterize the city's government long after other cities centralized and modernized their administrative structures.[13] Even as some realignments resulted from Black St. Louisans' successful battles to gain representation in local elected office—reflected in particular by the ascent of William Clay Sr. from ward alderman and Democratic Party committeeman to a dynastic tenure in the US House of Representatives—local politicians' toolkit for progress did not stray far from visions of public-private partnerships using clearance and large-scale new construction projects to summon jobs and people. While eminent-domain powers and the harnessing of federal urban-renewal funding enabled them to bring these visions to life, the outcomes invariably proved disappointing when it came to revitalization, with the costs staggering when accounting for the human toll.

Woven throughout the experience and perception of decline wrought by abandonment, overstretched and underfunded services, and distrust in leadership was the recognition that the urban crisis was a crisis of race relations and racial inequity, a point of acute instability that put the operations of the US racial caste system into high relief. St. Louis's racial demographics, Colin Gordon notes, were "starker and simpler" than those of its peers, with self-identifications other than white or Black remaining a "statistical blip" in population counts throughout the twentieth century. As the African American proportion of the city's population rose due to colossal white flight and the tail end of the Second Great Migration, contests over the city's future became deeply enmeshed with the trajectory of the local Black freedom struggle.[14]

Many observers have pointed to St. Louis's geographic and cultural underpinnings as a border city to explain its distinctive politics of race relations, echoing local civil rights luminary Margaret Bush Wilson's oft-quoted epigram that it is "a northern city with southern exposure." Given the multiplicity of borderlands produced by this confluence of places and people, overly general gestures toward North and South might obscure the complexities of the structural shifts coming to bear on the city in the mid-twentieth century, as well as erase ethnic community life beyond Black and white European.[15] However, as Clarence Lang underscores in his chapter here, this perspective does indeed capture something about the idiosyncratic mix of cultural factors that came into play as the crisis of US cities intersected with the intensification of the civil rights and Black Power thrusts.

These factors included the inexorable but uneven reach of Jim Crow in public life; an ethnically and racially heterogeneous working class, significant pockets of which were reached by labor and grassroots political organizations; a white elite determined to highlight its own interracial co-operation with the Black bourgeoisie; and African American middle- and working-class communities that crafted extensive networks of community institutions in response to the segregated terms of civil society. A *Wall Street Journal* correspondent's 1969 adoption of this border-city frame had a certain acuity, asserting that being located "squarely between the South and Midwest" meant "the worst of both worlds—Northern urban problems and old-line Southern racial attitudes"—for the city's African American populace.[16]

Certainly, Black St. Louis experienced the worst of both worlds when it came to the city's headlong leap into postwar renewal schemes that deepened racial disparities and converted significant portions of the built environment into wastelands. The city was perfectly positioned at midcentury to pounce on federal redevelopment policy, with planning technocrats ascendant in a network of institutions that were empowered to wipe away the presumed liabilities of the city's past. With the avowed mission of rectifying "substandard housing" and "obsolete districts," the city initially constructed public housing in tandem with mass clearance of districts characterized by municipal experts as incurable slums. When compelled to desegregate public housing under the landmark 1955 *Davis et al. v. The Saint Louis Public Housing Authority* federal court decision, its leaders invoked the language of liberal interracialism in self-congratulatory fashion. Nevertheless, it quickly became clear to working-class inhabitants of color that renewal functioned, in the words of local activist Ivory Perry, as "Negro removal with white approval."[17]

The late-1950s demolition of Mill Creek Valley, an African American neighborhood of some 20,000 residents, was one of the nation's largest such ventures of the postwar decades. The resulting barren acreage would become something of a "nonument" to the ongoing cycles of dispossession and forced migration of Black residents in spaces deemed blighted by civic powerbrokers. Less visible but also significant was the uprooting of city's Chinese community and the unhoused poor of its riverfront Hoovervilles in the downtown stadium and civic center projects.[18] Though the failures and miscalculations of these schemes were much in evidence soon after their execution, policymakers held close to the logic of bulldozer-driven renewal, even if the demolition of Pruitt-Igoe's thirty-three public housing towers from 1972 to 1976, dubbed "public housing's Vietnam" by one national pundit, marked the end of any politically viable ambition to use these mechanisms to secure social-democratic ends.[19]

Figure Intro.2 The staggering scale of the late-1950s Mill Creek Valley clearance project is apparent in this May 1965 aerial view, looking westward with Union Station visible in the bottom right. *Photo by W. F. Jud, from the Alfonso J. Cervantes Mayoral Records, Department of Special Collections, Washington University in St. Louis*

Something of the worst of both worlds could be seen too in the shifting skirmish lines of racial de- and re-segregation, which followed a more tangled path than present-day media renderings of a straightforward "Delmar Divide" of North Side and South Side, Black and white, might reveal. The fight for open housing produced such landmark federal court victories as *Shelley v. Kraemer* (1948), *Jones v. Alfred H. Mayer Company* (1968), and *United States v. City of Black Jack, Missouri* (1974)—all cases originating in the St. Louis region. Yet the metro area's racial geography remained stubbornly separate and unequal, with each of these cases offering documentation of the immense social and legal barriers facing prospective residents of color throughout majority-white areas of the city and its suburban periphery. In 1970, the residential segregation index in St. Louis was the highest among eighteen major northern cities.[20] A product of white-supremacist government planning and policymaking, this phenomenon also reflected neighborhood-level attitudes among the many whites who chose either to fight racial integration or to flee to suburban refuges. Characterizing this sentiment, one area housing expert told the *New York Times* in 1966, "There

12

isn't a white neighborhood anywhere in St. Louis that you could have a colored family move in without it falling apart at the seams."[21]

Given these conditions, the Black freedom struggle provided the most sustained arena of organizing efforts for progressive change in the 1960s and 1970s. As Heidi Ardizzone's chapter reminds us, the city had a deeply rooted history of effective civil rights agitation, a history obscured by factors that range from white-owned newspapers' embargo of reportage on early postwar boycott efforts to a subsequent politics of memory that has enshrined the post-1954 struggle in the Deep South as the template for understanding the movement writ large. Those roots nourished a network of St. Louis labor and social welfare organizations invested in racial equity and community betterment. Bringing together long-standing institutions like the Urban League and the National Association for the Advancement of Colored People with shorter-lived ventures like the Tandy Action Council of the Teamsters Union, this network fostered a range of liberal community organizing efforts. In turn, it became a springboard for more radical forms of action and institution building in the 1960s and 1970s, evident in the career arcs of such local activist innovators as Ivory Perry and Percy Green, some of whose efforts are narrated in the pages that follow.

Though the local Black freedom struggle stood as a bellwether for a range of liberal and leftist activism in the region, the dramatic transformations being wrought upon the city and its region set the terms and served as the inescapable milieu for almost every local social movement of the period. Often, scholarship on this era interprets social movements in a primarily national context, describing them in reference to landmarks such as the March on Washington, *The Feminine Mystique*, Stonewall, Earth Day, the Moratorium to End the War in Vietnam, the National Black Political Convention, and so on. One merit of the chapters that follow, by contrast, is their insistence on the importance of locality, neighborhood, community institutions, and rooted social networks. As numerous contributors show, the protean nature of urban and suburban St. Louis in this era generated unique constraints, opportunities, and contexts for activists to navigate as they pursued their objectives.

St. Louis Activist Landscapes

As these structural, demographic, and economic changes unfolded, a distinctive activist landscape emerged, one that responded to the local conditions that surrounded it. By bundling together such a heterogeneous collection of writings on activism of this era, the present volume allows us to perceive in greater relief several features of this landscape that might not stand out so visibly if the chapters were encountered in isolation. Three facets come to the fore in multiple contributions that follow: the creation of new activist-oriented geographies as a crucial form of organizing work; the role of the metropolitan region's deeply embedded political and cultural conservatism in determining the tone and limits for progressive grassroots initiatives; and the importance of earlier legacies of activist work as foundations for campaigns of the 1960s and 1970s. Each merits a brief discussion.

As the chapters here make evident, a first element defining St. Louis's liberal and left-wing activism in this era is the importance participants attached to remaking segments of the city's social geography—and, particularly, to building a spatially grounded infrastructure for political dissent and alternatives to rigid forms of bourgeois normativity. The significance of locality, space, and cultural environments to progressive grassroots campaigns more generally has been insightfully described elsewhere by historian Finn Enke. Writing about 1970s feminist organizing in the urban Midwest, Enke emphasizes how ground-level participants in fact "*constituted* feminist activism by intervening in established public spaces and by creating new kinds of spaces"; conversely, they continue, "social geographies and built environments shaped activist communities as they emerged on the ground."[22]

Such observations apply equally well to St. Louis's range of social movements. On the one hand, these kinds of spatial interventions took on the greatest public resonance when highly visible existing sites, intended to symbolize an elite-friendly civic consensus, were temporarily transformed by activists into stage sets for contestation and struggle. As illustrations, one need only think of Percy Green and Richard Daly's iconic 1964 scaling of the unfinished Gateway Arch to indict racial discrimination in federal construction hiring, or the summer 1969 "Black Sunday" demonstrations held in the aisles of the Central West End's Cathedral Basilica as part of a nationwide campaign publicizing Christian churches' centuries-long complicity in slavery and racism.[23]

On the other hand, albeit less publicly, St. Louis by the late 1960s and early 1970s had witnessed the development of an intricate map of new social nodes and institutions, aimed in various ways at fostering oppositional forms of consciousness. This stretched far beyond the confines of formal organizational offices. As volume contributors demonstrate, it came to include an expanding set of cultural, residential, and commercial spaces in which progressive organizers, artists, and sympathetic broader circles could assemble, network, and share ideas.

For instance, St. Louis–area residents seeking out literature and events reflecting the impulses of the burgeoning Black Arts and Black Nationalist movements could visit various new Afrocentric bookstores such as the House of Umoja, the Black Smith Shop, and the House of Negro History on the city's North Side, or East St. Louis's House of Truth.[24] During the later 1960s, new community centers and experimental education initiatives, some partially funded by area universities or the federal War on Poverty, became meeting places for diverse groups of young activists concerned with racial and economic justice. In East St. Louis, these initiatives included IMPACT House and Southern Illinois University's Experiment in Higher Education; on the river's St. Louis side, examples included the Mid-City Community Congress, the Grace Hill Settlement House near the north riverfront, and the Black Culture Center, established by the city's short-lived Black Nationalist Party just north of Forest Park.[25] These and similar institutions initiated Black history classes or hosted speeches by local and nationally known Black liberation movement writers and intellectuals. Most enduringly, the Performing Arts Training Center, a major East St. Louis educational venture founded by legendary dancer and choreographer Katherine Dunham in 1967, became a bustling cultural entrepôt and offered regular performances by its student drum and dance troupes at activist fundraisers and park rallies on both sides of the Mississippi River.

Meanwhile, coffeehouses, performing venues, and other cultural spaces aligned with the lesbian and gay liberation movement began to dot the Central West End and the city's blue-collar Near South Side neighborhoods through the 1970s—supplementing the bar scenes that had long been a significant staple of the region's gay life. Progressive religious institutions such as the Central West End's Trinity Episcopal parish and Metropolitan Community Church congregation became hubs for events fostering LGBTQ community building and organizing.[26] At the same time, audiences with worldviews, artistic tastes, or commitments shaped by the New Left and campus-based counterculture could, by the end of the 1960s, find several vibrant outlets catering to their interests. Prominent in this regard were KDNA radio and Left Bank Books. Broadcasting from an old Gaslight Square house from 1969 to 1972, KDNA became a beacon of eclectic music and free-form talk aimed at left-of-center young listeners. Left Bank Books, founded by Washington University graduate students, opened its doors in the Delmar Loop area in 1969 before migrating to the Central West End eight years later. And shoppers at Left Bank's longest-lived Delmar location only had to walk a few steps eastward to arrive at the Peace Information Center, a storefront organizing hub founded in 1967. There, religious pacifists, antinuclear activists, SDS members, and other Vietnam War opponents developed resistance strategies, offered draft counseling, and circulated antiwar and anti-imperialist literature.[27]

Figure Intro.3 DJ at the KDNA studio, circa early 1970s. Advertising itself as "Radio Free Speech," the station promised to bring "unpolluted air" to its listeners. *From the Double Helix Corporation Records (S0199), State Historical Society of Missouri*

Figure Intro.4 The St. Louis Peace Information Center in 1968. The storefront here, at 6244 Delmar Boulevard, was the second of the center's three successive Delmar Loop locations. *From the St. Louis Peace Information Center Records (S0136), State Historical Society of Missouri*

Central to these distinct but intersecting networks, circa 1970, were several high-profile spaces that brought together political and cultural activists from divergent demographic or ideological backgrounds—making them outliers in such a rigidly segregated and socially segmented city. Two of the more notable examples were LaClede Town, a low-rise Midtown residential community just east of Saint Louis University, and the shorter-lived headquarters of the Black Artists' Group (BAG), established in a disused warehouse on Washington Boulevard near downtown's western edge.

Figure Intro.5 A view of LaClede Town during a late-1960s arts festival and concert series. The community's distinctive townhouse design is apparent in the background. *From the St. Louis City Planning Agencies Collection, Missouri Historical Society Library and Research Center*

LaClede Town, built on a 28-acre portion of the Mill Creek Valley "slum"-clearance project, achieved a national profile for successful racial integration—and a local reputation for bohemian free-spiritedness—soon after opening in 1964.[28] Residents included some of the city's best-known civil rights activists (including Percy Green and Ivory Perry), its most dynamic young performing artists (jazz musicians like Oliver Lake, Julius Hemphill, and Floyd LeFlore), and its most visible countercultural impresarios (including the complex's manager, Jerome Berger, and event organizer Jerry Faires). At LaClede Town's Circle Coffee House and the nearby Berea Presbyterian Church, avant-garde artists regularly mingled and tried out new techniques. Visitors could hear anything from Black Arts poetry to acid rock, or take in informal productions of politically oriented stage works such as *Viet Rock* and *Prayer Meeting.* By the late 1960s, area US congresswoman Leonor Sullivan had denounced the complex as a "hotbed of radicalism."[29] And less than half a mile to the northeast, the BAG headquarters building, in operation from 1969 to 1972, became home to a full calendar of experimental performances and informal meetings emphasizing Black cultural and political liberation. The same spirit infused stage offerings at BAG's other regular performance locale, the venerable but largely vacant Gateway Theatre in the declining Gaslight Square entertainment district. Yet simultaneously, as BAG co-founder Malinké Elliott recalled of typical audiences, the BAG and Gateway venues were two of the city's rare spaces "where you had Blacks and whites communing together . . . understanding where we each were coming from, and contributing to one another."[30]

A quickly sketched map such as this leaves out the city's plethora of similar yet more evanescent and informal spaces and institutions—including houses inhabited by small feminist collectives, campus-adjacent apartments that

Figure Intro.6 Exterior of the Black Artists' Group building at 2665 Washington Boulevard in 1969. BAG musicians James Jabbo Ware (left) and Julius Hemphill (center) are joined by visiting Chicago saxophonist Roscoe Mitchell. *Photo from James Jabbo Ware personal collection*

became social hubs for student protest leaders, and union halls periodically repurposed for radical political work. Several of these are compellingly described in chapters contained here, including those by Gretchen Arnold and Ilene Ordower, Clarence Lang, Mary Maxfield, and Rodney Wilson. In a more diffuse way, certain neighborhoods, too, acquired activist reputations of various flavors. For instance, as Susanne Cowan details in this volume, the Soulard neighborhood, several miles south of the downtown, became known in the early 1970s for its "hippie" enclave of do-it-yourself home renovators, envisioned by some as bearded warriors waging battle against demolition-obsessed municipal technocrats. The Jeff-Vander-Lou neighborhood in North St. Louis attracted national attention for confronting city powerbrokers through its activist experiments in community control and self-initiated service provision, approaches that drew from contemporaneous Black Nationalist principles.[31] Or the 1970s Central West End, with its grand early twentieth-century architecture, mounting vacancy rates, and physical deterioration, turned into a crossroads for LGBTQ communities and a home for offbeat storefront businesses projecting a countercultural ambience.

Given the locations namechecked above, it's worth speculating about the degree to which the calamitous postwar decline in real estate values, population, and building condition in many of these institutions' host neighborhoods paradoxically may have opened up opportunities for fresh activist geographies, specifically by making certain St. Louis locales affordable and accessible to dissident grassroots ventures that lacked financial capital. As the urban analyst Jane Jacobs, referring to affordability, put it in 1961, "Old ideas can sometimes use new buildings. New ideas must use old buildings."[32] This in turn raises the question of how the subsequent rise in property values in St. Louis's gentrifying central corridor and certain historic districts of the city's southeastern quadrant—oftentimes abetted by major tax subsidies for large private developers—may have limited activist geographies in the 1980s and beyond.

Gravitating to affordable neighborhoods, diverse groups of 1960s and 1970s left-leaning organizers inscribed overlapping oppositional geographies onto the St. Louis map. To proprietors, creators, and users, this small but tangible accumulation of activist-oriented spaces facilitated alternative approaches for envisioning the city's geography—alternative "mental maps" for moving through space, weighing political possibilities, and making sense of the region's social and spatial networks—that differed markedly from those purveyed by the typical tourist maps put out by the local convention-and-visitors bureau.[33]

Even as a fragile yet vital "spatial infrastructure" for movement building materialized and evolved over time, many participants in progressive grassroots initiatives understood themselves to be contending with a metropolitan region whose politics and culture remained exceptionally conservative. Resistance to change emanated from the corporate paternalism of self-interested area business and political elites and also from a growing collection of grassroots organizations inspired by the far Right. The local potency of conservative and reactionary forces—both as a reality and as a pervasive perception held by organizers of diverse stripes—constitutes a second major element defining the city's social-movement landscape of the era.

Leftist and liberal activists had no shortage of examples to point to. Perhaps most conspicuously, the region's rigidly policed residential racial boundaries gave liberal and radical organizers ample evidence of the fervent opposition to equity embraced by much of the white populace and leadership. In 1971, the US Commission on Civil Rights, pointing out the systemic racial discrimination in St. Louis's public- and private-sector housing and home-finance entities, predicted "little hope of reversing the trend toward increasing separation of the St. Louis metropolitan area into a poor, predominantly black central city and an affluent, predominantly white suburban ring."[34]

In the city itself, powerful corporate leaders maintained a tight grip over development priorities, allying with municipal officials to pour funds into downtown building projects while starving Black and working-class residential communities of resources—or, worse still, decimating such neighborhoods through a succession of top-down "renewal" initiatives. To many observers at the grassroots level, such leaders' sway over policymaking was symbolized by the existence of Civic Progress Inc., an organization of top local corporate executives which, as contributor Ezelle Sanford III contends here, "came to be associated with wealth and whiteness and antagonism to the concerns of Black St. Louisans."[35] The same social hierarchies were lavishly put on display in the annual public parades and televised balls of the elite, all-white Veiled Prophet organization, sparking the long-running protests chronicled in Thomas M. Spencer's chapter. Yet, in the face of all evidence to the contrary, city officials and business figures consistently downplayed the existence of interracial or class-based contestation. Instead, leaders projected a vision of St. Louis as a tranquil oasis of "cooperation, goodwill, and public voluntarism among Black and white professionals and elites," as scholar Clarence Lang has noted elsewhere.[36] Exemplifying this paternalism was Mayor Cervantes's 1968 directive, reported in the *St. Louis Argus*, that Black activists must now "adopt the new three R's—respect, restraint, and responsibility."[37]

At the same time, antiwar groups found it disturbing that the region's economy included a dense agglomeration of private-sector participants in the Vietnam War–era defense industry, as contributor Nina Gilden Seavey emphasizes. The influence of corporate leaders from military suppliers like McDonnell Douglas, the Olin Corporation, Mallinckrodt Chemical Works, and Monsanto extended well beyond the executive suite, with top figures playing guiding roles on the boards of local universities and major nonprofits. Meanwhile, in one indicator of ground-level sentiment toward US militarism, St. Louisans in June 1970 heard a local echo of New York City's infamous "hard-hat riot" of the previous month. Traversing one of the longest parade routes in St. Louis's history, a pro-war march of 45,000 mostly white participants, sponsored by nearly a hundred area union locals, progressed for four miles eastward along Lindell Boulevard, with some demonstrators violently attacking young antiwar protestors clustered on the sidelines.[38]

The 1960s nationally saw the genesis and rapid growth of the conservative movement known as the New Right, a cluster of constituencies and political forces that would eventually send Ronald Reagan to the White House. An entire book-length study could be written on the St. Louis area's importance to the New Right's burgeoning organizational infrastructure. Under the leadership of editor Patrick Buchanan and publisher Richard H. Amberg, the *St. Louis Globe-Democrat*, one of the city's two daily papers, articulated an agenda for this incipient movement while secretly aiding J. Edgar Hoover's FBI counterintelligence operations against the civil rights movement and New Left.[39] And starting in 1972, the anti-feminist organizations STOP ERA and the Eagle Forum—both headquartered at the Alton, Illinois, home of their founder, Phyllis Schlafly—became organizing juggernauts that would help to secure New Right electoral victories to come.

Schlafly's agenda was national in scope, and by the early 1970s she devoted little more than passing commentary to St. Louis–area politics. Yet the very propinquity of her political vehicles, paired with her ubiquitous media appearances, loomed large in the minds of many local grassroots feminists, as Arnold and Ordower explain in their chapter here. More broadly speaking, St. Louis's legal climate reflected the encompassing state's constrictive politics of gender and sexuality. Abortion was illegal for any reason in Missouri (as in most other US states) up until the US Supreme Court's 1973 *Roe v. Wade* decision; the state was one of fifteen that never ratified the proposed Equal Rights Amendment to the US Constitution; and statutes prohibiting "deviate sexual intercourse" between consenting same-sex partners remained in Missouri's criminal code until well after the *Lawrence v. Texas* Supreme Court decision of 2003.[40]

The radical Right also maintained a significant and visible presence in St. Louis, as historian Walter Johnson and others have documented. In the realm of institutions and publications, Gerald L. K. Smith and John A. Stormer ran their Christian nationalist and anticommunist operations from the region for parts of this period.[41] A White Citizens Council made headlines in the mid-1960s, nearly securing the use of downtown's Kiel Auditorium for Sheriff James G. Clark to "tell the other side of the Selma story" in the wake of atrocities committed against civil rights demonstrators there.[42] An active outpost of the American Nazi Party engaged in intermittent acts of terrorism against civil rights and antiwar institutions, including the Peace Information Center; it also staged a precursor to its infamous 1978 attempted march in Skokie, Illinois, with a truck procession down Cherokee Street under the protection of city police. Beyond these organizations, the region played host to a shadowy grassroots of hard-core far-right ideologues. At the Grapevine Tavern, a bar adjoining Benton Park owned by the family of James Earl Ray and a gathering spot for white supremacists, a bounty was reportedly offered for the life of Martin Luther King Jr.[43]

Given the climate described above, it should be no surprise that many of the left-leaning grassroots organizers and campaign participants whose words are quoted in this volume describe pervasive feelings of isolation and beleaguerment. Indeed, as they looked outward at their counterparts in other similarly sized cities, St. Louis activists toward the left of the political spectrum often shared a sense that they faced unique challenges: less extensive or persuadable constituencies for progressive political and cultural ventures, more obdurate and immovable opponents, an antagonistic exurban hinterland and state government, and a general day-to-day ambience of hostility to change.

This is perhaps one reason why several of the movement ventures described in the chapters that follow came into existence noticeably later than did parallel organizations in other US cities. For instance, St. Louis's first formally organized gay-rights group, the Mandrake Society (established in 1969), arrived nearly twenty years after the nation's first postwar "homophile" organization, the Mattachine Society, took flight in Los Angeles. The Metro St. Louis chapter of the National Organization for Women (NOW) didn't make its appearance until a half-decade after NOW's 1966 launch at the national level. Dozens of American universities had chapters of the left-wing campus group Students for a Democratic Society (SDS) before St. Louis's first chapter, initially tiny, emerged at Washington University in 1965. While St. Louis's ideologically diverse Black freedom activists consistently implemented assertive campaigns across the full period covered here, various other St. Louis manifestations of 1960s and 1970s social-movement cultures were smaller in participant numbers, more isolated, and sometimes more muted in tone and tactics than their counterparts in other major US metropolises.

Nonetheless, such feelings of besiegement could impel cross-group alliances or forms of rapprochement that may not otherwise have arisen. Terry Koch, an SDS leader at Washington University, later described this phenomenon to sociologist Rebecca Klatch: "What to me was wonderful about St. Louis was that if you were a poet, if you were a black jazz musician, if you believed in abortion rights . . . it was the same as being in the antiwar movement. You were all in it together because you're in St. Louis and you're surrounded by a bunch of rednecks."[44]

One might take issue with the class connotations of Koch's terminology for conservative opposition, and the comment overstates the degree to which local Black artists felt an unambiguous kinship with predominantly white leftist groups like SDS. Still, Koch is not alone among the era's activist veterans in emphasizing how the conservative tenor of the region sometimes, as a matter of necessity, fostered a sense of comradeship among progressives with highly divergent backgrounds and issue-oriented concerns. While an empirically grounded comparison would be hard to produce, this climate most probably was not as prevalent in cities with more extensive and highly elaborated taxonomies of activist communities. It may also be a reason why self-described liberals and radicals chose at least intermittently to make common cause on specific projects and campaigns, rather than allowing ideological differences always to put them at loggerheads.

A third feature worth noting about the city's activist milieu of this period is the degree to which local participants drew from local legacies of organizing and dissent inherited from previous moments and generations. In his groundbreaking biography of St. Louis activist Ivory Perry, scholar George Lipsitz points out how local 1960s and 1970s Black freedom organizers drew on "underground streams of resistance from the past," a collection of "sedimented community networks and associations" that survived and served to facilitate later activist interventions.[45] Several chapters included here ably testify to this phenomenon across multiple movements. These sorts of insights align with larger shifts in how 1960s American social movements are narrated by researchers. In US popular memory, a commonplace impression has long existed that the decade's signature activist movements emerged virtually from thin air, a wave of youthful discontent and insurgency unconnected to earlier histories of progressive social struggle. By contrast, research of recent years on 1960s movements nationwide has brought into view the continuities, enduring resources, and crossgenerational intellectual and organizational foundations that bolstered progressive change efforts of that era and its aftermath.[46]

Figure Intro.7 Feminist activists highlighted St. Louis's intertwined histories of labor organizing and women's movements as they participated in the successful campaign to defeat a right-to-work amendment to the Missouri state constitution in 1978. *Poster created by Barb Goedde; from Kayla Vaughan personal collection*

In civil rights scholarship, for example, the framework of the "Long Civil Rights Movement," a label coined in 2001 by historian Jacquelyn Dowd Hall, has markedly altered the traditional storyline.[47] Work following this perspective highlights the extensive, centuries-spanning push for Black liberation—and especially the labor-rooted racial justice activism of the interwar years—that preceded 1954's *Brown v. Board* decision and the 1955 Montgomery bus boycott. The latter events, once typically described as starting blocks for a postwar civil rights sprint, are now more often understood as milestones in a long-distance run that was well underway. Similarly, research on the modern environmental movement, which once identified the middle-class activism inspired by Rachel Carson's 1962 best-seller *Silent Spring* as a unique point of origin, has lately brought to the fore the preceding decades' worth of unsung organizing against what is now labeled environmental racism, often led by communities of Black women city-dwellers.[48]

Moreover, scholars of gay liberation have recently deemphasized the role of New York City's Stonewall Uprising of 1969 as a foundational moment, casting it as a culmination as well as a starting point, distinctive more for its role in sparking media coverage than as an originary event.[49] And much scholarship on US feminist movement building has called into question the traditional "wave" model of periodization.[50] The latter is a result, in part, of work by women's historians who have unearthed rich histories of women's mobilizations for gender equity unfolding *between* US feminism's so-called first wave, dominated by the long-running suffrage battle ending in 1920, and the second-wave upsurges of the 1960s.

Without a doubt, many younger activists of the 1960s understood there to be a yawning ideological and experiential gulf between themselves and their generational predecessors. Among numerous other factors, this reflects how postwar McCarthyism and conservative political repression, by constraining and stigmatizing public expressions of organized dissent during the late 1940s and 1950s, created what often appeared to be a hard break between New Deal–era activist generations and those of the 1960s. However, the connections between progressive organizing efforts of the former and latter periods were often as significant as the discontinuities.

Though often ignored in retrospective journalistic accounts, these cross-decade linkages were crucial in St. Louis, as emphasized by numerous chapters that follow. Heidi Ardizzone, for instance, discusses the overlooked influence of 1930s and 1940s Black Catholic integration advocates on the civil rights movement that took shape locally over the subsequent two decades. Or, in the late-1950s campaign against US nuclear-weapons testing by middle-class St. Louis women, Luke Ritter finds an important tributary for more avowedly radical feminist and environmentalist work of the late 1960s.

Reaching further back, contributor Ezelle Sanford III sees the city's inter-war tradition of community-based Black institution building under legal-ized segregation, which led to the creation of Homer G. Phillips Hospital, as key to the emergence of an expansive language of healthcare rights adopted by 1970s African American neighborhood organizers. In Ian Darnell's analysis, 1950s cultures of liberal religious interracialism amid widespread white flight helped lay the groundwork for neighborhood-based coalitions propelling the gay liberation drive of the early 1970s. And authors Gretchen Arnold and Ilene Ordower point to early postwar labor-movement work in largely female St. Louis union locals as a significant precursor to employ-ment nondiscrimination and anti-harassment agitation by Missouri wom-en's activists of the 1960s and 1970s. While their chapters address disparate activist initiatives, these and other contributors provide evidence of the local oppositional legacies that St. Louis organizers of the 1960s and 1970s had available to draw upon.

Volume Organization and Potential Future Directions

This collection assembles ten newly written chapters along with five piec-es previously published elsewhere, with the majority of the latter signifi-cantly revised for inclusion here. Until now, most of the five reprints have remained relatively inaccessible for general readers interested in St. Louis, and we hope their inclusion brings these pieces more fully into conversa-tions of the present moment.

The organization of the chapters, meanwhile, is undertaken in roughly chronological fashion, based on where each essay's historical "center of gravity" seems most firmly to sit. Thus, the earliest chapters give greatest weight to 1940s and 1950s pre-histories of movement-building activities that emerged more visibly at the start of the 1960s. Chapters in the middle portion address the late-1960s and early 1970s height of local antiwar agi-tation, the city's Black Power movement, and confrontational direct-action protest, as well as the coalescence and emergence into broader public visibility of gay liberation and disparate strands of feminist activism. In these chapters, covert containment and subversion efforts by state security agencies, most notably the FBI, also receive substantial attention. Chapters near the volume's end follow campaigns of the late 1970s into the start of the Reagan era, when St. Louis organizers had to contend with devastating federal and municipal austerity measures, invigorated white backlash against recent gains in integration and civil rights, and the extending reach nationally of anti-gay, anti-feminist, and anti-labor reaction. The final chapter, a dynamic collection of maps created by Monica Duwel and Elizabeth Eikmann, looks back over the entire volume and invites readers to explore spatial relationships among sites discussed throughout.

Some readers may initially feel disoriented by the decision to order chapters by chronology rather than though thematic groupings. We hope this is a productive disruption, one that allows readers to discover connections among contemporaneous St. Louis activist initiatives that are normally, and sometimes reductively, considered in isolation. Moreover, it seems critically important to avoid an artificial grouping of chapters by movement "type"— e.g., "the" feminist movement, "the" gay and lesbian rights movement, "the" civil rights movement—because this sort of framework risks reinforcing false conceptions that such activist projects were monolithic, fenced off from one another, or the products of entirely discrete demographic groups. Instead, many of this volume's contributors actively highlight dialogues (both conflictual and collaborative) across movements, while seeking to illuminate how activist mobilizations emerged from participants' experiences of multiple and intersecting forms of oppression.

For instance, Rob Gioielli stresses North St. Louis organizers' insistence that lead poisoning was simultaneously an environmental and a racial justice issue. Mary Maxfield points out how white South St. Louis lesbian activists' own experiences of violence motivated them to join alliances in support of Black organizers defending the existence of Homer G. Phillips Hospital. Keona K. Ervin identifies the visionary anti-carceral politics of St. Louis's chapter of the National Alliance Against Racist and Political Repression (NAARPR) as emerging from an activist network that spanned prisons, churches, union halls, Marxist study groups, and Black Nationalist community organizations. Clarence Lang's chapter shows how the compounding nature of race, gender, and class inequities provoked a "thunderous" welfare-rights movement among Black female public housing tenants, who "assertively voiced their right to social citizenship, autonomous households, and lives with dignity." This list could go on. The point, though, is that to slot any of these chapters exclusively under a single narrowly cast movement heading risks replicating the very forms of erasure and identity-based hierarchies that numerous organizers self-consciously struggled against. As scholars and activists have insisted elsewhere, forms of oppression—and therefore, necessarily, movements against them—intersect in different ways for different population groups, meaning that no inclusive liberation campaign can be fought out solely along a single axis of identity.

Despite the extensive ground covered by the chapters printed here, it would be a mistake to take this anthology as seeking to represent an all-encompassing overview of the disparate local groups pushing for progressive change during these decades. What is presented here simply constitutes a sampling of scholarship that currently exists or is now being done, rather than a compendium of all that should exist or needs to be done. And many readers will immediately identify significant local events, projects, issues, and populations that either are not explored between these covers or are mentioned only briefly. Examples that might pop to mind include St. Louis's groundbreaking 1969 rent strike in public housing, the vibrant Black student movement on area campuses, the range of coalitions throughout the region in opposition to the Vietnam War and military draft, cultural institution building by LGBTQ Black St. Louisans, and radical labor organizing emerging in tandem with the era's burgeoning public-sector union drives.[51] Meanwhile, readers interested in further exploration of Black working-class women's community-based organizing for economic empowerment in 1960s St. Louis—discussed here in illuminating fashion by Arnold and Ordower—will be well served by turning to Keona K. Ervin's important recent book, *Gateway to Equality*.[52]

Still, we hope that a volume of this nature—both wide-ranging and necessarily incomplete—will spur innovative future research on the complexity of St. Louis's activist pasts. In some cases, such projects might emerge because of tantalizing anecdotes or insights found between this volume's covers, as readers encounter stories that seem to crack open doors to new corridors of inquiry. In other cases, new paths may be inspired precisely by how this volume's table of contents makes more readily evident the areas not yet touched upon in existing scholarship.

Regardless, the materials collected here—both in terms of what the chapters do explore and in terms of what this anthology leaves unaddressed—seem to suggest at least three areas that may be particularly fruitful for future work. First is research that investigates more broadly the activist pasts of the entire metropolitan region. The chapters that follow, with a few notable exceptions, focus mostly on events and institutions located in various parts of the City of St. Louis. Yet organizers within this small slice of the metro area were oftentimes embedded in activist networks that extended well beyond city limits, and all of them fought against practices and institutions that weren't confined to a single municipality. Conversely, their counterparts in various parts of suburban St. Louis faced their own unique challenges, ones partly determined by the specific politics, culture, and demographics of their own locations within the region.

Hints of these stories already exist in research underway elsewhere. So, for instance, antiwar student groups at Meramec Community College—which was founded on rural land near suburban Kirkwood in 1964 and attracted many working-class matriculants—faced much different constraints than did their counterparts at wealthier four-year schools closer to the urban core.[53] Neighborhood activists in East St. Louis, organizing to fight the destruction of their communities under various freeway and urban renewal schemes, operated within a municipal political milieu distinct from that facing Black inhabitants to the Mississippi River's west.[54] Or, as liberal interracial groups such as the Freedom of Residence Committee agitated to open all-white suburbs of St. Louis County to Black residency, they faced different barriers and opted for different strategies than did integrationists in older neighborhoods of the city itself.[55] Numerous other examples could be named. Emergent scholarship like this highlights the fact that the region beyond the city proper has complex activist histories that are ripe for exploration. Such investigations may deliver an even richer sense of the networks in which the organizers mentioned in this volume were enmeshed.

A second area into which research on metropolitan activist histories could productively move relates to the multiplicity of racial, ethnic, and immigrant groups that inhabited St. Louis during these tumultuous decades. Nationally, the period considered by this volume saw the upwellings of the Chicano movement, Native activist initiatives such as the American Indian Movement, the Asian student movement and broader Asian American movement, and other 1960s and post-1960s antiracist coalitions that participated in "recentering and refiguring race" in the United States, as sociologists Michael Omi and Howard Winant have phrased it. Inspired in part by ongoing Black liberation struggles, such movements "irreversibly expanded the terrain of political conflict," Omi and Winant explain, and thereby "set the stage for a general reorganization of US politics."[56] Yet the

St. Louis political landscape, and retrospective accounts of its evolution, has traditionally been dominated by narratives centering on the Black/white dichotomy and the dialectic of oppression and resistance along that axis.

Across the entirety of the twentieth century, however, the St. Louis region has also been home to small but active and cohesive communities of Asian and Latinx (especially Mexican and Mexican American) inhabitants—something a tiny yet important body of recent scholarship addresses. For instance, Huping Ling, in her pathbreaking work on St. Louis's Chinese and Chinese American populations from the 1860s to present, identifies how this community fought to establish a political voice across successive generations, while insisting that its members be understood "not merely [as] passive victims of institutionalized exclusion" but also as "active agents" in shaping their own circumstances and the city around them.[57] And researchers such as Bryan Winston and Daniel Gonzales have recently explored the history of St. Louis's Mexican and Mexican American communities during the twentieth century's first half. As Winston finds, Mexican migrant communities in the cities and towns of Missouri and adjacent states "made culture and nationalism points of struggle to determine what their life would be like in the United States and what Mexico could look like if they ever returned."[58] The ways in which diverse constituents of these population groups—differentiated internally by class, gender, citizenship status, and other attributes—responded to and participated in St. Louis's experiences of the upheavals of the 1960s and 1970s is a direction worthy of future exploration.

A third potentially generative area for investigation involves the ways 1960s–1970s activists in St. Louis, like their counterparts in other cities, embraced the expressive realms of culture and the arts to make assertions about politics, social struggle, and community self-definition. In the realm of music alone, emerging genres such as free jazz, psychedelic rock, folk, and soul built imagined communities among their listeners and helped to "organize consciousness" within those audience groups.[59] And nationwide, participants in numerous of the era's progressive political ventures frequently put drama, poetry, dance, film, and other art forms to use as a way of critiquing existing institutional arrangements, re-envisioning social identities, or imagining alternative futures. In doing so, they created new constituencies and communities for their campaigns for social change.

This was certainly the case in St. Louis, where activist initiatives often unfolded in tandem with performance events, poetry readings, outdoor dramatic sketches, musical gatherings, arts festivals, and the like. Indeed, several chapters in this volume highlight the significance of such creative work. Lang, for instance, details the 1968 creation by young Black painters, working under an ACTION member trained in the visual arts, of the Wall of Respect mural at a street intersection northwest of downtown. While celebrating Black history through depictions of cultural and political luminaries, the mural also served as a summer rallying spot for performers and speakers.[60] And in Maxfield's chapter, several St. Louis lesbian-feminist organizers recall the catalytic effects of area concerts by artists from the 1970s women's music movement, both local and touring. Such events, Maxfield affirms, "effectively created a discursive space that had not previously existed."

With the St. Louis region as a focus, this relationship between the cultural and the more formally "political" has also recently been taken up elsewhere

Figure Intro.8 Young activists painting the early stages of the Wall of Respect mural at North Leffingwell and Franklin Avenues in July 1968. Figures depicted here are poet Amiri Baraka and abolitionist Frederick Douglass. *Photo by Bennie G. Rodgers, from the Rodgers Photograph Collection (S0629), State Historical Society of Missouri*

by scholars and documentary filmmakers, including George Lipsitz, Joanna Dee Das, Joyce Aschenbrenner, and Bryan Dematteis, each of whom has explored local artists and cultural institutions that allied their work to grassroots social movements of the 1960s and 1970s.[61] As all convey, the political work of the picket line, demonstration, march, or neighborhood organizing meeting can't be seen in isolation from the cultural work that often sustained activist communities while helping to bring into sharper focus a particular understanding of a given predicament or struggle. Chapters in this volume may provide helpful tools for those seeking to investigate this relationship in research yet to be done.

Whatever their topical differences, all these chapters tease out how particularities of the St. Louis region shaped activist projects and prospects. In doing so, they dovetail with an increasing curiosity among St. Louis general readers, journalists, contemporary activists, and public humanities practitioners about the metropolitan region's historical role as an environment for social-movement work and social justice battles.

For instance, energized in part by the 2014–2015 Ferguson uprisings, St. Louis communities outside academia have recently worked to unearth the city's position as a major midwestern center for 1960s and 1970s racial justice organizing while tracing the lineages that connect earlier phases to present-day iterations. This interest has emerged in tandem with a recent expansion of public history work on local social-movement cultures. A notable instance is the 2017–2018 exhibit *#1 in Civil Rights: The African American Freedom Struggle in St. Louis*, at the Missouri History Museum (MHM), which had its run extended, eventually to more than a year, due to popular demand. Other examples include ongoing initiatives like the St. Louis LGBT History Project. Founded in embryonic form in 2007, this tenacious community-driven effort aims to collect, preserve, and disseminate elements of the city's LGBTQ past, including activist stories and artifacts, that might otherwise be lost to time.

Yet the engrossment such projects have inspired among segments of the region's public represents something of a shift. As recently as 2002, the historian Kenneth Jolly felt the need to give the title "It Happened Here Too" to his first publication on St. Louis's late-1960s Black freedom struggle. The title's insistent assertion indicated the degree to which local activist histories had remained largely absent from local media output and public awareness over the preceding few years.[62] Similarly, MHM curator Gwen

Moore told the *St. Louis American* that, when she began devising the *#1 in Civil Rights* exhibit, she frequently heard erroneous claims that the city had no significant past of racial-justice organizing. Such traditions, Moore said, are "not how we tend to think about St. Louis."[63] In 2014, LGBT History Project founder Steven Brawley likewise pointed to the "largely unknown" status of local histories of lesbian, gay, and transgender community building and activism—"our very own special queer history"—as a reason for the urgency of his group's preservation and education efforts.[64]

Today, both activist communities and various grassroots public history initiatives are seeking to rectify such absences and to enrich St. Louisans' understandings of the region's histories of movement building for progressive social change. With their shared commitment to unearthing oppositional legacies of a particular generation and era, works by the authors in this volume can perhaps serve as a resource for that broader project of recovery. By revising our sense of the region's past, they can also expand our sense of the possibilities that the future may hold.

1. Generational Activism and Civil Rights Organizing in St. Louis

Heidi Ardizzone

ON AUGUST 9, 2014, LOCAL community outrage in Ferguson, Missouri, quickly evolved into protest in the long hours between the moment police officer Darren Wilson shot and killed local teenager Michael Brown and the time when Brown's body, first covered by a community member, was finally removed from the street where he lay. News of the event in this northern suburb of St. Louis spread quickly. Over the next weeks, clergy, students, scholars, reporters, and everyday people gathered daily to march, chant, yell, strategize, and organize to demand change. The police response quickly escalated and St. Louis became the center of the Black Lives Matter (BLM) movement, born in the aftermath of the Trayvon Martin shooting in Florida two years earlier. Even as police killings of unarmed Black people drew national attention elsewhere (Eric Garner in New York; Tamir Rice in Ohio), St. Louis and Ferguson remained a focus of national attention.

This national coverage routinely implied or directly expressed some surprise that the resurgence of the Black Lives Matter movement emerged from St. Louis, of all places. Why St. Louis, which had never had the kind of protest that demanded national attention? Even within St. Louis, the idea that a national movement might be ignited here seemed unlikely. In 1982, civil rights activist Ivory Perry agreed to work with historian George Lipsitz because "there were parts of the struggle that the general public knew nothing about." Perry realized that St. Louis's civil rights campaigns had been largely forgotten within a decade, and he wanted the younger generation to know this history.[1] Similarly, historian Clarence Lang noted that organizers he encountered in the mid-1990s related a common narrative that "the city was a cultural backwater and its black community politically timid." Lang's own realization that there were actually "deeply rooted traditions of black resistance" in the city led to his research on civil rights activism in St. Louis.[2] And while activists both old and young talked about the gulf between the civil rights generation and the BLM activists' strategies and goals, there is also a direct through-line that can be traced from Black St. Louisans' protests in the 1960s to some of the organizations that were front and center in the aftermath of Michael Brown's death.[3]

This chapter traces the trajectory of Black protest and organizing in St. Louis around civil rights issues in the mid-twentieth century, especially in the period of what scholars label the heroic Civil Rights Movement of the 1950s and 1960s. While recent scholars have roundly challenged traditional narratives of the neatly bracketed "1954–1968" chronology that defines the "heroic" era, these years still dominate our cultural memory of movement history. History textbooks continue to foreground the leadership of Dr. Martin Luther King Jr. and other clergy; the inspiration of Rosa Parks; the martyrdom of Medgar Evers; the Southern Christian Leadership Conference (SCLC); school desegregation battles; boycotts of buses, Woolworth's counters, and other segregated spaces; and challenges to voting restrictions. At the national level, this periodization erases the labor-based activism, sometimes radical and Communist-allied, of the 1920s and 1930s, as well as urban struggles against police repression, lynching, and racial violence. It also suppresses the extent of women-led organizing and the numerous grassroots efforts that predated and often set the stage for the iconic events of the 1960s.[4] But the 1954 Supreme Court *Brown v. Board of Education* decision, though itself a result of another civil rights campaign, certainly prompted a new chapter of activism both to enforce *Brown's* public school desegregation mandate and to expand its reach to challenge discrimination in other arenas such as voting, jobs, housing, public and private businesses and venues, and transportation.

Civil rights movements in St. Louis followed national patterns and shifts in some fundamental ways, yet they also hinged on some key moments and events that were particular to the city. Protests against hiring discrimination were ubiquitous in the US, but where else could such a movement feature two activists climbing halfway up a partially constructed metal arch that would soon become the region's iconic skyscraper landmark? Why would one of the earliest public "processions" highlighting Black participation in white-dominated institutions begin and end at Catholic churches in Midtown St. Louis? And while American business associations and political networks routinely excluded Black business owners and politicians, where else did it make sense to crash a debutante ball to point out such exclusions?[5]

But despite these remarkable moments, activism in St. Louis mostly looked much like activism elsewhere. Certainly, its history and shifting place in American regional and racial landscapes matter in the shape of racial structures and the resulting strategies and motives of activists trying to reshape their local terrain. Black St. Louisans engaged in interracial coalitions and demanded control of their resources, created parallel institutions to serve community needs even while campaigning for inclusion in white institutions, worked within the political structures that they always had some weight and stake in, and dreamed of radical change and rebellion. Writing a national story through just one city's story is hardly the goal here; instead, this chapter presents an overview of civil rights activism in St. Louis in the mid-twentieth century. The March on Washington Movement (MOW), the Congress of Racial Equality (CORE), and the post–World War II National Association for the Advancement of Colored People (NAACP) all had vibrant branches or local groups in St. Louis. And St. Louis activism led to several precedents of national significance, as well as contributing important individuals and ideas to national movements.

Through this overview of St. Louis's civil rights movement, I weave two arguments. First, I suggest that the St. Louis campaigns were as tied to and responsive to local and regional attributes as they were to tensions and shifts unfolding on the national stage. St. Louis is a specific place in African American history and experience, and its regional ambiguity and presumed insignificance shaped its impact. Second, my history illuminates the role of Black Catholics and their campaigns within the Catholic institutions in St. Louis as integral to the development of public civil rights campaigns. Saint Louis University (SLU), a Jesuit Catholic institution founded in 1818, is proud of its claim to be the first university in Missouri, and the first in any "former slave-holding state," voluntarily to desegregate, which it did in 1944. But this action is usually relegated to a paragraph or a footnote in civil rights histories. Here I argue both that SLU's integration was the result of an important yet overlooked civil rights campaign waged by Black activists, and that it was an inspiration and a model for other anti-segregation campaigns in the city.

Despite its significance, St. Louis's civil rights movement has been largely overlooked by national media and academics. In large part, this is because

St. Louis has been an understudied city in an understudied region. As such, the area simply wasn't on the national radar in the twentieth century. By the 1960s, St. Louis had long since lost the status it had held in previous generations as the fourth biggest city in the US. It dominated nineteenth-century steamboat ports for decades but then lost out to Chicago in its quest to be the midcontinent crossroads of twentieth-century travel and commerce.[6] Its postindustrial economic decline in the mid-twentieth century followed tragically familiar patterns of white flight and urban renewal at the cost of Black neighborhoods, making it "a poster child for the fall of the American city."[7] In the 1960s it won further infamy as the celebrated Pruitt-Igoe public housing complex, built in 1956, became part of a citywide rent strike and a center of Black Nationalist organizing just years before its demolition was begun in 1972.

This ragged reputation endured into the twenty-first century, as reflected in a 2012 BBC report on the "Delmar Divide" that dubbed St. Louis the "most segregated city" in America.[8] The city's stark demarcation between the poverty and structural blight of its northern neighborhoods and the relative wealth and whiteness of those areas just south of Delmar Boulevard extended to the North County suburb of Ferguson.

But as this volume and other recent scholarship attests, St. Louis matters, in both its past and present incarnations. Perhaps nowhere is this significance clearer than in the history of race, anti-Black structures, and Black American culture and survival. Missouri was brought into the United States in 1821 in the wake of a new federal law, the Missouri Compromise, that promised to keep congressional balance between states that had recently ended chattel slavery and those that still relied on it. The US Supreme Court's devastating 1857 decision in *Dred Scott v. Sandford*, which held that no person of African descent, whether slave or free, was a citizen or had the right to bring suit in federal court, began with Dred and Harriet Scott's suits winning their freedom in St. Louis courts. The Dyer Anti-Lynching Bill was named for the Missouri senator from St. Louis who introduced it in Congress in 1918 in response to white anti-Black violence the previous year in St. Louis and neighboring East St. Louis. St. Louis, then, was integral to the development of national policies on enslavement, Black citizenship, and basic human dignity and protections for African Americans. And it was it was integral, as well, in the twentieth-century civil rights movement, although rarely in ways that brought it to the foreground of national attention.

Black St. Louis and Activism before 1954

Understanding the patterns of St. Louis civil rights activism requires some background on St. Louis, on African Americans' experiences in the region, and on the origins of the discriminatory structures and practices that were the targets of activism in the 1950s and 1960s.

Pre–World War II activism in St. Louis was characterized by attention to labor issues and a focus on other Black working-class needs and concerns. It was often led by women, and it sometimes included alliances with radical leftists, even communists. Which is to say, it was defined by who was in the city and what their experiences and living conditions were. So, to understand that activism, we need to ask, who *were* Black St. Louisans and what were the racial patterns of the city leading up to the mid-twentieth century?

St. Louis was founded in the late eighteenth century as a French fur-trading outpost and named for a thirteenth-century French king. Africans and their descendants arrived in the region primarily as slaves and property. By the time the Louisiana Purchase brought the region into the US as a territory, about one-third of the city's population was enslaved. Their relative numbers diminished as the city grew, but St. Louis remained a major center of the domestic slave trade until the start of the Civil War. Before William Wells Brown escaped his own enslavement, his owner, who lived outside of the city, contracted him out to work on a Mississippi riverboat that carried goods back and forth between St. Louis and New Orleans. Brown's memoir recorded the human chattel often included on those journeys. After serving "the longest year I ever lived" in working for the slave trader, Brown confronted his owner ("a near relative of mine") who intended to sell him and offered to let him find a good master in St. Louis. Brown declared there were "no good masters" in St. Louis or the whole state, and made his first attempt to escape northward.[9]

As a slave-holding state that did not join the Confederacy, Missouri was not subject to federal emancipation until the war ended in 1865. According to Diane Mutti Burke, however, by that time most enslaved Missourians were "already effectively free."[10] In the aftermath of emancipation, many former slaves remained in the area, not an uncommon practice. In St. Louis, these freedmen and freedwomen and their descendants were largely Catholic, a legacy of the dominance of Catholicism among white owners and the strong presence of slave-owning Jesuits in the city and its environs. The Jesuit order had appointed one priest to minister to the Black Catholic population and celebrate the sacraments for them long before they built a dedicated "Negro parish" in 1860. By the early twentieth century, St. Louis had several Black parishes with attached schools overseen by Jesuits.

Like all major cities in the US, St. Louis had a population of free Blacks (often called free people of color) long before 1865. The economic and social gulf between those recently freed and families who were several generations out of enslavement was considerable, although there were many ties across that gap. One member of St. Louis's "colored aristocracy," Cyprian Clamorgan, documented and described many of his peers in 1895. Clamorgan described the "peculiar circumstances" of the highest "free colored people of St. Louis," whose connections to white family members and patrons may have provided early support, but who now "by means of wealth, education, or natural ability formed a peculiar class—the elite of the colored race."[11]

To add to this complex community, newcomers arrived in greater and greater numbers. St. Louis was primarily a rest station on the way further west or north for the first wave of migrants fleeing the US South. In 1879 these "Exodusters" had traveled northward on or along the Mississippi headed for Kansas, whose history of being an antebellum free state seemed to promise a better life. But many found temporary refuge in St. Louis, supported by the local Black population, which provided food, shelter, and "relief" to the exhausted migrants before sending them on.[12] St. Louisans could also make common cause across greater cultural divides: in 1904 a group of Africans hired for cultural exhibitions in the World's Fair disappeared for several days. They were found in a Black downtown neighborhood socializing with locals.[13]

Despite these examples of connections across the diaspora, the arrival of permanent migrants by the thousands in the Great Migration of the late nineteenth and early twentieth centuries often exacerbated tensions based on class, cultural, or religious differences. This was not uncommon. St. Louis was one of many destinations for African Americans seeking better prospects in the industrializing North and Midwest during this period. Most destination cities already had an "old settler" Black population whose presence predated the new migrants by generations and sometimes centuries.[14]

Like all migrant communities, the new Black St. Louisans were connected to friends, family, and a broader African American sensibility through personal networks, culture, music, and newspapers. St. Louis became a hub of Black American culture.[15] The "St. Louis Blues," one of pioneer blues musician W. C. Handy's most famous songs, memorialized a St. Louis woman who stole the singer's man. Numerous songs and stories dramatized the life and crimes of Lee "Stagger Lee" Shelton, a St. Louis carriage driver and dandy who murdered another Black man in 1895.[16] And in 1917, thousands of Black women, men, and children marched silently down Fifth Avenue in Manhattan to the somber beating of drums in protest against racist violence, most recently the attack on East St. Louis's Black business and residential neighborhoods which sent survivors fleeing across the river into St. Louis.[17] While the *Chicago Defender* played a particularly crucial role in uniting Black Americans in this secondary diaspora, St. Louis's Black population was large and stable enough to support a series of Black-edited newspapers of its own.[18] Two of these continued into the twenty-first century: the *St. Louis Argus*, established in 1912, and the *St. Louis American*, founded in 1928 in response to the conservatism of the *Argus*. Such newspapers both provided a record of and helped actively promote and create a sense of shared identity and purpose.[19]

Just as scholars of the long civil rights movement elsewhere have found crucial groundwork, and sometimes broader and more radical campaigns, in the generation before the heroic movement, so too have historians of Black St. Louis activism. Three significant recent studies focus on class as the (or one of the) most salient of the intersecting categories of identity and experience within St. Louis's Black communities. Priscilla A. Dowden-White examines two pre-1950s generations of Black activism in her study of the work of the Urban League, NAACP, and other "social welfare reformers" in St. Louis in the 1910s to 1940s. African American organizing and institution building worked in alliance with white political networks and institutions to secure jobs, fair housing, healthcare, and other basic civil rights. Black reformers in many locations worked closely with white allies during this period because of their limited political power and resources. In St. Louis specifically, the aldermanic system did allow some political voice in wards that had significant Black populations, and access to the vote was relatively open. Dowden-White argues that these generations set a civil rights agenda for the World War II and postwar generations.[20]

Clarence Lang agrees, but argues it was a frustratingly narrow agenda. His overview of civil rights organizing in St. Louis combines attention to the working-class and middle-class Black St. Louisans, starting from the labor activism of the mid-1930s and ending in the mid-1970s. Lang argues that this was the era when the Blacks in the working class began to set their own agendas, only to find their activism undermined by the constraints of the Black elite's priorities and strategies. For Lang, working-class definitions of civil rights, and the more radical protest tactics meant to advance them, did not gain ascendency in the movement until the mid-1960s.[21]

More recently, Keona K. Ervin revisited roughly the same period, focusing on Black women's organizing for workers' rights. Several major industries that emerged in early twentieth-century St. Louis targeted female workers for employment, and Ervin notes that more Black women than men moved to St. Louis during the Great Migration period. Among these working-class women can be found many of the city's more radical activists. Among the defining events of this era are the Funsten Nutpickers' strikes in St. Louis, led by Black women, who held the worst of the jobs shelling and preparing pecans for market. Their actions were openly supported by the Communist Party of the United States of America (CPUSA).[22]

While labor activism and reforms were clearly central to the development of the city's community organizing and drives for social change, Black Catholic St. Louisans also made strides in challenging segregation and discrimination within Roman Catholic institutions in the city and region. Like their secular or Protestant counterparts, they did so in part through networking with a national organization but also in developing their own local campaigns. The Federated Colored Catholics (FCC) was founded in the mid-1920s on the East Coast under the leadership of Thomas Wyatt Turner. The FCC advocated for integration of Catholic schools and the development of pathways for Black men and women into religious orders, especially the priesthood. Actively leading the organization in the late 1920s and early 1930s, Turner lost a power struggle over its leadership to two white priests in 1932.

In 1931, the annual meeting of the FCC came to St. Louis, where there was already a sizeable Black Catholic population ready for the changes it was advocating. St. Louis activists were becoming central to the FCC, and some already had personal connections to Dr. Turner, who was also no stranger to St. Louis. Early in his career, he had taught one year of biology at Sumner High School, then the one Black public high school in St. Louis. During his short time there he had made many friends, joined the board of the Black hospital being built, and had experienced discrimination in his faith home: being forced to sit at the back of a church during mass.[23] By 1931, he had been joined in the leadership of the FCC by two white priests, Father John LaFarge of New York and Father William Markoe, one of a pair

42

of brother Jesuits assigned to Black parishes in St. Louis. When they took over the FCC the next year, LaFarge and Markoe would change the name of the organization to the National Interracial Catholic Federation, assume the publication of an official newsletter (prompting Turner's resignation), and shift the movement to a white-led pro–civil rights organization.[24] But in 1931, Turner was still in control and played a substantial role in corresponding with local St. Louis organizers, including a young man named Charles Anderson, who was a St. Louis local and probably still a student at Sumner High School himself.[25]

The St. Louis conference was notable because it gave extended time and attention to the issue of job discrimination. Turner later noted with satisfaction that several speakers at the St. Louis meeting directly addressed labor concerns for Black Americans. More importantly, some of the resolutions of the FCC meeting, which included attention to equal opportunities and protections of Black workers, encouraged union organizing.[26]

One of the biggest events of the 1931 conference was a sermon given at the College Church on SLU's campus by Father John T. Gillard, who had been advising the Oblate Sisters in Rhode Island, the first African American women's Catholic order.[27] Gillard addressed a collection of five hundred clergy and laity who had processed from St. Elizabeth's, the most prominent Black parish in St. Louis, to the campus church at the southwest corner of North Grand and Lindell Boulevards. Gillard appealed to Blacks to convert to Catholicism. Their only other option, he argued, was socialism, which was not working out very well in Russia for the poor.

Father Gillard was followed by Father Louis Theobald, the first Black priest ordained in the US. Theobald was introduced by the president of Saint Louis University, whom he then put on the spot by denouncing SLU's discrimination against African Americans in admissions. It was a tense moment. Other administrators were in attendance, as were many of the Jesuits who staffed and made up the faculty of the Catholic university. FCC members hoped the public nature of the charge would ignite the Jesuits in attendance to action.[28]

Those hopes failed to reach fruition over the next few years, but some seeds had been sown. Charles Anderson, the high school student who helped organize the conference and sat in the audience that day, left St. Louis to attend Lincoln University, Missouri's leading Black institution of higher education. When he returned, he was hired to teach at his former high school. He applied to SLU to continue his education sometime between 1939 and 1941, without success. For the next few years Anderson led an open campaign to desegregate Catholic schools in the area, writing letters to local leaders, talking to Black parish members, and passing out leaflets outside of Sunday masses. Anderson also passed out flyers on SLU's campus, directly exhorting students to protest his and other Blacks' exclusion from their company. Anderson wrote to the archdiocese and was likely also known to the regional Jesuit provincial leader, who officially started SLU's internal consideration of desegregation in 1942. Anderson's apparent one-man campaign against segregation at SLU was in fact a group effort. Local Black businessmen paid for his supplies, his employer allowed him time off to stand on campus, and Black-published newspapers in the city supported his efforts and dubbed the arrival of the first Black students at SLU as "Charles Anderson Day."[29]

The role of Charles Anderson and other Black St. Louisans in SLU's desegregation has been largely forgotten. SLU's own institutional narrative features Father Claude Heithaus, a Jesuit teacher at SLU, who gave a sermon in February of 1944—two years after Anderson's campaign and after the Jesuits' provincial leader told the university to begin plans for integration. Published in both the campus paper and the *St. Louis Post-Dispatch*, Heithaus's sermon offers a rare public example from the often behind-the-scenes theological, moral, and social debates that took place at many Catholic institutions in this period. Heithaus exhorted the white college students in attendance to accept Black students, invoking Catholic global history, theological doctrines of Christian unity, and (like Father Gillard over a decade earlier) warning that African Americans would turn to communism if white Christians turned their backs on them.[30] By the fall of 1944, a handful of Black students were indeed enrolled in classes. Claude Heithaus was there to welcome them, although he soon complained publicly about the limitations on their involvement in campus activities: they could not live on campus, join social groups, or attend parties. His superiors chastised him and removed the wayward priest to a military chaplaincy. But Heithaus left evidence of his connection and indebtedness to a network of Black Catholics, as well as a few white priests, who advocated for the integration of parish schools and Catholic colleges and universities, along with jobs, fair housing, and human dignity.

Saint Louis University's desegregation also had an impact beyond its campus. While each private university was self-regulating, once SLU desegregated, other Catholic colleges in the area soon followed suit. Four miles west of SLU, students at the secular, private Washington University, especially in its School of Social Work, also began campaigning to open their doors to Black students.[31] They organized the Student Committee for the Admission of Negroes (SCAN) in 1947 and were working with labor activists when CORE, the first new organization of the heroic civil rights era, came to St. Louis.

Local Catholic K–12 schools were organized separately and under the direct authority of Archbishop John Glennon of the St. Louis Archdiocese. The campaign to desegregate them was less organized, but also connected to the Anderson-Heithaus SLU campaign. Jane Kaiser spearheaded this campaign and documented a meeting with Glennon about desegregating the city's parochial schools. In a very long letter to Claude Heithaus, turned over to the diocese at some point, she outlined her encounter with the archbishop, a meeting that did not go well. Glennon did not see any contradiction between the Roman Catholic Church's teachings on human unity and his own allegiance to "the social customs of the time." He berated Kaiser, first for ignoring the largess of Catholic charitable support for "Negro schools," then for not acknowledging the justification of separate educational systems. Beyond the local custom he cited, Archbishop Glennon believed that Black Catholics already got more than they deserved. He criticized African Americans in St. Louis because, he claimed, they "don't give the money, don't take care of their things. They should fix up their houses, paint their houses, mow their lawns, put curtains at their windows—you've seen how they live."[32] Glennon also complained about "Negro men on Grand St. [sic]"—the boundary between SLU's campus and the working-class African American district named Mill Creek Valley—trying to rape white women, and he let forth a diatribe against "miscegenation." As Kaiser left, threatening to go over his head or to the press, Glennon called her "impertinent, fallacious, fantastic, fanatic, and lacking in humility," and he dared her to "go write your little letters, tell your little press."[33]

Kaiser did write letters, with no immediate effect. But when Glennon unexpectedly died in 1946, his replacement was the response. The new Archbishop of St. Louis, Joseph Ritter, immediately ordered all St. Louis parochial schools to integrate in 1947. Ritter had already done the same thing in his previous posting in Indiana, so there is little doubt Catholic leadership moved Ritter into St. Louis at least in part for that purpose. Local opposition to his order was quick—and quickly quashed. Ritter had both the support of a significant portion of local white Catholics and the

45

power to threaten the excommunication of leaders of the opposition, a warning that he ordered to be read from pulpits by priests throughout the city.[34] This threat was effective: while a group of white Catholics opposing integration had already formed a Catholic Parents' Association, had held meetings, and had begun to organize a lawsuit against Ritter, they swiftly dissolved in the face of the loss of Catholic communion, community, and salvation. Black students were soon enrolled in several of the white parochial schools, and the Black schools were slowly phased out over the next few years.

By the end of World War II, then, St. Louis had seen some significant changes. Civil rights campaigns had begun, and organizations like the FCC, NAACP, Urban League, and CPUSA offered national resources and networks to local community leaders, reformers, and Black activists. The national trends and pressures of World War II that we understand as setting the stage for the civil rights movement of the 1950s and 1960s touched St. Louis as well. At the same time, there were already numerous organizations and networks within the city and its environs, and these drove the local movement as much, and sometimes more, than national turning points like *Brown v. Board of Education.*

St. Louis Activism during the Heroic Civil Rights Movement

Traditional histories of the civil rights movement usually bring the North into the narrative in the mid-1960s, when racial riots and rebellions began to break out, the Black Panther Party organized, and the Student Nonviolent Coordinating Committee (SNCC) broke with the SCLC and embraced the slogan and ideology of Black Power. Historians have emphasized that many of these movements were happening in cities throughout the North and Midwest long before the SCLC supposedly "brought the movement" northward to them in the mid-1960s.[35] King did visit St. Louis several times in the 1960s, including a 1964 talk at Saint Louis University. But the SCLC and its affiliated SNCC allies never brought their campaigns to St. Louis as they did elsewhere.[36] In St. Louis, however, the new era of civil rights organizing began with the development of a CORE chapter in the late 1940s, and it developed further through the 1950s and into the 1960s. Numerous organizations emerged, sometimes working in coalition, sometimes in conflicting directions, and often both simultaneously. While it is not possible to go into detail or even touch upon all of these, I try in this section to follow the major events of the 1950s and 1960s in St. Louis.

The Congress of Racial Equality (CORE), originally named the Committee for Racial Equality, was founded in Chicago in 1942 in the aftermath of the planned 1941 March on Washington (MOW), intended to protest Black exclusion from defense work. Inspired by Mahatma Gandhi's nonviolent resistance to British rule in India, CORE founders immersed themselves in labor activism and a theology and practice of civil disobedience, pacifism, and social change. With the war over and some concessions for defense jobs and military opportunities won from the Roosevelt administration in exchange for *not* marching on Washington in 1941, CORE mobilized an expanded civil rights agenda for postwar America.

The MOW Movement had also been very active in St. Louis, and St. Louis CORE quickly became the "most viable chapter in the entire CORE movement" in the early 1950s.[37] (It was founded so early that it continued to use CORE's original term "Committee," rather than "Congress," in its chapter name.) The St. Louis group worked closely with national MOW leader A. Philip Randolph and Theodore McNeal, another Brotherhood of Sleeping Car Porters and MOW organizer. CORE had some early successes in St. Louis, developing tactics in line with the national CORE philosophy of nonviolence, moral suasion, and respectable comportment during direct action.[38]

From 1949 to 1954, St. Louis CORE focused on desegregating restaurants, lunch counters, and other public facilities. CORE members lobbied business owners behind the scenes and held sit-ins at local department store and drugstore dining counters, independent restaurants, YMCAs and YWCAs, bus terminals in St. Louis and East St. Louis, and the Municipal Art Museum (now the Saint Louis Art Museum). These early sit-ins, which long predated the 1960s sit-ins at Woolworth's lunch counters led by CORE and SNCC, were studiously ignored by St. Louis's white newspapers and therefore never received national attention.[39] By 1952, CORE wrote up a proposal to work with department stores throughout the city to transition "from a racially segregated to an integrated society."[40] In addition to sit-ins, they developed a method of "controlled testing"—forging agreements, for example, to have an interracial group of CORE members and affiliates be served at Woolworth's once a week and gradually increase the frequency. This careful approach produced more early success for the group than did demonstrations. As one activist said, "Though the testing is presented to the manager as a means of education [for the public], we consider it more as a 'foot in the door,' making it easier to push him a little further. . . . We have discovered a damned good foot in the door tactic."[41]

This campaign lost traction by the mid-1950s. On the one hand, quite a few stores had opened their lunch counters to Black customers. On the other hand, some of the largest businesses simply refused to change their policies. Jobs were clearly the next major issue to take on, but CORE was not well suited for this task. Scholars August Meier and Elliott Rudwick suggest that CORE leaders were reluctant to step on the toes of organizations like the Urban League, which had long focused on job opportunities and fair treatment for Black St. Louisans.[42] For Clarence Lang, the tactics and focus of CORE, like those of the NAACP and other groups active in the 1930s and 1940s, were simply out of step with the experiences and needs of Black working people. As the ones bearing the brunt of hiring discrimination practices, working-class Black St. Louisans would finally enact the "mass-based insurgency" in the 1960s, breaking away from CORE and other older organizations to do so.[43] But CORE and its members continued to play a leading role in major events of the 1960s local movement, even as an increasing number of new organizations and strategies emerged, one that would both work with and challenge CORE's ideology and approach.

Interestingly, school desegregation was not a priority of the movement in the aftermath of *Brown v. Board of Education*. This was largely because the St. Louis Board of Education voted almost immediately to desegregate schools, and the process began in 1954. National attention turned to cities in the South, where local boards, mayors, or governors resisted compliance with the decision, cementing the narrative that only the Deep South still had segregation and the deep-seated racism to defend it. But *Brown v. Board of Education* combined four different local civil rights legal cases— ones challenging the constitutionality of segregated schools in Delaware, the District of Columbia, Virginia, and South Carolina—into a case named for the fifth location: Topeka, Kansas. Still, St. Louis's quick accession to the new law satisfied the requirement to dissolve an explicitly segregated system. The issue had been on the city's radar for over a decade, of course, with news coverage of the Catholic schools' desegregation in the 1940s. By 1954, then, St. Louis public school officials already had a local model for how integration could be enacted and had seen some of the shapes opposition could take.

But the city also had other ways to maintain a racial hierarchy. Like many northern and midwestern cities, St. Louis school districts were based on residential neighborhoods that were themselves built around overt racial restrictions.[44] New charges of "re-segregation" soon emerged, and school desegregation did become a target of activism by the early 1960s in St. Louis. By that point, the integration process had slowed nearly to a halt, and the increase in relative numbers of African Americans in St. Louis, as whites left the city and its public school system, exacerbated the obvious inequities remaining in the system. A coalition of organizations presented overwhelming evidence of continued segregation in 1963, rallying downtown when the board failed to respond. Despite continued efforts, little changed in the ineffective integration plan already in place in St. Louis.[45] In fact, St. Louis City and County continued to be in the process of desegregating in the 1980s, after a series of lawsuits and settlements that continued to be negotiated into the twenty-first century.[46]

In the local history of St. Louis's civil rights movement, the arguable climax was the 1963–1964 picketing and boycott of the Jefferson Bank and Trust Company, which morphed into a "general strike against racism." And the driving issue was jobs. For years, activists had been meeting with leaders of this large downtown bank about their failure to hire Black employees, especially outside of service positions. For years, bank leaders had made promises and done nothing. In summer 1963, CORE shifted to a demand that Jefferson Bank hire four Black employees (two smaller banks had recently hired two each) and gave a short deadline.[47] It was likely no coincidence that this gauntlet was thrown down just as four busloads of the established civil rights leaders from the area were headed to Washington, DC, to attend the long-delayed March on Washington. By the time the DC marchers returned, those who remained behind had already followed their ultimatum to the bank with a direct-action protest in defiance of a court restraining order naming CORE.

There had been several new faces and voices in CORE who contributed to this shift in strategy to a more combative action and the direct defiance of a court order. The most immediately visible was the new CORE chairman, Robert Curtis, a young Black lawyer with a long history in St. Louis antiracist organizing. His mother was the director of the People's Art Center, an interracial organization funded by the New Deal–era Works Progress Administration, that became a center for networking.[48] Curtis himself had been one of the few dozen Black children who entered the newly integrated public swimming pool at Fairground Park in 1949, only to be escorted out by police when white teenagers surrounded the area and soon escalated the confrontation into a violent riot that lasted twelve hours and brought out hundreds of whites looking for Black victims.[49] By 1963, Curtis was

Figure 1.1 Protests at Jefferson Bank and Trust in fall 1963. The center picketer's sign references Martin Luther King Jr.'s recent speech at the March on Washington for Jobs and Freedom. *From the Charles and Marian O'Fallon Oldham Papers (S1112), State Historical Society of Missouri*

one of many in St. Louis losing patience with the old-guard focus on interracial cooperation, respectable behavior and dress, and gradual, careful approaches to change. He wrote the letter threatening direct action against the bank.[50] The bank sought and received a court order prohibiting the organization from enacting its threatened actions against the bank, but the campaign went forward.

The Jefferson Bank protestors used tactics that, by then, had been successful in other locations: they began with a picket line of more than a hundred people outside the bank, with signs announcing their demand for "JOBS NOW" and the need for "Civil Rights" and "Freedom." Several groups then moved to block the front and back doors, in violation of the court order. In the confusion of the police response, several entered the bank, and suddenly the protest was inside. There they sat in, three rows deep in front of the tellers to block business, following a strategy set by nearby East St. Louisans in recent bank sit-ins.

Nine CORE leaders were arrested, including founding member and former chair Marian Oldham. When the trial began, the judge only grudgingly granted a few days for defense lawyers to prepare against charges not yet specified. The coalescence of St. Louis's white power structures became clear as white-published newspapers decried the actions of protestors and white prosecutors suddenly unveiled criminal, rather than civil, charges against the CORE activists. And a special prosecutor assigned to the case turned out to be an attorney for Jefferson Bank and the son-in-law of its president. Convictions, harsh sentences, and a refusal to allow bonds for defendants while their appeals were in process highlighted the collusion of St. Louis's economic, political, and judicial systems to punish activists and quell future protests. Over the next few weeks and months, more demonstrators were arrested not just on the picket lines, but in their homes late at night, for unrelated "crimes" like failure to pay off a loan.[51]

The lines were drawn, but they were not drawn in the same place for everyone. While some Black St. Louisans tried to focus on actions less likely to trigger further arrests, others jumped into the frontline, outnumbering CORE members. Students from local high schools, as well as from Washington and Saint Louis Universities, joined the picket lines. Local Black ministers appealed to congregants to join a general boycott of downtown stores, while Black doctors and other community elites made statements against the bank and supported or joined the pickets. The campaign became not only CORE against Jefferson Bank, but also, more broadly, Black St. Louisans united against white racism.

White religious leaders also began to speak up on behalf of the convicted civil rights activists. Missouri's Episcopal bishop, George L. Cadigan, issued a pastoral letter warning that the local "cleavage between Negroes and whites" had become so deep that the city might be "on the threshold of disorder and violence." Three hundred fifty Catholic religious leaders and members held a benediction service and then walked to the Civil Courts Building for prayers and to hear SLU law professor John E. Dunsford describe the lawbreaking of the demonstrations as a justified response to the "silent strangulation of Negro manhood with the rope of racism."[52] Black religious leaders had been consciously visible at the forefront of the SCLC, and their appeals to white peers to support them accelerated in the mid-1960s.

In November 1963, a coalition of city aldermen, CORE activists, local ministers, and other community leaders signed a statement protesting the harsh sentences of the CORE officers and other activists convicted of contempt of court. The statement also denounced the unjustifiable and

"deplorable statistics" documenting stark racial gaps in income, employment, and housing, all illustrating the impact of racism and discrimination
on Black life. On Thursday, November 21, the group then led an hours-
long march and protest which began at the Jefferson Bank and traveled
eastward to downtown's central business district. There, they marched in
a large square while entering and walking through five downtown department stores, "weaving through the aisles and around showcases, singing
and clapping." Signs and chants urged shoppers not to buy in stores that
refused to hire Black workers and called for a Christmas shopping boycott.
Upon completing their circuit, the group of more than fifty demonstrators
took over a major intersection at Sixth Street and Washington Avenue, still
singing, with some lying in the street directly blocking traffic (Fig. 1.2).
Police dragged protestors off the street and seven were arrested.[53]

Figure 1.2 CORE field secretary Winston Lockett blocking traffic at Washington
Avenue and Sixth Street downtown, leading to his arrest. The demonstration was part
of a CORE march on November 21, 1963, urging a Christmas boycott of downtown
retailers. *Photo by Rich Kurre for the* St. Louis Globe-Democrat, *from the collections of
the St. Louis Mercantile Library at the University of Missouri–St. Louis*

By now, the city's white-owned daily newspapers could no longer ignore civil rights activism. CORE's Christmas Boycott march was front-page news in the *St. Louis Post-Dispatch* the next day. But by the time the *Post-Dispatch*'s evening edition landed on subscribers' porches, President John F. Kennedy had been assassinated in Dallas, and the story of activists in St. Louis disrupting downtown shoppers, businesses, and traffic for several hours temporarily vanished from the press.

For activists, of course, the work continued. Long before Jefferson Bank ended the campaign by hiring six Black tellers in March 1964, the stakes of the standoff had already been evident. While the bank and the legal system fought back, dozens of other businesses had increased their hiring of Black workers into both skilled and semi-skilled positions, producing a 32 percent increase between 1963 and 1964.[54] By the end of the year, the US Congress had passed the 1964 Civil Rights Act. This victory provided support for ongoing campaigns against discrimination and racism, and Black St. Louisans began to turn to the myriad ways their education, work opportunities, residential choices, and recognition as full citizens and humans were still limited.

The next stage of civil rights in St. Louis would be characterized by a new organization: the Action Committee to Improve Opportunities for Negroes, with the dynamic acronym of ACTION. ACTION was founded by Percy Green, a local man from a working-class family, one of the few Black skilled workers at McDonnell Aircraft Corporation. Green was one of two relative newcomers to the movement who came to personify the next generation of St. Louis activism. The other was Ivory Perry, a literal newcomer to St. Louis from Arkansas, a Korean war veteran with an unstable work past and some trouble with the law.[55] Both Green and Perry joined CORE in the early 1960s, and found that they had shared concerns and social unease, as well as disagreements with the group's leadership about the best strategies and approaches to push for change.

Continuing the campaign for job equity in St. Louis, ACTION launched a series of direct-action protests against the lack of equal-opportunity federal hiring in the building of the now-iconic Gateway Arch and its accompanying underground museum. The most dramatic of these actions featured Percy Green and fellow ACTION member Richard Daly climbing up the unfinished Arch during a workers' lunchbreak and chaining themselves there for four hours, yelling down demands for more Black workers to be hired while police tried to figure out how to cut them down to arrest them

(Fig. 1.3). Although excoriated in the press and by some fellow activists as attention seeking, the "stunt" was part of a series of protests of the federal- and city-funded project. This campaign ultimately resulted in a federally mandated affirmative action plan for St. Louis.[56]

Figure 1.3 With its nonviolent theatricality, Percy Green and Richard Daly's iconic July 1964 protest of hiring discrimination at the unfinished Gateway Arch captured the confrontational turn of the local civil rights struggle in the wake of the Jefferson Bank protests. *Photo by Paul Ockrassa for the* St. Louis Globe-Democrat, *from the collections of the St. Louis Mercantile Library at the University of Missouri–St. Louis*

Other campaigns spearheaded by ACTION are highlighted elsewhere in this volume.[57] As in most places, the line between civil rights and Black Power organizing is often blurred. ACTION perhaps represents the clearest transition from one towards the other. Like later organizations more explicitly aligned with Black Power, ACTION consistently worked with the older civil rights and community organizations like CORE, the Urban League, and the NAACP, even as its members pursued campaigns that annoyed adherents to respectability politics.

Newspaper editor Nathan B. Young Jr. once claimed that "you could write the entire story of civil rights by going back to the history of the city of St. Louis."[58] St. Louis's civil rights history does present, as Young predicted, a microcosm of sorts of the national history of the movement. Civil rights organizing in St. Louis in the 1950s grew out of the labor movement of the 1920s and 1930s. CORE, once a new and radical organization with its post–World War II emphasis on nonviolent sit-ins, civil disobedience, and mass protest gave rise to more direct-action strategies by the mid-1960s and eventually movements that emphasized community self-sufficiency, cultural pride, and systemic change over integration and reform. During the turbulent years of the civil rights movement, St. Louis saw no stand-offs with police with firehoses and attack dogs; no eruptions of outrage that turned to destruction of property such as had made headlines in the 1960s in cities around the nation; no Black Panther Party chapter formed.

Finally, along with some with some quintessentially "St. Louis" moments, we've seen regional networks and patterns. Individuals, strategies, and organizations moved to and from St. Louis, Chicago, and East St. Louis, as well as to and from national meetings, events, and campaigns. St. Louis also shared the urban midwestern pattern of continued in-migration of African Americans seeking jobs, white flight from cities that drained municipal tax revenue, and eventually the Rust Belt experience of the 1970s and 1980s, with the loss of industries where affirmative action programs were just providing Black workers access to jobs. As the Black population of St. Louis increased both in numbers and proportion within the city, new organizations and leaders emerged. Some activists transitioned into ward and local political service, while others focused their efforts on Black cultural and artistic expression and community-based training. The impact of the 1960s civil rights movement, and the institutions and practices it targeted, are still with us in St. Louis.

Activist Generations and Ferguson: A Coda

In October 2014, activists gathered in St. Louis for a weekend of rallies, workshops, and action. While still centered on the ongoing legal and policy aftermath of Michael Brown's death, the focus expanded to include Vonderrit Myers Jr., an unarmed Black man killed by an off-duty police officer just south of SLU's campus in a neighborhood where faculty and some students lived. The proximity brought protestors onto campus in what turned out to be a week-long "occupation" by students and community members in tents in a central area by the Clock Tower.[59] Hours prior to the occupation's start, SLU's Chaifetz Arena hosted a panel of local clergy and older community leaders. A divergence between those on the panel and younger activists in the audience soon emerged. Unimpressed by the dignitaries' speeches, the activists began talking back and were given the microphone. Tef Poe, a St. Louis poet inspired to activism by Michael Brown's murder, criticized his elders for their inaction and rejected their attempts to school him and his generational peers on how to be an activist: "This ain't your grandparents' civil rights movement!" he exhorted.[60] The refrain was picked up because of how strongly it either resonated with or offended Americans' perceptions of both the contemporary Black Lives Matter movement and the civil rights campaigns of previous generations.[61] Some of the "grandparents" would agree there was a marked difference between the generations' movements, and continued to offer their own critiques of BLM for its alleged failure to follow the nonviolent politics of agape.[62]

Black Lives Matter certainly differs from the civil rights movement of the 1950s and 1960s in many ways. But it is also a direct legacy of preceding generations of activism and Black organizing in St. Louis. Despite generational gaps and ideological differences, there is a through-line of activism from the 1960s to the present. St. Louis's CORE chapter was founded in 1949, in part by labor activists who had been active in local campaigns in the 1920s to 1940s. CORE dominated the civil rights scene for almost a decade and a half. Disaffected CORE members then formed ACTION, which continued civil rights campaigns for jobs and fair housing. When ACTION began to fracture two decades later, some of its members formed the Organization for Black Struggle (OBS) in 1980. OBS is still active in St. Louis, and it was one of a handful of groups consistently visible and active in Ferguson and in the larger Black Lives Matter movement.[63] Younger and newer organizations were of course also formed out of the community protests that caught the world by surprise in August 2014. These deep connections between organizing projects across distinct historical moments demonstrate the civil rights movement in St. Louis as not just the work of a single decade or era, but rather as a multigenerational project whose relevance and importance endures today.

2. The St. Louis Baby Tooth Survey and Women's Environmental Activism

Luke Ritter

THE ABOVE-GROUND NUCLEAR WEAPONS TESTS conducted by the United States, Great Britain, and the Soviet Union between 1945 and 1963 revealed a dangerous disregard for the impact of man-made technologies on the environment. Few cities in the United States saw environmental activism as determined and influential as in St. Louis. The city may have ranked tenth on a list of the country's largest cities circa 1960, but it was first in environmentalism.[1] The concerned citizens and scientists of the St. Louis Committee for Nuclear Information (CNI) created a mid-twentieth-century marvel of grassroots environmental science: the Baby Tooth Survey (1958–1969). The Baby Tooth Survey collected more than three hundred thousand baby teeth from across the country for analysis in a lab at Washington University in St. Louis. One byproduct of nuclear explosions, strontium-90, followed the normal pathways of calcium and collected in cow's milk, which children consumed while their deciduous teeth formed *in utero* and early infancy. By measuring levels of nuclear fallout poisoning absorbed in the teeth of children born during the era of hydrogen bomb testing, the survey produced data that became instrumental in ending above-ground nuclear weapons tests. The Baby Tooth Survey's announcement of a thirty-fold rise in Sr-90 uptake in children since 1951 contributed to the swift passage of President John Kennedy's Nuclear Test Ban Treaty with the USSR in 1963.

American citizens who demanded a ban on nuclear weapons testing during the height of the Cold War with the USSR faced formidable resistance, especially since many Americans equated antinuclear sentiment with communism.[2] Maternalism turned out to be a useful tactic, activist Amy Swerdlow pointed out; a woman against nuclear arms "could not be ignored or attacked because she was doing it all in the name of a hallowed institution—motherhood."[3] Those involved in the Baby Tooth Survey represented a particular demographic: middle-class, white, stay-at-home moms in their thirties and forties with free time and a social mandate to actively campaign. For many of the nuclear women, "the decision to become active," explained historian Adam Rome, "came in response to an environmental threat that hit home."[4] St. Louis's nuclear women organized the world-renowned Baby Tooth Survey for the sake of their children, protested military intervention abroad, and eventually joined the movement for women's liberation. Not only did Americans become enlightened about the many interconnected environmental concerns related to the H-bomb, nuclear storage, industrial pollution, and pesticides, but they also recognized women's sustained role in raising consciousness and demanding governmental protections against devastating man-made technologies. The ideas and strategies developed over the lifespan of the Baby Tooth Survey directly influenced the emergent environmentalism and feminism of the 1960s.

Nuclear Fallout and the
Origins of Women's Environmental Activism

The very scientists who cheered on nuclear bomb production began to express grave concerns about the public health hazard of nuclear fallout once the Soviets acquired their own deliverable hydrogen bomb in 1953. The Atomic Energy Commission (AEC), a civilian-controlled federal agency established after World War II by the US Congress to manage nuclear facilities, focused its early fallout studies on one byproduct in particular, the radioactive isotope strontium-90 (Sr-90), for two significant reasons: it has a much longer half-life than any of the other radioactive substances in fallout (twenty-eight years), and it follows the normal pathways of calcium into the human body. In 1953 the AEC tasked its commissioner, Willard Libby, with conducting a massive analysis of milk supplies from various regions in the United States, theorizing that Sr-90 could circle the world for years before falling to Earth and absorbing into plants eaten by cows. Then Sr-90 could collect in cow's milk. In the 1950s, cow's milk was Americans' leading source of calcium, and so it followed that it might also be their primary source of exposure to this most dangerous radioactive isotope.[5] The AEC's research project, nicknamed "Project Sunshine," gathered data on Sr-90 in milk supplies after 1953. "Atomic energy," observed Barry Commoner, a leading environmentalist and biologist at Washington University in St. Louis, "had made its environmental debut."[6]

Figure 2.1 After the nuclear weapons tests began, scientists realized that milk was a likely source for human ingestion of strontium-90, an isotope that could be measured to assess levels of radioactive contamination. The US Public Health Service began gathering milk from ten cities, including St. Louis, to analyze it for Sr-90. *From the Arthur Witman 120mm Photograph Collection (S0732), State Historical Society of Missouri*

In 1955 the AEC selected the midcontinental city of St. Louis as one of the sites for the original studies. The early data showed that the concentration of Sr-90 in local milk rose in direct correlation to nuclear bomb tests. Near the end of 1956, the *St. Louis Post-Dispatch* ran weekly—and sometimes daily—stories on Sr-90 contamination. A journalist for the *Post-Dispatch*, William K. Wyant Jr., pointed out that by the summer of 1959, strontium-90 had become "a household word in St. Louis."[7] Concerned citizens worried about Sr-90's potential to cause bone cancer in children and genetic defects in infants.[8]

The AEC set the maximum permissible concentration (MPC) of radiation doses in the human body to 80 strontium units, which were nicknamed "Sunshine Units"; more than 80 was deemed detrimental to good health. In a report for the *Journal of Dairy Science* in 1958, scientists admitted nevertheless that any "permeation of radioactive isotopes might contribute to a small increase in genetic defects in children."[9] Other official statements were chillingly ambiguous.[10] AEC scientist Charles L. Dunham confessed to the arbitrary nature of the MPC threshold later in 1959: "It is a dose which . . . represents the greatest hazard that should be permitted under conditions to which the recommendation is applicable. Under different conditions, either a lower or a higher permissible dose may be more appropriate." The implication was that the federal government could consider fallout from nuclear weapons tests an acceptable public health risk under "wartime conditions." Meanwhile, Sr-90 levels continued to rise. In November 1958, St. Louis milk carried an average of 20.1 Sunshine Units, the highest recorded in the area to date.[11] St. Louisans who saw their city listed as a "hot spot" in both the newspapers and the available scientific literature demanded answers.

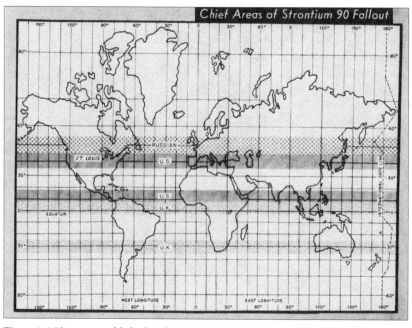

Figure 2.2 This map, published in the *St. Louis Post-Dispatch* on December 21, 1958, shows the widespread distribution of strontium-90 fallout from nuclear weapons tests conducted during the 1950s. *From the Newspaper Collection, State Historical Society of Missouri*

St. Louis women organized citizens' action groups and raised public awareness of the potential dangers of H-bomb testing. These middle-class, white women occupied a well-defined political niche dating back more than half a century on most urban matters related to cleanliness, the environment, and health.[12] Because most American women of this era identified as housewives and mothers, they considered political matters related to the home and children as their special domain. Indeed, as historian Carolyn Merchant has pointed out, women in the 1930s and 1940s "repeatedly called on the traditions assigned them by society" and "drew on a trilogy of slogans—conservation of womanhood, the home, and the child."[13] The

Women's Organization for Smoke Abatement, one of the most influential anti-smoke groups in St. Louis during the 1920s, adopted an outlook known as "municipal housekeeping," which held that the role of women as caretakers extended to the city at large as another kind of home environment requiring the particular scrutiny of nurturing women.[14] Environmental activist Henry Obermeyer urged women in 1933 to embrace municipal housekeeping because "mothers and home-makers the country over" stood to suffer the most from unclean and putrefying smoke, which crept into their houses, sullied their laundry, and inflamed their children's respiratory illnesses.[15] The intolerable black coal smog enveloping St. Louis during the 1930s compelled middle-class, white women to demand additional industrial regulations. The very identity of the city and its citizens turned on this remarkable crusade against smoke. "No city," historians Joel A. Tarr and Carl Zimring remark, "effectively controlled its heavy smoke until St. Louis did so in 1940."[16]

The H-bomb presented brand new public health concerns. This awesome new energy source not only wielded the power to destroy "any city in the world," as AEC chairman Lewis Strauss put it, but also posed an unprecedented set of global environmental hazards.[17] The battle was no longer against visible smoke spewing out of chimneys. Nuclear weapons imposed on the public at large an often invisible yet more frightening threat. The arms race with the Soviet Union incited the US government to mandate the manufacture and testing of ever higher-yielding atomic bombs. Meanwhile the fallout from these tests, though detonated in remote areas, circled the globe, shed invisible radioactive contaminants over skies and soil, and passed through the ecosystem into cow milk and human bone.

Women's heightened sense of urgency had a lot to do with the prospect of contaminated milk. Women, after all, were the primary caretakers of young children in the 1950s, and milk was children's top source of calcium; so many female activists came forward as mothers who were concerned about the health and safety of their children. "Mothers of young children besieged their pediatricians with questions," Commoner recalled in his autobiography. "Was there really any danger? Should they give their children less milk? What about the strontium-90 content of other foods?"[18]

The atom bomb had been shrouded in secrecy since its birth in the Manhattan Project. Even more disturbing was the mismatch between hand-waving statements from high-ranking government and military officials and the concerning scientific reports issuing from the AEC. Edward U. Condon, a former Manhattan Project physicist then at Washington University, began to speak out against nuclear armaments in 1956. "Nobody knows just when these nuclear tests will begin to damage civilization or their effects on generations unborn," he warned one St. Louis audience.[19] In that same year Gertrude Faust added nuclear fallout to the Consumer's Union's list of potentially dangerous chemical additives in consumer items "whose long range effect on the human body is completely unknown."[20] Faust, the president of the local branch of the Consumer's Union in St. Louis, pointed out that despite what some officials were telling the public, the data "clearly indicates some strontium-90 present in our milk supply." Faust organized one of the first petitions to St. Louis's health commissioners to investigate the amount of "radioactive materials in hydrogen bomb fall-out" in local milk. She gathered twenty-eight notable St. Louis women, including Edna Gellhorn, president of the League of Women Voters in St. Louis (Fig. 2.3), Marcelle Malamas of the International Ladies Garment Workers Union, and Virginia Warner Brodine, a lifelong activist, author, and founder of the Committee for Nuclear Information, to draft a letter first and foremost as mothers. "It appears that as we feed our children milk today, we are also feeding them radioactive materials," the letter read. "Not only our own children but our children's children may be affected physically and mentally by the radioactive materials which are now entering human organs for the first time." The letter emphasized that strontium-90 "enters plants used as food by cattle" and then "becomes part of our milk and enters the bodies of our children"—claims which Faust documented with certified scientific studies. Malamas, one of the signers of the original petition, "just sat down at the typewriter," one coworker recalled, "and began sending copies of [the letter] to everybody she knew all around the country."[21]

Health commissioners J. Earl Smith of St. Louis and Herbert R. Domke of St. Louis County acknowledged the problem, but pleaded a lack of funds for an official investigation. Domke suggested that federal agencies like the Public Health Service would "have to be involved." Faust and her team of volunteers then sent letters to officials in both Jefferson City, Missouri, and Washington, DC. She appeared in 1956 along with St. Louis scientists Walter Bauer and John Fowler before a special subcommittee on disarmament in the US Senate's Foreign Relations Committee, calling for a halt on H-bomb testing before Sr-90 levels rose beyond the MPC.[22] Faust even contacted Admiral Lewis Strauss of the Atomic Energy Commission directly, requesting information on Sr-90 testing. She found an ally in congressman

Figure 2.3 Prominent in the founding of the League of Women Voters in 1920, Edna Gellhorn had been a fixture among St. Louis activists for decades prior to the advent of atomic weapons. In her seventies she joined the antinuclear movement, lending extra gravitas to the organizational efforts of St. Louis's "nuclear women." *Photo by John Fischel, from the St. Louis, Missouri, Photograph Collection (P1151), State Historical Society of Missouri*

Frank M. Karsten who demanded more transparency from the AEC. In the summer of 1957, the US Congress held its first big hearing on the effects of radioactive fallout and eventually authorized the Public Health Service to investigate as they saw fit. Virginia Brodine, who had migrated to St. Louis from Los Angeles after her husband's political activities landed him on the studio blacklist, celebrated how antinuclear activism in St. Louis "was certainly one of the things that led to the testing of milk here and also in other cities."[23]

Meanwhile, the US Air Force continued to test massive bombs. President Dwight D. Eisenhower insisted that "the continuance of the present rate of H-bomb testing, by the most sober and responsible scientific judgment . . . does not imperil the health of humanity." Leading AEC figures such as Edward Teller, the Hungarian physicist who created the hydrogen bomb, and Admiral Lewis Strauss also issued statements denying the negative consequences of nuclear fallout. Six nuclear devices had already been detonated on Bikini Atoll by the beginning of 1956 when Eisenhower's administration approved Operation Redwing, which conducted seventeen more detonations on Bikini and Enewetak between May and July 1956.[24] The US Air Force conducted more controversial tests in Nevada the following year. Between 1945 and 1958, the United States, the Soviet Union, and Great

Britain tested a total of 190 atom and hydrogen bombs (US, 125; USSR, 44; Great Britain, 21). Radiation levels subsequently spiked in 1958 and 1959.[25]

Faust and her Consumer's Union joined forces with several other women's organizations in St. Louis in a grassroots political campaign to end nuclear testing. They hoped the United States would take the high road and stop testing first. Juanita Sherman, a local activist and the wife of a *Post-Dispatch* editor, Thomas B. Sherman, led a group with a clear mission and a straightforward name: the St. Louis Women's Committee for Ending Hydrogen Bomb Tests. Some also knew them as the "Eves against Atoms," a playful spin on the apparent antagonism between female activists and male military personnel responsible for building and testing nuclear weapons. The *Post-Dispatch*'s William K. Wyant Jr. recognized this "pioneer group" who "got into the conflict early" and "took a stand against testing." Between June and September 1957, they secured 1,154 signatures of St. Louis women backing the plea that all H-bomb tests be stopped "in the interest of world health and peace" and sent their petition to President Eisenhower. Sherman and the fifty members of the committee prepared pamphlets "listing the known biological facts on the effects of radiation and strontium-90" and made headlines when they sent a Mother's Day greeting card to Mamie Eisenhower on May 9, 1958, urging the First Lady to "join with other American mothers in an effort to end hydrogen bomb tests." The St. Louis branch of the Women's International League for Peace and Freedom (WILPF), a group composed largely of pacifist housewives and mothers, endorsed antinuclear activism. The president of WILPF at the time, Joy Guze, closely followed the information campaign of Faust and Sherman. Whatever "this means in terms of our children's health," one WILPF–St. Louis memorandum read, "we are grateful to Mrs. Faust for continuing to prod our congressmen into getting information. They have *all* shown surprising ignorance of the effects of H-bombs."[26]

St. Louis's nuclear women gained real star power when life-long activist Edna Gellhorn, who had shared the stage with Carrie Chapman Catt during the famous inaugural National Suffrage Association Convention in St. Louis in 1919, called for an immediate ban on nuclear weapons testing.[27] The League of Women Voters had focused on political issues upon which all women could unite, and although many of their campaigns included environmental concerns such as clean water and air, they stopped short of demanding that the US government diminish its national defense during the height of the Cold War. Gellhorn, at the age of seventy-nine, spoke out in 1957 "simply as a woman and a citizen . . . for those women who are becoming more and more concerned about the danger to our children from H-bomb tests."[28] Although scientists had not reached a consensus on how much radioactive exposure the human body could withstand, Gellhorn explained, St. Louis women were in agreement that they "do not want [children] to suffer in an experiment to find out how much strontium 90 (radioactive material) the human body can tolerate." She pleaded, "Children are no white mice or guinea pigs."[29]

The fear of nuclear war, which the men in the Civil Defense offices assumed would compel quartered housewives to "bunker in," had the opposite effect; it brought them out of domestic hiding and into the political limelight. Bonnie Hart, a mother of three, earned the moniker "Atomic Lady" for her relentless activism against nuclear weapons testing (Fig. 2.4).[30] After AEC commissioner Thomas E. Murray cavalierly suggested on a TV program that nuclear war was "likely," Hart published a piece detailing the likely reality of a nuclear attack:

> You could put together . . . all the death and suffering of the plagues of the middle ages, the despair and resignation of the 6,000,000 souls in Nazi Germany as they waited half starved to go in the furnaces or pits, the tears of every Mother who has had a child die in her arms . . . and all the rest of human misery since the beginning of time . . . add all these together and you have a better picture of a nuclear war than our leaders have the guts to give us—however inadequate.[31]

While the Office of Civil Defense of St. Louis at the time issued a family handbook with "tips" on how mothers might prepare for and survive a nuclear blast, Hart pointed out that nuclear warfare rendered bomb shelters and "civil defense" preparations almost entirely useless. A nuclear attack on St. Louis would be incomprehensibly disastrous, and with the advent of rapid intercontinental ballistic missiles, there was no point in running. "The understatement of the problem of surviving a nuclear war is so general and complete that it is almost sinister," Hart wrote in one widely disseminated newspaper article. She cited several absurdities in the Civil Defense literature, including the suggestion to use "water to wash the radioactive particles away" in the event of a nuclear blast. For Hart, this "sheer nonsense" indicated at worst a deliberate deception engineered at the highest levels of government, and at best a complete lack of awareness of the impact

Figure 2.4 Bonnie Hart, pictured here with two of her three children, Holly and Mark, earned the nickname "Atomic Lady" for her passionate stance against nuclear weapons. Hart led antinuclear letter-writing campaigns, wrote tirelessly to newspapers and public officials herself, and regularly engaged with call-in radio shows. *From the Bonnie Hart Papers (S0657), State Historical Society of Missouri*

nuclear fallout would have on the broader environment. For this reason, she forbade her daughter Holly to participate in the "duck and cover" nuclear bomb drills schools held in Belleville, Illinois. "She was making the point," Holly later remembered, "that it didn't matter if we were in the hall or where we were at, or even if we did survive, would we want to survive?" Yet there were environmental problems even closer to home. Hart also did not allow her daughter to drink St. Louis milk for fear of contamination. "I had to drink powdered milk," Holly recalled, "because of the strontium 90."[32]

The Committee for Nuclear Information and the Baby Tooth Survey

By 1958 St. Louis's nuclear women had raised public awareness of the environmental problems caused by H-bomb production and testing, appealed to the government to conduct in-depth studies of St. Louis's milk supply, and substantially contributed to the nationwide plea to ban nuclear weapons testing, which President Eisenhower offered to do for one year. That one-year ban on atmospheric testing stretched into three. Some suggested that Eisenhower's decision constituted a concession to the American mothers who pleaded for their children's safety. In the spring of 1958, antinuclear activists in St. Louis organized one of the nation's most prominent grassroots environmental awareness groups to date: the Greater St. Louis Citizens' Committee for Nuclear Information, or CNI.[33]

The CNI was unique for two significant reasons: for the first time it brought together scientific experts and everyday citizens to investigate socially relevant environmental matters and make scientific data accessible to the public; and women played an unparalleled role in forming and directing it. Precisely for these reasons, anthropologist Margaret Mead later dubbed CNI "a new social invention."[34] The group originated in March 1958 at a meeting of concerned citizens and scientists in Edna Gellhorn's apartment. Biologist Barry Commoner (Fig. 2.5) had been adamant that scientists bore a duty to inform citizens of probable environmental hazards. The information movement within the American Association for the Advancement of Science called upon scientists to responsibly interpret the facts in a way lay people could understand; at the time, the "single most important case," wrote Commoner's biographer, "was raising public concern over the hazards from atmospheric nuclear weapons testing." Scientists' attempts to inform the public about nuclear fallout thus became "a necessary tool for democracy and for environmentalism." Physicist John Fowler and pathologist Walter Bauer, both founders of the CNI and members of the faculty at Washington University, joined Commoner in the effort. After an extended series of discussions between the CNI's scientists and lay men and women at the March meeting, the founding group decided to provide "the basis of informed action," as CNI founder Brodine put it, rather than take a uniform stand against H-bomb testing. It was not that anyone in the group was opposed to activism. "We were saying that nobody knows, has the adequate information now," Brodine explained, "but when we find out what it is and get it out, then probably the whole organization will take a vote, are we or aren't we against the H-bomb."[35]

The first steering committee included several women and, interestingly, none of the founding scientists: Brodine, Gellhorn, Marcelle Malamas, Ralph Abele of the Metropolitan Church Federation (of which Gertrude Faust had been a vital part), and "a psychiatrist and a lawyer and two people from the union." The steering committee elected Commoner as the CNI's first president. The founding resolution of April 21, 1958, resolved to study the effects of nuclear fallout on the environment and to present scientists' findings to the public, since "decisions regarding the use of nuclear energy . . . are not now based, as they should be in a democracy, on an informed public opinion." The 185 diverse founders who signed the CNI's first

Figure 2.5 Barry Commoner speaks at the Committee for Environmental Information's 1970 annual meeting as folk singer and activist Pete Seeger looks on. A biologist at Washington University who served as the first president of the Committee for Nuclear Information, Commoner urged fellow scientists to keep the public well informed of the facts surrounding nuclear testing. *From the Committee for Environmental Information Records (S0069), State Historical Society of Missouri*

resolution included thirty-six doctors (most of them academic and nearly all men), nine Christian pastors (Catholic and Protestant), three rabbis, and ninety-three women, which meant that women composed just over half of the CNI's total membership. Forty-six of these founding women were married but listed without their husbands, thirty-five more were married and listed alongside their husbands, and twelve women on the roster were apparently not married.[36]

The CNI began disseminating information through its flagship journal, *Nuclear Information*. Brodine served as the journal's editor and became a sort of liaison between the scientists who wrote for it and readers who did not possess any background in science. Especially after 1959, *Nuclear Information* helped put St. Louis's nuclear women on the proverbial map, as interested activists, organizations, politicians, and scientists from around the world subscribed. Freelance writer Doris Deakin interviewed former pediatrician and self-described housewife Miriam Pennoyer about the potential connections between the Sr-90 in St. Louis's milk supply and rates of bone cancer and leukemia for an article titled "Mothers Ask—What Should We Feed Our Kids?" Pennoyer said, "We're finding that there are hot spots. The middlewest is one. We don't know why this is so."[37] Florence Moog, a biologist at Washington University, contributed an especially influential article in the September 1959 issue. Based on all the available data gathered on radioactive fallout for congressional hearings earlier that year, Moog described in a science-fiction format what an attack on St. Louis would be like. The report, "Nuclear War in St. Louis: One Year Later," became wildly popular. The CNI eventually distributed, in Commoner's estimation, forty-five thousand copies of that single issue. A company named Dynamic Films even approached the CNI about turning the manuscript into a movie, though a screenplay never materialized.[38]

Moog imagined two bombs striking St. Louis—one eight megatons, the other ten—and a worldwide total of seven thousand megatons exploding simultaneously. So powerful was the blast force in Moog's scenario that "east of Grand almost everybody was wiped out at once. From Grand to Big Bend some people survived the attack itself, but not many are still alive." Fires erupted as far as thirty miles away; people experienced third-degree burns twenty-two miles away. Radiation sickness and infection slowly worked on people in the metropolitan area, especially east of the city in Illinois, where the wind would likely carry the radioactive fallout. On the first day alone, Moog predicted five hundred thousand dead. But that was just the beginning of the devastation.[39]

Many experts had not properly described what a post–nuclear war world would look like, with no medical supplies available and the contamination of crops, food, and water within a hundred miles of the blast. Insects and rats would thrive in the absence of larger predators, making it even harder to produce uncontaminated food. The future of the human race seemed imperiled: worldwide, those who at first survived would develop blindness and cancer. There were sure to be genetic defects in children born to mothers exposed to large doses of radiation. Readers of the journal began to ask out loud if it was even possible to "win" a nuclear exchange with the Soviet Union. A follow-up article in the *Post-Dispatch* lauded *Nuclear Information*'s lesson that the "ecological damage" of nuclear fallout "alone could be disastrous." Far too many Americans dwelled on the immediate "holocaust of blast, fire and radiation" when perhaps they should consider "the disruption to the delicate balances of interrelationships which govern the survival of all living organisms."[40]

The CNI's most important innovation was the Baby Tooth Survey. The ingenious idea derived from biochemist Herman Kalckar's 1958 article in the international scientific journal *Nature*. Kalckar suggested that while collecting adult human bone for data analysis of Sr-90 uptake presented insurmountable logistical problems, scientists could conceivably collect enough deciduous teeth of children to get definitive results. The baby teeth of nine- and ten-year-olds in 1958 hypothetically contained a record of Sr-90 uptake, since they had formed *in utero* and early infancy precisely during the opening years of nuclear testing. At the time Kalckar published his article, the teeth of an eight-year-old born and raised in St. Louis contained a record of Sr-90 uptake in 1950; a seven-year-old, 1951; a six-year-old, 1952; and so on. Collecting these children's teeth would allow scientists to create a record of Sr-90 uptake in the human body. They could then trace spikes in Sr-90 levels to nuclear weapons tests, as well as compare regions and describe any "hot spots." Alfred S. Schwartz, a St. Louis pediatrician and vice-president of the CNI, believed scientists and citizens in St. Louis were up for the challenge; the city already had the basic infrastructure in place for starting such a survey, including a strong scientific community at Washington University and Saint Louis University and grassroots support from female activists.[41]

In 1959 the Atomic Energy Commission ceded its initial mandate to evaluate fallout damage to the Public Health Service, which awarded several large grants to the CNI to fund a world-class lab at Washington University's School of Dentistry in cooperation with the School of Dentistry at Saint Louis University.[42] The lab included a Geiger counter capable of precisely measuring twenty-five to ninety exfoliated and crushed baby teeth between two 250-pound steel plates, each carved out of the hull of a decommissioned World War I battleship.[43] By the time the lab at Washington University became operational in 1961, the head of the Baby Tooth Survey, Louise Zibold Reiss, declared: "Teeth can be collected on a large enough scale to get results," and "Analysis of deciduous teeth can provide information concerning strontium-90 deposition in bone." Reiss and her husband, Eric, helped found the CNI, and the steering committee elected Louise as the Baby Tooth Survey's first director.[44]

Once in effect, the Baby Tooth Survey clinched St. Louis nuclear women's leadership in the emergent environmental movement. At the outset, the CNI formed a subcommittee for the Baby Tooth Survey composed of five women and three men, including Barry Commoner and his wife, Gloria. They decided to organize the survey into a scientific advisory group and a public awareness campaign headed by Reiss. Reiss received funding for promotional fare and a few crucial staff members, including Sophia Goodman and Yvonne Logan. Still, she relied heavily on the efforts of "volunteer women," many of whom responded to calls for help on the women's pages of the *Globe-Democrat* and *Post-Dispatch*. Goodman, the executive secretary of the Baby Tooth Survey and mother, reported that there were numerous female volunteers, many of them "housewives who find the need to help others and feel our work is worthwhile."[45] Logan, also a mother, later became the executive director of the Baby Tooth Survey in addition to participating in the League of Women Voters and chairing the St. Louis Branch of the Women's International League for Peace and Freedom (WILPF).[46] She became instrumental in providing antinuclear activists in WILPF with up-to-date, scientifically verified information.[47] Reiss announced the full cooperation of the National Council of Catholic Women, who pledged to advertise the Baby Tooth Survey in the city's numerous Catholic schools, as well as the National Council of Jewish Women.[48] The Women's Auxiliary of the St. Louis Dental Association and the Junior League of Women donated their time collecting and cataloging teeth. Other female volunteers belonging to different educational programs and organizations spread the word—a vital accomplishment because the scientific advisory group required an estimated fifty thousand deciduous teeth per year.[49]

St. Louis's nuclear women took up the massive challenge of convincing hundreds of thousands of mothers of all races and creeds that scientists needed their children's teeth. Yvonne Logan, who succeeded Reiss as director of the Baby Tooth Survey, put it this way in one public service announcement: "Before that scientist can ever start to analyze baby teeth for strontium 90, a lot of you mothers and children have to help him." Here was one of the few scientific experiments geared towards mothers and their children. The May 1960 issue of *Nuclear Information* declared that the Baby Tooth Survey's Operation Tooth "is probably the only club in the world where children are an important part of the research team." Despite its novelty—or perhaps because of it—the response was "instantaneous and overwhelming," Barry Commoner recalled. The women at the Baby Tooth Survey managed to place donation forms in nearly every public and private school in the greater St. Louis area, as well as in many dentists' offices. Their media campaign targeted children in broadcasts on local television programs such as *Captain 11's Showboat, Romper Room, S. S. Popeye,* and *Wranglers' Cartoon Club.* Leading St. Louis newspapers published press releases on the CNI's need for baby teeth. The team at the Baby Tooth Survey also organized an educational program called Operation Tooth, which sent representatives to local schools for "tooth round-ups." Children who donated their teeth were asked to fill out a simple form identifying their residential background and age. In exchange they became members of the Operation Tooth Club, complete with an official certificate (Fig. 2.6) and a shiny button featuring a smiling child with a missing tooth. The caption read, "I Gave My Tooth to Science." In 1960, Mayor Raymond Tucker even declared the week of April 18 to be Tooth Survey Week. "Any child with a wobbly baby tooth is a person of consequence in St. Louis, Mo.," *Newsweek* announced to a national audience in its April 25, 1960, magazine issue.[50]

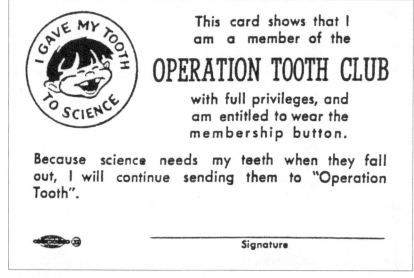

Figure 2.6 Children who donated teeth were welcomed into the Operation Tooth Club, receiving this membership card and the coveted "I Gave My Tooth to Science" button. Many donors also worked out special arrangements to continue receiving compensation from the Tooth Fairy. *From the Committee for Environmental Information Records (S0069), State Historical Society of Missouri*

Operation Tooth was a remarkably successful environmental campaign. Teeth started trickling in from all over the world, even though the Baby Tooth Survey initially sought teeth from within a 150-mile radius around St. Louis. Then came a deluge. By 1962, the survey reported 95,000 teeth collected. One year later, Sophia Goodman announced, "We have collected 127,000 teeth to date. Mothers and children accept it as part of the tradition—like the tooth fairy." By 1968, 287,000 baby teeth had been collected. Children everywhere were enthusiastic about the project. There was something giggly, profound, even empowering about the thought that their little tooth could help an adult scientist in a lab coat make important discoveries about nuclear bombs (little did they know their tooth was destined to be ground up into a powder and mixed in with a sample of forty or so other teeth). "This is my tooth. It is cute. Do you like it?" asked the Commoner's six-year-old son, Freddy, when he donated his tooth to science in 1959. "Today I lost my second baby tooth," wrote six-year-old Kent D. Votaw of Pasco, Washington, "and after my mommy read me the story of your campaign in our newspaper I wanted very much to contribute my tooth to your campaign."[51]

Some stoic children forwent their monetary reward from the Tooth Fairy for the sake of science. "I read in the paper about your Operation Tooth. I lost one of my tooth [sic] today," recounted Leslie Pierce of Lansing, Michigan, "and I decided to lose 50c and have that test done." One eleven-year-old donor from Decatur, Georgia, sent his tooth straight to Mayor Tucker's office in May 1960 after having read about Operation Tooth in an Atlanta paper: "As I want to be a doctor when I grow up I always put my tooth under my pillor [sic] for a dime but had rather the Scientists use this one." Tucker wrote back to the boy and enclosed a dime "so that you will not suffer any financial loss by turning this tooth over to the scientists rather than putting it under your pillow." Many mothers preserved the Tooth Fairy ritual by telling their children to write a special note and place it under their pillow with their tooth. "Dear Fairy, I would like to have a dime. But do not take my tooth," a young girl named Jill instructed the Tooth Fairy. "I am going to send it to siense [sic]." Young Don wrote the Good Fairy, "p.s. Please donate to science." Amy asked the "Good Fairy" to "Please send my tooth to Washington University."[52]

One of the biggest incentives for these young donors was the shiny Operation Tooth button they received in the mail. The pin bearing the slogan "I Gave My Tooth to Science" became a badge of honor. "I will be proud to wear the pin," declared Patty Hamley in June 1961, "and will tell [other] children about it." The buttons appeared on the covers of newspapers around the country and were coveted by children from afar. In May 1960, Peter Trapolino of Rochester, New York, asked the Baby Tooth Survey in earnest, "May I become a member of the Science Club too?"[53]

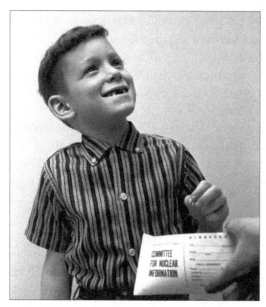

Figure 2.7 Seven-year-old Tommy Blumenthal of Clayton, Missouri, was one of tens of thousands of children who gave their teeth to the Baby Tooth Survey. *From the Arthur Witman 120mm Photograph Collection (S0732), State Historical Society of Missouri*

Once in full swing, the CNI and its tooth survey became a model not only for science-based public awareness campaigns but also for women's activism. Representatives of leading scientific research organizations and government agencies from across the United States expressed support for the CNI's work. The Division of Radiological Health of the US Public Health Service commended the CNI's journal, renamed *The Scientist and the Citizen* in 1961, for its "contribution toward greater understanding of the radiation problem, as it relates to the surrounding environment." Civil Defense offices found the publication invaluable. Senator Hubert H. Humphrey of Minnesota and other members of the Committee on Foreign Relations informed Virginia Brodine, the journal's editor, that the CNI's findings proved crucial to Humphrey's campaign to end the nuclear arms race.[54] Inspired by the success of the citizens of St. Louis, many environmental activists around the country began to express interest in forming their own baby tooth surveys to gauge Sr-90 levels in their communities.

Irene Hoglund, the chair of a Massachusetts branch of WILPF, recognized the St. Louis group's influence, writing to Sophia Goodman, "I find many young mothers who are concerned and want particularly to do something which might have a bearing upon their children. Many to whom I have explained your work are interested."[55]

In 1962, after the operation had been testing St. Louis–area baby teeth for a year, the Washington University lab's main supervisor, Harold Rosenthal, called for samples of teeth from other parts of the country sufficient for making comparisons. Women's groups such as the Ann Arbor Women for Peace in Michigan chose to send teeth they collected to St. Louis for analysis, rather than try to establish their own lab. Women from as far away as Alaska, California, and North Dakota also sent collections of teeth for analysis at Washington University. Their young donors received the much-desired buttons.[56]

The female-led Baby Tooth Survey inspired similar start-up tooth surveys in New York, Los Angeles, Montreal, Japan, and Germany.[57] The Montreal tooth survey originated with a grassroots group known as the Voices of Women. In 1960 this group formed the Citizens for Nuclear Disarmament, which followed CNI's lead in organizing both a team of science advisers and a Montreal Baby Tooth Survey directed by citizens. The appointed chair, Ethel Kesler, contacted Louise Reiss for information about the St. Louis operation, including specifics on the questionnaires for children tooth donors. Kesler informed Reiss on May 27, 1960, "We have gone ahead and made up our own questionnaire for distribution, using yours as a model." She added, "It will be necessary for us to have it translated into French as well." "Dans votre interet et celui de vos enfants aidez-nous a recueillir cette annee 50,000 dents de lait," read the first line of the Montreal Survey's first questionnaire, which featured a slightly altered version of the familiar smiling toothless child in the Baby Tooth Survey logo ("Will you and your children help us to collect 50,000 baby teeth this year?"). The Montreal survey sent its tooth samples to the Washington University lab and ordered ten thousand English-language "I Gave My Tooth to Science" buttons from a St. Louis manufacturer (in French, "J'ai fait don de ma dent a la science"). Kesler and the Montreal tooth survey continued to take cues from the original survey in St. Louis, its director Reiss, and its chairman of the Publicity Committee in 1961, Gloria Commoner.[58]

Even the Japanese Baby Tooth Survey of 1962 modeled its research and advertising on the St. Louis original. The Japanese organizers corresponded with Reiss, Brodine, and Goodman and based much of their organization's seminal study on reports in the CNI's *Scientist and the Citizen*. A nearly two-hundred-page Japanese-language study paid homage to the role of St. Louis's nuclear women on its front cover, which featured a picture of female American protestors. An American woman in the picture brandishes a sign bearing the message, "East & West Love Life [but] BOTH Don't Stop Testing"; another holds her child in one hand and a "Save Our Children!" sign in the other.[59]

Of the tooth surveys around the world, St. Louis's remained the largest and most successful. The findings of the St. Louis survey allowed CNI scientist Herman T. Blumenthal to announce a roughly thirty-fold rise in Sr-90 levels in children between 1951 and May 1963. Lab supervisor Harold Rosenthal later reported that the Sr-90 content in children had increased from 0.15 picocuries per gram of calcium in children born in 1950 to 4 picocuries for those born in 1960, in direct correlation to the increase in nuclear weapons testing during those years. "Although tooth surveys have been started in New York, Montreal and Tokyo," Goodman stated confidently in 1963, "ours is the only one making available data of this kind."[60]

Behind every one of these children's tooth donations and precious letters was a mother. "We wish it were possible for the unsung heroines (and heroes) of the study to come in for some kudos every time the Baby Tooth Survey is mentioned," one CNI newsletter announced. "We mean the MOTHERS (and fathers) who take the time and trouble to fill out the form, tape on the tooth, and mail it in."[61] Mothers taught their kids about environmental hazards and encouraged their children to help by donating their teeth. Many concerned mothers from across the country sent letters of their own requesting information on the survey's results, eager to discover whether their children were in danger.

A Political Sea Change

Murmurs of an impending women's strike for nuclear disarmament circulated in the media after a self-described housewife from New York City, Dagmar Wilson, urged housewives and mothers to protest nuclear weapons testing on September 22, 1961. Various branches of Wilson's organization, Women Strike for Peace (WSP), contacted the CNI in St. Louis to request information on potential connections between nuclear bomb tests and birth defects, mental disability, leukemia, and cancer. Although CNI did not take a political stance, many of its members supported Wilson's cause; Virginia

Brodine enthusiastically commended Wilson's work.[62] CNI scientist Eric Reiss, the husband of Louise Reiss, wrote to the health commissioner of St. Louis on October 25 that a "Russian superbomb" might spew radioactive iodine-131 across the United States. He recommended giving pregnant women and infants small doses of nonradioactive potassium iodide, a hypothetical preventive measure.[63]

On October 30, 1961, multiple seismographs of the US Geological Survey simultaneously recorded a shock that circled the Earth three times with a seismic body wave magnitude of 5.25. The Central Intelligence Agency quickly informed the president, John Kennedy, that the Soviets had detonated an H-bomb with an explosive yield large enough to shake the entire globe. The bomb was reported to be approximately fifty megatons, or 1,570 times the combined explosive yield of the atomic bombs dropped on Hiroshima and Nagasaki. Although President Kennedy guaranteed the American public in the days after the test that "No nuclear test in the atmosphere will be undertaken as the Soviet Union has done for so-called psychological or political reasons," many grew frightened by his additional pronouncement that "we shall make necessary preparations for such tests so as to be ready in case it becomes necessary to conduct them."[64] The Soviet test of October 30 and the dark subtext of Kennedy's statements frightened Americans into action.

On November 1, approximately fifty thousand American housewives went on strike in sixty cities around the country to end the nuclear weapons race. Women protested in downtown St. Louis; some brought along their infants in baby carriages. About eight hundred women in Washington, DC, picketed the Soviet Embassy and the White House. Several hundred in New York held demonstrations outside the Atomic Energy Commission office and the Soviet Union's offices at the United Nations. The *Post-Dispatch* reported that a couple of mothers donned "a placard shaped like a milk bottle and topped with a skull" that bore the caption "Milk: Death, Disease, Deformity."[65]

The political determination of self-described "housewives" in WSP came from a profound sense of maternity—what Catharine Stimpson has described as "feminine, not feminist."[66] According to WSP striker Amy Swerdlow, an educated, white, middle-class mother of four children, the "nuclear emergency" initially compelled her to join the picket lines. Swerdlow later remembered how Women Strike for Peace "helped me to find my own political voice and to act in my own name. It took me out of the suburbs . . . without feeling guilty about leaving my children. My justification for what some of us self-deprecatingly called 'movement jet-setting' was that WSPers had to leave the home to save it."

At first, many of the nuclear women embraced a relatively unthreatening, quasi-essentialist view that women *as women* were somehow more attuned to nature than the male leaders of the world—more nurturing, more sensitive to environmental damage, and thus better peacemakers. This was in line with traditional ideas about women's supposed maternal nature. As much could be seen in WILPF. For most of the 1960s, WILPF's leaders in St. Louis and at the national level spoke of "special fields where women can operate far more effectively than men. These are the fields of child care, education, consumers unions, to name only a few." The nuclear fallout crisis invoked each of these so-called "fields" as both motive and justification for feminine activism.[67]

Even so, such female-led outcries for halts on nuclear testing touted the promotion of women, rather than men, to political leadership roles as part of the solution. The very idea challenged the male-dominated US administration. In November 1961, this view—that the "woman's style" of handling the environment and foreign policy was bound to reap better results—became edgier. Not only were otherwise passive housewives and mothers now on the streets in protest, but WSP grew emboldened to simply bypass the government's typical diplomatic channels and send duplicate letters directly to the wives of the world's preeminent leaders. The letter writers urged Nina Khrushchev and Jacqueline Kennedy to "think what hope would gladden the world if women everywhere would rise to claim the right to life for their children and for generations yet unborn." Around the same time WILPF called a joint Soviet-American women's conference at Bryn Mawr, Pennsylvania, to collaborate with female Soviet activists, who they flew in for the occasion, on how women in both countries could bring about immediate nuclear disarmament. St. Louis's nuclear women continued to hold demonstrations against nuclear weapons testing, and in June 1963 the St. Louis branch of WILPF sent Yvonne Logan, a member of the National Board, to the highly publicized World Congress of Women in Moscow to inaugurate female-led peace diplomacy with the Russians.[68] The mood in Washington intensified as American leaders attempted an awkward balancing act between showing strength to deter Soviet aggression and compassion for the pleas of mothers who worried about their children's safety.

The Cuban Missile Crisis of October 1962 and several new findings of the CNI in St. Louis further animated antinuclear women's activism and forced another special congressional hearing on the effects of nuclear fallout in August 1963. At that very moment, the Baby Tooth Survey's long-awaited results came in. CNI's Eric Reiss informed the Joint Congressional Atomic Energy Committee that children residing in Nevada and Utah since 1951 had been exposed to dangerous amounts of fallout from about one-third of the ninety-nine atomic tests conducted in Nevada, especially since they received most of their milk from cows that pastured in contaminated areas. Reiss predicted a likelihood of at least twelve cases of thyroid cancer for every three thousand children who had lived in the area. The report sparked a firestorm of controversy around the country. "The St. Louis committee report is the first to assert," reported the *New York Times*, "that radiation exposures have reached levels at which there is general medical agreement that physical damage would result."[69]

Moreover, the St. Louis scientists demonstrated that much of the radiation had derived from more recent underground tests. Apparently, the United States' own underground tests were venting radiation into water, soil, and even the sky. A report in the *Wall Street Journal* stated that more than ninety bombs had been tested underground in Nevada since 1961; of this number, the AEC admitted that sixteen had resulted in venting, with five reaching the atmosphere. In at least one confirmed case in June 1962, "radioactivity in milk jumped in Spokane, Wash., following accidental venting of an underground explosion in Nevada."[70] This finding fueled an international crisis because Spokane was just one hundred miles south of the Canadian border.

Many Americans were outraged when they read the reports. In July 1963 the chairman of WILPF expressed deep concern about the AEC's outright denial that nuclear fallout had any measurable effects on humans: "As the levels of radioactivity increase in the environment and in the food we eat and feed to this nation's children—and the world's children—the tolerance of the human body for this poison does of course not increase accordingly. Merely announcing that higher levels of radioactivity are 'permissible' saves no child from leukemia nor any unborn baby from genetic damage."[71] In addition to testimony from St. Louis's CNI, Congress also heard from members of WSP, whose official statement of June 5, 1963, demanded "a nuclear test ban at once" on behalf of all "American mothers."[72]

On August 5, President Kennedy signed just such a test ban, which passed swiftly through the US Senate. CNI scientist Herman T. Blumenthal later estimated that if nuclear testing would have continued through 1965 at the same rate as in 1962, "there would have been a 100 fold increase in Sr 90 absorption by St. Louis one-year-olds." Effective October 10, 1963, the Nuclear Test Ban Treaty between the United States, Great Britain, and the Soviet Union became a testament to the growing political power of environmentally conscious and emboldened women. Many have attributed the test ban, at least in part, to the heroic efforts of women. Swerdlow believed that their "recognized contribution to the test ban treaty of 1963 . . . raised women's sense of political efficacy at a time when women were expected to exert their influence, not their power."[73] In this way, the Test Ban of 1963 proved to be a crucial turning point in the women's environmental movement.

The Legacies of Antinuclear Activism: Ecology and Liberation
With long-standing test bans in place, the antinuclear activists of St. Louis turned their attention to other important environmental and social issues. The CNI continued to support the Baby Tooth Survey until Washington University absorbed and ultimately discontinued the study in 1969. By then, above-ground testing had ceased long enough for the survey to record a dramatic decrease in Sr-90 uptake in St. Louis children, and scientists could safely assume, as long as the test ban remained in place, that levels of Sr-90 in Earth's atmosphere would remain negligible. Virginia Brodine encouraged the group to broaden its scope to other environmental issues. In 1963 the CNI announced its intention to tackle related environmental hazards. Malcolm Peterson of the CNI explained the connection: "Air pollution with smog; water pollution with industrial wastes; air, water, and food contamination with radioactivity are all examples of the way in which technological innovations have changed man's world." In this sense CNI took an "organizational initiative" in redirecting activists to other manmade chemical problems in the environment.[74]

In 1967 the organization elected to change its name to the Committee for Environmental Information (CEI), and the CEI renamed its journal *Environment* in 1969 to reflect broader aims. For Brodine, the organizational shift required "an enormous educational job." "I had just learned a little bit about radiation," she recalled in a 1972 interview, "now I had to learn about all these other things. . . . We set up scientific division committees. We had a very good air pollution committee. That was the first one.

We had a pesticide committee. . . ."[75] She elaborated on several left-leaning environmental policy suggestions in the journals *Air Pollution* (1972) and *Radioactive Contamination* (1975). Scientists of the CNI discovered that the common pesticide DDT (dichlorodiphenyltrichloroethane) was "more widespread than radioactive fallout," registering in the milk of nursing mothers up to "6 times the amount allowed in milk for commercial sale." The long-term effects on humans were not known at the time, and yet "One drop of toxaphene-DDT in 6,000 gallons," one fact sheet claimed, "will kill fish."[76] The CEI also investigated nuclear power plants and nuclear waste.

The nuclear women thus collectively forged a staging ground for the ensuing ecological and women's liberation movements of the 1960s. "Through participation in the WSP movement," Swerdlow has since suggested, "thousands of women who had identified themselves only as housewives found to their surprise that they could do serious research, write convincing flyers and pamphlets, speak eloquently in public, plan effective political strategies, organize successful long-range campaigns, and challenge male political leaders of the Left as well as the Right, to whom they had previously deferred."[77]

With a nuclear test ban in place, antinuclear activists pursued a new language to address the cultural and political concerns of the 1960s. The Women's International League for Peace and Freedom increasingly attended to Black civil rights, a "Mother's Lobby" protesting the Vietnam War, global nuclear disarmament, and "reclaiming" the environment in an "ecology crusade."[78] The roster of the St. Louis branch of WILPF doubled as a "Who's Who" list of antinuclear female activists in the city.[79] While many of these women pursued other issues after the Nuclear Test Ban Treaty of 1963, they uniformly supported WILPF through the 1960s and 1970s. WILPF members included early antinuclear activists such as Edna Gellhorn, Gertrude Faust, and Bonnie Hart; CEI leaders Virginia Brodine, Marcia Bauer, Gloria Commoner, Eleanor Blumenthal, Sophia Goodman, and Yvonne Logan; as well as Kay Drey of the Coalition for the Environment and Doris Bolef of WILPF's Scientific Contacts Committee.[80]

In addition to supporting the new ecology, many of the women in WILPF also gradually came to embrace second-wave feminism. Issue after issue of the organization's official newsletter, *Four Lights* (renamed *Peace and Freedom* after 1970), expected women to exert themselves as nurturing mothers, until in 1969 a shift in the organization's rhetoric revealed a new direction. Articles on the new "women's liberation movement" were featured in many issues after that. Former St. Louis branch member Doris Bolef, now speaking as the national vice president of WILPF, announced, "If we are to remain true to our pioneering heritage, we must change with the times . . . The black power and the women's liberation movements—both highly articulate, determined, and demanding changes in our political and economic system—has as much to teach us as we have to teach them." WILPF's president, Katherine Camp, also encouraged members to embrace the militant youths speaking up about gender and racial inequality on college campuses across America: "We must relate more intimately with the budding women's liberation movement here and around the world."[81]

After an October meeting in 1970, WILPF made "achieving women's liberation" one of its chief priorities, which meant supporting the swift passage of the Equal Rights Amendment. Women in WILPF were concerned by the lack of female representation in various sectors of American society. "Although women constitute more than half the population," one 1970 report claimed, "less than 3% of our national legislators are women"—and only 7 percent of doctors, 3 percent of lawyers, and 1 percent of engineers. The women of St. Louis, under the direction of longtime activist, Baby Tooth Survey director, and WILPF St. Louis chapter chair Yvonne Logan, made "Women's Liberation" and "Ecology" their top priorities for 1970. Betty Friedan's *The Feminine Mystique*, Margaret Mead's *Male and Female*, and Simone de Beauvoir's *The Second Sex* appeared on the organization's recommended reading lists. Contributors to the newsletter challenged women to think about their role in society. "Of course we are chiefly women," wrote Vice President Marion Edman, "but isn't that term taking on new meanings?"[82] In 1971, WILPF poured special energy into a commission for "Protection of the Environment," which focused on atomic energy and other pollutants, as well as a commission titled "Women's Liberation," which was devoted to fair employment, women's health, reproductive rights, and eliminating sexism.[83] Here was a kind of social activism that linked women and the environment in unique ways, such that "the devastation of the Earth" became synonymous with "the exploitation of women."[84]

Independent women, mothers, and housewives all campaigned tirelessly over the following years to secure the heritage of future generations. The nation's first ever Earth Day on April 22, 1970, became a roaring success and ultimately a significant moment in the history of the environment and women's activism. The Coalition for the Environment's local coordinator for Earth Week in St. Louis, Mrs. J. K. Street, considered Earth Day that year "an overwhelming success" because "millions of people, drawn from all segments of society, turned out . . . to peacefully demonstrate their environmental concern." A string of governmental regulations protecting the environment ensued, including the creation of the Environmental Protection Agency and the Clean Air Act.[85] Activists embraced the term "ecology" (from the Greek *oekologie*, or study of "home") to identify a way of thinking analytically about the relationships between human and nonhuman nature. As American women campaigned against environmental hazards, they also discovered a new sense of their place in nature and society.

3. The Gospel of the Gay Ghetto

Trinity Episcopal Church, the Urban Crisis, and the
Origins of Queer Activism in St. Louis

Ian Darnell

MORE THAN IN ANY OTHER single place, queer activism in St. Louis got
its start in the parish hall of Trinity Episcopal Church. Within months of
New York City's Stonewall Rebellion of June 1969 and through the early
1970s, the Mandrake Society—the city's earliest locally based gay rights
group—met at this handsome stone church in the diverse Central West End
neighborhood. Accompanied by the smell of incense and the sound of altar bells, members of the Mandrake Society discussed issues such as police
harassment, planned events such as drag balls, and otherwise strategized
about the group's mission to "equalize the status and position of the homosexual with the status and position of the heterosexual."[1] Trinity Episcopal
Church served as a home base for these queer activists as they helped lay
the foundations for a flowering of local gay and lesbian activism later in the
1970s and for the region's vibrant, visible, and politically influential LGBTQ
movement of subsequent decades.

Trinity did more than just provide a meeting space for the Mandrake
Society. By the start of the 1970s, a contingent of openly gay men worshipped at Trinity and were active in the life of the parish. At a time when
queer people faced intense social stigma and legal discrimination in St.
Louis and across America, Trinity welcomed them. The church even purchased advertising space in the newsletter of the Mandrake Society, announcing to its readers, "All people . . . including each of you . . . are invited
to attend all services in this historic Anglo-Catholic parish church whose
special mission is to serve the entire community."[2] In 1971, one local gay
activist told the *St. Louis Post-Dispatch*, "Trinity accepts people for what
they are."[3] Trinity was on the cutting edge of one of the most dramatic shifts
in America's recent social history: the integration of openly queer people
into mainstream community institutions.

This chapter seeks to explain how the Trinity Episcopal Church of the 1960s and 1970s came to serve as a sort of midwife of gay liberation in St. Louis. To do so, it focuses on the social transformations wrought by white flight and neighborhood decline in the post–World War II decades and on liberal Protestantism's response to this urban crisis. This approach reveals how Trinity's progressive attitude toward sexual difference was closely related to its atmosphere of racial integration and paralleled its support for the Black freedom struggle.

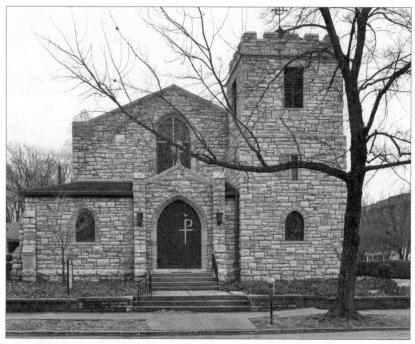

Figure 3.1 Trinity Episcopal Church in 2021, at the northeast corner of Washington and North Euclid Avenues, with the main church building looking much as it did in the 1950s. *Photo by Matthew J. Mancini*

The roots of Trinity's emergence as a hub of queer organizing can be traced to a pivotal moment in the early 1950s. Founded nearly a century before, Trinity had always been an exclusively white congregation, and its members had tended to be respectable professionals. In the years after World War II, however, the parish found itself amid a neighborhood that was rapidly changing because of a growing population of African Americans and an exodus of white families to the booming suburbs. Faced with plummeting attendance and uncertain prospects, Trinity's lay leadership was ready to close the doors of its long-standing Central West End building. During this era, many similar congregations in St. Louis and elsewhere in urban America dissolved or relocated to the suburbs. But Trinity took a different path.

One Sunday in 1953, many of the parish's remaining members met to decide Trinity's future. After hours of deliberation, they resolved to keep Trinity in place and to reaffirm its identity as a "neighborhood parish."[4] Through the remainder of the 1950s and the 1960s, members of Trinity in large measure achieved this aim—and in the process embraced a more inclusive vision of community belonging.

One dimension of this transformation was that the parish became racially integrated, with about a third of the congregation made up of African Americans by the mid-1960s.[5] Another was that Trinity became a community anchor in what one contemporary sociologist described as St. Louis's "gay ghetto"—an area of the city, roughly overlapping with the Central West End, with an unusually concentrated and visible queer population and a cluster of queer social spaces.[6] Trinity came to welcome gay members and to aid St. Louis's pioneering queer activists by extending the ethos of inclusion and neighborhood engagement that had led to its decision to stay in the city and to open the parish to African Americans.

As a racially integrated church in a substantially queer neighborhood, Trinity offers an atypical but illuminating perspective on St. Louis's urban history in the 1960s and 1970s. Exemplified by Colin Gordon's *Mapping Decline*, much of the scholarship on St. Louis and other American cities in this era focuses on social and spatial divides and tells stories grounded in loss and failure.[7] Indeed, dramatic population decline, racial conflict, and persistent segregation shaped urban life in these decades. However, Trinity's history evidences an important countercurrent. The processes usually interpreted as "urban decline" sometimes generated creative responses and catalyzed connections across social boundaries. Institutions in these changing neighborhoods could be sites of encounter and cooperation where community was reimagined in more inclusive terms. The racially mixed and gay-affirming congregation that emerged at Trinity—and the queer activism that the parish nurtured—are important alternative legacies of the demographic upheavals of this era.

This chapter joins other works that take stock of liberal (or ecumenical) Protestantism's often-overlooked impact on American history since World

War II. In 2011, historian of religion David Hollinger noted that scholars have been "slow to see" the role that liberal Protestantism played in forging a "more widely dispersed and institutionally enacted acceptance of ethnoracial, sexual, religious, and cultural diversity." Hollinger especially credited liberal Protestants' "egalitarian impulses and capacities for self-interrogation" as drivers of these changing attitudes.[8]

One crucial contribution of liberal Protestantism to progressive change in American society has been its support of gay and lesbian activism. From the beginning of the field of queer history, some scholars have noted, if only peripherally, liberal Protestantism's role in the rise of the movement. In his trailblazing 1983 account of lesbian and gay political organizing in the 1950s and 1960s, John D'Emilio gives passing attention to the sympathetic response of some Protestant clergy to the emergent homophile movement. He documents early instances of cooperation between ministers and activists, most notably the founding of the Council on Religion and the Homosexual in San Francisco in 1964.[9] More recently, Heather Rachelle White's *Reforming Sodom* explores debates between liberal and fundamentalist Protestants over the morality of homosexuality, demonstrating that some Christian thinkers were important defenders of the early gay and lesbian movement.[10]

Despite this scholarship, the positive contributions of religion generally and liberal Protestantism specifically tend to be overlooked in both popular and scholarly narratives of queer political organizing. This may in part stem from the prominence of conservative religious opponents of queer equality, from the Roman Catholic hierarchy to Anita Bryant to the show-stealing Westboro Baptist Church.[11] However, the present chapter and Chapter 8 in this volume, Rodney C. Wilson's study of the Metropolitan Community Church of Greater St. Louis, both demonstrate that religion was essential to the movement for queer liberation in St. Louis as it got off the ground in the late 1960s and 1970s.

What follows is a study of the liberal Protestant affirmation of sexual and racial diversity at the grassroots. It demonstrates how ideas about the proper Christian response to human difference and the crisis of America's cities found expression in the context of one remarkable neighborhood: the Central West End, St. Louis's racially liminal "gay ghetto" of the 1960s and 1970s. This convergence of place and principle set the stage for gay liberation in the St. Louis area.

Evangelizing the Inner City
Liberal Protestantism Responds to the Urban Crisis

Trinity's decision to remain in the urban core and to welcome the new Black residents of its neighborhood was one example of a national phenomenon. During the post–World War II era of urban decline, white flight, and mass suburbanization, many liberal Protestant clergymen and some lay people were preoccupied with taking a stand in the cities and making new converts there. They persuaded their denominations to invest considerable resources toward reaching out to "unchurched" city-dwellers and maintaining congregations in the urban cores. "One of the most exciting missionary opportunities of our age lies open to the Church in the inner city," concluded a panel of Episcopal priests from across the country in 1959. "The inner city," they declared, had become "the new missionary country."[12]

Liberal Protestant evangelism in cities had multiple, intertwined aims. On the one hand, members of missionizing churches sought to uplift dispossessed city-dwellers by providing them with cultural and educational opportunities and social services. On the other hand, these churches also sought to win souls for Christ and to shore up their respective denominations' influence in the urban cores.

In some ways, these urban churches resembled Protestant city missions and religiously affiliated settlement houses of the nineteenth and early twentieth centuries.[13] During the post–World War II decades, however, inner-city missionizing differed from previous eras in at least two important respects. First, the postwar liberal ideal of tolerance led to a more sympathetic posture toward cultural diversity. In particular, with the rise of the civil rights movement, these congregations vigorously condemned white supremacy and racial segregation, disavowing an earlier history of segregated houses of worship and complicity in Jim Crow.[14] Second, the demographic upheavals of the postwar era seemed to put mainline Protestant churches' very presence in the inner cities in jeopardy and infused the project of urban evangelism with great urgency. "Those of us who have studied and worked in the urban-industrial church are painfully aware of the crisis at hand," wrote Episcopal clergyman G. Paul Musselman in his 1960 call-to-arms, *The Church on the Urban Frontier.* "We feel that the Church must speak out soon and plainly if it is to save dozens of parishes which are becoming paralyzed by economic and sociological change." For Musselman, the Church was in "a race against time . . . to engage all its forces in what might well be a life or death struggle for many parishes." Meanwhile, a panel of Episcopal priests also warned, "Unless dioceses make a radical reassessment in their attitude toward [urban evangelism], our Church will lose the whole city."[15]

By the early 1950s, the Episcopal Church in St. Louis had already concluded that the declining population and changing racial makeup of the city required a sustained program of neighborhood evangelism. In November 1953, on the heels of Trinity's service of rededication, the Rev. Joseph G. Moore, director of the Unit of Research and Field Study of the National Council of the Protestant Episcopal Church, directed St. Louis's urban churches to reach out to their neighbors. Moore listed seven city congregations, Trinity among them, where "an intensive program of evangelism" in the surrounding neighborhood was "vital" and three others in or near the city where such efforts "would be useful." He recommended that priests at these churches organize committees of parishioners to "study the needs of their communities so that new neighborhood families can be brought into these congregations." Moore suggested several ways that Episcopalians in the city might attract new members: adult education programs; discussion groups; and parish-based programs for "the aged," "the underprivileged," and other "segments of the community" that lacked organizations of their own.[16]

Through the remainder of the 1950s and 1960s, the efforts of urban congregations to win converts and address neighborhood problems were of great concern to Episcopal leaders in St. Louis. The Missouri edition of the national Episcopal newspaper *Forth* published a regular column called "Church's Work in the City . . . Everyone's Problem and Responsibility." Alongside its headline was a sketch of the face of Christ set amid the St. Louis skyline. In the February 1955 installment of the column, a priest from one of the "town and country" parishes explained why suburban and rural Episcopal congregations should help finance the diocese's City Mission Society. "The whole shifting pattern of the cultural scene finds our cities becoming jungles of factory slums and waste-places over-housed with desperate people who have lost all hope," he wrote. "Their help must come from those who live outside . . . [from] those who can obey Christ's injunction concerning even the least of our brethren, and manifest their concern for those stranded on the wasting beaches of our big city streets."[17] The priest's comments suggest the dual purpose of the Episcopal Church's engagement with the urban core, which sought to alleviate the material poverty of city-dwellers while also ministering to their spiritual needs.

The 1956 film *The World Within* showcased the Episcopal Church in St. Louis's urban missionizing efforts as they were getting off the ground.

Filmed on location and based on an "original story" by William Matheus, a local parish worker, it tells the story of George, a white teenage boy growing up in "deep downtown St. Louis." Every day after school, George takes "a shortcut through the alley, past lidless garbage cans, overflowing ashpits, and through the aroma of backyard outhouses." At the end of his journey, he makes his way "up three flights of rickety steps" that cling "desperately to [the] worn brick wall" of a tenement house. George tells the viewer that this is "home—four families, thirteen kids, one outhouse. This is how my people live."

Stifled by poverty, tempted by crime, and bored by a life spent "on the street corner," George finds purpose, community, and faith at St. Stephen's House, an Episcopal congregation on the Near South Side (Fig. 3.2). Invited in one day by a friend, George begins to come to St. Stephen's regularly, taking part in handicraft classes and amateur theater and developing a passion for photography in the church's darkroom. "From the start, they treated me like an individual, someone important enough to care about," George says of the adult congregants. "Here I counted as someone, with a personality of my own."

Figure 3.2 St. Stephen's House, at Sixth and Rutger Streets, in the 1930s. Once a noted site of settlement-house activity, the Episcopal congregation was a leader in interracial ministry during the 1950s. In 1961, the church relocated to a new building a half-mile to the west and soon emerged as a significant center for civil rights and Black liberation organizing work. St. Louis Globe-Democrat *photo, from the collections of the St. Louis Mercantile Library at the University of Missouri–St. Louis*

At St. Stephen's House, George is also introduced to the Episcopal Church. While attending mass there and listening to the Gospel, he feels "wonderfully moved." Later, he is baptized and confirmed. After receiving the Blessed Sacrament, George "sense[s] that [he is] part of a worldwide communion, dedicated to building a better world in [Christ's] name." At the conclusion of the film, a grown-up George—smartly dressed in a suit and with carefully combed hair—returns to St. Stephen's to teach Sunday school to a new crop of boys from the neighborhood. "You know about institutions that have run away from the inner city," George observes, "but you know that St. Stephen's won't run away."[18]

It is difficult to say how accurately *The World Within* captured the perspectives and experiences of the neighborhood youths who came in contact with St. Stephen's in these years. It does, however, offer a clear picture of the hopes that liberal Protestants held for the kind of urban evangelism underway in St. Louis. *Now*, the newspaper of the Episcopal Diocese of Missouri, boasted that the "inspired Churchmen" of St. Stephen's were "following God's people where they go—bringing the Church and the good news of Jesus Christ!"[19]

In 1957, St. Stephen's set up a mission on the Near South Side near the Darst Apartments, a newly constructed public housing project intended for hundreds of poor Black and white residents. The mission was also near two other large public housing projects. The new mission at first took the form of a three-room chapel located in a converted corner flat, which had been renovated by volunteers. It opened its doors "for neighborhood use" in February with its first weeknight fellowship meeting.[20]

By May, members of St. Stephen's and the congregation's "new friends" in the neighborhood had begun to march through the streets to "bear witness to their Church and to their Lord and Savior." Every Sunday, congregants paraded along a winding, nine-block route from the congregation's mission near the Darst Apartments to St. Stephen's House itself. They carried banners and a processional cross, and along the way "the group [made] its rounds, stopping to call for friends at their home[s]." This weekly procession, reported *Now*, "acquaints people with their neighborhood, St. Stephen's parish and the Episcopal Church. It also serves as an icebreaker." A photograph accompanying *Now*'s article on the processions featured a group of marchers—Black and white, adults and children—filling a sidewalk. At its close, the article noted, "Episcopalians are not used to witnessing on street corners—some of us do not find it easy." But considering the pressing demands of urban evangelism, it concluded, "there are things the Church ought to be doing—at St. Stephen's House they are trying."[21]

Like Trinity during the same period, St. Stephen's succeeded in bringing African Americans into its congregation. A 1958 photograph of some members of that year's confirmation class suggests the church's racial mixture and ability to win new members. Of the sixteen people pictured, five are white and ten are Black. Most of the students preparing to enter the Episcopal Church are children; however, of the five adult initiates to the church, all are Black.[22]

Overcoming racial divisions, however, was not a simple task for congregations in changing urban surroundings. For example, the priests and congregants of the Episcopal Church of the Ascension struggled to relate to residents of their institution's racially transitioning neighborhood. Founded in 1888, Ascension had long been "one of the city's best known parishes" and a fixture in St. Louis's West End neighborhood, an area that sat at the city's western boundary north of Delmar Boulevard and was distinct from the Central West End. Postwar white flight transformed the neighborhood, however; the formerly white community had become "almost entirely Negro" by 1960. While there was "a strong nucleus of both old and new members in the nearby area of the church," most congregants had moved to the suburbs. Few of the new residents of the now "highly transient" neighborhood seemed interested in the parish. *Now* reported that the remaining members of Ascension had come to see that the parish's situation was on the forefront of "the most critical issue facing the American church today— the battle line of the Inner City." To "grapple in new and dramatic ways with the challenges before it," Ascension's members launched a "crash program of neighborhood evangelism" that sought to make the parish "relevant to its neighbor." At an "Institute on the Inner City" held at Ascension in January 1961, the Reverend Dr. David Cox asked the assembled parishioners to consider, "Why does the Church become separated from the people who live in the community?"[23]

Congregations that survived during the urban crisis tended to prioritize overcoming racial barriers. By the early 1960s, for example, St. Stephen's had begun to emphasize interracialism in its urban missionizing efforts. In May 1963, the congregation initiated "the most extensive door-to-door evangelistic endeavor ever conducted in [its] eighty-one year history." The "theme" of the project was "In Christ's Name We Meet Our Neighbors." Over three days, forty-eight volunteers from St. Stephen's and seven other

St. Louis–area Episcopal congregations visited hundreds of apartments in three predominantly Black public housing projects near the parish. "The goal of the callers," reported *Now*, "was to discover the names of persons in the immediate parish community who were unchurched, lapsed in their Christian commitments or seriously looking for a more meaningful experience with another Christian [denomination]." Of the 1,250 households that were contacted, "approximately 300 families and individuals indicated to Churchmen an interest to learn more about St. Stephen's and the Episcopal Church." *Now* noted that the dozens of volunteers who knocked on doors in the public housing projects "sought face-to-face contact with God's people of many racial, cultural, economic, and national backgrounds." The volunteers themselves, meanwhile, were both white and Black and from suburban and city parishes.[24]

St. Stephen's concern with diversity and efforts to overcome social divisions were widespread in contemporary liberal Protestantism. Church leaders recognized that the success of this endeavor would require that parishioners adopt an attitude of inclusion. George Cadigan, the bishop of the Episcopal Diocese of Missouri, captured this spirit of inclusion in a 1963 pastoral letter: "It must be made clear that our churches are open to every child of God." He then quoted a recent message from the national Episcopal Church's Presiding Bishop Arthur C. Lichtenberger (formerly bishop of Missouri): "Discrimination within the Body of the Church itself is an intolerable scandal. Every congregation (and every church organization) has a continuing need to examine its own life and to renew those efforts to insure its inclusiveness fully."[25] Although Cadigan's pastoral letter was prompted by the recent March on Washington and "the present racial crisis," it is noteworthy that its call for inclusion was not framed in specifically racial terms. Instead, it called for universal fellowship in Christ—"*every* child of God" was to be welcomed in the church.

"A Church in This Neighborhood"
Reconstituting Community at Trinity Episcopal Church

Founded in 1855, Trinity moved from near downtown St. Louis to the corner of North Euclid Avenue and Washington Avenue in the Central West End in 1935.[26] This neighborhood experienced dramatic demographic and social change through the course of the twentieth century.[27]

Since the end of the nineteenth century, the Central West End had been a bastion of St. Louis's well-to-do. Attracted by the area's distance from the bustling central business district to the east, people of means built their mansions in the neighborhood's grand private places. Seeking to control the processes of urban change, they employed restrictive covenants to keep out people and activities they regarded as undesirable.[28] For a time, they succeeded. Through most of the 1920s, the Central West End was eminently respectable and fashionable among St. Louis's white elites.[29]

The character of the neighborhood had already begun to shift by the time Trinity established itself in the neighborhood. Many affluent St. Louisans had begun to relocate from the Central West End and similar neighborhoods to new homes in St. Louis's first automobile-oriented suburbs, such as Ladue. The population beyond the city limits in suburbanizing St. Louis County grew dramatically in in the 1920s and 1930s. This contrasted with the city of St. Louis itself, where growth slowed in the 1920s, and the population decreased for the first time from one census to another in the 1930s.[30] "One must . . . appreciate the suburban growth that has characterized St. Louis County in recent years," the *St. Louis Globe-Democrat* reported in 1934. "More and more have men with the financial means necessary provided for themselves and their families sumptuous retreats in the country where, removed from turmoil of the city, they may enjoy a bucolic life, although their business interests remain in St. Louis."[31]

These processes accelerated after World War II, when many more of the neighborhood's remaining well-to-do white residents relocated to suburban St. Louis County. They were replaced by newcomers, both white and Black, who often moved into large single-family homes that had been converted into rooming houses.

The Reverend Arthur Walmsley, Trinity's rector during in the early 1950s, remembered that during his tenure "attendance was down [and] changes in the [Central] West End of St. Louis were drastically affecting Trinity and nearby congregations." "I recognized the crunch which the [Central] West End faced because of blockbusting tactics by real estate interests," Walmsley recalled, "practices which hurried white flight to the new suburbs and imposed unrealistic financial obligations on a majority of the colored . . . new residents of the neighborhood." The parish was in crisis.[32]

In 1952, the Rt. Reverend Arthur C. Lichtenberger, at the time bishop of the Episcopal Diocese of Missouri, asked Trinity's remaining members to keep the church in the Central West End and moreover to "expand its program, particularly with reference to the neighborhood." The parish remained in limbo for some time as its lay leadership considered

Lichtenberger's request. Then, in July 1953, Walmsley, another priest from a nearby parish, and "some thirty or forty" congregants—then nearly half of the parish's active members—assembled at the diocesan retreat center to consider the question, "What is the role of Trinity today?" At the end of the day, they decided to take up Lichtenberger's challenge and to renew their commitment the Central West End and its inhabitants. In September 1953, Lichtenberger held a "service of re-dedication" at Trinity to celebrate the launch of its new mission.[33]

Soon afterward, some Black Episcopalians who had moved to the neighborhood began attending early morning mass at Trinity. "As their comfort level grew," Walmsley recounts, they asked to join the parish. While several members of Trinity were active in local civil rights struggles and Walmsley himself had participated in Committee of Racial Equality (CORE) sit-ins at downtown dining establishments, other congregants were reluctant to integrate the church. "At a highly-charged vestry meeting," Walmsley recalls, "I stood firm on the principle that we did not count membership or communicant standing on the basis of race. To the everlasting credit of the people at Trinity, no one left over the matter."[34]

Having decided to remain in the city in 1953, Trinity became a neighborhood church in the years that followed, even as the Central West End became racially mixed and a hub of the region's lesbian and gay community life. Its success depended on the congregation's capacity to expand its vision of acceptable human difference and to adopt an inclusive vision of community. "Daily the church must service the people who are here," the Reverend Anthony Morely, then Trinity's rector, told a reporter for St. Louis Magazine in 1963. "Our job is not to determine who they shall be." The reporter observed that Trinity's communicants were indeed "a microcosm of the diverse community" of the Central West End.[35]

By 1958, five years after Trinity's lay leaders had voted to stay in the Central West End, about a quarter of the parish's members were Black.[36] While some of the new congregants at Trinity were Black Episcopalians who had approached the church on their own initiative, Trinity joined other urban Episcopal parishes such as St. Stephen's in a program of evangelizing the surrounding community. "The theology is this: we are a church in this neighborhood," Morely, who had replaced Walmsley two years before, told Now in 1960. "What can we do in it, with it, for it?" After conducting a "neighborhood survey," a committee of parishioners discovered that some seventy Black children lived within one block of Trinity and perhaps two hundred within two blocks of the church. The committee members determined that "a non-religious supervised recreation program . . . was needed, even strongly desired, by the Negro families living literally next door to the Parish." Volunteers from the parish organized a program of activities for neighborhood children, including ball games at nearby Forest Park and movie screenings, story hours, crafts, and games at the church.[37] Later, study halls, after-school tutoring sessions, and other programs were introduced.[38] Dozens of children participated in these activities at the church, which, according to *Now*, served as a site of "inclusive community life" in an area that otherwise had "very little" of it.[39]

As with the Episcopal Church's other efforts in the city of St. Louis during the 1950s and 1960s, Trinity's outreach to neighborhood youths seems to have been motivated both by concerns about the children's poverty and by a desire to recruit new members. On the one hand, the church sought to "broaden the horizons of the underprivileged," and, according to Charlotte Brown, a parish historian, "the church maintained a definite policy not to proselytize since many of the neighborhood families belonged to other denominations." On the other hand, Brown noted, "Whenever Fr. Morely took the little boys to the bathroom, he took them through the church and taught them to genuflect!" Meanwhile, in its coverage of Trinity's programs, *Now* referred to the neighborhood children as "potential parishioners."[40]

In any case, Trinity did attract some of its Black neighbors to the church. Trinity's success at surviving amid a changing urban neighborhood and at integrating its congregation drew accolades from outside St. Louis. In July 1965, *The Living Church*, a national Episcopal magazine, named Trinity a "Distinguished Congregation" and published a cover story on the parish. Trinity had been nominated for the honor by an "out-of-town visitor" who had attended mass there one Sunday morning. "It was one of the most inspiring experiences I have had," the visitor attested. "This is a completely integrated congregation that truly lives in its church." According to *Now*, "Careful investigation and research bore out the truth of [the visitor's] statement."[41]

The article in *The Living Church* reported that nearly a third of the parish's members were Black, "with children equally divided racially." By the time of the article's publication, Black members of the congregation had served on the lay leadership board, and Yolanda Williams, a Black woman who lived near the church, had taken charge of the church's after-school tutoring program. Photographs accompanying the article show Black and white members of the congregation standing beside each other in pews at mass. According to *The Living Church*, Trinity's congregation was also diverse in terms of class, occupation, and way of life:

> There are rich and poor, professionals and middle class of both races. In the parish are the principal of a high school in the wealthiest suburban school district, a couple of physicians engaged in research at Barnes hospital, a Negro psychiatric social worker recently honored by a St. Louis newspaper as a "Woman of Achievement," another Negro who operates a one-man print shop, and many disadvantaged of all ages.

"In short," the article concluded, "a description of the 'face' of the parish would read like a description of the 'face' of its community."[42]

Trinity and the Birth of Gay Liberation in St. Louis

The diversity of Trinity's neighborhood not only resulted from a substantial presence of African Americans. It also had to do with the rise of what some contemporary queer St. Louisans referred to as a "gay ghetto" in the Central West End. More recently referred to as "gayborhoods," "gay ghettoes" were urban neighborhoods characterized by an unusually large and visible concentration of queer residents and queer social spaces. A product of the social dynamics of the twentieth-century urban history, they resulted both from queer people's desire to claim space and build community and from discriminatory practices that tended to push gender and sexual minorities into marginal or transitional areas.[43]

Going back even before World War II, evidence suggests that there was a noteworthy presence of queer white residents in in the surrounding area. In the latter half of the 1930s, for example, Mabel Thorpe's Cocktail Lounge near the intersection of Olive and North Sarah Streets hosted popular floorshows by "female impersonators." These drew complaints from neighbors who objected to "indecent songs," and anti-vice crusaders pointed out that the entertainers violated St. Louis's municipal ordinance against "masquerading" in the clothes of the opposite sex.[44] The incipient queerness of the neighborhood in these years may have been related to its relatively high concentration of apartment buildings, rooming houses, and other kinds of multifamily rental housing—an environment that made the area more hospitable than other parts of the city to life outside of the strictures of heteronormativity.[45]

St. Louis Gay Lib presents **the** Social Event of the season... the annual

Valentine Party

Saturday ♥ Feb. 12 ♥ 8 PM

4530 McPherson

admission $1.00   door prize

Figure 3.3 The 1972 party referenced here, held at an apartment house just west of North Taylor Avenue, speaks to the Central West End's role as a hub for queer sociality and activism. *From the Laura Ann Moore Papers, Department of Special Collections, Washington University in St. Louis*

The neighborhood around Trinity solidified its reputation as St. Louis's "gay ghetto" in the post–World War II period. About sixty blocks in size, the area was described in 1972 by sociologist Laud Humphreys as a "bohemian community of high social and racial diversity" with a "high proportion of homosexual residents." A half-dozen gay bars operated in the neighborhood, including some so popular that they "lock their doors before midnight because they have reached the maximum number of customers allowed by fire-department regulations."[46] In 1969, a man arrested in the area for dressing in drag told a vice officer, "In this part of the city all the fellows are Gay."[47] While clearly hyperbolic, the man's statement is suggestive of the degree to which St. Louis's gay community had rooted itself in the neighborhood by the end of the 1960s.

The queerness of the Central West End in these years is suggestive of an important but often overlooked dimension of the post–World War II urban crisis: these years not only saw a change in the racial geography of the American metropolis, but also in its sexual geography. The migration of white families to the suburbs not only meant that many cities came to have proportionally larger African American populations, but also proportionally larger populations of unmarried, childless, and in many cases queer adults.[48]

There are intriguing hints that Trinity had already begun to cultivate ties to the queer community that surrounded it around the time that the parish committed to staying in the Central West End. In a 1999 reminiscence on his years as Trinity's rector, Arthur Walmsley recalled, "Trinity proved to be a remarkably resilient and creative community. We even had our own 1950s version of the blessing of same-sex unions when I was asked to preside at house blessings of a number of parishioners living in committed relationships; it's clearly inappropriate not to bless all the rooms in a house or apartment."[49] This statement suggests that during his tenure at Trinity, Walmsley was not only aware that there were queer people among his parishioners, but was also willing to affirm the holiness of their "committed relationships" by blessing their shared living spaces. At this point, however, these seemed to have been only tentative and private gestures.

From the mid-1950s onward, Trinity's neighborhood evangelism attracted queer white people living in the Central West End for much the same reason that it attracted Black families in the area. Indeed, much of the language used by Trinity's outreach was not framed in specifically racial terms, and most of the residents of Trinity's census tract remained white in the 1950s and 1960s. "We must be willing to explore new ways of attracting the interest of people who live in our neighborhood," the Reverend Morely told *Now* in 1963. "We want them to know who we are and why we're here. It's important to us that we find different ways of making it possible for them to discover the meaning of the worship we would share with them." To this end, Trinity organized adult discussion groups, musical performances, and theatrical productions at the church. In January 1963, Trinity held a "jazz mass" with a full band and children's choirs. "Special invitations to participate in this service [were] extended to all residents of the Trinity Church area," *Now* reported. A guest preacher from the diocesan cathedral was also invited to deliver a sermon at the service directed to non-Episcopalians who might be in attendance. "[Rev.] Morely and I are convinced that many people will come to this service out of curiosity who might otherwise never darken the doorway of Trinity Church, even though it is just around the corner from them," the preacher told *Now*.[50]

There was even a place where gay nightlife in the Central West End intersected with liberal Protestants' urban evangelism. In 1964, a coalition of St. Louis churches opened a coffeehouse called The Exit. It was located at Westminster Place and Boyle Avenue, six blocks east of Trinity in the Gaslight Square entertainment district. It was within easy walking distance of a number gay and gay-friendly bars and cafés. Open at night, staffed by volunteers from area churches, and hosting poetry readings and folk music performances, The Exit, as *Now* noted, attracted "hordes" of patrons, including many of the neighborhood's "Bohemian residents." "By flickering candlelight over cups of steaming coffee or tea or cocoa," *Now* reported, "they come together to talk, sit, listen, heckle, stare, make out, argue, quarrel in the knowledge that someone cares, cares who they are, cares what they are!" The Exit was a "Christian adventure" whose purpose was to introduce "students, beats, artists, drifters, the cautious and the curious" to "Christian people who . . . want to communicate the Gospel in meaningful new symbols." It was "the Church in the world" and "a stage where we can allow the Holy Spirit to act."[51]

The Exit hosted public discussions on controversial social and political issues of the day, including homosexuality. It also apparently attracted many queer patrons. In 1966, *The Phoenix*, a Kansas City–based publication that called itself as "the Midwest Homophile Voice," described The Exit as "half gay and half straight."[52] While at its core an evangelizing enterprise, The Exit also suggests how liberal Protestant churches of the era were willing to broaden their conception of morality and the limits of their community. Rev. Ed Stevens, one of the coordinators of The Exit, said that the patrons of the coffeehouse were teaching him and his staff "about what is common between us—that we share a humanness in which we all stand." *Now*'s reporting on The Exit does not condemn the "stimulating off-beat people" who frequented the coffeehouse. It is likely that some visitors to The Exit found their way to Trinity, located just a half a mile to the west.[53]

The Central West End's widely known status as a queer neighborhood, then, made it an unsurprising locale for an event that galvanized many gay St. Louisans for the first time to take public action against state harassment and repression. Shortly after midnight on November 1, 1969, officers of the St. Louis Police Department's Vice Division arrested a group of nine people who, despite being legally male, wore wigs, evening gowns, women's earrings, and high-heeled shoes. The arrests took place outside the Onyx Room, a bar in a gay nightlife district on Olive Street just east of North Grand Boulevard near the Central West End (Fig. 3.4). Those arrested were taken to the jail at police headquarters downtown and were charged with violating a municipal anti-masquerading ordinance, which prohibited cross-dressing. According to Laud Humphreys's first-person account of the night's events, the plainclothes officers had been waiting outside the bar where the men had gathered after a Halloween-night drag ball.[54]

Figure 3.4 The 3500 block of Olive Street looking west toward North Grand Boulevard in about 1963. The Continental Life Building is in the background to the right. This stretch of Olive Street was a center of queer nightlife from the 1930s to the 1970s. Shelley's Midway Bar and the Golden Gate Bar (later Golden Gate Coffee House) are visible on the left side of the street. The Onyx Room is farther down the street on the left. *From the St. Louis City Planning Agencies Collection, Missouri Historical Society Library and Research Center*

The Mandrake Society, "St. Louis's homophile organization," had been founded that April in an apartment near Trinity in the Central West End. Its purpose was to "equalize the status and position of the homosexual with the status and position of the heterosexual." Mandrake sprang into action immediately after the Halloween-night arrests. Outraged by the arrests, a group of "about two dozen homosexuals" congregated in the lobby of police headquarters to protest. Members of Mandrake were notified through a telephone chain that had been organized for such an occasion. Soon the group's president and Humphreys were on the scene to negotiate with the police and to help raise bail.[55]

In the following months, Trinity would offer critical assistance to Mandrake. The arrests deeply concerned many queer St. Louisans and attracted many new members to Mandrake. While only about twenty-five people had attended Mandrake's October 1969 gathering before Halloween, some 150 were at the first meeting after the arrests. One was the woman owner of a gay coffeehouse who was "concerned about the welfare of some of her boys . . . who had been arrested." Mandrake helped finance the arrested men's legal representation, and, three months after the arrests, the group's attorney succeeded in convincing a judge to drop the charges. By early 1970, Mandrake counted more than one hundred dues-paying members.[56] Throughout all of this, Trinity invited the Mandrake Society to hold its meetings in the church's parish hall, effectively making the church the administrative center of the city's nascent gay and lesbian movement.

Gay Liberation, Black Power, and Liberal Protestantism
Trinity in the 1970s

Ellie Chapman recalls that when she moved to the Central West End in the fall of 1969, she was "really struck by the diversity, because it was something new to me." Chapman had previously lived in rural Kennett, Missouri, where her husband, Rev. Bill Chapman, an Episcopal priest, had served as rector of a small, all-white congregation. While the Chapmans were personally committed to racial equality and social justice—their first date had been at a NAACP rally—the parishioners in Kennett chafed at civil rights activism. When Bill began to serve as co-rector of Trinity the following year, Ellie discovered something remarkable about this urban congregation. "Here we come to Trinity Church, St. Louis," she remembers. "There were a lot of Blacks . . . There were a lot of gays. A very active—I don't want to say 'cohort' of gay people, because they weren't a group as far as I could see. Just part of the congregation." Two members of the elected lay leadership board were openly gay men in the early 1970s, and Trinity had developed a reputation as the diocese of Missouri's "gay church."[57]

In this environment, Bill Chapman flourished as a priest and as a sort of community organizer. Through most of the 1970s, he served as part of a three-person Team Ministry along with Father Richard Tombaugh, a white academic with ties to nearby Washington University, and Father John Mason, a Black pastoral counselor.[58] Under their watch, Trinity attracted growing numbers of queer people while also serving as neighborhood anchor and hub of Black Power and gay liberation organizing.

For several years after the 1969 Halloween-night arrests, Trinity remained perhaps St. Louis's most important site of lesbian and gay political activism. It received coverage in the *St. Louis Post-Dispatch* for its "open door policy" toward homosexuals and also served as a meeting place for St. Louis's student-led Gay Liberation Front.[59] Chapman encouraged gay congregants to become involved in the life of the church by joining the choir or running for election to the parish's lay leadership board.[60] In these years, Trinity became a space where straight Christians met, got to know, and worshipped alongside out queer people. While this was sometimes a source of friction, members of the parish recall that this everyday mingling led many congregants to become newly sensitive to the concerns of lesbians and gay men and supportive of their movement.[61]

In the early 1970s, Trinity provided financial support to the Mandrake Society by purchasing regular advertising space in its newsletter, which was distributed in many of St. Louis's queer gathering places. Most of the other advertisers were local bars, cafés, and bathhouses that attracted queer patrons with the promise of a good time. The Onyx Room, for example, tempted readers of *Mandrake* with "drinks," "dancing," and "friends," while the after-hours Golden Gate Coffee House declared that "for fun and frolic," it was "the late-night place to be."[62] Trinity, however, used its advertising space to invite lesbian and gay St. Louisans to join an inclusive spiritual community. In March 1971, for instance, a full-page ad listed its weekly schedule of masses, which on Sundays were followed by refreshments and socializing (Fig. 3.5). The ad announced that the church was "open daily for private prayer, meditation, and visits before the Blessed Sacrament."[63]

During the 1970s, Trinity not only served as a center of lesbian and gay activism, but also of African American and interracial community life and political organizing. This was exemplified by the collaboration between Bill Chapman and Jesse Todd. As young man in the 1960s, Todd cut his teeth as an activist in the Zulu 1200s, a St. Louis Black Power group. In the late 1960s, Todd helped lead a campaign by the group to stage sit-ins in St. Louis–area churches demanding that they take responsibility for their role in facilitating white supremacy. The Roman Catholic Cathedral Basilica in the Central West End was among the houses of worship targeted by the campaign. When Todd entered Trinity's sanctuary to stage a sit-in during a Sunday morning service, he was invited to address the congregation to discuss his concerns. Shortly afterward, Trinity hired Todd to run some of the church's neighborhood programs, and he later became a member of the congregation himself.[64]

For several years, Todd served as director of the Concerned Citizens Community Center, which was in a building that Trinity rented adjacent

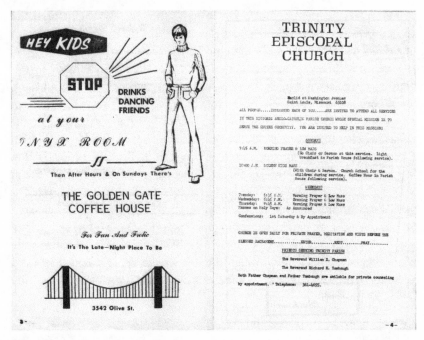

Figure 3.5 Ads for the Onyx Room and Golden Gate Coffee House, alongside an ad for Trinity Episcopal Church, in an early issue of the Mandrake Society newsletter, St. Louis's first locally produced gay periodical. *From* The Mandrake, *March 1971, courtesy of ONE Archives at the USC Libraries*

to the church. This facility held African dance classes, adult education classes, and meetings of a prison visitation program operated by the Black Panthers. The same space also featured pool and ping-pong tables, and for a time Trinity's Sunday school met there as well.[65]

Father Chapman was conscious of Trinity's unusual identity as a congregation that was both racially mixed and welcoming to gays, and he encouraged parishioners to think through how this fit into their lived experience of faith. In Lent of 1976, for example, he led a weekly series of discussions of "Christian Perspectives" on the following topics: "Sexuality and Vocation," "Sexuality and Ordination," "Race and Identity," "Race and Power," and "Race and Community."[66]

Trinity's support for both racial and sexual minorities emerged out of a common framework rooted in an inclusive vision of Christian community and a commitment to neighborhood engagement. However, Black Power and gay liberation activism at Trinity largely ran along parallel tracks, and openly queer people of color seem to have been mostly absent from the church in these years. This likely reflects the prevailing racial segregation of St. Louis's queer social spaces and emerging activist organizations.[67]

St. Louis's 1980 gay pride march illustrates of the progress made by lesbian and gay activists in St. Louis over the previous decade. On a bright, warm Sunday in April 1980, some five hundred people marched through the streets of the Central West End, St. Louis's "gay ghetto." Carrying banners and chanting slogans, the marchers made their way down Lindell Boulevard along the northern edge of Forest Park. Finally, they arrived at Washington University and staged an exuberant rally there for the cause of lesbian and gay liberation. That day's march and rally concluded a week of gatherings around the city that together made up what organizers called the St. Louis Celebration of Lesbian and Gay Pride (Fig. 3.6). While not strictly speaking the first pride celebration in the St. Louis region—smaller-scale pride events had occurred through the 1970s—the unprecedented size and visibility of the 1980 pride week made it a momentous turning point for the local community.

Figure 3.6 Organized by an ad hoc coalition of activist groups, the April 1980 Celebration of Lesbian and Gay Pride was a turning point for local LGBTQ communities. *From the Lisa Wagaman Papers (S0542), State Historical Society of Missouri*

Tellingly, lesbian- and gay-affirming religious leaders and religious institutions played key roles in making the 1980 Pride celebration a reality, and they had a prominent presence at many of the week's events. In fact, the Magnolia Committee—the ad hoc group that took charge of planning the march—held its meetings at St. John's Episcopal Church in the Tower Grove South neighborhood. Michael Allen, an Episcopal priest and dean of Christ Church Cathedral downtown, worked closely with the Magnolia Committee and was even remembered as its "chaplain." Meanwhile, the leadership of the lesbian and gay Metropolitan Community Church (MCC) of Greater St. Louis—founded in 1973 and by then operating out of a converted mansion in the Central West End—helped coordinate preparations for the Pride celebration, and the MCC hosted one of the week's largest events. Finally, Dean Allen of Christ Church Cathedral spoke at the rally after the march. Clad in black and wearing a clerical collar, Allen used his address effectively to align his church with the movement for lesbian and gay rights.[68]

Figure 3.7 Participants in the April 1980 pride march, formally dubbed "Lesbians, Gays, and Friends Walk for Charity," arrive at the steps of Washington University's Brookings Hall. Notable was the presence and participation of urban liberal Protestant leaders. *Photo by Wilbur Wegener, from the Challenge Metro Collection, Missouri Historical Society Library and Research Center*

Epilogue: A Legacy of Inclusion

Trinity's crucial role in St. Louis's queer community did not end with the 1970s. The church remained a hub of activism through the remainder of the twentieth century and beyond. Following the footsteps of the Mandrake Society, LGBTQ groups as varied as Pride St. Louis, Growing American Youth, and the Bisexual Alliance of St. Louis enjoyed the parish's spirit of hospitality toward progressive organizing and met at the church's facilities. Through the 1980s and 1990s, much of the day-to-day work of building a movement for LGBTQ rights took place at this old stone church in the Central West End.

In 1993, Trinity was the site of another turning point in the region's LGBTQ history. That February, St. Louis's first-ever forum for mayoral candidates on gay and lesbian concerns was held in the church's sanctuary. Some 130 community members filled the pews, and Trinity's large crucifix—depicting a triumphant Christ the King—was suspended above the candidates. The mayoral hopefuls, eager to win the votes of an increasingly powerful constituency, answered questions about AIDS policy, policing, and teaching public school children about same-sex parenting.[69] One of the candidates who participated that day, Freeman Bosley Jr., went on to win the election and to become St. Louis's first African American mayor, thanks in part to substantial gay and lesbian support.[70] It was fitting that this pivotal moment for LGBTQ politics in St. Louis—when the community first commanded the attention of aspirants to the city's highest office—took place at the church where the Mandrake Society had held its meetings and launched the local movement more than two decades earlier.

In the years after the start of the new millennium, Trinity perhaps came to have a somewhat lower profile in the St. Louis's LGBTQ community than it had had in the previous few decades—not because the parish had become any less accepting of queer people, but rather because its inclusive atmosphere and support for LGBTQ rights had become less exceptional. With legal milestones such as the nationwide legalization of same-sex marriage in 2015 and the increasing visibility in and integration of queer people into mainstream community institutions, it became clear that Trinity had been on the cutting edge of a profound cultural shift.

In recognition of the parish's momentous role in the history of queer activism in St. Louis, Trinity Episcopal Church was added to the National Register of Historic Places in 2019—the first site in Missouri added because of its significance to LGBTQ history.[71] On Pride Sunday in June

2021, parishioners and other community members gathered in front of the church to dedicate a historical marker highlighting Trinity's inclusion on the National Register. Among the speakers at the ceremony was Gregory Smith, a member of the parish and one of the young people whose arrest for cross-dressing on Halloween night in 1969 helped get the Mandrake Society off the ground. Young queer parishioners also offered reflections, attesting to an ongoing spirt of acceptance at the church. But perhaps the most notable speaker was Bishop Deon Johnson. Installed the year before, Johnson was the first Black and first openly gay bishop of the Episcopal Diocese of Missouri.[72] Before unveiling and blessing the marker, Johnson preached about a Christian faith that demanded radical inclusivity across the boundaries of race and sexuality. A half century before, in an era of urban crisis, this was a faith that had led Trinity Episcopal Church to re-define its relationship with its neighbors and to help birth gay liberation in St. Louis.

4. Black Power on the Ground

Continuity and Rupture in St. Louis

Clarence Lang

Introduction

A SEA CHANGE IS UNDERWAY in the field of "Black Freedom Studies."[1] Not only have numerous scholars engaged new chronological, geographical, and conceptual frameworks to complicate popular narratives of postwar Civil Rights struggles (1955–1966), but they have also critically reexamined, and rehabilitated, key figures, organizations, and institutions associated with Black Power (1966–1975). Far from simply provocative rhetoric, inarticulate rage, and self-defeating violence, Black Power encompassed a range of concrete, programmatic initiatives geared toward tangible—indeed, political—vision and goals. Yet, historians and social scientists have further to go in recovering these many legacies. While an earlier wave of scholars excavated the "indigenous" character of Civil Rights campaigns, the growing subfield that historian Peniel Joseph has characterized as "Black Power Studies" remains in need of more local treatments that foreground the groups and activists that seeded the soil for the Black Nationalist renaissance of the mid-to-late 1960s and early-to-mid 1970s. As with the Black Freedom Movement writ large, Black Power achieved its successes, experienced its reversals, developed its various strategies, and encountered its myriad opportunities and constraints on the ground.[2]

Focusing on Black Freedom activism in the border-state city of St. Louis, Missouri, this chapter contributes to the ongoing historical retrieval of localized Black Power struggles and their genealogies. In one vein, this has an additive significance, for it helps augment a richer synthesis of Black Power. Using St. Louis as a case study of local movement trajectories, this chapter contends that the thesis of movement continuity must similarly be tested on the ground, with scholars paying attention to grassroots movements as

113

they developed and evolved over time and in response to changing social and economic circumstances. One challenge lay in assessing not only the political and ideological blocs that surged and receded within shifting Black activist communities over time, but also the uniquely *generational* schisms that emerged among freedom workers in different historical periods and defined the predominant forms of activism. In places like St. Louis, African American protest over the long haul of the Great Depression, World War II, early Cold War, and the high tide of the late 1950s, 1960s, and early 1970s, was defined by historically specific leadership, strategies, constituencies, objectives, and popular understandings of "freedom." Thus, I trace the city's Black Freedom struggle from the 1930s to the 1970s to illustrate that while Black Power was consistent with preceding (and subsequent) efforts, it was nevertheless a distinct historical moment reflecting both continuity and change in the African American experience. Moreover, as the following section discusses, localizing Black Power studies requires establishing the importance of place and its effects on social (racial) relations and political economy.[3]

The St. Louis Context

Located at the nation's center, St. Louis was a cultural and political transition point between the Northeast, Midwest, and the South, and embodied "a microcosm—often in exaggerated terms—of national trends."[4] The city was typical of a border-state environment; yet, what constitutes a border state is both simple and elusive. At its most basic, the concept identifies the slaveholding states—Missouri, Maryland, Delaware, West Virginia, and Kentucky—that did not secede from the United States during its Civil War. At the same time, it speaks of other ways in which these states were both southern and conspicuously "non-southern." Their relatively small Black populations contrasted with the large numbers of African Americans who resided in the former Confederacy, particularly in its cotton-producing areas. Likewise, the ethno-religious diversity of white border-state residents—the product of European immigration during the late nineteenth and early twentieth centuries—departed significantly from the demographic homogeneity characteristic of most southern whites. Border-state Black people participated in regular electoral politics, where the Democratic and Republican parties "shared" a plurality. This differed from mass Black disfranchisement and white Democratic hegemony in the South. The breadth and depth of industrial mass production vis-à-vis the

South also distinguished border-state cities, as did the uneven civic cultural influences inherited from Dixie.[5]

Located along the Mississippi River, near its confluence with the Missouri River, St. Louis City had been a vital center of steamboat commerce. After the war, it became a rail link between eastern financial interests and the conquered western territories drawn by the Market Revolution into an evolving national economy. The "Gateway City" also became a supplier of finished goods to the West. The city not only developed an industrial base, but also, similar to Chicago and Detroit—two of its midwestern neighbors—housed an active labor union movement. The heterogeneity of its European immigrant population (primarily German and Irish), and the immigrants' Catholicism, were heavily inscribed in many of St. Louis's civic, as well as religious, institutions. This Catholic presence was even more the case, given St. Louis's Spanish and French colonial origins. Consistent, too, with a border-state typology, the city had small numbers of African Americans: Black St. Louis had grown dramatically following the Civil War, but in 1880 it only comprised 22,000 out of a total city population of 351,000. This factor, alongside Republican-Democratic contestation, had much to do with why Black St. Louisans retained the vote even after ex-Confederates redeemed the South. White leaders fostered a public perception of interracial cooperation and used discourses of racial "civility" to maintain Black subordination, with outright brutality as an unspoken corollary. Incorporated into municipal and state patronage politics, St. Louis's emergent Black leadership relied on white paternalism to tap political appointments and public employment and services.[6]

Jim Crow permeated St. Louis's institutional life. Missouri state law protected segregated public education and prohibited intermarriage; most public accommodations, aside from libraries and public transport, also enforced the color line. The same applied to residential settlement. In 1916, white voters passed the nation's first residential segregation ordinance achieved through a popular referendum. (Just one year later, major race riots erupted across the Mississippi River in East St. Louis, Illinois, similarly emblematic of white resistance to Black migration and mobility during the Great War.) While a US Supreme Court decision later nullified the law, it nonetheless set a precedent for private restrictive housing covenants. Thus, while Black St. Louisans lived in clusters around the city, their area of settlement and growth became rigidly confined to older, declining areas near the downtown business district and central riverfront. African Americans were equally constricted in local job markets, where they were overwhelmingly employed as domestics and common laborers. Unusual even for African Americans in southern cities, St. Louis's Black workers were excluded from the skilled building trades and most professional crafts.[7]

From the Great Depression to the Early Cold War

These conditions generated a range of indigenous Black cultural, social, and political institutions, including the Civic Liberty League, and local chapters of the Urban League, Negro Business League, and the National Association for the Advancement of Colored People (NAACP). While ministering to African Americans' immediate needs, many of these organizations also helped ignite popular struggles for racial reform. During the 1930s, Black St. Louisans waged community campaigns for more recreational space, schools, and relief and employment. The Colored Clerks' Circle, working with the city's Housewives League, led efforts for the hiring of African American delivery drivers and dime store sales staff. African Americans also comprised a particularly visible and militant core of the Unemployed Councils organized by the American Communist Party, and their involvement in downtown demonstrations and street fights with police helped goad city hall into establishing a formal public relief structure. Assisted by the Trade Union Unity League, Black female nutpickers and rag and bag factory laborers organized a massive, though short-lived, movement for wages and working conditions.[8]

Through the "Popular Front" vehicle of the American Workers' Union, Black workers fought for equity in the emerging federal New Deal programs. The St. Louis Urban League, whose Industrial Department was an unlikely hub of radicalism during this period, supported the self-organization of Black construction and hotel workers, motion picture projectionists, janitors, and domestics. St. Louis's Negro Workers' Council, created in 1934, challenged the monopoly on skilled work held by white tradesmen of the American Federation of Labor; after 1936, Black organizers helped fortify a burgeoning Congress of Industrial Organizations, especially in the steel industry where they had a strategic foothold. St. Louis's branch of the National Negro Congress, though small and dependent on the Urban League, nonetheless was a convergence of Black community-based mobilization, left-wing politics, worker self-organization, and industrial union militancy.[9]

The popular upsurge also affected the city's electoral politics. George Vaughn, Jordan Chambers, and David Grant—a young attorney involved in the Colored Clerks' Circle—were among a rising new coalition of Black politicos who helped engineer a white Democratic sweep of local municipal offices, including the mayoralty and the Aldermanic Board. By 1937, 60 percent of the city's African American voters had defected to the party of the New Deal. Chambers, elected committeeman of the heavily Black Nineteenth Ward, ascended as the city's principal Black Democratic boss. St. Louis's decentralized, weak-mayor system of government allowed Black ward-level politicians like "Pops" Chambers to exercise far greater power than was possible in machine-run cities like Chicago.[10]

As depression gave way to war and industrial regeneration, the March on Washington Movement galvanized Black communities against racism in defense production and the armed forces. Spearheaded by the Brotherhood of Sleeping Car Porters (BSCP) and adopting the vocal anticommunism of BSCP president A. Philip Randolph, the group generally eschewed any association with radicalism in favor of a militant liberal racial reformism. Highlighting the contradiction of maintaining Jim Crow at home while fighting fascism abroad and using the imminent threat of disruption, the coalition leveraged a presidential executive order and the creation of a Fair Employment Practice Committee (FEPC). Yet, the March on Washington Movement was a grassroots project that continued throughout the war, sustained by active local committees that assumed the weight of actually implementing the federal decree. St. Louis's affiliate, led by Grant and local BSCP President T. D. McNeal, staged several marches to force the hiring and upgrading of Black workers at McDonnell Aircraft, US Cartridge, and other firms. As public transport and communications were deemed war industries by the White House, demonstrators also pressed for the employment of Black men as streetcar and bus drivers and picketed the Southwestern Bell Telephone Company for white-collar jobs for Black women. By the spring of 1943, March on Washington activists boasted of having won more than 8,000 jobs for African Americans in the city.[11]

The mayor's office, maneuvering to staunch the tide of Black militancy, avert the race riots that had erupted in cities like Detroit and Philadelphia, and preserve the city's image of interracial civility, created a race relations commission. But in areas where city hall failed to act, politicized citizens were more than willing. In 1944, a coterie of women associated with the local March on Washington committee, NAACP, and labor union auxiliaries formed the Citizens Civil Rights Committee, which conducted a series of sit-in protests at the segregated lunch counters of the major downtown department stores. Stemming from the women's ties to the Christian pacifist Fellowship of Reconciliation, these were among the earliest sit-in demonstrations in the nation.

Following the war, Black activists persisted in their efforts to dismantle American racial apartheid—for instance, lobbying for a permanent national FEPC. Yet, in a postwar climate of heightened US-Soviet rivalry and perceived threats to internal security, "communistic" demands for racial equality invited unwanted attention from federal, state, and local authorities. This is not to say that Black freedom workers ceased drawing the potent linkages between racial and economic justice. The Civil Rights Congress, active in St. Louis and East St. Louis, engaged in protests against police brutality and Black unemployment in 1949 and 1950. In 1952, the St. Louis Negro Labor Council (NLC), similarly connected to a national united front of progressive trade unionists, veteran left-wing organizers, and members and "fellow travelers" of the American Communist Party, gained attention through its lengthy boycott of the city's main Sears, Roebuck and Company store. One of its leading figures, Hershel Walker, was a former Young Communist League member and a veteran of St. Louis's unemployed movement. The early Cold War, however, had a chilling effect on forms of Black militancy that had been possible during the Depression and World War II. Certainly, the protests of the NAACP and Congress of Racial Equality (CORE) during this period were carried out by a small number of committed activists, who at best achieved short-lived and piecemeal reforms.[12]

Just thirty people walked the NLC's picket line, due in no small part to the fact it had been named in the US Attorney's Subversive Organizations list. The NAACP, CORE, and the Urban League all refused any involvement with the demonstrations, and the council was largely ostracized in St. Louis's Black public sphere. Harassed by police, and hounded by the charges of subversion from conservatives and Cold War liberals, Black and white alike, the NLC's national body was forced to dissolve less than six years after its birth. (A similar fate befell the Civil Rights Congress.) Hence, the late 1940s and early 1950s comprised a moment of rupture in the Black Freedom Movement, particularly in the development of its radical flank.[13]

Civil Rights in St. Louis

As bus boycotts in Baton Rouge, Montgomery, and Tallahassee, Florida, helped push matters of racial justice to the forefront of the national agenda, Civic Progress, Incorporated—an organization of the city's major industrial and civic leaders—touted a proposal to revise the municipal charter. The plan unwittingly ignited the "heroic" period of postwar Civil Rights struggle in St. Louis.[14] For many African Americans, the proposed new charter's provisions reducing the Aldermanic Board and enlarging the scope of at-large elections directly undermined the electoral strength of a growing Black populace. Between 1940 and 1950, 38,000 African Americans had migrated to the city; by 1956, they comprised approximately 180,000, or well over 20 percent of the city's population. Given the charter's silence on civil rights and fair employment guarantees in municipal employment and projects, and given that the city was entering the throes of a protracted downtown-area renewal, the proposal threatened to strip Black people of their collective power in public decision making at the very moment they were poised to wield substantive influence at the polls.[15]

At a time when the NAACP was on the defensive in the South and often recoiled from mass protest in the North for fear of accusations of communism, St. Louis's branch launched a successful grassroots opposition to the charter's passage, one involving Black ward politicians, beauticians, taxicab drivers, unionists, and clergy. It is noteworthy that the NAACP's president at this time was Ernest Calloway, a veteran union organizer and high-ranking official in Local 688 of the powerful International Brotherhood of Teamsters.[16] Calloway, a newcomer to the city, was of the same generation as individuals like Grant and McNeal; yet, he was part of a nascent cohort of mainly young activists, like Margaret Bush Wilson and William L. Clay, who emerged out of the NAACP's community mobilization campaign.

The anti-charter moment of the late 1950s is also historically significant because it illustrates how early Civil Rights activism, including the initiatives outside the South, responded to quality-of-life issues beyond ending Jim Crow accommodations. Victory over the proposal set in motion a modern Black mass movement for better jobs and wages, meaningful electoral power, equitable education and housing opportunities, Black communal stability and urban redevelopment—as well as an end to segregated facilities. Local Black freedom workers articulated this agenda in a comprehensive "Negro Proclamation." At the cutting edge of this activity were two NAACP affiliates—the Job Opportunities Council and the NAACP Youth Council—which often collaborated with St. Louis CORE. St. Louis's unit of the Negro American Labor Council (NALC), subsequently led by Calloway, was also involved in aggressive action against job discrimination.[17]

Cold War liberalism was not the only framework activists employed in response to racist exclusion. Muhammad Mosque No. 28, which had grown dramatically since the early 1950s, represented a persistent Black Nationalist vision. Spurning the Civil Rights strategy of nonviolent direct action, members of the Nation of Islam (NOI) questioned the desirability of racial integration. Such messages resonated with many Black St. Louisans. Some 3,500 people gathered at the city's municipal auditorium in August 1962 to hear NOI leader Elijah Muhammad deliver the apocalyptic prediction that the "rule of the white man over the Black man" was coming to an end. Malcolm X, Muhammad's national spokesman, addressed the crowd at the same event (Fig. 4.1), and he also drew a sizable audience during an early 1963 appearance. An effective organizer, Malcolm had been planting the seeds of a secular Black Nationalist rebirth since the late 1950s.[18]

But the NOI stood at the margins of Black protest (and fell out of favor altogether with many Black activists after Malcolm's assassination). As

Figure 4.1 Malcolm X speaks at the Kiel Auditorium on August 12, 1962, for a Nation of Islam rally attended by an audience of 2,000. Seated behind him are Elijah and Clara Muhammad. *Photo by Edward L. Meyer for the* St. Louis Globe-Democrat, *from the collections of the St. Louis Mercantile Library at the University of Missouri–St. Louis*

120

the tempo of Civil Rights struggle quickened in the South, the thrust of insurgency in St. Louis similarly became more robust, with CORE at the forefront. Many Youth Council members, hampered by their parent organization, defected from the local NAACP to CORE in the early 1960s. Appeals for a "fair" share of jobs became demands for "full" employment as definitions of Black "freedom" evolved. African Americans were negligibly employed in banks, retail stores, and grocery chains; soft drink, dairy, bread, and brewing companies hired them as neither plant workers nor driver-salesmen. Racial inequality also defined the hiring policies of the city's utility companies and major industrial firms. With one in every three Black St. Louisans employed in unskilled work or household service, African American families earned an annual income of $3,000 in contrast to $6,000 for whites. Another result of economic disenfranchisement was a high rate of Black unemployment. Between 1958 and 1964, Black unemployment stood at more than 10 percent, with one of every six Black youth absent from the formal labor force. The problem was especially acute for Black men. Still, the fact that women had an easier time finding work did not mean they were better employed. In 1960, 62 percent of Black women in paid labor earned $1,999 or less. Suitably, women anchored most Civil Rights projects, despite the fact that gender equity was not an explicit basis of organization. However, the nature of many jobs campaigns implicitly promoted the expansion of employment available to Black women, albeit within the confines of "women's work"—retail, telephone operative, and petty clerical work.[19]

St. Louis's Civil Rights movement reached its peak in 1963–1964, when CORE activists launched mass disruptions at the Jefferson Bank and Trust Company in response to its hiring practices. The campaign assumed the form of a "general strike" against city hall, downtown businesses, and other institutions that deposited their receipts at the bank. CORE, once a small, predominantly white middle-class organization philosophically sworn to nonviolence, changed dramatically as younger, working-class Blacks swelled its membership, questioned nonviolence, leaned closer to Black Nationalism than to liberalism, and contested for leadership. The increasingly militant character of CORE's civil disobedience and mass arrests elicited criticisms from older activists like Calloway and then–state senator McNeal, who the "Young Turks" dismissed as "Uncle Toms." The dispute revealed the straightforwardness of a grassroots rank-and-file who, facing structural unemployment, had no abiding allegiance to the rules of civility that had governed relations between Black and white leadership. Intergenerational schisms also underlay the hostilities. Many of the critics, having come of age during the 1940s or earlier, had been schooled in earlier paradigms of militancy that adhered to legal boundaries. For veteran activists, the Jefferson Bank boycotters represented a form of protest they neither understood nor appreciated. Mass protests eventually dented racial apartheid in the bank's employment practices, but this success was contradictory. It splintered local movement forces, exacerbating CORE's internal differences over tactics and goals while changing the complexion of the group's leadership.[20]

A major outgrowth of this disaffection within CORE was the formation of the Action Committee to Improve Opportunities for Negroes (ACTION) in 1964, chaired by Percy Green, an ex-gang member and McDonnell Aircraft Company worker. Composed initially of CORE dissidents, the

Figure 4.2 Ronald Gregory, brother of comedian Dick Gregory, arrested during one of the Jefferson Bank demonstrations, October 7, 1963. *Photo by Paul Ockrassa for the* St. Louis Globe-Democrat, *from the collections of the St. Louis Mercantile Library at the University of Missouri–St. Louis*

group first came to public attention after Green and Richard Daly, a white member, climbed the base of the unfinished Gateway Arch and secured themselves more than 125 feet above workers, police, and other demonstrators. The highly visible protest, spanning four hours, was designed to draw attention to the exclusion of Black workers by unions and contractors from skilled work at a federally funded project (Fig. 4.3). ACTION quickly gained a militant reputation for its flamboyant, yet meticulously planned, nonviolent guerilla theater waged against the local construction industry and the metropolitan area's other major employers. A purely local organization, ACTION nevertheless informs a broader history of the postwar Black Freedom Movement. Focused primarily on "More and Better Paying Jobs for Black Men," its leadership was characteristic of the ways in which Black "freedom" during this period imagined the redemption of a Black "manhood" premised on the patriarchal, male-headed household. This paralleled an emergent thesis of cultural pathology that attributed Black poverty rates to the dominance of Black matriarchy in African American communities.[21]

Figure 4.3 Activists Percy Green and Richard Daly at the Gateway Arch on July 14, 1964, the day they climbed the partly constructed monument to protest racial discrimination in federal construction hiring. *Photo by Paul Ockrassa for the* St. Louis Globe-Democrat, *from the collections of the St. Louis Mercantile Library at the University of Missouri–St. Louis*

Like a number of other local groups around the nation, ACTION also constituted a vital bridge between the civil rights movement and what would soon come to be labeled "Black Power." At a time when national organizations such as CORE and the Student Nonviolent Coordinating Committee (SNCC) were adopting the policy that white members should organize antiracist campaigns in their own communities, ACTION remained stubbornly interracial. Yet, its top leadership positions were self-consciously reserved for African Americans only, under the presumption that Black activists deserved to play the central role in their own struggles for self-determination. Members adopted many Black Nationalist flourishes common to the period, including military berets, army field jackets, and dark sunglasses. Influenced by third world revolutionary movements, the organization even established a youth auxiliary known as the ACTION Guerrilla Force. And while adhering to a strategy of nonviolent action, members were not philosophically opposed to self-defense. As a number of scholars have illustrated, this was not atypical of Civil Rights activists. However, it is noteworthy that ACTION's leadership went beyond a pragmatic support for defensive violence, and actually made preparations for a time when revolutionary violence might be historically necessary: Members regularly participated in military training in forest preserves outside the city. When viewed as organizational transition points from "Freedom Now" to "Black Power," indigenous groups like ACTION reveal organic linkages between the two phases.

From "Freedom Now" to "Black Power" in the Gateway City

It is noteworthy that a number of elder activists—mainly Cold War liberals who had survived the anticommunist purges of the late 1940s—were put off by what they regarded as Black "separatism." Existing organizations like the NAACP and Urban League rejected the concept with equal vehemence. Even senior Black Nationalists like Elijah Muhammad were out of step with their junior counterparts. Although the NOI continued to attract members, it remained tainted by Malcolm's death and its general aversion to political engagement. Not only were the Black Muslims politically suspect, but many young activists also found them culturally reactionary. Steeped in a nineteenth-century paradigm of Black Nationalism that echoed Western discourses of "civilization" and regarded sub-Saharan Africa as backward, Muhammad publicly lambasted beards and "afro" hairstyles as "germ-catchers." Fruit of Islam members, adhering to strict codes of "respectability" with their clean-shaven faces, closely cropped hair, and conservative suits and bowties, likewise stood in stark contrast to their peers in dashikis, sandals, earrings, and dangling African jewelry. Moreover, at a time when Black women were beginning to assert (proto) feminist identities and interests within movement organizations, the NOI held fast to patriarchal ideals.[22]

In St. Louis, as elsewhere, Black Power sprang from numerous changes in the movement's landscape. Foremost were the remarkable, if qualified, successes of Civil Rights activism. These included the attainment of greater Black representation on the St. Louis school and aldermanic boards by the end of the 1950s, and T. D. McNeal's election, in 1960, as Missouri's first Black state senator. With the passage of a public accommodations ordinance in 1961, activists finally achieved a major goal many had been seeking since 1948. The 1963 March on Washington had powerfully symbolized Black demands for full citizenship and helped yield national legislation that included the 1964 Civil Rights and 1965 Voting Rights acts and the advent of the federal "War on Poverty."

These reforms exposed, at the same time, deepening racial inequalities. Automation eroded Black advances in semi-skilled operative jobs, leading one sociologist to ruefully contemplate, "Who needs the Negro?"[23] Despite the defeat of the Civic Progress–touted charter in 1957, large-capitalist prerogatives had prevailed in directing the path of urban redevelopment. Beginning in 1959, the demolition of St. Louis's central-city Black enclave, Mill Creek Valley, displaced some 20,000 Black St. Louisans. Many moved north of downtown or took up occupancy near the central business district in the massive Pruitt-Igoe homes and other federal housing projects. The relocations tightened the spatial containment, and the racialized poverty, of the Black community: in 1960, for instance, 70 percent of the city's 214,337 African Americans lived in or near old, decaying housing. White St. Louisans retired to the suburbs of St. Louis County, with private capital and federal welfare programs following them. Because its boundaries had been frozen since 1876 (when voters approved home rule), St. Louis City's government lacked the power to annex economically thriving adjacent communities.

Moreover, bitter experiences of arrests, beatings, church bombings, and assassinations—and the unreliable nature of the Kennedy and Johnson administrations as Civil Rights allies—helped to sour younger activists on the idea that they could end racism, poverty, and militarism through American liberalism. They became deeply critical of local antipoverty agencies like St. Louis's Human Development Corporation (HDC), which, while supportive of popular participation in principle, resisted genuine popular control. Premised on correcting the defective behavior of the Black urban poor rather than structural racial inequalities, many Johnson-era Great Society programs trained younger Black workers for declining or obsolete jobs.

The pervasive influence of Malcolm X and the inspiring examples of third world revolt and revolution also conditioned profound strategic, tactical, and ideological transformations among young African Americans. Drawing from the contemporary examples of Malcolm, Robert F. Williams, and formations like the Deacons for Defense and Justice—as well as from a longer history of Black armed "self-help"—activists publicly (re)asserted and popularized discourses of self-defense. Civil Rights workers also critically reevaluated the place of white organizers in the movement and formally adopted long-term "community organizing" projects. As part of this strategy, existing organizations, such as SNCC, attempted to expand their base beyond the South, where their activities had been concentrated before the demise of legal apartheid. Further, Black radicalism and (inter) nationalism, while certainly present during the early Cold War, discovered new mass constituencies as it journeyed from the movement's margins to its center in the mid-to-late 1960s. Thus, when SNCC organizer Willie Ricks and chairman Stokely Carmichael popularized "Black Power" in 1966, they spoke to the particular frustrations, concerns, and idealism of movement activists at a specific historical moment. Further, while individuals such as James Forman, Floyd McKissick, Queen Mother Audley Moore, and Detroit's Reverend Albert Cleage Jr. attest to Black Power's crossgenerational appeal, the slogan nonetheless had its greatest appeal among younger militants.

Yet, as many scholars have noted, "Black Power" lacked real definition and therefore was broad enough to embrace a wide range of framing processes and diffuse activities. "Negroes" became "Black." The "white power structure," "crackers," "honkies," and "pigs" emerged as negative condensation symbols that sought to explicitly reveal, and delegitimate, the institutions and practices of white racial control. Many Black people adopted the "afro" and other African-derived hairstyles and clothing, assumed new names, and engaged in new social practices and symbolism, as in learning Swahili and raising fists in the "Black Power salute." The Black urban working-class rebellions that shook most major US cities between 1963 and 1968 spoke even more dramatically to these tectonic political shifts. St. Louis often escaped national attention in the media coverage of "riots" because of the relatively small scale of its disturbances; yet, recovering the many narratives of revolt in midsized and small cities like St. Louis illustrates how truly widespread the phenomenon was. In early July 1964, police responding to a fight between two siblings, touched off an hour-long civil disorder on the near north side of the city. Officers dispersed a crowd of rock- and bottle-throwing Black youth with tear gas and arrested three people. Thirty minutes after the clash ended, about forty-five demonstrators marched to the nearby Lucas Avenue police district station, whose officers were particularly known for violent treatment of Black citizens in their custody. After someone hurled bricks through two station windows, officers drove the protestors away with police dogs.[24]

Scattered neighborhood disturbances occurred again in June 1965, following the shooting of a seventeen-year-old burglary suspect, Melvin Cravens. The Black community reacted in outrage over the news that the youth, unarmed and with his hands cuffed behind his back, had died from a gunshot to the back of the head. In October 1965, nearly a hundred Black youth ran along Delmar Boulevard—a street which marked the north-south dividing line between Black and white St. Louis—smashing automobile and store windows. A similar outbreak occurred in September 1966, following a CORE demonstration at the St. Louis Police Department's downtown headquarters. A group of teenagers, shouting "Black Power," tossed garbage cans in the streets and broke car windshields. One group smashed the plate-glass windows of a laundry. Firefighters responding to false alarms were pelted with flying glass and stones, as were uniformed police.[25]

Civic officials prided themselves on the fact that St. Louis did not experience the mass uprisings that shook Kansas City, Chicago, Detroit, and most other major US cities following the assassination of Martin Luther King Jr. in April 1968. This was not altogether true, for minor disturbances did occur in several Black neighborhoods. Yet, several factors intervened on the side of the status quo. Local news media, fearing the spread of disturbances, avoided coverage. Meanwhile, leading members of CORE and the Mid-City Community Congress (discussed below) worked to quell further unrest. Also, St. Louis Mayor Alfonso J. Cervantes—seeking to direct the anger of the Black populace and drawing on the city's culture of "civility"—helped craft an interracial, ecumenical coalition that sponsored what became a 30,000-person eulogy procession and prayer service under the auspices of city hall.[26]

More serious rebellions occurred immediately east of the Mississippi River in neighboring East St. Louis. In early September 1967, SNCC Chairman H. Rap Brown spoke before a crowd of 1,500 people at East St. Louis's Lincoln High School. Following the speech, he gave another, more impromptu presentation atop a police cruiser outside the school. That evening, disturbances erupted in the city's downtown. At least 200 people were involved in white-owned property destruction and looting, as well as firebombings. Several residents were arrested, and a nineteen-year-old was shot to death as he fled police in a stockyard parking lot just outside city limits. The following day, thirty people marched to the police headquarters; looting continued sporadically into the following evening, requiring the intervention of more than one hundred state and city police officers.[27]

But reducing Black Power to Black rebellion against police and other symbols of white authority and power buttresses its oversimplification as unorganized, violent rage. To the contrary, Black Power had institutional moorings. Certainly, it transformed CORE and ACTION. By 1965, most of St. Louis CORE's mainly white founding members were gone as a result of organizational schisms, both local and national. A year later, the national CORE, like SNCC, formally endorsed a version of "Black Power." In 1966, when the region's Bi-State Transit System purchased a local service car company with the intention of dismantling it, CORE began a boycott. Less expensive than Bi-State fare, and more extensive in their routes, service car companies had served a disproportionately African American clientele. CORE subsequently organized its own network of "Freedom Cars" to transport Black patrons. Negotiations with Bi-State Transit ended the boycott in March. Not surprisingly, the Gateway City became a test site in 1967 for CORE's national program, "Black Power, a Blueprint to Success and Survival," which focused on strategies of Black control of community institutions.[28]

ACTION's history committee, chaired by Luther Mitchell, became another vehicle for institutionalizing Black Power. A veteran of Chicago's South Side Community Art Center, Mitchell coordinated the production of weekly questionnaires on African American history, which were delivered along routes in Black neighborhoods. At a moment when the Black Studies movement was developing in many college and university communities, residents eagerly consumed the pamphlets and waited for the answers to run in the following week's edition. These experiences provided the entrepôt for Mitchell's involvement in a community-driven mural project that would bring art and history to the public. Working with activists and artists, Mitchell helped oversee the painting of the "Wall of Respect" at the intersection of North Leffingwell and Franklin Avenues, near the Pruitt-Igoe projects (Fig. 4.4). Initiated in the summer of 1968, the mural featured a color collage of faces that included Jomo Kenyatta, W. E. B. Du Bois, Malcolm X, Martin Luther King Jr., and Muhammad Ali. Marcus Garvey's famous appeal, "Up You Mighty Race," underscored the images. After its completion, the wall became a popular gathering space for political speakers, organizers, and cultural workers.[29]

Black Power Organized: A Local View

Besides transforming existing groups, Black Power also inspired new institutions, networks, and organizational forms. The opening of the Black-owned Gateway National Bank in 1965 simultaneously refuted the endemic racism in St. Louis's banking industry, provided a source of credit and loans for working-class African Americans, and announced the arrival of a burgeoning new Black entrepreneurial middle class. The Committee on Africa, also founded in 1965, mainly attracted students and faculty from Saint Louis University and Washington University, both private schools. The committee's goal lay in connecting Black St. Louisans to other people of African descent, mainly through educational forums and cultural programming, and providing aid to African liberation movements. *Proud*, a monthly publication also established in St. Louis during this period, was consistent with numerous periodicals around the nation geared toward audiences of the new Black Nationalism. Similarly, the Association of Black Collegians, which staged building takeovers in 1968 at Saint Louis University, Washington University, and Forest Park Community College, was part of a wave of militant Black student unions that emerged at historically white institutions of higher learning when, following the urban riots after King's death, African Americans were first admitted in substantive numbers. In St. Louis, as elsewhere, campus-based Black insurgency led to the creation of Black Studies curricula and programs, among other reforms.[30]

Southern Illinois University's Experiment in Higher Education (EHE), located in East St. Louis, likewise became a regional hub of Black Studies and Black Arts ferment. The EHE contained the Performing Arts Training Center, helmed by the internationally renowned choreographer and anthropologist Katherine Dunham, and enjoyed ties to poet Eugene B. Redmond, whose Black River Writers Press was central to popularizing

Figures 4.4a and 4.4b The Wall of Respect mural as shown in a 1969 ACTION poster. The Wall became home to weekly rallies, poetry readings, dramatic sketches, and jazz performances in summer and fall of 1968. *Courtesy of the St. Louis Public Library Special Collections*

the new aesthetic through chapbooks, published fiction, and spoken-word recordings. As scholars like Benjamin Looker and James Edward Smethurst have reminded historians, the Black Arts movement was not confined to the East and West Coasts, but also blossomed in the nation's interior. According to Looker, the Black Artists' Group (BAG), founded in St. Louis in 1968, was particularly illustrative of this point. Heavily influenced by Chicago's Association for the Advancement of Creative Musicians, the collective sought to raise a Black social consciousness through multimedia works of poetry, dance, theater, visual arts, and free-jazz music; at its peak in 1969–1970, BAG had over fifty members. Headquartered in a renovated industrial building in the city's declining Midtown area, the group staged performances in churches, storefronts, public housing centers, public schools, and sidewalks of Black working-class communities, and ran a free youth arts academy (see Fig. 4.5).[31]

Figure 4.5 Black Artists' Group actor and playwright Vincent Terrell, wrapped in chains to symbolize bondage, performs in a dramatic sketch before a downtown audience circa 1970. *Photo by Bennie G. Rodgers, from the Rodgers Photograph Collection (S0629), State Historical Society of Missouri*

In some instances, antipoverty programs provided bases for Black Power organizers. Certainly, the EHE, as well as East St. Louis's Project IMPACT—geared toward cultural and recreational outlets for Black youth—were beneficiaries of federal funds. Another was St. Louis's Jeff-Vander-Lou (JVL) Community Action Group, which was formed in 1966 in the heart of the Black neighborhood bounded by Jefferson, Vandeventer, St. Louis Avenue, and Natural Bridge Road. The JVL focused mainly on housing rehabilitation and the corollary opportunities of Black employment and homeownership these projects generated. The group also developed a medical clinic. The Mid-City Community Congress (MCC), established that same year, similarly promoted Black community control. The MCC's autonomous youth "action arm," the Zulu 1200s, took shape in November 1967 under the leadership of Vietnam veteran Clarence Guthrie. The group's name spoke clearly of an agenda of reconnecting to the African past and raising Black cultural consciousness. Its members, operating out of the MCC's Delmar Boulevard office, were involved in initiating the Wall of Respect project and other educational programming.[32]

The Black Liberators, formed in 1968 soon after King's assassination, were perhaps the city's most daring new organization. Charles Koen (Fig. 4.6), the Liberators' founder and "prime minister," had, at sixteen, been chairman of the Cairo Nonviolent Freedom Committee, a SNCC affiliate in southern Illinois. Sometime after graduating from McKendree College, he had moved to the East St. Louis area, where he led school protests. Although new to the area, he had become a spokesman for East St. Louis's Black Economic Union, an umbrella organization made up of antipoverty, youth, and cultural organizations, and the Imperial Warlords and Black Egyptians, two local gangs. An experienced and dynamic organizer, Koen had recruited heavily from the Egyptians and Warlords to build the Liberators, and he envisioned the new group as a vehicle for a metropolitan-wide Black militant youth alliance. The Liberators, in fact, developed a statewide influence in Illinois, though its actual membership ranged between 150 and 300 people. At the invitation of the Reverend William Matheus, a white ACTION member, the newly formed organization, in addition to maintaining headquarters near Pruitt-Igoe, used St. Stephen's Episcopal Church as a regular base of operations.[33]

In appearances, the paramilitary Liberators patterned themselves after Oakland, California's Black Panther Party for Self-Defense, which had formed two years earlier. Members sported black berets and leather

Figure 4.6 Charles Koen (center), founder of the Black Liberators, gives a press conference at the Wall of Respect in September 1968. At the far right is the group's attorney, Robert Curtis. St. Louis Globe-Democrat *photo, from the collections of the St. Louis Mercantile Library at the University of Missouri–St. Louis*

jackets, held weekly military drills, published a short-lived newspaper, *The Black Liberator*, ran a free breakfast program for children, and worked closely with white antiwar student activists at Washington University. (The Liberators supplied draft counseling to Black youth fighting military conscription.[34]) Curiously, female recruits did not belong to the organization, per se, but rather to a women's auxiliary. This fit the group's self-image as a band of warriors, an identity centered largely on a masculinist vision of heroism. The Liberators' platform, a manifesto of radical Black Nationalism, demanded an end to anti-Black police violence and capitalist exploitation and called for Black pride and draft resistance to the war in Vietnam. Like the Panthers, they also drew immediate media attention through well-publicized and audacious acts. In August 1968, the Liberators approached the mainly white Franklin Avenue Businessmen's Association about making donations to the group, as well as hiring its members as night watchmen. The protection plan, which the merchants rejected, was both an obvious fundraising ploy and a step toward the group's other goal of supplanting police authority in the Black Franklin Avenue area they patrolled. That same month, the Liberators provided an armed escort to the embattled

Black congressman from New York, Adam Clayton Powell Jr., whom they had invited to town for a speaking engagement. A standoff between police and Liberators occurred as Powell attended a rally at the Wall of Respect. As the situation threatened to erupt into gunplay, Powell's aides spirited him away, and the small Liberator delegation dispersed. Police arrested two members on weapons violations charges.[35]

Other Black militant leaders, like Green, deemed the Liberators' activities "adventurist," a reckless invitation to a police showdown for which its young, relatively inexperienced rank-and-file were ill prepared. Such criticism reflected more than just the fact that Green was a movement veteran who viewed such tactics as politically immature, or that he regarded the upstart Liberators as competitors. While Green regarded nonviolence in purely practical terms—and though he had played a role, locally, in the shift to what became labeled "Black Power"—his discomfort with the Liberators' activities speaks to how Black Power initiatives could differ dramatically from their Civil Rights antecedents. It is telling, moreover, that while the Liberators were a source of frustration for someone like Green, they apparently provided a model for *younger* African Americans. The Black Nationalist Party (BNP), which formed in 1969, was a similar avatar of Black revolutionary politics. Like the Liberators, the BNP conducted separate community patrols of police. With funding from the city's HDC, the group also ran a short-lived Community Variety Store.[36]

Although organizations such as the Liberators and BNP were regional and local in character, they have broader significance in understanding the crosscurrents of Black Power. For instance, given Koen's preexisting ties to SNCC, one may view the Liberators as consistent with SNCC's earlier, abortive efforts to form organizations under the insignia of the Black Panther in Philadelphia and other cities. (This was conceived as an outgrowth of the Lowndes County Freedom Organization, or Black Panther Party, organized by SNCC activists in Alabama in 1965–1966.) It is notable, also, that the Liberators developed at a time when SNCC and the Oakland-based Panthers had been attempting to forge an alliance. To the extent that the Liberators imitated the Black Panthers (who experienced explosive growth in 1968), it suggests that historians cannot evaluate the impact of a national organization like the Panthers simply on the basis of its chapters and known members. Rather, in localizing Black Power, we must also factor in the other numerous community groupings that readily adapted Panther platforms, programs, and stylizations to their specific conditions.[37]

The close ties between the Liberators and Zulus are also historically revealing. At the outset, both organizations shared members and engaged in joint activities. These multiple connections between the Liberators and the Zulus call into question the long-running bifurcation between "revolutionary" and "cultural" nationalists that has characterized descriptions of the encounters between nationally known groups like the Panthers and the US Organization. The Liberator-Zulu relationship supports the arguments made by historians such as Komozi Woodard and Scot Brown that the two Black Nationalist "camps" were not as diametrically opposed as the national Black Power narrative—told primarily through the deadly Panther-US feud—suggests. Clearly, real ideological differences existed, as on the question of forming coalitions with white radicals; and police agencies had different evaluations of the respective threat each tendency posed to the status quo. Still, revolutionary nationalists were not dismissive of cultural work, just as cultural nationalists were not glibly "apolitical." In the relatively tight-knit activist community of a midsized metropolis like St. Louis, it was common for Black Freedom workers to participate simultaneously in "political" and "cultural" organizations, including ACTION, the Zulu 1200s, CORE, BAG, and the Liberators. Certainly, this overlap did not necessarily make organizational relationships harmonious—the small geographical space and density of interactions in a small city like St. Louis could in fact exacerbate battles over "turf" and differences of personality and ego among titled leaders. Yet, the frequency and multiplicity of relationships among African Americans here may equally have mitigated the sort of intense intra-movement conflicts that elsewhere turned deadly.[38]

The Black United (Liberation) Front
The Liberators and Zulus were part of a larger bloc of local organizations known as the Black United Front (later renamed the Black Liberation Front). Other members included CORE, ACTION, the Mid-City Community Congress, the Jeff-Vander-Lou action group, and, after its formation, the Black Nationalist Party. In the spring of 1968, soon after King's murder, the alliance presented Mayor Cervantes with a fifteen-point mandate calling for upgrades of Black municipal workers, city contracts for Black businessmen, greater efforts to recruit Black police officers, and a massive restructuring of the Model Cities program. That fall, students at the predominantly Black Vashon High School rioted after administrators eliminated a prom queen candidate because of her afro hairstyle. Students and members of ACTION,

the Liberators, and the Zulus met with school officials to negotiate a series of student demands, including the adoption of Black Studies curricula and the creation of a student advisory committee.[39]

The mainly male leaders of this local Black Power bloc, however, soon found themselves supporting players in the increasingly militant activity of Black women and mothers receiving public assistance and living in St. Louis public housing. Signs of their growing dissatisfaction had been evident in 1967, when nine women and their children staged a ten-day, round-the-clock sit-in at the HDC offices. Having recently completed an HDC training program in electronics assembly, the women were frustrated by their inability to find employment—the result, they claimed, of racial discrimination practiced by McDonnell and fourteen other firms, as well as the HDC's hollow promises of job placement. That same year, sixty demonstrators, the majority of them Black women, picketed the offices of the St. Louis Housing Authority, calling for rent reduction, better janitorial services and pest control, and greater tenant representation on the housing authority board. These rumblings of discontent had turned thunderous as these women, drawing on their identities as mothers, public housing tenants, and aid recipients, more assertively voiced their right to social citizenship, autonomous households, and lives with dignity. In laying claim to entitlements independent of any male breadwinner, they implicitly rejected masculinist discourses that assigned them a secondary or entirely passive place in the Black Freedom Movement—and projected a new one rooted in "welfare rights."[40]

In May 1968, two hundred public housing residents had marched to city hall to dramatize the need for jobs at a minimum wage of two dollars, a reduction in public rents, reforms in Missouri's means-tested welfare system, and the investigation of seventy-six caseworkers accused of unethical practices. Organized by the locally formed League for Adequate Welfare, the marchers walked twelve abreast with the Zulus and ACTION's Guerrilla Force serving as parade marshals. Holding signs with such pronouncements as "Idle Hands, Empty Stomachs, Hot Weather = Riots," demonstrators played on the white public's anxieties about urban rebellion to further goad city officials into action.[41]

The breaking point came in February 1969, though not in the form of a street uprising. When the housing authority announced its second rent increase in two years, more than 1,000 tenants of the city's six public housing developments launched a general rent strike. Their central argument, artic-ulated by leaders like Jean King (Fig. 4.7), was that rents should not exceed a quarter of a family's income. Initially, the protest did not constitute even half of the Gateway City's 7,800 public housing residents; yet it became the largest of its kind in the nation ever, effectively commanding the attention of housing authority staff, the mayor's office, and even the White House. While the St. Louis Housing Authority faced the prospect of bankruptcy, the strikers picketed city hall. Federal officials, anxious about the direc-tions the insurgency could take, intervened to settle the crisis. Not since the 1930s, when African American women laborers staged strikes in St. Louis's food-processing industry, had Black working-class women so boldly demonstrated their autonomy from the male-centered leadership that had characterized most periods of local activism. ACTION, the Liberators, and the Zulus all lent support to the strike, and St. Stephen's Episcopal Church (the stronghold of Matheus, a prominent ACTION member, and a hub of Liberator activity) became the strikers' headquarters. Community organiz-er Buck Jones, the St. Louis Legal Aid Society, and the Teamsters Local 688 also aided the strikers. A settlement with city officials, reached in the fall of 1969, acceded to the strikers' main demands, which included rent reduc-tions, the establishment of tenant management boards, and better upkeep and policing of the housing developments. Nationally, the rent strike helped influence the passage of the Brooke Amendment to the 1969 Housing Act, which placed a ceiling on public housing rents and provided subsidies for rent reductions.[42]

Black Power activists' involvement in women's struggles for fair public housing rents and adequate welfare payments illustrates the grassroots or-ganizing that defined local Black Power initiatives, which historians like Matthew J. Countryman and Yohuru Williams have described. Consistent with Rhonda Y. Williams's work on Black female public housing activists in Baltimore, this episode also contradicts narratives of a Black Power move-ment that was thoroughly masculinist and anti-woman. This is not to say that male organizers like Green or Koen were pro-feminist, or that they did not idealize the patriarchal, male-centered household (or even that female public housing and welfare rights activists did not harbor the same ideals). The point, rather, is that viewing Black Power mobilizations on the ground reveals that the actual praxis of both were more nuanced than any public pronouncements from national, or even local, figures.[43]

Figure 4.7 Jean King initially organized with a tenants' group, the Peabody, Darst, Webbe Movements for Better Living. She emerged in 1969 as the visionary behind a citywide rent strike protesting public housing conditions and policy. *Photo by Paul Ockrassa for the* St. Louis Globe-Democrat, *from the collections of the St. Louis Mercantile Library at the University of Missouri–St. Louis*

Police and FBI Repression of Black Power Militancy in St. Louis

As is well known in national narratives of Black Power, activists were also targeted by police agencies. The Liberators, arguably the city's most radical Black Power organization, weathered the brunt of this harassment locally. A long history of police abuse in Black St. Louis communities directly influenced the formation of the Liberators, and authorities frequently harassed, provoked, and arrested members through discriminatory uses of existing ordinances. Yet, the Liberators' own tendencies toward "adventurism" may have further inflamed the harassment. In early September 1968, a violent series of incidents unfolded after Koen and four other young men were arrested following a dispute with police about an unlaminated license plate. Gunmen fired shots through the front window of the infamous Lucas Avenue police station, where the five had been taken. Gunshots were also fired into the home of Fred Grimes, a Black police lieutenant and Lucas Avenue station watch commander. Assailants, too, firebombed the office of a Black realtor who served on the Board of Police Commissioners.[44]

In rapid succession, a barrage of gunfire destroyed the window of the Liberators' headquarters, and unknown assailants ransacked their office and set their patrol car ablaze (Fig. 4.8). (A witness later claimed to have seen Lieutenant Grimes fire a shotgun blast through the Liberators' office window.) That same evening, police rounded up twenty-one people affiliated with the Liberators, as well as the Zulus, for questioning. Claiming that the spate of shootings and firebombings was the result of a Liberator–Zulu feud, the president of the police commissioner board, Mayor Cervantes, and Missouri governor Warren Hearnes endorsed a police crackdown on both groups. The chain of events reached a crescendo on September 13, 1968, when Koen and Leon Dent, another key Liberator, were seriously injured while again in custody at the Lucas Avenue station (police had arrested them on traffic charges). Dent suffered facial lacerations, while Koen's skull and both hands were fractured. Disputing charges that they had assaulted officers, the two activists claimed that police had beaten them with brass knuckles and clubs in the basement of the station house. A broad coalition of Black Power, student, and antiwar organizations came to the

Figure 4.8 A period of armed conflict between the Black Liberators and the St. Louis city police culminated in the destruction of the Liberators' headquarters and patrol car, as well as dozens of arrests, in September 1968. St. Louis Globe-Democrat *photo, from the collections of the St. Louis Mercantile Library at the University of Missouri–St. Louis*

Liberators' defense. Congressional hopeful William Clay, a veteran of the Jefferson Bank boycott and the 1957 charter fight, telegrammed US Attorney General Ramsey Clark to investigate the police station incident. In October, Koen, Green, and Joel Allen of the Washington University Students for a Democratic Society (SDS) were plaintiffs in a lawsuit seeking an injunction against the police harassment of local Black and antiwar activists.[45]

Public criticism of police actions made the department more circumspect in its dealings with Black Power organizers, but it did not qualitatively change police activities. Nor did the outcry even begin to address the larger campaign of state terror directed at St. Louis's Black Liberation Front by the Federal Bureau of Investigation (FBI). FBI director J. Edgar Hoover had updated his anticommunist crusade in August 1967, when the Bureau launched its Counterintelligence Program (COINTELPRO) to undermine Civil Rights, Black Power, and New Left organizations. Expanded in March 1968, COINTELPRO operations instigated police raids, arrests, and assassination, bankrolled informants, maintained surveillance of individuals and groups, and fed negative stories about activists to cooperative newspapers. The *Globe-Democrat*, a consistent foe of Civil Rights and Black Power activism, had in fact been one of the five newspapers selected by the FBI to spread propaganda about local and national movement figures.[46]

The Bureau also circulated phony correspondence and seemingly anonymous cartoons to spread distrust and paranoia and exploit the latent friction within and between organizations like the Liberators and Zulus. In November 1968, the FBI distributed an unsigned flyer (Fig. 4.9) praising the Zulus and criticizing the Liberators for, among other things, "work[ing] with white college honkies" and dressing like "honkie truck drivers and motersycle cats [sic]." The circular, noted an internal Bureau memorandum, "is purposely slanted to give the impression that the Zulus may have had a key role in its preparation although this is not stated." The widely disseminated flyer fed claims by St. Louis police that the two groups were engaged in a war. The FBI similarly weighed the possibility of promoting animosity between the Liberators and ACTION. Observing that the two organizations were drawing closer together, an FBI memorandum, dated January 8, 1969, declared that the Bureau was looking into plans that would "frustrate any strong degree of cooperation" between the groups. However, a succession of costly arrests in 1968 and the indictment of Koen and Dent on charges of assaulting police had effectively hampered the Liberators' ability to function as an organization by the end of 1969, despite its publicized merger with SNCC the previous fall. The group faded steadily from the St. Louis scene—as did the Zulu 1200s, who were largely defunct by the spring of 1969.[47]

Figure 4.9 FBI COINTELPRO flyer, anonymously circulated in St. Louis in November 1968. By praising the Zulu 1200s (whose work it appeared to be) and disparaging the Black Liberators, the leaflet's creators aimed to stir divisions among activists. *FBI Records, COINTELPRO, "Black Extremist,"* 100-448006, section 4

The Bureau concentrated its attention on ACTION, which, according to a September 1969 memorandum, was "the only Black group of any significance other than the NOI [Nation of Islam]." FBI documents reveal that by early 1970, the agency was developing a plan against an unnamed white female active in ACTION. Through apparent surveillance, agents learned that her husband, who was uninvolved in the group, was threatened by the woman's close interactions with Black men. The Bureau mailed him a phony letter, signed by "A Soul Sister," intimating that his wife had had multiple affairs with ACTION members. The couple soon separated and divorced, and Bureau correspondence noted approvingly that the woman's political involvement waned. In localizing the story of FBI counterinsurgency, scholars may recognize how these operations were symptomatic not only of the harassment of thousands of little-known local individuals and organizations around the nation but also of the FBI's monitoring of entire Black communities. It was not until November 1975 that the US Senate Select Committee on Intelligence disclosed the full extent of these tactics against the progressive social movements of the period.[48]

Conclusion

Considered over time, and on the ground, the Black Freedom Movement has shown a durable continuity. But it has also been marked by change, in terms of leadership, constituencies, dominant ideologies, and strategies and tactics—as well as shifting structures of US capitalism and modes of racial control. As anticommunist harassment during the early Cold War and FBI counterinsurgency during the late 1960s attest, Black freedom workers have encountered moments of political rupture that disabled radical tendencies while promoting, or at least sparing, others. What is striking about the Black radical tradition is not its impermeability to repression but rather its ability to reemerge at different historical junctures, despite attempts to suppress it. While Black Power followed numerous antecedents, including a long history of Black Nationalism, it nonetheless represented the agendas of a particular generation who experienced the successes and failures of postwar, popular Black struggles. Black Power Studies has expanded historians' knowledge and appreciation of this period of the late twentieth century— the weaknesses and setbacks, as well as the triumphs and enduring legacies. As Black Freedom scholars retrieve more local narratives of Black Power (and their precursors), the richer will be our engagement with past, and present, transcripts of African American resistance.

A Postscript—March 2022

Since I first published this work in 2010, the scholarship on Black freedom struggles in twentieth-century St. Louis has continued to expand. Beyond my own book, *Grassroots at the Gateway* (2009), the literature has included *Winning the War for Democracy* (2014), David Lucander's study of the March on Washington Movement of the 1940s, highlighting the key role of local St. Louis organizers like T. D. McNeal in Black mass protest during World War II. From the standpoint of the late 1960s through the mid-1970s, Lucander's work is a reminder of the many local antecedents to the Black Power militancy that emerged over the decades after the war. Along similar lines, Keona K. Ervin's *Gateway to Equality* (2017) particularly foregrounds Black women's leadership in the fight for racial and economic justice between the 1930s and 1960s, and, much like works by Rhonda Y. Williams (2015) and Ashley D. Farmer (2017), renders more powerfully visible the ways they set the agendas for local activities associated with Black Power. Moreover, in Walter Johnson's wide-ranging history, *The Broken Heart of America* (2020), the city and region are the focus of a broader exploration of the nation's intertwined narratives of racism, violence, and exploitation.

Alongside scholarly books and articles, documentary films like *The Pruitt-Igoe Myth* (2011) historicize the significant role that St. Louis played in national debates about public housing, suburban development, and racial exclusion. *Whose Streets?* (2017) similarly captures contemporary forms of Black St. Louis grassroots activism that echo the late 1960s while also depicting emerging traditions that reflect Black freedom demands shaped by racialized mass incarceration and other evolving realities of the twenty-first century.[49]

Indeed, the most consequential development since this chapter first appeared in print has been the consistently fraught relationship between Black St. Louisans and law enforcement. This of course mirrors national patterns of Black criminalization, racial profiling, and the militarization of police tied to the "war on drugs" and the spectacular growth of the US prison system since the 1980s. In 2013, Black Missourians were 66 percent more likely than whites to be stopped by police, even though the latter were more likely (26 percent) to have contraband than their Black counterparts. That same year, African Americans in Ferguson—a suburb in the county surrounding St. Louis City—constituted 80 percent of traffic stops and 92 percent of police searches in that community. This record formed part of the backdrop to the police shooting death of 18-year-old Michael Brown during a local pedestrian stop in August 2014.[50]

When civil disturbances flared in Ferguson, harkening back to the Black urban uprisings of the 1960s, police reacted with an overwhelming show of force, deploying military gear and vehicles as they occupied the streets. In turn, these local events were a catalyst for a national wave of popular "Black Lives Matter" solidarity rallies and demonstrations, campus insurgencies beginning at the University of Missouri at Columbia, news coverage by international media, and the eventual intervention of the US Department of Justice. Despite the many resonances with the 1960s, these events unfolded during the second term of the nation's first Black president, and the sharp divergence reflected the ironies of post–Black Power elected officialdom.

Still, what emerged from the Justice Department's 2015 report on the Ferguson Police Department was an exposé of the practice among law officers and the municipal court (at the behest of local government) of using overzealous traffic stops and excessive court fines to generate revenue—a combination that drowned Black residents in arrests, imprisonment, and catastrophic financial debt. "Ferguson," then, became not only a metonym for national discourses about racist police violence and Black resistance, but also a modern signifier of longstanding regional legacies of racial segregation and economic inequality rooted in the proliferation of municipalities in St. Louis County, political fragmentation and parochialism, and protective localism.

But while many of the conditions underlying the violence in Ferguson were unique, the overall relationship between Black communities and law enforcement was far from singular. When George Floyd died at the hands of police in the Upper Midwest metropolis of Minneapolis in 2020, another massive wave of "Black Lives Matter" protests ensued. This time, the insurgency was aggravated by the responses of an unabashedly white racist presidency and its laissez-faire approach to the perils of a deadly global pandemic. Nevertheless, in St. Louis, the Midwest, and elsewhere, "Black Lives Matter" has helped to bring to the center of Black politics a range of groups that have inhabited the margins in the decades since the 1960s. This category encompasses those with minimal work histories in declining formal economies and extensive jail records for nonviolent offenses in illicit economies, as well as those who may openly identify as lesbian, gay, bisexual, transgender, or queer.

As in a previous historical moment when "Negroes" became "Black," the current period has fostered space to further expand and recognize multiple and intersecting Black identities. Yet, despite the stridency that "Black Lives Matter" evokes, the slogan implicitly appeals to a white recognition of Black humanity rather than asserting an ethos of Black self-determination wherein Black personhood is presumed. It remains to be seen how present-day movement activists will resolve such political and ideological contradictions; but, as in the past, the fundamental work invariably will occur locally—that is, on the ground.

5. Surveillance and Subversion of Student Activists, 1967–1970

Standoff in St. Louis

Nina Gilden Seavey

Prologue

I COME TO WRITE THIS essay in a manner that is unique for a university professor. This chapter is at once personal in its motivation and narrative style, and yet professionally guided in its rigor. Perhaps this is fitting. I am not your typical academic. Rather, I am a documentarian with an academic title: Research Professor of History and Media and Public Affairs at George Washington University. As such, I don't come to the practice of history in the same way as most historians—that is, by engaging in scholarly debate about the interpretation and reinterpretation of ideas and events filtered through an ongoing historiographic context. Rather, I engage history as both a storytelling mechanism and as a means of expressing larger truths about the human experience. I like to think of this study and presentation of history as *accessible*, intended to spark the interest and imaginations of all with whom I come into contact, whether through my films, podcasts, or writings.[1]

With that approach in mind, let me embark you, as readers, onto the journey of this chapter with a simple story. As I said, this is personal: my father, Louis Gilden, was a civil rights attorney in St. Louis during the 1960s and 1970s (Fig. 5.1). He had a client, a twenty-two-year-old student named Howard Mechanic. Mechanic was arrested and indicted on federal charges stemming from his involvement in a riot in which an Air Force Reserve Officers' Training Corps (ROTC) building was burned to the ground on the campus of Washington University in St. Louis on the night of May 4, 1970. For his involvement in this protest, Mechanic was charged under Section 231 of the Civil Obedience Act of 1968.[2] He was not charged in the burning of the federal building itself, but rather, was alleged to have thrown a cherry bomb (an exploding firework) at a policeman during the riot. The police officer was not injured. Mechanic denied having ever thrown the cherry bomb. At trial, Mechanic was found guilty. He was sentenced to five years in federal penitentiary and levied a fine of $10,000. Appeals to higher courts were denied and on May 26, 1972, when he failed to appear to serve his sentence, a warrant was issued for his arrest. Mechanic was officially a federal fugitive.

Figure 5.1 The chapter author with her father, civil rights attorney Louis Gilden, in 1980. The whereabouts of Gilden's vanished client, Howard Mechanic, became a much-discussed mystery in the Gilden household. *Author's personal collection*

While Mechanic's life on the run for the next twenty-eight years as he fled his wrongful conviction is an interesting story unto itself, what motivated my research was my father's sense that there was something else that was at play that affected, either directly or indirectly, Mechanic's trial.[3] Simply put, there was too much about Mechanic's indictment and conviction that didn't add up.

The riot at Washington University was but one of hundreds of outpourings on college campuses in the wake of the murders of four students at Kent State University on May 4, 1970. In the hours and days that followed, four million students protested, buildings were burned, and many students were arrested.[4] When my father made inquiries to his legal colleagues across the nation, he could not find other students outside of St. Louis who were being brought up on similar federal charges. This was worrisome and puzzling to him.

146

The evidence presented at trial was scant. The prosecution called nineteen witnesses. Only one, Donald "Dick" Bird, swore under oath that he had seen Mechanic propel a firecracker in the direction of the policeman. And that assertion varied over time in its details from one statement to another.[5] In spite of the lack of corroboration for Bird's testimony from any of the other eighteen prosecution witnesses, the government pursued its case with a vengeance. And they were successful. What had been planned as a two-week trial ended in four days. The jury deliberated for just under an hour before rendering the guilty verdict. Howard, feeling himself the victim of an unjust conviction and assuming the worst from the rest of the criminal justice system, fled even before the US Supreme Court refused to hear his appeal.[6]

The fact of Howard's flight created a story of mythic proportions in my family. Frequently my father would ask, "Whatever happened to Howard Mechanic?" and we would spend many dinner hours speculating as to his whereabouts and his fate. But what nagged at my father—and then me— was how peculiar it was that the conviction on these never-before-levied charges had been successful in the first place.

Howard wasn't the only student charged with a federal crime at Washington University in the wake of the ROTC burning.[7] He was simply the only one who fled. Howard's disappearance for nearly three decades kept his and the others' inexplicable convictions more present than they might otherwise have been. Once the acquittals had been issued or the sentences served, the cases' resonance would most probably have faded, except for the gnawing fact of Howard's long absence. Always in search of an historical narrative that reflects on a larger truth, a decade ago I decided to explore my father's hunch that something didn't quite add up about what was set into motion on the night of May 4, 1970, in St. Louis, Missouri.

To uncover that truth, I needed more information about the government's activities in St. Louis, and in the lives of these students, before and after the Kent State murders. I started small, requesting FBI files on Howard Mechanic, my father, and several other leaders in antiwar and civil rights activities in St. Louis under the Freedom of Information Act (FOIA). I also began to collect files from former students, many of whom had previously requested their own files in the late 1970s and 1980s and who were willing to share them with me. The more files I garnered, the more the avenues for inquiry opened and my FOIA requests increased. In the documents garnered early in my research, I began to see patterns in the activities of federal agents and their confidential informants. I found numerous reports about students who were consistently under surveillance as targets of the FBI's secret long-standing neutralization and subversion plan: COINTELPRO. And I discovered evidence of government collaborations against students by the Department of Justice, the FBI in Washington, DC, and the Bureau office in St. Louis as early as 1967.

The more information I found, the more FOIA requests I made—until I had accumulated 358 official inquiries. The government denied or obfuscated on all of them. Upon advice of my attorney, we combined these FOIA requests into a single lawsuit, *Seavey v. Department of Justice et al.*, which included as defendants the FBI, the CIA, and the National Archives. In two separate judgments handed down in May and July 2017, Judge Gladys Kessler ruled on both the access and speed with which the government would be required to respond to my requests. And she was unequivocal about the importance of this work:

The basic purpose of the Freedom of Information Act [is] to open agency action to the light of public scrutiny. At this present difficult time in our country's history, it is important as never before, that the American public be as educated as possible as to what "our Government is up to."[8]

Now, thousands of documents were released each month over a three-year period, yielding a total of 150,000 records. Many of these documents had not been part of other congressional, journalistic, or historical inquiries into COINTELPRO, so they have added to the canon of information shaping what we know about the program. What I came to learn was that, indeed, my father's intuition was correct. There was much more at play than he, Mechanic, and the other defendants and their attorneys could possibly have imagined at the time. Unbeknownst to the small band of protestors at Washington University, St. Louis had become a proving ground for the government's assault on the antiwar and civil rights movements. That insight about the role that St. Louis played as a crucible for the nation is the focus of this chapter. But before we get to what these documents contain, it will be instructive to provide some background and context so that the meaning and import of this discovery can be more fully understood and appreciated.

PART ONE
The FBI and the Roots of the War on the New Left

The Battleground

On May 10, 1968, FBI Director J. Edgar Hoover did something extraordinary. He wrote a memo to all Special Agents in Charge (SAC) of Bureau offices nationwide that, on the face of it, resembled so many others. During his thirty-seven-year reign, the Director would, from his desk at the Seat of Government, issue thousands of memoranda—official and unofficial missives that acted as his tentacles controlling the broad expanse of the Bureau. Some dispatches were personal notes of congratulation upon a marriage or the birth of a child, others were critical notes of censure citing even the smallest infraction that intended to humiliate the recipient, and still others were meticulous directives in ongoing investigations, as if the Director himself were on the ground supervising the daily activities of his agents. Hoover's hold on the ten-thousand-man agency was absolute, tight, and unforgiving. This memo, while couched in the bureaucratese of which Hoover was the master, was most notable for its lack of specificity, its broad-brush call to action, and its uncharacteristic vagary as to the expansiveness of its tactics. On May 10, 1968, J. Edgar Hoover called for a full-scale assault on America's youth. It was called COINTELPRO New Left. The Director's words were unambiguous as to their intent:

> Effective immediately, the Bureau is instituting a Counterintelligence Program directed against the New Left Movement and its Key Activists. All offices are instructed to immediately open an active control file, captioned as above, and assign responsibility for this program to an experienced and imaginative Special Agent who is well versed in investigation of the New Left and its membership.
>
> The purpose of this program is to expose, disrupt, and neutralize the activities of the various New Left organizations, their leadership and adherents. . . . The devious maneuvers and duplicity of these activists must be exposed to public scrutiny through the cooperation of reliable news media sources, both locally and at the Seat of Government. We must frustrate every effort of these groups and individuals to consolidate their forces or to recruit new or youthful adherents. In every instance, consideration should be given to

disrupting the organized activity of these groups and no opportunity should be missed to capitalize upon organizational and personal conflicts of their leadership.[9]

The Counterintelligence Program, COINTELPRO for short, was Hoover's fifteen-year effort to subvert those he identified as America's enemies. The program's absolute secrecy guaranteed its long duration, and Hoover's control over the day-to-day strategy and tactics of its execution defined its potency as a weapon against its targets. In this new, expanded, phase of the program Hoover was clear about the priority the initiative was being assigned in the conduct of an agent's duties: "Law and order is mandatory for any civilized society to survive. Therefore, you must approach this new endeavor with a forward look, enthusiasm, and interest in order to accomplish our responsibilities. The importance of this new endeavor cannot and will not be overlooked."[10] If local SACs had any doubt as to their personal accountability for neutralizing this somewhat ill-defined target, Hoover's final admonishment made it clear that they, themselves, would be monitored and held responsible for significant tangible results on a mission where nothing less than America's institutions and ideals were at stake. His was a tall yet ambiguous order. But without a doubt, no man in the FBI wanted to find out what the dark side of Hoover's implied threat looked like should the director perceive a misstep in his work. In St. Louis, SAC Joseph Gamble and, later, his successor, SAC J. Wallace LaPrade, would find energetic and imaginative approaches for executing this new frontline offensive.

Between 1968 and 1971, Hoover used the latitude afforded to him from the full cloak of secrecy inherent to COINTELPRO to codify and press his expectations of agents assigned to New Left activities. In numerous subsequent memoranda, Hoover's presence hovered as field agents scurried to meet his ever-growing demand for intelligence, analysis, and subversion of the "depraved nature and moral looseness" of America's youth movement.[11] The most detailed directive came from Hoover on July 5, 1968, in which he outlined twelve "suggestions to be utilized by all offices." Some of the proposed actions included the use of targeted propaganda as he instructed agents to prepare anonymous defamatory leaflets for distribution on college campuses. The leaflets were to be illustrated with photos of Students for a Democratic Society (SDS) leaders using the "most obnoxious pictures" or, in others, with defamatory cartoons. Hoover observed, "ridicule is one of the most potent weapons we have against [the New Left]."[12] Other instructions suggested the authoring of anonymous "poison pen" letters describing the depravity of New Left adherents to be sent to university administrators, wealthy donors, members of legislatures, and parents of the students.[13] Moreover, the use of "cooperative press contacts" to write articles and editorials minimizing the size and effect of New Left activities was strongly encouraged.[14]

But perhaps the most forceful of Hoover's instructions was directed towards fomenting discord and paranoia among New Left leaders and their followers.[15] Hoover perceived abundant possibilities in this arena, but success would be reliant upon effective and active instigators of such divisions. Therefore, the recruitment of confidential informants (CIs) to garner additional relevant intelligence and to spearhead the execution of surveillance and subversion activities was critical. The philosophical and tactical underpinning for the use of these informants was to "enhance paranoia. . . and further serve to get the point across that there is an FBI agent behind every mailbox."[16] In order to engender this level of induced mistrust, the universe of agents and their surrogates needed to be greatly expanded to infiltrate the daily lives of New Left activists endlessly and insidiously. One memo articulates a key tactic for the recruitment of these CIs, noting that "the use of marijuana and other narcotics is widespread among members of the New Left" and that agents should be on heightened alert for opportunities to encourage local authorities to arrest students on drug charges."[17] Consequently, a favored and effective method for encouraging students to turn on one another was the promise of forgiving or lessening criminal charges in return for active cooperation.[18] The ubiquity of marijuana and other drug use on college campuses provided ample opportunities for a steady stream of foot soldiers dragooned into Hoover's war of subterfuge.

New Left Domestic Counterintelligence in Context

So as not to overstate the significance of Hoover's May 10, 1968, memorandum, a brief history of the COINTELPRO will help to frame the program more rightly as "evolutionary" rather than "revolutionary." There had been active domestic counterintelligence programs since the mid-1950s. Initially, COINTELPRO was focused on the Communist Party of the USA (1956) and the Socialist Worker's Party (1961); it then progressed into the infiltration of the Ku Klux Klan (1964), expanded into the Black Nationalist movement (1967), until it finally landed on the New Left (1968). Hoover considered all these groups a threat to national security, and once each was so identified, he afforded himself great latitude in determining how to eliminate that threat.

What defined COINTELPRO was threefold: its iron-clad secrecy, its avoidance of any accountability within the federal government, and participants' total lack of introspection as to the legal and ethical implications of the tactics they employed. COINTELPRO was a tightly guarded secret even among Bureau personnel within field offices.[19] Many agents had no notion of the program's operations, even in small offices. In Washington, DC, COINTELPRO went undisclosed to Congress, the Department of Justice, and the President of the United States for decades.[20] Indeed, it was not until 1975—three years after Hoover's death—that key aspects of the program were finally revealed. That year, Congress launched its first major investigation into the program, conducted by the Senate Select Committee to Study Operations with Respect to Intelligence Activities (known more familiarly as the Church Committee, named for the committee's chairman, Idaho Democrat Frank Church). During COINTELPRO's productive years, evidence of domestic intelligence gathering was well-known by many government officials, but Hoover made certain that the sources and methods that yielded those results remained both secret and without independent oversight. Therefore, even as COINTELPRO was monitored with a cool military precision from the Seat of Government, the program was frequently without tether in its ambition and tactics in the field. When William C. Sullivan, Hoover's Director of Domestic Intelligence and the man considered the main architect of COINTELPRO, was deposed in 1975 by the Church Committee, he succinctly framed the contours of the program:

> This is a rough, tough, dirty business and dangerous. It was dangerous at times. No holds were barred. The issue of the law or ethics was secondary to the ill-gotten gains. Never once did I hear anybody, including myself, raise the question: "Is this course of action which we have agreed upon lawful? Is it legal? Is it ethical or moral?" We never gave any thought to this realm of reasoning, because we were just naturally pragmatists. The one thing we were concerned about was this: "Will this course of action work, will it get us what we want?" We did what we were expected to do.[21]

152

COINTELPRO's long, successful history of fighting America's domestic "enemies" led Hoover to the May 10, 1968, memorandum inaugurating COINTELPRO New Left. In one critical sense, however, this effort represented an entirely new phase in the program. Unlike previous FBI targeting of groups framed as domestic threats, COINTELPRO New Left was not so much focused on an organization as it was an assault on an ideology. There were literally and figuratively card-carrying members of the CPUSA, the SWP, the KKK and the Black Panthers. These were organizations that had named leaders, organizational headquarters, and chapters throughout the country. But the New Left had few such formal identifiers. There were organizations such as Students for a Democratic Society (SDS), but the followers of New Left ideology expanded far beyond that sometimes rag-tag organization. Instead, Hoover's understanding of the "New Left" was an amorphous mix of countercultural, frequently long-haired young people with a variety of liberal ideas on politics, sex, drugs, and other life-style choices. These were primarily students on college campuses who, in the Hooverian world view, were being surreptitiously guided by outside communist forces hellbent on undermining the very fabric of American society. As he noted:

The Bureau has been very closely following the activities of the New Left and the Key Activists and is highly concerned that the anarchistic activities of a few can paralyze institutions of learning, inductions centers, cripple traffic, and tie the arms of law enforcement officials all to the detriment of our society. The organizations and activists who spout revolution and unlawfully challenge society to obtain their demands must not only be contained but must be neutralized.[22]

With the notion of the "New Left" hard to characterize other than a vague sense that an FBI man was supposed to know an adherent if he saw one, the targets of this neutralization effort needed to be made more identifiable. Who exactly was this New Left enemy? On May 28, 1968, just two weeks after Hoover's initial missive, the SAC of the FBI's New York field office offered the embraced answer to this question: such a figure could be identified by an "aversion to work," a "Jewish liberal background," and "anti-establishment dress and ideology."[23] While not a severely delimiting factor, such characterizations offered some general focus—and perhaps a rationale—for the FBI's plan of attack.

In the Company of the FBI

Before coming to understand the scope and breadth of the Bureau's assault on the New Left specifically in St. Louis, it is important to provide even more context, as the FBI was not the only agency of surveillance and subversion on college campuses. To surveil college students nationwide the Department of the Army created Operation Garden Plot, the Central Intelligence Agency launched Operation Chaos, the National Security Agency hosted Operations Shamrock and Minaret, and the Internal Revenue Service formed Operation Leprechaun. These named operations, as well as others in the Office of Naval Intelligence, the Secret Service, and many other federal agencies, were involved in the collection and dissemination of intelligence on student activists around the nation. In addition, local law enforcement, in this case the St. Louis County Police, had their own police intelligence units that prowled meetings, demonstrations, and other informal gatherings of civil rights and antiwar agitators.[24] Indeed, the coverage of the many quotidian activities of progressives was so extensive that America's most trusted newsman, Walter Cronkite, reported that "There were so many agencies involved in the surveillance of antiwar activities that, at times, spies would trail spies."[25]

While Cronkite's remark might seem tongue-in-cheek, it was an apt characterization of the expansion of the intelligence infrastructure in defense, foreign, and domestic agencies of the government, each one contributing its own unique expertise and area of specialization. For example, from 1967 to 1973 the CIA's Operation Chaos amassed some ten thousand files on individuals and over one hundred domestic groups, within a computerized index system known as Hydra.[26] Because the CIA had particular interest in Americans' relationships with foreign adversaries, the agency surveilled US mail flowing to and from countries of interest (also known as "covert mail coverage") in Operation HTLINGUAL.[27] The most direct interaction the CIA had with students on college campuses was found in Project Resistance, a program devoted to collecting background information on student groups the CIA believed posed threats to their facilities and personnel at home and abroad. In 1968, information collected from Project Resistance was merged with intelligence from the FBI, and was then collated at the CIA's Targets Analysis Branch, all resulting in detailed Situation Reports and a comprehensive calendar of demonstrations and meetings.[28]

The most influential FBI partner, however, was the Department of the Army, specifically Military Intelligence—and, most specifically in the case

154

of St. Louis, Military Intelligence Unit 113 (MI-113). MI-113 was part of a nation-wide effort to collect, analyze, and disseminate intelligence on antiwar activities that came under the umbrella of Operation Garden Plot. The Army's efforts under this program from 1965 to 1970 were particularly fruitful, resulting in twenty-five million index cards on individuals (this number comprised one-eighth of the American population at the time), eight million personality dossiers, 760,000 reports on organizations, and provision, on average, of 12,000 daily responses to information requests. Spearheading the Army's efforts were 1,000 plain-clothed military agents who collected domestic intelligence and fed it to the FBI, other military branches, local police, and a variety of federal agencies such as the Secret Service, the US Passport Office, and the Civil Service Commission.[29] MI-113, which included both Missouri and Illinois, was considered the Army's lead domestic intelligence unit, having successfully handled operations during Chicago's 1968 Democratic National Convention. It proved, therefore, to be a powerful partner to the FBI in St. Louis.

One particular asset not afforded to the FBI, from which the CIA and MI-113 benefited greatly, was the ability to operate undercover. CIA and MI agents grew their hair long, wore "hippie clothing and beads," and attempted, as best they could, to fit in with the crowds of students surrounding them. In the case of the Army, many of the undercover agents were of essentially the same age, having only recently been drafted or volunteered for service, so blending in was less of an acting challenge. Hoover, on the other hand, expressly forbade his agents to adopt the demeanor and dress of the students, relying instead on a developed network of confidential informants that allowed penetration into the lives of the targets.[30]

Despite the differing approaches to intelligence gathering, all the agencies worked closely with one another to share, compare, and provide analysis. Most documents received through *Seavey v. Department of Justice* indicate this extensive collaboration among intelligence agencies. As was the norm nationwide, the St. Louis Bureau office provided near daily carbon copies of their intelligence reports to many federal agencies but most frequently to MI-113 and the CIA. And these agencies reciprocated. Of course, such efficient and thorough collaboration among agencies meant that the accumulated information gathered about New Left adherents was staggering. By the end of COINTELPRO, the FBI possessed 6.5 million investigative files and 58 million index cards that filled three floors of the FBI building and 7,500 six-drawer filing cabinets.[31] Given the acquisition and flow of information and analysis derived from the two interagency methods of operation—one undercover and one penetrative through the use of confidential informants—Walter Cronkite's reporting on the extent of government surveillance of civil rights and student activists proves more accurate than hyperbolic. The efforts of the St. Louis office of the FBI were well-positioned at the epicenter of this multi-pronged approach to intelligence gathering and subversion that led the midwestern city to a place of particularity in the history of dissent—one that devolved poorly to those caught in the middle of the tug-of-war between social activism and the government's law-and-order imperatives.

PART TWO
Government Surveillance and Subversion
in St. Louis: A Midwestern Saga

St. Louis: The Unexpected Battleground
in the War against the New Left

When J. Edgar Hoover's trusted lieutenant, Cartha DeLoach, wrote a book-length apologia defending his former boss nearly twenty-five years after the director's death, he cited one incident that, above all others, represented a defining moment in the FBI leader's search for the consummate New Left poster child. The opportunity presented itself on August 24, 1967, during a speech delivered by then–Washington University student body president, Devereaux (Dev) Kennedy, at a conference at the Center for the Study of Democratic Institutions in Santa Barbara, California. DeLoach reported on the scene as it played out in Southern California that day: "The New Left leaders of these nationwide demonstrations and riots were quite explicit in telling their followers and the general public their alarming intentions. Devereaux Kennedy, student body president at Washington University, made his desires clear:

> I want student power to demand "revolutionary reforms" that can't be met within the logic of the existing American system. I'm going to say loudly and explicitly what I mean by revolution. What I mean by revolution is overthrowing the American government, and American imperialism. . . . This is going to come about by black rebellion in our cities being joined by some white people. They have access to money, and they can give people guns, which I think they should do. They can

engage in acts of terrorism and sabotage outside the ghetto . . . and they can blow things up, and I think they should.[32]

Kennedy's articulation of the goals and tactics of the New Left in an influential public forum—advocating the mixing of races in a unified armed assault on the status quo—was just the kind of apocalyptic scenario that gave Hoover ammunition to expand what were already penetrative COINTELPRO actions against specific organizations and to target them more broadly towards the nation's eighteen- to twenty-two-year-old college students.

Years later, reflecting upon his noteworthy speech, Kennedy recalled: "I remember there was a lot of loose talk about 'revolution this' and 'revolution that.' But understand that I had no idea how controversial it would be at the time because I wasn't looking up to see all the people who were recording this and listening to it. So, I had no idea that that was that controversial."[33] At least in Kennedy's current recollection, his talk of revolution didn't imply the same imminent threat of violence for him that it did for the FBI informants and conservative press who attended the conference. No matter what his actual intentions, Kennedy's speech allowed Hoover to draw the battle lines for his war on the New Left.

Soon enough, Kennedy and his fellow students at Washington University in St. Louis found themselves in the FBI's crosshairs. Within days of Kennedy's Santa Barbara appearance, a report was solicited from the St. Louis Police Intelligence Unit on his activities. Undercover local law enforcement sent back a detailed report quoting a statement Kennedy had made on September 19, 1967, asserting that he was a "revolutionary but had not preached the overthrow of the government, but if the revolution came, he would 'gladly join in.'"[34] The St. Louis FBI office quickly responded by making Kennedy a target of investigation.[35] His name was added to the Security Index and a "Main File" was opened on him.[36] Now, thorough investigations of Kennedy would be conducted that would come to ensnare others in his orbit; the names and activities of all of Kennedy's known contacts came under the microscope of the FBI's St. Louis field office.

Kennedy's speech was seen by Hoover as a manifesto for other students across the US, and his words became enshrined in the FBI's iron-clad institutional memory. They were frequently quoted in memoranda as the rationale for more aggressive surveillance and infiltration of all those with a New Left ideology. In short, Dev Kennedy's comments, and others like them, became the rallying cry in Hoover's world of suspicion about the motives, tactics, and intents of America's counterculture. That Kennedy's words were recalled with such clarity and precision by DeLoach over two decades after he had uttered them is evidence of the indelible imprint that the unwitting Washington University student-body president had made on those in the FBI's Seat of Government. Within the year, they provided both a motivation and a rationale for Hoover's May 10, 1968, memorandum and its detailed follow-up instructions.[37]

Even in spite of Kennedy's inflammatory speech and the FBI spotlight that it unwittingly focused on St. Louis—and on Washington University in particular—it may seem anomalous that students from this frequently ignored "fly-over state" should find themselves elevated onto the national stage. If anything, Washington University in St. Louis seemed, in the mid- to late 1960s, a relatively quiescent and insular place to go to school. The main campus sits at the intersection of University City and Clayton, the first suburbs just over the line separating St. Louis City from St. Louis County. The long promenade of crisscrossed brick pathways was surrounded by late nineteenth- and early twentieth-century academic buildings, all modeled on the august courtyard configurations of Oxford and Cambridge. The administration's aspiration to turn the institution from a commuter college of the pre–World War II era into a world-class university by focusing heavily on its science and engineering departments ultimately paid off, earning Washington University the moniker of the "Harvard of the Midwest."

Dissent of the kind that Kennedy was espousing was rare on campus.[38] Indeed, his role as student-body president resulted not from broad student support for his views but instead from an astute political calculation that the student body was so apathetic to issues and governance that his candidacy wouldn't meet much of a challenge. Indeed, he later reflected, he "won in a landslide . . . because there was really no opposition."[39] So, nothing in this midwestern academic enclave offered a whiff, at the time, of significant activist dissent. But given the political and cultural make-up of Missouri, the WU student protests that did occur came to take on a distinct and outsized meaning.

St. Louis: The Fertile Terrain of Conservatism
Missouri's reputation as a socially and politically conservative state pales in comparison to the iconic images of racism and repression from the Deep South: the blasting of Bull Connor's water hoses on protestors and

the unleashing of attack dogs on women and children in Birmingham, the beatings of the Freedom Riders in Mississippi, and the grisly work of lynch mobs in Louisiana. These kinds of vivid images don't exist in our collective historical memory of St. Louis. Yet the seeming absence of these more violent acts does not make the border state of Missouri immune to the reactionary impulse that gave rise to these notorious incidents just a few hundred miles to the south. Two examples of Missouri's activist hard-line conservative political core include the city leaders' backlash against the 1963 protest against discriminatory hiring practices at the Jefferson Bank and Trust Co. in St. Louis and Missouri congressman Richard Ichord's use of his chairmanship of the Committee on Internal Security (previously known as the House Un-American Activities Committee) to unmask SDS members as "extremists bearing the banners of communism, anarchism, and nihilism."[40] Historian Walter Johnson locates St. Louis as a bastion of conservatism in the immediate postwar era, when the literal construction of the city codified segregation. "[The] 1947 *Comprehensive City Plan* provided a beginner's guide to building a racist city—incising and intensifying existing differences of race and class in the physical form of the built environment," Johnson notes. Local activists dubbed 1950s and 1960s urban-renewal clearances of Black neighborhoods as "Black removal by white approval." These planning initiatives cemented the bifurcation between the city's haves and have-nots.[41]

It was within this context that St. Louis and its surrounding communities constructed their own particularized version of radical conservatism, one that differed from its counterparts in the Deep South but was no less punishing. Built on the foundations of segregation, the city was home to a deep pool of conservatives from which St. Louis chose its judges and elected its representatives to Jefferson City and Washington, DC. The people who built the city's economic fortunes in the war industries likewise were conservatives.[42] They initially focused their antagonism on civil rights activists and then later turned to antiwar protestors. Students at Washington University, many of whom arrived from afar to attend this now world-class university, were unprepared for the ferocious midwestern border-state rules of engagement.

The discord that grew between the counterculture students at Washington University and surrounding conservative communities crept in slowly and sat there, festering. Such was the case when, on February 14, 1968, a group of seventy-five students and faculty fixed their sights on a Dow Industries recruiter visiting the WU campus. Dow was a primary manufacturer of napalm, the incendiary defoliant dropped in bombs, that caused severe burns and asphyxiation among civilians and military personnel who came in contact with it. The company frequently recruited on the WU campus, given the university's renowned engineering and science programs. On that day, activists sang songs, chanted, and presented the recruiter with a petition signed by three hundred individuals who were opposed to his presence on the campus. The crowd was ultimately so disruptive to the recruiter's efforts that he was forced to terminate the day's scheduled interviews at 10:40 a.m. and was hastily escorted from campus to ensure his safety.[43] From the protestors' perspective, this "action" was an effective encounter but not a directly combative one—a way of expressing their anger about the war but not one that would invite police intervention.

While these kinds of targeted protests against war-industry representatives were not uncommon on many campuses, what made them more significant at Washington University was the direct connection between the recruitment efforts and the vested economic interests of the university. The Board of Trustees at Washington University was dominated by CEOs and chairmen of companies directly involved in supplying materials to support the war in Vietnam, and many of those companies were headquartered in St. Louis. For example, the Chairman of the Board of Trustees, Charles Allen Thomas, was the Chairman of the Board of Monsanto Corporation, maker of another controversial Vietnam-era defoliant, Agent Orange. Also represented on the Board were Harold Eugene Thayer, CEO and Chairman of the Board of Mallinckrodt Chemical Works, which, like Dow Chemical, produced napalm; John Olin, President of Olin Industries, an enterprise formed from the combination of the Winchester Repeating Arms Company and Mathieson Chemical, which manufactured armaments and ammunition for the Vietnam conflict; Sanford McDonnell, Chairman and CEO of McDonnell-Douglas Corporation, the largest supplier of US military planes during the war; and Clark Clifford, former Secretary of Defense during the Johnson Administration, under whom America's involvement in the Vietnam conflict had significantly escalated.

Taken as a whole, this commitment to government contracts and contacts within the Department of Defense and war-related industries had been a significant factor in transforming Washington University from the small commuter college it had been in the 1950s to the powerhouse in higher education which it had become by the late 1960s. Therefore, understanding the significance of the Dow Chemical recruiter's February 1968 flight from campus requires an appreciation of the high-level, vested interests of Washington University leaders and of the institution itself. The students themselves may or may not have recognized the broader context of their actions. "It's as if those protests were in the middle of a military base and they [the students] thought of those protests as being in the middle of their campus where they went to school. And instead, from the standpoint of the FBI or even the administration of Wash. U., it looks as if they're there right in the middle of some sort of strategically essential asset."[44] The threat of interruption to the school's defense-industry relationships was therefore unacceptable—a position echoed by the conservative community surrounding the university—and this context helps to explain the larger drama that later played out on the campus.

The most visible symbol of the war-related presence on campus was the Reserve Officers' Training Corps (ROTC) program. Throughout the 1960s and 1970s, Washington University hosted both the Air Force and Army ROTC, offering college credit for programs that acted as a pathway into the ranks of the officer corps. The WU ROTC programs were housed in Quonset huts situated on the edge of campus (Fig. 5.2). These were simply made, oblong, tin structures in which junior officer candidates would take courses in military science and strategy. In the open spaces nearby, cadets received their outdoor training, such as marching in formation and other physical-education exercises. The two Quonset huts became a magnet for dissent as they provided the campus's most consistently accessible and visible representation of the Vietnam War.[45]

Prior to late 1968, most of the anti-ROTC activities on campus were confined to small protests that included taunting the cadets while they marched in formation or mounting guerrilla theater pieces intended to mock the ROTC exercises.[46] The tenor of these ridiculing, but harmless, protests changed when, at 4:00 a.m. on December 3, 1968, a WU security guard witnessed Michael Siskind (Fig. 5.3), a WU senior, and another unnamed individual place a Molotov cocktail on the window ledge of the Army ROTC building. Siskind's accomplice escaped arrest by quickly departing before the security worker arrived from the perch from which he had been

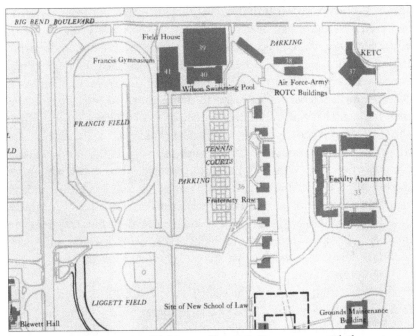

Figure 5.2 Detail from a 1966 Washington University campus map, with the western edge at the top. The ROTC buildings are near the top right, close to the intersection of Big Bend Boulevard and Millbrook Boulevard (now Forest Park Parkway). *From the Publications–Student Union Collection, Department of Special Collections, Washington University in St. Louis*

standing guard, leaving Siskind standing alone with the still-intact incendiary device in hand.

Within days of his arrest, Siskind admitted to having made the weapon, noting that he had intended to set fire to the interior of the ROTC building to "wake up the people."[47] While pleading guilty to his own involvement, Siskind steadfastly refused to identify his accomplice, a fact that continued to frustrate the St. Louis FBI and local federal prosecutors long after his conviction.

At the time of his arrest, Siskind was found to have an SDS membership card in his wallet, signed by Terry Koch, leader of the Washington University chapter of the national leftist student organization. This small but significant detail provided the prosecution team with a novel idea intended to make an example of Siskind as a warning for other

Figure 5.3 Michael Siskind as pictured in the *Globe-Democrat* on December 5, 1968. "W.U. Student in Bomb Case Carried SDS Card," ran the accompanying headline as Siskind became the first student activist in the US charged with sabotage. *Photo by Ralph Hyer for the* St. Louis Globe-Democrat, *from the collections of the St. Louis Mercantile Library at the University of Missouri–St. Louis*

"card-carrying revolutionaries." Normally, such an aborted attempt by a first-time offender would be prosecuted as attempted arson by the county prosecutor, potentially resulting in little more than a slap on the wrist. With this arrest coming just months after Hoover's May 10 COINTELPRO New Left call to action, the St. Louis FBI field office seized on Siskind's plight as an opportunity. Local agents and the US Attorney for Eastern Missouri, Veryl Riddle, took a far more aggressive prosecutorial stance, levying charges under the Federal Sabotage Statute—a crime that carried a maximum penalty of thirty years in prison and a $10,000 fine. In a documented conversation with Riddle, St. Louis FBI Special Agent Spurgeon J. Peterson articulated the potential this crime presented when he noted that the New Left across the US was "responsible for 20 similar events" and that prosecuting Siskind for breaking a federal law would "do much to curtail future acts of anarchy against the U.S."[48] Writing from Washington, DC, Assistant Attorney General J. Walter Yeagley initially cautioned Riddle that the evidence to support a sabotage conviction was weak, especially since the incendiary device had not gone off and intent to harm would be difficult to prove.[49] But in spite of those initial misgivings,

Yeagley, too, eventually seized the unique opportunity that Siskind's circumstance presented. He noted:

This case may have far-reaching ramifications in view of the number of ROTC facilities which have already been the objects of violence and the probability that additional violence of this type can be expected in the future. Moreover, this is the first case to be brought under the revised [sabotage] statue, and the resulting case law could have a substantial effect on future cases under the sabotage statues.[50]

The prosecutors' problem, however, remained unchanged. Evidence in the case was thin. Instead of yielding to that reality, Yeagley spurred the FBI to widen its inquiries to include the development of peripheral and circumstantial evidence to bolster the sabotage charge and to ensure its wider impact on student activism. He directed the FBI to "undertake an immediate intensive investigation to develop evidence of any pre-act or post-act statements made by [Siskind's name redacted] or other activities on his part which would tend to establish his specific intent."[51] Evidence produced didn't need to be specific to the crime, but rather could be used to corroborate an impulse to engage in or justify such a crime. That legal construct seemed sufficient for the federal and local prosecutors.

Hoover had made the penetration and subversion of the New Left one of his highest priorities; field agents' careers could be made or broken based upon its successful execution. Siskind's arrest was seen by the St. Louis office as a prime opportunity that would score needed points with the director. They had an iron-clad conviction (Siskind had been caught in the act) and a local prosecutor willing to use federal law—for the first time— as a bludgeon against an activist. The St. Louis office bet that the reliably conservative judges in Missouri would see the broader implications of this case to levy a harsh sentence, one that would send a chill through the spines of Siskind's compatriots. These were the kinds of "tangible outcomes" that Hoover would reward with congratulatory notes in personnel files and with promotions. These were results that could motivate COINTELPRO New Left agents around the nation.

Equally important for the future of COINTELPRO New Left was Assistant Attorney General Yeagley's directive to the FBI to expand its investigative work into the collection of allied, but not direct, evidence. Although he wasn't aware of COINTELPRO and couldn't imagine the extent of the surveillance and subversion already underway, Yeagley unknowingly endorsed the use of evidence that was, in the later words of COINTELPRO's chief, William C. Sullivan, frequently gathered without regard to ethics, morality, or legality. Allowing agents to present at trial such potentially unrelated and circumstantial information collected from COINTELPRO's clandestine activities gave them license to use statements and actions in support of the broader goal of "law and order" in its most strident form. Should this investigative overreach result in a successful conviction in the carefully watched Siskind test case, Hoover's field agents would have the judicial imprimatur they sought to "imaginatively" collect and interpret evidence. To their delight, the federal grand jury returned an indictment on the sabotage charge, and the noose around the necks of student activists tightened. And then as hoped, three months after Siskind's arrest, Judge Roy Harper outlined what he perceived to be at stake in this oddly consequential sabotage case in which no bomb had ever gone off. The *St. Louis Post-Dispatch* related Harper's remarks:

"My information is that you were a user of drugs and a member of the Students for a Democratic Society which is committed to destroying the system of government that made our country great." Judge Roy Harper continued that he had presided over the trial of a group of Communists charged with the violation of the Smith Act several years prior and that "the group you belong to is committed to the very thing they were." Judge Harper went on, "Society is entitled to protection."[52]

He then sentenced Michael Siskind to five years in a federal penitentiary. It was the first time that sabotage charges involving the destruction of "war utilities" had successfully been levied since World War II. It was such a momentous conviction that Walter Cronkite reported it that night on the *CBS Evening News*.[53]

What is most interesting about the Siskind conviction and its ultimate impact was not simply that the twenty-one-year-old student had been successfully prosecuted for a fizzled bombing attempt under what were the harshest possible federal charges in modern US history, nor that the SDS card in his wallet played a significant factor in the prosecutorial strategy, nor that his lot seemed to be tied to a band of communists who had appeared before Judge Harper years before and with whom Siskind had no possible connection, nor that, in spite of his dire prospects, Siskind did not provide information about his accomplice in return for leniency. No, what is most telling comes from comments J. Edgar Hoover made in a lengthy memo he wrote to Joseph Gamble, SAC of the St. Louis Bureau Office, commending his and his agents' efforts. Hoover wrote:

> The guilty plea entered by [Siskind's name redacted] to the charge of the violation of the sabotage statute marks a decided change, particularly on the part of the Department in the manner in which such cases may be handled in the future. This case ... [is one] in which your Division and the Bureau can be justifiably proud. All future violations should be vigorously pressed in order that they may result in prosecutive action.[54]

And even more pointedly as to the anticipated future FBI efforts in St. Louis was Hoover's final comment:

> This marks the first time that the Sabotage Statute has been utilized. Prosecution in this matter was initially authorized by the US Attorney at St. Louis, much to the consternation of the Department [of Justice] which had no choice but to follow through on the prosecution.[55]

While Hoover may have overstated Assistant Attorney General Yeagley's initial concerns about the lack of evidence in Siskind's sabotage case, he saw an opportunity in the ability of the St. Louis Bureau to work collaboratively with a far more aggressive St. Louis US Attorney to procure stringent federal convictions for crimes that would otherwise have been relegated to local or lesser federal charges, even if that meant challenging the legal wisdom of the Department of Justice itself. Investigative ingenuity could be married with prosecutorial brashness to yield what Hoover saw as his goal: a way to stem the tide against a progressive ideology that he found anathema.[56] In St. Louis, Hoover had found the right mix of political and cultural conservative activism to suit his purposes. Moreover, entrenched economic interests on the Board of Trustees ensured that the dominant voices in the university's administration would not necessarily object when investigative and prosecutorial innovations were needed to quash student dissent. And now Judge Harper had delivered case law that would reward even the thinnest of evidence with the harshest of convictions. St. Louis was, indeed, fertile ground for Hoover's war on the New Left.

166

Hoover, not one to rest on his laurels nor to miss a moment to instruct his local agents, articulated the next steps in this battle to SAC Gamble:

Consider contacting campus sources for the purpose of obtaining full details regarding demonstrations or disturbances at Washington University which were directed toward the war in Vietnam or, specifically, against ROTC training. Determine ringleaders of such disturbances for consideration as possible suspects in this matter. . . . All informants and sources at the Washington University campus should be contacted or recontacted in this matter for assistance in identifying the unknown subject [Siskind's accomplice] of this case. . . . In connection with the foregoing, it should be kept in mind that public knowledge and publicity relative to [redacted—presumed to be Siskind's] plea of guilty may encourage individuals interviewed to be of assistance in this matter.[57]

Even with the victory on Siskind's sabotage charge and sentencing, the FBI was still searching for the identity of his accomplice. The prospect of garnering Hoover's approval for bagging such a prize catch would prove motivational for his field agents, and there were numerous potential suspects on the Washington University campus on whom they could focus their investigative efforts. The cloak of secrecy inherent in COINTELPRO New Left, coupled with the ever-expanding use of infiltrative confidential informants, would soon lure many students into the FBI's net.

Targets, Tactics, and Tangible Results

SAC Joseph Gamble fully appreciated St. Louis's centrality in Hoover's assault on the New Left. Just two weeks after the Director's May 10, 1968, call to action, Gamble responded by identifying four central targets for the St. Louis Bureau COINTELPRO activities: Action Committee to Improve Opportunities for Negroes (ACTION), Students for a Democratic Society (SDS), St. Louis Draft Resistance (SLDR), and the Committee to Support Draft Resistance (CSDR).[58] He identified ACTION as a "racial-type organization" formed as an off-shoot of the local chapter of the Congress of Racial Equality (CORE), separating from that organization because the latter was "not militant enough."[59] He further observed that that the latter three organizations were centered at Washington University and Saint Louis University. Having identified his four main targets for neutralization,

Gamble seized on Hoover's suggestion of using relationships with the press to maintain a steady drumbeat of anti-activist public sentiment and noted, "The feeding of well-chosen information to the St. Louis *Globe-Democrat*, a local newspaper whose editor and associate editor are extremely friendly to the Bureau and the St. Louis Office, has also been utilized in the past and it is contemplated that this technique might be used to good advantage with this program."[60] In fact, this relationship had been a productive, familiar one for the FBI long before 1968. In 1962, the FBI had selected the conservative morning St. Louis newspaper as one of five press outlets for disseminating propaganda aimed at discrediting Dr. Martin Luther King Jr. and his organization, the Southern Christian Leadership Conference.[61] Recalling his tenure as *Globe-Democrat* assistant editorial-page editor from 1961 to 1965, well-known conservative activist and eventual Nixon aide Patrick Buchanan later noted:

A great admirer of J. Edgar Hoover, the publisher [of the *Globe-Democrat*] was in regular contact with the FBI and we were among Hoover's conduits to the American people. Through Amberg [the publisher] the FBI channeled us constant information on local Communists and radicals. The bureau's penetration of the extreme left in St. Louis was truly something to behold. Truly, speaking of the Far Left, J. Edgar Hoover could say, with near biblical certitude in those years, that "Where two or three are gathered together, there I am amongst you."[62]

SAC Gamble's commitment to using the local press as a method of shaping public opinion about New Left activities was made with the full confidence of a receptive welcome and was but one action on the horizon. "St. Louis will carefully analyze these organizations under these programs in an effort to affect [sic] the disruption of the New Left and specific suggestions of Counterintelligence action will be submitted for approval by separate letter," Gamble promised.[63] With Hoover's demand for "tangible results" to be reported every ninety days, SAC Gamble and his successor, J. Wallace LaPrade, got busy making good on the promise that St. Louis, located in the fertile proving ground of midwestern conservatism, offered Hoover in his mission to neutralize the New Left.[64]

The activities of the St. Louis Bureau of the FBI dedicated to disrupting the activities of the New Left fell into three categories: 1) development of confidential informants to increase penetrative surveillance; 2) disruptive efforts intended to undermine activists and their protests; and 3) creation of a prosecutorial environment in which examples could be made of students in well-publicized cases as a way to create a chilling effect on the activities of others.

Crucial to the success of the second and third goals was the successful fulfillment of the first: the development of a pool of information garnered through a reliable network of informants. We do not know how the St. Louis office of the FBI was able to develop their base of CIs; they may have used the coercive means of trading cooperation for reduced or forgiven criminal charges, as referenced above, or other inducements may have been provided to solicit cooperation. But we do know that activities of student activists on the Washington University campus were monitored closely by a trove of human infiltrators with code names such as Dave, Jed, Ivan, Edna, Gill, Mike, Stella, Fran, Nick, Otto, Ross, and Kip, among many others whose monikers are still redacted from documents.[65] What one gleans from their reports is the wealth of information made possible by the proximity of these informants to their intended targets.[66] For example, several reports provide details on potluck suppers attended by activist leaders Terry Koch, Larry Kogan, Howard Mechanic, and many others in the local chapter of SDS.[67] These events were small, intimate gatherings frequented by a close-knit group of friends, so the presence of the CI speaks to the extensive penetration into the inner circle of the activists' social fabric. These up-close reports of daily life afforded the Bureau a wealth of information that spoke not only to the activities of these twenty-somethings but also insight into their motivations, their habits, their random musings, their financial circumstances, and sometimes their sexual activities.

The information garnered through confidential informants was augmented by the insights offered by confidential sources. These were frequently individuals who voluntarily came to the FBI with information or who, under questioning by Special Agents, unwittingly revealed previously unknown information. Taken together, these informant and source reports offered a rich profile of just what the FBI believed it was looking for in terms of student intentions and activities.

An excellent example of the way in which information from these sources worked to support the COINTELPRO New Left mission can be found in the wake of the February 1970 burning of the campus Army ROTC building. This was the same building targeted by Siskind in his failed arson attempt fourteen months earlier. The Army's continued training presence on campus increasingly chafed student activists and led them to do more than protest. Sometime after midnight on February 23, some person or group broke the ROTC building's windows, threw in several Molotov cocktails, and successfully burned the structure to the ground. The arsonists were never identified or apprehended. The continued mystery surrounding the identities of those who were responsible frustrated the agents of the St. Louis Bureau of the FBI, earning them palpable impatience from Hoover.[68] The incident intensified the call for increased scrutiny of student suspects by the Bureau, local law enforcement, and federal prosecutors by whatever means necessary. Someone was going to be held to account, and the Siskind conviction was proof enough that direct evidence was not a prerequisite for severe prosecution and punishment in Missouri.

In the FBI's network of suspicion, confidential informants and sources could provide sufficient innuendo and circumstantial fodder for the arson

Figure 5.4 An exchange of views after Washington University student protestors disrupted outdoor ROTC drills on March 23, 1970. Facing the camera is Army ROTC cadet Dennis Guilliams. *Photo by Jim Carrington for the* St. Louis Globe-Democrat, *from the collections of the St. Louis Mercantile Library at the University of Missouri–St. Louis*

investigation. Details provided by these various sources offer crucial insight into the influences on the FBI's pursuit of the case. In a report covering the period from February 23 to March 4, 1970—that is, the days in the immediate aftermath of the Army ROTC burning—the following information was noted:

[Name redacted] stated that a second confidential source, who smokes "grass" and is considered a student radical, had advised him that . . . Howard Mechanic left his apartment at 6015 Pershing, St. Louis at approximately 11:00 PM on the night of February 22, 1970. [Redacted] told the source that MECHANIC returned at about 1:00 A.M. February 23, 1970 and he [MECHANIC] stated he had "just torched the ROTC building."

[Name redacted] stated that the source was very nervous about the situation and that he did not want to get further involved. He agreed, however, to recontact the informant and attempt to get him to develop more information.

[Name redacted] was contacted on February 25, 26, and 27, 1970 and on each occasion he indicated that he had been able to recontact the informant. It was suggested [by name redacted] that it might be advisable to put his source directly in contact with Agents of the FBI. He agreed to do this, providing the source had no objections.

On March 5, 1970 [name redacted] advised that he had re-contacted his informant and that the latter was very scared. [Name redacted] stated that the source had no additional information to offer and that he did not want to talk to FBI Agents. [Name redacted] advised that he would maintain contact with the informant and continue to provide the FBI with any information developed.[69]

In another summary report, additional insights were offered:

On March 2, 1970 [redacted] (protect by request) provided the following information: [Extended redaction], St. Louis, Mo. and has [redacted] on Tuesday evenings an individual by the name of HOWARD MECHANIC. On the evening of February 24, 1970, MECHANIC appeared anxious to talk about a fire that had occurred at Washington University February 23, 1970. [Redacted] remarked to MECHANIC, "You did a good job on the ROTC building," and MECHANIC did not reply but instead smiled. MECHANIC stated that he was attending a meeting at Washington University that same night at 8:30 P.M. and was of the opinion that all the students at Washington University (WU) needed to bring them together was an incident like the ROTC fire.

[Redacted] told MECHANIC that [redacted] thought it was a very professional job and probably not done by students and MECHANIC grinned and said, "Do you really think that?"[70]

And finally, in a summary note:

On February 28, 1970 [redacted] telephonically contacted [redacted] and [redacted] stated that [redacted] had been at HOWARD MECHANIC's apartment when [redacted] had called MECHANIC earlier on February 28, 1970. [Redacted] stated that he felt that the fire at Harris Teachers College and the fire at WU's ROTC Building were both political in nature. [Redacted] stated that in his opinion whoever started the fires worked in teams and that the teams were very small in number so that if FBI informants were to attend meetings of organizations they would not find out about the team and their activities.[71]

What we learn from the compilation of these reports is telling. First, we are privy to the various layers of information—some of it coming from a known informant or a source who is speaking to an unofficial source who is admittedly anxious at the prospect of having these discussions. Other information is being plied from the contact time and time again. Second, we are witness to the extraordinary intimacy of these interactions. These are reports that emanate from interactions within Mechanic's home, in one-on-one conversations, and, in one case, overheard as a private telephone conversation. That's as close as a source could get; the reports come as a function of small group interactions, collected by people who knew their targets well as friends. Third, we are privy to the importance not just of direct information of criminal conduct, but of reported impressions, mannerisms, affect, and non-verbal responses that were weighted as heavily as the reportage of facts. In this context, Mechanic's demeanor became, for the agents of the St. Louis field office of the FBI, telling evidence of his culpability. Finally, the observation that the arsonists worked in small groups so that informants who attended larger organizational meetings would not know of their activities bears witness to the success of Hoover's intention of creating an environment of fear of an "FBI agent behind every mailbox." Clearly the students knew they were being watched in larger meetings, yet they had no notion of the level of penetration into their innermost circle of friends.

The assumption that there might be informants in their wider orbit obviously weighed heavily on the activists. Was it a deterrent? Obviously not. The Army ROTC building was torched and burned to the ground by one or more unnamed individuals on the night of February 23, 1970. And, given the extraordinary secrecy of the perpetrators, no one was ever brought to justice for the destruction of that federal facility. In the absence of serious leads, the more specious pieces of information took on greater importance as the unsolved crime dragged on and Hoover's impatience became more pronounced. Filling the vacuum were bits and pieces of uncorroborated, impressionistic, and anonymous information about presumed or likely suspects. But those bits of information served as powerful weapons in targeting young activists.

In what was a giant leap of COINTELPRO-led deduction, on April 17, 1970, a memorandum from the SAC Cleveland asserted that "HOWARD LAWRENCE MECHANIC has been developed as the chief suspect in the above-captioned incident [the February 23, 1970, Army ROTC bombing] and may also be the accomplice of [redacted—presumed to be Siskind] who was apprehended in the act of attempting to firebomb the ROTC building in December 1968 and is currently serving a five-year prison term."[72] Mechanic was now suspected of a successful federal bombing and was potentially identified as the unnamed accomplice in the Siskind attempted bombing.

No proof was required for these suppositions, and further investigation had not yielded any confirmation or corroboration. But the confidential informant report noting a "smile," a "grin," and an unconfirmed hearsay "confession" was all the evidence the St. Louis agents needed. Now Howard Mechanic was unknowingly positioned as the FBI's central target. Mechanic's ascendance to the top of the FBI's list of "persons of interest" was but one example among many others on the Washington University campus. As a targeted group living in the shadow of COINTELPRO New Left—which was now operating at full throttle, in total secrecy, and without restraint since its introduction nearly two years earlier—student activists would soon find themselves, unwittingly and without preparation, on a collision course with the federal government.

The Epic Encounter—May 4, 1970

President Richard Nixon's April 30, 1970, announcement of the expansion of the Vietnam War with the bombings of Cambodia and Laos was met with shock by students on college campuses across America. Nixon had stated his intention to withdraw from the Southeast Asian conflict during the 1968 presidential election; his escalation was received as a betrayal and immediately ignited the activist tinderbox. Students began planning nationwide protests against Nixon's policy, and it was no secret that May 4 was the intended date for this unified national expression of anger.

When the May 4, 1970, early morning edition of the *St. Louis Globe-Democrat* hit its readers' front steps, it contained an editorial vilifying the student protestors at the University of California at Berkeley, at Stanford University in Palo Alto, California, and at Hobart College in Geneva, New York. But that was the predictable editorial posture for the hardline conservative newspaper. What was noteworthy, some might say "prescient," about

Figure 5.5 Holmes Lounge, opening off of the Washington University Brookings Quadrangle, frequently served as the planning headquarters and staging point for student demonstrations. Here, activists have temporarily renamed it "Ho Chi Minh Lounge," after the Communist North Vietnamese leader. *Photo by Jack Fahland for the* St. Louis Globe-Democrat, *from the collections of the St. Louis Mercantile Library at the University of Missouri–St. Louis*

the op-ed, titled "Criminals on Campus," was its specific praise for Ohio governor James Rhodes's activation of the state's National Guard to quell student unrest on the Ohio State University campus. Later that morning, the Guard would move some 140 miles to the west of OSU to Kent State, where they would have a fateful encounter with student protesters.[73] Ohio campuses, like so many in the Midwest, were frequently overlooked as national bellwethers by the media and political cognoscenti. But *Globe-Democrat* publisher Richard Amberg knew that the Midwest was at the epicenter of the war between the status quo and the nation's youth movement. Indeed, with insider's informatioin provided by the FBI the *Globe-Democrat* frequently and intentionally fanned those flames of civic unrest. The newspaper wasn't the cause of what happened the night of May 4, 1970, on the Washington University campus, but, like a mob egging on a schoolyard bully, it eagerly stood on the sidelines yelling "Fight! Fight! Fight!"[74]

At 12:24 p.m., several hours after the *Globe-Democrat*'s public statement of support for Governor Rhodes, four students at Kent State University were shot to death by twenty-eight members of the Ohio National Guard. The guardsmen fired approximately sixty-seven rounds over a period of thirteen seconds, killing the four students and wounding nine others. Some of the victims were protestors. Others were simply passersby and onlookers. It didn't matter; all were swept up in the onslaught by National Guardsmen in an act that quickly became a defining, seismic moment of an era. The photograph of a young girl kneeling over the dead body of one of the victims became the iconic image representing the violent schism that existed between the World War II "Greatest Generation" and their college-aged offspring.

The murders ignited violent protests on college campuses across the nation, and Washington University in St. Louis was no different. Again citing St. Louis as a city of note on the national stage, Walter Cronkite's report on the ripple effect of the Kent State murders observed: "Shooting deaths of four students at Kent State University aggravated campus tensions elsewhere. Other campus fires burned an ROTC building at Washington University in St. Louis while students chanted, 'Remember Kent.'"[75] The student protestors made good on that promise to honor their fallen comrades. That night a mob burned the Air Force ROTC building, the last remaining vestige of the military's presence on the campus, to the ground (Fig. 5.7).

When viewed in the history of antiwar dissent, what is remarkable about the ROTC burning is the extraordinary extent to which the St. Louis office

Figure 5.6 Students mass in the Brookings Quadrangle during a term upended by the escalation of resistance to the campus military presence. *Photo by Roy Cook for the* St. Louis Globe-Democrat, *from the collections of the St. Louis Mercantile Library at the University of Missouri–St. Louis*

of the FBI was immediately ready to capitalize on it as a high-visibility prosecutive opportunity. Michael Siskind's conviction and unique sentencing on sabotage charges a little over a year before emboldened the federal agents. The names Mechanic, Kogan, Kennedy, Koch, and a host of others were already well known to SAC Gamble's successor, J. Wallace LaPrade. Their daily activities had been documented and formed what was now considered a reliable profile of a revolutionary pattern, thanks to a multiplicity of intimate confidential informant reports. The presumption of their guilt in the still-unsolved Army ROTC burning three months earlier steeled the FBI's resolve. Given all the accumulated intelligence and the suppositions that sprang from it, Mechanic was considered a prime suspect among the 3,000 individuals who rioted and destroyed the Washington University Air Force ROTC building on the night of May 4, 1970.

There was already a restraining order in place prohibiting Mechanic, Kogan, Koch, and others from protesting on campus, so the students knew they were violating a local injunction by simply attending the rally.[76] What they didn't know was that the Department of Justice had a powerful new arrow in its quiver that would now be aimed directly at them: the Anti-Riot

Figure 5.7 Firefighters arrive as Washington University's Air Force ROTC building burns in the early morning hours of May 5, 1970. The photo dominated the front page of the *Post-Dispatch* under the lead banner headline "Protesters Burn ROTC Building." St. Louis Post-Dispatch *photograph; reprinted by permission of Polaris Images*

Figure 5.8 Howard Mechanic and William Bothwell (handcuffed together) and Margaret Murphy jubilantly leave the St. Louis Court of Appeals on June 15, 1970. The three had just posted bond in advance of their appeal of convictions for violating a restraining order against "disruptive activities" on campus. These legal proceedings were separate from the federal charges Mechanic and others would face. *Photo by Bob Diaz for the* St. Louis Globe-Democrat, *from the collections of the St. Louis Mercantile Library at the University of Missouri–St. Louis*

Provisions, also known as the Civil Obedience Act, of the 1968 Civil Rights Act. While the 1968 Civil Rights Act is best known for establishing federal fair-housing practices, this lesser-known provision authorized the levying of federal charges against protestors who impeded the work of firefighters and policemen in the conduct of their duties during a civil disturbance.[77] Legal precedent was still needed to formulate the case law around the use of this statutory weapon. What better locale to flex this prosecutorial muscle against student unrest than in the city where groundbreaking sabotage charges had already been successful? St. Louis was, again, to be the crucible for this judicial test, supported by the intricate network of COINTELPRO-provided intelligence and innuendo upon which to build a potential case. Both the St. Louis office of the FBI and local federal prosecutors were confident that the political and cultural environment would produce juries receptive to arguments breaking this new legal ground. Further, law enforcement officials felt sure they would have the full backing of Washington University's trustees, whose vested interests supported an end to the chaos. And finally, they relied on the recent history of the Siskind conviction to know that Missouri judges would allow the thinnest of evidence to levy harsh sentences.

Standing in the dark at the edge of the rioting crowd that night was Daniel Bartlett, the new US Attorney for Eastern Missouri and Walter Yeagley's successor. Was his presence by accident or design? We don't know. But from his vantage point he bore witness to the burning of Air Force ROTC building. Bartlett had known since March that there were plans to levy these new federal charges against someone, but he didn't know who. The plan had been hatched after the Army ROTC building had burned in February and just a few weeks prior to the fire's destruction that he was now watching unfold before him. Nixon's Assistant Attorney General for Civil Rights, Jerris Leonard, had called upon Hoover to encourage aggressive St. Louis Bureau investigations to pave the way for levying the novel charges.[78] All the local FBI agents and Department of Justice attorneys were waiting for was an opportunity. With the riot playing out before his eyes, Dan Bartlett recognized this as his moment.

Howard Mechanic, Larry Kogan, Napoleon Bland, Joel Achtenberg, Michael Rudofker, and Joe Eisenberg walked onto the WU campus that night having no notion of the trap that had been laid for them. Whatever their actions, no matter how specious the criminal case against them might be, they had fallen directly into the grasp of the FBI and federal prosecutors in Washington, DC, and in St. Louis. And the results were breathtaking. Without the federal government ever having to prove the question of whether they, themselves, even actually burned the ROTC building, Bland, Eisenberg, Rudofker, and Achtenberg were each sentenced to ten years in federal penitentiary on sabotage charges. Mechanic and Kogan were the first defendants ever to be convicted on a violation of the 1968 Civil Obedience Act. Both were sentenced to five years in federal prison and ordered to pay a $10,000 fine.

The Aftermath

Most of those arrested and convicted on federal charges in the wake of the May 4, 1970, burning of the Air Force ROTC building on the Washington University campus would serve variants on their initial sentences or would later be acquitted after years of appeals. Both Eisenberg and Kogan served their mitigated sentences in the Psychiatric Ward of the United States Medical Center for Federal Prisoners in Springfield, Missouri. Neither of them ever showed signs of psychological impairment or overt distress, except perhaps as one would expect from having been ensnared in a trap laid by the state and federal law enforcement. Napoleon Bland, the only Black defendant, served the longest sentence—seven of ten years on a sabotage charge for his involvement in acts for which no evidence of his participation was offered at trial.

The only defendant who didn't serve his sentence was Howard Mechanic. He fled and lived underground for twenty-eight years as a fugitive. It was Mechanic's flight, the focus of which will be explored in greater detail in the next chapter of this volume, that kept this miscarriage of justice alive. Had Mechanic not disappeared for nearly three decades, these misbegotten arrests and inexplicably harsh sentences might have simply faded from our collective memory, lost in the blur of so many of Hoover's excesses. But my father's consistent refrain—at holidays, when the FBI would come to query him about Howard's disappearance, and sometimes for no reason at all, out of the blue—was "Whatever happened to Howard Mechanic?" His query kept this as a burning question that begged to be answered. My father didn't live long enough to know the results of my investigation. Perhaps that's for the best as he would have been dismayed that my ten-year search for the truth uncovered a surprising number of nefarious government operations intended to subvert the civil rights of Mechanic, his co-defendants, and thousands of others across the nation. He believed in the courts and our system of justice, so he had no concept of what he was up against when he argued his defense for Mechanic and Kogan. As my father had initially suspected, and I later confirmed, St. Louis was the only city in the nation where these federal charges had been levied. As such, none of us could have imagined the central role that St. Louis came to play in the larger history of the suppression of dissident voices in the US.

In the wake of the 1970 burnings of both the Army and Air Force facilities, the ROTC program was moved off the Washington University

Figure 5.9 Washington University students hide their faces from photographers as concerns about targeting of students by law enforcement agencies grow in the wake of the Kent State murders and the burnings of ROTC buildings on the WU campus. *Photo by Bob Diaz for the* St. Louis Globe-Democrat, *from the collections of the St. Louis Mercantile Library at the University of Missouri–St. Louis*

campus.[79] This relocation took the ROTC program away from being a convenient target of student opposition to the war. It didn't stop protest against ROTC facilities and, indeed, the building on Forest Park Boulevard was bombed and burned on March 9, 1971.[80] But the relocation did diminish the more regular, sometimes daily, assault on ROTC activities by those who intended to end military education on their college campus.

After the trials and convictions of Mechanic and others, on-campus dissent among all activists was even further muted. Statements from the FBI and federal prosecutors had demonstrated their confidence that sentences this harsh would send a chilling message to activists across the nation. And indeed, this strategy worked. In the ongoing surveillance and subversion of student activists after May 4, 1970, one confidential source noted that "some individuals had attempted to organize the Washington University this Spring 1971 for radical activities but that the vast majority of Washington University students opposed what was being done in this direction for several reasons, including the Federal charges that were brought against individuals involved in the burning of the ROTC Building during the summer of 1970 and the penalties which were levied against these individuals."[81] Mission accomplished.

Twenty-eight days after this particular report was filed, J. Edgar Hoover, worried that the disclosure of COINTELPRO and its tactics would embarrass the FBI and permanently tarnish his legacy, sent a memo ending the secret war on his enemies: "Effective immediately, all COINTELPROs operated by this Bureau are discontinued. These include COINTELPRO–Espionage; COINTELPRO–New Left; COINTELPRO–Disruption of White Hate Groups; COINTELRPRO–Communist Party, USA; Counterintelligence and Special Operations; COINTELPRO–Black Extremists; [and] Socialist Workers Party–Disruption Program."[82] Hoover's decision came too late for the students from Washington University, all of whom were now sitting in prison or fighting in the courts for their freedom, or who, like Howard Mechanic, was on the run as a federal fugitive from justice.

6. The Saga of Howard Mechanic

Carl Boggs

HISTORY OFTEN FOLLOWS SOMETHING OF a dialectical pattern—power be-gets resistance, war generates blowback, and so forth. In 1960s America, it was a brutal imperialist war in Indochina—the bloodiest in US history—that gave rise to some of the largest and most incendiary protests this coun-try has ever seen. There was, at the same time, a crucial third part to this dialectic: massive governmental repression designed to quell those protests. Much is known about the war and the deep opposition to it, far less about the nefarious work of the FBI and kindred intelligence agencies to crush not only the antiwar movement but other forms of social revolt. Howard Mechanic, a student at Washington University in St. Louis during the early 1970s and protestor against the war, was one of those caught in the sprawl-ing web of what we nowadays call the "deep state."

Thanks to the remarkably diligent and patient efforts of one activist, film-maker, and investigator, that state of affairs could dramatically change. In 2018, Nina Gilden Seavey won a landmark federal lawsuit to gain access to a vast collection of files held by US intelligence agencies that for years infiltrated, probed, and sought to disrupt anti–Vietnam War mobilizations of the 1960s and 1970s. There can be no doubt: security-state attempts to destroy or at least impair those mobilizations were considerably more ambitious—and more effective—than generally believed.

Widespread student antiwar protests at Washington University peaked during the years 1969 to 1972, the very time I joined the political sci-ence faculty after finishing graduate work at the University of California, Berkeley. In those years Wash U had become a cauldron of militant New Left politics, mostly revolving around student anti-ROTC protests that led to the torching of one ROTC building, a familiar target of antiwar fervor on campuses throughout the US. An organization called the Washington University Liberation Front, or WULF, had formed to channel student activism toward common strategic objectives.

From the vantage point of fifty years later, it seems worth briefly noting what that era signified: unfathomable violence met by fierce resistance. The Vietnamese referred to their protracted struggles as the "Resistance War against America," when a poorly developed country took on—and defeated—the world's leading superpower and military machine. Estimates of Vietnamese deaths spanning the years 1960 to 1975 vary greatly, some reaching as high as 3.8 million. Beyond that, the costs were staggering: fifteen thousand hamlets destroyed, twenty-five million acres of farmland ruined, one and a half million farm animals killed, every city north and south virtually leveled. The war generated 200,000 prostitutes, 900,000 orphans, 180,000 disabled people, more than one million widows. Nearly twenty million gallons of herbicide had been dropped in South Vietnam alone, its long-term effects still felt in a terrible legacy of cancer, birth defects, and other afflictions.

As for the US, its ruling elites spent roughly $1.4 trillion (in 2019 dollars), deployed nearly three million troops, and suffered more than fifty-eight thousand battlefield deaths. The war gave rise to the largest, most sustained, and most militant protest movements in American history, an impact still reverberating across American society. What happened at Wash U in those days turned out to be a microcosm of these movements—a saga that would shape Howard Mechanic's life forever.

On May 4, 1970, some three thousand Washington University students—along with a scattering of professors and community activists—marched on the *second* ROTC center where prospective Air Force officers were being trained for military service. The marchers had been angered by President Richard Nixon's sudden expansion of the war into Cambodia. That anger was intensified by events unfolding earlier the same day at Kent State, where the National Guard opened fire on defenseless protestors, killing four and wounding nine. I was one of those marchers, along with Howard, looking to quickly reach the edge of campus, site of the ROTC facilities. Like other spontaneous outpourings across the country, the protest quickly turned combative and violent: within minutes *this* ROTC structure was also burned to the ground. Firefighters were repelled by a fusillade of rocks and other projectiles. The episode reinforced an antimilitarist upsurge that would not recede until the end of the academic year.

Law enforcement reaction was swift: twelve protestors were arrested and charged with various (mostly nebulous) crimes and banned from campus. Six were convicted of charges associated with "rioting." A new law was invoked for the first time—the 1968 fascist-sounding Civil Obedience Act passed by Congress to broadly target activists who might be deemed to "interfere with public safety." Speaking at the Pentagon three days before the anti-ROTC events, Nixon had lauded patriotic American troops fighting in Vietnam (roughly half a million at that point) while mocking "these bums, you know, blowing up the campuses."[1] The uniquely harsh crackdown in St. Louis was clearly meant to send a message across the nation: the lives of antiwar resisters could be ruined, or at least severely disrupted, with one arrest.

If Nixon famously adopted a hard line toward opponents of an increasingly unpopular war, so too did FBI director J. Edgar Hoover, who ordered a nationwide campaign to infiltrate and derail what by 1970 had become one of the largest social movements of any type in US history. In the lengthy course of this repressive campaign the Pentagon and FBI, along with cooperative state and local agencies, had assembled files on an estimated twenty-five million Americans. The "deep state" had now established its own menacing trajectory.

The FBI's notorious COINTELPRO program was maintained full force during these years. Begun in 1956 to harass and round up Communists, the program later targeted the usual suspects: Civil Rights activists, socialist organizations, Black Panthers, the Nation of Islam, and sundry New Left groups. Hoover ordered his phalanx of agents to "expose, disrupt, misdirect, discredit, neutralize, or otherwise eliminate" all manifestations of popular revolt. Illegal surveillance, then as now, was the norm. The FBI worked in close partnership with the NSA, CIA, and Pentagon, while the CIA carried out its own subterranean work under the provocative heading Operation CHAOS. COINTELPRO was terminated in 1971, but nobody believed that decision had much of an impact on the well-entrenched FBI *modus operandi*.

One of the Washington University students arrested was Mechanic, accused of throwing a cherry bomb during the anti-ROTC actions and charged under that 1968 Act. Mechanic was sentenced to the maximum five years in federal penitentiary but, having exhausted his appeals, in 1972 decided to flee underground rather than face extended incarceration. He ended up in Scottsdale, Arizona, under the pseudonym Gary Tredway and managed to carry on a relatively "normal" life for nearly three decades before being discovered and reported (in 2000) by a probing local reporter who had interviewed Mechanic/Tredway when he was running for the Scottsdale city council.

Figure 6.1 Howard Mechanic (center) at US District Court on October 29, 1970, where he was sentenced to a five-year federal prison term. About seventy-five young Mechanic supporters attended. *Photo by Bob Diaz for the* St. Louis Globe-Democrat, *from the collections of the St. Louis Mercantile Library at the University of Missouri–St. Louis*

Wanted as a "fugitive" by the FBI, Mechanic had been described as "armed and dangerous." Arrested and sent back to prison, he remained behind bars for less than a year before being pardoned by President Bill Clinton on his last day in office, January 20, 2001 (the same day Clinton pardoned another erstwhile fugitive, Patricia Hearst). For a president who gave us NAFTA, a draconian crime bill, media deregulation, the Balkans war, and the abolition of Glass-Steagall, this had to be perhaps the greatest achievement of his administration.

Mechanic's liberation from federal confinement gained impetus from a dedicated campaign waged by friends, colleagues, and others, including a contingent of antiwar folks involved in the Washington University events at the time of Mechanic's first arrest. Celebration segued into a momentous "reunion" at the university in April 2001, which brought together activists from around the country, some (including myself) given "defenders of peace" awards from "the friends of Howard Mechanic."

Much like student radicalism itself, the dynamics of political repression at Washington University had rather deep roots. A mid-sized liberal-arts institution known for its enlightened atmosphere and progressive faculty, the space for truly subversive action narrowed drastically when it came to opposing the war, however immoral that war had been widely viewed by 1970. The stark reality was that the university was dominated by such corporations as McDonnell-Douglas and Monsanto, both with headquarters in St. Louis, along with Olin Industries and the Mallinckrodt Chemical interests. The CEOs of these huge contractors all sat on the WU Board of Trustees, while Sanford McDonnell was simultaneously chair of the Board of Trustees and chair of the board at McDonnell-Douglas. The *St. Louis Globe-Democrat,* once home to such arch-conservatives as Pat Buchanan, relished publishing front-page "exposés" of campus radicals. In the end, freedom would have its definite limits.

During my seven years at Washington University, I had the privilege of several visits from neatly attired FBI agents to my office, classrooms, and political gatherings that had become almost routine in those days— including a rather harmless film festival I had organized in 1973. After the second anti-ROTC protests, two of these operatives set out to intimidate me with supposedly incriminating photos. More outrageous, it turned out that a close graduate student and friend (and "research assistant") had been doubling as a federal informant. Infiltration of the New Left was far more pervasive than anyone imagined at the time. We knew that Nixon was hellbent on destroying the antiwar movement, but we were somewhat naïve when it came to the extraordinary level of federal spying and sabotage, much of it surely aided and abetted by the university hierarchy. Amid the turmoil, Sanford McDonnell denounced me in a speech for being strangely ungrateful to my generous corporate paymasters, then called for my dismissal—a wish that would soon enough come true, thanks in part to a compliant university administration.

We have nowadays come to realize that surveillance-state intrusions into the political activities of American citizens have become nearly Orwellian in scope, though we remain in the dark about much of its origins and early history. To gather new sources of information, the filmmaker Seavey was forced to tangle with those very bureaucratic fortresses set up precisely to insulate and defend the power elite. Seavey earlier noted that the feds had been releasing just five hundred pages of files monthly—this following 386 separate FOIA requests, quite likely the most ambitious such initiative in US history. "At that rate, it would take 60 years to get all the records," lamented Seavey. At one point she was hoping for a more reasonable five thousand pages a month—an amount that would appear to reflect an enormous record of political activism or, perhaps more likely, the extent of authoritarian security-state initiatives to track and monitor every sign of social protest.

For Mechanic, whose sacrifices in opposing a criminal war remain part of his everyday life to this day, the original punishment of five years (based on faulty evidence) was cruel and unusual by any reckoning. Meanwhile, the Civil Obedience Act has reportedly never been used to indict or convict anyone since it was unveiled to snare Mechanic.

Mechanic's underground ordeals were hardly unique, but they might well have brought more protracted hardship and grief than most other cases. Famous Weather Underground activist Bernardine Dohrn voluntarily surfaced in 1980, but she was allowed to plead guilty to aggravated battery and jumping bail, fined $1,500, and placed on three-year probation. David Fine, who planted a homemade bomb at the University of Wisconsin in 1970, killing a physicist, was apprehended in 1976 and spent less than three years in prison. When Abbie Hoffman (alias Barry Fried) emerged in 1980 after six years in hiding, he was given a perfunctory one-year sentence and set free in four months. For simply hurling a cherry bomb (which he stoutly denies), Mechanic was given the maximum five years.

A former colleague at Washington University, literature professor Carter Revard—who put up his house as collateral for Mechanic's 1970 bond—said many years later that he had no regrets; he would have been happy to step forward again. In April 2000, Revard told reporter Lisa Belkin in the *New York Times Magazine*: "They gave him five years for throwing a cherry bomb while they were handing out Medals of Honor for dropping napalm on civilians. I think the people who should be in jail are the people who prosecuted him."[2] To that Revard could have added a tight circle of Harvard-educated imperial elites, liberal champions of technowar, who orchestrated the Indochina horrors from the outset and never expressed any regrets—or apologies.

It could be argued that for American society the Vietnam War never really ended; its tortured legacy pervades both American domestic politics and foreign policy to this day—as does the most far-reaching national security apparatus in history. In *Vietnam and Other American Fantasies*, H. Bruce Franklin refers to "Vietnam's defeat of the mightiest war machine the world had yet known," adding: "Looking backward, historians of the future may recognize that this war machine was . . . the most stupendous achievement of American culture. By defeating this war machine, the people of Vietnam not only exposed the myth of its invincibility but also ignited a series of wars within the culture that created it."[3]

7. "Whacking the Elephant Where It Hurts"

The Veiled Prophet Organization, ACTION, and
Economic Justice in St. Louis, 1965–1980

Thomas M. Spencer

DECEMBER 22, 1972, WAS A cold and snowy evening in St. Louis. Inside cavernous and warm Kiel Auditorium, the festivities at the Veiled Prophet Ball were right on schedule. At about 10:30 the matrons had completed their part of the program, and the last maid of honor, Beatrice Busch, was making her way around the stage. The Veiled Prophet of Khorassan, dressed in ornate robes and wearing a silky veil and gold crown, watched the proceedings from his throne. The several thousand spectators, most of whom had been in their seats for more than three hours, were growing restless. The Queen of Love and Beauty, the queen of the Midwest's oldest and most public debutante ball, was to be named next, and then it would all be over until next year.

Suddenly a woman in the balcony shouted, "Down with the VP!" and scattered leaflets, which fell on the spectators below. Quickly the auditorium's security guards carried her out. Then, to the left of the stage, there was a much more serious noise. A woman had apparently fallen from the balcony. A man went over to see whether she had been hurt, and after a few words with him, she disappeared through the right stage door. Since the woman seemed unhurt—and had fallen out of a section reserved for housekeepers and other servants anyway—all eyes returned to the stage where the Veiled Prophet was preparing to name his queen.

Next, just as Miss Busch completed her pattern around the stage, the woman who had fallen was somehow standing next to the Veiled Prophet. Before anyone could stop her, she removed the Prophet's crown and veil to reveal the face of Tom K. Smith, an executive vice president for the Monsanto Company. Surprised and angry, Smith quickly recovered the crown and veil and replaced them as if he could still hide his identity. The Bengal Lancers,

191

the Veiled Prophet's private honor guard, roughly dragged the woman back-stage by her arms, neck, and feet. For the first time in the twentieth century and only the second time in the ball's ninety-five-year history, the Veiled Prophet's name became public knowledge. Despite the rather bizarre inter-ruption, the ball went on as usual, as if nothing had happened.[1]

The unveiling of the Veiled Prophet at his ball in 1972 represented the crowning achievement of the civil rights group ACTION. From the years 1965 to 1984, ACTION protested at all events connected with the Veiled Prophet celebration. Although ACTION's targeting of the Veiled Prophet debutante ball may appear frivolous, the issues involved—economic justice in the form of jobs for minorities—were quite serious. Despite their denials, the Veiled Prophet organization clearly found it necessary to respond to the challenge by ACTION.[2] Over the next several years many major changes occurred in the Veiled Prophet organization.

ACTION, which stood for Action Committee to Improve Opportunities for Negroes, was an unusual organization in the late 1960s. The group's goals represented a sort of practical middle ground—neither accommoda-tionist nor nationalist. The story of ACTION offers a local case study of a group that was ahead of its time in emphasizing economic opportunities and in employing "theater-of-confrontation" tactics. Moreover, ACTION was an exception to most of the generalizations that have been made about civil rights groups during this period; unlike other organizations, the St. Louis group remained integrated and viewed white members as valuable assets. While national civil rights groups such as the Congress of Racial Equality and the Student Nonviolent Coordinating Committee battled over the issues of Black nationalism and separatism, ACTION advocated a more economically centered and practical set of immediate goals.[3]

In contrast to the recently founded ACTION, the Veiled Prophet or-ganization had been a St. Louis institution for nearly a century by 1972. Fashioning themselves after a New Orleans carnival society, the Mystick Krewe of Comus, a group of prominent white St. Louis businessmen found-ed the Veiled Prophet organization in 1878. The Veiled Prophet organiza-tion formed largely in response to a general strike by workers the summer before, when workers had both symbolically and physically gained control of the streets. A Veiled Prophet (or Grand Oracle), who "shall preside and be recognized as infallible," presided over the organization.[4] It is not public-ly known how the Veiled Prophet was (or is) chosen, only that he has always been a successful local businessman.

Figure 7.1 The Queen of Love and Beauty and her court glide through downtown St. Louis as part of the October 1951 Veiled Prophet Parade. *Photo by Boleslaus Lukaszewski, from the Lukaszewski Photographs Collection, Saint Louis University Archives*

The organization, which is still in existence, annually puts on the Veiled Prophet Parade and Ball. In the nineteenth and early twentieth century, the parade consisted of a group of related tableaux, each depicting a scene that fit in with the theme for that year. For example, the first parade's theme was the "Festival of Ceres" and included floats depicting various Greek and Roman Gods as advocating capitalist values. The parade's primary social function from the outset was to be a show of physical power. Parading along on the tops of floats, the members laid claim to the streets. Depicting themselves as royalty set above their social inferiors, the members tried to reinforce the social hierarchy. The other primary social function, which had been to provide "acceptable" entertainment and to provide cultural messages advocating capitalism for the working class and poor of St. Louis, no longer seemed a necessary part of the parade by the 1960s. The St. Louis elite no longer felt an overwhelming need to preach a capitalistic and moral gospel to their workers. For example, the 1966 theme, "Sports," and the 1967 theme, "A Salute to the Wonderful World of Disney," brought with them less moralistic cultural baggage.[5]

Founded to control courtship, the Veiled Prophet Ball has become a rather anachronistic debutante ball for the daughters of St. Louis's wealthiest families.[6] The ball primarily consists of the presentation of matrons and maids, followed by the crowning of the "Queen of Love and Beauty." Like the selection of the Veiled Prophet, it is not publicly known how the organization chooses the "Queen of Love and Beauty."[7] Since 1981, the Veiled Prophet organization has also been responsible for the annual Veiled Prophet Fair—a large Fourth of July carnival.[8]

Civil rights scholars describe the period between 1965 and 1975 as a sort of "middle period" that was "something completely different" from the earlier national activism of the civil rights groups of the early 1960s and the more radical activism of groups in the late 1970s. Civil rights scholars have yet to study the period in much depth, and few case studies of local grassroots civil rights organizations have been undertaken. During this period most civil rights groups shifted their goals. Some historians have argued that by 1965 the "classical" phase of the civil rights movement—which James Ralph has defined as "the destruction of the legal foundations of racism in America"—had ended. As Ralph put it, the "passing of one era inaugurated a troubling time of transition" in which civil rights workers "insisted that equal results, not equal treatment, become the standard of public policy." ACTION is a prime example of this ideological thrust on the part of civil rights organizations. Members of ACTION believed that the struggle for basic civil rights was mostly finished and that the important struggle for economic rights remained ahead. As Martin Luther King Jr. contemplated whether he should pursue an economically based campaign in Chicago, ACTION pursued just that in another large midwestern city, St. Louis.[9] In short, ACTION offers historians a chance to study a local civil rights group that advocated economic justice in a midwestern city during the little-studied "middle period" in the civil rights struggle.

Originally founded by Percy Green and a few members of the St. Louis chapter of CORE's employment committee in April 1965, ACTION was, in Green's words, "committed to direct-action protest," by which he meant confrontation with specific opponents with specific goals in mind.[10] The St. Louis Jefferson Bank protests in 1963 divided the St. Louis chapter of CORE. The chapter subsequently abandoned the idea of direct-action protests.[11] Green and several members of the employment committee, a growing faction inside CORE that called for more direct-action activities, felt betrayed. "CORE was apprehensive," Green told a reporter in 1970. "The members had battle fatigue or something, I guess. We needed a group that would be a spark for change in St. Louis."[12]

ACTION's primary goal, in the words of former member Jane Sauer, a white female, was "to obliterate racism through economic justice, through jobs," and "through communication with the upper echelons of St. Louis in order to promote change."[13]

Specifically, ACTION advocated more and better-paying jobs for Black men. ACTION activists believed this focus on job opportunities for Black males would be the most beneficial course to follow because men were the primary breadwinners for their families in the Black community at that time. As Percy Green explained, the members of ACTION "thought that would cut down on the risk factor of Black men running the risk of committing burglaries, you know, cut down on the criminal approach to getting money to feed their families and so forth." Members of ACTION believed that Blacks had a right to equal and well-paying employment opportunities, which were central to a good quality of life. Sauer explained ACTION's economic views this way: "It's up to you whether you want to buy a house. But you have a right to have a job that will let you buy that house. It's your right to have a grocery store that has better produce . . . you have a right to own a car, shop wherever you want. And the only way to have these things is to have a job."[14] For ACTION activists, civil rights coexisted with economic rights. African Americans needed the civil rights legislation passed in the mid-1960s, but this legislation meant little if they could not find jobs to sustain themselves. True freedom and economic liberation involved being able to support a family. African Americans needed jobs that would provide for a family's basic economic survival.

Unusual for the time, ACTION remained an integrated group. For many ACTION members, integration represented a tactical move. Police were less likely to brutalize whites or charge them with crimes. Jane Sauer said that ACTION

used white people as a protection. When they arrest a white person they don't know what they've got. It's different when they pick up a Black—they can be sure that he has no status. When they picked me up they didn't know what they had. I came from a highly educated professional family. They didn't know—what was her family going to do if we rough her up? It wasn't like a poor Black man who couldn't afford to hire a lawyer or, worse yet: "the *Post-Dispatch* might cover it if we roughed her up."[15]

For Jacqueline Bell, a Black female member, working in an integrated group reflected the real world, a world in which Blacks and whites lived together and needed to work together. When asked why ACTION remained integrated, Percy Green replied that "our thinking was that the whites in our organization were very productive and what we were primarily interested in was performance."[16]

All members of ACTION had to agree to one thing: The organization would always have Black leadership. Green felt that "Black folks had the right to make mistakes for Black people rather than to have white people make mistakes for them." Whites certainly did play integral roles in the organization, but a Black leadership made the important decisions. As Green said, "One way to find out whether one was still tainted with racism was if one could accept Black leadership." In fact, ACTION members believed that Black leadership was therapeutic for whites.[17]

ACTION's protest tactics demonstrated that locally based groups during this middle period of the civil rights movement did not choose just one tactical approach. ACTION's goal of better-paying jobs for Black men required members to use both nonviolent direct-action sit-in protests similar to those of national civil rights groups of the early 1960s and "guerrilla street theater" or theater-of-confrontation protests reminiscent of radical feminist groups in the late 1960s. ACTION's location in a conservative midwestern city forced the group's members to use a combination of tactics to further its goals. ACTION's protests had to be physically unthreatening because, according to Margaret Phillips, a white female former ACTION member, "St. Louis is a very conservative place. The far-out, fringy kinds of behavior never percolated here."[18] However, ACTION's tactics at the different Veiled Prophet events evolved over time. While the first Veiled Prophet protests in the middle 1960s were nonviolent sit-ins meant to disrupt the parade, protests in the 1970s mixed sit-in tactics with guerrilla street theater, in which symbolic acts (e.g., the unveiling of the Veiled Prophet) played a central role.

In addition to protesting at the Veiled Prophet Ball and Parade, ACTION tried to achieve economic and social justice through protests at large corporations in St. Louis. ACTION targeted these employers because, unlike smaller businesses, their businesses would not be economically threatened by a single successful protest. Members of ACTION believed that these large employers owed a special duty to the community to promote equality in hiring practices. The businesses targeted by ACTION included McDonnell-Douglas, Wonder Bread, Southwestern Bell Telephone, Laclede Gas Company, and the Union Electric Company. These protests often involved picketing, sitting-in, pouring syrup and animal excrement on company equipment, and, in the case of McDonnell-Douglas, breaching their security.[19] ACTION members generally considered these protests against corporate employers as central to their goal of increasing minority employment opportunities. For most ACTION activists, the Veiled Prophet protests remained something of a sideshow.

At the same time, ACTION picketed other organizations, most notably Roman Catholic churches and Protestant churches of all denominations (both Black and white), as well as Jewish synagogues. ACTION members believed the churches had failed to provide moral leadership on civil and economic rights issues. ACTION members also researched the property holdings of the Catholic Church in St. Louis and found the church was one of the city's largest slumlords. Protests involved picketing, interrupting services, and, on a few occasions, reading speeches to the church's members.[20]

Figure 7.2 ACTION members (from left to right) William Matheus, Percy Green, Cecilia Goldman, and Luther Mitchell at a June 1969 press conference addressing the group's Black Sunday demonstrations at area churches. *Photo by Paul Ockrassa for the* St. Louis Globe-Democrat, *from the collections of the St. Louis Mercantile Library at the University of Missouri–St. Louis*

Like radical groups of the late 1960s, ACTION often staged protests that were examples of theater-of-confrontation tactics. "Percy has a genius for guerrilla street theater," said Margaret Phillips. By "guerrilla street theater," ACTION activists meant that they tried to get their point across visually and vocally, without touching or harming people. "As we all know, you can send out the most beautifully worded press statement and it will fall flat," Phillips said. "But you do something theatrical, and all the press are there." Street theater effectively pointed out injustice to those who may have been insulated from it by race or class. "Hey, when something hurts, you've got to scream ouch!" Phillips contended. "You don't need a medical degree to scream ouch. We were just screaming ouch." The ultimate goal was to raise the viewers' consciousness—to alert them to the economic injustices perpetrated on minorities.[21]

Like the New York Radical Women's Miss America Protest in 1968, in which a sheep was crowned "Miss America," many of ACTION's protests were confrontational and symbolic but not physically threatening. One notable St. Louis protest involved burning a dollar bill, which symbolized the Protestant establishment's values, in front of an Episcopal church congregation on a Sunday morning.[22] Unlike the more extreme groups, ACTION members were not advocating a radical redistribution of power; they only demanded the moderate goal of equal economic opportunity. Unfortunately, their message was sometimes difficult to discern.

A prosopography of ACTION members is nearly impossible. ACTION brought together people of many different educational and social backgrounds: It included men and women of nearly every conceivable age and many different ethnicities—white Washington University professors, a few radical labor activists, young college-educated women, young Black men and women still in high school, and many others. Nevertheless, ACTION never grew to be very large: At most the group had an active membership of a little over fifty people. There were as many or more "unofficial members"— often members of Washington University's faculty or administration—who sent in regular financial contributions. ACTION consistently had more Black members than white members. White members made up between 35 and 40 percent of ACTION's membership.[23]

In summing up ACTION's activities, Barbara Torrence, a white former ACTION member, asserted that the group's members "found it was relatively easy to get appointments [with the CEOs of large companies] but it was really hard to get anything beyond that. You know the old joke about the elephant—first you've got to get his attention. To get his attention, you whack him where it hurts—after you've tried everything else."[24] One of the better ways ACTION found to "whack the elephant where it hurts" involved attacking something he held dear. That something was the Veiled Prophet organization's parade and ball.

Why did the parade during this period rapidly become just a few hours of relatively frivolous entertainment? Robert Tooley, who began working for the Veiled Prophet organization in 1969 and became Den Superintendent in 1973, argued it was the result of a conscious effort by the parade makers to change the philosophy of the organization with regard to the parade's themes. Tooley believed "a parade float is a sort of entertainment for children, should be aimed at children. That's my idea. In other words, you can't teach anyone any part of history by a parade float that just crosses by for twenty seconds."[25] Tooley's background included working for the Scruggs, Vandervoort, and Barney department store designing animated Christmas window displays for twenty-six years. Tooley claims he sincerely wanted to please children with his parade floats.

Despite Tooley's contention that the Veiled Prophet Parade's floats conveyed no meaning, many ACTION members were profoundly affected by the annual parade as children. "As a kid my recollections of the Veiled Prophet," said a founding member of ACTION, Judge Johnson, "were that it came through the heart of the Black community. I guess we were protesting even then and didn't know it. We would take our beanshooters and shoot at the VP. We thought it was time for the VP parade, let's go shoot at the VP." White ACTION members who had grown up in St. Louis had similar early memories of the Veiled Prophet. "As a child I remember being taken down to see the Queen of Love and Beauty," said Jane Sauer.

> I remember the big parade that went through the city that was supposed to be the gift given by the regal folks who inhabited the upper echelons of the city, and it was there for us poor folks to come look. You could gaze at these people, and they had floats to entertain you. It was charity. You were down lower—much lower. This is real charity— "we parade ourselves down Main Street in front of them and they can bring their lawn chairs and watch us." I still have strong feelings about that image. I remember watching from my childhood the Queen of Love and Beauty wearing a gown like a fairy princess, and I can remember very vividly being told "Jewish girls don't do that." They don't

go to this ball. World War II is over, but Jews are not allowed in a lot of places.

The exclusive practices of the Veiled Prophet organization seemed even more obvious to a child in the Black community. Judge Johnson said that the Veiled Prophet celebration "symbolized elitism and exclusionariness [sic]" to the African American community in St. Louis, "because when you get a parade coming through and there's not one Black, you had to think, 'Why is this parade coming through?'"[26]

For most members of ACTION, the Veiled Prophet celebration symbolized racism and white control of St. Louis's economy. Members of the Veiled Prophet organization held the purse strings at most of the corporations where ACTION protested. Jane Sauer believed "the VP embodied the white power structure of this city. It involved their children. It really did—the white male heads of state, heads of corporations, the city fathers, the whole myth of city gentry, the whole myth of an establishment, of regalness, of blue-bloodedness. It was the figurehead of everything we were against. It was for many years a white, Anglo, Episcopalian thing to do."[27]

Political anthropologist James Scott argues that in societies there exists both a public transcript and a "hidden transcript," forged in secret away from the prying eyes of powerful elites. Scott further contends that, in times of major social upheaval, open acts of defiance by subordinate groups are viewed as possible and even necessary. ACTION's protests were an example of a "hidden transcript" of a subordinate group becoming public.[28] But this time, the Veiled Prophet organization would have trouble answering a challenge to its authority. The seeming acquiescence of the St. Louis community since World War II had lulled many in the organization into a false sense of security about the organization's popularity and standing in the community. They would make a big mistake by dismissing ACTION's position as representing the feelings of only a small minority. Once ACTION had brought the hidden transcript out into the public arena, their message would prove to be very powerful.

The Veiled Prophet represented the perfect target for ACTION—for both tactical and strategic reasons. Protests against the Veiled Prophet would draw a great deal of media attention. Sauer felt the Veiled Prophet "was like a precious child of this city. Because of that, it was something that the media wanted to defend. Of course, the editors wanted their tickets, and it was a big social deal." ACTION also targeted the Veiled Prophet

Parade and Ball because it furthered its goal of more jobs for Black men. Green declared that "after we attacked all of the big industries we found out that all of the CEOs of these industries were also members of the Veiled Prophet. So, we felt that attacking the Veiled Prophet was a strategic move. The CEOs of these firms were showing how racist they were because they were associating themselves with a racist organization socially. Their mental and moral fiber is tied to this." Many activists viewed the protests at the Veiled Prophet as a way to hit all of the CEOs at once. Jacqueline Bell believed that the Veiled Prophet protest represented "an opportunity to protest against twenty different corporations about their racism in their hiring practices" and "their institutional racism in all promotional and wage practices."[29]

ACTION's public statements made clear that, because the Veiled Prophet organization used Kiel Auditorium for the ball, the city's political leaders were closely linked to the white power structure. "The Veiled Prophet symbolized the power they had access to, at public expense," said Margaret Phillips. "That was a big point. For years they did it at the Kiel Auditorium, a taxpayer-supported auditorium." Many ACTION members believed one of their greatest achievements was getting people of all races to realize that, by having the ball in Kiel Auditorium, their tax dollars indirectly supported the organization. ACTION also made a public issue of the fact that the city spent a great deal of money on police protection for the ball.[30]

ACTION wanted two things from the Veiled Prophet organization. First, ACTION members wanted the CEOs in the Veiled Prophet to begin to hire more minority workers, and second, they wanted the Veiled Prophet organization to disband. They felt the money spent on this celebration, both public and private, would be better spent on something more helpful to the community as a whole.[31]

ACTION protested the Veiled Prophet celebration every year from 1965 to 1976. Most of these protests involved picketing the ball and disrupting the parade in some way. Typically, a group of ACTION members disrupted the parade by lying down in front of the parade floats while other activists passed out leaflets explaining the reasons behind the demonstration. The protest would continue until the police arrested the protestors. For instance, members acted out a scene—often as "nurses" or "doctors of social healing"—in the street in front of the floats until the police arrested them. On a few occasions members chained themselves to floats. In these protests the activists held up the parade until authorities cut their chains and arrested them. The goal was for protestors to distribute as many leaflets as possible to the crowd and, eventually, for someone to get arrested—usually for "disturbing the peace."[32]

The approach to the Veiled Prophet Ball varied somewhat each year, though some things stayed consistent. Every year, ACTION picketed the ball with signs that read, for example, "VEILED PROFITS" or "VP = KKK." ACTION's ball protests also included sending Blacks to try to gain admission with legitimate or phony tickets. Police arrested some activists and charged them with "disturbing the peace" for these attempts at gaining admission.[33]

One of the more interesting protest activities of ACTION was the Black Veiled Prophet Ball, a parody of the Veiled Prophet Ball. In this event, members of ACTION elected a Black Veiled Prophet. Green contended that ACTION used the Black Veiled Prophet Ball "to mimic the white Veiled Prophet." "We always used to say we'd like to challenge the white VP on the battlefield of justice," Green insisted. "Their queen was Love and Beauty, and our queen was called the Queen of Human Justice. We invited the white VP to the Black VP, and we demanded the Black VP to be in their functions and be seated next to the white VP." Needless to say, the white Veiled Prophet never showed up to meet the Black Veiled Prophet. The annual Black Veiled Prophet celebration became a popular festival for the African American community in St. Louis during the early 1970s. Green argued that this event was primarily intended "to make a mockery of the white Veiled Prophet, a symbol of St. Louis's racism and oppression." In no way did the Black Veiled Prophet celebration indicate that ACTION wanted Blacks to become a part of the Veiled Prophet organization.[34] The Black Veiled Prophet celebration, like the 1968 Miss America protest by radical feminist groups, was a public lampoon—an artful use of guerrilla street theater.

The events of October 2, 1965—the first Veiled Prophet protest—showed the early tactics of ACTION. "There were three of us: Maryann, an Episcopal intern; and me; and a young Black guy, sweet kid," said Barbara Torrence. "When the queen's float went by, we were to get in front of the float and stop the parade. We knew we were going to be arrested." The activists laid down in front of the float until the police arrested them. Then the protestors went limp. The two white women were detained by police immediately. Lost in the confusion, the young Black activist was not arrested. Once apprehended, the police subjected Maryann and Torrence to the usual tactics: They were taken down to the city hospital to be checked out because they had supposedly "resisted arrest." The police employed this tactic whenever they dealt with ACTION's protestors. When Torrence heard she would be charged with resisting arrest, she remembers saying "What! We had just gone limp. I couldn't see how going limp could be called resisting arrest!" Once the activists returned to the city jail, the police refused several bonds. As usual, ACTION had people waiting at the jail to bail out the demonstrators, but the prosecutor's office would not accept any of the bonds— including one from Torrence's husband, who had put their house up as a property bond. Torrence began to feel as if they "were in enemy territory." Finally, the prosecutor accepted a bond from a middle-class Black couple who had no tangible connection with ACTION. The prosecutor tried to charge Torrence and Maryann with eight different offenses but finally settled on three, including resisting arrest. Torrence and Maryann pleaded guilty and received a year's probation. The court waived their fine.[35]

This first Veiled Prophet protest gave insight into both the early aims of ACTION and those of the police authorities who arrested them. ACTION had a simple plan: Disrupt the parade. The group used tactics that had been successful for civil rights groups throughout the country during the 1950s and 1960s. The ultimate goal was to make people stop and think, to raise people's consciousness. Members of ACTION hoped that consciousness raising would convey their double message to the middle-class white audience: economic rights for Black men and the end of the Veiled Prophet organization. In the early years of the Veiled Prophet protests, ACTION attempted to draw attention to themselves and the Veiled Prophet organization by staging protests that did not physically threaten the members of the Veiled Prophet organization. As members of ACTION wanted, the police responded by arresting the activists. The police then tried to frighten the activists by charging them with many crimes and refusing legitimate bonds. However, when the cases made their way to court, most of the charges were dropped, and the fines were often waived.[36]

The Veiled Prophet organization itself did several things in reaction to ACTION's protests. First, the Veiled Prophet queen and maids ceased to take part in the parade after 1967. This move was an expression of concern on the part of the Veiled Prophet membership that the ACTION activists might do something to harm their daughters. In 1968 the parade no longer went into downtown St. Louis, staying in the relatively safe Central West End. Furthermore, the parade now avoided African American neighborhoods entirely.

In 1969 the parade moved to the daytime, and the Veiled Prophet himself did not participate between 1969 and 1973. Despite many official denials, the move to daylight hours was directly tied to ACTION's protests and the increasing animosity toward the parade among many working-class and Black St. Louisans. As Tooley recalled, the parade was moved to the daytime because "we started having an awful lot of trouble at night—a lot of protests against the VP and so forth." In fact, the animosity was reaching a fever pitch by 1968 when, according to Tooley, "one of the drivers, who was driving the float [in] the last nighttime parade, said he remembered seeing something sailing through the air, and he said it looked like a pie pan, and the next thing he knew he woke up in the hospital with fourteen stitches in the side of his head." As Rusty Hager, the 1995 Veiled Prophet Fair chairman, admitted, "Security for any nighttime event is always a problem."[37] The 1968 parade was the last nighttime parade in the organization's history. Every Veiled Prophet Parade since then has taken place in daylight. The tradition of the Veiled Prophet Parade as an evening event—a tradition of ninety years—had come to an end.

The switch to a daytime parade led to several important changes regarding the personnel on the floats. Tooley recalled that at this time they began "using women on the floats. Before that, it was men dressed as women, always just members of the order riding on the floats, and the krewe were ugly enough in the nighttime, let alone in the daytime. We had to go to girls on the floats."[38] In 1969 city school students also began riding on the floats. The Veiled Prophet members thought it would be harder for ACTION's protestors to argue that the parade was exclusive with these additions to the parade's participants. Also, the addition of women and children on the floats made it less likely that anyone in the crowd would throw objects at the passing floats.

Women were also allowed into some of the organization's functions and facilities for the first time during this period. In the 1970s the organization finally lifted its rule barring all women from its "Den."[39] Therefore, by the 1970s the organization had begun to rethink some of its rules regarding membership and participation in the group's activities.

The organization also made changes in the ball. Beginning in 1970 the ball was moved to the Friday night before Christmas.[40] The change in date was an attempt to disassociate the October parade, which was still viewed by many people as a positive civic event, from the ball, which was becoming increasingly unpopular with many St. Louisans as a tasteless show of wealth. By having the ball during the Christmas season, it no longer seemed so closely linked with the parade. Because the ball was held on the Friday before Christmas, a large number of St. Louisans would be away or busy enjoying their Christmas holidays, thus lessening public attention and criticism. It was apparent that the organization's members thought the ball remained their private party, separate from the more civic-oriented parade.

The protest at the Veiled Prophet Ball in 1972 showed major changes in ACTION's strategy. Having disrupted the parade and picketed the ball for seven straight years, members of ACTION felt they needed to step up their attack on the organization. No matter how creative the parade demonstrations, they had no direct effect on the members of the organization itself. Similarly, by ignoring the picket lines and quickly dashing inside, members of the Veiled Prophet organization arriving at the ball minimized their contact with ACTION's message. However, that did not mean that the members were oblivious to what was going on around them. As Tooley remembered, one of them came in very exasperated and asked him, "Do you know that these Blacks are marching in the street here?" He replied, "Yeah, I know. They're protesting." The VP member complained: "I had to bring my fifteen-year-old daughter by them, and they were shouting 'Fuck the Veiled Prophet!' at the top of their voice, and I don't think that's right." Tooley responded, "Well, we don't think it's right, either, but that's the way it is."[41] Despite many official denials, ACTION certainly got the Veiled Prophet membership's attention . . . if only for short periods of time.

In 1972, members of ACTION obtained four tickets to the ball. Barbara Torrence's neighbor had given her two tickets, which she subsequently gave to ACTION. Percy Green claimed to have gotten the other two tickets from "a VP person—it was a vice president that was very, very high up in the organization." To this day, Green will not identify that person: "that was the understanding, because he would be decimated if it ever got out." ACTION's plan involved getting three white women into the ball and somehow unveiling the Veiled Prophet. Green and members of ACTION had been saying they would "unveil the Prophet" for years, but no one took them seriously.[42]

Gena Scott, Jane Sauer, and Phyllis Knight used three of the tickets to get into the balcony. "I think the idea sounds so simplified, but the symbolic goal was to unmask the VP," Scott remembered. "I did not set out personally to do it, but I knew that anyone who had the opportunity to take that thing off would have—because it was a symbolic gesture. You could write about it. It was more of a class issue. I think a lot of people got a tickle out of it."[43]

Unmasking the Veiled Prophet would show him to be not some "mythical figure," but merely a wealthy white male in the white male power structure. By unveiling the Prophet, ACTION wanted to show that the Veiled Prophet organization was not a kindly civic group but a supporting strut of St. Louis's ever-present white male power structure. Secondarily, ACTION wanted to embarrass the Veiled Prophet organization by conspicuously infiltrating the extensive security employed by the organization.

Scott, Sauer, and Knight's tickets were in the upper balcony in the section generally reserved for house servants or, as Sauer said, "friends of no importance." "We were told how to dress," Sauer remembers. "Not too fancy, but like it was a big night for us. And so, we did it. This was theater—it was grand opera. We wore wigs. We wore—neither Gena nor I wore makeup at the time—but we wore makeup for this. We got heels and stockings and so forth. We had a whole background of who we were if we were caught. We sat away from other people—we couldn't strike up a dialogue with anyone."[44]

Although the women had been told how to get into the ball and how to be inconspicuous, they had no idea how to bring about their main objective. "The goal was to unveil the Veiled Prophet," Sauer said, "but once I got in there and saw how high that balcony was, I said no way we're going to do anything like this!" But then Gena Scott saw a three-inch electrical cable that came from the roof of the building and went down into an electrical box on the floor. "We sat there for over an hour while they just had the matrons and maids parading around," Scott said, "and each one was timed at about two minutes and thirty seconds to go around and get to the microphone and be announced as 'Mrs. August A. Busch,' etc."[45] The three women split up into different parts of the auditorium, and Sauer waited for Scott to begin her move toward the cable.

As Scott neared the cable, Sauer began throwing leaflets over the balcony and shouting "Down with the VP!" The police quickly converged on Sauer and very roughly carried her out—she missed the rest of the performance. Knight's actions were not clear at this point. But Scott swiftly climbed over the balcony and grabbed the cable. As she was about halfway down, the cable broke loose from the ceiling. Fortunately, the cable, which had run diagonally from the roof to the stage, swung Scott out onto the first set of steps to the stage. "And that's where I landed," Scott said. "Later on, I learned I had three crushed ribs. I had the wind knocked out of me. I imagine I fell about fifty feet. I remember thinking: 'I didn't die, I can still go on.'"

At this point, an official came over to ask Scott what had happened. She responded that she had fallen out of the balcony and needed to get back to her seat. She moved toward the stage door, where a man met her. She told him that "someone just fell over there" and pointed in the direction she had just come from. The man headed in that direction, allowing Scott access to the stage door. Scott made her way from the back of the stage through all the flats. Suddenly Scott found herself behind the Bengal Lancers—the Veiled Prophet's honor guard. "There were about three rows of people all dressed up in costume like Arabian Knights or what they think Arabian Knights looked like, with swarthy skin. I thought it was so interesting that they had darkened their skin—you know, with these Aryan features." Scott nudged her way through the Lancers by saying she had an important phone call and, before she knew it, she was standing next to the Veiled Prophet.

> I didn't look at him [the Veiled Prophet] directly because I was looking out front to see if anyone was going to stop me and no one was, and so I just reached over and pulled off his veil. It was loosely attached. It was a very silky gossamer, like a silk-stocking feeling. So, I pulled it down and held it in my hand. Of course, I didn't have any plans with what to do with it afterwards, which was unfortunate—what I might have done with the veil, or carried it to the front or something. But I could feel flashes—so I knew that pictures were being taken.[46]

Immediately grabbed and carried backstage by members of the Bengal Lancers, Scott now felt the pain of her broken ribs. Until then, Scott insisted, the pain had been pushed back in her mind. "And the pain now was not so much because I had taken that fall," Scott said. "They then dragged me over the triangular supports of those slats, and I remember thinking, 'Boy you're really angry.'" After having her ribs taped at a local hospital, police arrested Scott at around one o'clock in the morning in the halls of the hospital. At about four, the authorities released Scott from jail and gave her a court date. The Veiled Prophet organization later dropped the charges of disturbing the peace and destruction of public property (the cable) when it became obvious that, in order to prosecute Scott, they would have to reveal the name of the Veiled Prophet. Although there were photographs clearly showing his face, Smith still refuses to admit he was the Veiled Prophet in 1972. Sauer was also charged with disturbing the peace, but this charge was dropped as well.[47]

In November 1973, ACTION filed a class-action suit claiming that the city's rental of Kiel Auditorium for the Veiled Prophet Ball was "tantamount to renting a public building as a private club, in violation of city law." Shortly afterward, the organization announced it was moving the ball from the Kiel Auditorium to the Chase Hotel. The last ball held in Kiel was in December of 1974. ACTION proclaimed victory.[48] Moving the ball to the Chase was more than likely a response to both ACTION's lawsuit and the unveiling in 1972. By moving to a private facility, the Veiled Prophet organization took away one of ACTION's major and most effective arguments about the annual celebration. The organization moved the ball to the Chase's much smaller Khorassan Room, which would be easier to secure against ACTION's protests.

The last two major demonstrations at the Veiled Prophet Ball took place in 1975 and 1976. In 1975, Patrick Dougherty, an ACTION activist and former University of Missouri–Columbia faculty member, climbed onstage in the middle of the presentation of the maids and unfurled a banner that read "ACTION protests the racist VP." Dougherty's relatively mild form of protest was more an example of ACTION's mid-1960s nonviolent confrontational tactics than it was of the strategies of the 1970s. Dougherty, whose background included several demonstrations of this type (one of which cost him his job at the university), was not interested in performing guerrilla street theater. Removed roughly from the ball by two police officers, Dougherty was charged with disturbing the peace. The court later dismissed the charge when neither of the police officers appeared in court to testify against him.[49] Compared with the demonstration tactics used in the ball disruptions of 1972 and 1976, Dougherty's tactics in the 1975 demonstration appear anachronistic.

The demonstration at the 1976 Veiled Prophet Ball has been called "the death rattle" of ACTION by one of its former members and "going too far" by another.[50] The plan involved a "cry-in" against racism. On December 23, 1976, ACTION activists Annette Foster and Jessie Baker climbed onstage at 8:30 p.m. shortly after the Veiled Prophet was announced. The two activists ran across the stage spraying tear gas into the air, trying carefully not to spray it directly into anyone's eyes. Jacqueline Bell, an ACTION member at the time, claimed that ACTION chose the tear gas because "basically it was a unique gesture." Although the police claimed that the tear gas "was a paralyzing gas," Green insisted it was a commercial tear gas. Bell said the gas was "very harmless" and argued that it got into

Figure 7.3 When this photo of Percy Green was taken for a newspaper profile in 1975, years of contentious engagement had taken their toll on both ACTION and the Veiled Prophet organization. *Photo by Bob Moore for the* St. Louis Globe-Democrat, *from the collections of the St. Louis Mercantile Library at the University of Missouri– St. Louis*

the spectators' eyes when the security guards grabbed Foster and Baker, causing the spray nozzles to be pointed toward the crowd. Because the two ACTION members lived outside of St. Louis and the police had no information on them, the police and the Veiled Prophet organization tried to make it seem as if ACTION had hired the two protestors. The Veiled Prophet organization and the police insinuated that the women were outside agitators or, at least, non–St. Louisans. Foster, found guilty nearly two years later of spraying a chemical irritant at a policeman, was sentenced to six months in prison.[51]

By 1976 ACTION had trouble garnering publicity. The "cry-in" at the ball that year had merely been an attempt to draw public attention and had skirted the edge of violence. Whereas the other protests had clearly defined goals, this protest appeared to be nothing more than a simple grab for publicity at any cost. To spray an irritant into the air and then claim that it was the security guards' fault for getting the substance into people's eyes was a dubious assertion.

Until its disbanding in 1984, ACTION continued to protest at the Veiled Prophet Ball, Parade, and at the Fair, when it began in 1981. The 1976 tear gas incident severely damaged ACTION's credibility with the media and the public and had violated the major tenet of St. Louis public activism: Demonstrations should never be physically threatening. After 1976, ACTION was unable to garner much public attention at the Veiled Prophet protests and quietly faded away.

In 1979, the Veiled Prophet organization allowed its first Black members—three doctors—to join. When asked if they were admitting Black members in response to ACTION's protests, former Veiled Prophet Tom K. Smith—despite much evidence to the contrary—said that the Veiled Prophet organization

> hardly recognized ACTION. But we weren't aware that as much change was taking place in the community. Unfortunately, we didn't have time to keep up with the kind of changes that an institution like ACTION would like to see. We have Black members now because the city began to change. There were social changes. As Blacks became more active in business, they became members. We didn't think about them [ACTION]. I was too busy. Not that I wasn't interested. I just didn't have time.[52]

Ronald Henges, a longtime Veiled Prophet organization member, put it even more strongly: "I don't believe the protests—I don't believe Percy Green influenced the organization any more than just having more security. That's all. . . . He got publicity, and that's what he wanted and if he felt that was helpful to his cause then he accomplished that. As far as influencing any change in the VP organization, Percy Green can't take any credit for that." However, the St. Louis press certainly saw a connection between this decision and ACTION's protests. Reporters called ACTION headquarters on the day the Veiled Prophet organization announced it had admitted Black members. When asked about that day, Jacqueline Bell said that "the press called us down there saying ACTION will no longer be protesting at the Veiled Prophet because they have admitted Black members. I said, 'Hey, you guys have missed the point! We weren't trying to integrate the damned thing. You missed what we were trying to do.'"[53]

The Veiled Prophet organization was in fact responding to ACTION—but in an unanticipated way. In January of 1978, William H. Webster, a St. Louis native and federal judge, was nominated to become director of the Federal Bureau of Investigation. At his confirmation hearings, much was made of his membership in several exclusive all-white clubs—including the University Club, the Noonday Club, the St. Louis Country Club, and the Veiled Prophet organization. ACTION member Jacqueline Bell even testified about the nature of the Veiled Prophet organization. In a line designed to get press attention, Bell claimed the elites in the organization were "heavyweights" who "auctioned off their daughters among themselves, showing no respect for women" and that "we observed that there were judges and other Big Brother types in this clan."[54]

Webster was eventually confirmed in February after assuring the Senate Judiciary Committee that he would monitor these four clubs and, if he detected any indication of racial or religious discrimination, he would resign. In September of 1979, the Black members were initiated. In the article in the *Post-Dispatch* announcing the initiation (the only time in the organization's history initiates were ever publicly recognized), the spokesman for the organization admitted that the initiation committee had taken Webster's problems in getting confirmed into account and argued that "many members of the Veiled Prophet do not want to be vulnerable to the charge of racism" any longer.[55]

That the papers considered this a solution shows the way newspapers routinely distorted ACTION's pro-employment message all during that time. Both the *Globe-Democrat* and *Post-Dispatch* obscured ACTION's goals in their stories. None of the stories about the Veiled Prophet protests mentioned ACTION's employment goals. The newspaper press depicted ACTION as a group of radical militants who advocated evil subversion of the current social order. The *Globe-Democrat* published many damning editorials—many of which were written by then-editorial writer Patrick J. Buchanan—attacking ACTION as a small group of dissidents who were spoiling the annual celebration for everyone.[56]

Many ACTION members insisted that a large portion of the reporting of their protest activity had been cut by copy editors to match the newspaper owners' political and social agendas. When asked about the coverage of the Veiled Prophet demonstrations, two prominent former *Post-Dispatch* employees agreed with the ACTION members, contending that a great deal of content was cut by the editorial staff from the Veiled Prophet protest stories.[57]

One of the more telling examples of the press's bias was the coverage of the unveiling of the Prophet in 1972. In spite of the fact that everyone in the Kiel Auditorium saw Tom K. Smith and that there were probably one hundred pictures taken of his unveiled face, neither of the St. Louis daily newspapers ran Smith's name in its account of the unveiling. Evarts Graham, the assistant managing editor at the *Post-Dispatch* in 1972, stated that "the managing editor told me not to print it." Perhaps Tom K. Smith explains it best himself. Smith contended that "the *Post* and *Globe* appreciated the assets the Veiled Prophet organization had brought to St. Louis and the activities of the VP. So, they withheld the name out of respect—telling the name would have been destructive to St. Louis." This unwillingness on the part of the newspapers to follow the dictates of journalistic practice likely stemmed from two sources: the fact that prominent members of the editorial staff at both newspapers were members of the Veiled Prophet organization and that the newspapers counted on the members of the organization for a large portion of their advertising revenue. It was not until the next month, when the *St. Louis Journalism Review* published Smith's name, that the public knew the Veiled Prophet's identity.[58]

While Smith may contend that he and other Veiled Prophet members "hardly recognized ACTION" and "didn't think about them," the experiences of some former activists suggest otherwise. A few weeks after Gena Scott unveiled the Prophet in 1972, her car was bombed in front of her apartment. In the year following the protest, Scott's apartment was also vandalized several times. Several of the former activists interviewed for this study reported receiving threatening phone calls during their time with ACTION.[59] All of their stories taken together attest to the fact that some St. Louisans not only had enough time to think about ACTION activists, but they also had enough time to devise ways to harass the activists as well.

Throughout the 1960s and 1970s, Percy Green was the target of much harassment. During ACTION meetings in the mid-1960s, Percy Green's wife often received phone calls telling her that her husband had been killed. After being laid off by McDonnell-Douglas in 1964, Green applied to be rehired in late 1965. The management at McDonnell-Douglas claimed that Green's participation in protests at their plant during 1965 proved he was a "disruptive person" and refused to rehire him. Over the next ten years, Green—backed by the Equal Employment Opportunity Commission— pursued a discrimination suit against McDonnell-Douglas all the way to the United States Supreme Court.[60] While the corporate executives in the

Veiled Prophet organization may not have "recognized" ACTION, they clearly "recognized" Percy Green when he applied for a job. Despite thirty years of trying, Green has never been given another job at a major St. Louis corporation.

Some harassment of ACTION activists was directed by the FBI as a part of its COINTELPRO program. FBI agents—alerted by someone to the supposedly subversive nature of ACTION—frequently tormented activists. In 1970, the St. Louis office of the FBI "authorized an anonymous mailing from a soul sister" to Jane Sauer's estranged husband, Richard Simon. The letter, actually written by a male FBI agent, accused Sauer of marital infidelities with Black men. Four months later, a memorandum written by the St. Louis office of the FBI to J. Edgar Hoover gloated that "while the letter sent by the St. Louis Division was probably not the sole cause of the separation, it certainly contributed very strongly."[61]

Like ACTION, however, the Veiled Prophet organization was itself in dire trouble by the late 1970s. In 1978, Veiled Prophet membership was at an all-time low. Young St. Louis businessmen saw no reason to join. When asked about resignations during this period, all one "source close to the organization" would say was that "there were so many." One of these resignations was Charles Polk, an executive of the Baldwin Regalia Company. "In those days," Polk explained, "the crowds just kept diminishing. The VP wasn't perceived as a civic organization. It wasn't serving the interests of St. Louis. . . . A lot of money was being wasted on one party and a parade."[62] Public interest in the celebration itself dropped. The parade and ball were no longer covered by the media very closely. Television coverage of the ball had ended by the middle 1970s. The parade, although it was still televised, saw its attendance figures begin to drop precipitously. The organization was beginning to wither away; it seemed to be in its death throes by the late 1970s.

The Veiled Prophet celebration, once a cherished city tradition, was meeting a great deal of popular resistance and the members of the organization did not know what to do about it. In fact, some of the sons and daughters of members began to feel that the ball had outlived its usefulness. In an article that summed up the malaise of the 1970s for the Veiled Prophet organization, Curtis Wilson recounted interviews with debutantes who told him they agreed with Green that elitism was wrong and that the ball represented elitism. Wilson even spoke with one former maid who told him the ball was "a farce" and that "this kind of exhibition has got to go." Another maid described her experience with the ball as "much ado about nothing" and told him "I don't plan to have my daughter in it." The ultimate indignity for the organization was an interview with Dr. William H. Danforth, Chancellor of Washington University and a longtime Veiled Prophet organization member, who told Wilson his two daughters (aged twelve and fourteen) were already asking him if they would be presented at the ball. "I don't know what to tell them," he told Wilson frankly.[63] As of the late 1970s, the disbanding of the Veiled Prophet organization appeared to be imminent.

However, the end was not nigh. Through the creation of the July Fourth weekend VP Fair in 1981 (later called Fair St. Louis), the Veiled Prophet would eventually come up with a more effective event as a *raison d'etre* for the organization. This celebration gave the organization a marginally better community orientation and probably saved it. It would remain a viable organization largely due to its continued success as a place to make business contacts and little else. The VP Ball and Parade would continue largely unchanged well into the twenty-first century. Surprisingly, it was not until 2021 when a very different and strange scandal involving a Hollywood actress and a former Queen of Love and Beauty from 1999, Ellie Kemper, would finally lead to major changes in the celebration, including the dropping of the Veiled Prophet from the parade as well as numerous vague promises to reform the organization.[64]

Did ACTION's Veiled Prophet protests ultimately improve employment opportunities for minorities in St. Louis? Green did not think so. He believed "these individual companies still carry on racial discriminatory practices although not to the same degree as before. The level of tokenism has gone up to some degree but not enough to say that they are fair in their employment practices." However, ACTION's protests did change employment practices at some companies—those companies targeted for direct-action protests throughout this period. "We saw McDonnell's figures change," Jane Sauer said. "Who knows why? Maybe it was federal law. Maybe what ACTION did fed back in there somewhere."[65] Regardless, all of the former ACTION activists agreed that large-scale changes in employment practices in St. Louis did not occur as a result of any ACTION protests. The most obvious failure of ACTION's protests is the fact that the Veiled Prophet organization still exists.

Margaret Phillips senses why ACTION remained unable to achieve many tangible goals. She argues that ACTION "had no concrete plan that would help—just in effect screaming 'ouch!' . . . Maybe the problem was we just got stuck in a rut of protest and when somebody said, 'What do you suggest?'— we'd retreat. Which isn't saying a whole lot more than just 'jobs.'" Phillips believes ACTION needed more comprehensive positions on a broad range of issues as well as possible solutions to the problems that faced St. Louis.[66]

On the other hand, ACTION did compel the Veiled Prophet organization to move the ball from the publicly funded Kiel Auditorium to the Chase Hotel. However, the move from Kiel Auditorium also stole a great deal of ACTION's thunder and may have sounded the death knell of the organization. A large number of St. Louisans seemed to have been perfectly willing to allow the Veiled Prophet organization to continue its ostentatious debutante ball as long as public facilities were not used. When asked in 1993 about the achievements of the Veiled Prophet protests, Percy Green had additional victories in mind:

The victory was that it was our staying power that encouraged the VP to do the many different things that they have done to try to discredit our claims. The victory is in that they had to discredit our charges by making these other moves: having the VP Fair, taking the ball off television. If you look at the time we started our campaign, many changes have happened. They do still get the police department to lie and say what the crowds at the fair are, they aren't as big as they claim they are. They still get the news media to cover the parade. They've tried to separate the VP from the parade to some extent (only a couple of floats are from the VP): they try to give the impression that it's a community affair. They still try to bring in the white communities from other places: St. Peter's, St. John's, Cape Girardeau, but I don't think it's working.[67]

Green and other former ACTION members see their victory in the fact that the Veiled Prophet organization had to change in response to ACTION's protests. Despite denials by current and past members, the Veiled Prophet organization did bow to pressure and modify its ways, albeit not to the extent that most ACTION members would have liked.

Does the story of ACTION fit comfortably into the history of local Black activism during this period in America? In some ways, but not in others. ACTION's employment-oriented goals were indeed similar to those of other local groups studied by scholars, such as the Coalition of United Community Action (CUCA) in Chicago during the late 1960s. CUCA,

215

which protested against discrimination in the Chicago building trades during 1969, favored more menacing tactics, embodied in the slogan, "You own the trades—We own the match—build or burn."[68] The membership in these groups, like the national groups, tended to be all-Black; few, if any, whites participated.

Unlike other local groups studied by scholars during this "middle period," ACTION is exceptional in that its protests raised the public consciousness on some very important issues. Although large-scale changes in employment practices did not come about, ACTION's successes demonstrated that an integrated group devoted to nonviolent tactics could change some minds in a conservative midwestern city like St. Louis. While the Veiled Prophet protests did little to further ACTION's employment goals, these protests showed many St. Louisans that their tax dollars were indirectly supporting an elitist and, at the time, racist institution. ACTION's protests against corporate employers made some white St. Louisans stop and ask themselves an important question: Did minorities have equal opportunity to well-paying jobs with these major corporations? This raising of the public consciousness on a few vital issues was perhaps ACTION's most important achievement. Unfortunately, most white St. Louisans at the time seem to have rejected ACTION's employment goals.

In spite of ACTION's success in consciousness raising, the reasons for ACTION's decline did fit the explanations offered by civil rights scholars. Unlike other groups, ACTION's decline was slow and steady and linked to the steady rise of white backlash against civil rights groups during the late 1960s and 1970s. As James Ralph has argued, whites became "disturbed when civil rights crusaders guided the traditional quest for equality into more private realms of American life." Ralph maintains that while whites "applauded the southern black drive for basic political and civil rights," they dismissed the Chicago Freedom Movement's goal of ending housing discrimination "as an illegitimate demand that threatened their right" to make certain "basic, private decisions." Whites in St. Louis felt the controversy over the location of the Veiled Prophet Ball in the early 1970s was a "legitimate" public concern about basic civil rights (involving either equal access to or proper use of public facilities). At the same time, many in the white community rejected ACTION's employment demands as a separate issue that fit into the "private decision" realm. After the ball was moved from Kiel Auditorium, the white community turned a deaf ear to ACTION's Veiled Prophet protests and to ACTION's other more employment-oriented protests as well. By the late 1970s, after a decade of increasing white back-lash against civil-rights advocates, an overwhelming majority of white St. Louisans viewed ACTION's employment demands as an illegitimate infringement on their rights. Consequently, ACTION's demise was not quick and explosive like that of other civil rights groups during this period. ACTION did not, in the words of J. Mills Thornton, die "like a fire deprived of oxygen."[69] ACTION's flame, like an abandoned campfire, slowly flickered and burned out.

8. "The Seed Time of Gay Rights"

Rev. Carol Cureton, the Metropolitan Community
Church, and Gay St. Louis, 1969–1980

Rodney C. Wilson

*I took a cork out of a bottle, I think, that had so much energy, and so much
giving in it that it spilled out all over St. Louis. . . . I don't deserve any more
credit than somebody scattering a bunch of seeds.*

Carol Cureton, November 13, 1994

ON JUNE 27, 1993, ST. LOUIS mayor Freeman Bosley Jr. spoke to gays, lesbians, and their supporters gathered in Forest Park at the concluding festival
of Lesbian and Gay Pride Month. He offered this assurance: "I want you to
know today that if anyone comes for you, I'll speak up." The crowd of thousands cheered, understanding that Bosley, by announcing his position as a
heterosexual ally to the city's homosexual minority, had just made history.
That same day, Mayor Bosley announced that he would appoint longtime
human rights activist Laura A. Moore to the Civil Rights Commission, the
panel which oversees the city's Civil Rights Enforcement Agency; this action made Moore the first openly lesbian or gay person ever appointed to
citywide office.[1]

Bosley became the first St. Louis mayor to positively acknowledge his gay
and lesbian constituents. Before Bosley, the only city-sanctioned authorities
to meet with homosexuals in Forest Park were police officers determined
to arrest them for actual or perceived violations of city ordinances. A journey twenty-five years into the past from the date of Bosley's speech illustrates some of the evolutionary and revolutionary changes that created a
homosexual community with sufficient clout to beckon the mayor to a gay
pride festival.

In the late 1960s, St. Louis possessed no publicly visible gay community,
and for the most part heterosexual St. Louisans viewed homosexuality as

sinful, sick, or criminal. Patrons of gay institutions lived in fear of police raids and, along with most homosexuals, feared public exposure of their private lives.[2] In explaining why this changed and why gays and lesbians began creating open communities in the 1970s, historians have focused on several factors, including post–World War II urbanization, the 1960s climate of political and sexual liberation, and the Stonewall Rebellion of 1969. Urbanization, for example, was crucial to the development of gay meccas; historian Margaret Cruikshank states that the anonymity provided by crowded urban environments "created possibilities for living permanently outside of the traditional family structure."[3] Equally, the increasing acceptability of birth control, divorce, and out-of-wedlock cohabitation created an environment in which all forms of sexuality, including homosexuality, became far less taboo than they had been previously. Furthermore, women's liberation sanctioned women's desire to live separately from men and to choose women as partners—"women's liberation told women that they could be heterosexual, homosexual, bisexual, or asexual and that these choices were equally valid." Finally, coming in the midst of the social turbulence of the 1960s, bar patrons' refusal in June 1969 to cave in to police harassment at the Stonewall Inn in New York City's gay district sparked a gay liberation movement across the country; Stonewall—an episode often compared with the 1955 refusal of Rosa Parks to relinquish her bus seat to a white man—has been called "the shot heard round the homosexual world."[4]

All these factors played an important role in the national gay civil rights movement and made more probable the rise of gay rights movements in cities throughout the United States. In St. Louis, however, an institutional catalyst was needed for the creation of a public gay presence. The Metropolitan Community Church, a consciously gay and lesbian Christian fellowship, provided the missing element. This avenue for gay resistance was unavailable before 1968, when defrocked Pentecostal preacher Troy Perry founded the Universal Fellowship of Metropolitan Community Churches (UFMCC) in Los Angeles. Such a church-based liberation movement particularly appealed to residents of St. Louis, a conservative midwestern city bordering the "Bible Belt." From 1973 to 1980, the Metropolitan Community Church of Greater St. Louis (MCC) played a leading role in creating and sustaining a publicly recognized homophile movement.

Some organizational activity did occur before UFMCC minister Carol Cureton founded MCC in St. Louis in 1973. In April 1969, for example, eight St. Louisans gathered to form the Mandrake Society, which was loosely connected to the Mattachine Society, a national homophile organization founded in Los Angeles in 1950 by teacher and artist Harry Hay. By the end of the summer of 1969, the organization had only eighteen dues-paying members, who met twice a month at Trinity Episcopal Church in the Central West End.[5]

Following the arrest of nine men in drag outside the Onyx Room, a gay bar on Olive Street just east of North Grand Boulevard, on Halloween night in 1969, Mandrake members were alerted via the phone chain they had established for just such emergencies. By 3:00 a.m., two dozen activists had arrived at St. Louis police headquarters to work for the release of the men, who had been charged with illegal masquerading, despite the fact that it was Halloween. Unable to solicit the help of the St. Louis chapter of the American Civil Liberties Union, Mandrake alone aided in the men's defense. Ultimately, the city dropped all charges.[6]

This "mass" arrest of homosexuals stirred some homosexual St. Louisans to action; the November meeting of Mandrake, coming the month following the arrests, saw 150 in attendance; by January 1970, approximately one hundred people had joined the St. Louis Mandrake chapter.[7] Within a few weeks of the new year, however, a conservative coup at a Mandrake Society election ousted from the board the student activists who had founded the organization. The conservative takeover involved suburbanites who wanted a less visible, less confrontational organization. Mandrake's effectiveness as an institution for social change diminished following the installation of the new leadership, and within a couple of years the organization faded away.[8]

In the fall of 1970, a few gay students at Washington University—some of whom had been among the activist leaders removed from the board of Mandrake—formed a Gay Liberation Front, perhaps the first student homophile group in the Midwest.[9] That organization also fractured under tensions between confrontational radicals and moderates who wanted to maintain respectability while working for gradual change. In the spring of 1971, the Gay Liberation Front split; it dissolved completely by the end of the year. The following year, a handful of gay men organized Gay Patrol, a group that patrolled the parks attempting to prevent gay-bashing incidents. However, Gay Patrol never amounted to more than a handful of individuals, and it also folded in the mid-1970s.[10]

Finally, in the early and mid-1970s, a group called the Lesbian Alliance began promoting lesbian-feminist causes; among its many activities was publication of a booklet entitled "Homophile Community and the Law:

Rights We Don't Have," which was distributed to various organizations including the Eastern Missouri American Civil Liberties Union. The Lesbian Alliance, however, also folded in the mid-1970s without having successfully focused the attention of St. Louis at large on the needs of the homosexual community.[11]

Besides these few exceptions, St. Louis's gay landscape prior to 1973 consisted of little more than "the baths, bushes and parks," according to one gay man who has lived in St. Louis since the early 1960s. His partner of twenty-nine years and a resident of St. Louis since 1964 affirmed, "You could be gay, but you had to be in the closet." Gay bars were the prime method of contact with other gay people during this period, but they "had no political activity within them," according to Lisa Wagaman, a resident of St. Louis since 1972.[12] Fear of exposure caused gay and lesbian St. Louisans to remain an invisible minority. The creation of a public gay organization in the gay-oppressive atmosphere of 1960s St. Louis would have been difficult, according to two gay men who remember the period: "We [gays and lesbians] were not ready for that. We couldn't have coped with it. It was still too new then."[13]

Then came MCC, which assumed a role similar to that of other religious institutions active in American social movements, from the African American civil rights movement to the peace movement. As one student of the role churches played in the African American civil rights movement explained, as the "source of . . . universal humanistic values," religion often provided "strength that can come from believing one is carrying out God's will in political matters."[14] Additionally, according to sociologist Laud Humphreys, who both studied and participated in the St. Louis gay rights movement in the late 1960s, gay churches, "due to the nation's tradition of religious freedom . . . enjoy[ed] some protection from legal and social stigma."[15]

Given this history, it was possible for gay churches to overcome the fears of gays and lesbians to create a strong, vocal organization. Gay churches could provide protection (tax-exempt even) for gay political and educational work. This was certainly the case with MCC, which provided an institutional base for many of the organizing activities undertaken by the St. Louis gay community. As Wilbur Wegener, a St. Louis resident since 1962, contends, MCC not only provided "a place to meet" but allowed gay St. Louis to safely "come together under the cover of religion.[16] It was the Reverend Carol Cureton who brought this opportunity to St. Louis, arriving to found

MCC only weeks after anti-homosexual militants bombed the first UFMCC church in Los Angeles, where Cureton had received her training.

Born in Poplar Bluff, Missouri, in 1946, Cureton graduated from Poplar Bluff High School in 1964 and from Southeast Missouri State College in 1968 with a degree in biology and chemistry. Shortly after commencement, she moved to Los Angeles and married a man she had met the previous year; her marriage ended in divorce in 1971. Following her divorce, she embraced her lesbianism, but not knowing where to meet other lesbians, she felt "very alone, and very isolated and very afraid—not able to talk to another human being on this earth."[17]

Ultimately, she contacted the Gay Women's Services Center in Los Angeles, later remembering her arrival at the first meeting as "the most frightening moment in my life." Shortly thereafter she came across a small advertisement announcing the service schedule of MCC–Los Angeles tacked to a bulletin board at the Gay Women's Services Center.[18] Cureton had been raised with a sense of religious conviction but had cast it aside during college, partly in the spirit of rebellion and, she recognized many years later, partly due to her sexual orientation. With the option of attending a gay and lesbian fellowship, she decided to return to church.

She felt filled with anxiety on her first Sunday at MCC–Los Angeles: "I was afraid I wouldn't fit in, afraid that it would be just like any other church that I ever walked into, afraid that the police would be outside taking my

Figure 8.1 Rev. Carol Cureton, first pastor of the Metropolitan Community Church of St. Louis. *Photo by Wilbur Wegener, 1975, from* Gateway Heritage *15, no. 2 (Fall 1994)*

license number down."[19] But when the service ended, she was satisfied that she had found a church to which she could belong without lying or compromising her sense of self. That Sunday was a "great, fun, joyous experience." Comfortable with UFMCC's theology and its affirmation of gay and lesbian individuals as Christians, Cureton began attending services regularly. Shortly thereafter she became a member of the UFMCC's Exhorter (student clergy) program and soon made her way to St. Louis.[20]

On arriving in St. Louis, Cureton commenced missionary work in the local gay and lesbian bars, distributing her card to patrons and posting flyers announcing the organization of a church that would not discriminate against homosexuals. Committed to calling St. Louis homosexuals out of their closets and into the first consciously gay and lesbian church fellowship in American history, Cureton also hoped to encourage homosexuals to become more public in demanding their rights as citizens of the United States. To make this possible, she wanted to build a community whose members could more freely present themselves in the "overground" as both homosexuals and Christians.[21]

Cureton also approached area churches in search of a meeting place. After several churches refused her the use of their sanctuaries, the Berea Presbyterian Church at 3010 Olive Street (Fig. 8.2), a racially integrated church with progressive leadership, approved her request to hold services there. The first homosexual church meeting in the history of St. Louis occurred at that church at 2:00 p.m. on October 28, 1973. Ten people were present.[22]

Many early members of MCC in St. Louis stumbled upon the flyer announcing the creation of the church while spending an evening in the local gay bars. Lisa Wagaman recalled: "I had a strong religious background from a child, and felt it was something missing in my life. . . . When I heard about MCC I decided that was a place where I could go and I would feel comfortable—and I was."[23]

Other gays and lesbians were reluctant to attend MCC. Recalling bar raids and other forms of police harassment, they feared reprisals for appearing in daylight at a "homosexual" church. Indeed, four months after the church was organized, Cureton reported that some prospective members "still fear that a cop will be outside the church door taking down names."[24] Nevertheless, as news of the church spread, the number of people attending services grew.

Figure 8.2 Interior of Berea Presbyterian Church, at 3010 Olive Street, in 1969. The Midtown congregation, long active in civil rights advocacy, offered its sanctuary for the first meeting place of the city's Metropolitan Community Church. *From the Mac Mizuki Photography Studio Collection, Missouri Historical Society Library and Research Center; reprinted by permission of SmithGroup*

Operating as an open secret for five months, MCC's first widely publicized meeting occurred on March 11, 1974. That evening, the UFMCC's founder, the Reverend Troy Perry, addressed a group of nearly three hundred, the largest gathering of St. Louis gays and lesbians outside of a social function to that time. Declaring that "God does not want you to change that part of you which he created," Rev. Perry encouraged audience members to go forth into the community at large as witnesses to that fact. Never before had homosexuals in St. Louis been encouraged so boldly to leave a gay-friendly environment to mingle, as homosexuals, in the non-gay world.[25] That evening five people embraced Perry's and Cureton's revolutionary understanding of God's love, coming to the altar to dedicate their lives to Christ as gay Christians. The next day, stories on the service ran in both the *St. Louis Post-Dispatch* and the *St. Louis Globe-Democrat.* Under the headline "Homosexuals Gather for Church Meeting," the *Post-Dispatch* reported that the congregation responded to Rev. Perry's sermon with "Amens" and "Praise the Lords."[26]

MCC preached the born-again experience and performed full immersion baptisms for new members. Although raised a Southern Baptist, Rev. Cureton quickly adopted an ecumenical liturgy to accommodate members from all religious backgrounds. In a letter given to visitors, MCC described itself as an "ecumenical Christian Church with a ministry of special emphasis toward the Gay Community." However, no person would be excluded from its services, regardless of "age, sex, national origin, race, socio-economic status or sexual preference."[27] Cureton's 1975 Easter Sunday sermon provides a good example of MCC's message in the early years: "So we have through our history, victims of religion, not victims of God—victims of people and religion . . . but God does not turn anyone away. . . . [MCC] must proclaim to the world that He is risen. Let us proclaim it anew to everyone without exclusion," preached Cureton, "to the person in the bars, to the person behind the closed doors of this community, gay and non-gay alike."[28]

MCC's mission, however, extended beyond the construction of a spiritual community. It became a growing social and political organization for the area's Christian and non-Christian homosexuals, individuals described as "Friends of MCC." Wilbur Wegener, for example, considers himself an atheist, yet he was an early supporter of the church. According to Wegener, the creation of a gay church provided a safe and effective way for the St. Louis gay and lesbian community to make its presence known, and the existence of the church strengthened individual lesbians and gays in such a way that many of them began the difficult process of publicly acknowledging their homosexuality.[29] Once they had done so, gay and lesbian St. Louisans increasingly began to involve themselves in the gay rights struggle. As MCC member Galen Moon wrote to the *Post-Dispatch* in the autumn of 1974:

> In St. Louis you have a thriving unity of the Metropolitan Community Church with a growing outreach program aimed at helping the gay people in the area into their full rights as citizens. As the thousands of gay people in the area join together in the effort to enjoy lives free of the oppressions and discriminations we now suffer from the press, the clergy and the government, their needs and rights will have to be honored. This letter is only the beginning of public airings of our resentment and refusal to continue to silently suffer harassment and abuse.[30]

According to the Milwaukee-based *GPU News*, a publication of that city's Gay People's Union which sent correspondents to St. Louis to experience the church firsthand, MCC had sparked a sense of community and by the fall of 1974 had emerged as the "spiritual, social and political center" of St.

Louis's gay community: "As a sense of community grows, sparked by MCC, there can be little doubt that more will come." Creating a community of gays and lesbians had been, of course, Cureton's mission when she arrived in St. Louis less than a year earlier.[31]

The community created by MCC was not one in which all gay St. Louisans participated; many of the area's gays and lesbians never attended a service. The congregation overwhelmingly consisted of white working- or lower-middle-class urbanites. While some Black St. Louisans joined MCC, their numbers were small. And, with exceptions (Galen Moon, for example, was in his seventies), most MCC members were in their early twenties to mid-forties.[32]

Although church membership consisted of nearly equal numbers of women and men, in the 1970s MCC was a women-led congregation: Cureton's primary supporters in the church's leadership were women. The board of directors carefully maintained gender equity; however, some male MCC members felt that the church was too oriented toward lesbians and that on occasion men's issues were overlooked. Others active in the lesbian community at the time, Laura A. Moore, for example—who was never involved with MCC—believed MCC to have been "very male dominated." According to Moore, MCC was not that attractive to lesbians, while it did create "excitement in the male community."[33]

Figure 8.3 Lesbian activist Laura A. Moore, who in the mid-1970s co-authored the pamphlet "Homophile Community and the Law: Rights We Don't Have," shown in 1973. *Copy courtesy of Janice Gutman (photographer unknown)*

On December 23, 1974, with nearly 150 worshippers, the church left Berea Presbyterian Church and moved to its own building at 5108 Waterman Boulevard (Fig. 8.4). The acquisition of this property from the St. Louis Theosophical Society "mark[ed] the first time in Missouri that any self-proclaimed homosexual group has owned its own facilities."[34]

The dedication ceremonies took place in mid-1975. Once again, UFMCC founder Troy Perry addressed the St. Louis congregation, urging its members to express their homosexuality publicly and to be proud of who they were: "Gay liberation is knowing who you are, and what you are, and knowing that you have every right to exist in this time and this period in this Universe, and you don't have to apologize to anybody for that. That's real liberation. . . . That's exactly the attitude that you have to have in Missouri. Don't let them off the hook for a minute."[35]

MCC's three-story Victorian building became the nearest thing to a gay community center St. Louis had ever known. To passersby it looked like just another Central West End residence. Inside, however, it housed a large auditorium that comfortably seated about 250 people as well as additional meeting rooms and offices on each of the three floors and in the basement. These gay-friendly rooms served as the birthplaces of several gay and lesbian institutions in St. Louis.[36]

The most successful organization to emerge from MCC was the Metropolitan Life Services Corporation (MLSC). Created as an organization

Figure 8.4 A 2021 photo of 5108 Waterman Boulevard, which served as the first permanent home of the city's Metropolitan Community Church congregation. *Photo by Matthew J. Mancini*

dedicated to gay liberation, MLSC was envisioned as a secular MCC. Although the organization later changed its name to Mid-Continent Life Services Corporation to avoid a lawsuit from Metropolitan Life Insurance Company, MLSC originally associated itself with the Metropolitan Community Church by using the word "metropolitan" in its name. Formalizing the connection between the two organizations, the MCC board pledged its support for MLSC, approved MLSC's name and mission, and offered the organization office space in the church's basement.[37]

Within a few months of its mid-1975 organizational meeting, MLSC commenced publication of a newsletter called *Prime Time*, which kept readers up to date on all national and local events that affected homosexuals. It created the first guide to St. Louis's gay and lesbian organizations, including a detailed listing and explanation of the meeting places in the various St. Louis parks and the precautions to take when visiting them ("Extreme caution is advised here, for the police occasionally use entrapment methods").[38] *Prime Time* also offered advice to its readers on other topics, like this admonishment which appeared in nearly every issue: "STRAIGHT OR GAY, IF YOU'RE PROMISCUOUS, GET A BLOOD TEST EVERY 90 DAYS!"

MLSC's greatest contribution to St. Louis's gays and lesbians, however, was the establishment of the Gay Hotline. For the first time ever, any St. Louisan with a phone could contact homosexuals in the area through the Gay Hotline. The first Sunday of operation, 232 calls were made to the number advertised in the personals column of the *Post-Dispatch*; the following week, MLSC members answered an average of 188 calls per day.[39]

Overwhelmed by the community's interest, MLSC soon moved from Waterman to its own facilities at 4746 McPherson and later to 4940 McPherson (Fig. 8.5). During its years on McPherson, MLSC organized St. Louis's first gay community center. The Center, as it was called, opened its doors each day from 9:00 a.m. until 11:00 p.m. and provided services ranging from rap sessions and counseling services to a community library, a community bulletin board, an MLSC Blood Bank program, Friday night feminist women's coffeehouses (called "Womenspace"), and Saturday night mixed-gender coffeehouses, scheduled so as not to interfere with MCC's Friday night coffeehouse. In addition, any night of the week, lesbian and gay St. Louisans could attend the Center to play pool, pinball, and other games, eat at the snack bar, dance, listen to the jukebox, and occasionally enjoy live music.[40]

Figure 8.5 A 2021 photo of 4940 McPherson Avenue, once home to the Metropolitan (later Mid-Continent) Life Services Corporation. *Photo by Matthew J. Mancini*

The Center's activities did not supplant the community work carried on by MCC, which also provided a variety of programs for gay St. Louisans. In addition to worship services, MCC sponsored Bible study groups, a women's counseling group, peer counseling groups, Alcoholics Together and Al-Anon, rap sessions, a youth group, a lending library, and a Christian social action committee. Additionally, MCC's Friday Night Coffee House served as an alternative to the bars. Bill Cordes, a leader in the gay community since the late 1970s and the founding owner of the St. Louis gay and lesbian bookstore Our World Too, remembers the MCC coffeehouse as "a big thing in the community for a long time."[41]

As Lisa Wagaman explained, MCC provided the "impetus for the community—to get things going." In addition, MCC confronted the non-gay world on behalf of all gay St. Louisans. Wagaman asserts: "If there was something going on in the gay community, if there was some gay issue, the focus was always on MCC—what are they doing about it? What does MCC say about it?"[42]

The need for an organization that would speak out on behalf of the gay and lesbian community was never more apparent than in 1977, when singer Anita Bryant led an attack against homosexuals in Florida. Believing that "militant" homosexuality threatened the very foundation of American society, Anita Bryant and other conservative leaders in Dade County, Florida, organized the Save Our Children campaign to reverse a pro–gay rights county commission vote that had added sexual orienta-tion to Dade County's non-discrimination policies. Bryant appeared on Christian evangelist television shows, including Pat Robertson's *700 Club* and Jim and Tammy Bakker's *PTL Club*, where she explained: "We are in the middle of a battle that the Lord opened my eyes to. . . . Homosexuals want to come out of the closet. We are not against homosexuals, but we are against the act."[43]

The Save Our Children initiative campaign galvanized gays and les-bians across the country. In St. Louis, MCC, MLSC, and other gay and gay-friendly organizations mobilized against the anti-homosexual agenda of Anita Bryant and her allies. And, in fact, the struggle against Bryant boosted gay and lesbian organizing in St. Louis. According to Bill Cordes, it provided "a training ground for a lot of people who became [St. Louis] activists later." The events in Florida created the realization that St. Louis needed a "unified community of gays" to begin "networking" with com-munities in other cities in order to defeat such measures.[44] While existing gay-friendly organizations mobilized, Rick Garcia also founded the St. Louis Task Force for Human Rights, specifically geared toward raising money for pro-gay forces in Dade County. A thousand people attended one task-force fundraiser, a benefit screening at the Maplewood Theatre on Manchester Road of a film about homosexuality, *A Very Natural Thing*.[45]

Despite mass pro-gay mobilization throughout the country, the Save Our Children initiative passed, repealing Dade County's sexual orienta-tion protection with 69.3 percent of the vote. In response, New York, San Francisco, and Chicago anti-discrimination forces held mass rallies and candlelight vigils, where participants shouted gay rights slogans.[46] Two days after the June 7, 1977, election, MCC hosted St. Louis's Second Annual Gay Pride Rally. The standing-room-only crowd of over three hundred was addressed by Rev. Cureton, four leaders of the St. Louis gay community, and two out-of-town leaders, including Rev. Troy Perry, who had just come from Florida where he had spoken out against the Anita Bryant campaign.

While acknowledging the serious setback, the speakers at the rally expressed their continued determination to win human rights for gay people. In her introductory remarks, Rev. Cureton declared that "your very presence here is a statement that the election in Dade County . . . does not mean that gay people are going back into the closet!" The crowd cheered.[47]

The predominantly gay and lesbian audience responded loudly to Rick Garcia's announcement that "solidarity . . . is the key . . . to gaining our rights. No legislator is going to give us our rights. We have to take those rights. We have to stand up and be counted. We have to say, 'We are here. We are good. We are important. And we deserve what is ours! Human rights are God-given rights!'"[48]

Jim Alexander, board member of Dignity–St. Louis (an organization of St. Louis Catholic homosexuals founded in 1974, which met once a month at MCC) also addressed the crowd. A transplanted Bostonian, Alexander sounded eerily like Senator Robert Kennedy the night he comforted the crowd in Indianapolis following the assassination of Martin Luther King Jr. Provoking a deep sense of reverence among the crowd, Alexander spoke of the events of the past week: "This past week has been a week of many emotions, many different emotions: It's been a week of despair and despondency and anger and maybe even of hope." He ended with a prophecy: "We are presently in the seed time of gay rights. We're planting the trees . . . that will eventually bear fruit for our future generations."[49]

Septuagenarian Galen Moon, founder of MLSC, declared: "I've known loneliness and I've known ridicule." Looking upon the newly formed gay groups in St. Louis, he commented: "I dream now of all gay groups and individuals getting together . . . and getting rid of the lies and myths . . . and coming out on top." Moon ended his exhortation by encouraging the gay and lesbian people of St. Louis and Missouri to continue to work to "change the situation in this state."[50]

The last speaker was the featured guest, Rev. Troy Perry. Declaring that "gay people have come to a crossroads in our country," he spoke defiantly and with boldness: "If we don't rock the boat, things aren't going to change in America. . . . Every time the Anita Bryant forces go around and try to say we can't hold jobs, maybe tomorrow we all ought to quit working and bring this country to its knees! . . . Gay people are not going back to the closets. . . . We're going to have a non-violent revolution in this country and we're going to smother the Anita Bryants in love!"[51]

Figure 8.6 Rev. Troy Perry, founder of the Universal Fellowship of
Metropolitan Community Churches, in 1970. *Photo by Pat Rocco, from
the Pat Rocco Collection, courtesy of ONE Archives at the USC Libraries*

Cureton closed St. Louis's Second Annual Gay Pride Rally, agreeing that
the "gay movement for human liberation" would ultimately prove successful: "We're going to be a free people!" She called the audience to its feet; the
rally ended with a loud, soul-felt rendition of all four verses of "We Shall
Overcome."[52]

A few weeks after this rally, the *Post-Dispatch* ran a lengthy article on
the gay and lesbian movement in St. Louis. The author wrote that lesbian
and gay St. Louis was "not nearly so well-organized as their counterparts

in Washington, San Francisco, New York or Boston"; nevertheless, because of the recent organizational accomplishments of St. Louis's homosexuals, "Anita Bryant's antihomosexual Save Our Children crusade could turn out to be the best thing that has happened to the St. Louis homosexual community in years."[53]

However, the 1977 Gay Pride Rally proved to be the last large political event hosted by MCC for many years. Four months after the rally, Cureton departed St. Louis to serve the UFMCC in Los Angeles as clerk of the Board of Elders. Lisa Wagaman recalls Cureton's departure as "traumatic" for the church. According to Wagaman, "a lot of people left MCC because of Carol Cureton's leaving."[54]

Over the next three years, MCC had three ministers; the lack of continuity within the church made it nearly impossible to present a united front to the gay community and the rest of St. Louis. MCC continued to serve as a meeting place for gay groups, including the Catholic organization Dignity–St. Louis, Washington University's student group, and many others. As the decade closed, however, they no longer took an active part in building the community.

In addition to the pastoral turmoil at MCC, the year following the Dade County defeat was not kind to gay and lesbian America or gay St. Louis. In 1978, Anita Bryant launched a nationwide campaign to repeal laws and ordinances designed to protect lesbians and gays from discrimination. Within months anti-gay rights forces were successful in Wichita, Kansas; St. Paul, Minnesota; and Eugene, Oregon. In November 1978, George Moscone, mayor of San Francisco, and Harvey Milk, San Francisco's first openly gay supervisor, were assassinated by the only San Francisco supervisor who voted against their non-discrimination ordinance for gays and lesbians.[55]

In St. Louis, the Task Force for Human Rights folded a few months after the Dade County defeat. The Mid-Continent Life Services Corporation ceased publication of *Gay St. Louis* (its successor to *Prime Time*), and in March 1978 moved to a smaller location at 10 South Euclid in an attempt to stay afloat financially. In October 1978 MLSC formally voted to cease operations, and the first self-proclaimed gay community center in St. Louis faded into history. Also, in October 1978 a young gay man was shot in the back of the head in Forest Park; he was found dead hours later.[56]

While MCC's leadership stabilized in 1980 with the arrival of the Reverend P. Thomas Jordan, it never regained its primary position in the community. During his tenure Jordan deliberately steered the church away from politics, and MCC ceased to act as a religious/political institution and became more narrowly religious. As Jim Thomas described the transformation, MCC "turned . . . inward [and] became more churchy. There really was a withdrawal from a sense of social ministry and going much more back to a sense of Christian evangelical ministry."[57]

Furthermore, MCC abandoned the Waterman location in 1984, removing itself from the Central West End, an area of the city where gays and lesbians often gathered. MCC moved to Lafayette Square into a church on 1120 Dolman, previously home to the St. Mary's Assumption Ukrainian Rite congregation. Some viewed the new location as less safe than the Central West End, and as the new building had much less space for meeting rooms than the Waterman church, the move ended MCC's de facto role as a community center. Subsequently, MCC lost (or left) its position as community leader. Without an activist MCC and in the face of other setbacks, the gay communities of St. Louis floundered in the early and mid-1980s.[58]

Nevertheless, MCC accomplished much during its early years. As a focal point for the gay communities of St. Louis, MCC provided the impetus necessary to foster a visible, above-ground community of gays and lesbians. Cordes comments that

> MCC played a very crucial role in the beginnings of the community here because . . . it was the first non-bar space that had a telephone and an address and someplace you could go that wasn't a bar, that wasn't a post office box. It was a gathering place for those people who couldn't drink or couldn't go into the bars or didn't like them or wanted to be able to have a conversation where the music wasn't blaring. It gave a different direction than the bar did. . . . MCC . . . became a community center, a networking center; it was where we politicked. It provided space for the hotline when nobody else would. It was a catalyst for community organizations to start. It was an essential part of this community growing. . . . They have been the catalyst for an awful lot going on in this community.[59]

Several gay institutions of lasting importance began during MCC's period of community activism. Washington University's Concerned Gay Students (Fig. 8.7), a re-emergence of their student group, organized Gay Pride Week on its campus in 1979. In April 1980, the city's first Gay Pride March was held (Fig. 8.8). *No Bad News*, a newspaper aimed at the gay

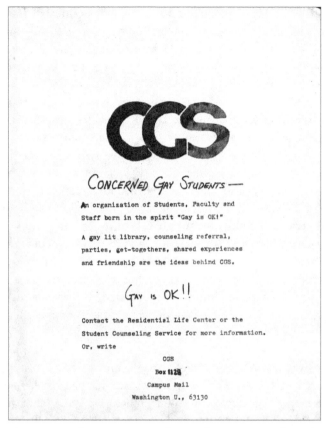

Figure 8.7 Washington University's Gay Liberation Front, formed in 1970, had dissolved within a year, but it was succeeded in 1976 by the group Concerned Gay Students (later Concerned Lesbian and Gay Students), which organized a campus Gay Pride Week in 1979. *From the Bruce Janis Student Papers, courtesy of ONE Archives at the USC Libraries*

communities, was founded in 1980; a year later, in October 1981, the first issue of the *Lesbian and Gay News-Telegraph* (then called the *Gay News-Telegraph*) hit the stands, distributing five thousand copies.[60] Its editor, Jim Thomas (Fig. 8.9), who entered St. Louis's gay community in 1977 during what he refers to as "Dade County Summer," was destined to become a leader of the gay community from the early 1980s onward. Thomas contends that "merely . . . the fact that [MCC] existed . . . was of absolutely vital importance. . . . You were thankful that they were there whether you

Figure 8.8 Marchers traverse the Central West End in St. Louis's April 1980 gay pride march and rally, formally titled "Lesbians, Gays, and Friends Walk for Charity." *Photo by Wilbur Wegener, from the Challenge Metro Collection, Missouri Historical Society Library and Research Center*

Figure 8.9 Jim Thomas, chair of the committee that organized the 1980 gay pride march and founder of the *Lesbian and Gay News-Telegraph*, pictured in 1979. *Reprinted by permission of Jim Thomas*

wanted to attend their church or not, or believed the way they did. It just had such a symbolic importance."[61]

MCC was not solely responsible for creating an open gay community in St. Louis. Without question, the social and political changes in America during the 1960s and 1970s impacted all of St. Louis, including gay St. Louis. The civil rights movement, the women's movement, the national gay rights movement, and post-pill, pre-AIDS sexual liberalization all played a role in creating the possibility of an open gay community and, in fact, made MCC possible. Nevertheless, MCC provided the necessary catalyst. When it arrived, the city's gay landscape was practically barren. After a seven-year role as a creating and sustaining institution of the gay community, MCC backed away; nevertheless, the "children" of MCC lived on and struggled for gay rights throughout the 1980s. By 1993 they had mustered the degree of political clout and social legitimacy that made it possible for them to bring the mayor to Forest Park. It was the Metropolitan Community Church of the 1970s, however, that wrote the first lines on the mayoral invitation.

9. The Limits of Middle-Class Activism

Neighborhood Organizing in St. Louis

Susanne Cowan

LIKE OTHER SOCIAL MOVEMENTS IN the 1960s and 1970s, neighborhood organizing employed protests and advocacy to try to change policies related to social injustice, such as racial segregation and affordable housing. In a time when many social activists were challenging the authority of the federal government, neighborhood organizers questioned "technocratic top-down decision making."[1] Instead, they aimed to develop more local forms of governance and to replace large-scale government projects with small-scale self-help improvement efforts. Neighborhood organizing was particularly common among the "new middle class," a group of young, educated professionals who challenged the values of commercialism and conformity endemic to the 1950s suburbs, and who moved into cities in the 1960s and 1970s looking for new, more authentic and diverse experiences.[2]

However, unlike many of the leftist groups associated with activism during this period, the political orientation of neighborhood organizers was less overtly progressive. Across the United States, neighborhood organizing was embraced by both the Left and the Right as a rejection of big government and an effort to reinvigorate local voluntary institutions as sites for democratic engagement.[3] On the ground, neighborhood organizing often focused on conserving the status quo by supporting homeownership and protecting property values. While neighborhood organizing was an important part of the activist movements of the 1960s and 1970s, it was also limited in its scope of reform by virtue of its focus on addressing the needs and values of the middle class.

As in many other cities across the county, neighborhood organizing took hold in St. Louis in the 1960s and 1970s. At that time, white flight was depleting St. Louis's population as residents fled the crime and disinvestment

239

of the city to the presumed safety of the suburbs. But some middle-class residents in the region chose to stay or to move back to the city, often joining together in neighborhood associations to build communities and improve urban amenities. Around the city of St. Louis, dozens of neighborhood associations adopted activism to improve the quality of the built environment and the social services in their area.

Some of these groups employed the more progressive social ideas of their time to challenge established modes of city planning. In the face of urban planners who believed urban decline was inevitable, neighborhood associations used bottom-up social organizing to reverse decades-long practices such as redlining, which divested from low-income areas, and slum clearance, which demolished dilapidated houses. Instead, they aimed to promote homeownership in shrinking neighborhoods and to rehabilitate rundown homes to bring life back to the inner city. Organizers in St. Louis neighborhoods like Skinker DeBaliviere and Soulard fought banks, real-estate agents, and government agencies as they tried to create liberal enclaves for inclusive urban communities. But these community groups, mostly composed of white middle-class residents, also faced internal conflicts as neighbors disagreed about how to address urban problems. These divisions within the community highlighted demographic differences between residents of different classes and races.

In Skinker DeBaliviere, a neighborhood undergoing a change in racial makeup, a group of white residents chose to stay and to try to build an integrated community. In their outreach materials and local histories, the longtime residents celebrated how their choices to stay had helped to "save the neighborhood."[4] They did this by trying to improve the social and physical infrastructure of the area and to retain and attract white buyers to an integrating neighborhood. Yet residents disagreed on the economic development priorities of the neighborhood. While white middle-class homeowners valued the aesthetic improvement and redevelopment of the neighborhood to increase property values, low-income Black renters preferred spending funding on social services to ensure educational and job-training opportunities for children and young adults. Despite the neighborhood's rare feat of achieving an approximately fifty-fifty Black-white racial balance for more than fifty years, disagreements over economic development spending caused rifts in the community.

In Soulard, neighborhood organizers began their mission to preserve the historic working-class neighborhood by trying to stop bulldozers and by expressing outspoken resistance to government slum-clearance programs. Labeled as "hippies," the young long-haired activists tried to reverse decades of planning theories about the inevitability of urban decline by promoting self-help programs to protect and restore historic homes.[5] Over time, as an increasing number of middle-class homeowners gained more sophisticated knowledge of bureaucratic systems, their local neighborhood organizations strategically employed government programs to help provide services and protect historic homes. However, the two neighborhood organizations in Soulard took two distinct approaches to economic stabilization: private redevelopment through home restoration and infill development through subsidized government housing projects. This philosophical divide, exacerbated by demographic differences, led to combative relations between the groups from the late 1970s to early 1990s. Both groups contributed to the revitalization of the area, successfully attracting back-to-the-city middle-class homebuyers. But neither group could fully engage the low-income residents as equal participants in community organizing.

In both case studies, middle-class neighborhood organizers promoted some progressive ideas, countering the redlining and slum-clearance models of urban redevelopment to promote economically or racially diverse neighborhoods. However, these neighborhood associations did not represent a united community; they hid deeper demographic and ideological divides exacerbated by differences in race and class.

Neighborhood Organizing as
Protest against Government Planning

While neighborhood organizing existed in many forms in St. Louis in the early twentieth century, it took on a unique form in reaction to the changes of the 1960s, serving as a means both to protest government action and to facilitate self-help. After World War II, planners had started a series of large-scale urban redevelopment projects around the country. In St. Louis, this included the modernization of downtown and the construction of highways connecting the city to the suburbs. Redevelopment also involved clearance of industrial areas and dilapidated housing such as in Mill Creek Valley, and the construction of public housing on the Near North and Near South Sides, including large high-rise projects like Pruitt-Igoe and Darst-Webbe.

Community members did not have much say in these projects, even though they often cut through their neighborhoods, demolished their homes, and dislocated residents. Early urban redevelopment laws, like the

federal Housing Act of 1949, had not provided any means for community input. While later amendments contained in the 1954 Housing Act did
mandate "citizen participation," in reality the policy was largely implemented by "rubber-stamp" commissions that did not reflect true democratic
processes.[6] During this period, neighborhoods were often caught off guard
by redevelopment projects, which were approved without much publicity—
sometimes years or decades before implementation. Many urban neighborhoods, such as those in St. Louis, had very little relationship with city
government, lacking close connections with their aldermen, and thus did
not have a clear process for lodging their complaints.

In the 1960s and 1970s, neighborhood organizations grew up around
the country as a means of protesting these types of government programs.
Planning historian Suleiman Osman calls the 1970s "The Decade of the
Neighborhood"; at that time, a backlash against "objective," top-down
planning shifted favor toward the subjectivity and intimacy of local decision making.[7] In 1976, Milton Kotler, executive director of the National
Association of Neighborhoods, declared that "there's a new recognition
that the country's not going to be saved by experts and bureaucrats" but
by "the grassroots and the neighborhoods."[8] This loss of trust in government and empowerment of local organizers led to a boom in neighborhood associations.

In St. Louis, neighborhood organizing surged in a variety of different
neighborhoods, including middle-class residential areas facing the first
signs of urban decline, older areas near downtown starting historic preservation movements, and areas in the north experiencing racial demographic change. By 1972, the mayor's office knew of ninety neighborhood
associations in St. Louis that met on a monthly or more frequent basis,
varying in size from twenty to 250 members; some had been started by
the residents, others were "initiated with assistance" from the city, but all
operated independently.[9] Most of the neighborhood groups seemed to take
a liberal rather than radical approach, focusing on equal opportunities
rather than redistribution of resources. While some groups directly addressed social policy, many neighborhood groups started as Improvement
Associations which aimed to maintain aesthetic standards. Other groups
began as Restoration Groups aiming to promote renovation of historic
homes. While not all neighborhood associations were politically oriented,
these groups were part of a national movement of citizen participation in
urban planning.

Nationally, community organizing in the 1960s was often characterized by protest and resistance to official planning schemes, like protests to stop freeway construction or campaigns to protect historic buildings.[10] In the field of planning, one of the most memorable organizers was Jane Jacobs, who helped organize protests against the urban renewal plans of Robert Moses in Greenwich Village in Manhattan. She participated in local groups that fought the extension of Fifth Avenue through Washington Square Park and the demolition of Penn Station. Her dismissal of the expertise of urban planners and her support of the benefits of historic neighborhoods made her a figurehead for grassroots preservation movements.

Another of the most well-known community organizers in the 1960s and 1970s was Saul Alinsky, who helped relatively small groups in their quest to gain power to protect their interests against powerful institutions. His first book, *Reveille for Radicals* (first published in 1946 and issued in revised form in 1969), became standard reading, spreading his strategy for organizing, building leadership, and winning against the odds. Alinsky urged community groups to employ dramatic approaches like picketing, demonstrating, and filing lawsuits to surprise and weaken their enemies. Yet he was pragmatic and sought out allies, willing to work with anyone who could support the cause, even if they held different ideologies. His techniques successfully empowered "have-not" groups to win greater access to limited resources. However, like other interest-based approaches, his strategy accepted that a success for one group meant a loss for another group, sometimes just as disempowered. His pragmatic approach focused on one local condition at a time, rather than more holistic, ideological, or long-term goals. Alinsky's second book, *Rules for Radicals*, published in 1972, focused less on "have-nots" than on organizing the middle class, the "have some, want more's," as Alinsky called them. Adopters of this approach argued that all citizens were disempowered by the concentration of power under corporations.[11] This approach fit well with the goals of middle-class neighborhood organizers, who, despite being financially stable, saw themselves as hindered both by governments and by businesses such as banks in their work to improve their neighborhoods.

In the 1970s, community organizing shifted away from more radical strategies. Veering away from the provocative approaches of the 1960s, which had often centered on public demonstrations, neighborhood groups adopted more cooperative, behind-the-scenes approaches to working with governments and businesses. Organizations acknowledged the need for skill and expertise in organizing, and worked to train themselves on how to facilitate meetings, use publicity and marketing, and delegate tasks to match the abilities of their members.[12] During this period, neighborhood organizers gained greater knowledge about the contextual conditions shaping their struggles. Many developed sophisticated understandings of the legal, policy, and financial structures that shaped problems like redlining, urban renewal, and redevelopment. Organizers used this knowledge to work with banks and city agencies to develop new approaches. Rather than working from an obstructionist stance of "not-in-my-backyard," they tried proactively to promote the types of programs that would reinforce their goals.

Neighborhood groups used their collective power with elected officials to try to influence planning professionals and change policies in their favor. In St. Louis, this approach was noticed as early as 1966, when Lucius Cervantes, brother and assistant to the mayor, Alfonso J. Cervantes, noted a lack of protests in the summer of 1966; he said that neighborhood groups were veering away from Alinsky-style confrontations to "overthrow the power structures" and instead realizing that a "positive approach" creates "harmony and progress throughout the community."[13] This statement alone cannot represent the larger ethos of community organizing in St. Louis, which certainly went through periods of protest and confrontation. This quote does show that, even during times when their counterparts in other regions of the nation were organizing protests, many neighborhood groups in St. Louis were trying to work within the system rather than in opposition to it. By combining tactics that opposed and collaborated with government, these community groups had a significant impact on planning policies and programs in St. Louis in the 1970s.

Organizing Integration in Skinker DeBaliviere

In Skinker DeBaliviere, this more cooperative approach to neighborhood organizing can be seen in the way residents tried to achieve racial integration by balancing the promotion of liberal social ideals with the protection of property values for middle-class homeowners. In the 1960s, the neighborhood of Skinker DeBaliviere, located in the northwest of the city, experienced demographic changes as the neighborhood became more racially diverse. In the early twentieth century, the area had included two middle-class white neighborhoods, Rosedale Skinker and Washington Heights. After World War II, many white homeowners chose to move to the suburbs lured by cheap, modern, single-family houses. As they left, the new buyers in Skinker DeBaliviere chose to rent out or subdivide homes for lower income groups, first white rural migrants and later Black households.[14] Starting in 1963, dislocated Black residents from areas such as Mill Creek Valley, targeted for urban renewal, moved out of the old industrial core of the city westward into Skinker DeBaliviere and adjacent neighborhoods. Many new arrivals moved to the Triangle area in northeast Washington Heights, where renters found cheap apartments.[15] The area also attracted Black homebuyers who settled in the semi-detached homes elsewhere in Washington Heights (Fig. 9.1).[16]

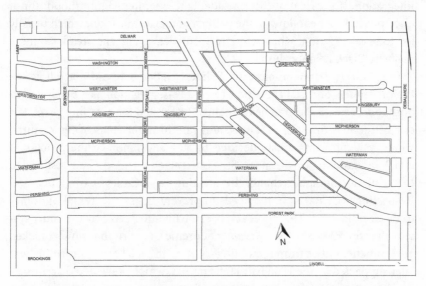

Figure 9.1 This map of Skinker DeBaliviere shows how the railroad tracks divide the neighborhood into two segments, isolating the mostly Black residents of the "Triangle" in the northeastern corner. The east side of the neighborhood, from Des Peres Avenue to DeBaliviere Avenue (including the Triangle), is called Washington Heights. The west side of the neighborhood, from Skinker Boulevard to Des Peres Avenue, is called Rosedale Skinker. *Adapted from Cultural Resources Office map, City of St. Louis, 2010*

By 1970, Black residents accounted for 55 percent of the population of Skinker DeBaliviere, with a higher percentage of Black households living in Washington Heights than in Rosedale Skinker.[17] As is typical in other similar neighborhoods, the racial transition triggered redlining, a discriminatory lending guideline practiced by banks and by the Federal Housing Administration that relied on color-coded maps, marking in red those districts deemed to be unsafe for mortgage lending. While presumably based on the age and the condition of the housing, this designation was also frequently based on the racial and ethnic identity of the residents. Redlining diminished the ability of homebuyers to qualify for mortgages on homes in the area, decreasing property values.[18] Like in other cities, many white residents who feared losing home equity, or were "unable to accept the changes" in the racial demographics, left the area in "white flight" to the suburbs.[19] Between 1960 and 1970, the white population of Skinker DeBaliviere decreased by 50 percent.[20] The area had experienced racial integration, the arrival of Black residents to a white neighborhood. But it also appeared to be following the pattern of racial transition, which usually led to re-segregation, when white residents leave, and the area becomes a majority Black neighborhood.

Despite this demographic shift, Skinker DeBaliviere did not follow the typical models of racial transition toward re-segregation as a Black neighborhood. Instead, the area has remained integrated for over fifty years. For one of the first times in St. Louis, and rare in other areas of the country, white residents consciously decided to stay and embrace the process of racial integration. In the past, St. Louis neighborhoods had responded to racial demographic change by creating new Codes, Covenants, and Restrictions (CCRs) in home deeds to prevent the sale or rental of homes to Black residents.[21] This approach became unenforceable by the court system after the 1948 *Shelley v. Kraemer* Supreme Court ruling, which blocked government entities from upholding CCRs with racial bias. This ruling was later supported by the 1968 Fair Housing Act, which prevented discrimination based on race in the sale, rental, or financing of housing. While neither of these decisions ended housing segregation, they limited the options for neighborhoods to overtly organize discrimination. Without the same tools available to prevent integration, white homeowners in places like Skinker DeBaliviere had to choose between fleeing to the suburbs or staying in an integrated neighborhood.

Those residents who chose to stay formed the Skinker DeBaliviere Community Council (SDCC) to try to maintain racial balance in the neighborhood. This group formed in 1965 when two earlier neighborhood associations, Washington Heights Neighbors and Rosedale Skinker Improvement Association, combined forces with three local churches and nearby Washington University. With funding from the university, the SDCC hired a full-time staff member. In 1970, the SDCC also opened a new office at 6008 Kingsbury Avenue in a shopfront in the "heart of the neighborhood."[22] From here, they worked to expand and create new marketing campaigns, real-estate policies, social programs, and redevelopment projects to combat urban problems in the neighborhood.[23]

The approach the SDCC employed to achieve integration was to encourage whites to stay. This group's efforts fit within a strategy known as "managed integration," which was used in other urban areas across the United States.[24] This approach to integration tried to manage racial balance through careful targeting of new residents instead of leaving integration up to market forces, which were negatively affected by discriminatory banking and real-estate practices. In *Making Good Neighbors*, Abigail Perkiss describes the approaches to managed integration in Philadelphia's Mount Airy neighborhood as part of a commitment to emerging ideas of "liberalism" among whites in the face of the civil rights movement. This liberal approach, which emphasized the right to equal opportunity rather than equality of outcome, paralleled the approach Skinker DeBaliviere took toward promoting integration.[25]

While the neighborhood organizers responded to integration, they did not aim to fight it or stop it. The first Director of the SDCC, Jim L'Ecuyer, noted that some people wanted him "immediately, within two to three weeks, to stop the trend of integration in the neighborhood." The group, racially integrated from the beginning, committed to proceed in the opposite direction. L'Ecuyer emphasized, "We were going to promote integration at any cost, meaning integration was going to work here, or it wouldn't work at all."[26] To that end, Skinker DeBaliviere aimed to become a model for other neighborhoods, arguing that the area could successfully integrate and maintain property values through what local organizer and historian Jo Ann Vatcha calls the "triumph of hope and a lot of gumption."[27] She recounts how, in the face of white flight, a substantial group of white homeowners "refused to participate in this panic" and instead "pulled together" uniting "residents black and white" to form community organizations that fought to make the "community safe and secure and see that its historic housing could be made available to all races." White "stayers" in Skinker DeBaliviere, like those in other cities, expressed pride in their unique choice to "do the right thing," seeing themselves as exceptional for following their "moral imperative" rather than economic self-interest.[28] This kind of rhetoric seemed to claim that hard work and good values could overcome white flight and structural racism (see Fig. 9.2).

Figure 9.2 A sketch from the May 1976 issue of the *Skinker DeBaliviere Times* shows how the neighborhood imagined itself: as a harmonious racially integrated community. *Reprinted by permission of* The Times of Skinker DeBaliviere

Those who stayed often explained their decision as reflective of their liberal values. Some claimed that all the racists had already left and that the inhabitants who had stayed "were those who believed in integration."[29] A brochure produced by the SDCC called integration "interesting and challenging" and praised the area's "wonderful blend of people from varied economic, social and religious backgrounds."[30] While some people may have genuinely believed in the ideology of integration, others expressed a less idealistic, more pragmatic stance. Leaders like the president of the Washington Heights Neighbors group encouraged all residents to help promote neighborhood integration "whatever their personal feelings may be."[31] The organizers of a housing project said the goal was "not just civic pride" but to "save the neighborhood and make a profit at the same time."[32] For those who stayed, their social mission also served their practical interests in protecting their home values, providing an urban lifestyle, and ensuring like-minded neighbors.

For some neighborhood organizers, the idea of integration embraced a diversity of race but not class. The SDCC identified its power to improve the neighborhood as based in members' own middle-class identity. One resident argued, "we have a large black and white middle-class community with unlimited potential and energy to tackle the economic and racial barriers that seem to hang-up our city and indeed our nation."[33] This focus on the benefits of middle-class organizers seems to show a bias toward those of the same economic class. Like in other integrating neighborhoods around the country, the SDCC promoted an integrated middle-class neighborhood, promoting racial diversity and economic homogeneity.[34] This group's intentional promotion of middle-class values can be seen in several aspects of their policies to try to "stabilize" the neighborhood, including preventing white flight, attracting new middle-class homebuyers, and redeveloping the dilapidated areas of the neighborhood.

Preventing White Flight

The SDCC aimed to promote integration by preventing white flight and the seeming inevitability of racial transition and re-segregation, which they knew had occurred in many other neighborhoods. While most white residents in St. Louis thought real-estate values inevitably decrease during racial transition, the members of the SDCC recognized that this could be a self-fulfilling prophecy; moving to avoid loss of home values for oneself caused loss of value for the next neighbor to sell. In contrast, the members of the SDCC hoped to halt that cycle of real-estate value freefall by engaging with a more rational rather than emotional understanding of the effect of racial transition on home values.

An editorial in the December 1966 Washington Heights Neighbors newsletter lamented the fact that true integration rarely existed in St. Louis and hoped to institute a new pattern. Using knowledge of the Chicago School and related sociological and economic theories, the author acknowledged the concern that integration of formerly white neighborhoods led to racial transition, and thus to re-segregation or "dis-integration" into all-Black neighborhoods. Instead, the author argued that an ideal form of integration should "reflect the overall community mixture" in St. Louis, this being about 40 percent Black residents and 60 percent white residents. To achieve this type of integration in St. Louis, the author proposed that the neighborhood should ensure "equal opportunity" for Black and white homebuyers in any area.[35] Reversing the typical civil rights logic of integration, which argued for the need to open up new housing markets to Black residents, the author instead asserted that integration requires ensuring that white households are able to buy and finance houses in transitioning neighborhoods. This would help to create true integration by keeping and replacing white residents in the neighborhood as Black residents moved in. The SDCC adopted this approach to encouraging white homeownership as a central tenet of their group.

To encourage white homeowners to stay, neighborhood organizers first had to prevent the panic that caused white flight. Members of the SDCC and their member organizations, Washington Heights Neighbors and Rosedale Skinker Improvement Association, promoted positive images of the neighborhood to try to reassure and retain existing residents. Even those who did not flee expressed concern about lower home values and the continuing desirability of the neighborhood for white residents. In the first year of transition, the Washington Heights Neighbors newsletter tried to calm fears, noting that, despite the rise of integration, the neighborhood's "assets" would "continue to attract those people who aspire to our high standards."[36] A 1967 letter from the president of Washington Heights Neighbors tried to shore up confidence, saying that, despite the changes in recent years, the organization was "not about to give up the fight against the problems of urban blight and decay."[37] Using programs to maintain the area's aesthetic character, the Washington Heights Neighbors tried to promote an image of stability and safety in the neighborhood.

While the SDCC boosted the morale of homeowners, those same homeowners remained the targets of blockbusting, a technique by which realtors tried to encourage or capitalize on white fears for their own profit. In blockbusting, a real-estate agent uses the sale of a home on a block to a Black buyer to convince other white owners that the area is poised on the precipice of rapid racial change and that they should sell immediately to stave off financial losses. The Skinker DeBaliviere neighborhood experienced the usual unsavory real-estate practices and scare tactics, including phone calls warning residents that their homes could drop in value.[38] Out of fear that too many real-estate signs might encourage panic and cause lower home prices, the SDCC also promoted policies such as banning the display of for-sale signs. Though many other cities across the nation employed this technique, it was not particularly effective.[39]

In many cities, whites who moved reported that it was not to escape integration so much as to avoid losing home equity. To counter these fears, the Washington Heights Neighbors tried to create a mentality of collective strength and joint responsibility. The speed of racial transition and the exploitative real-estate practices of blockbusting depended upon white homeowners panicking and selling. While all neighborhoods experience a certain percentage of turnover annually, which would allow for slow racial transition as people happen to move out, re-segregation often occurs when an abnormal number of people sell their homes all at once. Washington Heights tried to overcome this by discouraging residents from moving. For example, an editorial by the president tried to persuade homeowners not to sell, saying, "A home presently owned and occupied cannot be sold to anyone." This argument tried to stifle the fears that could lead to flight, and the theory that racial transition, once begun, unfolds inevitably.

However, the editorial also emphasized the shared responsibility of residents, saying "if you stay it will be a better neighborhood."[40] Again trying to squelch white flight, the president argued that the Washington Heights Neighbors members should not "run away from problems" and that they needed to continue to "work out their problems together in a genuine spirit of common purpose."[41] The SDCC took an even more aggressive stance, drafting a letter and phone-call script which tried to guilt residents into participating in improvement programs to stop the "creeping cancer" of decline. They asked, "Do you care at all what happens to your property values?" or are you the kind of person who is "completely unwilling to look after his own vested interests?"[42] These types of outreach approaches aimed to stem what one SDCC consultant called the "psychological withdrawal" in which residents "extricate their emotional investments" in the place, a condition which they feared would lead to exodus.[43]

By holding homeowners accountable as participants in, rather than victims of, the process of neighborhood change, the Washington Heights Neighbors and SDCC hoped to inspire homeowners to remain invested in the neighborhood and to act unselfishly when making choices about selling their home. These techniques often appeared in neighborhoods that tried to prevent integration, but they were rarely successful due to the high natural turnover rate in the United States. An average of 5 percent of households in the nation move each year, even in racially and economically stable neighborhoods.[44] For that reason the SDCC augmented their work seeking to prevent flight with strategies aimed at attracting new buyers.

Attracting New White Middle-Class Homebuyers

Nationally, areas adopting "managed integration" had greater success attracting new "replacement whites" than in preventing white flight.[45] The SDCC tried to encourage new white residents by developing a real-estate market that would attract new homebuyers. The SDCC knew some homeowners would sell, and that white middle-class people would not move to the area if real-estate agents and banks prevented them from purchasing and financing homes there. Several homebuyers reported difficulty convincing realtors to show them homes in Skinker DeBaliviere or getting mortgage loans for homes there. Because few realtors were willing to work in the neighborhood, the SDCC set up a Residential Service in 1970 to provide self-help real-estate services. [46] Two residents passed their real-estate licensing exams and started showing properties on a "nonprofit and non-discriminatory basis." In their first two years they assisted in eighteen sales. [47]

To promote sales of homes to new white homebuyers, the SDCC engaged in advertising campaigns. The Residential Service not only tried to provide traditional real-estate services but it also worked to market the neighborhood by projecting a "clear definition of the character" of the neighborhood. [48] An SDCC flier followed similar logic, promoting the neighborhood for its city-living, affordability as a "good buy," and its cultural diversity as an "integrated urban community." [49] Unlike nearly any other neighborhood in the city, Skinker DeBaliviere celebrated its racial diversity as an amenity.

The SDCC touted its success at encouraging homeownership, especially among white households. The May 1967 newsletter described "the bright side of the housing picture," celebrating the sale of two homes to "white families." This fact is used to counter the growing perception and fear of racial change, with the article insisting, "This area is stable!" [50] Jim L'Ecuyer echoed similar sentiments a month later when he reported that twenty white families had moved into the neighborhood during the previous year, calling it a "real inspiration if we are to stabilize the neighborhood." [51]

This attitude continued for years, and white homeownership became a measure of neighborhood success. In 1972, *The Paper* published an article called "White Influx," which touted the Residential Service as a key factor in the success of recruiting new white residents. [52] These types of programs to promote and celebrate white homeownership were common in other integrating areas of cities like Chicago. [53] Using the number of white homeowners as a metric for successful integration shows the ambiguities of managed integration programs; in order to encourage diversity, these programs focus on meeting the needs of white middle-class homebuyers rather than Black renters or Black homebuyers.

Overall, this multifaceted approach, including confidence building, marketing, and real-estate interventions, helped to slow but not stop white flight and natural turnover in Skinker DeBaliviere. The area experienced another 37 percent decrease in white residents between 1970 and 1980. However, Blacks also left the area in equal proportion during this time, and the area lost 36 percent of its overall population. Besides depopulation, census data also showed other signs of decline in the area, including high vacancy rates and a loss in overall housing units likely due to demolition.

Nonetheless, some areas of the neighborhood achieved a level of stability. The western area, Rosedale Skinker, which had higher homeownership levels at the beginning of integration, increased its homeownership rates in the 1970s. This area also resisted re-segregation, retaining a higher percentage of white residents.[54] Overall Skinker DeBalievere could rightfully claim to be an integrated neighborhood, but that diversity did not ensure either equity of power and resources or a unified culture.

Cultural and Philosophical Divides

A schism developed among residents of Skinker DeBaliviere about how to invest in revitalization of the neighborhood. This schism occurred geographically between Rosedale Skinker and Washington Heights; but it also appeared along class lines between middle-class homeowners and lower-income renters, and along racial lines between Black and white residents.

In part, this schism developed because the white home-owning minority in Skinker DeBaliviere remained actively involved in local leadership, with the power to shape the neighborhood's character, to influence the development agenda, and to set the tone of local race relations. The SDCC struggled to bridge key cultural and socioeconomic differences between the residents. While early Black residents, especially Black homeowners, assimilated into the white community, as the Black population grew, tensions and divisions between the different demographic groups grew in tandem.

As in many integrating neighborhoods, some of the first Black residents in Skinker DeBaliviere bought homes and belonged to the middle class. By 1970, the US Census showed that there were hundreds of Black homeowners in the area. These Black homeowners shared many social and economic characteristics with the existing white homeowners. They participated in neighborhood associations at similar rates to whites and experienced acceptance by the white homeowners. In Skinker DeBaliviere, this acceptance led the SDCC to welcome Black members and elect Black leaders, including two SDCC presidents: Virgil "Jack" Wright, who served from 1970 to 1980, and professor Jim McLeod, who served from 1987 to 1988.[55] Librarian

Charles M. Brown, a Black community leader, called the neighborhood "one of the most peacefully and productively integrated areas in America's most racist city."[56]

However, as the Black population grew, so too did the number of poor Black renters. Nearly double the percentage of Black families were below the poverty line compared to white families. These class differences triggered conflicts over perceived cultural differences. Many SDCC members stereotyped and criticized the lower-income residents of the neighborhood. A master's student in Urban Design at Washington University, Durwin Gerald Ursery, conducted interviews with residents and recorded in his thesis the racial tensions among community members. He noted that residents expressed concerns about the people of "different ethnic backgrounds having different modes of behavior."[57] In particular, local interviewees critiqued the mostly Black residents of the Triangle, with one saying they were "enmeshed in a life-cycle that is dysfunctional to the welfare of the whole community."[58] These views appeared not only in statements by the rank-and-file membership but also in those by leaders. The director of a local survey conducted by the SDCC noted, "The black has not learned the white middle-class lifestyle. One has to understand that to the black person . . . barbequing at 2 am, drinking beer and having a few laughs is not unusual. Their idea of cleanliness and social relationships is somewhat different from whites."[59] These quotes by residents, including SDCC leadership, may demonstrate the more extreme views of a few outliers, but they also show the way some residents were stereotyping and judging the values and choices of Black residents, implying that they were less appropriate than the values and behaviors of white residents. These stereotypes also emphasized class differences, valorizing middle-class lifestyles over those of lower-income residents.

This class difference also led to differences in the values, goals, and methods of community development for the neighborhood. The geographic and demographic groups in the area adopted two distinct approaches to improving the area. Residents in the single-family blocks west of the tracks, in the Rosedale Skinker area, expressed more interest in redevelopment projects to fight physical decay by improving the appearance of the neighborhood. They focused on "reversing the increase in crime, stopping further blight of buildings, holding the line on the white move out rates," in response to maintaining property values.[60] This approach did not always align directly with race; some local Black leaders supported the

SDCC's real-estate-based approach. But most Black residents, especially those in the apartment blocks in the "economically deprived" Triangle area of Washington Heights, preferred improvements to the public schools, youth programs, and job training.[61] Black residents were less concerned with the "poor living conditions" of buildings than with "the social state of the people."[62] They thought the most useful interventions would be "aid and assistance" to those most in need.[63] Their concerns revolved around providing services for their children, including "education, trade skills, day care," and safe places to play.[64] One social worker, Dorothy Garrett, tried to represent this point of view, encouraging the SDCC to give more attention to the needs of the under-served Triangle area. She especially advocated for a greater demographic distribution of funding for housing, noting that most programs focused on the wealthier Rosedale Skinker area.[65] This split mentality between investing in physical development of buildings versus investing in human development through services became a major fault line in the Skinker DeBaliviere neighborhood. While these were not necessarily completely opposing or mutually exclusive goals, they served to divide the ideological and pragmatic focus of the group.

These two different viewpoints and the lack of communication and understanding between the two communities in Skinker DeBaliviere came to a head as the neighborhood began larger-scale redevelopment projects in the late 1970s and 1980s. The city redevelopment agency, working with local aldermen and the SDCC, started to consider projects that would redevelop "problem areas" in Washington Heights, including renovation of several buildings of apartments at Nina Place. In 1979, Washington Heights Neighbors initially supported the Nina Place project. The project aimed to ensure diverse representation, with 40 percent of the Redevelopment Corporation Board composed of Black residents.[66] But by 1984, Washington Heights leadership opposed the project due to the dislocation of forty families by eminent domain. One resident, Ethel Sawyer Adolphe, charged that the decision to blight the entire block was motivated by "racism and greed." The debates over the Nina Place project strained racial relations in the neighborhood. Those who opposed the project, especially Black community leaders, reported being "criticized for speaking out."[67] The debates over the Nina Place project, along with other issues about the mission and power structure of the SDCC, led Washington Heights Neighbors to vote to leave the SDCC, saying the organization no longer pursued projects helpful to their members. While some Washington Heights residents decided to participate in SDCC as individuals and were welcomed by the SDCC, this secession demonstrated the level of division within the community.

Over time, the economic, cultural, and value divide between class and racial groups led to an increasingly fragmented neighborhood. Despite the attempt to use the SDCC to create a "general forum of all the residents," the organization did not represent a single unified community, but two communities with increasingly divergent interests.[68] Their opposing approaches to neighborhood improvement led to a fight for resources and power. White middle-class community organizers more effectively leveraged their political power to accumulate economic resources to achieve their vision for the neighborhood. While social workers and activists advocating for the needs of low-income residents protested the SDCC's urban plans, they failed to shift resources to services or to stop redevelopment projects that dislocated Black renters. The initial liberal goal of the SDCC to promote integration had inspired innovative and progressive strategies to overcome segregation and discrimination in housing policy, yet by the 1980s the focus on redevelopment had undermined some of the more socially inclusive objectives of their community organizing. Cooperation with official planning empowered neighborhood organizers to wield resources to enact change, but not always in a way that represented the diversity of interests of the neighborhood.

Organizing to Prevent Slum Clearance

In Soulard, located just south of downtown St. Louis, organizers faced similar demographic divides, in this case between economic classes rather than racial groups. Like in Skinker DeBaliviere, different class identities aligned with different approaches to development. While the community groups in Soulard aimed to reverse the unjust impacts of redlining and redevelopment, their focus on self-help approaches tended to prioritize traditional middle-class values for homeownership, sometimes at the expense of the needs of low-income renters. The anti-government approach at times reified the logic of the capitalist real-estate market, prioritizing homeownership over federally subsidized affordable housing. In this way, neighborhood organizing in Soulard shifted over time from progressive and combative in the early 1970s to more institutionalized in the 1980s.

As one of the oldest neighborhoods in St. Louis, Soulard faced extensive decline and disrepair by the 1960s and 1970s. For many decades, it had been one of the poorest white neighborhoods in St. Louis, with derelict homes, vacant lots, and crime. With an average building construction year of 1889, the area faced many calls for improvements by the early twentieth century.[69] The 1907 *A City Plan for St. Louis* designated the area a "slum" and proposed it as the location for a new civic center. But even after improvements to the local park, that area continued to attract low-income residents into dense, overcrowded housing.[70]

The area faced a series of problems through the rest of the twentieth century. In the 1920s the neighborhood, once a center of the brewing industry, faced economic hardship during Prohibition, which closed or transformed many local businesses, eliminating a major source of employment. In the 1930s, the area faced redlining, which curtailed mortgage opportunities and property investment. Many homes were left vacant or were partitioned and rented, with little maintenance by the landlords. After World War II, planners expressed concern about the dilapidated housing. In 1960, only 19 percent of the neighborhood's buildings, then on average seventy years old, were deemed structurally sound.[71] The buildings required repairs that the owners and tenants could not afford.

Soulard also faced major physical changes as the area was cut off from nearby neighborhoods by redevelopment (Fig. 9.3). First the area was isolated by the demolition of Bohemian Hill to build the Third Street Expressway. Further clearance for the Darst-Webbe housing project dislocated residents to the northwest of the neighborhood, further undermining social connections within the local Czech community.[72] Some Black residents were also dislocated by the clearance of the adjacent Kosciusko neighborhood and industrial area. Bounded by these projects around its edges, the center of the neighborhood also faced demolition. Census data show that nearly 60 percent of its buildings, a total of 3,607 structures, were torn down between 1940 and 1970.[73] Another 25 percent of homes remained vacant, accounting for 673 of the remaining 2,708 structures.[74] Only a small fraction of the structures in Soulard remained by 1970.

Once a cultural enclave for multi-ethnic European immigrants, the neighborhood in the postwar period also experienced demographic shifts that led to a change in social character. In the nineteenth century, Soulard had been the most dense and diverse neighborhood in the city, housing

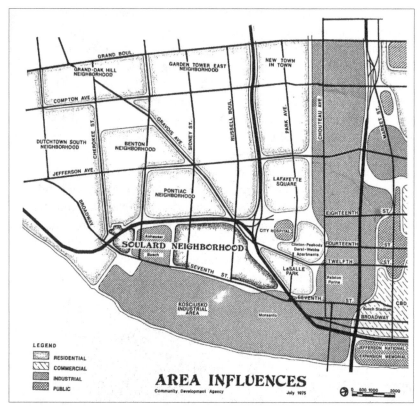

Figure 9.3 This map of Soulard, with the west at the top, shows how the neighborhood is isolated from other residential areas by the highway and industrial areas, which cut through historic communities. *From* Soulard Restoration Plan, *by the Community Development Commission, 1975*

immigrants from over a dozen countries, especially from Eastern and Southern Europe. But between 1960 and 1970, more than 43 percent of the population left as upwardly mobile second- and third-generation families moved to the suburbs in search of new and affordable housing.[75] While the neighborhood did not undergo racial changes like those taking place in North St. Louis, the change in religious affiliation and social networks left churches underutilized and homes unwanted.

Many of the new people to move into the neighborhood between 1950 and 1960 were white rural migrants fleeing a six-year drought in the Ozark farmlands and looking for work in the city.[76] The cheap apartments in Soulard served as a first foothold for new arrivals to St. Louis. Like the previous residents, many were poor, with one-third of Soulard residents living below the poverty line.[77] However, unlike the immigrants before them, they did not make long-term ties or set up community organizations or churches in the neighborhood; they saw the neighborhood as a means to an end, rather than an enduring investment.[78] This gave the neighborhood a reputation as a "second-class place" and the city's "most transient area."[79] This lack of community involvement left city officials mostly unchallenged as they went about the business of urban renewal. The media—like later restorationists—often portrayed these new arrivals negatively for their "general apathy" to neighborhood issues.[80]

In the late 1960s, the back-to-the-city movement and the historic preservation movement brought more new residents to the Near South Side area, this time from the middle class. While rehabbers had first showed up in the nearby Lafayette Square, the more affordable and quirky homes of Soulard also began to draw attention, offering a greater variety of housing types and styles, especially of modest working-class character (Fig. 9.4). This brought a consistent trickle of new middle-class homebuyers to the neighborhood. Mostly young and idealistic, sometimes with skills in the building trades or

Figure 9.4 The 3302–3324 block of South Ninth Street, representative of Soulard, showcased a variety of house types, including a grand three-story mansion with a mansard roof and a more modest two-story home. It also contained a vacant lot, a typical gap in the streetscape. Soulard restorationists aimed to preserve these blocks from further demolitions. *Library of Congress Prints and Photographs Division*

social work, these new residents didn't just want to fix up their own homes; they wanted to improve the neighborhood.

Some of these new residents energized the Soulard Neighborhood Improvement Association (SNIA) in 1969 to try to bring a sense of stability to the area.[81] SNIA members included mostly educated middle-class former suburbanites, but often those active in countercultural movements. The group included people of a variety of ages and professions, including "Vietnam Veterans, couples with young children, federal state employees, administrators of federal or state funded poverty programs, and zealous social reformers," as the *St. Louis Post-Dispatch* noted in 1972. The members brought "missionary zeal" to their work, with romantic and nostalgic attitudes towards architecture and urbanism.[82] Their leader, Robert "Bob" Brandhorst, possessed a Harvard-educated intellectualism, sarcastic humor, and bushy beard that signified both the privilege and the rebellious attitude of the young SNIA organizers.[83] SNIA members brought their knowledge and energy to the task of revitalizing this neighborhood in decline.

Stopping the Bulldozer

SNIA began their mission to preserve the historic working-class neighborhood by trying to stop bulldozers and expressing outspoken resistance to government slum-clearance programs. The group opposed redevelopment head-on by fighting demolitions, boarding up vacant homes to save them from the elements, and trying to restore existing homes. By 1972, SNIA leaders had established a headquarters, soon dubbed the Soulard Neighborhood Center, in an unheated and sparsely furnished basement at 716 Geyer Avenue, which soon attracted a daily stream of phone calls and walk-in visits from residents and prospective rehabbers.[84] Labeled by the newspapers as "hippies" with a lack of "diplomatic skills," the young long-haired activists tried to reverse decades of planning theories about neighborhood decline by promoting smaller self-help programs rather than large federal projects.[85]

This task often brought them into conflict with city officials and other landowners, sometimes in dramatic standoffs. Joyce Sonn, a SNIA leader, claimed that to stop demolition, "some of us had to sit on bulldozers."[86] Speaking to a *St. Louis Post-Dispatch* reporter in 1971, Brandhorst recounted another conflict. He was working with a group of his neighbors to board up a vacant building to protect it from arson and vandalism when a bulldozer began to knock down the house next door. They were surprised because he believed the mayor had given them an oral promise that the city would stop demolition in the area until the city and the neighbors could develop a plan for how to manage rundown buildings, but they didn't have any proof in writing. They begged the bulldozer operator to hold off on removing the house until they could straighten things out with the city; the wrecker stopped for the day but came back a few days later and completed demolition.[87]

This is just one of many demolitions that Brandhorst and SNIA tried to fight. In this case, the demolition had been ordered by Mel Bottoms, the head of the Special Demolition Project, who was administering a grant for demolition that included 140 buildings in Soulard, among others around the city. In his office hung a map of the city with black pins marking those homes scheduled for demolition, replaced by yellow pins after they were torn down. An editorial in the *St. Louis Post-Dispatch* described the dispute between Bottoms and Brandhorst. It depicted Brandhorst as a "hippie" who hoped to save every building he could as part of efforts to preserve the "old time flavor" of the neighborhood.

The editorial author seemed to vilify Bottoms, comparing him to a "bomb wing commander" conducting "saturation bombing" of the "target." This depiction drew on longstanding metaphors comparing slum clearance to aerial warfare dating back to at least World War II. Though not explicit, the use of the metaphor here likely drew comparisons to the US bombing approaches in Vietnam and the antiwar activism which aimed to stop that destruction. The article also emphasized the bureaucratic momentum for officials who had "federal money burning a hole in the city's pocket," and thus chose to tear down buildings because "it would be foolish not to spend it."[88] The article's contrast between Brandhorst's on-the-ground knowledge and personal investment versus Bottoms's technocratic and pragmatic detachment emphasizes the way neighborhood activists pitted themselves against municipal institutions and top-down decision making.

This conflict about how best to rehabilitate neighborhoods—whether through preservation or demolition—was symptomatic of a larger shift in neighborhood planning in the 1970s. While many planning agencies still focused on top-down clearance and large-scale redevelopment for declining neighborhoods, the historic preservation movement had inspired many bottom-up neighborhood organizing efforts to protect and restore dilapidated homes. Activists like Brandhorst and Sonn would continue to fight demolition projects for the next decade. But their confrontational style was critiqued by some more established preservation professionals at the time who hoped to work with officials rather than merely obstructing their work.[89] This image of a "hippie" protestor stopping the bulldozer and demonstrating against an overly bureaucratic government agency is part of a romanticized image of community organizing from the 1960s and 1970s. But the neighborhood groups in Soulard experimented with a more diverse set of approaches, beyond protests, for revitalizing their neighborhood.

Building Community Resources

Besides its work in stopping demolitions, SNIA also worked to improve the quality of life for the existing mostly low-income residents. With its partner nonprofit organization, Youth Education and Health in Soulard (YEHS), SNIA provided philanthropic services to children and the elderly through twenty different social programs.[90] They often held fundraisers for projects such as a breakfast program for poor school kids, an outreach program for the elderly, and craft and learning programs.[91] YEHS worked to create an alternative high-school equivalency program that taught construction trade skills to provide strong job training.[92] SNIA even set up cottage-industry and craft enterprises to help residents supplement their incomes.[93] While many of these activities fit into traditional philanthropic work, some showed a communitarian philosophy to look for solutions outside of capitalism or state welfare programs.

Beyond helping those already living in the neighborhood, the organizers also wanted to attract new residents. SNIA tried to recruit new residents to the area by hosting house tours, ethnic festivals, and street fairs to promote the unique character of the neighborhood.[94] This type of activity also became one of the main tools of the Soulard Restoration Group (SRG), formed in 1974 by those focusing on historic preservation. Inspired by the nearby Lafayette Square Restoration Group, the SRG organized homeowners to share knowledge, recruit new homebuyers, and coordinate political activities. The SRG ran several house tours each year, in spring, fall, and winter, which drew visitors from across the region. Like leaders in Skinker DeBaliviere, they hoped to attract middle-class homebuyers to move back to the city and help restore the historic homes of the neighborhood.

SRG also began to take the lead on historic preservation efforts. Once homebuyers had purchased one of the neighborhood's Victorian structures, they could turn to the SRG for help with ideas on how to renovate and for guidelines on maintaining its historic character (Fig. 9.5). The SRG newsletter shared success stories as well as challenges, providing humor, support, and guidance for new homeowners.[95] SRG also took a strong role in formalizing the historic preservation of the neighborhood. SNIA had successfully applied as a National Historic District in 1972. In 1975, SNIA and the SRG worked together to list the district locally with the City of St. Louis. They collaborated on a plan for preservation, setting up design codes and proposals for neighborhood amenities and public spaces. A student at

Figure 9.5 Restorationists work in August 1977 to rebuild the interior of a historic home in Soulard, using their sweat equity to turn abandoned properties into livable homes again. *Photo by Bob Moore for the* St. Louis Globe-Democrat, *from the collections of the St. Louis Mercantile Library at the University of Missouri–St. Louis*

Washington University led a collaborative process to balance different goals in the district plan.

But the SRG knew that a plan and a hundred homeowners wouldn't be enough to save the neighborhood. They needed to be constantly vigilant to protect structures from demolition. The SRG fought government agencies and local nonprofits like the Boys Club and churches, trying to stop the destruction of any viable historic structure.[96] With so many buildings already demolished, they saw every remaining building as an asset that needed to be protected. They spent much of their time in hearings and lawsuits. While they were rarely successful in stopping demolitions, they mourned every loss.

The SRG also stayed informed and active in pursuing policy approaches to bring funding sources to the neighborhood, especially to promote opportunities for mortgages. The SRG worked with local banks, local government, and federal programs to promote home lending in the area. The SRG was well informed on national programs to make loans available to buy or restore historic homes, such as the Federal National Mortgage Association pilot lending program and other programs conducted by the National Trust and the FHA.[97] The SRG also worked with local banks and city officials on the St. Louis Mortgage Plan, which set aside $3 million from local banks for mortgages in "those areas of the city with the greatest need" with the assistance of Community Development Association (CDA) block grants to provide a partial loan guarantee.[98] Although this program led to thirty loans, the Aldermanic Housing and Urban Development Committee cut the CDA funds, and many of the loans were not in the target areas.[99]

Over time, both SNIA and SRG had gained more sophisticated knowledge of bureaucratic systems. The less romantic work of hearings and policy advocacy doesn't provide the dramatic image of the protest that is so emblematic of the activist movements of the 1960s and 1970s, but it was this day-to-day work that made the biggest changes in stopping clearance and promoting reinvestment.

Conflicts over Preservation versus Infill Development

By the late 1970s, the presence of two community organizations in the neighborhood had started to create conflict, as each approached neighborhood improvement though a different philosophy. As the SRG took leadership in resident recruitment and historic preservation efforts, SNIA and YEHS focused increasingly on social services including affordable housing. In some ways this division of labor created a symbiotic relationship to meet the neighborhood's diverse needs. However, it also led to fights over the direction that Soulard should take.

The SRG had a similar demographic profile to SNIA, being mostly middle-class educated newcomers. But the SRG and later homebuyers in the 1980s tended to be more professional than those who arrived in the 1960s. Using the stereotypes of the time, while SNIA might have been called hippies, the SRG fit in the category of young urban professionals, or "yuppies." SRG included lawyers, engineers, teachers, and small business owners. The SRG rallied around homeownership, and often used their position as taxpayers as leverage to demand attention from politicians and city agency staff.

The tensions between these two groups appeared nearly as soon as the SRG had formed in 1974. The first activity of writing the Historic District Plan led to conflicts between SNIA and SRG on which group would take the lead in creating it, as well as on the content of the code. Members of the two groups refused to work together and attend the same meetings. SNIA members wanted to keep codes loose to allow for affordability, while SRG members wanted strict codes to protect the homes and maintain high aesthetic standards. While they found a relatively good compromise at the time, the issue reignited fifteen years later in the early 1990s, when the SRG sought to protect the architecture and SNIA advocated on behalf of low-income residents.[100]

Other debates developed through the late 1970s and 1980s about affordable housing. SNIA hoped to use federal grants and programs to build subsidized infill housing including Section 8 rentals on vacant lots to provide low-income residences and to reestablish the density and street continuity of the prewar neighborhoods. SRG opposed the developments, concerned they would be aesthetically incompatible, redirect resources that should be invested in restoration to new construction, and attract new low-income residents to the area. The SRG argued that Soulard already had a higher percentage of low-income residents than other areas of the city, and that the city had promised to disperse affordable housing, rather than concentrating it in the inner city.[101] This debate avoided outright discussion of race, but also hinted at racialized fears of the nearby Darst-Webbe public housing project and attracting more welfare families to the area.

These debates opened a larger concern about whether Soulard was experiencing gentrification. Gentrification is the replacement of lower-income groups, often renters, with higher-income groups, often owners. Gentrification can often displace low-income residents, making it hard for low-income residents to find homes nearby. SNIA argued that low-income renters, such as older "ethnic" residents of Eastern and Southern European background, were being displaced by homebuyers.[102] However, SRG said many of the homes were empty and abandoned and that there were plenty of cheap homes for low-income residents. SRG, while first acknowledging that gentrification or displacement might be occurring, began to staunchly defend their activities by denying that their homebuying was having any negative effect or that they should change their approach.[103]

Throughout all the debates it is clear that the neighborhood had several distinct interest groups: low-income renters, who were mostly older prewar residents or newer rural migrants, and newer middle-class homeowners, themselves divided by philosophy. SNIA sometimes vilified the SRG, claiming they wanted to exclude low-income groups. While the SRG denied these claims, it did sometimes show unconscious bias towards these groups, denying the struggles of the older poor and critiquing the purported apathy of the newer poor. On the other hand, SNIA portrayed itself as the champions of the poor, but was sometime critiqued as paternalistic. Most of the SNIA members were middle-class, and while they spoke on behalf of the poor and tried to engage the poor, they were "not representative" of low-income residents.[104] Some SRG members accused SNIA and Brandhorst of having political motives and personal stakes in the subsidized housing projects, and questioned Brandhorst's philanthropic intentions. While low-income residents sometimes showed up at city meetings or were interviewed in the newspaper, the neighborhood leadership was dominated by middle-class residents.

Both the SRG and SNIA represented a certain white middle-class demographic, typical of neighborhood organizers across the city in the 1970s. City planners often conflated these groups, especially by equating the SRG with the neighborhood as a whole and by assuming its members represented the interests of all residents. However, like in Skinker DeBaliviere, these groups—while successful at working with city agencies to achieve change—were not democratically elected leaders; they accounted for only a small minority of the population and did not exemplify the typical resident of the neighborhood.

Conclusion

Neighborhood organizing in St. Louis in the 1960s and 1970s responded to the many changes taking place in the city. Some neighborhood organizing aimed to preserve the status quo and freeze change, to keep the social and aesthetic character of the neighborhood the same, preventing decline, disinvestment, or racial transition. But other neighborhood organizing, like in Skinker DeBaliviere and Soulard, took a more activist approach, fighting unfair and unjust government policies or real-estate practices. Both neighborhoods successfully fought redlining and white flight, attracting middle-class residents to the city. In the end, both neighborhoods maintained economically diverse populations with affordable rental opportunities. But in both cases the racial and class identity of the organizers, mostly middle-class whites, led to organizing approaches that prioritized their values and perspectives, while perhaps unintentionally or unconsciously disempowering other classes or racial groups. While middle-class white organizers tried to speak and act for the good of other groups, they did not successfully create organizations that allowed for equal participation and an equal voice for lower-income residents.

Nonetheless, neighborhood organizing in St. Louis still constitutes an important part of activism in St. Louis and nationally. By challenging the unjust policies of government agencies and businesses, neighborhood organizers have helped to end some of the most harmful forms of housing discrimination, such as redlining and slum clearance. By challenging experts in urban planning, neighborhood organizers improved the transparency and inclusiveness of government processes, pressuring agencies to create new avenues of participation for residents to shape local decisions about the built environment. Neighborhood organizing in St. Louis, as elsewhere in the country, was part of a larger shift in the 1960s and 1970s to engage citizens more actively in local governance and self-help solutions to social problems.

10. "We Were on a Mission"

Feminist Activism in St. Louis in the 1960s and 1970s

Gretchen Arnold and Ilene Ordower

Introduction

MOST EARLY HISTORICAL ACCOUNTS OF second-wave feminism in the 1960s and 1970s focused on the actions of self-identified feminists in large urban areas on the East and West Coasts.[1] Their dominant narrative was that these feminists propelled a national, top-down strategy of women's activism, creating organizations such as the National Organization for Women (NOW) along with a handful of smaller, more radical organizations such as "Redstockings" in New York City that had nationwide influence. As a result, many people have assumed that places in the Midwest like St. Louis were feminist backwaters during that time. What we argue in this chapter is that, in fact, there was significant women's activism in the St. Louis metropolitan area that at times was not only in the vanguard of the feminist movement but also a leader in innovation. For example, St. Louis activists created a model for stand-alone reproductive healthcare services that was widely adopted around the country once abortion became legal nationwide in 1973; local women labor activists were at the forefront of pressing for women's interests and leadership in organized labor; and St. Louis gave birth to one of the two earliest grassroots men's groups to address domestic violence.

To date, no one has systematically attempted to explain how this level of activism developed in St. Louis. We hope this chapter will start to fill this gap. Feminist historians in recent years have come to appreciate that feminist activism takes different forms in different places because it is embedded in people's everyday lives—activists' goals, strategies, and identities are uniquely affected by local conditions.[2] So, it should come as no surprise that activism looked somewhat different in a large midwestern city like St.

Louis. This is not to say, however, that the better-known coastal feminist groups did not influence the goals and strategies of activists in St. Louis—they did. In addition to the general dissemination of ideas that occurred through the modern mass media, educational institutions also played a role. The St. Louis metropolitan area is home to a relatively large number of universities and colleges that bring in a steady stream of new ideas, which then spread from the students and faculty to the local population. In the 1960s, these ideas included those from coastal feminists that challenged traditional patriarchal arrangements.

However, there were important differences between feminist activism in St. Louis and what was happening nationally. Some of these differences can be traced to the cultural and political context of St. Louis. The Midwest is a more culturally conservative part of the country with tangible southern influences. In Missouri, there is a clear political divide between the more progressive and cosmopolitan urban populations of St. Louis City and St. Louis County, on the one hand, and the rural areas of the state, on the other; the latter exert disproportionate political influence in the state legislature and tend to have more in common culturally with the southern Bible Belt. In addition, approximately 30 percent of the population in the city of St. Louis (excluding surrounding counties) in 1980 was Roman Catholic, with parochial schools and parish activities playing a central role in many families' lives and giving the Catholic Church broad influence.[3] And during the 1960s and 1970s, the antifeminist activist Phyllis Schlafly, whose home base was in the St. Louis metro area, cast a large shadow over feminists' attempts to gain support among the population and to get legislation passed at the state level.

This raises the question, then, of how feminist ideas and actions developed in spite of, or in response to, the obstacles presented by this relatively conservative midwestern political and cultural context. It also presents an opportunity to explore how the feminist movement developed at the grassroots in seemingly unlikely places and how it has exerted such a widespread and lasting impact on US society for the last half century.

Our Approach

In this chapter we tell the largely untold story of feminist activism in St. Louis during the 1960s and 1970s. We conducted original interviews with sixteen different people who were activists for women's issues at that time and obtained three more activists' interviews in local archives. We gathered information from archival collections at the Missouri Historical Society and the State Historical Society of Missouri to verify, add detail, and fill in gaps in the interview transcripts. And we combed books and other academic works for relevant material written specifically about social and political activism in St. Louis.

In any analysis of a social movement, one must draw boundaries around what counts as part of the movement and what does not. Drawing boundaries is especially contentious when analyzing American feminism because it has never coalesced around a single, unified definition. Most analysts today agree that the feminist movement in the US (and across the globe) has been characterized by "multiple, intersecting streams of women's activism" driven by women in diverse political communities.[4] As a result, there has been a lively debate about whether to include as part of the movement those women who actively pursued goals articulated by feminists but who did not themselves claim the feminist label. We have chosen to take the more expansive approach used by, for example, Finn Enke in *Finding the Movement*. Enke makes a convincing case that feminism was developed and spread both by those who explicitly identified as feminist and by those who did not, including women who organized around progressive issues commonly understood as rooted in race, class, and sexuality. A similar argument is made by Annelise Orleck in *Rethinking American Women's Activism*. Orleck reconceptualizes the history of feminism as one comprising diverse and often conflicting streams of activism, much of which has been carried out under the banner of other social movements, such as labor and civil rights, that have previously been treated by historians as separate movements.

Following in these researchers' footsteps, we sought out not only self-identified feminist activists, but also feminist activism located in other social movements. We looked for collective actions intended to challenge authority and gender hierarchies in a variety of contexts and using a range of practices. Using this information, we describe the configuration of activist groups that were part of the movement landscape in the St. Louis metropolitan area working on women's issues in the 1960s and 1970s. We detail the issues that drove that activism at the community level and how they came to the forefront. And we explain how it was that activists from different social locations came together around these different issues and goals, and why some of these grassroots campaigns were able to have notable successes.

The Broad Landscape of Feminist Activism in St. Louis

In some ways, feminist activism in St. Louis mirrored the conventional history of second-wave feminism first developed by Jo Freeman in 1975.[5] In Freeman's account, two main "branches" of the feminist movement had formed by the early 1970s. The first was a group of predominantly white, younger, well-educated feminist activists, many of whom were self-identified lesbians, who were active primarily around cultural and social issues. These feminists considered themselves "radical" in the original sense of the term: namely, as tackling the root of the problem—in this case, eliminating women's oppression by dismantling the cultural and social practices fundamental to patriarchy, especially those in the family and personal life. The second group was composed of (often, but not always) older, mostly white, middle-class professional women who devoted much of their energy to promoting more progressive laws and electoral politics. These women have often been labeled "liberal" because of their efforts to ensure women's equality with men in public life by advocating for women's individual rights within existing economic and political institutions. Recognizable versions of both groups had developed in St. Louis by the early 1970s.

Freeman's account, however, largely excludes the efforts of working-class women, poor women, and women of color to bring about both greater political and economic equality for women as well as changes in gender relationships in the home. For example, in *Gateway to Equality: Black Women and the Struggle for Economic Justice in St. Louis*, Keona K. Ervin brings to light the previously ignored but vibrant history of African American women's organizing around workplace issues. Ervin's work shows that by the 1960s, St. Louis was a rich site of activism by Black women who were challenging gendered hierarchies in the workplace even when they did not necessarily identify themselves as feminist.[6] They organized in racially segregated groups as well as with white women in integrated groups to push for changes in employment practices that directly affected women, including reforming labor unions and workplaces.[7] We actively sought information about women's labor activism to include in this chapter.

In addition, in a city long segregated along Black-white lines, there was an active NAACP that, in the late 1950s, had been energized by civil rights organizing in the South. Clarence Lang shows in *Grassroots at the Gateway* that the social and professional networks of Black women were its most critical base in St. Louis, although these women often downplayed their public activism "in deference to prevailing gendered ideals of female domesticity."[8] Like Ervin, Lang argues that much (although not all) of their activism around gender issues focused on workplace issues and took place within the labor movement. By the 1970s, however, there was a sizeable group of African American women in St. Louis who were also active in the local Black Nationalist movement and who, over time, took on many of the same issues around which white feminists were mobilizing. We also included this group of women in our research.

This broad description of four relatively distinct groups, however, is only part of the story of feminist activism in St. Louis, and it in some ways obscures another equally important aspect: the fluidity with which many activists from these groups came together in ever-shifting formal and informal collaborations to pursue common interests. Historians of US feminism have tended to focus on the disagreements and conflicts among the various groups active around women's issues, giving accounts that often leave the impression that there was little interaction or overlap between them. Yet, as Stephanie Gilmore has argued in *Feminist Coalitions*, women's activists have often worked alongside social justice activists beyond those in their own organizations.[9] Gilmore demonstrates that, while feminist activism is undoubtedly influenced by nationwide movement campaigns, it nonetheless unfolds at the local level and coalesces around the interests and injustices that affect people's daily lives. This process brings together activists from different locations in the broader social movement community who not only have a stake in these issues but also recognize that their strength is magnified if they work with other groups. And, as this chapter will show, it was often the collaboration of these different groups in common struggles that led to the remarkable successes they enjoyed.

The Radical Feminists

The radical feminists in St. Louis in what Freeman dubbed the "younger branch" of the women's movement were, like those in East Coast cities, composed heavily, although not exclusively, of self-identified lesbians.[10] Similar to developments in other midwestern cities documented by Enke, many St. Louis lesbians in the 1960s had been finding one another by participating in softball teams and patronizing specific bars.[11] Starting in about 1970, however, a robust, active lesbian-feminist community developed, centered on a loose group of perhaps ten (not all simultaneous) communal houses where many lived, first in the Central West End neighborhood and then in South St. Louis.

This network was predominantly composed of professional or pre-professional white women, although there were also a few men.[12] For example, in one house in the 4300 block of Westminster Place, there lived a law student, a PhD candidate in English, an Asian studies scholar, a doctor, a farmer, and a dancer. One member of this community, Kayla Vaughan, had moved to St. Louis from Louisiana in 1969 to attend Washington University, and she helped give a southern flavor to the social life of these houses. Residents hosted a series of house parties and fancy-dress women's balls that were open to all women because, as Vaughan told us tongue-in-cheek in 2020, "we knew that all women were really lesbians."[13] She described the origins of the balls this way:

> I'm from the South, so there's a tradition in the South of a lot of hospitality, and valuing entertaining. Ladies' tea parties. We had mock ladies' tea parties. But I would say that I was an influence on the balls. I think they were my brainchild, actually. We would dress up big time. People would go to Goodwill, they would get fake pearls, some people would wear tuxedoes. They were fabulous parties! Candles, and great music and wonderful food. They were just knockout parties, they were great. They weren't all the time, but maybe once or twice a year. But other than that, yes, there were parties [at the houses] constantly on into the mid-1970s. But the balls I'm referring to, these were women's balls with a theme. Like we would have the Victoria Woodhull and Tennessee Claflin Ball. Or the Emma Goldman Ball.[14]

This community took seriously the feminist mantra of women's self-help through mutual aid and gave birth to several all-women's businesses, including a piano-tuning business, a printing press, and a car-repair collective.[15] Similar to lesbian-feminist communities on the coasts, a portion of these women felt that lesbians should not have any interactions with men. And like the radical feminist groups in New York City, these St. Louis feminists also specialized in disruptive action intended to "dismantle the patriarchy." As Vaughan explained:

> Then we formed a group called the West End Feminists, and we mostly did guerrilla actions, like we made up stickers that said, "This exploits women," and stuffed them everywhere, because everything did. We did pregnancy testing. When the Food Co-op started in the [Delmar]

Figure 10.1 "Fancy-dress" ball-goers in 1976, at the feminist collective house at 4367 Westminster Place. *From Kayla Vaughan personal collection (photographer unknown)*

Loop, they had a refrigerator, so we advertised in *The Outlaw* for people who wanted pregnancy testing. So, we went to this chemist and got these things and learned how to do pregnancy testing because they weren't on the market. It was no big deal; he explained what we had to do. So, we had people drop their urine off in the Food Co-op refrigerator *[laughing]*, and we did free pregnancy testing. We collected money for abortions for people. And this was before it was legal [in Missouri]. We drove all over St. Louis delivering money for people's abortions. We went to abortion demonstrations and made a lot of drama, a lot of flags, a lot of signs. We did a lot of sort of guerrilla theater, and we did a lot of disrupting things. Mostly we were just crazy, and we had a lot of fun. But we were on a mission.[16]

These feminist activists also targeted institutions. For example, some formed the successful Committee to Promote Women in the Skilled Trades and used protests and threats of legal action to force a local trade college, Ranken Tech, to admit women in the mid-1970s. Some formed the equally successful Committee to End Sterilization Abuse in 1975 to force Washington University to stop training doctors to sterilize women outside

Figure 10.2 Graffiti affirming "lesbian love," painted outside of the Playboy Club on Lindell Boulevard circa 1973, captures the guerrilla spirit and underground style that characterized the city's feminist collectives. *From Kayla Vaughan personal collection (photographer unknown)*

the US.[17] Some of these activists helped establish St. Louis's first rape crisis center and then the city's first battered women's shelter, the Abused Women's Support Project, on Lafayette Avenue in South St. Louis.[18] And some later helped found the city's first legal abortion clinic, Reproductive Health Services.[19]

However, these feminists did not limit their activism to women's issues. According to our interviewees, they were often ongoing participants in a variety of social justice movements at the time, with overlapping memberships and collaboration among different groups and causes. For instance, many we spoke with talked about their involvement in the prolonged 1970s struggle to prevent the closure of Homer G. Phillips Hospital, a nationally renowned Black teaching hospital that was a source of great pride in the Black community. The effort by the local white political establishment to close "Homer G." was regarded by many African Americans as well as white activists to be an especially egregious symbol of whites' racism against Blacks; it sparked years of protests, some of them violent. Another example of cross-movement collaboration was when some feminists performed poetry and music with members of the Black Artists' Group (BAG). BAG was a multidisciplinary arts collective that, from 1968 to 1972, included dance, theater, visual arts, and creative writing and was known for its artists' convergence of free jazz and experimental theater.[20] The collaboration with BAG served as one conduit to get these feminists involved in civil rights actions, although it was not the only pathway.[21] Many feminists were also actively involved in anti–Vietnam War protests. Sondra Stein, one of the self-identified radical feminists who moved to St. Louis in 1968 and was active in several local social movements at that time, told us,

> All of these pieces—there was much more fluidity at that time. There was a lot of connection between all these different pieces going on; it wasn't one or another. There was the cultural piece, which brought people together, the political piece, and . . . the welfare rights, and the civil rights [pieces]. There was still antiwar stuff going on. And the women's movement piece. All of those pieces were developing and integrated, [with] much more overlap of people.[22]

This claim was echoed by another member of the lesbian-feminist community, Margaret Flowing Johnson, who told us, "The intersections of all the movements dancers were kind of connected."[23]

Figure 10.3 Dancers from the Black Artists' Group (BAG) rehearse. Occasional readings and performances with BAG members allowed some feminist activists from outside the collective an avenue for cross-organizational collaboration. *Courtesy of Portia Hunt*

This overlapping activism was driven not just by the urgency of local struggles but was also consistent with socialist-feminist thinking, one of the predominant strains of feminist thought at the time. Zuleyma Tang-Martinez, who went to college at Saint Louis University from 1963 to 1967 and later learned about feminism in graduate school at the University of California–Berkeley, described socialist feminism this way:

> I always considered myself a socialist feminist and what I mean by that is I take into account the economic cultures of the societies we live in and how that influences the treatment of minorities. For me, I think the most important part of identifying as a socialist feminist is the fact that we don't prioritize women's oppression over everything else and that we feel that racism, antisemitism, you know, all of these other "-isms" should be right up there in the work that we do.[24]

This broader, intersectional perspective was echoed by another of our interviewees, Laura Cohen, who moved to St. Louis in 1976 and immediately joined one of the lesbian-feminist collective households. Asked why so many self-identified lesbians in St. Louis became involved in issues of reproductive rights and violence against women, Cohen said:

> I think that it came down to that sort of political analysis, of women's role in society. Even though whatever choices I made in my personal life, that I may not be in that situation, you could understand it as a woman. And it was also part of the whole antiracism thing, which of course any woman can be a victim of that. And the Take Back the Night movement that was going on at that point, too.. . . It was feminism, *that* was the analysis. The lesbian part was just the other aspect of it, but it wasn't the core part.[25]

The intersectional character of feminist thinking was also embodied in the Women's Self-Help Center, which was established in 1977 by a handful of radical feminist activists. For decades, the Self-Help Center, described in greater detail later in this chapter, was an important mechanism for bringing together activists from different social locations by serving as a central clearinghouse for information about, and connections to, a wide range of activist projects in the St. Louis area.

Women's Rights Activists

Alongside this more radical feminist community, and often overlapping with it, there was an even larger cohort of women's rights activists working to change politics and laws—what Freeman referred to as the "older branch" of the feminist movement.[26] A number of organizations served as vehicles for their activism. Several chapters of NOW in Missouri worked primarily on passage of the Equal Rights Amendment (ERA), but, according to some people we spoke with, the St. Louis–area chapter didn't attract enough members to be effective on its own.[27] The local Women's Political Caucus (WPC), on the other hand, was one of the more active mainstream groups. According to Sally Barker, who had recently finished a master's degree in political science at Washington University and was organizing a rent strike as an intern for the Teamsters Union, the group got its start after a speech by Bella Abzug in 1971 at the local Jewish Community Center.[28] A handful of women, previously strangers to one another, were so inspired by her talk that they decided to organize as a group to work on electoral politics, and they in turn invited women they knew to join. This organization, which remains active to this day, regularly attracted twenty to thirty women to its monthly meetings; after a few months, the members decided to join the national WPC that was forming at the same time.

Barker told us they undertook two projects to launch the organization:

One was to find a state representative district where we could run a woman, and that woman would sponsor the ERA and she would step forward to be the leader in Jefferson City [the state capital] for ratification. The other project was to get women elected as delegates to the 1972 Democratic Convention.[29]

Although Barker now believes they were "kind of naïve, thinking 'OK, we're just going to go out and find a woman candidate,'" they did locate one, Sue Shear, who was willing to run in a suburban district that lacked an incumbent. Through a combination of Shear's tireless door-to-door campaigning, her son's computer skills organizing data about the district, and the help of many women volunteers, she won and went on to serve successfully in the state legislature for twenty-five years.[30] The next candidate the group helped sponsor was an African American woman who did not win election, but in the process she introduced WPC leaders to a dynamic African American union activist, Ora Lee Malone, who joined the group and got them involved in city politics as well.[31] The local WPC went on to have a successful track record of recruiting, mentoring, and helping women candidates run for local boards and commissions, get appointed to judgeships, and win statewide offices, including Harriett Woods, who eventually was elected Lieutenant Governor of the state.[32]

The Women's Political Caucus was just one of the more mainstream women's organizations whose members were active in a wide range of what they considered feminist causes. The ERA and abortion rights were two of the more visible campaigns, but these organizations also worked on issues like the minimum wage and pay equity, child care, poverty among women and children, housing for low-income older adults, access to contraception, adult education for low-income women, violence against women, and healthcare.[33]

Even though Missouri was one of the states where the ERA was never ratified, the issue did serve as a catalyst for significant coalition-building activities among feminists. There were African American sororities that

Figure 10.4 A pro–Equal Rights Amendment rally inside downtown's Christ Church Cathedral on February 26, 1977. The rally, organized by the region's NOW chapter, followed a march through snow and sleet from the Arch to the cathedral. *From the National Organization for Women, Metro St. Louis Chapter Records (S0175), State Historical Society of Missouri*

actively worked with other groups for passage, as well as the organization Federally Employed Women, which was largely African American. Other groups included local branches of the Coalition of Labor Union Women, the American Association of University Women, the National Women's Political Caucus, the League of Women Voters, Planned Parenthood, the Older Women's League, the National Abortion Rights Action League, the Missouri National Education Association, and the National Council of Jewish Women. Once time ran out to pass the ERA in 1982, those who had been involved across the state formed the Missouri Women's Network to keep the momentum going. According to one of its founders, Margo McNeil, "During the next ten years, we had thirty or forty organizations that were active members, and we would follow legislation in Jeff[erson] City" to advocate for women's interests.[34] Coalitions like this one were instrumental in spreading feminist ideas through mainstream organizations, a mechanism that scholar Stephanie Gilmore points to in explaining how the feminist movement was arguably the farthest-reaching social movement of the twentieth century.[35]

In his history of the feminist movement in Missouri, John C. Deken argues that, in St. Louis, the conventional distinction between the movement's younger, more radical branch and the older, more rights-oriented branch was, to some extent, a false dichotomy: "The yin-yang relationship between 'rights' and 'liberation' activities helped ensure a blurring by the mid-1970s."[36] Like in other places, the radical feminists had raised new issues—including abortion, wife beating, rape, and lesbian inclusion—that were then picked up by the mainstream rights activists and incorporated into their understanding of feminism.[37] Our research bore this out. The people we spoke with and the peers they described embraced a variety of activist strategies and pursued a number of social justice outcomes rather than working on just a single issue or with one movement organization at a time.

Just as important was the nature of social networks in St. Louis. St. Louis was (and still is) a city of intersecting social circles. The metropolitan area, which at that time included more than two million people, was large enough to include people from a wide variety of backgrounds, interests, and spheres of life, yet small enough to nurture overlapping social networks that could create ready-made bridges between groups. Then as now, when two St. Louis inhabitants meet for the first time, they can often find someone they both know in common. When it came to social movement activities in the

Figure 10.5 Organizers highlighted four quality-of-life issues in a day of programming commemorating International Women's Day: child care, healthcare, housing, and domestic violence. Rebuffed from participation, anti-abortion protestors drew headlines away from the event by staging sit-ins that day at two nearby abortion clinics. *From Kayla Vaughan personal collection (creator unknown)*

1960s and 1970s, these overlapping networks facilitated communication between seemingly disparate groups and enhanced the spread of information about upcoming movement actions, which was especially important in a pre-internet era. These overlapping social networks made collaboration and combined activism more likely as long as any underlying philosophical or political disagreements remained below the surface. So it is no surprise that, by the mid-1970s, activists from both the more radical and the more rights-oriented branches of the feminist movement had come together to form what they called the Women's Rights Action Group to work on a variety of political issues affecting women, including providing escorts for women entering abortion clinics.[38]

Labor Activism on Women's Workplace Issues
St. Louis has long been a heavily unionized city. Fueled by the immigration of German socialists and radical democrats to the city in the mid-1800s, St.

Louis became the site of a strong labor movement that "relied on a base of community support and networks in ethnic and neighborhood solidarity."[39] At a time when most nationwide labor unions were predominantly male and often discriminated against women and racial minorities, there was a strong current of support locally for including all laboring people in the struggle for workers' rights.[40] The huge garment manufacturing industry that developed in the city after the turn of the twentieth century served as the locus of labor organizing by women and led to a series of unions whose membership was predominantly women and which were active in promoting women workers' interests. One of these was the Amalgamated Clothing and Textile Workers Union (the Amalgamated), whose local membership of around two thousand in the 1960s was composed mostly of women working in the garment industry. Another was the Office and Professional Employees International Union, Local 13, which had been chartered in St. Louis in 1945.

In the early 1970s, a loosely organized group of white women who self-identified as feminists sought to support other women (and men) who were attempting to unionize their workplaces. They had previously been involved in picketing and other actions on behalf of women workers involved in the Baden Bank strike and in attempts to unionize service jobs at Jewish Hospital, among other employers. One of these activists, Marcia Cline, had recently returned to St. Louis from graduate school in upstate New York and was working at the Westinghouse Electric factory. As Cline remembered:

> So, a lot of us were involved with trying to support women, trying to unionize existing [businesses]. It was a time of many demonstrations. . . . [T]here was a demonstration every day. There was antiwar, civil rights, women's rights, all kind of picket lines and strike lines, etc. It was always constant, but a rather exciting time also. . . . So, there was a group of us who were very involved. Some of us may have been involved with NOW, but we were really more interested in working-class women. And of course, we were all white and we were trying to unite with Black women too, which . . . was an important thing for us and them.[41]

In March of 1973, local women labor activists, both Black and white, organized a "huge conference of women workers" held for two days at a

Teamsters facility in St. Louis, bringing in nationally recognized women union leaders as speakers. Hundreds of people showed up. At this conference they met Ora Lee Malone, a well-known, powerful local Black woman labor activist who was the first African American business representative for the Amalgamated.[42] Several participants in this conference went on to meet monthly afterwards, including Malone, "who really was the guiding light for forming the local Coalition of Labor Union Women (CLUW) chapter here," as one fellow activist recalls.[43] According to Cline:

> This was a group of Black and white union women working together, trying to do something together. Meeting regularly, talking, and not being dominant one way or another but just trying to work together on mutual problems. [For example,] a lot of UAW [United Auto Workers] women came to this newly founded women's organization with the news that a lot of the young women who were working in the [nearby Chrysler] plant were from rural areas. The probationary period was ninety days, so a lot of these women were being propositioned and told that if they didn't sleep with their supervisor, union guy, or whoever it was, they wouldn't make their probation and they'd be fired. So, that was a huge issue at the time that we took on.[44]

A year later, in 1974, the CLUW formed as a national organization, and these women established the CLUW's St. Louis chapter, which is still going strong today. They worked not only on workplace issues, including securing the right of women to be hired as their unions' business representatives (a particularly important position), but also on addressing other needs of working women, including minimum-wage laws and access to contraception. As Cline put it in 2020, "[By then,] I was an organizer for service workers. They are suddenly 'essential' [during the COVID-19 pandemic], but back then, they were just pitifully underpaid and under-resourced. There were just a lot of crying needs out there."[45] To meet those needs, these activists worked with a wide range of other groups with similar goals, including local clergy and the Coalition of Black Trade Unions. Cline told us they considered coalition work to be essential: "We weren't just trying to do everything on our own. . . .. There's an awful lot of people who came together whenever there was an issue" to be addressed.[46]

According to our informants, this coalition of Black and white women held together even in the face of potential racial tensions that split so many other interracial groups apart. As Cline remembers, "We had strong leadership from Black women, and we were focused. . . . Alice Moore Jones [a Black union activist] was terrific that way, getting people to focus on the issues and not getting off on a tangent."[47] The kinds of things that *did* cause people to leave the group were conflicts over support for abortion rights.[48]

Like elsewhere, the ERA was controversial among women labor activists in St. Louis not because of disagreements about women's rights but because many feared it would undermine protective labor legislation for women (which, ironically, was eventually eliminated without passage of the ERA). We spoke with Joan Suarez, who since the 1950s had been involved with the labor movement in several different states and moved to St. Louis in 1964 to take a job with the Amalgamated. Suarez told us about debating the ERA with members of feminist groups: "That was not a very popular position to take in those groups. . . . Yeah, I had some meetings that were pretty rough."[49] Other than that, according to Suarez, the Amalgamated and most of its members were very supportive of the issues that the feminist movement was raising, including reproductive rights.

Many, although not all, labor unions in St. Louis actively promoted a number of progressive causes in the 1960s and 1970s. For example, when a new educational director for the Urban League moved to St. Louis in 1964, he contacted the Amalgamated to coordinate their efforts. According to Suarez, who was the union's Midwest educational director at the time:

The Civil Rights Act had been passed now, and our shops in lots of parts of the region where African American women had been hired for the pressing rooms (the dirtiest jobs in the factory) now had an opportunity to get to sewing machines. That was considered a real progressive step because they were on piecework and could make more money.[50]

So the Amalgamated invited the Urban League to add education about Black history to the agenda of its regular educational sessions about things like contracts, the grievance procedure, and the history of the union.[51]

Few if any analysts would claim that organized labor has been a consistent vehicle for the promotion of women's interests, especially if those interests were perceived as conflicting with men's, but we did find additional evidence of support for women in predominantly female unions. Nearly all labor unions until the 1970s had educational arms to teach their members about current political issues and how they affected their interests as workers. Suarez told us about going to textile plants in small towns in rural Missouri and Arkansas in her role as the Amalgamated's education director and asking for volunteers in each union local to serve as a legislative reporter. Then she talked the union into paying for one hundred of these "reporters" to go to the state capitol to talk with their legislators about basic workers' issues such as workers' compensation and unemployment insurance.

> It was probably the first time that any of those folks had ever met their elected official who was responsible for their pay and their disability pay. . . . The legislative reps who were at that meeting talked about that weekend for a year and a half. . . . I think it made them feel like whole people, like they have some influence and some power. That is what it was all about, to get them to begin to develop their sense of power. And at the same time to know what values they held and what the issues were all about.[52]

This anecdote illustrates a kind of feminist consciousness raising intended to help individuals make connections between their personal lives and the larger political and social forces that shape them, echoing the era's feminist slogan that "the personal is political." In other words, Suarez and other feminists engaged in labor organizing as another type of feminist activism. Roz Sherman Voellinger, who left the feminist Women's Self-Help Center in 1978 to become a union organizer for the Service Employees International Union and later the United Hatters, Cap and Millinery Workers International Union, echoed this sentiment:

> It was primarily low-wage women workers. I remember feeling like I know there are women here who are in abusive situations, and I felt that through the union they were being given a voice. They were low-wage women who worked really hard, especially the ones in the nursing homes, and then . . . sewing machine operators and such. It was a lot of Black women, and the employers were pretty domineering and dismissive and did not really treat these women with dignity and respect. I'm making a generalization, but I felt like through our work with the union, these women were able to have a voice and to speak up and to be empowered. In my view of things, that light filters into your

whole world, right? To be in a situation where either at home or at work you're being dominated is quite oppressive. So, to find your voice and be able to speak up and be active through the union was a real positive. So, I really threw myself totally into that work and believed in it wholeheartedly as a way to empower workers as a whole.[53]

Most mainstream labor unions, such as the United Auto Workers, have had a considerably less progressive record when it comes to protecting and promoting the interests of women and racial minorities, especially in industries where the jobs have traditionally been held predominantly by white men. Unions often failed to protect the interests and safety of women and Black workers while also making it difficult for women to play a role in union governance. Pushing back against this pattern, St. Louis Black Nationalist activist Jamala Rogers told us her group's goal was not only to protect Black women's interests but also to get them into leadership positions in unions, which they did:

When you're talking about women's employment, you are going to come face to face with the discrimination of unions, not just against Black folks but against Black women. The Organization for Black Struggle was founded in 1980, and we had a number of members that were represented in the three big auto industries. So, we were very influential in helping them to deal with those issues. A lot of them were not part of—well, they were part of UAW, but the UAW in many ways was not addressing the issues that they felt. So, most of them had caucuses. . . . And [eventually] they became leaders in the union, which was, even now, very difficult to find women in leadership because of the union hierarchy.[54]

These examples show a convergence of efforts and goals between self-identified feminists, labor activists, and Black liberationists who all regarded workplace issues and labor unions as key components in their respective struggles on behalf of women and racial minorities. What would become the St. Louis chapter of the Coalition of Labor Union Women was both a direct outgrowth of this convergence and a catalyst for further collaboration in the decades to come. Alongside the CLUW, activists worked in individual labor unions to promote women's interests—both workplace and otherwise—and establish a foothold for women's leadership. While their efforts yielded results in some cases, especially in those unions with predominantly female memberships, their struggles, like those of the feminist movement, are still ongoing.

Black Women's Activism

While the Black Nationalist and Afrocentric organizations in St. Louis in the 1960s and 1970s did not advocate an explicitly feminist agenda, their activism included campaigns that were clearly intended to advance the empowerment of Black women. The activist quoted just above, Jamala Rogers, also helped found the St. Louis chapter of the Congress of Afrikan People (CAP) in 1972. She told us, "So, understanding what feminism was, it wasn't quite there yet, [we] didn't have the language for it. But I knew that there were certain oppressions that women faced that men did not face. In fact, those oppressions were coming from men."[55]

Like other Black activists around the country at that time, Black women activists in St. Louis tended to take a holistic approach to Black women's liberation and to focus on multiple intersecting issues at the same time. One of the predominant issues for Black residents in St. Louis in the 1960s and 1970s was subsidized housing, which "basically was impacting women and children."[56] There was a very active tenant organizing campaign in public housing led by women like Loretta Hall, Jean King, and Bertha Gilkey, including a successful rent strike in 1969 that captured national attention. These women, in turn, took activists like Rogers under their wings and taught them how to step into leadership roles in community organizing. According to Rogers, local Black Nationalists put sustained effort into developing women's leadership capacities for very practical reasons:

> One of the things we found very early on was women are the first ones—they get out there and they want to do it, but there's so much that's pulling them back, back—whether it be the men in their lives, the children in their lives, the job. So, eventually they just receded into the background. That's a fight that I've been fighting for a very long time. "You're supposed to be out here, find out who can support you to be out here because we need your expertise, we need your charisma, we need your energy, we need your passion, we need all of that." So, just making sure that women are prepared for the roles that they want to take on is very important.[57]

Some of the other issues the local CAP chapter took on included the FBI's attacks on Black political leaders (such as members of the Black Panther Party) as well as everyday police violence and repression targeting Black people and poor Black neighborhoods, and welfare rights. Their strategies included demonstrations and protests, but also educational forums to help people understand the systemic origins of repressive laws and policies. Rogers notes:

When you talk about particularly women's issues, I remember within our social organization, the CAP, we had specific sessions for women only, learning about relationships, learning about systems of oppression, political education, all of that was in there. . . . [S]ometimes there were issues of domestic abuse. There were issues of employment or health issues. So really, just looking at people's lives in a more holistic way and what you need to do for yourself in order to continue to participate [in the movement] was important. Particularly around children and making sure they were safe and protected. And there was a view about how the community takes care of children so that women can be more politically active. In the early days of the CAP, we actually had a collective daycare, so that freed up women to participate.[58]

Even though their efforts were aimed at the empowerment of Black women, Rogers told us, "In the early 1970s, I definitely didn't consider myself a feminist. In fact, in the Black liberation movement there was some resistance to even the term because then it was like this whole white-women-led movement that didn't really consider the issues of Black women."[59] Rogers herself, however, came to reframe her activism after attending the World Conference on Women in Nairobi, Kenya, in 1985:

Women of color were definitely calling themselves feminists in other parts of the world. Then we were like, "Whoa. . . Maybe we've been too narrow in our thinking, or we've let the way the movement has developed here define how we look at feminism." Because there's nothing wrong with the word "feminism" or the concept of feminism, so why is it that we're not embracing it? So, when women from the Francophone African countries were calling themselves feminists, [and] women of Asia would consider themselves feminists, then I started to rethink that whole piece.[60]

Rogers illustrated some of the tensions between white women and women of color in the women's movement with the example of white women calling for "pro-choice" reproductive policies while, for women of color, the issue went beyond abortion to include the broader concept of "reproductive justice," a term indicating the ability to control one's fertility and to have and raise children if one chooses. Still, they found issues on which to collaborate. Rogers remembered participating with white women in actions to raise awareness about violence against women in the 1970s:

> I think about that time in 1976 when Take Back the Night started, and we were part of organizing those in St. Louis. You start to look at, OK, violence against women is not some kind of phenomenon that exists in one person's home. This is a global phenomenon, and it is attached to a system of patriarchy that you could do that to women and get away with it. I remember being part of those marches for a number of years.[61]

She and others also took action to raise awareness about violence against women in the Black community:

> It was also during that time that we began to look at rape in the Black community . . . , which was rarely talked about. I remember we took out a full-page ad in the *St. Louis American* [a leading local Black newspaper] and got a lot of signatories about, like, how you can start to talk about rape in the Black community. The thing about rape and prosecution and reporting, it means that you get ready to send a Black man into a [criminal justice] system that you are already opposed to. So, it created a bit of a contradiction for women who wanted to be safe but had no place where there could be a real resolution of the situation. Because you didn't want to call the police, or you didn't want to send that person to prison because you know what happens to Black men in prison. But we at least had the conversation, like "Let's talk about it. Let's make sure if you don't report, that you're getting the services you need and the support you need, both emotionally and medically."[62]

When asked whether Black women in St. Louis supported the ERA, Rogers told us that getting the constitutional amendment ratified legislatively was not a priority for the groups she was involved in, but that they did support the principle of equal rights for women. And after an initial period of skepticism, she and others were more actively involved in pushing for access to contraception:

> In the Black liberation movement, the whole notion of birth control was looked at as some form of genocide. So, for women of conscience, and informed women, we had to then begin to look at how to educate not just women but our community about birth control and the role it could play, not just in better planning but allowing women to participate [in the movement] more fully. I'm going to tell you, when you have children, that becomes your full-time job . . . [so] you're probably not going to be as involved as you would like to be. So, just putting that into perspective and educating people about it was one of the primary issues. In the mid-1970s, we were part of helping to found the National Black Women's United Front, and some of those issues actually came up. Birth control, reproductive rights, and those kinds of things.[63]

By the 1980s, Rogers said, the momentum had grown to the point where

> . . . we were part of a lot of those marches, women's marches, both nationally and statewide. So, all of those things helped to create a space where women could talk to each other. You're talking to somebody you don't necessarily work with, but you're working on the same issues. . . . [Y]ou could see the growth; each time we came together, there was more awareness, more participation by women, and you could literally see the progress that was being made on that front.[64]

Rogers highlights specific issues that helped to bridge the divide between Black Nationalist women and white feminists: namely, combatting sexual and domestic violence against women and promoting women's reproductive rights, including access to birth control. White feminists had pinpointed these problems as evidence of men's oppression of women, while Black women's concern with them—and their reframing of access to abortion as just one part of reproductive justice for women—took a separate but simultaneous path in St. Louis as it did in other parts of the country.[65] And even though the two groups remained largely organizationally distinct in St. Louis, there were instances in which activists came together to push for progress on these and other fronts.

Obstacles to Cross-Racial Feminist Activism

Given their overlapping interests, why wasn't there more sustained activism uniting Black and white women around women's issues in St. Louis? St. Louis has long had a well-deserved reputation as a very segregated city. Jamala Rogers traced the unique quality of the racism here back to the Dred Scott case, which was adjudicated multiple times at St. Louis's Old Courthouse beginning in June 1847. The eventual St. Louis Circuit Court decision against Scott was later upheld when the US Supreme Court ruled in 1857 that Black people had no claim to the rights of US citizenship, whether they were enslaved or free. As a young Black woman in the 1960s, Rogers moved to St. Louis from Kansas City and

> immediately I felt the difference. . . . The racial relationships were different, even the way Black people looked at themselves was different. I know I was often told, as I was asserting my Blackness, that I must not be from here because I was acting different than most people. . . . Any time you have a court decision [like the Dred Scott decision] that says there is no rights that you have that we have to respect, that permeates every fiber of your being as well as every level of interaction you have, whether it be on the government level or a social level. It's just hanging there, and I could see how people would respond to that.[66]

Rogers believes that oppressive race relations were so "embedded and ingrained" in the perspectives of both Blacks and whites in St. Louis that, if a Black person like Rogers objected to something another person just did, "it's almost like it's impossible for them to understand that because it's been such a part of who they are and how they've operated, that it's just a mystifying thing for them to understand."[67] She used this characterization to describe not only offensive behavior on the part of whites but also the tendency by Blacks to conform to unwritten rules of behavior, such as downplaying their objections in order to avoid ruffling another person's feathers.

Rogers's perception is echoed in a 1973 interview with another leading Black St. Louis activist, Ora Lee Malone, who moved to the city from Alabama. Malone's description of racism in St. Louis was this:

> St. Louis was not different from Alabama, other than voting, and I actually believe St. Louis is worse than Alabama is now, as far as the attitudes of the people is considered. You have such hidden prejudices

in St. Louis that you don't run into in Alabama. You'd never run into such deep-seated hatred between Blacks and whites in the South. They never had any . . . because of the living patterns in the South. . . . [Y]ou have integrated housing, and they played baseball together, and they knew each other. . . . As Dick Gregory says, "In the South, they don't care how close you get if you don't get too big, and in the North they don't care how big you get, if you don't get too close." And that's about the size of it.[68]

Whether because of the legacy of the Dred Scott decision or the long history of racial segregation in the St. Louis metropolitan area (which was enforced and exacerbated by nearly a century of municipal zoning and other laws), or more likely a combination of both along with other factors, cross-racial organizing among activists of all stripes was difficult to pull off, but not impossible.[69] So while many of the activists we spoke with mentioned intermittent collaborations across racial lines, such as white women protesting the closing of Homer G. Phillips Hospital and Black women helping organize the first Take Back the Night marches, most echoed Jamala Rogers's assessment that there was "not so much" cross-racial organizing.[70]

Organized Religion and Religious Groups

St. Louis is in a part of the country that is culturally conservative, so it should not be surprising that organized religion played a significant role in people's lives in the 1960s and 1970s. What may be less obvious, however, is that the route many women took to feminism was through the religious groups to which they belonged. For many of the activists with whom we spoke, whether they were Protestant, Catholic, or Jewish—the three dominant religious groups in the region at the time—getting involved in their church's or synagogue's women's groups was a stepping-stone to becoming a feminist activist. For example, Margo McNeil told us that, after moving from Cincinnati to Missouri in 1978, she joined a Methodist church in a St. Louis suburb, and the church happened to be having a session on the ERA that she attended:

And leaving that session, I talked to one of the ladies who was presenting and said, "You know, in Ohio I was a teacher." The year before I had my first child, they [Ohio] passed the ERA. And because they passed the ERA, I was able to continue teaching the entire year. [Before that,]

I would have had to quit the first semester of my pregnancy. . . . So, I said, "It was a very good thing for me, I would like to help Missouri pass the amendment." So, she put me in touch with a NOW chapter. . . . Then I volunteered for a task force on the ERA.[71]

According to historian Ann Braude, the role of religion in supporting second-wave feminism has been overlooked both by historians and by feminists, leaving the impression that religion and feminism are inherently incompatible.[72] In fact, however, many mainstream Protestant religious groups embraced feminist ideas starting in the 1960s, including support for the ERA, the legalization of abortion, and the ordination of women. According to Braude, "By 1969 the language of women's liberation could be heard at the national meetings of most liberal Protestant denominations."[73] In 1963, Betty Friedan's *The Feminine Mystique* was required reading for national leaders of the United Methodist Women, whose goal was to spread ideas about women's liberation to average, middle-American women.[74] McNeil's experience attending a session on the ERA at her new Methodist church, then, was part of this larger trend rather than an anomaly.

Jewish women involved in the St. Louis section of the National Council of Jewish Women had long been active working on issues affecting women and families, although they did not take explicitly feminist stances until the 1980s. Still, in the 1960s and 1970s, they did organize groups of their members to work on issues that affected women and children, including foster-care legislation, expanding the availability of child care, and tightening licensing regulations to ensure child care was safe. They were also instrumental in securing funding for the first federally subsidized housing complex for low-income older adults in the St. Louis area, the majority of whom are women.[75]

There were also Catholic religious women's orders in St. Louis that played an important role in the local feminist movement. In 1969, Roman Catholic sisters around the country had established the National Coalition of American Nuns to support feminist issues across orders and diocesan boundaries. Then in 1972, the Leadership Conference of Women Religious, which was another broad coalition of nuns, placed women's issues at the center of their agenda.[76] In 1977, the Sisters of Loretto order decided to send five of their members across the US to explore and work on women's issues. Two of them were sent to St. Louis.[77] Through contacts they made at the Women's Self-Help Center, these two sisters got involved in starting a women's credit union, did volunteer work in a new lesbian bookstore (the Women's Eye bookstore at Clayton Road and Yale Avenue in the inner-ring suburb of Clayton), and taught gynecological self-examinations for a weekly women's clinic at the People's Clinic. As a result of the relationships they established through these activities, they later were instrumental in helping to found the first battered women's shelter in St. Louis.[78]

The Young Women's Christian Association (YWCA) was another religiously based organization (albeit an ecumenical one) that played an important role in local feminist activism. In 1979, the St. Louis branch of the YWCA took over a rape crisis hotline run on a shoestring by feminist activists and provided the funding, training, and volunteer resources to turn it into a full-service rape crisis center.[79] The YWCA of Greater St. Louis still operates this center as of 2022.

Forging Feminist Collaborations across Social Differences
Women's Health: Contraception, Abortion, and Routine Clinic Care
Abortion access was arguably the first high-profile feminist issue that St. Louis activists organized around. According to Cynthia Gorney's history of the abortion wars in the US, starting in the early 1960s, there was a groundswell of concern in medical and pastoral circles around the country about the toll that botched, illegal abortions were taking on young women's lives and fertility.[80] Small networks of clergy and medical personnel sprang up in cities around the country, including St. Louis, to steer women to local abortionists who would provide medically safe, albeit illegal, abortions. By 1967, at least a thousand clergy members nationwide had formed an organization called the Clergymen's Consultation Service on Abortion, which shared strategies for how to avoid coming to the attention of law enforcement.[81]

In St. Louis in the mid-1960s, a young psychologist, Gwyn Harvey, had set up a suicide hotline and recruited a local nurse, Judy Widdicombe, to volunteer to help answer the phone. Harvey and Widdicome discovered that most of the calls were not about suicide per se, but instead were from women asking for information about where to get an abortion. In 1968, Harvey and Widdicombe started working with the local informal network of clergy and medical personnel to provide referrals to local abortion providers.[82]

When abortion became legal in New York City in 1970, the group's modus operandi shifted: instead of referring women to local (illegal) abortion providers, they provided counseling and assistance to pregnant women to travel to New York City to obtain an abortion. Judy Widdicombe set up a dedicated crisis pregnancy hotline, and the demand was overwhelming.[83] One of our interviewees, Vivian Zwick, who was a young college graduate and mother at the time, worked as a volunteer on this hotline out of a house in a working-class neighborhood in the suburb of Maplewood, serving as a facilitator to help women travel to New York. Zwick described the highly organized and choreographed process involved:

> Somebody told me about this woman, Judy Widdicombe, who was get-ting people together to do this, and I was in the second group of [about eight or nine women] that she trained. . . . We were taught everything from the word go. We were taught how to counsel. We were taught how an abortion was done. . . . We used to send people on the early morning plane, and then they would be met at LaGuardia . . . by a man who knew you were from St. Louis. You had to know the password, which changed every week. . . . Everybody that we sent was someone that we had already counseled, someone who knew where they were going, what was going to happen to them. . . . They came back on a flight [the same day] at around dinner time. [For those women who didn't feel well on the return flight, Judy] got very friendly with some of the stewardesses and told them what she was doing and to watch out for these people . . . and she found a number of really good people who were willing to help these women.[84]

According to Zwick, information about the service was spread widely not only by word of mouth but also by a number of obstetricians/gynecologists in the St. Louis area who were concerned about their patients' health: "We were so busy we didn't know whether we were coming or going. It was in-credible how busy we were."[85]

When abortion became legal nationwide in 1973 with the US Supreme Court's *Roe v. Wade* decision, Widdicombe was prepared to establish the first abortion clinic in St. Louis, Reproductive Health Services (RHS). Widdicombe knew she wanted a free-standing clinic near a major hospital and bus line, a multistory building with other medical offices, and volunteer counselors working closely with paid staff. She took procedure and design ideas she liked from the abortion clinics she was familiar with, honing and expanding them to create a warm medical environment.[86] Widdicombe and others set up RHS in a nondescript office building on the northeast corner of Euclid Avenue and West Pine Boulevard in the Central West End neighborhood.

Figure 10.6 Judith Widdicombe, reproductive rights activist and founder of St. Louis's first legal abortion clinic following *Roe v. Wade*, pictured in 1973. St. Louis Globe-Democrat *photo, from the collections of the St. Louis Mercantile Library at the University of Missouri–St. Louis*

Widdicombe used certain innovations to ensure that the clinic and staff were respectful and considerate to the patient. She had pictures mounted on the ceiling in medical rooms so patients had something to look at. Each patient had a clinic counselor with her during the entire procedure, and the patient was sitting up when the doctor entered the room and introduced himself.[87]

In the late 1970s, RHS developed an optional Significant Other Program for the boyfriends, mothers, or trusted family member or friend who might accompany a patient into the clinic. They would be invited to sit around a conference table, were informed about the procedure and the medical issues to look for at home, and were encouraged to talk through their fear, guilt, hostility, or grief so that they were better able to comfort the patients after the abortion procedure. The counseling protocol and Significant Other Program eventually became national models for good care in abortion services.[88]

Violence against Women: Hotline, Women's Self-Help Center, Shelter for Battered Women, Orders of Protection, and Men's Collective

The Rape Crisis Hotline

One of the first feminist efforts to respond to violence against women in St. Louis was launched by members of the feminist collective house on Westminster Place in early 1973. One of the house's residents, Kayla Vaughan, had just learned about the rape of a medical student in her social circle. Knowing that "no one was serving rape victims," Vaughan, Marjorie Sable, and Ruth Harper decided to take action by starting a rape crisis hotline.[89] They had a phone installed in the ballroom on the third floor of the house, posted leaflets with the phone number near the Washington University campus, and advertised the number in the student newspaper and other local leftist publications. Their plan was simply to talk with the women who called and provide a supportive, nonjudgmental ear; they would also be prepared to accompany callers to the hospital or police if they requested it. After consulting with a lawyer and arranging for training by a psychologist, they recruited volunteers to stay in the ballroom around the clock to answer the few phone calls they received. A few months later, when they moved to a space above the People's Clinic, the phone began to ring in earnest. In the summer of 1973, knowing they were leaving town to attend law school, Vaughan and Harper approached the Phyllis Wheatley branch of the local YWCA, whose staff agreed to take over the hotline. Under the Y's leadership, this rudimentary hotline developed into the highly regarded St. Louis Women's Resource Center that today provides a hotline, 24-hour crisis intervention for victims of sexual assault, survivor support services, educational outreach to the community, and advocacy for victim's rights.

The Women's Self-Help Center and the Abused Women's Support Project

The Women's Self-Help Center, which for decades was arguably the most influential second-wave feminist organization in St. Louis, was started in

1976 by three recent graduates of Washington University. While students, they had begun a Women's Resource Center on campus that became the locus for a wide range of feminist activities, including a campus-based women's coffeehouse and consciousness-raising sessions or "rap groups."[90] One of these women, Louise Bauschard, had a particular interest in women's health, so Resource Center leaders visited some women's clinics in San Francisco, bringing back information on how to do gynecological self-exams that they shared with St. Louis women. Another member, Roz Sherman Voellinger, had in 1973 done a student internship with the national NOW office in Washington, DC, and brought to St. Louis knowledge of the latest feminist ideas and debates, such as the hotly contested issue of whether feminist organizations should be structured as cooperatives or as hierarchies. Members established a music series called Red Tomatoe that brought nationally known women artists such as Cris Williamson to town for concerts. At the same time, they started laying the groundwork for a women's credit union, which eventually opened in 1977 under activist Debra Law's direction.[91]

The group moved off campus in 1976, forming the independent Women's Self-Help Center at a location on North Newstead Avenue. As Sherman Voellinger told us, "We were just going in a lot of different directions":

> We initially just started out that we were going to be this broad-based, everything-to-all-women kind of resource center. We really were very excited. The Women's Self-Help Center, the self-help aspect really originated with the women's health [initiative]. That was the verbiage that was being used with regard to women's health. Then we decided that it applied broad-based and really was our underlying philosophy. When we started out, we were just taking this "everything" campus center to the community. . . .[92]

Their idea was to establish an organization that would connect women with one another and with community resources so that women themselves could take action to solve a wide range of problems in their lives.

The Women's Self-Help Center quickly became the hub for different networks of people wanting to get involved in women's issues. While the founders considered themselves feminists, not everyone who was involved did. Over time, the staff, volunteers, and women seeking help came from a variety of different social, racial, economic, and political backgrounds. As Sherman Voellinger described it, "During the time I was there, we covered the whole spectrum of individuals who were involved."[93] For example, after a few articles about the new Women's Self-Help Center were published in local newspapers, participants were contacted by a group of well-to-do suburban women who wanted to help, and who ended up holding successful fundraisers for the organization. Because of its social location at the intersection of many different groups of activists and constituencies, the Women's Self-Help Center was instrumental in the development of a number of feminist projects over the next few decades, especially those having to do with violence against women.

Once established, it didn't take long for the Women's Self-Help Center to become overwhelmed by the number of calls from battered women asking for help. This was when they discovered that there were few resources available for these women in the community. So by the end of the organization's first year, they stepped in and started working with abuse victims "in a very focused way," as Sherman Voellinger put it.[94] They expanded their staff with grants from SLATE (the St. Louis Agency on Training and Employment), the St. Louis Community Trust, and the Monsanto Fund, and established a hotline for battered women, through which they documented the need for battered women's services.[95] Sherman Voellinger recounted how, with few established models to follow, they developed protocols for providing crisis intervention, support, alternative housing, and legal counseling for these women. Some of the staff had social work backgrounds, which helped them formulate initial questions to ask women callers and clients. However, Sherman Voellinger notes, the founders did not want to make counseling or therapy the focus of their work:

A lot of social work students wanted to get involved and do private counseling and working with women. But we [the founders] were seeing this from the political/cultural/social point of view and were very adamant about that. . . . We were very focused on trying to address the crisis parts, which meant find a safer place, to be able to help however we could to get this woman into a situation where she could try to change her trajectory. We probably were actually very light on the personal counseling part of it. . . . [We] were looking at the factors of, "What does society say about women and relationships with men, and how does this play into why women are in the abusive situations that they are?" We really focused a lot on that. But, at the same time, we were desperately looking for what could be done to help them in very practical ways.[96]

Several different local groups in this moment were coming to the same realization that there was a crisis of domestic abuse in the community but few sources of help for the victims. The Women's Self-Help Center became the primary site where these groups coordinated their efforts and launched new initiatives. For example, armed with the realization that healthcare providers were often the main point of contact for battered women, Bauschard and Sherman Voellinger held in-service trainings for nurses at City Hospital about myths and facts surrounding family violence, intervention strategies, and housing alternatives.[97]

Initially, the activists at the Women's Self-Help Center used their personal contacts to find people who were willing to house battered women and their children in their own homes. Among them were the two Sisters of Loretto who had been volunteering with organizations they discovered through the Women's Self-Help Center. Sister Mary Louise Denny and Sister Virginia Williams then contacted five or six other orders of Catholic women religious and together they began to provide emergency housing for battered women at their orders' houses and at a retreat center. Denny told us they thought of this as an "underground railroad" of sorts.[98]

After a few months, the sisters realized that this was not an ideal solution for the battered women, according to Denny. Most of the houses were in predominantly white, suburban areas of St. Louis County, and the largely urban, Black women who were seeking help, and who were often traumatized, frequently felt isolated and stranded in these locations. The Sisters of Loretto happened to own an old, fully furnished Victorian house in the city that was standing vacant, and the two sisters proposed that the order donate the building to be used as a shelter for abused women and children. The order agreed.

Denny and Williams called for and received about twenty volunteers from a wide variety of women's advocacy groups in St. Louis, including the Women's Self-Help Center, the lesbian community, communities of women religious, and other individual activists. Denny told us they formed a working board and, having learned only rudimentary things from shelters in other cities, mostly made it up as they went along, developing policies, operating procedures, lists of needed resources, and a fundraising plan.

They opened the doors of the St. Louis Abused Women's Support Project in early 1978, and soon secured three VISTA volunteers for staff and hired a shelter director. The initial board members, who were all white but from different walks of life, remained actively involved in the day-to-day running of the shelter for those first few years. From the start, the shelter served a predominantly African American population of women and children, a pattern that still holds. Under its current name of The Women's Safe House, it continues to serve as a leading feminist organization that advocates for battered women in St. Louis to this day.

Missouri's Adult Abuse Law

While activists were organizing the hotline, shelter, and other programs to assist battered women, legal advocates were working to establish civil orders of protection for battered women. The increasing numbers of battered women who sought help from Legal Services of Eastern Missouri (LSEM, formerly known as the Legal Aid Society) quickly discovered that the legal options available to them were insufficient for addressing their situations.[99] In the early 1970s, most police departments' responses to domestic violence were grossly inadequate to protect victims, and momentum was building among legal advocates in many states to reform the laws about partner abuse. By the late 1970s, four states had adopted legislation providing civil orders of protection for abused spouses, but each one had significant drawbacks.[100] So, LSEM attorney Nina Balsam, with assistance from local lawyers and law students, took the lead in drafting state legislation for Missouri that would incorporate the strengths of each of the existing laws while avoiding their weaknesses. LSEM then convened a coalition of nine different organizations across the state (four of them from the St. Louis area), and this group was able to get Missouri's Adult Abuse Remedies Act passed in 1979.[101] At the time it was passed, this law was considered a national model for establishing legal protections for domestic violence victims. The coalition that pushed through its adoption decided to formalize the relationships its members had developed by establishing the Missouri Coalition Against Domestic Violence.[102]

RAVEN

Another way in which activists in St. Louis were at the forefront of nationwide attempts to reduce domestic violence was the development of a men's collective to work with men who batter.

The catalyst for establishing the collective came in 1977 with a loosely organized group of male graduate students at Washington University who were involved in a variety of leftist social causes. According to Don Conway-Long, who was working on his PhD in the history department, they were encouraged enough by the number of pro-feminist and gay-affirmative activist groups in St. Louis to organize the Fourth National Conference of Men and Masculinity at the university that fall.[103] The conference inspired some of the participants the following January to start the St. Louis Men's Projects, an umbrella group for a variety of initiatives, including a Fathers' and Children's Group. One pro-feminist strategy the men adopted was to provide child care for many of the feminist women's events around town. In the process, they engaged with the women who started the Women's Self-Help Center and who, according to Conway-Long, "told us to get off our ass and do something. 'You say you're supportive of [our efforts to help battered women], so work with the men.'"[104]

A group of about six men took this charge seriously and set out to form what became RAVEN (Rape and Violence End Now). At the time, there was very little published about domestic violence from a feminist perspective, and nothing about how to get men to stop being violent with their partners, so they had to create their own approach. They started from the premise that conventional therapy was not the solution, mirroring how feminist advocates had rejected therapy as a remedy for battered women's problems. Instead, they believed that men needed to challenge other men's violence. But deciding exactly how to do that was not easy, according to Conway-Long:

> We met unbelievably often. . . . Always, constantly meeting, meeting, meeting. We even had "RAVEN East" in the old bar north of Left Bank Books. . . . We processed and processed and processed, just like the early feminist groups did. I mean, you talk yourself to death to figure out what one thing means, right? That's what we did. We often talked, but I guess we were inventing much of the analysis.[105]

At the same time, men's groups to confront men's violence against women had formed in two other cities: AMEND in Denver and EMERGE in Boston. EMERGE had developed theories about men's violence that had much in common with those developed by RAVEN, so these two collectives worked together to create a national network to disseminate their ideas about how men could do antiviolence work. Operating on the philosophy that they should take their lead from feminist women's groups, RAVEN members also attended some of the earliest conferences put on by the National Coalition Against Sexual Assault and the National Coalition Against Domestic Violence, where their presence was controversial but tolerated.[106]

By the fall of 1978, RAVEN had expanded to a collective of about a dozen men, and in October they started holding groups for men who batter. The protocol they developed for the groups, Conway-Long remembered, called for two members to lead the discussion as they challenged the participants about their attitudes and behaviors:

> Consciousness raising was certainly part of it, but it was also confrontation about the use of violence and trying to educate an overall attitude about how to see women. Clearly, men being able to do violence to someone means you cannot see them as a human being, right? It was a lot of, "How do you get that? How do you put together loving someone and controlling them in this way? That's about *you*, not them." [We also developed] alternative behaviors to striking out. . . . We had all kinds of safety planning.[107]

RAVEN grew quickly, with as many as thirty men joining the collective and the weekly groups drawing an average of a thousand men a year throughout the remainder of the 1970s and early 1980s. The men who sought help were almost always "woman-mandated," that is, their women partners obtained RAVEN's number from a battered women's program and threatened to end the relationships if the men didn't seek help. The collective continued to support local feminist groups by helping local battered women's shelters move furniture and lobbying for passage of Missouri's adult abuse law in the state capital. It remained the most influential local organization for working with abusive men until well into the 2000s.[108]

Conclusion

The account we give in this chapter shows that feminist ideas in St. Louis were disseminated to a wide variety of social groups in no small part because activists were involved in multiple social justice struggles rather than with just one. This is consistent with Gilmore's claim that it was "through the strength of difference and diversity of many voices, ideas, and actions" that the feminist movement became one of the most consequential of the twentieth century.[109] Feminist ideas were spread across not only politically radical organizations but also mainstream religious, political, and social organizations. This was especially the case with the fight for the ERA, which drew in groups like the League of Women Voters, Federally Employed Women, the Older Women's League, and the Missouri National Education Association to participate not only in the initial mobilization for passage but also in the Missouri Women's Network for decades following the ERA's defeat.

The feminist movement's success in St. Louis depended in important ways on collaboration with other activist groups that was driven by multiple factors simultaneously. The intersecting social circles that characterize St. Louis facilitated personal connections and communication across different walks of life, including raising awareness about local issues and recruiting people to attend upcoming political events. The increasing influence of socialist-feminist thinking called attention to intersections of gender with class and race and facilitated ideological connections with other causes, including labor and civil rights. The urgency of local struggles like the planned closure of Homer G. Phillips Hospital and the looming deadline for passage of the ERA in Missouri mobilized many people to work across traditional divisions of race and class. And the presence of the Women's Self-Help Center served as a central clearinghouse for information and collaboration, and as an entry point into the feminist movement for people throughout the metro area.

Throughout our research, we found that when activists were able to initiate change outside of existing social institutions, they moved relatively quickly and effectively, as they did to establish the Abused Women's Support Project shelter, the Reproductive Health Services abortion clinic, and the men's collective RAVEN. In hindsight, it is remarkable that when activists saw a need, they simply took action with few, if any, models to follow—which also may have led to more innovation than might have occurred otherwise. Even some of our interviewees remarked on being naively unaware of potential obstacles, such as when the group that would become the local chapter of the Women's Political Caucus decided its first task was to get women elected to local and state offices. While not all activists' efforts panned out, a striking number of them did.

On the other hand, if activists had to work through established institutions, their efforts took longer to produce effects, if they did at all. Activists' track record of getting legislation passed in the Missouri legislature, where the rural parts of the state wielded substantial influence, was mixed: they lost the fight for the ERA but were successful in passing some of the most progressive laws to protect victims of domestic violence in the country at the time. Struggles on behalf of women in organized labor did yield advances by women into leadership positions in some unions, but the process was slow and the results uneven. Labor and Black activists could not assume that the people they were trying to mobilize already possessed a developed political consciousness, as could the radical and liberal feminists. Confronted with this situation, they sometimes had to back up and do basic political education first: one of the key strategies some of them used was to educate their constituents about how politics works, how existing laws and policies affected them personally, and how to change the system that had produced them. We saw this in the political education of women workers undertaken by Marcia Cline and the political education and mentoring of Black community members spearheaded by Jamala Rogers.

Perhaps the most surprising discovery that we made in researching the history of feminist activism in St. Louis is the progressive role that religion played in an otherwise culturally conservative part of the country. Mainstream Protestant, Jewish, and Catholic groups disseminated feminist ideas to their members, helped recruit new activists to the movement, and were instrumental in establishing new organizations that promoted feminist goals. For example, the YWCA took charge of the rape crisis hotline, the Sisters of Loretto Catholic women's religious order provided the house for the first battered women's shelter, and the local chapter of the National Council of Jewish Women participated in the political advocacy group, the Missouri Women's Network, that grew out of the fight for the ERA.

Most significantly, a legacy of the activism we document was the institutionalization of new advocacy groups like the Missouri Coalition Against Domestic Violence, the Coalition of Labor Union Women, the Women's Political Caucus, and others. Over time, many of these local groups evolved into, or joined, national organizations to amplify their efforts, and they are still active and effective in advocating for progressive change on issues that affect women in 2022. While it is often overlooked, many of these social-change organizations that have had a lasting impact on American society depended in significant ways on feminist activism not just in major coastal cities but also in places like St. Louis.

11. Is Ivory Perry an Environmentalist (and Does It Matter)?

Rob Gioielli

DURING THE LATE 1960S AND early 1970s, Ivory Perry worked tirelessly to try and address one of the biggest harms facing thousands of families in St. Louis: childhood lead poisoning. He gave interviews, organized meetings, and led sit-ins and rent strikes. Most importantly, he worked to prevent children from getting sick, and, if they did get sick, he made sure they and their families did not have to return to their toxic homes.

Before his work on lead poisoning, Perry had been a well-known "foot soldier" in local civil rights struggles in the 1960s. He has a local park named after him in the North Side's Visitation Park neighborhood, is well remembered by many former colleagues and friends for his commitment to social justice, and was the subject an excellent biography by George Lipsitz, a pioneering scholar of American Studies who taught in St. Louis in the 1980s. Perry was tragically murdered by his son in 1989 during a domestic argument.

Perry is an important figure in recent St. Louis history, but he is primarily remembered as a civil rights activist. But shouldn't we also consider him an environmentalist? Childhood lead poisoning is one of the most significant environmental issues of the twentieth and twenty-first centuries, one that affects millions of Americans, particularly the poor and people of color. So, the questions posed by this chapter are: Is Ivory Perry an environmentalist? And does it matter?

When we tell stories about social movements in postwar America, especially those that we associate with "The Sixties," we often rely on preconceived notions about who the activists were, and which issues they were concerned about. These conceptions, oftentimes derived from contemporaneous images and media, do not reflect the diversity and complexity of

307

the movements themselves. The civil rights movement, for instance, was not led solely by Martin Luther King Jr., but was a national, primarily grassroots movement that engaged millions of Americans in thousands of sit-ins, boycotts, and other forms of protest, mostly nonviolent, but sometimes not. The flower children protested against the Vietnam War, but so too did middle-class mothers and veterans who had served in the war.[1]

There is a similar discord between the memory and reality of the environmental movement, which is often collapsed into the wave of protests in and around the first Earth Day and associated with white, middle-class college students. But the reality was far more diverse, as Americans of almost every stripe engaged in environmentalism in some way, looking to find ways to clean up local parks, pass air pollution legislation, and limit their children's exposure to toxic chemicals. Documenting and understanding this complexity is important for several reasons. Over the past half-century, the narratives and institutions of American environmentalism have been dominated by middle-class and elite whites, actors who have a particular orientation to environmental issues that often crowds out divergent voices. This has an impact on politics and policy both directly and indirectly. Storytelling is a powerful tool within social and reform movements. It allows individuals and groups to connect to issues and make claims that the larger population and governing bodies recognize as valid. A history of environmentalism that includes folks like Ivory Perry helps lend more legitimacy and salience to claims made by contemporary environmental justice activists, who can argue that concerns about inequality and environmental racism have been present since the emergence of the modern movement.

Perry's story, and the larger history of anti-lead activism in St. Louis, also reveals the missed opportunities of modern environmentalism. Since the 1990s, major environmental institutions have faced criticism that their staffs, boards, and leadership are almost exclusively white and middle-class; that their orientation is reformist, accepting of existing social inequalities, and overly focused on preserving particular visions of "wild" nature; and that their preferred policies oftentimes infringe upon the rights and livelihoods of marginalized groups. This criticism has intensified in recent years, as the racist history of conservation and the wilderness preservation movement has become more widely known, and as climate-justice activists show how rising temperatures and sea levels will disproportionately harm the poor and racial and ethnic minorities in all parts of the globe.[2]

Within this context, lead-poisoning activism in St. Louis represents an intriguing case study in alternative pathways. Perry and others in the city's anti-lead movement were directly shaped and supported by the work of one of America's most important environmental activists, Barry Commoner, who was at the time a professor of biology at Washington University in St. Louis. During the late 1960s and early 1970s, a diverse network of activists, scientists, and—most importantly—community members developed around and through Perry and Commoner. Although primarily focused on childhood lead poisoning, they also worked to develop an alternative environmental politics that was focused on the concerns of central-city Black residents and the environmental inequalities and injustices they faced. Their movement is a vital and important part of the heritage of environmental activism not only for St. Louis, but also for the entire country.

The Destruction of St. Louis

The decades after World War II were beneficent to metropolitan St. Louis, the region that takes up eleven counties in Missouri and Illinois. But for the city itself, the postwar period was a disaster. Its population declined by half between 1950 and 1990, with the city losing 230,000 people in the 1950s and 1960s alone. Hemmed in by a boundary fixed in 1876, the city that had been densely settled during the first part of the century saw a massive outflow of people and capital. City leaders responded with an extensive urban renewal plan that focused on rebuilding the city center, clearing land for industry, and housing the city's poorest residents.[3] Despite early successes during the 1950s, by the 1960s it was clear that the benefits of renewal efforts, and the region's economic growth, would not be distributed equally. Middle- and upper-class whites from the suburbs would reap many of the rewards, while working-class and poor African Americans in the central city would be left out.

Depictions of these developments, particularly in American popular culture and media, tend to portray them as the "decline" of the city and the "rise" of the suburbs. And in relative terms, this portrayal is correct. St. Louis's suburbs were wildly successful in the postwar era, while the city declined precipitously. But this narrative naturalizes urban economic and social fortunes, making them seem inevitable. According to this story, the only force that acted upon cities was the capitalist market, which, although cruel, knew the best way to allocate resources. But the decline of St. Louis and scores of America's older industrial and commercial cities was not inevitable. The transfer of capital, jobs, and population (and, with that, economic and political power) from St. Louis to its suburbs was the result of a series of conscious decisions made by governments, corporations, private institutions, and individuals. The most important of these were governmental policies that subsidized the growth of suburban areas, making them extremely attractive to both large corporations and individual consumers. When these are layered in with the decisions of a myriad of private and public institutions, St. Louis and other cities were subject to a host of economic, cultural, and political forces that, when viewed from the perspective of history, doomed them to failure.

Within this context, "destruction" is a more appropriate description for the fate of America's postwar cities than decline, and it is especially apt when considering anti-city policies and decisions as well as their physical impact. But a purely spatial analysis of the postwar city, and especially of St. Louis, is inadequate. Both individual and institutional actors privileged the suburbs over the city because of racial factors. Racial discrimination that was supported and reinforced by racialized housing and credit markets severely restrained Black housing choices. In the early twentieth century, realtors and housing developers appropriated and adopted the ideas of social scientists who argued that racially and ethnically homogeneous neighborhoods led to urban harmony. These ideas became national policy with the creation of the Home Owners' Loan Corporation and the Federal Housing Administration during the New Deal period, and they were widely adopted on the local level, including in St. Louis.[4]

The loss of value that whites believed would occur if they had African American neighbors was not just the result of racial fear, but also of financial, legal, and political structures that privileged white suburbs over Black cities. It was virtually impossible for any applicant, white or Black, to get a standard home loan in many urban neighborhoods until the 1970s. This not only suppressed home values in many Black neighborhoods, but also created a direct connection between Blackness and declining real estate value in the minds of many whites, especially in what were considered "transitional" neighborhoods. By racializing suburban housing markets, the US federal government and local actors created financial incentives for whites to keep Blacks out of their neighborhoods. This policy not only kept Blacks out of the suburbs, but it also starved urban areas of capital for home construction, purchase, and renovation. The infamous "redlining" maps of the mid-twentieth century were important because they showed not only where Blacks could and couldn't purchase homes, but also where banks would lend money. This is vital for understanding the rapid decline of St. Louis's housing stock.

This lack of credit constricted Black housing options in several ways. Middle- and working-class Blacks who wanted to purchase or rent homes, even in majority African American communities, found it hard to get loans, or they had to pay inflated interest rates, well above what suburban whites were paying. The apartments and other rentals that were available were often owned by white, absentee landlords. Many of these buildings were older and had been subdivided into small, inadequate apartments during World War II and the immediate postwar years when St. Louis, like most American cities, faced a severe housing crunch. In the tight housing markets of the 1940s and early 1950s, landlords saw these properties as good investments. But as the suburbs opened to whites, and the remaining available tenants increasingly were poor African Americans, the value of the properties declined rapidly. Repairs and renovation were not a priority, and, by the 1970s, many landlords were abandoning properties or even hiring arsonists to collect insurance money.[5]

This was the housing situation that many African Americans faced in St. Louis during the postwar decades: new suburban areas that were virtually walled off and older urban areas almost devoid of available capital. But conditions were not static. In the 1950s, city leaders targeted two traditional African American neighborhoods—the waterfront and Mill Creek Valley—for large-scale urban renewal projects, forcing existing residents to move. Joining the evicted in the search for housing were thousands of new St. Louisans. The Great Migration of African Americans from the rural South to urban centers across the country continued in the postwar years. Like previous migrants, these newcomers were attracted by better economic, political, and educational opportunities outside of the nation's Black Belt. Many were also pushed out. The mechanization of cotton production meant that those jobs that were available to Blacks—primarily as sharecroppers—were quickly disappearing.[6]

Migration and urban renewal thus put tremendous pressure on remaining Black neighborhoods on the north side of St. Louis, and combined with white flight to the suburbs, led to rapid racial turnover in neighboring white areas. But many poor Blacks still faced limited housing choices, especially in the 1960s. Although housing activism would eventually open the suburbs to Black homebuyers, the fruits of these efforts would not be available

311

until the 1970s and later. There were extensive public housing projects in St. Louis, including Pruitt-Igoe (Fig. 11.1), a sprawling complex of thirty-three buildings, but this was not a panacea. Pruitt-Igoe, like many projects built in the postwar era, was plagued by mismanagement. Moreover, federal money only subsidized construction, not maintenance and upkeep, causing a fiscal crisis and leading to a maintenance backlog and rapid physical deterioration. In 1969 tenants organized a successful rent strike to force the city to fix the issues and address residents' concerns, but the structural deficiencies were too great, and Pruitt-Igoe was demolished in the late 1970s.[7]

Figure 11.1 The Pruitt-Igoe public housing complex, shortly after the 1972 demolition of three of its thirty-three towers. *From the George Wendel Collection Photos, Saint Louis University Archives*

The public housing rent strike was St. Louis's most notable housing movement during the late 1960s and early 1970s, but it was not the only one. Other activists focused on the private market, and their targets—hundreds of absentee landlords and property owners, but also city inspectors and housing regulators—were more diffuse and difficult to hold accountable. It is within this context that childhood lead poisoning became a major issue in St. Louis. But the focus on lead poisoning was not automatic. Black activists and residents received key assistance from the federal government, local social service agencies, and a major research university. Without this institutional support and scientific expertise, the lead poisoning campaign might never have emerged.

"The New Jeremiah"

By the early 1960s, St. Louis's civil rights movement could mark some major achievements, including solidifying Black political power and expanding job opportunities. After these successes, several St. Louis's Black activists took positions within the city government or in local branches of federal government agencies. On one level, this was a process of institutionalization, whereby the state officially recognized new issues and concerns, and former political outsiders became part of the bureaucracy. But the movement of activists from private citizens to government employees was not full-scale cooptation. Many appropriated the resources of government institutions to continue their activist work, advocating on behalf of the Black poor. One of the best examples of this in St. Louis is Ivory Perry.

The son of an Arkansas sharecropper and a Korean War veteran, Perry was a factory worker who became active in the local chapter of the Congress of Racial Equality (CORE) in the early 1960s. More than just a foot soldier, but less than a national leader, Perry was one of thousands of dedicated and skilled local organizers and activists who were the backbone of the American civil rights movement, participating in and leading important protests against police brutality and job discrimination. In 1966 he was recruited to become the housing coordinator for the Union-Sarah Gateway Center, a community office for the St. Louis Human Development Corporation, which was the local office coordinating federal War on Poverty programs. With no training, education, or experience as a social worker, Perry did not appear to have any qualifications for helping community members solve their various housing problems. But within the context of federal antipoverty programs in the 1960s, his experience as an activist, along with his knowledge of the community, was just as important as official training or expertise in social work.[8]

Named more for a map quadrant—the area between Union Boulevard and North Sarah Street on the north side of St. Louis—than for a locally recognized community, the Union-Sarah Gateway Center served the heart of St. Louis's Black community in the late 1960s and early 1970s. Although this area included the Ville, which was still one of the city's most prosperous African American neighborhoods, there were also significant pockets of poverty. According to the 1970 census, the average family income for the area was less than $7,000 per year, compared to $12,700 in Florissant, a major suburban city. Roughly 20 percent of families in the community lived below the poverty line; many of them were recent migrants from the South or recent transplants who had been evicted from homes in the Mill Creek Valley urban renewal zone. They rented rooms in row houses and other homes that had been divided and subdivided into apartments during and after World War II, dwellings that had been beaten up by years of deferred maintenance. This was one of the few areas of the city where Black families could find an apartment, and where rents were cheap.[9]

Within this context, Perry's official title might have been housing coordinator, but his job description was more like housing fixer. Much of his work focused on helping poor African American families deal with the day-to-day challenges of finding decent housing in a heavily segregated and rapidly deteriorating part of the city (Fig. 11.2). He negotiated rents and contracts, badgered recalcitrant landlords, and, if necessary, took them to the city's housing court to make necessary repairs. Perry helped families fight evictions and, if they were kicked out, he helped them find emergency housing. Every day, Perry faced the results of structural racism that forced many African Americans to live in the city's most rapidly deteriorating neighborhoods. It is within this context that he received help from one of America's most prominent environmental scientists and learned about the dangers of lead poisoning.

It's hard to get more famous that being on the cover of *Time* magazine, and that's where Barry Commoner was in the spring of 1970. Two months before the first Earth Day, a striking image of Commoner, with his face split between an illustration of verdant utopian greenery on one side of the page and gray, dystopian environmental destruction on the other, appeared with the caption "The Emerging Science of Survival." Six months earlier the magazine had profiled Commoner and four other scientists, whom the editors dubbed "The New Jeremiahs," popularizers of the science of ecology who were raising concerns about the impact of technology on modern life. This prominence was not sudden for Commoner; he had been working for years to raise awareness about the dangers of modern technology.[10]

Raised in Brooklyn, Commoner found his way to Washington University in the late 1940s to work in the college's botany department. He came to public prominence in the late 1950s through his work with the Committee for Nuclear Information (CNI). Scientists had been raising concerns

Figure 11.2 Ivory Perry, far right, with residents of Enright Court Apartments in 1973. Perry was helping them to organize a rent strike to force the landlord to address multiple maintenance issues. *Photo by Bob Moore for the* St. Louis Globe-Democrat, *from the collections of the St. Louis Mercantile Library at the University of Missouri–St. Louis*

about the health impact of nuclear fallout since the 1940s, but Cold War McCarthyism created a chilling environment for critique of the emerging military-industrial complex. As an alternative, scientists such as Commoner championed full and robust scientific communication. They argued that in a democratic society, access to accurate data was vital for citizens to make informed decisions. In St. Louis, the CNI, an alliance of Washington University scientists and middle-class women, pioneered a particularly effective way to communicate the potential harm of nuclear testing with the Baby Tooth Survey. Beginning in 1958, the CNI collected thousands of children's teeth from St. Louis and around the country. Spectral analysis of the teeth showed a marked increase in strontium-90, an isotope that is only released through atmospheric nuclear explosions. The survey was able to show that the fallout from tests in Nevada became embedded within the bones of St. Louis children thousands of miles away. The published results of the survey helped push public opinion against nuclear testing, leading to the eventual adoption of the 1963 Partial Nuclear Test Ban Treaty.[11]

Commoner and other members of the scientific information movement portrayed themselves as unbiased experts who simply wanted to educate the public. For Commoner, the test ban was rousing proof that, given complete and accurate information, people will make the correct choices about technology and its risks. In the 1960s, he expanded these efforts on both a personal and professional level. In 1966 he published his first book, *Science and Survival*, which provided accessible case studies of how modern technology was harming the natural world and posed a threat to human life. In the same year, he led a group of Washington University scientists to create a new interdisciplinary research lab, the Center for the Biology of Natural Systems. CBNS, as it was known, was funded by a $4.5 million grant from the US Public Health Service, the first major federal funding in the field of what would become known as environmental science.[12]

Commoner and the other members of the CBNS said they were engaged in basic, not applied, science, but they wanted to see some real-world results and address social problems. With this end in mind, the center created the Environmental Field Program (EFP) in 1969. Funded by a grant from the Kellogg Foundation, the EFP was designed to connect their research to the

Figure 11.3 Barry Commoner, speaking at the Arch for an April 1980 Earth Day event. *Photo by John Dengler for the* St. Louis Globe-Democrat, *from the collections of the St. Louis Mercantile Library at the University of Missouri–St. Louis*

greater St. Louis community. Wilbur Thomas, a young African American scientist who was also committed to civil rights, was hired to be the program's director, overseeing several projects each year. A staff of graduate and undergraduate students assisted Thomas, and they received technical support from the rest of the center. In the first year, the program conducted field studies on air and water pollution, rat infestation, lead poisoning, and infant mortality in the St. Louis area. The stated goal of the studies was to make "the resultant scientific information available to community groups and to representatives of operational agencies in a form that would enable them to develop appropriate courses of action toward resolving some of the critical problems, as well as promoting greater understanding of the nature of environmental problems."[13]

The program's lead-poisoning field study, completed in August 1969, proposed that the EFP work with the Human Development Corporation (HDC) to create a master plan for dealing with lead-poisoning victims, including finding funds for treatment, replacement housing, and building repair. In particular, the EFP wanted to develop programs at the Yeatman Gateway Center, which was also on the North Side and had a federally funded community health center. The study was unequivocal in identifying the source of the problem and the only real long-term solution: "Since the cause of childhood lead poisoning is known to result mainly from unlivable environmental conditions in slum housing, an effort [must] to be made to eliminate those conditions."[14] The study also identified people at the HDC, including Ivory Perry, with whom the EFP would work on the lead poisoning issue.

Childhood lead poisoning became a major problem in postwar American cities because of the widespread use of lead-based paint during the interwar period. Made by combining acidized lead with oil, lead paint was popular because of its bright white shine, durability, and low cost. Although early occupational health experts, such as Alice Hamilton, had highlighted the toxicity of lead in high doses, paint corporations argued that it was harmless for home use, and they marketed the paint heavily in the 1920s. By the 1930s, however, public health experts in Baltimore found that children in low-quality rental housing, which often had peeling paint and plaster, were susceptible to poisoning at doses much lower than those for adults in industrial settings. Poisoning in children not only caused severe illness and occasional death, but also long-term developmental disorders and mental handicaps. By the 1950s, experts argued that poisoning often reached epidemic levels in neighborhoods with decrepit housing stock not only because lead paint chips were readily available but also because of the sociology of "slum" life. They argued that malnourished children found the paint chips sweet tasting, and that poor, overworked (and, it was often implied, negligent) parents could not prevent ingestion. Thomas, Perry, and allied St. Louis activists were part of a wave of urban doctors, public health activists, and community residents from cities across the country that would change the epidemiology of childhood lead poisoning beginning in the late 1960s. They countered that a focus on the behavior of parents or children who lived in slum housing was blaming the victim. The cause of childhood lead poisoning was not the poor families but the structural factors that forced poor and minority families to live in slums in the first place.[15]

In the early twenty-first century, local activists and organizations in St. Louis resurrected and celebrated Perry's earlier work, arguing that he was a pioneer in the struggle for environmental justice.[16] As deserved as these portrayals are, they attribute the entire effort to eradicate lead poisoning to Perry. As with other popular discussions of civil rights and social justice histories, the focus on an individual hero ignores the complex networks and institutions that fostered and supported activists. For the civil rights movement, for example, Black churches, schools, and colleges in the Jim Crow South provided vital training, funding, and spiritual and moral support. Ivory Perry and other urban activists in cities around the country used similar support networks to fight lead poisoning. As an employee of the HDC, Perry was able to pursue a variety of different types of activist work while supported by the resources of a federal agency. To engage in environmental activism, he needed access to scientific expertise and knowledge. Thomas and the EFP provided city residents with a direct pipeline to the resources of a major research institution and a program focused on applied environmental health.

This support was vital. The city of St. Louis had its own regulatory and bureaucratic infrastructure for housing, public health, and medical issues, but none of it was designed to address lead poisoning. There were no testing programs or penalties for owning properties with lead paint. Many local doctors did not look for the symptoms of lead poisoning when examining sick children. Perry said even some Black doctors were hostile to the lead poisoning issue, seeing him and other activists as outsiders and agitators. But the research support of the EFP gave Perry the evidence he needed to speak with confidence on the issue.

"Black Survival in Our Polluted Cities"

After he began working with Thomas, Perry paid his own way to a conference on lead poisoning in Chicago, where a few years before the city government had begun its own testing program. He then raised the issue of lead poisoning at a local conference on low-income housing in 1969 and got the tentative support of the St. Louis Board of Aldermen, which led to the passage of the city's first lead-poisoning ordinance in April 1970.[17] But the original law was flawed. It split enforcement responsibility between two city offices. The health department was responsible for testing paint chips and blood samples taken from children at hospitals and community health centers. If a child had high blood-lead levels, then the health department directed the building division to conduct a home inspection. Building inspectors then had to do a complete survey of the house and a title search before the health department could bring the owner in front of a judge. This process took two to three months, and its sluggish pace proved exasperating to concerned citizens and activists. Over the course of 1970, frustration began to build. Many children had been diagnosed with lead poisoning and had undergone the painful treatment, chelation therapy, to remove the lead from their bodies. But families often had no choice but to return the child to their current home. If the landlord had not successfully removed the lead, the child would often be re-poisoned.[18]

In response to the molasses-like speed of the city's enforcement procedures, Perry and other HDC and War on Poverty workers began to organize around the lead poisoning issue. In addition to Perry, a group called the People's Coalition Against Lead Poisoning (Lead Coalition) arose out of the Yeatman Community Health Center, which was also in the city's predominantly African American North Side. The primary spokesmen and organizers of the Lead Coalition were Robert Knickmeyer, a medical social worker, and Larry Black, Yeatman's housing coordinator.[19] Starting in the fall of 1970, the Lead Coalition engaged in a series of confrontational tactics to highlight the dangers of lead poisoning and the city government's apparent unwillingness to deal with the issue. The first of these was a rent strike by Carrie McCain, whose granddaughter, Dorothy Nason, had been poisoned multiple times by the lead paint in her apartment at 2503 Glasgow Avenue on the North Side. She held back her rent from her landlord, Dorenkemper Realty, which managed the property for owner Charles Liebert. She was eventually evicted, and Legal Aid defended her in court, arguing that she had a right not to pay rent until Liebert made the necessary repairs.[20]

Though limited in number, rent strikes were an effective tool to force landlords to take action, and they show the commitment of the parents and families of poisoned children.[21] Many of them were already living on the margins; if not, it would have been easier for them to find safer housing. They had already incurred pain and heartache when their children were poisoned, and they were putting themselves at further risk by withholding rent from their landlords. But they judged the risks as preferable to the alternatives. "Paying more rent would be like having someone shoot you with a gun one time, and then paying him to shoot you again," Carrie McCain said.[22] Other tenants withheld rent as a personal protest, and not part of a larger campaign. Vatra Tanner lived in an apartment at 2820 Gamble in the Carr Square neighborhood on the North Side. She repeatedly asked her landlord, Block Brothers, to make repairs, but they refused. According to a social worker from the Red Cross who was assisting with her case, the owners allowed the property "to deteriorate to the point where it was almost uninhabitable." Her children became poisoned from the flaking lead paint, so she started to withhold rent to help pay for their medical bills, and because, as she told a city building inspector, she did not want to subsidize "the poisoning and sickness of her own children." Tanner was threatened with eviction, but she eventually got the city to prosecute the landlord under the lead ordinance.[23]

While the Lead Coalition tried to highlight the problem of unresponsive landlords, Perry tried to improve awareness of lead poisoning in local communities, and he spent much of 1971 raising money for a more comprehensive testing program. The city's three testing centers were inaccessible to those families that really needed the tests, he argued. Lead poisoning resulted from structural problems that required larger solutions, but children needed testing now. "[Housing] is the long range goal, but the present thing to do is have children screened, because children who may be subjected to lead poisoning don't have time to wait on long term programs," Perry told a newspaper reporter. His fundraising was not an effort to replace the city government's public health responsibility but rather to push municipal leaders to act. "It costs $250,000 for lifetime care of a mentally retarded person suffering from lead poisoning," Perry said. "But the city is spending only $50,000 a year for prevention and cure."[24]

City officials cited a growing budget deficit when activists attacked them for the lack of money for lead testing, but it was also a matter of funding priorities. Mayor Alfonso Cervantes, in office from 1965 to 1973, was a pro-growth Democrat who focused on downtown redevelopment. He understood the city's changing racial dynamics and worked to address the concerns of the Black community, but his administration, and the health department in particular, did not place lead poisoning high on its priority list. "All I can say is that the health division is doing the best it can with limited resources. I don't have the answer of how you raise $16 million," Health Director Dr. William Banton said in a newspaper article. He was referring to the city's $6 million budget deficit for 1971 and a projected $10 million deficit for 1972. He added that, although lead poisoning was a serious problem, he felt the city's high infant mortality rate was a more important issue.[25]

The budget crunch facing St. Louis was common in American cities during the 1960s and 1970s. A declining tax base from residential and in-dustrial flight and increasing crime and poverty put many older cities in a fiscal squeeze, all while they continued to attract poor Americans who needed more services, not fewer. Federal programs, such as the War on Poverty and Model Cities, were designed to address these issues by funding social services and community redevelopment. But, despite the claims of conservative critics, the amount of money spent was never that high com-pared to the need, and in 1972 the Nixon administration shifted federal funding altogether with its New Federalism programs, which removed the strings from federal dollars and let cities decide how they were going to spend the money. In St. Louis, this meant large downtown projects like a new convention center. Such projects were supposed to spur economic de-velopment, but many advocates for the poor saw them as direct subsidies to large corporate interests that ignored the immediate problems of city residents, including lead poisoning.[26]

By 1971, the efforts of Perry, the Lead Coalition, and other activists had helped make lead poisoning a community-wide issue. But once it entered the public forum, different constituencies tried to define the problem, and offer solutions, in different ways. The Ad-Hoc Committee on Lead Poisoning, created to advise the health department, was a group of doctors and social workers that was not as confrontational as the Lead Coalition and other activists. They did not seek to place blame on any one institution or group of people for the lead-poisoning problem. "If we are to eradicate this hazard, the entire community must assume responsibility and mobilize for its immediate elimination. Lead poisoning will not dissipate without a vig-orous, sustained, multi-faceted attack," they wrote in a public statement.[27]

In general city officials, medical department bureaucrats and many doctors viewed lead poisoning as a management and educational issue, one that could best be addressed by educating parents and doctors and getting children treated. But Perry, Thomas, and other activists, residents, and victims understood lead poisoning differently. To them, lead poisoning was not simply an unfortunate fact of ghetto life. It was the specific result of social forces—in particular, discriminatory and racialized housing markets—that exposed African Americans to certain environmental hazards. Childhood lead poisoning was the most tragic, but far from the only, hazard facing the residents of Black ghettos, they argued. They saw and understood that environmental hazards were not distributed equally and placed lead poisoning within this specific framework. This perspective was the direct result of the work of Wilbur Thomas. His job at the EFP was to create and oversee programs that transferred scientific knowledge from the scientific experts to government agencies. But, on his own time, Thomas pursued a more expansive vision, one that tried to transfer the knowledge of the laboratory to the people at large—in particular, to poor and working-class African Americans who, because of their race and class position, lacked access to this expertise.

In February 1970, Thomas spoke at Southern Illinois University in Edwardsville, the major university on the Illinois side of the St. Louis metropolitan area. The speech, entitled "Black Survival in Our Polluted Cities," was reprinted in *Proud* magazine in April, in honor of the first Earth Day (Fig. 11.5). The piece argued that, far from being a distraction from issues of civil rights and poverty, which many national Black leaders claimed, the "current emphasis on 'saving the environment'" was an important issue for inner-city African Americans, albeit in ways far different from those discussed in the mainstream press. Thomas argued that racist economic and political structures forced inner-city Blacks to bear a "double burden" of environmental threats. "The nitty gritty issues relevant to Blacks is [sic] simply the fact that a disproportionate number of Blacks are exposed to more environmental health hazards than non-Blacks in addition to the regular burden. Exposure to additional hazards such as lead poisoning, infant mortality, air pollution and land pollution, and rat control are all indigenous problems to most Black communities." Thomas had little faith that existing institutions would solve urban environmental problems, so Blacks must work on their own. "The message is loud and clear that if we want to achieve the kind of ecological quality and

Figure 11.4 Wilbur Thomas (right) with Dorothy Smittee and her mother, Mrs. Smittee. Dorothy had been diagnosed with acute childhood lead poisoning a year before. The photo ran in *Proud* magazine. *From the Publications–Student Groups Collection, Department of Special Collections, Washington University in St. Louis*

appropriate master strategy, provisions must be made for Blacks to save their community environment."[28]

After the publication of "Black Survival," Thomas edited a regular feature for *Proud* over the next two years entitled "Black Ecology." Unlike the city's Black-owned weekly newspapers, the *Argus*, *Sentinel*, and *American*, *Proud* was geared towards younger readers. According to *Proud*'s publisher, Ernie McMillan, one of the monthly magazine's goals was to "reach out to the young, Black person and help him in finding his rightful place here in the Greater St. Louis community." Articles focused on music, the arts, and fashion, but also on local political and economic issues, especially those that related to jobs and housing. In general, *Proud*'s editorial content reflected a broader shift in Black culture during the late 1960s. Instead of emphasizing integration and gaining access to America's mainstream (and white-dominated) political and economic institutions, Black activism became more focused on developing the cultural, social, and economic strengths of the community. This led to "Afrocentrism" and other celebrations of Black music and arts, but also to political efforts that were simultaneously more radical and pragmatic. Especially in American cities, Black Power meant activism directed towards economic issues that immediately

Figure 11.5 An unnamed child pictured with "Black Survival in Our Polluted Cities," an article by Wilbur Thomas about urban environmental issues published to coincide with the first Earth Day. *From* Proud *magazine, April 1970*

affected Black families as well as gaining control of municipal political institutions.[29]

This context is important for understanding Thomas's column and its success in framing environmental issues. While many Black leaders and intellectuals were arguing that environmentalism was a distraction from larger issues of economic justice, by focusing on immediate problems Thomas successfully took what others dismissed as a "full-stomach," almost utopian politics and adapted it to the pragmatic concerns of urban Blacks in the early 1970s. Thomas geared the "Black Ecology" articles towards educating African Americans about the environmental and health problems that faced their community. Most stories focused on how African Americans were the victims of specific types of urban environmental threats, which themselves were the result of racism and discrimination.[30]

In addition to "Black Ecology" in *Proud*, Thomas also helped found and advise the St. Louis Metropolitan Black Survival Committee. Led by Freddie Mae Brown, like Perry a social worker with the Union-Sarah Gateway Center and a self-described "fat Black woman who wants to help people," the goal of the committee was to organize and educate at the grassroots level. As part of the first Earth Day on April 22, 1970, the committee wrote and performed a play entitled "Black Survival: A Collage of Skits," designed to educate local African Americans about inner-city environmental issues.[31]

The skits opened with a group of Black college students contemplating what they will be doing for an upcoming break. They come across a friendly professor, who says that he will be joining a pollution protest and asks the students to join him. They blow him off, with one student saying, "I heard about the movement for a better environment and I feel like it's a cop-out from dealing with the real problems which are education and employment. No, that just ain't my bag. I let you and whitey take care of that." After the professor leaves, the students engage in a discussion about what they are going to do during the semester break. Several of them comment how they would rather stay on campus (located in "Pleasantville") than visit their inner-city homes and neighborhoods. Eventually, they realize that environmental problems do affect African Americans. After the students track down the professor and agree to help organize some protests, the play transitions into a series of sketches that explore DDT, lead poisoning, solid waste and garbage, rat bites, and air pollution. In the last sketch, after his mother is hospitalized with a respiratory ailment, a teenage boy launches into a final soliloquy lamenting the causes and impact of environmental racism.

Within this context, the utility of lead-poisoning activism for Black St. Louisans becomes apparent. From air pollution to poor housing to rats, Blacks in St. Louis faced numerous environmental hazards. But the impact of those issues on Black health was cumulative and hard to quantify. Childhood lead poisoning was different. It constituted an acute illness that, with a simple test, doctors could diagnose and trace back to a specific cause. This was evidence—verifiable proof—of how dangerous the slums could be, with manifestly innocent victims.

"The People Couldn't Pay More Rent, So I Sold It"

In 1972, St. Louis revised its lead ordinance to consolidate the efforts of the health department and the building division. Previously, owners had two months to fix problem properties, and two separate city offices had to co-ordinate the repairs. The changes put the entire system under the control of the health department director, and activists, politicians, and public health workers all considered that a significant achievement. But it could still take two months to completely remove the lead from a house. Seeing no way around the bureaucratic problems—the city lacked the funds to create a truly streamlined program—the Lead Coalition jumped on a provision that allowed the health department to appeal to the courts for immediate action. This led to "Court Injunctions to Save the Children," a campaign

325

coordinated by the Lead Coalition. In addition to forcing the city to act, the campaign also highlighted the hostility of landlords and threw the devastation of the city's housing market and housing stock into sharp relief.[32]

The campaign began in the fall of 1972 and lasted several months. The coalition wrote an open letter to Cervantes and then began to pressure city attorney Robert McNicholas. After his initial refusal to issue injunctions against landlords, the Lead Coalition staged a sit-in in his office to force him to deal with the issue. Knickmeyer, Perry, and other activists were joined by several children and their mothers, including Veronica Harris. Her daughter, Ethel, was being treated in Cardinal Glennon Hospital for her second bout with lead poisoning. They sat near Sheila Brewer and her mother. Young Sheila, who had recently been hospitalized for lead poisoning for the fifth time, was the poster child for the "Court Injunctions to Save the Children" campaign. Although lead paint had finally been removed from Sheila's home, her parents and activists worried about the children in the forty-three other apartments in her building.[33] The action against McNicholas yielded few results. The city attorney was an obstinate and combative adversary who argued that it was not the job of his office to enforce the lead-paint ordinance. A month later, the Lead Coalition decided to focus on Dr. Helen Bruce, the city's health director. After a sit-in and a rally, Bruce and the Cervantes administration relented, and agreed to start using injunctions to force landlords to fix up properties that were shown to have lead paint.[34]

This was a breakthrough for lead activists and, over the next year, the city made significant progress in enforcing the lead ordinance. By 1974, Bruce was able to show activists that, although the city had taken only sixteen landlords to court, they had prepared cases on more than one hundred, and the enforcement effort appeared to be having an impact. According to her records, about twenty-five homes and apartments were being detoxified under city order every month.

By most metrics, this is evidence of a very successful local social movement. Over the course of three years, activists had forced the city to acknowledge the problem, to pass a series of laws, and to engage in robust enforcement. But why did childhood lead-poisoning rates, especially in certain North Side communities, remain so high? It was because the city was engaging in what was called at the time "spot detoxification" and what experts today would call secondary prevention. Once a child was diagnosed as having been poisoned by lead, the city had the ability to force a landlord to make repairs. But, even then, they only fixed the obvious problems—flaking paint, holes in the plaster—rather than removing lead from the entire building. This meant that poisoned children returned to a lead-filled home, and the risk of poisoning for new tenants would still be very high.

This reality reflected the intersection of epidemiological and economic assumptions by city officials and North Side landlords. Most property owners placed the blame squarely on tenants themselves. "The children wrecked the faucets and furnaces," real-estate investor Louis Eisenstein told a local newspaper reporter. "They cracked plaster off the walls and ate it. I was forced to spend more than $500 to repair the damage. The people couldn't pay more rent, so I sold it." The assumption that many landlords made was that poor Black families did not take care of the properties, which led to the decrepit conditions. "Lead poisoning doesn't happen in my south St. Louis properties. Where there is good housekeeping, it does not occur," Paul Brune, one of the more combative landlords, said in the same article, his reference to the city's majority white South Side a not-so-subtle racial comment.[35] Even those who were less openly racist made assumptions about Black children having pica, a desire to eat non-food products, or being malnourished. "It seems that the basic problem is the fact that ghetto children have over a number of years developed a craving for plaster and actually dig this plaster out of the walls so that they might eat it," Walter Stradal, head of the local real-estate board, wrote in a 1971 letter to a local paint manufacturer to inquire about inexpensive wall coverings.[36]

These comments make it easy to portray landlords, property owners, and real-estate executives as the bad guys in the lead-poisoning morality tale, and they often played right into the hands of activists who were eager to cast them as evildoers. But the knee-jerk use of the slumlord label does not fully explain the structural problems facing certain sectors of the St. Louis housing market. By the 1960s, private capital, in the form of loans for new real-estate development and mortgages for individual homebuyers, privileged the suburbs. Large banks and smaller savings-and-loan associations saw newer suburban areas as a much better risk than older areas in St. Louis. It was hard to get any sort of real-estate investment capital in St. Louis, and the situation was especially dire in African American neighborhoods.

Central-city landlords and property owners were subject to these very same forces, albeit in a way that affected their businesses, not their health and that of their families. Despite these realities, however, these real-estate professionals still tried to absolve themselves for their complicity by arguing that central-city communities were victims of "decline" or "the market." Blaming the inviolate powers of free-market capitalism naturalized and obscured the forces—racialized housing markets, federal infrastructure and mortgage subsidies for the suburbs, and racial hostility from neighboring white communities—that created postwar ghettos. By making the reality of the central city appear as destiny, real-estate investors simultaneously rationalized their own losses and defended themselves against attacks that they were "slum lords" milking people for profit.

Invoking the invisible hand of capitalism was not the only way that landlords and property owners shifted responsibility for lead poisoning away from themselves. Arguments that children craved lead paint or that "it comes down to housekeeping"—implying that Black women could not keep their homes clean or supervise their children—placed the blame for lead poisoning on Black parents and families. Despite the covert, or, more often, overt, racism in these arguments, they are consistent with the era's epidemiological conclusions regarding childhood lead-paint poisoning. Until the early 1980s, the prevailing view in medical, public health, and popular discourses was that lead-paint poisoning was caused by the active ingestion of lead paint chips. This perception allowed landlords and realtors to argue that lead poisoning was caused by a general lack of cleanliness and hygiene among African Americans. Most residents and activists argued the other side of this epidemiological coin. They acknowledged that the cause of lead poisoning was often ingestion of paint chips, but argued it was ultimately the consequence of children residing in structures in such decrepit condition, and not the fault of negligent mothers.

This was the value of Wilbur Thomas's scientific expertise, but also his general environmental critique, to St. Louis's Black community, especially those who were concerned about lead poisoning. By arguing that childhood lead poisoning was broadly an environmental problem and placing the blame for that problem on racism and discrimination, Thomas provided the victims of lead poisoning with a strong counterargument. The problem was not their behavior as parents, or their children's behavior. Thomas's scientific expertise allowed Black St. Louisans to make scientific and public-health claims, which, combined with activism, forced the city to take lead poisoning seriously. In addition, by embedding these claims within a certain type of environmental politics, Thomas's expertise allowed them to argue that conditions outside of their control, not their behavior, had caused the problem.

"A Tent City Is Better Than
Having Children Live in Leaded Buildings"

The realization by activists, concerned doctors, and public health advocates that the city was enforcing its lead ordinance but that conditions seemed to be getting worse nonetheless led many to realize that they had run headlong into a massive structural problem: the rapid collapse of St. Louis's urban housing infrastructure. "It would be ideal if we could require that all lead paint be removed from a dwelling. This, unfortunately, is simply not economically feasible, and would result in eviction of tenants, and the boarding, or demolition of the dwelling, becoming the rule rather than the exception," Bruce wrote to Ad-Hoc Committee member Robert Karsh in 1974.

The cost of removing lead from a dwelling was $2,000 to $4,000. If the city forced the issue with landlords, they would just evict the tenants and abandon the building, because the repairs were not worth the expenditure, Bruce argued.[37] Even with spot detoxification, about 5 percent of owners required to make upgrades already simply abandoned their properties, and that rate would skyrocket if the city enforced complete detoxification, lead-poison control service director Gilbert Copley told the regional health planning board in 1975. "If required to detoxify, some owners would just abandon the building, leaving families to go to another lead infested structure," Copley said. "The city is trying to reach a balance between making it safe but not so expensive owners will foreclose." This balance, between housing availability and a leaded environment, was not something board members were willing to accept. "A tent city is better than having children live in leaded buildings," one health board member commented.[38]

St. Louis did not choose a tent city, and lead poisoning remained a significant problem. In 1975, the Centers for Disease Control (CDC) lowered the threshold for lead poisoning from 40 to 30 micrograms per deciliter of blood. This new definition caused a spike in the number of local poisoning cases. Larry Black called for emergency funds to deal with the problem, accusing city officials of dealing with the problem by ignoring it. "Now that health officials are agreeing with what we have been saying all along—that children suffer from lead at lower levels than those for which they were being treated—health officials should go all out to solve this problem. The longer they wait, the more lives will be lost," Black said. Two years later, when the CDC ranked American cities with the highest rates of lead poisoning, St. Louis was number one. Both doctors and activists admitted that this dubious distinction was based largely on the city's chosen method of lead control, secondary prevention. "The approach to childhood lead poisoning in the city of St. Louis and nationally is a classic case of 'closing the barn door after the horse has run out,'" commented an editorial authored by the Saint Louis University Department of Community Medicine.[39]

Primary prevention, removing all lead from a residence, was preferable, but, as the threshold for lead poisoning lowered and knowledge about the affliction increased, the cost of complete removal became onerous. Lead poisoning did not just come from hungry children eating flaking paint. Lead was in the dust and embedded in the walls. St. Louis made the choice for secondary prevention because primary prevention was expensive. They also viewed private property laws as paramount, which allowed owners and landlords to engage in convoluted ownership and lease agreements that helped them duck lead paint laws. And the city was loath to use the full force of the law against all owners and landlords. Politicians knew that a commitment to remove lead from all buildings without an accompanying housing plan would deepen the city's already severe housing crisis. With costs mounting, city officials and residents began to accept the leaded environment, and activism waned. In one year, the coalition lost two of its most important and confrontational leaders. Ivory Perry retired from activism in 1973, and Robert Knickmeyer moved to New York to take a job teaching social work. Larry Black remained involved for a couple more years, but government tolerance for activism by public employees working within Great Society programs dwindled over the course of the 1970s, and the goal of the Gateway Centers became service delivery, not organizing the poor.[40]

With no tools available to fix the city's myriad housing problems, politicians instead chose to leave it up to the dysfunctional and poorly capitalized private market. This meant that there would be no solution to the lead-poisoning problem, only management. In five years, lead poisoning became an endemic disease, instead of a health emergency. With the city settling for management rather than prevention, many residents voted with their feet. During the 1970s and 1980s, St. Louis continued to lose population. Not just whites were leaving now; African Americans fled as well. Population decline only increased the downward pressure on the housing market. Landlords and owners continued to abandon buildings, and the city began to acquire its current landscape of boarded-up homes and empty lots, especially on the North Side.[41]

Conclusion

Childhood lead poisoning is still a major problem in American cities, with evidence accumulating that it has caused an ever-widening panoply of mental-health and social problems. When the federal government banned leaded gasoline in the early 1980s, epidemiologists noticed a sharp decrease in the blood lead levels of all Americans. Further research showed that levels once thought to be tolerable were in fact poisonous, and even minor exposure could cause long-term mental and developmental disorders in children under five years of age. With this new understanding in hand, some public health and criminal justice researchers have begun to look retrospectively at the relationship between environmental lead concentrations and crime rates. What they have found is startling: there is a direct correlation between high levels of lead exposure in a city and that city's violent crime rate. People who are exposed to lead as children are more likely to commit violent crimes as adults, and when lead exposure rates go down (as they have with the banning of leaded gasoline) violent crime rates go down about twenty years later. Environmental health experts and criminal-justice reform advocates hope these data will bring increased attention to the lead problem. Poisoning and exposure rates in poor, central-city areas remain high, but the issue receives little publicity, primarily because, as groundbreaking researcher Herbert Needleman told the *Baltimore City Paper* in 2005, "it's a Black problem."[42]

Lead poisoning's continued existence as an endemic and destructive disease should not detract from its importance to urban environmental activists, or from their work in trying to address this issue. In St. Louis, at least, lead poisoning was not just a way to foment activism, but also a proxy for the variety of hazards and risks imposed on people by postwar urban abandonment—risks that individually were small but collectively were enormous. By itself, an abandoned park, potholed street, vandalized building, or missed garbage pickup might not bother the average city dweller. But when all the risks and hazards were present, they sent a message to African American residents that the rest of the city did not care about their neighborhoods and that city leaders were content to let them fall into disrepair. When those poor conditions crept into the home—with rat and roach infestations, insufficient plumbing, and plaster falling off the walls—many residents either voted with their feet by moving or worked with a social worker or legal aid attorney to have the landlord fix the problem. For many in early 1970s St. Louis, the final push towards protest and activism was seeing their child, grandchild, or friend's child poisoned by lead paint. This reality, and the knowledge that almost all the city's Black children were at risk, was what fed lead-poisoning activism in St. Louis and similar protests in cities across the country.

The piecemeal, accretive nature of urban environmental problems in St. Louis is one of the key factors that made them so hard to organize against, and what makes them so hard to fit within our standard narratives of environmental activism. We expect there to be a factory, dump, incinerator, or dirty well that the community realizes is poisoning them, and against which members then mobilize to address the issue. These sorts of movements are easy to publicize and much easier to organize. Community members have one corporation or government agency they can put the "black hat" on, and try to enforce the law against. But childhood lead poisoning, and the other attendant environmental issues of the postwar city, are excellent examples of what scholar Rob Nixon calls "slow violence."[43] There is not one major poisoning incident or destructive event, but a day-by-day creation of an ever more toxic environment. Childhood lead poisoning looks much different than other types of environmental problems and disproportionately impacts the poor and marginalized around the globe. They simply can't afford to live in healthier neighborhoods, don't have access to comprehensive healthcare that could diagnose chronic issues, and lack the scientific knowledge and expertise that makes it much easier to stake out environmental claims.

This is why the story of childhood lead poisoning activism in St. Louis is so important and instructive. War on Poverty and social-service agencies like the Union-Sarah Gateway Center and the Yeatman Community Health Center provided infrastructure to support healthcare workers and activists like Ivory Perry. They also provided key institutional partners for scientists like Wilbur Thomas, who brought the resources of a major private university and a commitment to an expansive definition of environmentalism that looked to address the specific concerns in the city's Black, central-city residents. Together they were able to forge a movement that, even if it did not solve the problem of childhood lead poisoning, made significant gains in improving the health and well-being of a significant number of city residents.

This is why I believe it is important to call Ivory Perry an *environmentalist*— and the lead-poisoning movement an *environmental* movement. To do so helps us to think expansively about the history of environmentalism, and to move beyond a story that has focused on the concerns of the middle class and elites, usually white men. This is not to create an inclusive story for its own sake. It is to help us see the missed opportunity of an environmentalism that actively worked to address inequalities and toxic issues that fall disproportionately on the poor and marginalized, but also impact us all. It is also important because social movements are built on storytelling. Storytelling allows activists and community members to explain to themselves and each other what motivates them and commits them to social change. But history matters as well. Being able to connect your story to a lineage of activists who looked like you and fought against similar issues not only lends legitimacy to a contemporary claim, but also fosters faith that your work falls within a necessary and valuable tradition. This sort of history is important for all forms of activism, but it is especially necessary for environmentalism, as the threats from climate change become ever more severe and will weigh most heavily on the most marginalized members of our national and global communities.

12. "Save Homer G. Phillips and All Public Hospitals"

African American Grassroots Activism and the Decline of Municipal Public Healthcare in St. Louis

Ezelle Sanford III

ON AUGUST 17, 1979, MONTHS of escalating protests reached their zenith as the City of St. Louis completed its consolidation of public hospital services. This action effectively closed Homer G. Phillips Hospital, a formerly segregated African American municipal teaching institution in the Ville, a historic neighborhood of North St. Louis. Hundreds of largely African American community activists gathered on hospital grounds not only to protect the beloved institution, but also to prevent the removal of hospital services from an emerging medically underserved community.

For much of the twentieth century, St. Louis maintained two segregated municipal general hospitals—Homer G. Phillips and Max C. Starkloff. In the Jim Crow era of racial segregation, sick African Americans could not access care in segregated white hospitals, or in some cases, like Starkloff, were subjected to basement "colored wards." To accommodate African Americans migrating from southern states, in 1919 St. Louis opened City Hospital No. 2 in the abandoned downtown Barnes Hospital.[1] City Hospital No. 2 freed Starkloff Hospital (then named City Hospital No. 1) to treat white patients exclusively.[2] Though a meager improvement to Starkloff's "colored wards," the fifty-year-old building was dangerous and unsuitable for patient care upon its opening. African American civic leaders demanded that the city provide more suitable hospital services for its growing African American population. Opening in 1937 as the successor to City Hospital No. 2 (1919–1937), Homer G. Phillips Hospital solidified its place in Black St. Louis as an important municipal employer, community center, economic engine, healthcare provider, and above all else a nationally renowned training ground for African American medical specialists, nurses, and allied health professionals. "Homer G.," as it was affectionately called,

335

emerged as one of the largest general hospitals in the nation and the largest segregated hospital administered by and for African Americans.

Figure 12.1 A wide-angle view of the chaotic clash between St. Louis police and Homer G. supporters on August 17, 1979, the day that hospital services were consolidated. St. Louis Globe-Democrat *photo, from the collections of the St. Louis Mercantile Library at the University of Missouri–St. Louis*

On that August day in 1979, Dr. Mary Tillman, a local pediatrician who began her career as a Homer G. intern in 1960, drove to the hospital to begin her shift. As she approached, she noticed the swarm of police officers, some of whom were mounted on horses, others on foot armed with clubs, pistols, shotguns, and dogs. One police officer approached her vehicle with his nightstick drawn and told her to turn around.[3] But she could not abandon her premature infant patients who remained in the hospital's Pediatrics Department behind police lines. The families of Dr. Tillman's patients had not yet been informed that their children, like all other remaining patients, would be transferred to an undisclosed local hospital. She could not call them, because the hospital's switchboards were disabled.[4] Of that infamous day, Dr. Tillman remembered that the police were "prepared for war," and she needed to secure her patients' safety amid the tumultuous scene.[5]

The "siege," as community organizer Walle Amusa would later describe it, was a coordinated surprise attack.[6] Anticipating protests, municipal leaders did not notify hospital and community officials of their intentions to

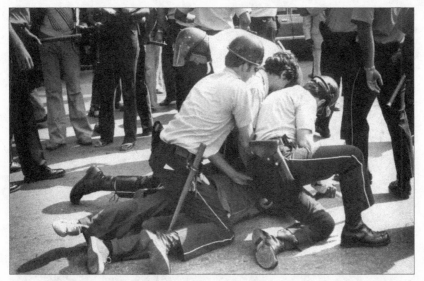

Figure 12.2 Three St. Louis police officers subdue a Homer G. advocate protesting the hospital's closure. *Photo by Jim Rentz for the* St. Louis Globe-Democrat, *from the collections of the St. Louis Mercantile Library at the University of Missouri–St. Louis*

close the hospital that day. Police explained their presence in peace-keeping terms, though it was clear that their motivation was to curtail direct action protests, indicated by the violent arrests of many supporters and activists.[7]

The Ad Hoc Committee to Save Homer G. Phillips Hospital—organized by health workers, including registered nurse Zenobia Thompson, a celebrated health activist in the 1970s and 1980s—mounted a barricade of hospital furniture. An elderly woman sitting in the hospital's front driveway, participating in the sit-in effort to block police access and thus prevent patient transfers, spoke to a news reporter, reflecting, "It's a modern way— close your hospital and your health centers instead of putting Blacks in the gas chambers or in the furnace."[8] Eliciting the violent images of the Nazi-led Jewish Holocaust, she communicated the very real fears rippling through Black St. Louis.

Though Homer G. was taken both by surprise and by force that day, grassroots activists were also prepared for battle. A *St. Louis Argus* editorial titled "No Surprise" noted that it was "commonly said: 'They've been tryin' to close Homer G. for years.'"[9] As St. Louis's financial status worsened amid deindustrialization and suburban expansion, the city's management of two general hospitals became untenable. Both hospitals continued

337

Figure 12.3 A view of the impromptu furniture barricade erected by Homer G. staff and activists to prevent patient transfers in late July of 1979. *Photo by John Bloomquist for the* St. Louis Globe-Democrat, *from the collections of the St. Louis Mercantile Library at the University of Missouri–St. Louis*

operating after the city desegregated public accommodations in 1955, though they stood as testaments to Jim Crow's legacy. Successive mayoral administrations from Raymond Tucker in the 1950s to John Poelker in the 1970s recognized that fact, but also understood that any action to close the hospital would be accompanied by political consequences. That is, until Mayor James Conway in the late 1970s instituted a plan to consolidate public hospitals and ultimately to move the city away from the hospital business altogether.

To grassroots activists, hospital consolidation was not a path to equitable healthcare. Instead, it threatened to exacerbate existing racial health disparities. By 1979, Homer G. was the only remaining hospital in the predominantly African American North Side. Activists also asserted that its closure would have dire economic and social consequences in the Ville neighborhood, placing the hospital's closure amid the city's strained history of race relations and urban blight. Activists mounted years of public awareness campaigns, petitions, protests, and coalition building between civic and civil rights organizations in opposition to the city's decision to close the hospital.

From the perspective of health activism, the confrontation on August 17, 1979, was the climax of a multi-decade political struggle for Black St. Louisans' ability to access affordable quality healthcare, one that began in the 1950s as the city desegregated its hospital facilities and ended in the mid-1980s as both public hospitals closed. The movement to save Homer G. Phillips Hospital—and, later, all of St. Louis's public hospitals—responded not only to local debates about municipal citizenship, deindustrialization, and privatization, but also to major national transitions in healthcare: the eradication of racial segregation and the demise of publicly funded hospitals in favor of the federally funded insurance programs of Medicare and Medicaid.[10]

This chapter takes seriously the mobilization of Black St. Louisans to preserve a healthcare institution that, for much of its forty-two-year history, provided much-needed but segregated care. Their fight was not one to preserve the medical "color line." Rather, their fight demonstrated the limits of desegregation and the power of economic forces combined with public policy that threatened to perpetuate racial health disparities after Jim Crow's demise. More importantly, this chapter calls attention to health as a terrain for political struggle, one that framed inequity in its starkest terms: life or death.

This local struggle can be denoted in three successive waves. The first arrived in the wake of St. Louis's ostensible desegregation of public facilities in 1955, as questions swirled around the continued viability of the formerly segregated hospital. The second occurred in the 1970s, as municipal leaders debated, planned, and ultimately consolidated in-patient services at Max Starkloff Hospital. Both activists and city leaders mobilized economic language—the city blamed its financial situation for the move to consolidate, while activists largely demonstrated concern for the poor and working classes, emphasizing economic need over racial identity. Finally, the third wave occurred in the face of Homer G.'s closure, as Black citizens worked not only to reopen Homer G. but did so using the language of health planning and health rights. These activists proposed their own municipal health plan and a radical vision for the future of public health in St. Louis.

Activists' efforts ultimately failed in the 1980s. Though unsuccessful, activists deployed their "Black radical imagination"—that is, the radical "desires, hopes, and intentions of the people" who dared to think beyond the realm of possibility, as historian Robin D. G. Kelley described it in *Freedom Dreams: The Black Radical Imagination* (2003).[11] There, Kelley argued that "the desires, hopes, and intentions of the people who fought for change cannot be easily categorized, contained, or explained."[12] Whether or not these activists achieved their goal to save Homer G. Phillips Hospital, it is important to understand their motivations in historical context. From this perspective, centering the work and vision of grassroots activists, it is evident that their understanding of the hospital consolidation plan differed significantly from that of municipal leaders. That understanding reveals two competing visions of municipal healthcare, with competing priorities promoted by those in power and by activists who envisioned healthcare as a human right. Amid a national transition from segregated to desegregated and increasingly privatized care, these activists forcibly inserted their own perspectives and demands to shape the future of public hospital care in St. Louis, ultimately reshaping municipal politics. By the 1980s, Black St. Louisans were no longer marginal actors in the municipal decision-making process. Rather, they became active participants.

"A Haunting Refrain": Black St. Louisans Respond to Rumors of Hospital Consolidation in the 1960s

The 1960s marked major transformations in American healthcare. Hospital utilization declined as patient stays shortened. Public health reformers began to emphasize primary and preventative services over more expensive hospital care. At the same time, operational and healthcare service costs began to rise. Cities like St. Louis, competing with suburbs for residential taxpayers, struggled to manage and finance increasingly complicated and expensive public hospitals as they had in the past.

Meanwhile, American healthcare largely desegregated across racial lines following the 1963 *Simkins v. Moses H. Cone Memorial Hospital* US Fourth Circuit Court of Appeals case and the 1964 Civil Rights Act. While *Simkins* overturned racial segregation in public hospitals and Title VI of the Civil Rights Act legislated hospital desegregation, the Social Security Act of 1965 and the newly created Medicare program served as the enforcement mechanism.[13] To receive funds for Medicare services, hospitals were required to comply with the Civil Rights Act by desegregating hospital wards.

But the transformation to desegregated care raised new challenges for formerly segregated *and* public hospitals. Medicare funding promoted rapid racial integration, but also expanded where Medicare and, later, Medicaid

recipients could receive care. Public hospitals could no longer serve a captive pool of poor and minority patients. Instead, these hospitals competed
with their private counterparts. While public hospitals struggled to generate revenue in the new economy of healthcare, private hospitals thrived
under the new financing structures. Homer G.'s continued operation sat at
the intersection of these twin crises, and, in the 1960s, it was increasingly
evident that the hospital's future was precarious.

In St. Louis, both hospital desegregation and municipal economic anxieties provided a powerful rationale to "get out of the hospital business."[14]
Because Homer G. was funded by the city, it was the victim of political
whims of successive mayoral administrations. Rumors of Homer G.'s closure
circulated long before the 1960s. One Saint Louis University administrator
described the dilemma as "a haunting refrain thru the years, precipitated
yearly by the [city] budget hearings."[15] Though this "haunting refrain" re-
surged throughout Homer G.'s somewhat troubled existence, by the 1960s
these rumors slowly crystallized as municipal leaders began exploring how
to effectively desegregate and divest from public healthcare.

Though hospital desegregation was mandated by federal law in the mid-
1960s, St. Louis desegregated its general hospitals in 1955 by the order of
Mayor Raymond Tucker, a Democrat who served three terms from 1953
to 1965. Starkloff and Phillips shifted from race-based admissions policies to residency policies. Because the city had yet to rectify its history of
residential segregation even after the US Supreme Court's 1948 *Shelley v.
Kraemer* decision, which deemed racially restrictive covenants in housing
deeds to be unenforceable in the courts, the two hospitals remained de facto segregated.

As the city struggled to maintain its two public hospitals, African
Americans resisted. They acknowledged that the municipal hospital system
was created by the city's early-twentieth-century embrace of racial segregation. Yet, Homer G. continued to provide much-needed services for African
American working and poor people concentrated in North St. Louis. An
exasperated Dr. Walter Younge, Associate Director of the Department of
Internal Medicine at Homer G., expressed his anger to the *Cleveland Call
and Post*: "You don't tear down an institution just to prove that you're integrated."[16] Black St. Louisans articulated the hospital's multiple roles in the
community beyond health functions. It was a large employer; it attracted
visitors and their money, supporting the local economy; and it was a means
by which residents engaged with municipal governance and politics. In

their eyes, Homer G. and all public hospitals continued to fulfill multiple vital roles in their communities.

Initial rumblings of the hospital's closure can be traced to 1961, though they reached their peak between 1963 and 1964. That year, the Board of Aldermen excluded Homer G. from the city's official budget. Reacting to public outcries, the board proposed an inquiry into both municipal hospitals. Endorsed by representatives from Washington University and Saint Louis University medical schools, the Aldermanic report favored consolidating the two municipal hospitals.[17]

Mayor Raymond Tucker tacitly supported the board's conclusion. In a 1963 memo, the dean of the Washington University School of Medicine, Dr. Carl V. Moore, wrote, "after considerable discussion in which the Mayor repeatedly stated that he was in favor of combining the two hospitals ... he asked Dr. Gilmore ... to come up with specific recommendations."[18] Local university administrators advised municipal leaders behind closed doors, though "took no side" publicly.[19] Privately, however, both St. Louis medical schools supported the merger—the deans of both medical schools served on various committees and commissions between the 1960s and 1970s that recommended hospital consolidation.

According to a summary of St. Louis hospital studies up to 1964 written by Director of Health and Hospitals Dr. Herbert Donke, the first inquiries began in the early 1950s.[20] In each case, hospital inquiries were prompted by reports of inefficiency, budgetary, and staffing concerns. As Donke's summary noted, "the question of 'must there be two hospitals when it is hard to staff one?'" was a perennial interrogative.[21] It is evident that the quick and quiet demise of racial segregation in healthcare at the local and national levels generated a sort of historical amnesia among health planners and municipal leaders. In fact, St. Louis's history of segregated healthcare was rarely, if ever, cited in municipal plans to explain *why* the city maintained two general hospitals.

Reacting to the Aldermanic inquiry and swirling rumors of hospital closure, the Homer G. Phillips Hospital Interne Alumni Association, an international physicians' organization of Homer G.'s internship and residency alumni, held an emergency meeting in October of 1964.[22] They told the St. Louis press that there was a "hidden effort" to close the hospital.[23] In addition, they declared, "We have authentic evidence that there have been at least three meetings between representatives of the mayor's office and heads of both universities regarding the future of Phillips."[24] The alumni association condemned the consolidation effort and went as far as to say that city administrators were conducting a smear campaign against the hospital. Dr. James Aldrich, President of the National Medical Association (the African American counterpart to the segregated American Medical Association) from 1960 to 1961 and member of the St. Louis Mound City Medical Forum (the local subsidiary of the National Medical Association and counterpart to the white St. Louis Medical Society) joined forces with the Homer G. Phillips Hospital Interne Alumni Association, appointing a Citizens' Committee to study the city's plan. Dr. James Whittico, Homer G. general surgeon and former intern and resident, was appointed chairman of that committee. It planned to "go into the community" and "arouse" it about the proposal.[25]

News of these closed-door meetings spread through the African American community, promulgated in part by Black doctors and the local press. Though no official plan had yet been publicly discussed or implemented, the mere specter of Homer G.'s closure catalyzed community mobilization. A flurry of letters and petitions from African American community members, citizens' committees, neighborhood blocks, civic organizations, and religious-affiliated auxiliaries flooded the mayor's office.

Nearly two hundred signed petition form-letters were also sent. Each letter began, "We view with horror the proposal to close Homer G. Phillips Hospital. We ask that instead, two new hospitals be added for the west end of St. Louis. We ask also that the St. Louis Citizens be treated at the hospitals according to their needs and their rights instead of with contempt."[26] The letter described how the deteriorating conditions of both public hospitals led to a pervasive problem of indigent St. Louisans avoiding care. The letter ended with a call to the people: "our rights are going to be taken from us by scheming politicians. Everyone protest the closing of Homer G. Phillips Hospital before it is too late. . . . We must keep our hospital."[27]

The specter of hospital consolidation was understood as a ploy to close Homer G. and therefore an infringement upon Black St. Louisan's rights to affordable quality healthcare and ultimately the right to a healthy life. While the US does not guarantee citizens the right to healthcare, the St. Louis City Charter mandated the provision of healthcare for the indigent.[28] At this time the language of "health rights" began to emerge nationally, coinciding with much broader movements for racial, women's, and LGBT equality. This letter, however, did not just refer to the right to healthcare; it referred also to other rights of Black and working people in the city that had been trampled. For example, the letter compared the threat to Homer G. with the fate of Mill Creek Valley, a downtown neighborhood with high concentrations of African American and poor residents that was destroyed in the late 1950s as one of the nation's largest urban renewal projects.[29]

African Americans also demanded an expansion of St. Louis's public hospital system rather than the contraction that hospital consolidation promised. Additionally, they demanded that these hospitals provide better service, and to not be treated with contempt, as comedian Dick Gregory had. Gregory, who grew up in St. Louis, wrote of Homer G. in his first autobiography, *Nigger* (1964).[30] Gregory described an episode where a physician slapped him while he was waiting to be treated. This story was repeated in his subsequent autobiographies, though Gregory's perspective evolved from one of resentment to championing the cause to save the hospital.

By the mid-1960s, both city hospitals were severely underutilized, understaffed, and underfunded, prompting some to ask why the rumored consolidation plan focused on closing Homer G. The Baptist Pastors Council of St. Louis wrote a letter to the mayor, stating, "we are in a quandary, why no thought has been publicly advanced to merge City Hospital #1 [Starkloff] into Homer G. Phillips Hospital since the indigent population has apparently shifted westward."[31] Homer G. advocates argued that the hospital was desperately needed and asked why an alternative plan could not be advanced to preserve the institution that continued to carry the burden of indigent care.

One letter from the Les Bonnes Amiee Study Club highlighted how Homer G.'s closing would not only impact the community but also those who trained and worked at the facility. They collectively wrote, "because of the Negro physicians, nurses, and others who would be greatly disturbed by the merger of Homer G. Phillips and City Hospital No. 1 [Starkloff] we ask you to give them consideration."[32] Homer G. had long been a training ground for health professionals who, because of racially segregated education and training, faced limited career opportunities. While many positions began to open for Black health professionals in the 1950s into the 1960s, some were still off-limits. The American Medical Association, for example, did not bar racial discrimination policies for membership until 1968.[33]

A Homer G. laundry room attendant named George Harvey wrote a poignant letter to the mayor outlining continuing inequities between the two municipal hospitals, even as some services were already consolidated. He began, "My dear Mayor Tucker, as a citizen of St. Louis, I want to express my opposition to the controversial issue of the consolidation of Homer G. Phillips Hospital with City Hospital #1 [Starkloff]." Harvey described how both laundry and mental health services were already consolidated. He noted that three hundred dirty diapers were sent from Homer G. to Starkloff's laundry,

> and instead of returning [the] same to Homer G. Phillips Hospital they received old, thread-worn diapers in their place. . . . [T]here can be no economy on life itself. The location and transportation involved are a great danger to the patient in need of medical care. . . . I have watched Homer G. Phillips grow from a 4-million-dollar institution to a 12 million dollar medical center. This is a community-civic issue, not racial nor partisan. . . . it is purely of the basis of community service and preservation of life itself, receiving medical care and services.[34]

In these letters, citizens appealed to the mayor as the city's chief public health officer, while also affirming their own municipal citizenship and right to care. Within the body of many handwritten protest letters, African Americans proudly included their addresses. Citizens' correspondence articulated deeper connections to the hospital—that is, that access to it was not a privilege. It was a guaranteed right. Taking the hospital away, as perceived by Black St. Louisans and articulated in the form protest letter above, would be an infringement on their rights as defined by the city.

Responding to the more than two hundred protest letters, Assistant to the Mayor Robert Osborne wrote, "The City administration will certainly not support any proposals for major changes in our present hospital system unless such proposals have been carefully and thoroughly studied and found to be sound."[35] Both local private medical schools and the city administration equivocated in the face of Black resistance, privately advancing consolidation efforts while publicly advocating the status quo. They embraced emerging health planning efforts to maximize operational efficiency while minimizing costs. At this initial stage, however, the nascent plans for municipal hospital consolidation lacked transparency, fueling rumors and fears about Homer G.'s impending closure. To those community activists following the story in the local press and in Board of Aldermen hearings, this equivocation seemed duplicitous.

African American St. Louisans were not wholly unified in their response to these rumors. To some, the hospital represented a time that had since passed, one of substandard but purportedly equitable separate institutions. These individuals pointed to the declining quality of healthcare, the rise of emergency care due to crime-related violence, the flight of African American health workers to expanding opportunities, and an increasingly dilapidated and insect-ridden physical infrastructure. Amid the growing tension between African American citizens and city leaders, Black St. Louisans disagreed amongst themselves about the hospital's future in the age of desegregation. As one NAACP official, Ernest Calloway, stated in *Jet* magazine, "giving up the hospital may be the price we have to pay for an integrated community."[36]

As the medical "color line" began to disappear in the 1960s, it was accompanied by growing municipal fiscal concerns as cities struggled to finance and operate public general hospitals. Homer G. stood at the intersection of these twin crises, though racial segregation largely framed Black St. Louisans' 1960s response. Homer G. was a social, economic, and political institution, the "crown jewel" of Black St. Louis, a pillar that supported the endeavors of the community. Amid these rumors, Black St. Louisans had to make a difficult choice—lose the institution in service of desegregation or maintain the institution to address continuing need.

The burgeoning fight to save Homer G. was easily incorporated into the decade's broad movements for social, economic, and political justice. More than a fight to preserve an important institution, this emerging struggle to save Homer G. became a battle for the right to healthcare, economic opportunities, the survival of urban communities, and, above all else, the survival of Black St. Louis. As Mr. Harvey described in the letter quoted above, it was ultimately a fight for the "preservation of life itself."

"Save Homer G. and All Public Hospitals" in the Desegregated 1970s
In the 1970s, St. Louis's "urban crisis" worsened as economic anxieties increased, taxpayers flocked to growing metropolitan suburbs, economic opportunities dwindled, and crime increased.[37] African American community leaders and grassroots activists coalesced into a vigorous campaign to "Save Homer G. Phillips." This slogan later expanded to include "and All Public Hospitals" as it became clear that the city was divesting from public healthcare altogether. Activists' efforts called attention to the unresolved legacy of racial segregation, its persisting consequences, and the eroding interest of local governments in the public good. They argued that city residents had

the right to public care—an overall resistance to the American healthcare system's ongoing privatization.

While the letter-writing campaign of the 1960s emphasized desegregation, local citizenship, and the local right to access care, the 1970s movement was framed in economic terms. Not only did city leaders blame the

Figure 12.4 Two unnamed young Homer G. supporters in August 1980, at a one-year commemoration of the hospital's closure, holding protest signs reading "Help! Save Homer G. Phillips" and "Priority Alert! Save Homer G. Phillip [sic] Hospital." *Photo by John Dengler for the* St. Louis Globe-Democrat, *from the collections of the St. Louis Mercantile Library at the University of Missouri–St. Louis*

municipal economy for its divestment from public hospitals, but also activists themselves criticized the city's economic framing while drawing upon their class status. They supported all public hospitals because they served poor and working-class people who still faced barriers to privatized care. Their choice to emphasize economic class also pointed to fractures within Black St. Louis as elites began to abandon the cause, while the movement became multiracial.

Throughout the 1970s, Homer G. received increasingly negative attention in the white St. Louis press. In October of 1972, for example, registered nurse Ussie Riley publicly resigned her position due to "poor medical care, unsanitary conditions and a 'rude, indifferent attitude to patients' by some doctors and nurses."[38] The publicity had a dual effect. It called attention to Nurse Riley's resignation while also highlighting the hospital's declining condition at a time when hospital funding was hotly debated among the city's Board of Aldermen and Board of Estimates and Apportionment.

A 1976 *Urban Health* article stated, "pressures to close Homer G. Phillips are not new, many Black St. Louisans agree. 'Homer G. Phillips has been closing virtually every year for the past 15 years.'"[39] Because the decision-making process was opaque,

Some Blacks in St. Louis express[ed] the opinion that recommendations to close Homer G. Phillips [were] a central part of an organized and deliberate move on the part of some forces in St. Louis to let the North side of the city fall into such a state of decay—a kind of benign neglect—that renovation is economically impossible. At such time, say some, the city would clear the area and develop it into the kind of setting which would attract Whites back into the city, but which would be priced beyond the reach of most Blacks.[40]

African American fears of a city-led conspiracy to drive them out were justified. Amid a robust urban renewal program and as the city planned to attract more residents, city officials consistently vowed to fix problems in African American communities while simultaneously exacerbating their structural roots. In 1975, city leaders employed the Team Four firm to produce an interim plan for the city. This plan proposed a policy of "depletion," a type of "benign neglect" by which municipal services and investments were cut off from communities deemed too far gone from any possible recuperation.[41] In essence, the plan proposed to isolate inner-city "ghettos" from necessary services so that they would collapse upon themselves.[42] The plan was never adopted, but it was published for review. The city's plan to close Homer G. was seen by many as yet another thread in overall attempts to divest from poor communities.

Homer G.'s closure was not inevitable—alternative plans were proposed by political leaders and community members—but by 1977 city leaders had become convinced that the only way to modernize public hospitals was to close them. After years of studies from outside experts, university administrators, and political leaders with limited community involvement and transparency, Mayor James Conway proposed a plan for "progress" and public healthcare modernization. James Conway was a businessman-turned-Democratic-politician who served as a Missouri state representative and senator from 1966 to 1977. Known as a reformer committed to revitalizing St. Louis, he served one term as mayor from 1977 to 1981.[43] Mayor Conway's 1977 consolidation plan would be deployed in three phases: Homer G.'s in-patient services would be combined with Starkloff's; the city would construct a new not-for-profit hospital that would coordinate with a network of federal and municipal community health clinics; and, finally, the city would close any remaining public hospitals.

The lack of transparency, combined with neglected acknowledgment of the legacies of segregation now entrenched within the city's public health system, fueled the animosity African American voters felt toward Conway, a white mayor. While the city expressed the economic need to divest from public healthcare, it implemented a vast downtown revitalization plan that same year.[44] Working-class African Americans perceived the city's health plan as one that did not prioritize their health needs.

Responding to the 1977 consolidation plan, coalitions between new and existing civil rights organizations were formed to protect the hospital. A unified group of clergy summoned the Southern Christian Leadership Conference (SCLC) to address the hospital closure as a civil rights issue.[45] Established groups including the Communist Party, union and labor organizations, the NAACP, the Urban League, and others from across the political spectrum agreed that the hospital's closing would be detrimental to the Black community's health.

A new organization, created by Homer G. allied health professionals, rose to prominence, the Ad Hoc Committee to Save Homer G. Phillips and

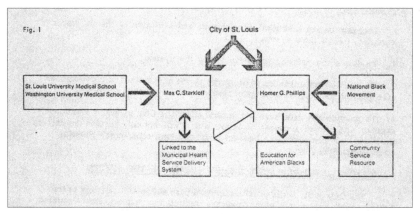

Figure 12.5 Diagram from the 1976 Pesch and Smith Report, a precursor to Mayor Conway's 1977 Hospital Consolidation Plan. This depicts how city leaders and hospital planners envisioned St. Louis's two public general hospitals and their integration into public health infrastructure. Notice how Homer G. is described—"National Black Movement, Community Resource, and Education for American Blacks"—while Starkloff is described by its university affiliation. *From LeRoy A. Pesch and Symuel H. Smith,* Report of the Study on Hospital Needs under the Jurisdiction of the City of St. Louis *(St. Louis: City Board of Estimates and Apportionment, 1976), 6.*

All Public Hospitals. The Committee described its purpose in three parts: "To utilize every legal and political means necessary and at our command to maintain Homer G. Phillips . . . To encourage by every legal and political means available to us improvements in the quality of healthcare for all poor people . . . to call upon the city, the state, and the federal government to increase and expand medical services."[46] Though nurse Zenobia Thompson did not establish the organization, she was quickly recognized among the movement's most visible leaders. In her eyes, this issue expanded beyond Homer G. to the plight of healthcare in urban America. She was aware of the larger transitions taking place, leaving inner cities, the poor, and African Americans specifically without hospital services. According to the *Journal of the American Hospital Association,* as cited in a *New York Times* article on the subject, more than two hundred hospitals had closed across the nation between 1975 and 1977.[47] Many of these were in the "inner city." Even as public hospitals were shutting their doors, the national crisis coincided with growing articulations of health as a human right.[48] Thompson, along with organizers Walle Amusa and Frank Chapman, later broke from the organization to form the more politically involved Campaign for Human Dignity,

350

which further linked the hospital debate to broad political discourses on labor organizing, as well as revolutionary liberation efforts informed by the multiracial local branch of the Communist Party.[49]

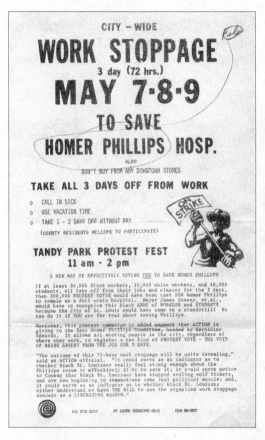

Figure 12.6 A 1979 flyer promoting a three-day "City-Wide Work Stoppage" to save Homer G. Phillips Hospital. Responding to the economic language mobilized by city leaders to justify Homer G.'s closure, activists employed an economic strategy of disruption to focus attention on the hospital issue. *From the James F. Conway Mayoral Records, Department of Special Collections, Washington University in St. Louis*

Supporters of Homer G. employed economic forms of protest, from shopping boycotts to work stoppages (Fig. 12.6), to demonstrate their opposition. One such campaign was a 1979 Christmas shopping boycott of the revitalized downtown district.[50] "Black St. Louisans," one protest flyer advocated, "either understand or have THE WILL to use the organized work stoppage concept as a LIBERATING WEAPON."[51] Commenting on the shopping boycott, Thompson stated, "We hate to hurt the small businessman but Conway is killing us."[52] Activists attempted to disrupt St. Louis's local economy, which civic elites had prioritized over the needs of poor and working people. A protest flyer from the Ad Hoc Committee outlined the situation: "We must come together—church, labor, and civil groups to save not only Homer G. Phillips and all public hospitals, but our constitutional right to live a decent and safe life."[53] Singing "We Shall Overcome," activists held a three-day City Hall sit-in. More than forty people were forcibly removed by police on resistance stretchers (Fig. 12.7). As they were removed, activists told reporters, "We will come back again and if necessary, close every city office to save Homer Phillips."[54] One activist threw a vial of blood on Mayor Conway's office door, leaving a note charging, "You have blood on your hands Jim."[55]

Figure 12.7 Activists occupying the offices of Mayor James Conway in City Hall on January 31, 1979, peacefully resist orders from St. Louis police to leave. They are carried out on passive-resistance stretchers. *Photo by Bob Moore for the* St. Louis Globe-Democrat, *from the collections of the St. Louis Mercantile Library at the University of Missouri–St. Louis*

Handwritten and typed letters along with numerous signed petitions also flooded Conway's office. These letters affirmed African American municipal citizenship and voting status. Citizens also wrote to their state and national representatives. The mayor often responded to the correspondence, politely conveying that writers were "misinformed" or "uninformed" about the hospital issue. The city appreciated the hospital as an economic and managerial problem. Black St. Louisans, on the other hand, appreciated it as a *survival* issue.

Alderman Freeman Bosley Sr., whose son would later serve as the city's first African American mayor (1993–1997), said, "the mayor is playing 'Russian Roulette' with the lives of a quarter million North St. Louis residents and he has to be stopped."[56] In Bosley's estimation, as the *St. Louis Argus* reported, "it will be a 'long, hot summer' if the hospital is consolidated, hinting at the possibility of street violence."[57] Bosley later alluded to the city's lack of transparency as he walked back his more extreme comments. He called for a biracial boycott of Starkloff Hospital, the historically white public hospital. He told reporters, "The purpose of the boycott organized by the People Organized to Win, POW, is to detour all the traffic of 'warm bodies and money' to a hospital anywhere else in the St. Louis Metropolitan area." Bosley's proposed boycott was a biracial effort including "groups such as ACTION, Elks, [and] Masons, . . . working toward the same purpose."[58] Like the work stoppages and boycotts, Bosley's attempt to divert "warm bodies" from Starkloff was also an economic protest. Diverting patients away from the municipal hospital meant diverting *money* away from the hospital.

With the help of prominent comedian Dick Gregory, Homer G. supporters achieved local, state, and national visibility. Gregory took an active role in the 1970s hospital movement, even drafting a letter to the Vatican petitioning the Pope to intervene. Gregory's previous autobiography, *Nigger*, had criticized Homer G.'s poor condition.[59] In a later autobiography, *Callus on My Soul* (2000), Gregory wrote, "the Hospital was a place where I had been treated badly as a child . . . but it took me all those years to understand what that hospital really stood for . . . what I failed to appreciate at the time was that Homer G. Phillips had some of the best doctors in the country, and definitely the best internship program."[60] Dick Gregory brought the struggle to save Homer G. to national and international attention, promoting boycotts of prominent St. Louis businesses, including brewing company Anheuser-Busch. These businesses were members of Civic Progress, a business organization formed in the 1950s by Mayor Joseph Darst to promote civic improvement and urban renewal.[61] Since then, the shadowy organization came to be associated with wealth and whiteness and antagonism to the concerns of Black St. Louisans.

Both state and federal governments responded to the mobilizations, amounting to failed bill proposals in the Missouri State Senate and in the United States House of Representatives. From the grassroots to national political bodies, Homer G. represented persistent racial discrimination and threats to Black survival. Responding to the protests, including a march from St. Louis to Jefferson City, state senator J. B. "Jet" Banks proposed Missouri

State Senate Bill No. 788, stating, "no person shall be denied services be-cause of inability to pay."[62] Banks further argued in a letter to colleagues, "because of the potential explosiveness of the situation, I ask that you use the power of your offices to withhold all . . . healthcare monies, from the City of St. Louis Department of Health and Hospitals, until the proposed . . . Consolidation Plans are submitted."[63] Responding to Homer G. protests among many others across the nation, US Representative Cardiss Collins, an Illinois Democrat, proposed an amendment to the 1965 Social Security Act to replace rapidly disappearing urban hospitals in many underserved communities.[64]

As the city moved to implement its plan, activists critiqued city leaders and deployed their "radical imagination" to envision the future of public health in St. Louis. Frank Chapman addressed the Ad Hoc Committee, saying, "So this is how the stage was set; those who wanted Phillips to close were for progress and those who wanted to keep it open were opposed to progress."[65] He continued,

> Mayor Conway's Health System Task Force does not give a scientific analysis of St. Louis' health problems in order to arrive at real solutions but to the contrary, they give us a politically contrived document that rationalizes what amounts to a plan of genocide dressed up and coded with euphemisms about progress. . . . Everybody knows that Homer G. has been an institutional anchor to the Northside Black Community, so in a very real sense to close Homer G. was to pass a death sentence on our community.[66]

Chapman among others saw the future of African Americans inextricably linked to the fate of this hospital. On the other hand, city leaders argued that the only way to modernize the St. Louis healthcare system was to shut the hospital down.

Not everyone in the African American community, however, ardently supported the hospital. In the age of desegregation, this seemingly unified constituency fractured across class lines: while the middle class could access new integrated opportunities, the working class could not. Organizers crit-icized the local NAACP for being too mild in its approach to the debate.[67] Congressman William Clay similarly attacked city religious leaders for not being more vocal.[68] The Black working class saw the hospital as a critical component to Black self-sufficiency and empowerment, ideals championed in the waning Black Power movement.

Days before Homer G. officially closed, leading grassroots activist Zenobia Thompson was knocked unconscious and forcibly arrested by two security guards after informing floor supervisors and Ad Hoc Committee representatives that the city was planning to take the hospital by surprise.[69] This effort, though thwarted by Thompson's actions, took place while many of the hospital's doctors were away at the annual meeting of the National Medical Association.

The city successfully closed the hospital on August 17, 1979. According to the *St. Louis Argus*, "the scene was reminiscent of 1960s protests as more than 100 people threw together an impromptu demonstration, successfully stalling an attempt to move equipment and furniture out of Phillips . . . to City [Hospital] . . . Throughout the morning [one protestor] moved from one side of the gate to the other, slowly and with dignity, telling all who would listen of how much the hospital meant to him."[70] The activists cried that, "Mayor Conway [h]as declared WAR on the North side and the Blacks in St. Louis. Either we STAND TOGETHER TODAY on this issue or we PERISH ALONE TOMORROW . . . as we did together in the 60s, make the commitment NOW and come be with us on the hospital grounds."[71]

Those who came to support Homer G. told reporters of the institution's importance to the community. One activist noted, "these people have saved my life again and again. I'd do anything, and I will be here as long as it takes. They won't close this hospital around me."[72] Another woman commented to a reporter, "all my children were born here, . . . I have eight children, you see them here with me. I will stay as long as it takes even if it's just me and these pictures. I was here when the vans came first and here I'll stay."[73] Reporters of the *St. Louis Argus,* the oldest African American newspaper in St. Louis and owned by former Homer G. medical director Dr. Eugene Mitchell, documented the day's organizing efforts. They wrote, "hundreds of employees and patients gazed from every window shouting support to the milling group below."[74]

The city's position was remarkably different. The Director of Health and Hospitals, Dr. R. Dean Wochner, noted to the *New York Times,* "the change at Homer G. Phillips Hospital is an effort to restructure our system to provide better healthcare for the 1980s. . . . Some people still think of health care as hospital care. . . . That's not correct. Today health care has got to be considered as a whole health system that addresses ambulatory, emergency, preventative care, mental and dental and longterm care, as well as hospitals. All over this country there are efforts to develop this kind of system."[75] Though St. Louis began the restructuring process, activists noted that such a vision could be achieved while Homer G. remained open. Homer G. was more than a health facility and the consequences of its closure would extend well beyond the realm of health.

Frank Chapman addressed protestors on closing day. "See, they [are] hitting us two ways," he said; "they are hitting us with a depression on one end and they are closing down our communities on the other end."[76] To Chapman and many other demonstrators, Homer G.'s closure was yet another instance in a long history of the city's divestment from Black communities, perpetuating and even exacerbating health, economic, and social disparities.

Working-class African Americans linked their survival, as a community, to the fate of the hospital. Chapman's comments went far beyond the health impacts of Homer G.'s closure. Losing the hospital had dire economic consequences for North St. Louis. According to civil rights lawyer and journalist Roger Wilkins, writing in 1979, "In the early sixties, black hospitals reported 75 percent more revenue and employed 200 percent more people than the 100 top black business firms in the country." Wilkins continued, "The hospitals that have replaced those removed from black communities have not usually placed blacks on the boards nor have they placed blacks in planning positions. In the entire country, there are only two black administrators of hospitals where the patient population is less than 50 percent black."[77] Homer G. was not only a social and medical anchor in the Ville, but it was also an economic anchor, "holding it together and providing employment for several hundred residents of the area."[78] Amid the urban crisis which hit North St. Louis particularly hard with Black unemployment, positions for janitors, cooks, and allied health personnel were crucial. With Homer G.'s closure, more than a thousand municipal jobs were lost or transferred.

"Reopen Homer G. Phillips Hospital": Working-Class Health and Political Activism in the 1980s

Activists' efforts to save Homer G. Phillips Hospital ultimately failed. But working-class Black St. Louisans did not stop demanding that the city provide access to quality and affordable healthcare. They shifted to a "Reopen Homer G. Phillips" campaign, transforming the community's grief into political action. This political issue ousted Mayor Conway and elevated a new mayor, Vincent Schoemehl. Activists sued in the courts, claiming that the hospital's closure was discriminatory. They radically reimagined the future of public hospital care in St. Louis and proposed an alternative vision to that of city leaders where Homer G. Phillips Hospital would again be fully functional.

Closing Homer G. had an immediate impact on Black St. Louisans' health and wellbeing. The Campaign for Human Dignity highlighted the consequences in a circulating pamphlet. It described a particularly egregious case: "It's now over a year since Homer G. Phillips Hospital was closed. Many people have died and many more are suffering. Recently a poor man Theotis Little was denied medical attention and turned away from Barnes Hospital with a steak knife in his back. Such repugnant and horrifying incidents are incredible. Mayor Conway must be held totally responsible. Homer G. Phillips Hospital must be reopened."[79] Though sensational, pamphlets like this generated by grassroots organizations made the case that Homer G. and other public hospitals remained necessary.

Even as public health reformers were beginning to embrace the principles of community-based primary and preventative care, institutions like Homer G. which had long histories of operating in this way were disregarded. Many of the Ville's aging African American population used the hospital as a "doctor substitute," using the hospital for primary care services.[80] They aimed to reduce the use of expensive hospital care in favor of primary care. Frank Chapman framed Homer G.'s closure as a threat to the future of Black St. Louisans and a form of racial genocide. A 1980 flyer circulated by the Ad Hoc Committee stated, "by his order, [Mayor James Conway] perpetuated the high crime of genocide against the Black Community" (Fig. 12.8).[81]

As stories of inequitable treatment at desegregated private hospitals spread, Homer G.'s defunct building sat as a visible scar in the Ville. It was a reminder not only of the community's loss, but of divestment from minority communities and a representation of the city's long-strained relationship with its Black citizens. The Campaign for Human Dignity, led by chemist and community organizer Walle Amusa, kept the pressure on the mayor.[82] The organization held a mock funeral procession from the grave of attorney Homer G. Phillips, the hospital's namesake assassinated in 1931.[83]

Activists pressured the city administration to reopen the hospital immediately after Homer G.'s services were terminated. African Americans did not simply respond to Homer G.'s closure with direct action. They took their fight to the courts. The activists were armed with attorney William Russell, who rose to local acclaim after he and his law partner Joseph McDuffie fought for school desegregation.[84] Immediately, the Campaign for Human

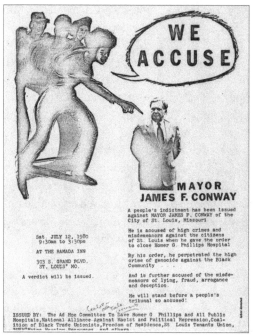

Figure 12.8 "We Accuse," a July 1980 protest poster by the Ad Hoc Committee to Save Homer G. Phillips and All Public Hospitals, proposes "a people's indictment" of Mayor Conway for racial genocide. *From the UMSL Black History Project Collection (S0201), State Historical Society of Missouri*

Dignity tried unsuccessfully to enjoin the hospital consolidation effort and to prevent the city from removing any further equipment.[85] In 1980, a district court judge refused to administer the injunction against consolidation since consolidation had already been achieved.[86]

In 1979, activists claimed that the city's hospital consolidation efforts were discriminatory.[87] The claim had to be investigated by the Department of Health, Education and Welfare's (HEW) Office for Civil Rights, the federal organization charged with investigating discrimination claims in healthcare.[88] Activists alleged that Homer G.'s closure violated Title VI of the Civil Rights Act of 1964 and unfairly discriminated against poor Black North Side residents.[89] This followed a 1966 complaint that the City of St. Louis violated federal law because it did not desegregate its two public hospitals quickly enough.

The seemingly paradoxical nature of the two complaints reveals the deep complexities surrounding the demise of segregated healthcare and its persisting structural consequences. Though such issues were intimately understood and experienced by working-class African Americans, city leaders were confused. Mayor Conway noted the irony in his letters to HEW officials, yet the department concluded that "The St. Louis Department of

Health and Hospitals is in violation of Title VI of the Civil Rights Act of 1964 because it has . . . continued and exacerbated the historic discrimination against Blacks by its failure to take the necessary affirmative actions in connection with its 1966 violation of Title VI."[90]

While activists' complaints proceeded in the background, slowly moving through federal bureaucracy and federal courts, the city was preparing for a 1981 Democratic mayoral primary between incumbent James Conway and an upstart candidate, alderman Vincent Schoemehl. Mayor Conway's decision to close Homer G. doomed his local political career. A young voter put it this way in her 1980 letter to the mayor: "Dear Mr. Conway, I am sure that you would like to continue being the mayor of St. Louis, Missouri, but I hope you're not re-elected if you must keep our hospital closed. I and many more people would like for you to reopen the Homer G. Phillips hospital."[91] The primary was widely seen as a referendum on Conway's move to close the hospital.[92] A significant turn-out of Black voters supported Vincent Schoemehl, who promised to reopen Homer G.[93] In April 1981, Schoemehl, at age 34, became the youngest mayor in recent St. Louis history.

An interfaith coalition initiated a petition campaign to put Homer G.'s reopening to a popular vote, garnering signatures from more than 15,000 registered St. Louis City voters.[94] The proposed charter amendment appeared on the January 1981 ballot alongside the Democratic primary for mayor. One newspaper reported, "The race for mayor will probably be a close one, and Alderman Vincent Schoemehl has taken this into account in his campaign. This week, in the wake of the success of the petition drive to revive the Homer G. Phillips Hospital issue, candidate Schoemehl advocated 're-consolidating' the two city hospitals . . . and putting Phillips back into full service."[95] The proposition almost passed. Though the proposition needed to be approved by 60 percent of voters, it received only 56 percent.[96] This failed proposition added to a growing list of activists' failures to save the hospital, but it had a more important impact. African Americans, particularly those who were poor and working-class, exerted both economic and political force to prioritize their demands. With the election of Vincent Schoemehl, based in part on this hospital issue, activists increasingly brought the political demands of African Americans to the front of St. Louis municipal politics.

Newly elected mayor Schoemehl felt the growing pressure of Black St. Louisans, a sizable proportion of the city's electorate and of his new constituents. In February of 1982, organizers criticized the mayor's inaction on the hospital issue: "Mayor Vincent Schoemehl Jr. has softened his original stand on the re-opening of Homer G. Phillips Hospital by saying he will await the outcome of a special study."[97]

Mayor Schoemehl had consistently supported reopening the hospital since his candidacy, but he asserted that Homer G. could never open from a municipal general-revenue account.[98] Doing so would once again add stress to the city's already challenging economic position. In April of 1982, Mayor Schoemehl detailed his new health plan, which included an operational Homer G., but the plan hinged on voter approval of a $60 million bond to improve the hospital's facilities.[99] Additionally, the plan appointed a nonprofit organization to manage hospital operations; clinical research and medical education would be eliminated; and a community-based board of directors would be established, ensuring that the reopened hospital would respond to community needs.[100]

Mayor Schoemehl gave the decision to reopen Homer G. Phillips Hospital to voters yet again. This plan elevated the voices of St. Louis voters—but the electorate was highly split. White voters on the city's South Side would not support using their tax dollars to reopen Homer G. Some African American voters, too, would not support the proposition. The plan also gave the mayor political cover. He would not make the final decision; voters would. The proposition was brought to St. Louis voters in November of 1982. Two-thirds of the votes cast were needed to pass the proposition, a tall order given that the city was highly divided racially and therefore highly divided on the issue of Homer G.'s reopening. The measure, almost expectedly, did not pass.[101]

Schoemehl soon found that his promise to undo the actions of his predecessor were easier said than done. Zenobia Thompson, still active with the Committee to Save Homer G. Phillips, told reporters, "Mayor Vincent Schoemehl, who promised to reopen Homer G. Phillips in six to nine months, has flip-flopped and abandoned his solemn campaign pledges to reopen Homer G. [Phillips] Hospital. As we observe this day, we renew our call to Mayor Vincent Schoemehl to put petty politics and excuses aside and fulfill the promises to those who are sick and dying in North St. Louis."[102]

The 1970s and 1980s movement to save Homer G. was a political primer and fueled greater activist efforts in St. Louis, including the 1970–1972 campaign to free scholar and activist Angela Davis from unjust imprisonment. This was especially true for Zenobia Thompson, whose activism eventually led her to join St. Louis's Communist Party. Davis, who spoke in St. Louis in the 1980s, used the Homer G. Phillips case in her speeches, stating, "under the Reagan administration, hospitals serving predominantly poor Black communities—including those with excellent trauma units, designed to treat victims of violence—were closed down. Such was the case with Homer G. Phillips Hospital in St. Louis, the largest teaching hospital for Black medical students in the country."[103]

As it became clear that Homer G. would not be revived, African Americans articulated visions of the future with and without the hospital. A protest poster authored by Black St. Louis artist Spencer Thornton Banks depicted in detail these two visions (Fig. 12.9). The poster's left side depicted the city's future vision of municipal healthcare as understood by activists. This possible future, in the minds of Homer G. supporters, was weighed down by "mire," "evil," and "political destruction" on the scales of justice. On the poster's right side, in contrast, an open Homer G. was accompanied by "faith" and "truth." Radiating with light, an open Homer G. was both a hopeful image for the future and the morally right choice. Like Frank

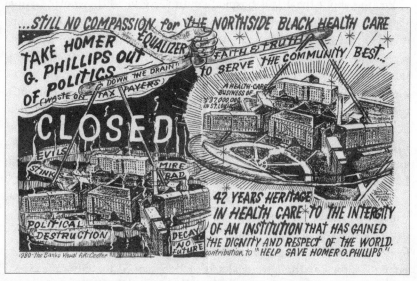

Figure 12.9 Save Homer G. Phillips poster, by St. Louis artist Spencer Thornton Banks. The 1980 illustration depicts two visions of Homer G.—one closed and one open—on a scale held by the "equalizer." *From the UMSL Black History Project Collection (S0201), State Historical Society of Missouri*

Chapman's speeches, Banks's art successfully juxtaposed these competing visions of progress for St. Louis's public healthcare infrastructure.

As local organizers became more familiar with the economic rationale behind the facility's closure, they proposed their own plans to keep hospital facilities in the city's North Side. Dr. Eugene Mitchell promoted his own plan to privatize the hospital, writing, "a recent study in St. Louis, for example, shows a steady declining Black doctor/patient ratio! . . . A plan which forever would end a division along racial lines in our town as we struggle together to plan our future."[104] Members of the Campaign for Human Dignity penned their own health plan for the city, one which also highlighted community involvement. This vision, proposed in an alternative People's Health Plan, provided that both municipal hospitals, the historically Black Homer G. and the historically white Max Starkloff Hospital, remain open to serve the city's poor and working-class populations. This plan argued that Homer G. could be maintained and operated with limited expense to the city. When that did not happen, and when health outcomes worsened on the city's North Side, African Americans remembered the closure of Homer G.

Writing about the 1970s hospital controversy in 1991, scholar George Lipsitz noted, "More than any other issue, the closing of Homer G. Phillips revealed that Black people and white people in St. Louis do not share the same understanding of the past, and as a result, they have different perceptions about the present and the future."[105] The struggle to reopen Homer G. hinged on divergent historical understandings; perhaps more importantly, these divergent histories generated dual visions for the future of public healthcare in St. Louis. As African Americans acknowledged, the struggle to keep Homer G. open was more than a concern over affordable healthcare access; it was also a fight for the survival of Black and working-class St. Louisans.

Though unsuccessful, the fight further demonstrated how African Americans used health as a terrain of political struggle. For nearly three decades, Black St. Louisans mobilized to save the institution, first in the face of hospital desegregation, then in the face of the city's divestment from public healthcare. Though racial segregation shaped the city's municipal healthcare infrastructure, by the 1970s African Americans joined with a multiracial coalition to save all public hospitals as a way of addressing the health needs of poor and working-class city residents. A new generation of activists, including Zenobia Thompson, Walle Amusa, and Frank

Chapman, utilized their "Black radical imagination" not only in terms of planning their resistance but also in imagining a new way to provide municipal healthcare. Though they failed, they ultimately forced their way into political and decision-making processes, marking Black St. Louisans as a powerful, vocal, and active constituency.

13. "Together We Can Make a Safe Home"

Space, Violence, and Lesbian Organizing in 1970s St. Louis

Mary Maxfield

THE WOMEN DO NOT REMEMBER the date, but they remember the scene: more than eighty concert-goers crammed into the Women's Building at Washington University in St. Louis for a performance by singer-songwriter Meg Christian. It would have been late 1978, perhaps early 1979, and Christian proved a substantial draw for feminists and lesbians in the area. One attendee, Margaret Flowing Johnson, described Christian as the crowd's "own traveling troubadour . . . a pixie like woman with a dimpled smile, powerful voice, and impressive guitar skills." Throughout the evening, Christian shifted from covers to original songs, including the fan favorite "Ode to a Gym Teacher." At the end of the concert, she covered "Fight Back," an anti-violence anthem written by fellow women's music icon Holly Near. Those in attendance "leapt to [their] feet and joined in the chorus— [their] voices filling the room."[1]

This moment relied upon a decade of lesbian organizing in St. Louis. The concert was hosted by Red Tomatoe Inc. (formerly Tomatoe Productions), a collective that produced cultural events for women, specifically lesbians. It was publicized in *Moonstorm*, the Lesbian Alliance magazine, which was printed by the Lesbian Alliance's in-house publishing imprint, Tiamat Press. Finally, it drew women from across and beyond the city, including members of the local lesbian collectives, volunteers from the feminist bookstore, and patrons of the women's bars.

The concert also inspired additional action. Invigorated by the call to "fight back! in large numbers," attendees felt further inspired to "[challenge] the oppressive conditions and [their] own acquiescence" to the status quo.[2] In the song's insistence that "together we can make a safe home," activists heard the possibility of eradicating violence against women, both within their individual homes and in their broader "home city" of St. Louis. For Johnson, that meant co-organizing the city's first Take Back the Night march, which was held a few months later on June 8, 1979. Along with fellow attendee Nan Cinnater, Johnson took the call to "fight back" literally, precipitating a one-thousand-woman march against battering and sexual violence that flooded the city's Central West End.

While memorable for many patrons, the Meg Christian concert is more representative than remarkable. Yet it effectively illustrates the networked approach of lesbian organizing in 1970s St. Louis. "Fight Back" encapsulates larger patterns of the era, both in its call to end violence against women and in its insistence on a collective response (that is, resisting in larger numbers rather than trying to do so alone). Indeed, the fact that Take Back the Night and other feminist anti-violence organizing emerged from within the lesbian community is neither incidental nor insignificant. Lesbians in St. Louis were well equipped to understand individual and systemic violence against women, in part because they were disproportionately targeted for such violence and in part because of their unusual location within city life. Unable safely to occupy public space, even to the extent of their white gay male counterparts, and unable safely to occupy their own homes, lesbian activists were especially aware of the ways that violence targets women in private and public spaces. As a result, they created hybrid spaces that simultaneously served public and domestic functions. The network of resources they built was always contested, yet they continued to maintain and expand resources in St. Louis for lesbians specifically, as well as for women at large.

At the same time, these mostly white activists and organizations struggled to cross racial barriers in this hypersegregated city and metropolitan region. Although many were committed to antiracist causes, building active and sustainable cross-racial coalitions proved difficult. Groups like the Lesbian Alliance remained majority-white throughout their operation, reflecting St. Louis's patterns of segregated interaction, as well as the racial dynamics of the larger lesbian-feminist and separatist movements during this period. Indeed, race and racism complicated the activism of these groups, particularly the anti-violence activism that defined much of their work. As lesbians, they experienced substantial violence, including harassment and surveillance by law enforcement. This experience conflicted with a dominant narrative that suggested police would "protect and serve" white women. Some white lesbians had contradictory relationships with police, whom they viewed as protective in certain instances and threatening in others. For other white lesbian activists, the same experiences led them to challenge, simultaneously, the patriarchal notion of women's need for male protection and the racist idea of Black men as inherently violent. Still, the intersections of racism and sexism—which influenced both the reality of "violence against women" and the discursive construction of that issue—remained difficult to challenge in practice. In considering these contradictions, this chapter pays critical attention to the concept of "public safety," building on work by Christina B. Hanhardt to contextualize the concept of LGBTQ "safe spaces" within broader public-safety initiatives influenced by progressive and conservative concepts of race, gender, and sexuality.[3]

More specifically, "Together We Can Make a Safe Home" examines how lesbian activists fought to take up space and challenge violence in 1970s St. Louis. It focuses primarily on organizing in St. Louis City's Shaw, Central West End, and Gravois Park areas, as well as University City's Delmar Loop and Clayton's DeMun neighborhood. Prior to gentrification, these areas drew organizers because they offered affordable housing near the local universities where leftist activism thrived. In its attention to these neighborhoods and the social landscapes developed within them, this chapter builds upon recent scholarship highlighting the spatial elements of movement building. In particular, "Together We Can Make a Safe Home" incorporates Finn Enke's assertion that spatial analyses can highlight the ways that activism exceeds identification. In other words, people participate in social movements without necessarily identifying as activists by, for instance, patronizing women's bookstores, attending feminist marches, or purchasing women's music. By analyzing these types of movement participation, Enke asserts, scholars can grapple more effectively with the true breadth of widespread movements.[4]

This chapter further argues that the cultural work undertaken within lesbian spaces—that is, the creation of periodicals, books, music, and so on—functions as a parallel space-making process. In this vein, the chapter draws on work by Kristen Hogan, Bonnie Morris, and other feminist scholars that examines cultural production by lesbians and feminists. As Hogan argues, physical sites such as bookstores become laboratories for creating new "relational practices."[5] And women's music recordings, Morris contends, created "a portable affirmation of self that had never before existed," transforming "a daily commute (or a trip across country, or just across town to visit homophobic relatives) into a personal lesbian concert space."[6] Reflecting those insights, this chapter argues that *material* spaces—while crucial components of movement building—also rely upon and facilitate the creation of *discursive* spaces, which often exceed and outlast material sites. Discursive spaces provide an alternative to material spaces when the latter are inaccessible or unsustainable. In a larger context in which women's spaces were often untenable, discursive spaces could maintain both individual spirits and network ties. Thus, a fuller understanding of lesbian and feminist history requires consideration of material and discursive spaces and of the networks forged on both planes.

Toward that end, this chapter highlights the work of the Lesbian Alliance, the lesbian bars managed by Muriel "Mac" McCann, and the first Take Back the Night march. Through oral histories and archival research, "Together We Can Make a Safe Home" unpacks how both physical and discursive spaces functioned to connect lesbians across the city, and argues that, while specific locations and organizations were often short-lived, the networks forged within them continued to operate long after the closings of doors. Although discrimination and violence limited lesbian access to space, St. Louis activists continued to "fight back," working together to remake the city into "a safe home," a room—and community—of their own.

Women's Houses: Lesbian Collectives in St. Louis

In the 1970s, the bulk of St. Louis's lesbian organizing took place within residential spaces, rented apartments and private homes that activists opened to other lesbians. These spaces served the same domestic purposes of heteronormative homes, providing shelter and intimate relationships. At the same time, they functioned as hubs for political conversation and planning. In this sense, women's houses served as both public and private spaces, respites from the larger city and meeting points from which activists might re-envision it.

Out lesbians in St. Louis founded at least four collectives, housed in private residences throughout the city. The city's first lesbian collective, the "Women's House," began in North County in the early 1970s, originating in a duplex on Plover Avenue, but quickly moving to a three-story house in the Central West End (4357 McPherson Avenue). Other collectives included July House (3540 Victor Street) south of Interstate 44, and two homes in the Shaw neighborhood, Cat House (3863 Botanical Avenue) and Thornapple House (3910 Botanical Avenue). Members of the collectives forged ties across the houses, maintaining romantic and sexual relationships and participating in political projects. Although some members valued a lesbian

368

separatist politics, the collectives also participated in a wider network of leftist organizing, working with other activists invested in fighting racism, capitalism, and the war in Vietnam.[7]

Figure 13.1 A July House event flyer, probably from the mid-1980s, gives a view into the social life maintained by the handful of lesbian collective houses founded in St. Louis City during the 1970s. *From the Laura Ann Moore Papers, Department of Special Collections, Washington University in St. Louis*

In fact, the Women's House was one of several leftist collectives located in the city during this period. Other group houses included the collective of Washington University activists who founded Left Bank Books, the collective that ran the independent radio station KDNA, and a collective recently returned from cutting cane in Cuba as part of the Venceremos Brigade, a leftist campaign to practice solidarity with Cuban revolutionaries and protest the US travel ban. However, the Women's House—as its name denotes—remained notable for its all-female population. The use of "women's" also necessarily coded the all-lesbian identity of the house. As former member Kris Kleindienst notes, the "Women's House" moniker simultaneously came from a feminist impulse to welcome all women and from a self-protective "fear of violence."[8]

Indeed, members of the Women's House and the other lesbian collectives experienced both individual and systemic violence. Collective member Clare Kinberg, then a student at Harris-Stowe State College, attended her student-teaching position with a black eye after being punched on a street corner. Barb Goedde, a former member of Cat House and Thornapple

Figure 13.2 Sue Hodes (right) and Janice Gutman explore gender through dress, on their way to a party in St. Louis. *Courtesy of Janice Gutman*

House, recalls cars "turned upside down" or left with tires stolen, as well as "innumerable gunshots" through the windows. Kinberg remembers youth in the neighborhood breaking "every window in [their] house with rocks," to the point that residents replaced the glass with plexiglass to protect it from shattering. "I was mostly terrified every day," Goedde says. "Not terrified, but . . . I'd come home, and I'd be like, *now* what is going to happen?" She describes a young neighbor who "loved to yell 'Barb is a fag' at the top of his lungs every time [she] walked into [her] house" and an occasion when the same expletives were painted on her garage door. Similarly, Kinberg recalls someone spray-painting "Clare is a lezzie" on her car in the early 1980s. Unable to remove the paint, Kinberg continued to drive the graffitied car to classes for another two years. Goedde also describes a particularly horrific incident that occurred one Halloween, when her harassers "stuffed a person, like a woman, and put a knife in her belly," covered it with fake blood, "and threw it on our porch." The harassment, she says, "just was endless."[9]

That harassment was not limited to neighbors. Lesbian activists also found themselves targeted for violence and surveillance by law enforcement, including the FBI. Lesbian Alliance member Diana Campbell recalls an FBI agent who "pushed [her] and pinned [her]" on a car, to intimidate her into giving her name and the names of other lesbians. Agents "knocked

370

on the door at Cat House" and showed up at activist Janice Gutman's home, after she moved to Wentzville, Missouri, from the Women's House. In Wentzville, the agents claimed to be in search of Susan Saxe, a lesbian activist on the FBI's "Most Wanted" list. "It was just an excuse for harassment," Gutman reflects. Years later, when Gutman gained access to her FBI file, she learned that—after the final residents of the Women's House moved—agents scoured the building, dug through the garbage, and opened a file for every name they found.[10]

The motivation for this FBI campaign remains unclear. Possibly, it grew from existing surveillance of activists involved with other organizations, extending to the Women's House as those activists joined the collective. For instance, it appears the FBI initially targeted Gutman based on her participation in the Venceremos Brigade, then continued to surveil her activities after she returned to the US. This is not to suggest, however, that lesbian and feminist activism did not draw suspicion in their own right. Since the Lavender Scare of the 1950s, the FBI viewed homosexual individuals as being at risk for blackmail by foreign operatives and therefore as threats to national security. The Bureau surveilled and infiltrated lesbian and gay organizations, including less militant groups such as the Daughters of Bilitis. Mere interaction with other gays and lesbians could result in sanctions, and lesbians were targeted doubly by anti-gay laws as well as those policing women's sexuality more generally.[11]

As David K. Johnson notes in his history of this era, the success of the FBI's Lavender Scare campaign ironically became its undoing, as "gay men and lesbians began to organize politically to challenge what they came to see as an unjust government policy."[12] This early gay liberation activism grew more radical by the 1970s, as lesbian organizers increasingly rejected ideas of lesbianism as pathological and began working to transform social institutions rather than to "pass" within them. For some of these activists, participation in antiracist, anti-capitalist, and anti-colonialist causes also led to increasingly militant tactics. In one case, those tactics landed them on the FBI's "Most Wanted" list, which made them targets of a nationwide search as fugitives.

In 1970, leftist activists Susan Saxe and Katherine Power participated in a series of bank robberies intended to help fund the antiwar movement. During a robbery in Brighton, Massachusetts, on September 23, 1970, one of Saxe and Power's accomplices shot and killed a police officer, Walter Schroeder. The shooter and two other partners were quickly arrested;

however, Saxe and Power went on the run. They also entered into a lesbian relationship. The two women lived in various lesbian communities across the United States, rarely revealing their true identities. According to feminist scholar Josephine Donovan, by 1975, the search for Saxe and Power had escalated "into a full-blown dragnet." The FBI questioned lesbians and feminists across the country, initially with the intent of locating the two fugitives. Ultimately, however, the interrogations "broadened to include questions about the lesbian community in general—who was in it, who was involved with whom, who were friends with whom, the tenor of their political beliefs, and the nature of their lifestyles and 'sexual preferences.'"[13]

The search for Saxe and Power, and the larger anti-lesbian campaign it justified, threatened lesbian communities across the country. The harassment and surveillance experienced by members of the Lesbian Alliance occurred within this context. Their recollections also emphasize the gendered, sexualized, and homophobic violence aimed at lesbians. "Private" homes were not safe from "public" violence. Lesbians, in any capacity outside the closet, threatened the public order, and were threatened in turn. Nevertheless, these women continued to organize. Before the Women's House "exploded into three different households," fourteen lesbians lived collectively within its walls. Together, they founded the Lesbian Alliance, *Moonstorm*, Tiamat Press, the Women's Eye bookstore, Tomatoe Productions/Red Tomatoe Inc., and the Women's Coffeehouse (later A Woman's Place). In collaboration with the bar scene, these efforts carved out space for St. Louis lesbians to live, connect, and organize.

Lesbian Alliance and *Moonstorm*

From within the collectives, lesbians in St. Louis continued to imagine a broader public space, through which they could connect with a larger population of lesbians and feminists. Toward that end, they began working to create physical spaces that women across the city, as well as women traveling through St. Louis, might contact or visit. At the same time, they began to develop alternative media, which created discursive spaces in which lesbians could connect. Efforts to secure physical and discursive space often occurred simultaneously and relied upon each other, as evidenced by the work of the Lesbian Alliance and their publication *Moonstorm*.

Members of the women's houses developed the Lesbian Alliance, in part, as a search for public space. According to a "herstory" of the organization provided in *Moonstorm*, in 1972 "a small group of women got together to talk about *finding a place* where women could meet for work, relaxation, and fun."[14] They named themselves the Lesbian Alliance and called the place they conceptualized "the Coffeehouse." Kris Kleindienst, who was living in the Women's House when the Coffeehouse began, describes it as an "informal" Friday-night affair involving candles and guitar music.[15] The event provided local women, few of whom were "out" as lesbians, with an opportunity to congregate outside the bar scene. The Coffeehouse also increased awareness of the Women's House within the broader lesbian community. In a 1994 interview with researcher Monietta Slay, Kleindienst describes the house on McPherson as a hub for lesbians traveling through St. Louis. She recalls that the "gigantic house"—a three-story building offering eight bedrooms—became akin to "a halfway house for women on the road. People would know someone who was traveling through, and they would stop, and sometimes they would stay, and sometimes they wouldn't."[16] When the Coffeehouse moved, it continued to "draw" lesbians from across and outside the city, functioning as a nexus where isolated and even closeted women could come together.

The Coffeehouse began in the early 1970s in the basement of the Women's House, but it outlived that collective, with organizers moving the event to a Soulard apartment and then to a former bar at the intersection of Miami and Louisiana bordering Gravois Park. As it expanded to offer a variety of social and support services, the Coffeehouse was renamed A Woman's Place. A Woman's Place provided a venue for a variety of events, including workshops, film screenings, and yoga, as well as the consciousness-raising "rap sessions" central to second-wave feminist practice. The Lesbian Alliance recognized the need for space within a broader context of discrimination, including housing and legal discrimination, that effectively—and at times explicitly—barred lesbians from gathering. In *Moonstorm*, Alliance members described a shared experience of "being trained not to get too close to other women."[17] The Coffeehouse provided a venue through which members and guests could resist that training, forming relationships with women, learning from one other, and establishing mutual respect.

In this sense, the function of the Coffeehouse, as a place "where women could meet," mattered at least as much as the space itself. Indeed, the Lesbian Alliance defined itself as a hub for creating connections, a "structure through which all women, especially lesbians, can get in touch with one another and together work toward common goals."[18] Toward that end, creating new discursive spaces—such as *Moonstorm*—proved as important as occupying physical locations. Not all women could feasibly visit the Coffeehouse. Closeted women risked "outing" and all women risked victimization. By subscribing to *Moonstorm*, or acquiring a copy at local feminist and leftist bookstores such as Women's Eye bookstore and Left Bank Books, women could plug into a larger network, sharing ideas, feelings, and events. For those able and willing to attend, publications like *Moonstorm* also mapped lesbian spaces and announced political actions. Through event announcements and service listings, the discursive space generated through the magazine functioned as a key into geographical spaces across St. Louis.

The Lesbian Alliance published *Moonstorm* from 1973 to 1980, shifting from a magazine to a newsletter format in 1978. *Moonstorm* effectively functioned as both a literary publication and a networking tool. According to contributors, *Moonstorm* provided a forum for "Lesbians to communicate with each other . . . sharing [their] knowledge, experience and feelings."[19] This included creative expressions, such as poems and drawings, as well as more practical services and support. The publication regularly featured individuals and organizations with "trades to trade" and "skills to share," ranging from guitar lessons and logo design to astrological readings and piano repair.[20] *Moonstorm* publicized local feminist and lesbian events, including softball games and Red Tomatoe concerts, and shared information about ongoing local and national social justice actions. The magazine encouraged readers to involve themselves not only in the creation of *Moonstorm* but also in the larger political projects in which it was embedded. In this sense, *Moonstorm* was more than a publication. It was a collective.

Indeed, the authors of *Moonstorm* continued to view themselves primarily as a collective, even as they worked to produce the magazine. In the August 1979 issue, the editors declared that *Moonstorm* is a "lesbian-feminist-socialist newsletter," in that its creators "put energy into uniting the lesbian community and giving each other support to be lesbians," "want to see all women have economic, political, and social power and control in their lives," and strive for "equal distribution of power and money and control among all people regardless of race, class, and/or sexuality."[21] In some ways, *newsletter* is the least crucial term in this description, as evidenced when the editors note—later in this passage—that they sometimes fail to publish on schedule as the result of investment in other political projects, such as creating a leaflet on abortion rights, designing displays for International Women's Day, or creating posters for the campaign against proposed right-to-work legislation. In this sense, *Moonstorm* functioned as an organization as well as a publication. As the writers note, "Moonstorm supports *other groups of people* who are working to put an end to . . . oppression," suggesting that the members viewed themselves critically—if not primarily—as an activist network.[22]

In this way, *Moonstorm* created a discursive network linking St. Louis lesbians, while also functioning as a political space for members. The magazine simultaneously met a need in the community and offered a means for enacting feminist theories in practice. Individual issues of *Moonstorm* often focused on themes (for example, the Collectivity issue of Spring 1976, the Food issue of Spring 1977, and the Violence issue of Fall 1977). In addition to researching, writing, and editing work on these topics, members of the *Moonstorm* collective also met for discussion, identifying their own standpoints and experiences, and working to make consensus decisions about the political identity of the publication and the materials it would include. Reflecting on this process, Janice Gutman describes *Moonstorm* as "the most collective experience [she has] ever had, particularly in writing." She notes that members tried to reach consensus about all magazine content, which resulted in "lengthy conversations" on each topic. On the one hand, this proved laborious; Gutman jokes that "it was amazing [the collective] got a publication out at all." On the other, Gutman appreciates "how thorough" collective members were. Barb Goedde, in her own recollections of the *Moonstorm* collective, agrees. "Everything was relevant," she says. "You had so much to fight for."[23]

Despite the difficulty, members of *Moonstorm* remained committed to consensus decision making, rotated responsibilities, and a work environment in which all contributors remained "in equal power relationships." In this sense, the group illustrated sociologist Francesca Polletta's claim that participatory democracy does not necessarily conflict with efficient progress and can in fact have tangible benefits for leftist movements.[24] Running *Moonstorm* as a collective reflected the group's larger political ethic, which understood the publication as "a process of recognizing and expressing our needs and values and of relating them to broader social issues."[25] Their commitment to "work together and [be] responsible to one another" extended to the broader community of St. Louis lesbians and women, including those who neither contributed to nor read *Moonstorm*. Indeed, the collective's decision to shift from a long-form magazine to a brief newsletter stemmed in part from their commitment to "reach more races and classes of women" and to create time for those involved with *Moonstorm* to increase commitments to other coalitions. They viewed the publication as a means to an end, rather than an end in itself.

For members of *Moonstorm* and the broader Lesbian Alliance, the real goal remained a larger liberation project rooted in lesbian-feminist-socialist principles. As a magazine and a newsletter, *Moonstorm* continuously emphasized the precarity of lesbian access to space and the need for women to commit—financially, politically, and personally—to the project of sustaining spaces for oppressed groups. This included organizing in solidarity with Black St. Louis activists, such as those opposing the racist closure of the city's only African American hospital, Homer G. Phillips in North St. Louis's Ville neighborhood. Lesbian Alliance members participated in the Ad Hoc Committee to Save Homer G. Phillips Hospital, which barricaded hospital entrances for two weeks in 1979 to save the North Side's only full-scale hospital. When the barricades failed, they joined Black activists in calling for a boycott of downtown businesses and urged *Moonstorm* readers to contact the mayor, demanding equal health care for poor and Black residents in the city.[26]

The Lesbian Alliance's work to radicalize access to St. Louis geography also included advocacy for spaces developed for and by women. Members sought access to male-dominated spaces, including Ranken Technical College. In the early 1970s, the organization ran a campaign that successfully pressured Ranken Technical College to admit female applicants. Two founding members of the Lesbian Alliance—Laura Ann Moore and Peggy Miller—became the first women admitted to and graduated from the program, respectively. They went on to found the Women's Car Repair Collective, regularly advertised in *Moonstorm*, which provided repairs and workshops "by women for women." In this way, the organization simultaneously worked toward multiple goals. They reshaped systems, such as college admission policies, which rejected women from technical careers. They empowered women with skills in areas where they were historically under-educated. And they created economic alternatives through which women could rely on each other for a variety of services, circulating capital among themselves rather than financially supporting men in the community.

This push for an alternative economy that centered women reflects the lesbian-feminist-socialist ethos that largely motivated the Lesbian Alliance. While not all members identified as lesbians, and not all lesbians identified as lesbian-feminists or socialists, the group maintained a lesbian-feminist-socialist politics, "[choosing] not to relate to men but to put energy and resources only into other women."[27] In this vein, members worked to create a variety of local institutions that served as decidedly feminist alternatives to mainstream and male-dominated spaces. These included a printing service, Tiamat Press; a bookstore, The Women's Eye; and a production company, Tomatoe Productions/Red Tomatoe Inc.

Figure 13.3 Mary Beth Tinker repairs a car outside the McPherson Avenue women's collective in 1972 or 1973. *Courtesy of Janice Gutman*

Figure 13.4 Activist Peggy Pullen participates in an egg hunt outside a lesbian collective in Wentzville, Missouri. *Courtesy of Janice Gutman*

Tiamat Press, Women's Eye Bookstore, and Red Tomatoe Inc.

As an organization, the Lesbian Alliance did not officially found Tiamat Press, the Women's Eye bookstore, or Red Tomatoe Inc. However, many of the same women involved in the Lesbian Alliance spearheaded and participated in these organizations, creating connections that effectively provided a network for lesbians and feminists across the city. Their efforts illustrate not only attempts to secure and maintain physical space in the city, but also to construct discursive space for women and lesbians. As Kleindienst emphasizes, in this pre-internet era, "the press was literally the press and whoever owned the printing presses" controlled the media. In that context, the lesbians who took charge of a printing press, a bookstore, and a women's music production company served vital roles both in creating a conscious community and in building "community as a conscious act."[28]

The Lesbian Alliance started Tiamat Press after a friend gave Diana Campbell part of her inheritance. Campbell used the money to purchase printing equipment, then completed a short apprenticeship with the two gay men responsible for printing the *Lesbian Alliance Newsletter*. She and other members of the collective purchased an offset printing press (Fig. 13.5), which they stored in the basement of Left Bank Books (then located near Skinker and Delmar). They called the press "Tiamat" after the Babylonian goddess of the sea and used their equipment to print *Moonstorm*, as well as political leaflets and a newsletter by prisoners. Tiamat Press operated on a sliding scale, asking customers to "pay according to what they had." Since they were "mainly printing for people who had nothing," the press rarely made a profit. For larger projects, such as posters against right-to-work laws and the closure of Homer G. Phillips Hospital, members of Tiamat sometimes made after-hours use of printing equipment at their workplaces. Laura Cohen and Clare Kinberg describe those projects as "guerrilla" actions, which resulted in prints that were from "Tiamat Press but not Tiamat Press's press."[29]

More often, however, the activists involved in Tiamat spent hours coaxing their old equipment to function. For projects like *Moonstorm*, they divided responsibilities like layout, typesetting, and stapling, in addition to creating illustrations and written content for publication. Campbell describes "constantly fixing the press" as the collective completed each job, buying time with rubber bands to complete a run.[30] Although the offset press required constant maintenance, Tiamat Press as an organization continued to function for more than a decade. After its initial operation from the basement

Figure 13.5 Lesbian Alliance member Diana Campbell became an expert in "constantly fixing" the offset press that Tiamat used to publish movement materials. *Courtesy of Diana Campbell*

at Left Bank, Tiamat operated out of spaces in Maplewood, Clayton, and University City, including its final location at 554 Limit Avenue, adjacent to University City's Delmar Loop, which it shared with another feminist institution, the Women's Eye bookstore.

Bev White, Chris Guerrero, Kate Kane, and Carolyn Walker opened the Women's Eye bookstore on May 14, 1976, in a building at the intersection of Clayton Road and Yale Avenue near St. Mary's Hospital. For the next twelve years, Women's Eye sought to provide a concrete physical space for feminists and lesbians. It functioned less as a bookstore and more as a community center, providing a venue for "groups that lack[ed] a place to meet."[31] In a 2011 interview, Laura Ann Moore (the same local activist who successfully challenged sex discrimination in Ranken admissions) explained that Women's Eye was "never meant to be a traditional business," but rather a space for women to explore "theory and practice."[32] At the same time, Women's Eye defined itself through the resources it could provide. A quality feminist bookstore, members believed, would provide a variety of quality feminist media.

The bookstore, however, struggled to find resources to enact this vision. In 1981, St. Mary's Hospital demolished the building where the bookstore was located to build a new parking lot, forcing Women's Eye to relocate. The bookstore moved a few blocks northward, to 6344 South Rosebury in the small commercial strip of Clayton's DeMun neighborhood, to share space with Tiamat Press. In 1983, both organizations moved to the Delmar Loop location on Limit Avenue (Fig. 13.6), where they continued to struggle for five additional years. Following the move to Limit, Women's Eye sent out a call for support, noting that the bookstore "seems to have a never-ending cash flow problem, . . . making it very hard to expand the stock of books, records, magazines, and newspapers that deserve to be in a feminist bookstore."[33] Like Tiamat Press, Women's Eye functioned as a collective; the bookstore was entirely volunteer-run and "very frugal"; yet they struggled to make rent.[34] As a result, both organizations closed in 1988.

The bookstore illustrates not only attempts to secure and maintain physical space in the city, but also attempts to generate discursive space for women and lesbians. In that vein, Women's Eye participated in a larger "bookwoman's" movement characterized by a surge in women's bookstores, feminist publishing houses, and books authored by women.[35] According to cultural historian Trysh Travis, the Women in Print movement "was an attempt by a group of allied practitioners to create an alternative communications circuit—a woman-centered network of readers and writers, editors, printers, publishers, distributors, and retailers through which ideas, objects, and practices flowed in a continuous and dynamic loop."[36] The Women in Print movement thrived throughout the 1970s and 1980s, alongside a burgeoning women's music movement that generated women-centric albums, record labels, and music festivals. Through the creation of feminist and lesbian media, those involved in the Women in Print and women's music movements effectively created a discursive space that had not previously existed. Increasingly, a woman cracking open a book or popping a cassette into her car's tape player could engage with other feminists and lesbians. Although these media relied upon public spaces,

Figure 13.6 A sketch of the Women's Eye bookstore in its third and final location, adjacent to the Delmar Loop, as published in the December 1982 issue of *Moonstorm*. *From the St. Louis Lesbian and Gay Archives Collection (S0545), State Historical Society of Missouri*

such as conference and concert venues, they also extended beyond those sites, entering and reshaping women's everyday lives in their homes, cars, and workplaces.

In St. Louis, the women's music scene relied on Tomatoe Productions/ Red Tomatoe Inc., the event production company cofounded in 1974 by Kris Kleindienst and Sue Hyde. Kleindienst and Hyde created Tomatoe Productions after receiving a call from Anneke Earhart, a high-school friend of Kleindienst's who had briefly lived in the Women's House before moving to Washington, DC. A skilled musician, Earhart ended up playing piano for a track on Meg Christian's *I Know You Know,* the first album released through the newly formed women's music label Olivia Records. Afterward, Christian, Earhart, and other musicians involved with the album wanted to tour. Earhart called Kleindienst about a stop in St. Louis, and Kleindienst agreed to set up a concert. She and Hyde worked with the fledgling women's studies program at Washington University to produce the event, participating in the first tour for the first album in women's music, a genre and network that would grow exponentially over the next decade.[37]

From then on, Kleindienst and Hyde "just kept [producing concerts] because there kept being more people"—that is, more women interested in performing and more women in need of events to attend. Kleindienst suggests that these concerts gave "women who would never go to a bar" or who would never think "'Oh, I might be a lesbian, maybe I'll go to a gay bar' a place to go and be around other lesbians." Once surrounded by other lesbians, these women often experienced a "watershed experience." In Kleindienst's experience, lesbian and feminist media—including music and books—offered women "a mirror . . . a way to put themselves in context" that could be "earth-shattering" and inspiring. After an event, women would come up to Kleindienst "with tears in their eyes . . . like they had come home."[38]

Figure 13.7 This Red Tomatoe stationery header, donated by cofounder Kris Kleindienst to the Missouri Historical Society, showcases one of the organization's several logos. *Courtesy Missouri Historical Society Library and Research Center*

Kleindienst's sense that the women in attendance at these concerts felt "like they had come home" again underscores the overlap of public and private space in lesbian experience. These women, attending a public event hosted at a private university, found access to a familial network parallel to—but distinct from—the heteronormative "home." Red Tomatoe concerts provided women who were perpetual outsiders with an opportunity to be "in" by physically coming "out." At the same time, these concerts did not require women to be "out," or even self-aware, as lesbians. Unlike the bar scene, the women's music movement also welcomed women who were not—or were not yet—lesbians. In this way, it also functioned as a bridge experience for women questioning their identities or struggling with coming out.

Between 1974 and 1982, Red Tomatoe hosted forty-two cultural events. Most were musical events produced through the women's music network. Hyde describes a "very lively . . . circuit of . . . relatively small production companies, producing relatively small events for . . . women musicians, all of whom were lesbians." Although Red Tomatoe events generally garnered audiences of seventy-five to two hundred women, the organization's largest event—a performance by Holly Near co-produced by the Coalition for the Environment—drew a crowd of more than a thousand women. Through announcements in *Moonstorm* (and later *The Gay News-Telegraph,* a gay and lesbian periodical that began publishing in 1981) and their own mailing list, Red Tomatoe effectively brought women together through concerts, dances, and other cultural events for nearly a decade.[39]

Spaces like these offered venues in which women could gain access to each other, as well as to new ideas and practices. Publications from Tiamat Press and books at Woman's Eye offered resources for women to explore or deepen their feminism. Red Tomatoe concerts, meanwhile, revealed a sizable local lesbian population and thus underscored the normalcy of lesbianism in two ways. First, the sheer prevalence of lesbianism challenged the idea of lesbians as deviant. Second, the overtly affirming lyrics of the women's music movement offered an alternative view, one in which women, feminists, and lesbians could be celebrated rather than reviled. At the same time, the larger culture continued to challenge these spaces through under-resourcing, discrimination, and outright violence. A Woman's Place—the community center that grew out of the Coffeehouse—and the local lesbian bars, Middle of the Road and Mor or Les, provide telling illustrations of these challenges.

A Woman's Place

The Lesbian Alliance created A Woman's Place as a community center "operated by and for women (primarily lesbian-feminists)." Activists envisioned A Woman's Place as a space that could be all things for all women: "The Woman's Place is your place," a blurb in the Lesbian Alliance newsletter declared in 1975. "If you want something to happen or if you want to help something happen call these women." A Woman's Place housed the Coffeehouse, as well as a host of community services, ranging from support groups and legal assistance to a library and recreation room. The space was intended as a hub for women to socialize, access resources, and plan direct actions. Yet, organizers struggled to maintain A Woman's Place in a larger context of financial precarity, discrimination, and violence. In this sense, the story of A Woman's Place illustrates how covert and overt forms of violence overlapped to target lesbian activists in St. Louis.[40]

After originating as the Coffeehouse in the McPherson women's collective, A Woman's Place moved to an apartment in Soulard, likely in or near 1906 South Twelfth Street. However, the group was forced out of that location in January 1974, when the building's owner decided to convert the space into a youth hostel. After learning of the landlord's intentions in the fall of 1973, the writers of *Moonstorm* published an update entitled "Back on the Streets Again," urging supporters to share "suggestions for locations, money and legal considerations . . . immediately."[41] Without alternatives, the Lesbian Alliance risked losing its primary meeting space within two months. Although the group had outgrown the apartment space, the search for a new venue offered a significant challenge. Reflecting on the search after the fact, members remarked that "no one wanted a group of homeless lesbians."[42]

Yet by March 1974, the Lesbian Alliance had successfully relocated to a two-story space on the southwest corner of South City's Gravois Park. The new location consisted of a former bar, which provided ample space for the Coffeehouse as well as for dances, film screenings, and other activities. An apartment above the bar offered an additional meeting space. From their new location, the Lesbian Alliance began hosting support groups. The legal group and the *Moonstorm* collective also found a permanent home for their services. In exchange for the organization's work repairing the space, the landlord offered the venue rent-free, with the option to purchase the building at the end of the year. "After much work fixing up the joint," declared a *Moonstorm* article, "the building is jumping with old activities and lots of new stuff."[43]

Yet, within a year, that building exploded. On January 30, 1975, an arsonist targeted A Woman's Place, firebombing the Coffeehouse and gutting the space. The fire compromised the building's roof, wiring, and plumbing, and smoke damage extended to the apartment upstairs. Some members of the Lesbian Alliance believed the landlord demolished the building for insurance purposes. Others suspected law enforcement personnel, including the city's Red Squad (a police unit that investigated leftist political and social groups) and the FBI. Laura Ann Moore, who lived a block from the building, arrived on the scene to find that someone had rifled through the organization's political files, increasing suspicion of police or federal involvement. To this day, the crime remains unsolved.[44]

Figure 13.8 This front-page drawing from the *Lesbian Alliance Newsletter* (vol. 2, no. 3) illustrates the rage, grief, and ongoing resistance of activists in the wake of the Coffeehouse bombing of January 30, 1975. *From the Lesbian Alliance of St. Louis Records (S0129), State Historical Society of Missouri*

Members' suspicions of the police and FBI were based on the ongoing harassment and surveillance they faced, including Campbell's experience of being pinned to a car by a federal agent and others' encounters with law enforcement officers outside Cat House. During the same period, lesbian activist communities in other cities, including Lexington, Kentucky, had been decimated by FBI infiltration and surveillance.[45] Some lesbian activists from other cities did escape prosecution by "hiding out" in St. Louis, although their fugitive status was generally unknown to others in the community.[46] In *Moonstorm*, Lesbian Alliance members highlighted the importance of "not letting the FBI intimidate [them] into destroying the solidarity of [their] community both nationally and locally." They also shared tips from the National Lawyers Guild to help women in the event "the FBI comes to your door." These included not answering knocks before identifying the caller; not letting law enforcement inside without a warrant; not speaking with officers or agents; writing down names, badge numbers, and descriptions; asking friends and family not to cooperate with law enforcement; and contacting the National Lawyers Guild for assistance. In brief, the column instructed activists to "Stay cool," "Stay calm," and "Stay silent."[47]

With the arson ten months after the move into A Woman's Place, harassment, discrimination, and violence had left the Lesbian Alliance's "new home" uninhabitable. Moreover, the destruction had been violent and purposeful, leading members to believe "continued use of that building would inevitably have resulted in continued harassment."[48] While initial reports of the fire in the Lesbian Alliance newsletter insisted that "[d]espite the setback spirit and energy are high," members also noted the challenge of finding and securing a new space.[49] Not only was the group increasingly acquainted with discrimination, but they also had minimal financial resources. The month before the fire, the Lesbian Alliance had warned supporters that they were "approaching a financial crisis" and only had resources to cover rent and utilities for the next two months.[50] After the bombing, the group's need for fiscal support multiplied. To continue unhoused, "make the search for a new home, and realistically consider buying or renting it," the Lesbian Alliance needed funds.[51]

The destruction of A Woman's Place illustrates the intersection of systemic and individual violence. While a single arsonist destroyed the space, that act also represented the culmination of an ongoing campaign of harassment. If the landlord was in fact culpable for the crime, his involvement exemplifies the violence with which those with resources responded to lesbian attempts to claim public space. Although the landlord's initial support of A Woman's Place may make his involvement unlikely, such support was often revoked without notice, in response to economic concerns or public anti-lesbian sentiment. Indeed, *Moonstorm* later reported that the YWCA, which initially offered to provide A Woman's Place three floors free of charge, abruptly changed its offer, instead quoting "an outrageous price" for a single floor of small offices, which lacked air conditioning.[52] In both instances, landlord support was tenuous and subject to change. Individual opinions on lesbian life and systemic disenfranchisement often interacted to ill effect.

The possibility of police involvement in the Woman's Place bombing further highlights this interaction, underscoring the climate of surveillance and criminalization, in which lesbians were targeted as threats to public safety, even while experiencing victimization. Moreover, the bombing exacerbated the group's already dire financial situation. While a better-resourced organization might have rebuilt or relocated, the Lesbian Alliance could do neither. Although the group continued to organize and publish through 1980, the fire was the final blow to a permanent public site. A Woman's Place, it seemed, was nowhere.

Deprived of public space, Lesbian Alliance members continued to congregate in apartments and other collective spaces. Members even squeezed into shared cars, shuttling each other from one neighborhood to another, to attend meetings. Still, the firebombing increased fear in the community. Barb Goedde recalls feeling "simply horrified" that there was "that much anger in the community." After years of harassment and violence, the bombing did not surprise many Lesbian Alliance members. Still, it highlighted the rage directed at their existence and their congregation. The bombing left the community shaken.[53]

Moonstorm, however, persevered. The magazine (and later newsletter) continued to promote local lesbian and women's events and to provide a space for women to express their experiences. *Moonstorm* also reported on the fire, and the financial and emotional toll it had taken on Lesbian Alliance members. In contrast, local publications such as the *St. Louis Post-Dispatch*, the larger of the city's two daily newspapers, made no mention of the fire or its criminal cause. In this sense, the discursive space erected by the Lesbian Alliance continued to function, even after the destruction of participants' physical space. *Moonstorm*, then, provided a *public sphere* for a community that had been violently deprived of *public space*. As conceptualized by political philosopher Nancy Fraser, the public sphere includes "arenas of citizen discourse and association."[54] Multiple public spheres can co-exist, and "private" concerns—such as those defined by sexism and heterosexism—cannot be extricated from this public discourse. Through *Moonstorm*, members of the Lesbian Alliance crafted an alternative public sphere that effectively linked and sustained members across distance. They also used *Moonstorm* to try to protect other jeopardized spaces, notably two lesbian bars run by Muriel "Mac" McCann.

Mac McCann, Middle of the Road, and Mor or Les

On a Sunday afternoon in May 1978, an urgent knock woke Mac McCann. Drawn by that "banging" fist and the sound of "hollering," McCann opened the door to her apartment. There, she found a fifteen-year-old girl, screaming and begging to be let inside. "Please let me in," the stranger screamed. A large man loomed behind her. McCann feared the man would follow and harm them both. She closed the door and secured a weapon before returning. In the thirty-second interim, she heard the man "pushing [the girl] around" and the girl's continued cries. McCann pulled the girl inside, then followed the man down the steps, threatening him. "If I thought I could have hurt him," she reflected in a September interview in *Moonstorm*, "I would have."[55]

The girl, a stranger to McCann, had been forced into a truck on the corner of South Grand Boulevard and Chouteau Avenue. The men inside had driven around for forty-five minutes, apparently searching for a location to rape her. When they tried to force her into an abandoned house, the girl escaped and began running from one doorstep to the next, desperately ringing bells to find safety. After McCann let her inside, she and the girl located the truck and called the police. Both McCann and the girl later appeared before a grand jury, convened to determine whether the men responsible would be indicted, and whether the charges would be child molestation or assault. During the proceedings, the prosecuting attorney brought up McCann's business, the lesbian bar Middle of the Road, which was located across the street from her apartment. Not long after, three men—including one of the men responsible for the assault—fired an air rifle through the windows of the bar.[56]

McCann called the police, who found and charged the men responsible that very night. The next morning, McCann returned to court, alongside a Middle of the Road patron who was shot trying to enter the bar but who sustained minimal injuries. Frustrated at being targeted, McCann pushed the state prosecuting attorney's office to fulfill its promise of protection. When this was refused, she went to the mayor's office. She emphasized ongoing issues related to a condemned property next to the bar, tying recent car burglaries and broken windows to the property, and to the overall unsafe climate illustrated by this girl's victimization. The result was not protection. Instead, McCann drew the attention of St. Louis's vice squad. On June 23, an undercover officer entered a private party at Middle of the Road. Twenty minutes later, additional officers arrived. They arrested McCann on charges including "no visibility." The window, shattered by the air rifle, had been boarded over, making it impossible to see inside. In effect, the police charged McCann for having been the victim of a crime.[57]

It would not be the last time. In March 1979, McCann opened a new bar, Mor or Les, at the Dutchtown neighborhood's 4135 South Grand Boulevard, just north of Meramec Street. By August, neighboring residents had begun circulating a petition opposing the presence of the bar. The petition jeopardized renewal of McCann's license, which was set to expire in September. A hearing was scheduled with the St. Louis Circuit Court judge for October, granting McCann and Mor or Les a temporary reprieve.

However, the license renewal became moot on September 11, when Mor or Les, like A Woman's Place four years earlier, fell victim to a firebomb. Firefighters on the scene reported "nothing but a ball of fire."[58] The blaze devoured the bar, as well as McCann's apartment upstairs. Two plastic gas canisters were found in the apartment, confirming suspicions of arson. Two days later, police charged McCann with the crime.[59]

A St. Louis Post-Dispatch article published the same day as McCann's arrest noted that McCann "turned herself in," that "investigators . . . had strong evidence" against her, and that "warrants would be sought" that day.[60] In contrast, while the building's owner, Bonita Stephens, was questioned several times, investigators saw "no prospect of her being arrested in connection with the fire."[61] The experience helps illustrate McCann's complicated relationship with local police. In a Moonstorm interview the autumn before the fire, McCann detailed asking the police to investigate the residents of a condemned neighborhood building for burglaries of her bar and home. She described "tremendous cooperation from the police" in investigating the burglary of the bar, but noted that her "apartment was a different story." In addition, the failure of the State to protect her as a witness frustrated McCann to the point that she "went over the mayor's office to raise some hell." McCann expected protection from law enforcement and local government. Indeed, she reaffirmed whitewashed narratives of the city that designate some areas as "tough neighborhood[s]" without considering the systemic racism and classism that affect the city's geography. At one point, McCann referenced "the problem of being in a racially mixed neighborhood," back-pedaling when the interviewer pushed her to consider whether integration is, in fact, a problem.[62] Previous experiences with police mediated by whiteness left her expecting law enforcement to protect her. As the white lesbian manager of a women's bar, however, she found herself protected in some situations and ignored or targeted in others. Although her interview obscures how racism and classism operate through policing, it highlights homophobia. The system of oppression that targeted her became increasingly difficult to ignore.

McCann's arrest outraged many local lesbians, who voiced strong support for McCann and criticized investigators for ignoring other possible suspects. In an article for Big Mama Rag, a Denver-based feminist periodical, columnist Judith Miller noted that "a series of phone threats" had been made against Mor or Les and that neighbors reported "three men [leaving] the scene in a pickup . . . a moment after the blaze erupted."

Another witness to the bombing claimed to have seen "the man who did it leaving the scene."[63] However, even after police—citing lack of evidence—declined to press charges against McCann, they pursued no other suspects. In *Big Mama Rag*, Miller questioned whether this decision left McCann "still guilty" in the eyes of the public. Indeed, McCann described feeling "crucified" by local news media and the police, who had "named [her] as the primary suspect" and positioned her as "the culprit" behind the blaze. McCann's recent move out of the apartment above Mor or Les proved a key detail in that narrative, with opponents presuming she left the space because she planned to destroy it. In fact, McCann had another reason for vacating the space. She moved in response to a bomb threat.[64]

In the wake of the fire and the arrest of McCann, patrons of Mor or Les and other local supporters formed the Concerned Citizens Against Violence (Fig. 13.9). The organization linked the bombing of Mor or Les with the neighborhood's sexist and homophobic response to the bar. While

Figure 13.9 About three dozen Mor or Les supporters, newly organized as Concerned Citizens Against Violence, gather outside the bar the afternoon following its fiery destruction to decry "this most immediate act of violence against women." Reading a statement at left is organizer Totty Dunham. St. Louis Globe-Democrat *photo, from the collections of the St. Louis Mercantile Library at the University of Missouri–St. Louis*

the local police sergeant who told the *Post-Dispatch* "South St. Louis just isn't ready for a lesbian bar" saw this response as a given, others took issue with the hostile climate.[65] Joyce L. Armstrong, the executive director of the American Civil Liberties Union of Missouri, argued in a letter to the *Post-Dispatch* that while news reports suggested "few South Side residents wished a fiery end" to Mor or Les, "few were prepared to live in harmony with the bar as a neighbor." Armstrong denounced the "cancer of discrimination" that resulted in a "disturbing pattern" of "intolerance" across differences, including those in sexuality, ability, and race.[66] Another *Post-Dispatch* reader, whose letter was published anonymously, noted that "the more [she] read concerning the feminist bar Mor or Les, the more convinced [she became] that women are the most helpless and harmless of all groups."[67] Comparing the firebombing of this women's space to the rape of individual women, this writer noted that "rape is often blamed on the victim" for reasons including "being in the wrong place," and "now the burning of a woman's bar appears to be blamed on the women themselves."[68] Another author, writing for *Sister Advocate*, a feminist newspaper in Oklahoma City, used the same metaphor: "If a woman is raped, she is accused of being in the wrong place or wearing provocative clothing. This women's space was accused of being in the wrong part of the city. Women have always been accused of being in the wrong place at the wrong time."[69]

For her part, McCann remained committed to continuing the fight. "Through all our history," she told *Big Mama Rag*, "women have been filled with guilt and fear, made to feel helpless in the face of constant injustices. I say no more." She urged readers to "stand up and fight," insisting "if we stand together we cannot be defeated." Yet, the closure of Mor or Les effectively ended McCann's career as a bar manager. The fire—and subsequent charges—signaled the end of eleven years managing lesbian bars and two decades in the business.[70]

Many lesbians felt that the firebombing of Mor or Les and the criminal charges against McCann constituted one more injury in a pattern of systemic harm. The destruction of Mor or Les was not an isolated incident, but the newest entry on a long list of offenses, including the destruction of A Woman's Place, the harassment of women in feminist and lesbian spaces, and the targeting of McCann following her testimony on behalf of the state's attorney's office. By conceptualizing the firebombing as an act of rape, women drew attention to the violence and trauma inherent in the crime, as well as the failed response of the criminal justice system. Like rape survivors, the women who operated lesbian spaces were viewed as criminals rather than victims. The harm committed against them was exacerbated by additional harm at the hands of a police force and judicial system that not only failed to protect and serve women and lesbians but also openly targeted them as a threat to the public order. Finally, the rape metaphor emphasized that the operation of power across the city was gendered in particular ways. Fifteen-year-old girls were forced into trucks, and lesbian bars were bombed. The streets were not safe for women; yet women's organizations were perpetually sent back into the streets. Not surprisingly, activists responded with a push to "take back" the streets for women.

Take Back the Night

Take Back the Night marches began in the early 1970s, as part of a larger effort to raise awareness around issues of sexual violence, create resources for survivors, and prevent further assaults. In the United States, the earliest known march occurred in 1972 at the University of South Florida. Similar "Reclaim the Night" marches occurred in European nations, including a West German event on April 30, 1977, and synchronous "Reclaim the Night" marches across England on November 12 of the same year. In St. Louis, the march developed as part of a growing movement to address and prevent violence against women through organizations such as the Women's Counseling Center and the St. Louis Abused Women's Support Project (later the Women's Safe House). The march simultaneously challenged women's inability to safely occupy public space and their experiences of "battering" within the home. In this way, it developed out of a specifically lesbian politics that understood the ways violence crossed barriers between public and private spaces.[71]

St. Louis's first Take Back the Night march developed in direct response to Meg Christian's performance of "Fight Back" at the Red Tomatoe concert in the Washington University Women's Building.[72] "Fight Back" provides a visceral description of the fear of physical and sexual violence that limits women's access to public space:

> By day I live in terror
> By night I live in fright
> For as long as I can remember
> A lady don't go out at night, no no
> A lady don't go out at night[73]

392

Near's lyrics also imply that the situation for women is worsening. She suggests that "nowadays a woman / can't go out in the middle of the day" either. In covering Near's song, Christian modeled her refusal to "accept the verdict" that public space simply does not belong to women and encouraged women to "fight back, in large numbers." Like most 1970s feminist theory and practice, the song insisted on a collective approach. Only by working "together" could activists remake their homes into safe environments.[74]

In her unpublished memoir, "Living a Surprising Life," Margaret Flowing Johnson describes the concert as a turning point, a moment in which her "habitual silences were irrevocably broken." Johnson left the concert moved and energized, "inspired" by the "enthusiasm and optimism" in the room, but unsure where to direct that energy. Direction arrived soon after, when word reached Johnson that another concert attendee, Nan Cinnater, wished to plan a Take Back the Night march in St. Louis. Johnson called Cinnater, and the two women began to organize.[75]

Cinnater and Johnson benefitted from university ties. Cinnater was the first full-time director of the Women's Center at the University of Missouri–St. Louis (UMSL), which opened in 1973.[76] Johnson had just been promoted to full professor at St. Louis Community College at Meramec. Johnson suggests these positions provided access to material resources—such as unmonitored printing privileges—that she and Cinnater would not have otherwise had (and would not have today in the same positions). Indeed, many of the lesbian and feminist events of the period relied upon local universities, specifically the newly formed Women's Studies programs at Washington University, Webster College, and the University of Missouri–St. Louis.[77]

Organizing for the Take Back the Night march also incorporated other standard practices of local lesbian and feminist activism. Like meetings for *Moonstorm*, Take Back the Night meetings took place in a private residence, a "beautiful home off Hanley" that Cinnater was renting. Meetings also encapsulated the energy of the era. Johnson describes weekly Saturday meetings in which thirty to fifty women "spilled off the sofas and chairs." Decision making was largely consensus-based, and women shared responsibilities. In retrospect, Johnson views the ease of organizing as one of the most memorable aspects of the experience. "Looking back," she feels "amazed . . . to realize how flawlessly the organizing occurred. Not once did a woman or subcommittee fail in their accepted task. Each of us was caught in a focused whirlwind of activity."[78]

Those activities included communication and outreach into the St. Louis community, a practice that relied upon the lesbian network established through organizations like the Lesbian Alliance and Red Tomatoe Inc. During the period, Johnson recalls, there were "lesbian events all the time." Organizers channeled their momentum through that network. They "went to every lesbian bar in town, and every lesbian dance, and every lesbian anything," leafletting and spreading word about Take Back the Night.[79] They also reached out to non-lesbian communities, contacting business owners and working to locate speakers and supporters. Johnson recalls a concerted effort to network with African American organizations. Although she and the other organizers "were all in the early stages of [their] own antiracist work" and "white privilege was a concept still in the future," the white activists were aware of the intersections between racism and patriarchy and strove to create an integrated march. Not only were these women clear that "violence against women crossed all race and class lines," they also "worried over the historical fact that white men upheld racist beliefs by claiming to protect white women from over-sexualized black men." As a result, they leveled their "rage . . . at the protection racket perpetrated by patriarchy which threatened women with the one fist while offering false protection with the other."[80]

They did not always succeed. Indeed, the Take Back the Night march reveals the complicated intersections of whiteness, feminism, and antiviolence activism. Months into the organizing effort and weeks before the scheduled march, three dedicated lesbian activists addressed the Take Back the Night meeting. They drew attention to the fact that they—like all the women assembled—were white, and called upon the group to cancel the march to avoid perpetuating racism. Johnson describes a "stunned, uncomfortable silence," which she eventually broke. "We have been planning this event for over six months," she recalls telling the women. "You've known about that all this time and been asked to participate. You chose not to. We've been working hard to ensure that the event is not racist, and we could have used your help with that. You're still welcome to join us, but we're not canceling the march."[81] The three organizers left the meeting, and the march was held, as scheduled, on June 9, 1979.

At 8:30 that night, more than a thousand marchers met for the rally in Forest Park. Although the park provided a "cruising" area for gay men, lesbians largely experienced the space as unsafe, and organizers specifically chose the venue to address that sense of danger, reclaiming the space as one

Figure 13.10 This poster, created for St. Louis's first Take Back the Night march in 1979, illustrates organizers' desire for interracial coalition in addressing violence against women. *From the Laura Ann Moore Papers, Department of Special Collections, Washington University in St. Louis*

that women could occupy. [82] They hosted a rally outside Steinberg Skating Rink that included speakers and performances, including a rendition of "Fight Back" performed by the St. Louis Women's Choir. Afterward, they marched onto Kingshighway and turned onto Lindell, then Euclid, before looping back to the park through the Central West End. They marched a total of 2.6 miles, facing taunts from some men, gathering additional supporters, and watching faces appear in windows as they passed. Men—including members of Rape and Violence End Now (RAVEN), a recently formed men's organization dedicated to stopping abuse and assault—participated in "supporting roles." The march was organized, enacted, and protected by women alone. "Can you believe it?" one marcher asked a *St. Louis Post-Dispatch* reporter. "We're walking in Forest Park at 11 pm."[83]

The *Post-Dispatch* described a diverse crowd, noting that the march included women "of all ages, of various races, and from all walks of life," including "girls no older than 8 or 9, college students, career women, homemakers, and grandmothers."[84] Others noted the disproportionate white presence in the crowd. In a 1980 *Moonstorm* article reflecting on the 1979 event, Clare Kinberg noted that "publicity for the march emphasized that the issue of violence against women crosses racial and class lines" and that the "mostly white planning committee made an effort to publicize in the Black media." However, she estimated that 95 percent of the attendance was white.[85] In contrast, African Americans comprised 45.6 percent of the St. Louis city population in 1980, according to the US Census.[86] For Kinberg, this discrepancy suggested that "groups . . . dominated by white feminists are not going to succeed in organizing events that Black women identify with," even when those events address issues that affect all women. "Since no other strategy for ending violence against women was presented," Kinberg argued, "'law and order' crackdowns can be the implied solution called for by this type of demonstration." This "implied solution" failed to address the systemic racism pervading the criminal justice system or the ways that this system could never "be seen as a solution to the violence in Black women's lives." Until racism in the white women's movement was addressed, "unified action by Black and white women" would remain an impossibility.[87]

At the same time, some white lesbian-feminists involved in Take Back the Night did challenge the role of "law and order" in addressing sexual violence. In the wake of events like the Woman's Place firebombing, lesbians and feminists in the city had little reason to view the police force as a source of safety. Although police cleared major intersections as marchers approached, they did not participate in the event or provide "protection," in large part because organizers viewed policing as a paternalist practice. As Johnson recalls, "We were trying to make a point that women should be able to go out at night without patriarchal protection."[88] While this emphasizes a particularly white experience of policing (as the police force's patriarchal protectionism rarely extends to women of color), it also illustrates the activists' concerns with challenging both the violence that targets all women and the white supremacist protectionism that seeks, specifically, to "protect" white women from "predatory" Black men.

The success of the march, as a cross-racial event, was debated at the time and remains debatable today. March organizers made attempts to publicize it in the Black community, include Black speakers, and consider racism in their analysis of sexual violence. The three white lesbians who pushed organizers to cancel the march likewise raised serious concerns about centering whiteness in the march. These efforts to network with Black women came to more successful fruition the following year, when the second annual march met up with a simultaneous Take Back the Night march organized by Black activists in East St. Louis. The two marches conjoined at the Gateway Arch, illustrating the possibility of interracial coalition in the fight against misogynistic violence. Decades later, the need for that kind of coalition remains.

Epilogue: Impermanence and Legacies

Most of the lesbian organizations described above did not survive the 1980s. *Moonstorm* ceased publication in 1981. Red Tomatoe Inc. hosted its last concert in 1982. The Women's Eye bookstore and Tiamat Press fared better, staying active until financial pressures forced simultaneous closures in 1988. Yet, by the decade's end, even the lesbian collectives that generated these organizations had dissolved. Several members of the Lesbian Alliance, for example, relocated to California and Washington, seeking more leftist and lesbian-friendly environments. Some eventually returned to St. Louis; others remained out of state. For example, after two years traveling between lesbian collectives in the United States and spending time abroad, Margaret Flowing Johnson returned to St. Louis to continue her activism in the area.[89] Months after the first Take Back the Night march, Johnson's co-organizer, Nan Cinnater, resigned her position at UMSL to pursue feminist organizing outside of a university context. She eventually moved to Provincetown, Massachusetts.[90]

The fact that so many key lesbian and feminist organizers relocated to the coasts underscores the difficulty of sustaining activism in a hostile climate. For many of these women, established leftist and lesbian environments, such as Seattle and Provincetown, provided a more livable alternative to remaining in St. Louis. Diana Campbell, who relocated to California in the 1980s and now lives in Seattle, says St. Louis "definitely still has a hold" on her, but was simply "a hard place to live." Campbell attributes that difficulty to the presence of "so many Republican and right-wing people," but adds that there has also "always been this force, resistance, and really good organizers and good organizing." She expresses admiration for the activists who have stayed, although even long-term St. Louisans note this environment's wearying effects on those with an ongoing commitment to change.[91] In a 1994 interview, Kris Kleindienst, who has remained active in St. Louis organizing since the 1970s, described St. Louis as "a small town on the urban scale," a city whose deeply embedded conservatism "lends a certain quality of challenge to any kind of change." At the same time, Kleindienst noted that "St. Louis is a great place to organize," because anyone willing to make the effort can become involved. "It's a great place to organize," she reiterated, "but a tough place to make a difference."[92]

The dissolution of the organizations and spaces that defined lesbian St. Louis in the 1970s attests to that difficulty. Nevertheless, the legacy of these organizations persists. In the 1980s, Red Tomatoe sold its mailing list to Wired Women, a women's music production company that hosted dances through the 1990s. Left Bank Books, a leftist bookstore co-owned by Kleindienst, celebrated its fiftieth anniversary in 2019 and remains a strong supporter of feminist and LGBTQIA+ organizing in the community. Take Back the Night events have continued since their inception, with the original rallies expanding to include workshops on domestic violence and sexual assault, including within the lesbian community. Other anti-violence resources, such as the Women's Safe House, remain open to this day.

In other words, while decades have passed since a St. Louisan attended a Lesbian Alliance meeting, walked into the Women's Eye bookstore, or danced at a Red Tomatoe concert, these organizations continue to influence lesbian and feminist cultures in the city. Failure to recognize the persistence of these networks risks reenacting in scholarship the same acts of erasure and violence that caused these organizations to "disappear" in the first place. Organizations have changed names, venues, and leadership, and particular projects have ended. Yet, the networks of women responsible for this activism continue the call to "fight back! in large numbers," and those numbers continue to grow.

14. The Time Is Now

Mass Defense, Coalitional Solidarity, and the St. Louis Chapter of the National Alliance Against Racist and Poitical Repression

Keona K. Ervin

At the victory party the evening of the verdict, our joy knew no bounds and our celebration no restraints. Yet in the echoes of our laughter and the frenzy of our dancing there was also caution. If we saw this moment of triumph as a conclusion and not as a point of departure, we would be ignoring all the others who remained draped in chains. We knew that to save their lives, we had to preserve and build upon the movement.

Angela Davis, *Angela Davis: An Autobiography*

CITING THE PERVASIVE PRACTICE OF militarized state violence against and political repression of Brown, Black, and working-class communities through deportation, ICE-led border patrol policing, Islamophobia, and police violence and murder, more than twelve hundred organizers gathered at the Chicago Teachers Union Hall on the night of November 22, 2019, to refound the National Alliance Against Racist and Political Repression (NAARPR). The Chicago and Kentucky chapters had remained active after the organization declined in the late 1980s, yet their members believed that a national movement was necessary to meet the challenge of a changing social order. Many agreed with this sentiment as hundreds of groups endorsed their call. The conference's opening event, "Rally on Human Rights: Democracy and Community Control of Police," featured speakers who represented the wide range of causes that had defined the organization's original founding in Chicago in 1973. For example, Michael Sampson, a cofounder of the Dream Defenders, and Jazmine Salas, the co-chair of the Chicago Alliance Against Racist and Political Repression, served as emcees, punctuating every speech with chants that expressed support for Puerto Rican, Filipino, and Palestinian national liberation and independence;

Black and Native Lives Matter movements; anti-imperialist struggles based in Latin America, Asia, and Africa; the freedom of political prisoners; an end to mass incarceration; and community control of the police as defined by the Chicago-based Civilian Police Accountability Council initiative. Local organizers Armanda Shackelford, the mother of Gerald Reed, who was wrongfully convicted of double murder based on a forced confession and had been incarcerated for nearly three decades; Aislinn Pulley of Black Lives Matter Chicago and the Chicago Torture Justice Center; and Frank Chapman, who joined the National Alliance in 1976 after serving a fifteen-year sentence at the Missouri State Penitentiary under a wrongful conviction, gave reflections that pointed to the significance of Chicago as an incubator for Black-, Brown-, and Left-led struggle. Chapman, now a lead organizer for the Chicago Alliance, highlighted the "revolutionary tradition" that the National Alliance had established nearly fifty years earlier. Angela Y. Davis gave the keynote address that evening, recounting the organization's history and making the case for a renewed NAARPR in a new century.[1]

The brainchild of Communist and former presidential candidate Charlene Mitchell, the National Alliance Against Racist and Political Repression was an outgrowth of the Free Angela Davis and All Political Prisoners campaign that Mitchell led.[2] Founders, members, and supporters believed that the most effective response to the "punitive turn" of the early 1970s—which witnessed the expansion of the carceral state; an economic crisis in which "more and more the burden of paying for inflation is placed upon the shoulders of working people and middle-class people"; rising costs of healthcare, housing, food, and utilities; systematic, state-led action to repress social movements; and the erosion of the social safety net—was the formation of the broadest possible alliance to defend the rights of ordinary people. A multiracial, multiethnic, transnational, and working-class-based solidarity organization designed not to replace grassroots constituencies but to amplify their ongoing work, the NAARPR defended the right to dissent as expanding surveillance of and mounting violence against antiwar, antiracist, anti-imperialist, and anti-capitalist movements posed serious threats.[3] The NAARPR's goal was to "build mass movements in defense of the rights of the people to organize and protest against injustice," as Frank Chapman put it.[4] In her reflection on the immediate aftermath of her legal victory against the State of California in 1972, in which she was charged with murder, kidnapping, and conspiracy, was placed on the FBI's "Most

Wanted" list, and faced the death penalty, Angela Y. Davis noted the strong sentiment among leftist radicals that the international movement to secure her freedom could only be true to its name should it constitute a beginning and not an end.[5]

In May 1973, between five hundred and seven hundred participants gathered to found the NAARPR, representing organizations and movements including the Puerto Rican Socialist Party, various political-prisoner defense committees, the Republic of New Afrika, the American Indian Movement, and the United Farm Workers of America.[6] Angela Y. Davis, longtime Kentucky-based white civil rights veterans Anne and Carl Braden, and Southern Christian Leadership Conference organizer, campus leader, and American Federation of State, County, and Municipal Employees leader Ben Chavis joined Charlene Mitchell, serving as founding members. Mitchell explained that the founding of the National Alliance revolved around three assumptions. First, systematic state repression of popular social movements was a defining mode of oppression. Second, basic needs were increasingly being unmet because states were rolling back social welfare programs as they allocated greater spending to law enforcement and the construction of new prisons and detention centers. Third, "massive, sustained and united struggle, [along with] multiracial and multinational [representation] in our leadership and at our base," was the only way forward.[7] At the forefront of solidarity movements in the late twentieth century, the NAARPR understood "alliance" in the broadest possible terms. It meant "unity that cuts across all barriers put up by those who fear change and want us divided."[8] Growing to nearly thirty chapters during its heyday, the National Alliance charted a path that merged anew civil rights, Black Power, Marxism, Black Left feminism, antiwar activism, and Third World liberation into a generative program of mass struggle.[9]

Inspired by earlier defense groups such as the Civil Rights Congress, which, during the 1940s and 1950s, took on high-profile cases such as those of Rosa Lee Ingram, Willie McGee, and the Martinsville Seven, original National Alliance members understood that the political climate of their time required a different set of approaches but ones no less committed to defending the freedom of those trapped by authoritarianism.[10] The organization focused much of its early effort on North Carolina because of the Tarheel State's high number of death-row prisoners, rampant white terrorist violence, anti-unionism (North Carolina was a right-to-work state), and political prisoner and self-defense cases such as those of the Wilmington

Ten (of which NAARPR founder Ben Chavis was a member) and Joan Little of Washington, North Carolina, who killed the jailer who had repeatedly sexually assaulted her.[11] Beyond organizing in North Carolina, the early National Alliance, headquartered in Chicago, supported high-profile political prisoners such as the Attica Brothers, the San Quentin Six, the Wounded Knee defendants, Puerto Rican liberation movement participants, Assata Shakur, Leonard Peltier, and Lolita Lebron, one of the five Puerto Rican Nationalists. Filing a UN petition in defense of political prisoners, support-ing the incarcerated by raising funds for their care and legal defense, and spreading the word about their cases, the Alliance won conviction reversals, removals from death row, releases, and settlements.[12]

For NAARPR organizers, growing political imprisonment was indica-tive of a larger set of concerning organizing principles by which the state operated because it reflected "the insidious lengths to which the system will go to destroy its severest critics and to cover up its victimization of oppressed minorities."[13] Political scandals such as Watergate and the result-ing findings of the US Senate's Church Committee, which uncovered deep and extensive violations of civil liberties by US intelligence agencies, were symptomatic of a larger problem of expanding, antidemocratic governmen-tal power. Members worked to abolish the death penalty, the militarization of the police, "all manner of repressive legislation," and state surveillance efforts such as the FBI's Counterintelligence Program, familiarly known as COINTELPRO. The organization supported workers' rights struggles, especially in the South, and resisted the closure of public institutions such as local clinics and state hospitals.[14] In addition to defending the liberation of political prisoners and labor's right to organize, the Alliance targeted repressive legislation, police crimes, hate groups, and the use of behavio-rial control and human manipulation and experimentation in factories, schools, and prisons. Members were also involved in the immigrant work-ers' rights movement, taking the position that "Latin, Caribbean, Arab and Asian workers without documents . . . [were] . . . exiled by political persecu-tion and economic depression from their original countries . . . [and were compelled to] toil at the worst jobs with the worst wages U.S. capitalism has to offer."[15]

Headquartered at the Peace Information Center, a shared office space for leftist antiwar organizations located on the Delmar Loop near North Skinker Boulevard, the St. Louis NAARPR chapter was among the more active local components of the mass defense group.[16] Growing from just over ten members to more than two hundred, and with an executive board of approximately thirty, the St. Louis NAARPR was a key local organization that became a political home to many of the Gateway City's most influential and active leftist organizers.[17] Hershel Walker of the Communist Party, USA; Walle Amusa of the All-African People's Revolutionary Party; Jim Anderson, the regional director of the Amalgamated Clothing and Textile Workers Union (ACTWU); Alice Windom of the Association of Black Social Workers; student activist and nurse Pam Talley; Lew Moye of the United Auto Workers; Saint Louis University student activist and campus leader Coraminita Mahr; Zenobia Thompson, a community organizer and a nurse at Homer G. Phillips Hospital; Gwen Giles, a Missouri state senator; Myrna and Leo Fichtenbaum, a radical Jewish couple, members of the Communist Party, USA, and longtime supporters of leftist causes in St. Louis; Yvonne Logan of the Women's International League for Peace and Freedom; and religious leaders the Reverend Sterling Belcher of Emmanuel Lutheran Church and the Reverend Bill Stickey of St. Stephen's Episcopal Church made up the local executive board.[18]

As local and national politics took a rightward turn, the "working-class-led black freedom movement" that had so deeply shaped St. Louis politics for three decades since the 1930s had lost its intensity.[19] Still, an active cadre of political dissidents, with deep roots in earlier liberation movements, built new organizations and created new struggles to address the distinct challenges of the moment. Holding no romanticized view of the 1960s, yet forging activist pathways in a time deemed by some as bereft of leftist struggle, the St. Louis Alliance fought to free political prisoners, reform the criminal justice system, challenge and end police violence and murder, defend the right of labor to organize, prevent deindustrialization, and stop the closure of public health clinics, hospitals, and access to public social services. The St. Louis NAARPR defined local leftist working-class struggle in a new age.[20]

Frank Chapman Jr.'s story reveals much about the emergence and work of the St. Louis NAARPR, particularly the organization's grounding in the fight to free the imprisoned. At the young age of nineteen, Chapman began serving a sentence of life plus fifty years in prison at the Missouri State Penitentiary in Jefferson City. Charged with murder and robbery and sentenced in 1961, Chapman returned to his St. Louis home fifteen years later after a long attempt by supporters to free him. While incarcerated, Chapman underwent a political awakening. Chapman founded Lifers Incorporated, a prisoners' rights organization, a Marxist-Leninist study group, and the first Missouri state prison branch of the NAACP. The "Collective," as members called it, aimed to establish a political education program for inmates. The NAACP Missouri prison chapter arranged prisoner education programs at a community college in Moberly, Missouri. It also desegregated sections of the prison, challenged discrimination in the allocation of prisoner job assignments, improved facilities by eliminating overcrowding, advocated for the release of more than thirty wrongfully imprisoned young men, filed suits against prison officials to hold them accountable for their wrongdoing, and defended prisoners' right to read socialist and Marxist literature. Studying radical political literature played an integral role in the formation of Black prisoners' political consciousness. From George Jackson, Angela Davis, and Mumia Abu-Jamal to Attica Prison organizers, access to Marxist writings, in particular, offered a blueprint and hope for freedom.[21] Of his first encounter with Karl Marx's writings, which were passed to him by a white prisoner jailed because of his trade-union activities, Chapman recalled, "In clear and concise language Marx and Engels set out before me the true meaning of history and where I fitted in as an oppressed person and as a member of the working class. . . . Marx showed me the revolutionary side of my misery. I was no longer helpless, now I could consciously be part of a revolutionary movement designed to empower the wretched of the earth."[22]

A Missouri state representative, DeVerne Calloway, worked with Frank Chapman to investigate prisoner abuse at the Missouri State Penitentiary. At the invitation of Lifers Inc., Calloway visited the state prison, meeting with Chapman and others to witness firsthand and discuss the institution's horrific conditions and the abuse that wardens routinely inflicted on inmates.[23] Calloway was moved to action by the stories of Black prisoners who sent her letters about the facility's deplorable conditions. Calloway likely would have heard stories like the one shared by prison organizer Dean Johnson, who wrote the St. Louis NAARPR branch to request "your support [for] and proper publicity" about the effort to have Warden Donald W. Wyrick removed. Johnson described Wyrick as a "psychopath and an archracist who actually relished imposing brutality and dehumanization against blacks." Johnson detailed Wyrick's support for the National White People's Socialist Party—a white supremacist inmate collective also known as the Nazis—that Wyrick "uses . . . as his henchmen." A member of the Nazis "attempted to murder the Black editor of the prison newspaper," and the editor was hospitalized with multiple stab wounds. The perpetrator was not placed in maximum security as was customary. Black prisoners, on the other hand, were routinely thrown into maximum security cells on the mere suspicion that they were engaged in "Black militant" politics, Johnson explained. Like Chapman, Johnson also detailed the targeting of Black prisoners who were studying Marxist literature and other radical political philosophies.[24]

Figure 14.1 Activist leader Hershel Walker (1909–1990), pictured here in 1956, contributed to several generations' worth of St. Louis labor and racial justice campaigns, including co-founding the region's NAARPR chapter and its predecessor, the local chapter of the Angela Davis Defense Committee. St. Louis Globe-Democrat *photo, from the collections of the St. Louis Mercantile Library at the University of Missouri–St. Louis*

St. Louis Communist Party leader Hershel Walker (Fig. 14.1), whom Chapman deeply admired and called his "political father," organized the Frank Chapman Defense Committee in 1969.[25] Through his contacts, Walker put Chapman in touch with a lawyer, Arley R. Woodrow, who agreed to represent Chapman. The year was 1971. Woodrow believed that because Chapman had been committed to a state mental hospital and later escaped, he was largely "incompetent to stand trial." Furthermore, the court did not include this information in the official record, nor did it mention that Chapman was beaten into a confession. Because Chapman had undergone such an intensive self-education process in prison—becoming well-versed in Marxist philosophy, dialectical idealism and materialism, history, and law—Woodrow made Chapman his co-counsel. Having filed a motion for Chapman's post-conviction release, Woodrow prepared the case as Chapman traveled to the St. Louis City Jail where he awaited trial. Back at the same courthouse where he was sentenced to life plus fifty years in prison a decade earlier, Chapman once again stood before the judge. Outside the St. Louis Circuit Court room, local members and supporters of the movement to free Angela Davis, who was captured, jailed, and was awaiting trial after having been convicted for murder, conspiracy, and kidnapping by the State of California, held signs that read "Free Angela Davis and All Political Prisoners." The judge denied Chapman's motion for release, and Chapman returned to the City Jail and, later, the Missouri State Penitentiary.[26]

Perhaps unexpectedly, upon returning to Jefferson City, Chapman felt a newfound hope in the possibility of his release. Inspired by the Attica Prison Rebellion—a "well thought out rebellion," as Chapman remembered, that took place in September 1971—he drew strength from the incarcerated workers whose collective action and political education demonstrated what he and his comrades could foment in the US heartland.[27] Chapman's most important wellspring of inspiration, however, came from the National United Committee to Free Angela Davis and All Political Prisoners, which had become a truly mass international defense organization. The membership of the St. Louis–based Frank Chapman Defense Committee overlapped with those who formed the St. Louis contingent of the Free Angela Davis movement, which would eventually develop into the St. Louis NAARPR. Like many political prisoners, Chapman wrote articles for supportive publications like *Freedomways*, the Black Left periodical edited by the Black Communist couple Esther Cooper and Jim Jackson along with John Henrik Clarke, all of whom were New York City–based supporters of the Chapman Defense Committee.[28]

In the wake of the 1971 Attica Prison Rebellion, Black, Brown, and Indigenous prisoners across the country were targeted by wardens and prison guards who were determined to avoid having their own facility become the latest stage for an uprising. Chapman's insistence that his plans only involved fighting his case in the courts were ignored by Missouri State Penitentiary officials. They were convinced that Chapman and others were plotting a mutiny. Guards mercilessly stripped Chapman of his clothing, beat, isolated, and segregated him, and forced other prisoners to view the violent spectacle. Missouri prison officials then relinquished Chapman to the authority and jurisdiction of the Kentucky State Penitentiary. Known as the "Castle on the Cumberland," the prison was founded in the late nineteenth century by Confederate State Brigadier General Hylan Benton Lyon. A maximum-security prison, the Castle typically became the new facility for prison organizers who had led and inspired insurgent actions or uprisings, including work stoppages, hunger strikes, or damage to property.

At the Kentucky State Penitentiary, Chapman met Louisville Black Panther Party member William Darryl Blakemore, the only member of the Louisville Seven sentenced to ten years on a weapons charge.[29] While there, he also met the Tinsley brothers—Narvel, 22, and William Michael, 18—who were convicted of murdering two police officers.[30] The brothers' case garnered widespread attention in the state of Kentucky and among civil rights organizers, including Anne Braden, the longtime activist who, with her husband Carl, put Kentucky on the proverbial map of racial justice causes. The Tinsley brothers put Chapman in touch with Braden, who met with Chapman and explained that she, along with Angela Davis, who had recently been acquitted on all charges, were forming a national group based in Chicago to extend the defense work performed by the National United Committee to Free Angela Davis and All Political Prisoners. The new group, called the National Alliance Against Racist and Political Repression, would function as a consortium of leftist organizations. Hershel Walker was instrumental in organizing a St. Louis chapter. In touch with National Alliance leaders, he shared the details of Chapman's case, and the new group agreed to support it.[31]

After spending eleven months in the Kentucky State Penitentiary, Chapman moved back to Missouri, where he would finally begin to take classes at the newly organized prisoner-education program at Moberly Community College. Just one day following Chapman's return to Jefferson City, the parole board permitted Chapman to enroll in Moberly Community College's associate-of-arts degree program. Should Chapman attain an associate's degree and then go on to earn a bachelor's degree through the study release program for prisoners at the University of Missouri–Rolla, the parole board would grant his official release. White St. Louis–based radicals, some of whom held affiliations with Washington University, supported

Chapman by helping to raise tuition funds. For example, environmentalists, communists, and Black freedom movement supporters Virginia and Russell Brodine were members of Chapman's defense committee.[32] To convince the parole board to grant Chapman's weekend furlough, the Brodines shared a list of supporters from Washington University with officials, including the name of a dean from the institution.

Frank Chapman spent one weekend in St. Louis in 1973, having been granted a furlough to raise money to continue his studies. The three-day trip provides a window onto the relatively small yet influential interracial leftist collective in St. Louis City. Hershel Walker picked up Chapman at 9 a.m. sharp in Moberly and drove him two-and-a-half hours to St. Louis. Walker first took him around the city for a meal with friends and family and for TV and radio interviews with local Black journalists and an interview for *Proud*, a magazine founded by Ernie McMillan in 1970. Walker then took Chapman to the Brodines' house, which was on Westminster Place, a wealthy white enclave in the city's Central West End neighborhood. At a gathering there, journalists from Black newspapers and periodicals like the *St. Louis Argus* and the *St. Louis American* were joined by "movement lawyers," including those who represented political prisoners or activists and organizers, as well as by unionists, socialists, communists, academics, representatives from the American Friends Service Committee, the National Conference of Black Lawyers, and college campus groups, environmentalists, higher education administrators, and leaders of the St. Louis Black liberation movement, including Percy Green.[33] Those who gathered that evening raised an estimated $10,000. The following day, Chapman met with DeVerne and Ernest Calloway, a formidable local couple with deep ties to the St. Louis Black freedom struggle. DeVerne held formal political office while Ernest was a leader of the local Teamsters Union and a professor of urban studies at Saint Louis University. Having raised enough funds, Chapman entered the University of Missouri–Rolla in the fall of 1973, months following the founding of the NAARPR and a chapter in St. Louis.

While a student in Rolla, Chapman forged political ties with St. Louis organizers. Traveling to his home city each weekend, Chapman participated in Marxist study groups, efforts to win employment opportunities for Black youths, prison reform campaigns, and the fight to abolish Missouri's death penalty. Chapman worked with the Missouri Coalition to Abolish the Death Penalty and with organizations like the Lutheran Mission Association. He also gave lectures and talks on prison reform, speaking, for instance, at Washington University's Institute for Black Studies.[34]

In December 1975, Chapman graduated *cum laude* from the University of Missouri–Rolla.[35] Joe Scoggins, a Black social worker and educator who routinely connected with groups like ACTION and the All-African People's Revolutionary Party, drove Chapman to St. Louis on the day of his official release. In St. Louis, Chapman lived with Dan and Nina Cole, a Jewish couple that had joined his defense committee and had pressed a Washington University dean to award Chapman a scholarship to pursue graduate study in anthropology. Through the Coles, Chapman met Leo and Myrna Fichtenbaum, also an activist Jewish couple.[36]

For the three years since its founding, the NAARPR had supported Chapman, joining the effort to free him. At a 1977 Raleigh, North Carolina, demonstration organized in support of the freeing of the Wilmington Ten, organizers raised Chapman's release to demonstrate what could be accomplished with mass effort.[37] There, with North Carolina as a focal point, the Alliance's effort to defend the Wilmington Ten became one its most important early causes. The ten defendants faced wrongful convictions on arson and conspiracy charges.[38] In an open letter addressed to President Jimmy Carter and written from his jail cell in North Carolina, Ben Chavis used his own case to demand the freeing of all political prisoners. "As only one of many American citizens who has been unjustly imprisoned not because of criminal conduct but as a direct result of participation in the human and civil rights movement in the United States," Chavis wrote, "I appeal to you, President Carter, to first set a national priority of freeing all U.S. political prisoners."[39] To support the Wilmington Ten, whom the court initially sentenced to a combined 282 years, members of the St. Louis NAARPR wrote letters, spread the word about the case, and raised money to help pay legal fees.[40] St. Louis members traveled to attend the Raleigh demonstration. In fact, forty St. Louis supporters traveled to North Carolina's capital, more than the number of people who traveled from Chicago, where the NAARPR was founded.[41]

In addition to Chapman and Walker, Coraminita Mahr, a Saint Louis University undergraduate and graduate student, was a campus leader and lead organizer of the St. Louis NAARPR.[42] Like many US Black radicals, Mahr traveled to Cuba, spending two weeks there as a representative of the National Alliance. Mahr briefly met with Fidel Castro, cane-field workers, and members of women's organizations. Expressing "solidarity with the

Figure 14.2 Unidentified NAARPR demonstration in downtown St. Louis, in support of the Wilmington Ten political prisoners, circa 1977–1978. *From the National Alliance Against Racist and Political Repression, St. Louis Branch Records (S0582), State Historical Society of Missouri*

colonized peoples' struggles around the world and in South Africa," Mahr shared stories of the St. Louis movement.[43]

Frank Chapman Jr.'s freedom was but one case of imprisonment to which the St. Louis NAARPR dedicated its time and resources. Others included the Missouri Nine—Archie Dixon, Clifford Valentine, Conrad Adkins, Robert Johnson, Robert X. Gales, Robert X. Toney, Michael Shephard, Cornell Jackson, and George Williams—who were Black men charged with murdering a prison guard at the Missouri State Penitentiary on January 20, 1975. They were supported by the Committee to Free the Missouri Nine, which was essentially an ad hoc organization created by members of the St. Louis NAARPR.[44] Confined within a maximum-security unit or solitary confinement, the Missouri Nine were physically abused and deprived of access to basic provisions.[45] By the spring of 1975, charges against seven members of the group had been dropped. The two remaining members, George Williams and Cornell Jackson, remained in custody and faced trials in June. The case of the Missouri Nine aligned with the NAARPR's definition of "political prisoner," a definition adopted at the NAARPR founding conference in May 1973:

> A political prisoner is one who because of his or her political activity or ideas is arrested and tried whether on direct political charges . . . or on trumped-up, framed criminal charges as are most of the civilian cases today. Further, those that, because of their refusal to take part in aggressive, genocidal wars of imperialism, by resisting the draft, refusing to go fight or go A.W.O.L. rather than take part in such wars are court-martialed, are also political prisoners. The term would also apply to those who actively resist racism and denial of civil liberties within the military.[46]

Workers engaged in militant actions at the site of production, including incarcerated workers, were two groups the alliance identified as those routinely targeted by the state.

Twenty-four-year-old Rayfield Newlon, sentenced to die in the gas chamber on January 4, 1980, for the April 1978 murder of Mansfield C. Dave, a store owner in Kinloch, Missouri, was the first person to receive a death sentence in Missouri since the state reinstituted the practice in May 1977.[47] Botched examination processes fit into the pattern of "racist frame-ups" that Walle Amusa (Fig. 14.3) identified in his remarks at the Political Prisoners workshop of the NAARPR national convention in St. Louis in November 1977.[48] Officers seemed to have insinuated that Newlon had a drug problem. Franz D. Williams and Walter Lee West, both of Kinloch, were sentenced to life in prison and ten years in prison, respectively, along with Newlon, who was the third to be convicted of murder.[49] Newlon arrived at the Missouri State Penitentiary in late November 1979 after receiving his sentence from St. Louis County Circuit Court judge James Ruddy, and was at this point under the authority of prison warden Donald W. Wyrick, the subject of inmate Dean Johnson's 1974 letter to the St. Louis NAARPR. Wyrick told reporters that the facility did not have a death row, so Newlon would be placed in solitary confinement.[50]

Addressing police abuse and murder cases filled St. Louis NAARPR organizers' time. On July 7, 1980, five police officers beat to death twenty-three-year-old Dennis Benson while eyewitnesses pleaded for his life.[51] The officers repeatedly struck Benson on the head and on other parts of his body with nightsticks and flashlights. No officers were charged or

Figure 14.3 Walle Amusa, a member of the NAARPR board and leader in the Campaign for Human Dignity, which organized for the reopening of Homer G. Phillips Hospital. St. Louis Globe-Democrat *photo, from the collections of the St. Louis Mercantile Library at the University of Missouri–St. Louis*

penalized. By the end of July, NAARPR members had filed a petition with US Attorney Robert D. Kingsland's office, demanding an investigation into the murder by the US Department of Justice.[52] Widely covered in most St. Louis newspapers and on radio and television, the Benson case compelled hundreds to write letters to President Jimmy Carter, US Attorney General Benjamin Civiletti, Missouri Governor Joseph P. Teasdale, and St. Louis Mayor James F. Conway.[53] A small group of St. Louis Alliance members picketed the federal courthouse in August 1980.[54] Benson, beaten while handcuffed, succumbed to his injuries two days following the attacks.[55] The St. Louis NAARPR called for the suspension of the police officers who were involved in the incident during the investigation into Benson's murder. The organization also demanded that the officers who killed Benson be prosecuted and that the intimidation and harassment of witnesses to the murder be stopped.[56]

Figure 14.4 NAARPR representative Zenobia Thompson (center), with activist Marie Tarr (left) accompanying, confronts St. Louis Circuit Attorney George Peach on September 30, 1980, over his handling of the police killing of Dennis Benson. *Photo by John Dengler for the* St. Louis Globe-Democrat, *from the collections of the St. Louis Mercantile Library at the University of Missouri–St. Louis*

To continue their protest, members of the St. Louis NAARPR later stood outside the office of St. Louis Circuit Attorney George Peach at a demonstration in October 1980. Lead organizer Zenobia Thompson (Fig. 14.4) explained to reporters, "The Internal Affairs Division of the Police Department conducted a truncated investigation. The five police officers refused to cooperate with their own Department's investigation, and yet they remain on the force. To add insult to deep injury, George Peach threatens to close the book on this case, under the guise of 'inability to find witnesses.'"[57] The Police Crimes Task Force of the St. Louis NAARPR delivered about five hundred petitions to Mayor Conway's office in September 1980.[58] Pam Talley and Zenobia Thompson, co-coordinators of the task force, published an open letter to Lieutenant Colonel Atkins Warren in the *St. Louis Argus.* The two leaders wrote that "police brutality and the use of deadly force by police officers is widespread in North St. Louis and has approached epidemic proportions."[59] The cases of Frank Chapman, the

Missouri Nine, Rayfield Newlon, and George Benson joined many others, including those of J. B. Johnson, Nathaniel Butler, Gerald Garrett, and Glen Amerson. In the St. Louis NAARPR chapter's early years, defending the lives of those mistreated by the criminal justice system took up the bulk of the group's activities.

While fighting for the liberation of political prisoners formed a great part of its work, from its inception and throughout its heyday the St. Louis NAARPR also placed great emphasis on the struggle to defend the right of workers to organize and to receive a living wage and decent working conditions. From legislation designed to constrict worker control to the politics of the National Labor Relations Board, court-issued injunctions against striking, the passage of the Taft-Hartley Act of 1947, which weakened unions, and the increase in the number of right-to-work states since the 1940s, it was clear that the labor and trade union movement faced some of its most severe challenges by the 1970s.[60] Noting the deterioration of worker control, wages, job opportunities, benefits, and the conditions under which most workers suffered, and the concomitant concentration of profit in the hands of a few, founder Charlene Mitchell often took special note of the primacy of labor in mass struggle. "We should learn well," she wrote, "the lesson that labor is always the first target in periods of sustained repression."[61] Rising corporate power, in partnership with state power, threatened to trample the working class, so for workers—and, in a much larger sense, for US citizens as a whole—"a strong, vibrant trade union movement is vital to the safeguarding and extending of democracy," Mitchell explained. Deeply concerned about the loss of foundational constitutional rights such as protection from illegal search and seizure and the right to free speech and free assembly, the St. Louis Alliance waged war against "the dictatorship of the corporations at the workplace." The group acknowledged and organized around the notion that Black and Brown workers "receive[d] the brunt of the repression" and that "all workers become its victims in the end." Urging trade unions to establish independence from corporations and clarifying that it was not the Alliance's aim to replace trade unions, leaders organized their work around the principle that "the defense of labor . . . [was] the frontline of the defense of democracy."[62]

The St. Louis freedom movement of the twentieth century was defined by working-class issues such as access to decent, safe, and affordable housing, good jobs, quality food, a robust public transportation system, and social services. Coalitions among Black freedom movement builders, activist trade unionists, and political radicals kept economic justice at the forefront. In strategic ways, the St. Louis NAARPR became a key player in a vigorous labor struggle in a moment when, for many, the death knell of the trade union movement was sounding. In fact, the St. Louis Alliance developed a reputation for being strong on labor issues.[63]

Union members played an active role in the St. Louis Alliance, as members made local labor struggle one of their key causes. Frank Chapman Jr. wrote articles and book reviews for the *St. Louis Labor Tribune* and the *Missouri Teamster*. Iron workers, construction workers, auto workers, and Teamsters were Alliance members. Chapman estimated that approximately one-third of St. Louis Alliance members were also members of trade unions. White unionists like Doug Lincoln of the ACTWU and autoworker Steve Holland, along with Black unionists such as Kenneth Jones, Lew Moye, and John May, were active participants. The St. Louis NAARPR helped to organized warehouse workers in St. Louis and built a local solidarity campaign to support striking white coal miners in Kentucky. Chapman traveled to Kentucky to meet with the workers, who were in a standoff with the National Guard and Kentucky state troopers. The miners had gone on strike after twenty of their coworkers were killed in an explosion. Chapman became friends with one striker, inviting him to speak at a National Alliance conference in New York City where members raised money for a strike fund.[64]

The most important St. Louis Alliance victory on the labor front was the defeat of the Missouri right-to-work ballot initiative, Amendment 23, in 1978. The St. Louis NAARPR played a major role in this historic victory, avoiding the fate of states such as North Carolina, which had been an earlier target of national Alliance campaigns. A coalitional effort, the struggle to defeat the right-to-work bill brought together organizations like the Coalition of Black Trade Unionists, the A. Philip Randolph Institute, Service Employees International Union Local 50, the Teamsters, the ACTWU, the International Association of Machinists, the United Auto Workers, and local social workers and religious leaders.[65] Reflecting upon the struggle to defeat right-to-work, Frank Chapman Jr. recalled, "We won the struggle to defeat the ultra-right in their attempt to turn Missouri into a right to work state. We helped to build a mass campaign to defeat the anti-union, fascist right-to-work gang and scored a resounding victory. It was a great moment and the most valuable lesson we learned is that labor united with the African American community can be an unbeatable alliance in fighting the ultra-right."[66]

Far less successful was the effort to stop deindustrialization. As Charlene Mitchell noted, "Those who believe the runaway shop is a southern problem have things mixed up. The runaway shop is a northern problem; it is one of the chief methods for breaking the strength of organized labor in the North."[67] Thousands in St. Louis had joined the Committee to Stop Plant Closings to hold demonstrations and urge politicians to take action. NAARPR members were actively involved in the effort to roll back the tide of devastating urban job loss. The loss of industrial jobs devastated working-class communities. General Motors, for example, closed not long after voters rejected Amendment 23, stripping the city of an estimated ten thousand jobs.[68]

Solidarity with workers on strike across the country was yet another staple of the St. Louis Alliance's activities. For example, striking poultry workers of Sanderson Farms in Laurel, Mississippi—mostly Black women— received support from the Alliance when they took action in February 1979. The International Chemical Workers Union supported the striking workers, and the St. Louis Alliance distributed flyers that asked the public to boycott Miss Goldy Chickens that were produced by Sanderson Farms.[69] Similarly, St. Louis NAARPR members lent their support to workers in North Carolina who struck at J. P. Stevens, the second-largest textile manufacturer in the country. St. Louis Alliance members supported national boycotts of companies selling J. P. Stevens products, urging St. Louisans to refuse to buy anything from the company's extensive list of products, which included sheets and pillowcases, towels, blankets, carpets, linens, and hosiery.[70] Organizing southern workers, in a region where anti-unionism ran deep, was of critical importance, and the size of J. P. Stevens made it a focal point. "It is no exaggeration to say," Charlene Mitchell said, "that the organization of J. P. Stevens is the key to textile; the organization of textile is the key to southern labor; and the organization of southern labor is the key to a healthy trade union movement as a whole." The ACTWU eventually prevailed against J. P. Stevens, winning union recognition at North Carolina textile mills.[71]

The third major front of the St. Louis NAARPR's work was protecting public hospitals. Not long after the city announced its plans to close Homer G. Phillips Hospital, one of the premier Black hospitals in the country that had opened in 1937 after a long battle to secure city funds, the St. Louis

NAARPR formed the Ad Hoc Committee to Save Homer G. Phillips and All Public Hospitals.[72] The grassroots organization engaged in direct-action protests to try to stop the closing.[73] An estimated one thousand Black St. Louisans worked at the hospital, and many more had been born there. The St. Louis Association of Black Social Workers, aldermen Freeman Bosley Sr. (whose son would become the city's first Black mayor) and Clifford Wilson, and the Coalition of Black Trade Unionists joined the St. Louis NAARPR to stop the closing.[74] Local white trade-union participants such as Jim Anderson (ACTWU), who was elected to the NAARPR Executive Board in 1979, Gus Lumpe and Harold Gibbons (Teamsters), and a few "white leftist rank and filers" supported the campaign.[75] St. Louis NAARPR members Frank Chapman and Coraminita Mahr were actively involved in the effort to save Homer G. Phillips; however, the member at the forefront of the struggle was Zenobia Thompson. A nurse and an employee of Homer G. Phillips, Thompson worked tirelessly to explain to the public why the closure would have a devastating impact on Black St. Louis.

The national NAARPR joined the National Conference of Black Lawyers and the United Church of Christ Commission on Racial Justice in issuing a formal petition to the United Nations Commission on Human Rights, charging the United States with violating the human rights of Black American citizens. In the statement, writers highlighted the fact that racism was not simply a violation of Black Americans' constitutional rights; it was also an all-out threat to the very survival of Black people. On the theme of survival, the position statement read, "We not only live at a time when it is becoming increasingly difficult for working people and the poor to live decently but we also must recognize that racism works diligently to see to it that when jobs are scarce Black people are the most unemployed and that when under the guise of budget cuts and 'savings' public hospitals are closed down, the death rate and illness rise to the sky for Black people." The statement called the move to close Homer G. Phillips Hospital a form of Black genocide: "Let us make no mistake about it; the crucial issue on the closing of Homer G. Phillips is genocide; it's the pronouncement of a death sentence on an entire community."[76]

The position statement also directly challenged conservative forms of Black Power that assumed the form of Black capitalism and privatization. It denounced arguments that favored turning Homer G. Phillips into a private, Black-owned hospital. Writers argued that making it private would give the mayor and business leaders an incentive to declare bankruptcy. "Blind, short-sighted self-interest continues to misguide us. For example, there are those who have this pipe dream of transforming Homer G. Phillips into a private institution that will be Black controlled. This is not the way to break the monopoly of white male doctors and administrators. In fact, this plays right into the hands of the Mayor and big business because once Homer G. Phillips goes private then they can force it into bankruptcy." The position statement insisted on framing the effort to close Homer G. as an assault on the public and the rights accorded to citizens: "Our struggle to save Homer G. Phillips must be a struggle to save public hospitals. We must see the right to adequate health care as a human right."[77]

The final three decades of the twentieth century are not typically years that register in popular or scholarly imaginings of the freedom movement, which I define as not just the civil rights movement, but also Black Power, peace struggles, anti-carceral or abolition politics, workers' rights organizing, and queer and feminist liberation. Yet, some of the most widely influential moments in freedom movement history happened during this time, and St. Louis was a key site of this political unfolding. Recently, historians have begun to uncover a dynamic period defined by robust political activity.[78] We are finding ways to think expansively about what constituted the freedom movement not by rethinking the 1960s, which has been done by many, but by examining the history of the movement's forgotten later years. Chronicling the evolution of mass struggles and campaigns designed to turn back the tide of growing state repression of popular social movements, this chapter has offered a history of a local attempt among leftist organizers to combat rising political repression and the dramatic growth of the carceral state. The story of the National Alliance Against Racist and Political Repression offers a political genealogy of leftists who meaningfully engaged in coalition politics to contest patriarchal, capitalist, imperialist, and racist systems. It shows how mass defense struggle of the 1970s and 1980s understood anti-carceral politics in expansive ways.

15. Where It Took Place

Mapping *Left in the Midwest*

Monica Duwel and Elizabeth Eikmann

IN KATHARINE CORBETT'S BOOK *In Her Place*, a guide to St. Louis women's history, the author emphasizes place as both a social construct and a physical space. Focusing on the geography of place, Corbett writes, "Physical settings sometimes help explain past events but almost always help give them a tangible immediacy."[1] Consideration of physical place through the act of creating and consuming maps can not only offer us insight about the intersections of history, culture, identity, and activism, but also can enrich our experiences with those very places in the contemporary landscape. As the present volume asserts, progressive activism and movement building did in fact happen here, in the midwestern metropolis of St. Louis. The maps that make up this chapter take that claim literally, illustrating exactly *where* in the city that "here" was.

The maps found on the following pages identify places where progressive activist movements of 1960s and 1970s St. Louis were built and sustained. They are organized into three categories: *Activist Institutions and Community Sites*; *Marches and Parades*; and *Protests, Sit-Ins, and Demonstrations*. It is important to note that neither these categories nor the sites mapped therein are meant to be comprehensive or exclusionary. Rather, the map content is limited to places and events that are directly addressed by the volume's contributors. Thus, individual sites as named within the preceding chapters determined the physical boundaries and thematic focus of each map. In addition, the *Activist Institutions and Community Sites* maps are not representative of a specific date or singular year, but rather are inclusive of the roughly twenty-year period addressed by the volume. Readers should therefore be aware that the individual sites appearing on a singular such map did not necessarily exist simultaneously.

The five *Activist Institutions and Community Sites* maps represent places mentioned in this volume that were significant to activist organizing, community building, and resource sharing, including organizational headquarters, frequent meeting sites, businesses patronized by progressive or activist-oriented clienteles, and private residences. Four of the maps in this collection focus on St. Louis City as divided into the broad areas of Northeast and Southeast St. Louis City, Midtown and its vicinity, and the Central West End. The fifth map, covering an area identified as the Western Central Corridor, focuses on sites surrounding the city-county boundary line.

The five maps in the *Marches and Parades* collection illustrate the specific pathways activist organizations took through the streets of St. Louis in their calls for attention to injustice by way of protest marches and celebratory parades discussed by the volume's authors. And the final map set, *Protests, Sit-Ins, and Demonstrations*, details the specific sites where activists held occupations and sit-ins, waged protests, and organized rallies that receive coverage in the preceding chapters.

This chapter joins a growing group of projects that seek to place St. Louis histories and cultures on a map in a variety of creative ways. Colin Gordon's books *Mapping Decline: St. Louis and the Fate of the American City* (2008) and *Citizen Brown: Race, Democracy, and Inequality in the St. Louis Suburbs* (2019) use maps to scrutinize the effects of urban change over time.[2] John A. Wright's *Discovering African American St. Louis: A Guide to Historic Sites* (1994 and 2002) maps more than four hundred sites relevant to the history of Black St. Louisans, many of them previously unrecorded in published works.[3]

Increasingly, scholars are using mapping techniques to understand social movements with respect to the physical spaces in which their activism took root and grew. Take, for example, *Mapping LGBTQ St. Louis: 1945–1992*, an interdisciplinary initiative led by Andrea Friedman and Miranda Rectenwald at Washington University. *Mapping LGBTQ St. Louis* utilizes digital mapping technology to document the region's lesbian, gay, bisexual, trans, and queer community histories and cultures, specifically tracking change and movement over time.[4] The maps included in this chapter will, we hope, be a valuable contribution to this established scholarly tradition and serve readers with yet another way to interact with St. Louis history and culture as seen on a map.

In the volume's earlier pages, one can read about the who, what, when, and why. In this chapter, one can experience the *where*. The physical spaces and places central to the activists and organizations whose stories make up this collection, when viewed on a map, offer a unique approach to understanding more fully the histories of St. Louis's progressive social movements during this volume's two-decade timespan. Yet the value of this project lies not only in its illustration of new historical perspectives but also in the possibilities it offers for readers to appreciate these physical spaces in fresh ways in the present moment. Ideally, these maps will provide readers with a richer sense of place and a new lens through which to understand the importance and power that it holds.

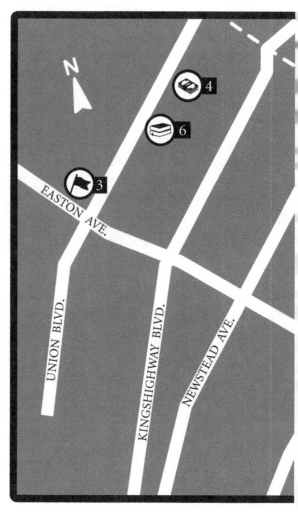

Activist Institutions and Community Sites: *Northeast St. Louis City*

1. ACTION headquarters—4154 N. Newstead Ave. (address circa 1969)
One of several successive headquarters used by the direct-action civil rights group, which split from CORE in 1964 to pursue a more aggressive style of nonviolent protest: Intro. and Chs. 1, 4, 7

2. Black Smith Shop—4167 Fair Ave.
Bookstore and coffeehouse, open from 1968 to the early 1970s, with literature, posters, and art emphasizing Black culture and politics: Introduction

3. CORE headquarters—1502 Union Blvd.
Office and meeting site, from the mid-1960s through early 1970s, for St. Louis's groundbreaking chapter of the Congress of Racial Equality: Intro. and Chs. 1, 4, 7

4. Gateway National Bank—3412 Union Blvd.
Commercial bank founded in 1965, by and for Black St. Louisans, as a community-generated response to redlining and other racist lending practices: Ch. 4

5. Grace Hill Settlement House—2600 Hadley St.
Long-standing social-service center that, during the late 1960s, administered federal antipoverty programs and hosted art and poetry events by activist Black performers: Introduction

6. House of Negro History—3014 Union Blvd.
Bookstore and book distributor, established in 1968, carrying literature on African American history and freedom struggles: Introduction

7. House of Umoja—1742 Division St. (first of two locations)
Afrocentric store owned by activist Mattie Trice, offering Black-authored books, African art and clothing, and courses on diasporic Black cultures: Introduction

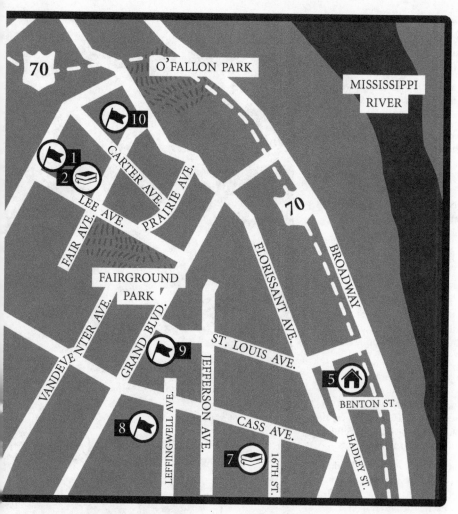

8. Jeff-Vander-Lou (JVL) Inc. offices—1346 N. Leffingwell Ave.
Headquarters for JVL's neighborhood empowerment work, including Black employment and homeownership initiatives and operation of a medical clinic: Intro. and Ch. 4

9. People's Coalition Against Lead Poisoning headquarters—2730 N. Grand Blvd.
Organization founded to fight environmental racism in St. Louis and based at the Yeatman Community Health Center: Ch. 11

10. St. Louis Urban League offices—4401 Fair Ave. (one of several locations)
Home starting in 1966 for the long-standing civil rights body, whose moderate stances left it sometimes aligned but other times at odds with young 1960s Black freedom activists: Intro. and Chs. 1, 4, 10, 12

Activist Institutions and Community Sites: *Southeast St. Louis City*

1. Cat House—3863 Botanical Ave.
Lesbian-feminist residential and activist collective: Ch. 13

2. Women's Coffeehouse—around 1906 S. 12th St.
Bar-scene alternative for lesbian patrons, founded in the Central West End's Women's House and located here in Soulard before moving again in 1974 to A Woman's Place: Ch. 13

3. July House—3540 Victor St.
Lesbian-feminist residential and activist collective: Ch. 13

4. Magnolia Committee meeting space—3664 Arsenal St.
Regular planning spot, using St. John's Episcopal Church, for the coalition organizing St. Louis's first pride march, held in 1980: Ch. 3

5. Metropolitan Community Church—1120 Dolman St.
Second permanent home of activist church serving LGBTQ worshippers after the institution left the Central West End for the Lafayette Square area: Ch. 8

6. Mor or Les—4135 S. Grand Blvd.
Lesbian bar and community institution, whose 1979 destruction by arson catalyzed a concerted activist response: Ch. 13

7. Soulard Neighborhood Center—716 Geyer Ave. (mapped here); then 2021 Menard St.
Basement office and walk-in facility run by the Soulard Neighborhood Improvement Association as home for anti-demolition agitation and education: Ch. 9

8. St. Stephen's Episcopal Church—1400 Park Ave.
Successor to St. Stephen's House, opened in 1961, and a frequent meeting site

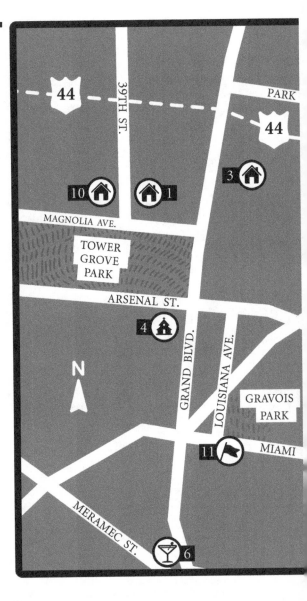

for ACTION, the Black Liberators, and organizers of the 1969 public housing rent strike: Chs. 4, 14

9. St. Stephen's House—520 Rutger St.
Episcopal congregation and social-service provider, founded in 1897, that became a

426

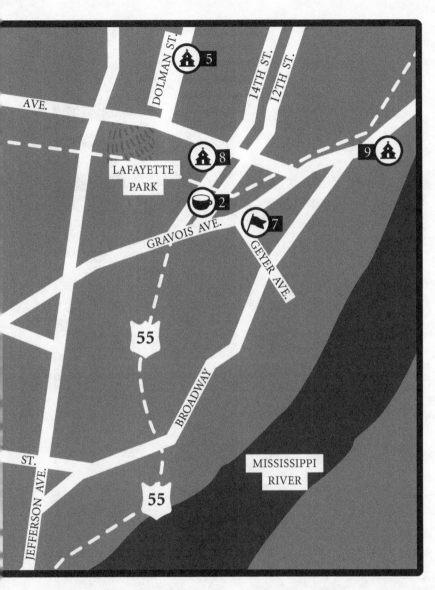

1950s center for interracial programming and outreach by liberal urban Protestants: Ch. 3

10. Thornapple House—3910 Botanical Ave.
Lesbian-feminist residential and activist collective: Ch. 13

11. A Woman's Place—intersection of Miami St. and Louisiana Ave.
Headquarters of the Lesbian Alliance, third home of the Women's Coffeehouse, and provider of space for political organizing and social events before its destruction by arson in 1975: Ch. 13

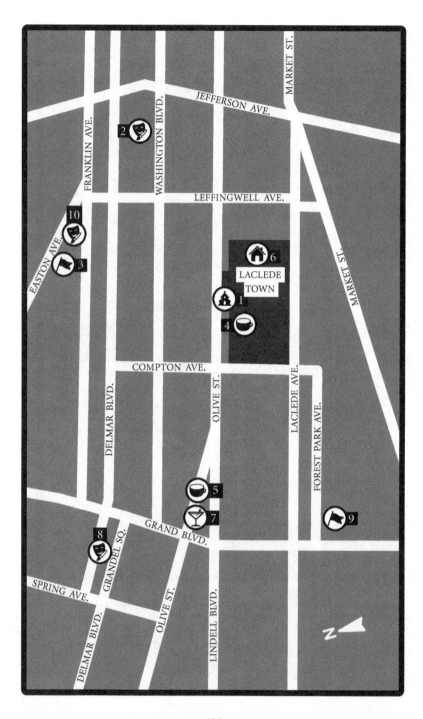

Activist Institutions and Community Sites: *Midtown and Vicinity*

1. Berea Presbyterian Church—3010 Olive St.
Multiracial congregation active in local civil rights struggles and temporary initial meeting place of the city's Metropolitan Community Church for gay and lesbian churchgoers: Intro. and Ch. 8

2. Black Artists' Group (BAG) building—2665 Washington Blvd.
Disused warehouse repurposed by BAG for a constant schedule of multimedia performances, youth classes, and political meetings from 1969 to 1972: Intro. and Chs. 4, 10

3. Black Liberators headquarters—2810 Easton Ave. (now Dr. Martin Luther King Dr.)
Office and gathering spot for the Liberators, a 1968–1969 activist and paramilitary group that partially modeled itself on Oakland's Black Panther Party: Ch. 4

4. Circle Coffee House—100 Cardinal Pl.
Social center in LaClede Town and host to avant-garde jazz, poetry, folk music, and "the more anarchistic of the younger generation," as the *Post-Dispatch* put it: Introduction

5. Golden Gate Coffee House—3542 Olive St.
Late-night gathering place for gay patrons, which advertised in the Mandrake Society's newsletter and was part of an LGBTQ nightlife district in this block of Olive: Ch. 3

6. LaClede Town—bounded by Olive (N), Ewing (E), Laclede (S), and Compton (W)
Low-rise, affordable rental community that attracted countercultural, activist, and arts-oriented residents while garnering national attention for its racial diversity: Introduction

7. Onyx Room—3560 Olive St.
Gay bar and site of the 1969 Halloween-night arrests that inspired public protests by the newly formed Mandrake Society: Chs. 3, 8

8. People's Art Center—3657 Grandel Sq.
Interracial education and arts organization, founded with New Deal federal support, that trained, hired, or featured influential Black visual artists until its demise in 1965: Ch. 1

9. Teamsters Council Plaza—300 S. Grand Blvd.
Affordable housing development and meeting site for community organizing projects of Teamsters Local 688, including union support for the 1969 public housing rent strike: Chs. 4, 10

10. Wall of Respect—intersection of N. Leffingwell Ave. and Franklin Ave.
Outdoor mural featuring portraits of influential Black figures and a regular activist gathering place following its July 1968 inception: Intro. and Ch. 4

Activist Institutions and Community Sites: *Central West End*

1. The Abused Women's Support Project training site—4501 Westminster Pl.
Frequent meeting location at Second Presbyterian Church for this advocacy organization, founded in 1978 by a coalition of feminist groups: Chs. 10, 13

2. The Exit—444 N. Boyle Ave. (mapped here); then 4283 Olive St.
Gaslight Square coffeehouse, run by a liberal church coalition, that attracted a diverse and often LGBTQ clientele: Ch. 3

3. Gateway Theatre—461 N. Boyle Ave.
Gaslight Square theater repurposed in 1969 for various performance series by the Black Artists' Group and Katherine Dunham's Performing Arts Training Center: Introduction

4. KDNA radio—4285 Olive St.
Alternative community radio station in Gaslight Square, offering eclectic music, political programming, and a fervently anticommercial ethos: Intro. and Ch. 13

5. Left Bank Books—399 N. Euclid Ave. (final of three locations)
Progressive independent bookstore that arrived in the neighborhood in 1977 after eight years on the Delmar Loop: Intro. and Chs. 10, 13

6. Metropolitan Community Church—5108 Waterman Blvd.
First permanent home for St. Louis congregation with a mission to serve gay and lesbian churchgoers and a hub for LGBTQ activism and community building: Intro. and Chs. 3, 8

7, 8, 9. Metropolitan Life Services Corporation—4746 McPherson Ave. (7); then 4940 McPherson Ave. (8); finally 10 S. Euclid Ave. (9)
Secular outgrowth of the Metropolitan Community Church and a dynamic community center for LGBTQ patrons: Ch. 8

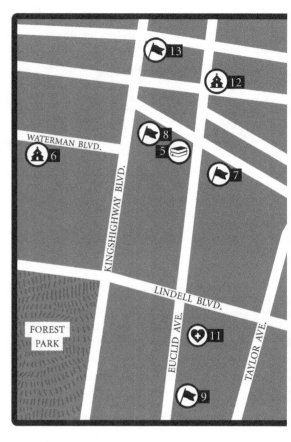

10. Mid-City Community Congress headquarters—4005 Delmar Blvd.
Business, church, and block-group alliance promoting Black community empowerment and home base for the group's youth affiliate, the Zulu 1200s: Intro. and Ch. 4

11. Reproductive Health Services—100 N. Euclid Ave.
St. Louis's first legal abortion clinic, opened in 1973 by longtime reproductive rights advocate Judith Widdicombe: Ch. 10

12. Trinity Episcopal Church—600 N. Euclid Ave.
A center for LGBTQ organizing and an early meeting place of the Mandrake Society, the city's first "homophile" activist group: Intro. and Ch. 3

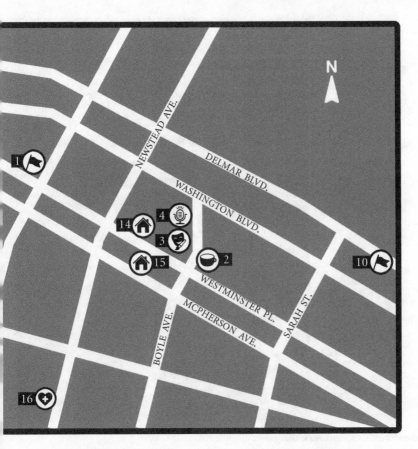

13. Union-Sarah Gateway Center—4957 Delmar Blvd.
Local office administering federal War on Poverty programs and a home base and source of organizers for neighborhood-based racial-justice initiatives: Ch. 11

14. Westminster House—4367 Westminster Pl.
Lesbian-feminist residential and activist collective: Ch. 10

15. The Women's House—4357 McPherson Ave.
Lesbian-feminist residential and activist collective, claimed as the earliest among such 1970s residences, and first home of the Women's Coffeehouse, a gathering spot for lesbian patrons: Ch. 13

16. Women's Self-Help Center—8129 Delmar Blvd.; then 27 N. Newstead Ave. (mapped here)
Feminist institution offering services for women, including "rap sessions," counseling, self-defense classes, and support for domestic violence survivors: Ch. 10

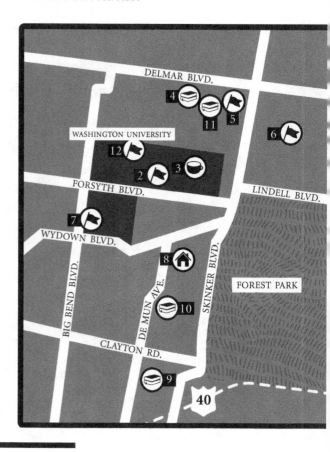

Activist Institutions and Community Sites: *Western Central Corridor*

1. Black Culture Center—5585 Pershing Ave.
Black Nationalist Party gathering spot, with music hall and library, established in 1969 and used by activists and youth largely from the West End neighborhood: Intro. and Ch. 4

2. Center for the Biology of Natural Systems—Rebstock Hall, Washington University
Innovative environmental science lab, directed by Barry Commoner, that supported community groups combating lead poisoning and other environmental inequities: Ch. 11

3. Holmes Lounge—Ridgley Hall, Washington University
Social hub and staging ground for antiwar and student-movement activism, especially during the student campaign to eliminate institutional ties with the ROTC program: Ch. 5

4. Left Bank Books—559 N. Skinker Blvd.; then 6254 Delmar Blvd. (mapped here)
Progressive bookstore, founded by Washington University graduate students in 1969, that was a Delmar Loop anchor until its 1977 move to the Central West End: Intro. and Chs. 10, 13

432

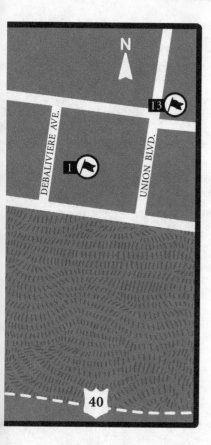

7. South 40 dormitories—Washington University
Regular meeting and recruiting area for campus activist groups, including Students for a Democratic Society and other left-wing and antiwar organizations: Intro. and Ch. 5

8. St. Louis Women's Committee for Ending Hydrogen Bomb Tests meeting site—306 DeMun Ave.
Regular meeting site, at the home of committee leader Juanita Sherman, for women's group pressing political leaders to adopt a nuclear-weapons test ban: Ch. 2

9, 10, 11. The Women's Eye—905 S. Yale Ave. (9); then 6344 S. Rosebury Ave. (10); finally 554 Limit Ave. (11)
Independent bookstore that functioned as a feminist and lesbian community center from 1976 to 1988: Chs. 10, 13

12. Women's Building—Washington University
Frequent meeting and event space for 1970s activist groups, including the campus's Gay Liberation Front and Feminist Coalition, and host to women's music concerts: Ch. 13

13. Yalem Human Development Center—724 Union Blvd.
Host to numerous mid- and late 1960s events put on by the St. Louis Committee on Africa, highlighting African anticolonial struggles: Ch. 4

5. Peace Information Center—6217 Delmar Blvd; then 6244 Delmar Blvd. (mapped here); finally 606 Eastgate Ave.
Delmar Loop storefront and meeting space, used for coordinating local antiwar initiatives, offering draft counseling, and mounting events opposing US militarism: Intro. and Ch. 14

6. Skinker DeBaliviere Community Council office—5858 Delmar Blvd.; then 425 DeBaliviere Ave.; finally 6008 Kingsbury Ave. (mapped here)
Liberal neighborhood group seeking to promote residential racial integration, stem white flight, and develop models for multiracial cooperation: Ch. 9

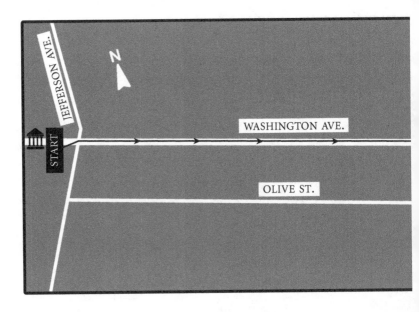

**Veiled Prophet Parade and Protest—
Saturday, October 7, 1967**
Ch. 7

ACTION protests along the Veiled Prophet
Parade route became an annual event. Here,
picketers at Jefferson Avenue and Olive
Street displayed slogans such as "Black Men
in Vietnam, Not in the Veiled Prophet,"
while others inserted themselves behind
a marching band at 22nd Street before
police intervened.

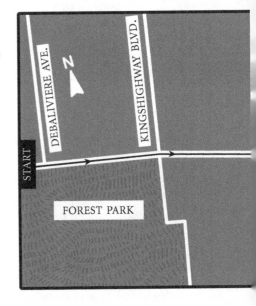

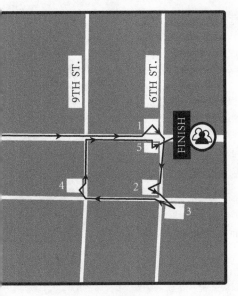

CORE Christmas Boycott March—
Thursday, November 21, 1963
Ch. 1

Protesting harsh sentences for Jefferson Bank protestors and downtown business support for the bank, CORE members marched through five downtown department stores, urging a holiday-season boycott. Demonstrators finally blocked traffic at Washington Avenue and Sixth Street, leading to seven arrests.

1: Stix, Baer & Fuller
2: Famous-Barr
3: Boyd's
4: Vandervoort's
5: Richman Brothers

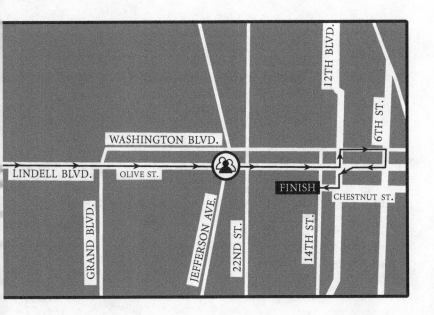

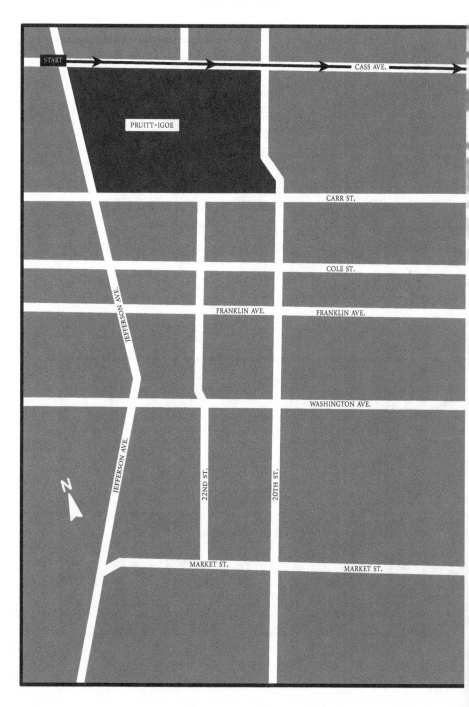

**League for Adequate Welfare
March—Sunday, May 12, 1968**
Ch. 4

Approximately 200 participants, mostly
North Side public housing residents,
traveled from Pruitt-Igoe to the city hall
mayor's office, bearing demands that elected
officials institute job opportunities for poor
St. Louisans and expand subsidies for food
and rent. The procession signaled the public
emergence of a vigorous welfare rights
movement in St. Louis.

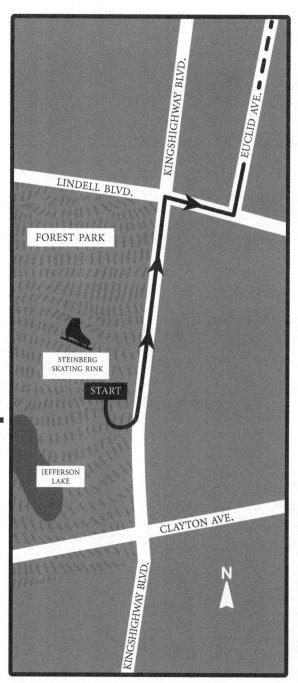

Take Back the Night Inaugural March—Saturday, June 9, 1979
Chs. 10, 13

More than 1,000 participants marched from an opening rally at Forest Park's Steinberg Skating Rink through the residential streets of the Central West End. The event emerged from a wider climate of local feminist and lesbian organizing against sexual and gender-based violence.

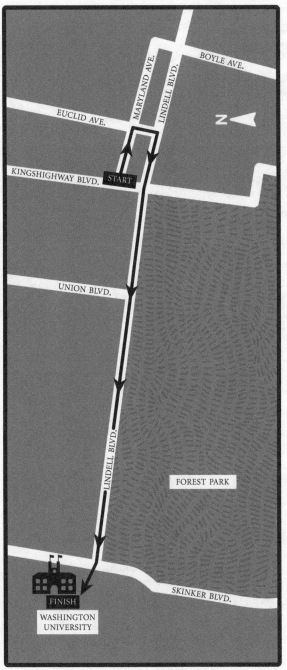

**First St. Louis Pride March—
Sunday, April 20, 1980**
Chs. 3, 8

Officially titled "Lesbians, Gays, and Friends Walk for Charity," the procession capped a week of events dubbed the St. Louis Celebration of Lesbian and Gay Pride. Participants began at Maryland Plaza and finished with a mass rally on Washington University's Brookings Quadrangle.

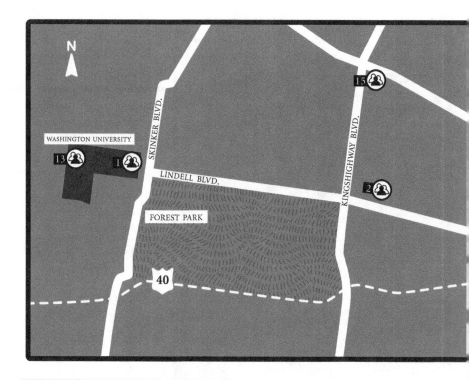

Protests, Sit-Ins, and Demonstrations

1. Brookings Hall, Washington University—1 Brookings Dr.
Site in December 1968 of an eight-day accounting office occupation by about forty Association of Black Collegians members, whose "Black Manifesto" outlined ten racial-equity demands for school officials: Ch. 4

2. Cathedral Basilica—4431 Lindell Blvd.
The most visible of many summer 1969 "Black Sunday" protest sites, where ACTION and allies called attention to Christian denominations' involvement in slavery and racism: Intro. and Chs. 3, 4

3. Christ Church Cathedral—1210 Locust St.
Host in February 1977 to a major pro–Equal Rights Amendment rally, led by the local NOW chapter, following a march through icy streets beginning at the Arch: Ch. 10

4. City Hall—1200 Market Street
Site for three days of sit-ins and protests in early 1979, leading to dozens of arrests, by Homer G. Phillips Hospital defenders including healthcare workers and two aldermen: Ch. 12

5. City Jail—124 S. 14th St.
Nightly assembly and vigil point, through much of October 1963, for hundreds of demonstrators supporting the Jefferson Bank protestors imprisoned inside: Introduction

6. Civil Courts Building—10 N. 12th St. (now Tucker Blvd.)
Prayer and candlelight vigil locale in October 1963, with 350 Catholic clergy and laypeople decrying harsh contempt-of-court sentences given to Jefferson Bank picketers: Ch. 1

Continued after page turn

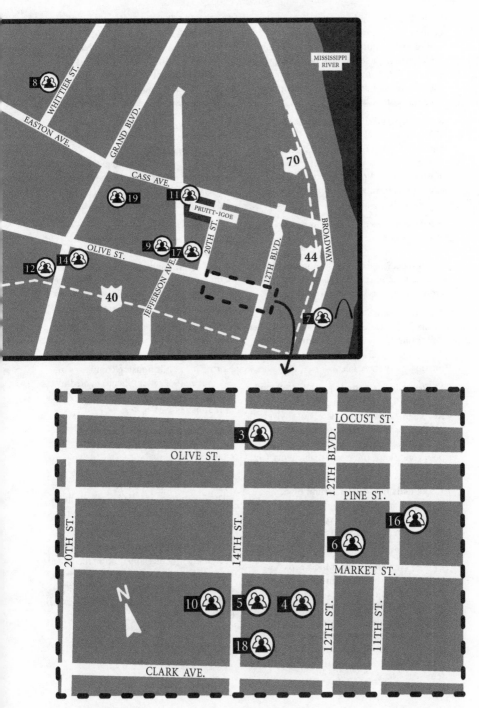

7. The Gateway Arch—1 Wharf St. (now N. Leonor K. Sullivan Blvd.)
Unfinished monument transformed in July 1964 into a stage set for dissent, as Percy Green and Richard Daly climbed the north leg to highlight rampant hiring discrimination: Intro. and Chs. 1, 4

8. Homer G. Phillips Hospital—2601 Whittier St.
Site of fierce August 1979 protests, including improvised barricades against police, by advocates defending the revered Black community institution against closure by the city: Chs. 10, 12, 13, 14

9. Jefferson Bank and Trust Company—2600 Washington Ave.
Target of months of picketing and nonviolent civil disobedience starting in August 1963, by CORE members demanding hiring and promotion of Black employees: Chs. 1, 4, 7

10. Kiel Auditorium—1401 Clark Ave.
Venue for the December 1972 Veiled Prophet Ball, infiltrated by ACTION members who unveiled that year's "prophet" to indict racism by city elites: Ch. 7

11. Pruitt-Igoe—bounded by Cass (N), 20th (E), Carr (S), and Jefferson (W)
Key staging area for the successful citywide public housing rent strike of 1969, which saw tenants organize against mismanagement, poor conditions, and unaffordable rents: Chs. 4, 11

12. Ramada Inn—303 S. Grand Blvd.
Setting for an all-day "people's tribunal," held in July 1980 by an activist coalition dubbing Mayor James Conway's closure of Homer G. Phillips Hospital an act of genocide: Ch. 12

13. Reserve Officers' Training Corps buildings, Washington University—Big Bend Blvd. near Millbrook Blvd. (now Forest Park Pkwy.)
Target of frequent student protests against the university's military ties, until both the Army and Air Force ROTC buildings were burned down during the spring 1970 semester: Ch. 5

14. Ritter Hall, Saint Louis University—220 N. Grand Blvd.
Home to the Arts and Sciences dean's office, occupied in April 1969 by members of the Association of Black Collegians, who called for Black Studies curricula and action against harassment of Black students: Intro. and Ch. 4

15. Sears, Roebuck, and Co.—1408 N. Kingshighway Blvd.
Department store facing an extensive 1952 boycott and picket effort by the St. Louis Negro Labor Council, as part of a nationwide campaign against racism in hiring: Ch. 4

16. Southwestern Bell Telephone Company—1010 Pine St.
One of several settings for 1943 pickets and demonstrations led by the local March on Washington Movement affiliate, calling for fair employment for Black women: Ch. 4

17. St. Louis Housing Authority—2031 Olive St.
Office picketed by sixty tenants of four North Side public housing complexes in November 1967, after officials denied requests such as better upkeep and a rollback of rent increases: Ch. 4

18. St. Louis Human Development Corporation (HDC) offices—1321 Clark Ave.
Scene in August 1967 of a ten-day sit-in by nine women and twenty children, after HDC job training resulted in no employment amid anti-Black hiring discrimination: Ch. 4

19. Vashon High School—3405 Bell Ave.
Predominantly Black institution facing fall 1968 protests urging student empowerment and Black Studies courses, with ACTION and the Black Liberators providing support: Ch. 4

About the Contributors

Heidi Ardizzone is an Associate Professor of American Studies at Saint Louis University, where she teaches courses on civil rights, race and citizenship, St. Louis and the Midwest, and social movements. Previous publications include "Fatherhood and Father Figures in Barack Obama's Early Presidency," in *Race and the Obama Phenomenon: The Vision of a More Perfect Multiracial Union* (2014), ed. G. Reginald Daniel and Hettie V. Williams; *An Illuminated Life: Belle da Costa Greene's Journey from Prejudice to Privilege* (2007); and, coauthored with Earl Lewis, *Love on Trial: An American Scandal in Black and White* (2001).

Gretchen Arnold is Associate Professor Emerita of Women's and Gender Studies at Saint Louis University. Her research interests include social movements and violence against women, and she has published several articles about US movements to end violence against women.

Carl Boggs received his PhD at the University of California–Berkeley and then taught political science at Washington University from 1969 to 1977. During that time, he was instrumental in bringing the important work of Antonio Gramsci to the US in a series of articles and two books. While at Washington University, he was involved in the antiwar protests, the McDonnell-Douglas Project, the St. Louis *Outlaw*, the Telos Group, and various environmental groups. Since then, he has taught at several universities, including UCLA, USC, Antioch University, and Carleton University in Ottawa. He is the author of twenty-five books along with hundreds of articles, essays, and reviews. Since the 1990s, he has been a regular contributor to the journal *CounterPunch*.

Susanne Cowan is an Associate Professor at the School of Architecture at Montana State University. Her research focuses on the impact of community organizing and participatory design processes on neighborhood planning. Cowan is currently working on the manuscript of a book titled *The Neighborhood Renaissance: Community Organizing and Uneven Development in St. Louis*. She began this research on St. Louis as a Postdoctoral Fellow at Washington University. Cowan has previously published about St. Louis in her chapter "Whose Neighbourhood? Identity Politics, Community Organizing, and Historic Preservation in St. Louis" in the book *Whose Tradition? Discourses on the Built Environment* (2017).

Ian Darnell is Curatorial Assistant for LGBTQIA+ Collections at the Missouri Historical Society. He is working on an exhibition about the queer history of the St. Louis area, scheduled to open in June 2024 at the Missouri History Museum. Darnell has been a longtime volunteer contributor to the community-based St. Louis LGBT History Project, and he served as Senior Research Associate for *Mapping LGBTQ St. Louis*, a digital-humanities project sponsored by Washington University's Divided City Initiative. Prior to his current role, he worked as assistant to the director of St. Louis's Griot Museum of Black History.

Zackary Davis (he/him/his), a photo researcher for this project, is a PhD student in the American Studies department at Saint Louis University, interested in cultural memory, histories of US capitalism and empire, and pop culture. Born in northern California and raised in north Texas, he went on to complete his undergraduate degree with majors in American Studies, History, and English at the University of Texas at Austin before moving to St. Louis. In his free time, he can be found reading poetry or poring over a game of chess.

Monica Duwel, graphic designer and illustrator for this volume's maps chapter, is an illustrator and a creative. She earned a BFA in graphic design from Missouri State University. Duwel currently works as a Senior Graphic Designer in Marketing and Communications at Washington University in St. Louis, where she collaborates with campus partners and students on print and web projects.

Elizabeth Eikmann, researcher for the volume's maps chapter, is a Postdoctoral Fellow in the Study of St. Louis in the American Culture Studies Program at Washington University in St. Louis. Her research focuses on the relationship between visual culture, gender, and race. Eikmann's current project explores the construction of whiteness and womanhood in the photographic works of St. Louis women.

Keona K. Ervin, a native of St. Louis, is Associate Professor and Director of Gender, Sexuality, and Women's Studies at Bowdoin College. Ervin is the author of the award-winning *Gateway to Equality: Black Women and the Struggle for Economic Justice in St. Louis* (2017). A recipient of the Career Enhancement Fellowship from the Institute for Citizens and Scholars, she has published articles and reviews in *International Labor and Working-Class History*, the *Journal of Civil and Human Rights*, *Souls: A Critical Journal of Black Politics, Culture and Society*, *New Labor Forum*, and the *Los Angeles Review of Books*.

Rob Gioielli is an environmental and urban historian based at the University of Cincinnati. His research and teaching focus on the intersections of race and sustainability in the modern American city. He is the author of *Environmental Activism and the Urban Crisis: Baltimore, St. Louis, Chicago* (2014) and is currently working on a project about how racism and suburban sprawl are destroying the planet. His research has been supported by the Rachel Carson Center for Environment and Society at the Ludwig Maximilian University of Munich, Germany, and in 2021–2022 he was a Mellon/ACLS Community College Fellow.

Amanda L. Izzo, volume co-editor, is an Associate Professor of Women's and Gender Studies at Saint Louis University. She is the author of *Liberal Christianity and Women's Global Activism: The YWCA of the USA and the Maryknoll Sisters* (2018). Her research focuses on US women and twentieth-century social movements.

Clarence Lang is Susan Welch Dean of the College of the Liberal Arts and Professor of African American Studies at The Pennsylvania State University. He is the author of *Grassroots at the Gateway: Class Politics and Black Freedom Struggle in St. Louis, 1936–75* (2009), and *Black America in* *the Shadow of the Sixties: Notes on the Civil Rights Movement, Neoliberalism, and Politics* (2015). A co-editor of two other volumes, he has published in the *Journal of Social History*, the *Journal of African American History*, the *Journal of Civil and Human Rights*, and the *Journal of Urban History*.

Benjamin Looker, volume co-editor, is an Associate Professor in the American Studies department at Saint Louis University. His most recent monograph is *A Nation of Neighborhoods: Imagining Cities, Communities, and Democracy in Postwar America* (2015), recipient of four professional-association book awards. Recent and in-progress projects examine housing and integration in the Great Society–era US city, Filipino theater and activism in Ontario, and the contested role of 1960s urban arts institutions and arts education.

Mary Maxfield is a Postdoctoral Fellow in Women's and Gender Studies at Saint Louis University (SLU), focusing on lesbian/queer community formation, technology, and space. Mary holds a PhD in American Studies from SLU, an MA in American Culture Studies from Bowling Green State University, and a BA in Creative Social Change from Fontbonne University. Previously, Mary's academic work has been featured in *Feminist Media Studies* and *Frontiers: A Journal of Women Studies*. A 2021 Lambda Literary Emerging Writers Fellow, Mary has a strong commitment to bridging academic and creative work, as well as to forging and sustaining queer networks. Learn more at *marymaxfield.com.*

Ilene Ordower, a former Missouri state representative, has been active for many years through her political and nonprofit organization work in women's issues, including domestic abuse, reproductive rights, ERA, and homeless and low-income senior housing. She has produced award-winning documentary videos on obtaining orders of protection and on children of women in prison. Ordower has served on nonprofit as well as government boards, such as the Missouri Arts Council, the Citizens Advisory Committee on Corrections, and the St. Louis County Boundary Commission.

Luke Ritter is an Assistant Professor at New Mexico Highlands University. He is the author of *Inventing America's First Immigration Crisis: Political Nativism in the Antebellum West* (2021). Ritter received his PhD in

American history from Saint Louis University. In 2017, he appeared as a featured speaker at Troy University's TEDx Conference. He is the author of numerous articles published in the *Journal of American Ethnic History*, *American Nineteenth Century History*, the *Journal of Early American History*, and the *Missouri Historical Review*.

Ezelle Sanford III is an Assistant Professor of History at Carnegie Mellon University, where he specializes in the history of modern medicine and public health, African American history from emancipation to the present, and twentieth-century United States history. He is working on a book project, *Segregated Medicine: How Racial Politics Shaped American Healthcare*. He obtained his PhD in History and History of Science from Princeton University and is an alumnus of Washington University in St. Louis. Sanford's writing has been featured in academic and popular publications and has been recognized by numerous awards.

Nina Gilden Seavey is an Emmy Award–winning documentarian with an over thirty-year career in the nonfiction world. Seavey is the Founding Director of The Documentary Center at The George Washington University. She holds the academic rank of Research Professor of History and Media and Public Affairs. Seavey's documentaries have won numerous awards, including five national Emmy nominations (one statue awarded), the Erik Barnouw Prize for Best Historical Film of the Year, and the Peter C. Rollins Prize for Best Film in American Culture, among others. She has received many professional accolades, including being named one of the top fifty professors of journalism in the US, and she was named a "Woman of Vision" by Women in Film and Video. More information about her work can be found at *seaveymedia.com*.

Thomas M. Spencer is Dean of the Honors College and Professor of History at Texas A&M University–Kingsville. He is also the editor of, and a contributor to, the University of Missouri Press titles *The Other Missouri History: Populists, Prostitutes, and Regular Folk* (2004) and *The Missouri Mormon Experience* (2010).

Rodney C. Wilson was the first openly gay public-school teacher in Missouri to be granted tenure and is the founder of October's annual LGBTQ+ History Month. He holds two graduate degrees—in history and in religion. Wilson's teaching career of thirty years has included secondary, correctional, ESOL, ABE, and community college instruction. He has published many essays on politics, religion, and LGBTQ rights and history; has received recognition awards from the National Education Association and the Human Rights Campaign; has been named a Missouri Trailblazer by the Missouri State Museum; and is the subject of the documentary short film *Taboo Teaching: A Profile of Missouri Teacher Rodney Wilson* (2019).

Notes

Introduction: Building Progressive Social Movements in St. Louis

1. Neal R. Peirce, *The Great Plains States of America: People, Politics, and Power in the Nine Great Plains States* (New York: W. W. Norton, 1973), 48–63. One might contrast this view with local press boosterism such as "The New St. Louis: A Swinging Town," *St. Louis Globe-Democrat Magazine*, May 17, 1970, 7–12.

2. Richard E. Edgar, *Urban Power and Social Welfare: Corporate Influence in an American City* (Beverly Hills, CA: SAGE, 1970), 10.

3. Ernest Patterson, *Black City Politics* (New York: Harper and Row, 1974), 119–20.

4. Harry G. Campbell, "Black Students at St. L. U. Takeover [sic] Dean's Office," *St. Louis Argus*, May 2, 1969; "'I Am a Man,'" editorial, *St. Louis Sentinel*, May 3, 1969. For charges of student docility, see, for example, John P. Willson, "Apathy Distinguishes Students, Faculty, and Administration," *Focus/Midwest* 7, no. 45 (1969): 37–39.

5. Charles Kimball Cummings, "Rent Strike in St. Louis: The Making of Conflict in Modern Society" (PhD diss., Washington University in St. Louis, 1976), 411.

6. "Radio: McGovern, Connally in Panel Interviews," *St. Louis Post-Dispatch*, Jul. 23, 1972.

7. Doug Rossinow, *Visions of Progress: The Left-Liberal Tradition in America* (Philadelphia: University of Pennsylvania Press, 2008), 2–3. Rossinow argues that the left-liberal tradition, a "political zone where liberalism and radicalism overlapped" to produce an "ambitious reform politics," disintegrated with the onset of the Cold War; chapters here, however, hint at its endurance on the local level across subsequent decades.

8. James Neal Primm, *Lion of the Valley: St. Louis, Missouri, 1764–1980*, 3rd ed. (St. Louis: Missouri Historical Society Press, 1998), 475; Colin Gordon, *Mapping Decline: St. Louis and the Fate of the American City* (Philadelphia: University of Pennsylvania Press, 2008), 223.

9. Primm, *Lion of the Valley*, 497.

10. Robert A. Beauregard, "Shrinking Cities in the United States in Historical Perspective: A Research Note," in *Shrinking Cities: International Perspectives and Policy Implications*, ed. Karina Pallagst, Thorsten Wiechmann, and Cristina Martinez-Fernandez (New York: Routledge, 2014), 38.

11. Gordon, *Mapping Decline*, 10.

12. A. J. Cervantes, with Lawrence G. Blochman, *Mr. Mayor* (Los Angeles: Nash Publishing, 1974), 132–37.

13. Lana Stein, *St. Louis Politics: The Triumph of Tradition* (St. Louis: Missouri Historical Society Press, 2002), xv.

14. Gordon, *Mapping Decline*, 11.

15. Adam Arenson and, less comprehensively, Walter Johnson call attention to the neglected regional dimension of the West as definitive of St. Louis as a border city. See Arenson, *The Great Heart of the Republic: St. Louis and the Cultural Civil War* (Cambridge, MA: Harvard University Press, 2011); Johnson, *The Broken Heart of America: St. Louis and the Violent History of the United States* (New York: Basic Books, 2020).

16. Ronald A. Buel, "Race, Welfare, and Housing in St. Louis," *Interplay*, Oct. 1969, 45.

17. Johnson, *Broken Heart of America*, 351.

18. Gordon, *Mapping Decline*, 168–69.

19. Quoted in Joseph Heathcott, "The Strange Career of Public Housing," *Journal of the American Planning Association* 78, no. 4 (2012): 370.

20. Douglas S. Massey and Nancy A. Denton, *American Apartheid: Segregation and the Making of the Underclass* (Cambridge, MA: Harvard University Press, 1993), 47.

21. Unnamed expert quoted (ca. 1966) in Norman M. Bradburn, Seymour Sudman, and Galen L. Gockel, *Side by Side: Integrated Neighborhoods in America* (Chicago: Quadrangle Books, 1971), 3.

22. Finn Enke, *Finding the Movement: Sexuality, Contested Space, and Feminist Activism* (Durham, NC: Duke University Press, 2007), 4–6, emphasis added. Geographer Juan Herrera makes a similar point, noting that "the movements that consolidated in the 1960s . . . were anchored by the goal of transforming aggrieved communities into vibrant and self-sufficient places." Herrera, *Cartographic Memory: Social Movement Activism and the Production of Space* (Durham, NC: Duke University Press, 2022), 6.

23. For descriptions of these events, see, for example, Robert J. Moore Jr., "Showdown under the Arch: The Construction Trades and the First 'Pattern or Practice' Equal Employment Opportunity Suit, 1966," *Gateway Heritage* 15, no. 3 (Winter 1994–1995): 30–43; and Amanda L. Izzo, *Liberal Christianity and Women's Global Activism: The YWCA of the USA and the Maryknoll Sisters* (New Brunswick, NJ: Rutgers University Press, 2018), 181–82.

24. The collective cultural importance of these bookstores is emphasized by poet Eugene B. Redmond, transcript of interview by Benjamin Looker, Aug. 7, 2002, compiled in *Interviews on the Black Artists' Group (BAG) of St. Louis* (s.l.: s.n., 2004),

268, Department of Special Collections, Washington University in St. Louis. For further details, see Robert L. Joiner, "Only Black Book Store in City May Be Closing," *St. Louis Post-Dispatch*, Mar. 14, 1971; "House of Umoja," *St. Louis Model City Voice* 1, no. 2 (Jul. 24, 1968): 3, Missouri Historical Society Library and Research Center (hereinafter MHS), St. Louis.

25. On the Black Culture Center, see Gerald J. Meyer, "Inside Black Militants' GHQ," *St. Louis Post-Dispatch*, Mar. 22, 1970.

26. On Trinity Episcopal Church's role in local LGBTQ movements, see, along with Chapter 3 in this volume, Katie Batza and Michelle Diedriech, "Trinity Episcopal Church," National Register of Historic Places Registration Form (Washington, DC: National Park Service, 2019), available at https://mostateparks.com/sites/mostateparks/files/TrinityEpiscopalChurch.pdf.

27. Also within steps of Left Bank Books and the Peace Information Center was the office of leftist newspaper *The Outlaw* (1970–1972), at 554 Limit Avenue, which hosted events for antimilitarist, feminist, and gay liberation groups. Exactly a decade after *The Outlaw*'s demise, the same address became the final home of feminist bookstore The Women's Eye, as detailed in Chapter 13 of this volume. On the newspaper, see Devin Thomas O'Shea, "Remembering the *Outlaw*, STL's Premiere 1970s Counterculture Publication," *Riverfront Times* (St. Louis), Jan. 6, 2022, https://web.archive.org/web/20220217222010/https://www.riverfronttimes.com/stlouis/remembering-the-outlaw-stls-premiere-1970s-counterculture-publication/Content?oid=36910661. For other alternative St. Louis newspapers of the era, see Underground Press Syndicate, *Underground Newspaper Collection*, microfilm collection (Wooster, OH: Bell and Howell, 1970–1986), containing scattered issues of the *St. Louis Free Press*, *Green Egg*, *The New Hard Times*, *Saint Louis Today*, and *Xanadu* (formerly *The Daily Flash*).

28. On LaClede Town, see Eric P. Mumford, "American Urban Housing and Racial Integration before 1968," in *Segregation by Design: Conversations and Calls for Action in St. Louis*, ed. Catalina Freixas and Mark Abbott (Cham, Switzerland: Springer, 2019), 48–52; and Benjamin Looker, "Neighbourhood Exceptionalism and Racial Liberalism in the Great Society City: Integration as Civic Showpiece at St Louis' LaClede Town," *Urban History* 49, no. 2 (May 2022): 401–34. The acreage figure given here excludes the adjacent LaClede Park complex and the early 1970s LaClede Town expansions known as Operation Breakthrough East and West. On the counterculture and LaClede Town, see, for example, Robert K. Sanford, "Hippie Here Has 2 Jobs and 6-Room Townhouse," *St. Louis Post-Dispatch*, Jul. 17, 1967.

29. Sullivan quoted (ca. late 1960s) in Ellen Sweets, "The Late, Great LaClede Town," *St. Louis Post-Dispatch*, Nov. 30, 1997.

30. Malinké Elliott, self-recorded cassette tape of memories about BAG, Feb. 2001, held at MHS. On other activist-related events at the Gateway Theatre, see, for example, "Lester to Speak for Liberators," *St. Louis Sentinel*, Jan. 18, 1969.

31. For examples of regional and national coverage of Jeff-Vander-Lou initiatives, see Michael Watson, "Jeff-Vander-Lou: Against All Odds," *FOCUS/Midwest* 12, no. 75 (1976): 18–22; Bernard Garnett, "Weaver's Bold Plan to Help Black Ghettos," *Jet*

Magazine, Jan. 4, 1968, 18. Our thanks to Michael McCollum for identifying these articles for us.

32. Jane Jacobs, *The Death and Life of Great American Cities* (New York: Vintage, 1961), 245.

33. The mental maps reference is inspired by Kevin Lynch, *The Image of the City* (Cambridge, MA: M. I. T. Press, 1960).

34. US Commission on Civil Rights, *Hearing before the United States Commission on Civil Rights: Hearing Held in St. Louis, Missouri, January 14–17, 1970* (Washington, DC: Government Printing Office, 1971), 579.

35. For a sociological study of Civic Progress Inc.'s influence during this period, see Edgar, *Urban Power and Social Welfare.*

36. Clarence Lang, *Grassroots at the Gateway: Class Politics and Black Freedom Struggle in St. Louis, 1936–75* (Ann Arbor: University of Michigan Press, 2009), 12.

37. Cervantes quoted in "Recognition, Repentance and Reward Being Sought by Negro Group Here in Confrontation with Mayor," *St. Louis Argus*, May 17, 1968.

38. "Some Violence at March Backing War," *St. Louis Post-Dispatch*, Jun. 8, 1970.

39. Johnson, *Broken Heart of America*, 330–31; and Chapter 5 of this volume.

40. Jordan Carr Peterson, "The Walking Dead: How the Criminal Regulation of Sodomy Survived *Lawrence v. Texas*," *Missouri Law Review* 86, no. 3 (2021): 20–22. Missouri likewise became the first state to ban abortion after the US Supreme Court rescinded *Roe v. Wade*'s protections in June 2022.

41. Johnson, *Broken Heart of America*, 329–30.

42. Robert H. Collins, "Selma Sheriff to Speak at Meeting Here," *St. Louis Post-Dispatch*, Nov. 9, 1965. See also "Citizens Council Contract for Kiel Meeting Canceled," *St. Louis Post-Dispatch*, Nov. 11, 1965; Neil R. McMillen, *The Citizens' Council: Organized Resistance to the Second Reconstruction, 1954–64* (1971; repr. Urbana: University of Illinois Press, 1994), 150–51.

43. Johnson, *Broken Heart of America*, 334–35. On terrorist activities, see, for example, Robert H. Collins, "Nazi Unit Reported in Area," *St. Louis Post-Dispatch*, Jun. 9, 1969; Robert H. Collins, "Harassment Target List Found in Suspect's Car," *St. Louis Post-Dispatch*, Jun. 15, 1969; Robert H. Collins, "Peace Center Gets New Death Threat," *St. Louis Post-Dispatch*, Jul. 6, 1969; and, more generally on the area's far Right, Group Research Inc. Records, Columbia University Archives, New York, NY, boxes 3, 6, 20, 35, 60, and 90. On the Grapevine Tavern and the FBI's failure to investigate evidence of conspiracy in the assassination of King, see Nina Gilden Seavey, *My Fugitive*, produced by Pineapple Street Studio, podcast, MP3 audio, https://shows.cadence13.com/podcast/my-fugitive, esp. episode 8, "The Conspiracy," May 18, 2021; Wendell Rawls Jr., "Panel Convinced Bounty Induced Ray to Kill King," *New York Times*, Nov. 17, 1978.

44. Koch quoted in Rebecca E. Klatch, *A Generation Divided: The New Left, the New Right, and the 1960s* (Berkeley: University of California Press, 1999), 141.

45. George Lipsitz, *A Life in the Struggle: Ivory Perry and the Culture of Opposition*, rev. ed. (Philadelphia: Temple University Press, 1995), 229, 212.

46. See, for instance, claims in Dayo F. Gore, *Radicalism at the Crossroads: African American Women Activists in the Cold War* (New York: New York University Press, 2011).

47. Jacquelyn Dowd Hall, "The Long Civil Rights Movement and the Political Uses of the Past," *Journal of American History* 91, no. 4 (Mar. 2005): 1233–63. For the 2001 usage referenced here, see Jacquelyn Dowd Hall, "Broadening Our View of the Civil Rights Movement," *Chronicle of Higher Education*, Jul. 27, 2001. For a counter-perspective, see Sundiata Keita Cha-Jua and Clarence Lang, "The 'Long Movement' as Vampire: Temporal and Spatial Fallacies in Recent Black Freedom Studies," *Journal of African American History* 92, no. 2 (Spring 2007): 265–88.

48. See, for example, Dianne Glave and Mark Stoll, eds., *To Love the Wind and the Rain: African Americans and Environmental History* (Pittsburgh: University of Pittsburgh Press, 2006); Sylvia Hood Washington, *Packing Them In: An Archaeology of Environmental Racism in Chicago, 1865–1954* (Lanham, MD: Lexington Books, 2005).

49. See, for example, Elizabeth A. Armstrong and Suzanna M. Crage, "Movements and Memory: The Making of the Stonewall Myth," *American Sociological Review* 71, no. 5 (2006): 724–51; Emily K. Hobson, *Lavender and Red: Liberation and Solidarity in the Gay and Lesbian Left* (Oakland: University of California Press, 2016); Marc Stein, *Rethinking the Gay and Lesbian Movement* (New York: Routledge, 2012); Aaron Lecklider, *Love's Next Meeting: The Forgotten History of Homosexuality and the Left in American Culture* (Oakland: University of California Press, 2021).

50. For one of many texts engaging in this debate, see Nancy Hewitt, ed., *No Permanent Waves: Recasting Histories of U.S. Feminism* (New Brunswick, NJ: Rutgers University Press, 2010).

51. Though the rent strike is discussed only briefly in this volume, it has received substantial attention elsewhere. See Michael Karp, "The St. Louis Rent Strike of 1969: Transforming Black Activism and American Low-Income Housing," *Journal of Urban History* 40, no. 4 (2014): 648–70; Lipsitz, *A Life in the Struggle*, ch. 6; Cummings, "Rent Strike in St. Louis"; and Daniel Blake Smith, producer, *Envisioning Home: The Jean King and Richard Baron Story*, documentary film (Winchester, KY: Eppic Films, 2012).

52. Keona K. Ervin, *Gateway to Equality: Black Women and the Struggle for Economic Justice in St. Louis* (Lexington: University Press of Kentucky, 2017), ch. 6.

53. Steven G. Collins, "Does This Matter to Us? The Response to the Kent State Shootings at St. Louis Community College" (conference paper, Southwestern Social Science Association 99th Annual Meeting, San Diego, CA, Nov. 2, 2019).

54. Michael C. Brickey, "Remaking Space, Shaping the Struggle: Urban Planning and the Civil Rights Movement in East St. Louis, Illinois, 1958–1974" (MA thesis, San Diego State University, 2017).

55. Amanda L. Izzo, "'To Help Them Brush Aside the Limitations That Hold Them Back': Ruth Porter, Liberal Interracialism, and St. Louis Community Organizing in the Civil Rights Era," *Missouri Historical Review* 115, no. 3 (2021): 201–25.

56. Michael Omi and Howard Winant, *Racial Formation in the United States*, 3rd ed. (New York: Routledge, 2014), 161.

57. Huping Ling, *Chinese St. Louis: From Enclave to Cultural Community* (Philadelphia: Temple University Press, 2004), 21.

58. Bryan Winston, "Mexican Corridors: Migration and Community Formation in the Central United States, 1900–1950" (PhD diss., Saint Louis University, 2019), 226; Daniel Gonzales, "A Gateway to the East: An Exploration of St. Louis' Mexican History through the Built Environment," *Confluence* 10, no. 2 (2019): 31–41.

59. The quoted phrase is adapted from an assertion specifically about Black liberation struggles in Paul Gilroy, *The Black Atlantic: Modernity and Double Consciousness* (Cambridge, MA: Harvard University Press, 1993), 36.

60. The Wall of Respect's importance to young Black artistic and activist communities is emphasized in East St. Louis poet Eugene B. Redmond's tribute to the mural: the poem "Wedge Wall, Huge Hand," in Redmond, *Sentry of the Four Golden Pillars* (East St. Louis, IL: Black River Writers, 1970), 11–14.

61. George Lipsitz, *Footsteps in the Dark: The Hidden Histories of Popular Music* (Minneapolis: University of Minnesota Press, 2007), ch. 5; Joanna Dee Das, *Katherine Dunham: Dance and the African Diaspora* (New York: Oxford University Press, 2017), ch. 8; Joyce Aschenbrenner, *Katherine Dunham: Dancing a Life* (Urbana: University of Illinois Press, 2002), ch. 10; Bryan Dematteis, dir., *The Black Artists' Group: Creation Equals Movement*, documentary film (2020).

62. Kenneth Stuart Jolly, "It Happened Here Too: The Black Liberation Movement of St. Louis, MO," working paper, Benjamin L. Hooks Institute for Social Change, University of Memphis, 2002, https://www.memphis.edu/benhooks/pdfs/jolly.pdf. A notable exception to this absence is George Lipsitz's award-winning 1988 book, *A Life in the Struggle: Ivory Perry and the Culture of Opposition* (Philadelphia: Temple University Press, 1988), republished in revised form in 1995.

63. Moore quoted in Kenya Vaughn, "Hugely Successful Missouri History Museum Civil Rights Exhibit to Close Next Week," *St. Louis American*, Apr. 5, 2018.

64. Brawley quoted in Lindsay Toler, "St. Louis' Gay History on Display at Cherokee Street Gallery before Big Move to Museum," *Riverfront Times* (St. Louis), Jan. 29, 2014, https://web.archive.org/web/20150921122926/https://www.riverfronttimes.com/newsblog/2014/01/29/st-louis-gay-history-on-display-at-cherokee-street-gallery-before-big-move-to-museum. One element of this work was the publication of Steven Louis Brawley, *Gay and Lesbian St. Louis* (Charleston, SC: Arcadia Publishing, 2016).

1. Generational Activism and Civil Rights Organizing in St. Louis

1. George Lipsitz, *A Life in Struggle: Ivory Perry and the Culture of Opposition*, rev. ed. (Philadelphia: Temple University Press, 1995), 2.

2. Clarence Lang, *Grassroots at the Gateway: Class Politics and Black Freedom Struggle in St. Louis, 1936–75* (Ann Arbor: University of Michigan Press, 2009), vii.

3. Melissa Ford, *A Brick and a Bible: Black Women's Radical Activism in the Midwest during the Great Depression* (Carbondale: Southern Illinois University Press, 2022).

4. Jacquelyn Dowd Hall, "The Long Civil Rights Movement and the Political Uses of the Past," *Journal of American History* 91, no. 4 (Mar. 2005): 1233–63; Danielle McGuire, *At the Dark End of the Street: Black Women, Rape, and Resistance—A New History of the Civil Rights Movement from Rosa Parks to the Rise of Black Power* (New York: A. A. Knopf, 2012).

5. The ball was being held by the Veiled Prophet (VP) organization, a group that combined Mardi Gras traditions, masonic-like secrecy in membership and meetings, and an annual veiled local leader as the Prophet in pseudo–Middle Eastern dress. The veiling was both literal and figurative, as only a handful of VPs have been publicly identified, one of whom was a police commissioner.

6. Jon C. Teaford, *Cities of the Heartland: The Rise and Fall of the Industrial Midwest* (Bloomington and Indianapolis: University of Indiana Press, 1994), 15–16, 35–38. The story of St. Louis's loss of dominance over transcontinental railroads is also told in greater detail in Adam Arenson, *The Great Heart of the Republic: St. Louis and the Cultural Civil War* (Cambridge, MA: Harvard University Press, 2011), 65–81, 180–81.

7. Keona K. Ervin, *Gateway to Equality: Black Women and the Struggle for Economic Justice in St. Louis* (Lexington: University Press of Kentucky, 2017), 176.

8. Franz Strasser, "Crossing a St. Louis Street that Divides Communities," BBC News, Mar. 14, 2012, available at bbc.com/news/av/magazine-17361995.

9. William Wells Brown, *Narrative of William Wells Brown, A Fugitive Slave* (Boston: Anti-Slavery Society, 1847), ch. 5, accessed at https://www.gutenberg.org/files/15132/15132-h/15132-h.htm.

10. Diane Mutti Burke, *On Slavery's Border: Missouri's Small Slaveholding Households, 1815–1865* (Athens: University of Georgia Press, 2010), 267.

11. Cyprian Clamorgan and Julie Winch, *The Colored Aristocracy of St. Louis* (1895; Columbia: University of Missouri Press, 1999), 45.

12. Historian Bryan Jack points out that the significance of this first exodus from the South was in the freedom for Black populations to move as and where they willed. The willingness of Black St. Louisans to rally around the needful visitors reflected their shared interest in the freedom of mobility. Bryan M. Jack, *The St. Louis African American Community and the Exodusters* (Columbia: University of Missouri Press, 2007), 111–13.

13. "Black Amazon to Rescue of Kaffirs," *St. Louis Post-Dispatch*, June 2, 1904, 4. Michael Brickey, now a PhD candidate in American Studies at Saint Louis University, brought this episode to my attention. See also Susan Curtis, *Colored Memories: A Biographer's Quest for the Elusive Lester A. Walton* (Columbia: University of Missouri Press, 2008), 233–45.

14. Davarian Baldwin, *Chicago's New Negroes: Modernity, the Great Migration, and Black Urban Life* (Chapel Hill: University of North Carolina Press, 2007), 9–10.

15. In his introduction to an anthology of Black St. Louis writers, Gerald Early claimed St. Louis to be an "important site of African American letters," though "predictably neglected." Early, ed., *"Ain't But a Place": An Anthology of African American Writings about St. Louis* (St. Louis: Missouri Historical Society Press, 1998), xviii.

16. Cecil Brown, *Stagolee Shot Billy* (Cambridge, MA: Harvard University Press, 2003), 37–47.

17. St. Louis had also seen a rash of white violence against Black people, business, and neighborhoods in 1917. Although the Silent Protest Parade was billed as a response to the East St. Louis Riots of that year, its planning predated the worst of the riots and its initial focus was the broader pattern of lynchings and other white violence against Blacks in the US. Cicely Hunter, "A Blaring Silence: "The Silent Protest Parade of 1917 and Its Historical Influence on Activism" (PhD diss., Saint Louis University, in progress).

18. James R. Grossman, "Blowing the Trumpet: The *Chicago Defender* and Black Migration during World War I," *Illinois Historical Journal* 78, no. 2 (Summer 1985): 82–96.

19. Two additional newspapers came and went in the early twentieth century: *The Palladium* (1903–1907) and the *Western Messenger* (1916–1917). Yet another, *The Sentinel*, was established in 1968, an even more radical voice into the twenty-first century.

20. Priscilla A. Dowden-White, *Groping toward Democracy: African American Social Welfare Reform in St. Louis, 1910–1949* (Columbia: University of Missouri Press, 2011).

21. Lang, *Grassroots at the Gateway*, 180–85.

22. Ervin, *Gateway to Equality*, ch. 1.

23. Thomas Wyatt Turner, *From Sharecropper to Scientist: A Memoir of Thomas Wyatt Turner, Ph.D.*, ed. Marilyn Wenzke Nickels (Middleton, DE: s.n., 2018).

24. The most in-depth history of the FCC and this triangle of Catholic activism is still Marilyn W. Nickels, "The Federated Colored Catholics: A Study of Three Variant Perspectives on Racial Justice as Represented by John LaFarge, William Markoe, and Thomas Turner" (PhD diss., The Catholic University of America, 1975).

25. Turner Papers, Moorland-Spingarn Research Center, Manuscript Division, Howard University, Washington, DC, Series E "Federated Colored Catholics of the United States (FCC)," Box 153:12, folders 3-4: "Seventh Annual Convention, St. Louis."

26. "Catholics Pass Resolutions to Better Labor Conditions," *Chicago Defender,* Sep. 26, 1931, 2.

27. Diane Batts Morrow, "'To My Darlings, the Oblates, Many Blessings': The Reverend John T. Gillard, S.S.J., and the Oblate Sisters of Providence," *US Catholic Historian* 28, no. 1 (Winter 2010): 1–26.

28. "Catholics Close Big Annual Session in Missouri City," *Chicago Defender,* Sep. 12, 1931, 2.

29. Daniel J. Ladd, "History Lessons," *Universitas: The Magazine of Saint Louis University,* Spring 1995, 14–17; "First Negro Students at Catholic University," *St.*

Louis American, n.d. 1944, in "Blacks at SLU" vertical file, Saint Louis University Archives; Charles Anderson to John J. Glennon, Aug. 25, 1943 (plus previous correspondence on other issues in May and June 1943), Archbishop John Joseph Cardinal Glennon Papers, 1834–1984, Archdiocese of St. Louis, Archives and Records, Record Group 01 E 05.4 "Correspondence—Negro Apostolate."

30. Jack Maguire, "Race Prejudice Denounced: Jesuit Says Christ's Teaching Must Prevail," *University News* (Saint Louis University), Feb. 11, 1944; "St. Louis U. Students Asked to Back Admitting Negroes," *St. Louis Post-Dispatch*, Feb. 11, 1944. Heithaus's anticommunist argument was highlighted in several of the contemporary press reports of his sermon.

31. There are a few pieces of evidence that SLU students played some role in these movements and in the general push to desegregate Washington University, which, despite having accepted at least a few Black students in the nineteenth century, developed a strong whites-only policy in the twentieth century. See Amy M. Pfeiffenberger, "Democracy at Home: The Struggle to Desegregate Washington University in the Postwar Era," *Gateway Heritage* 10, no. 3 (Winter 1989): 17–18. Pfeiffenberger does not make any argument about the influence of SLU on the Washington University movement, but does cite several references to participants in the debates doing so, and quotes from the letter of a SLU student.

32. Jane Aileen Kaiser to Claude H. Heithaus, SJ, Nov. 18, 1944, 1, Archbishop John Joseph Cardinal Glennon Papers, 1834–1984, RG-01-E-05.4.

33. Ibid., 3. I tell a more detailed version of Jane Kaiser's history and her confrontation with Glennon in the introduction to my forthcoming book, *The Color of Blood.*

34. Tim O'Neil, "Sept. 21, 1947: Parents Protest after St. Louis Catholic Schools Are Integrated," *St. Louis Post-Dispatch*, Sep. 21, 2021, 34.

35. Jeanne Theoharis brilliantly argues both for a re-periodization of the movement and for greater attention to the role of racism in the North, with Komozi Woodard in Brian Purnell and Jeanne Theoharis, eds., *The Strange Careers of the Jim Crow North: Segregation and Struggle outside of the South* (New York: New York University Press, 2019) and Jeanne Theoharis, *A More Beautiful and Terrible History: The Uses and Misuses of Civil Rights History* (Boston: Beacon Press, 2018). The excellent *Eyes on the Prize* documentary series is a perfect example of the narrative of a southern-focused heroic civil rights movement. Its narration refers to King bringing the movement to Chicago in 1964. See Henry Hampton, producer, "Two Societies, 1965–1968," a 1990 episode of *Eyes on the Prize* (Alexandria, VA: PBS Video, 2006).

36. Kenneth S. Jolly, *Black Liberation in the Midwest: The Struggle in St. Louis, Missouri, 1964–1970* (New York: Routledge, 2013), 73–75.

37. August Meier and Elliott Rudwick, *CORE: A Study in the Civil Rights Movement, 1942–1968* (New York: Oxford University Press, 1973), 74.

38. Mary Kimbrough and Margaret W. Dagen, *Victory without Violence: The First Ten Years of the St. Louis Committee of Racial Equality (CORE), 1947–1957* (Columbia: University of Missouri Press, 2000), 11–13. Several St. Louis leaders and members also went on to play important roles in the national organization.

39. Meier and Rudwick, *CORE*, 47–48, 54–56; William H. Freivogel, "Press Flubs First Draft of History of Race," *Gateway Journalism Review* 49, no. 356 (Winter 2020): 22–26.

40. St. Louis CORE, "A Plan for Establishing Equal Restaurant Service in St. Louis Department Stores," Apr. 1952, repr. in Kimbrough and Dagen, *Victory without Violence*, 3–5.

41. Billie Ames to A. C. Thompson, Dec. 13, 1950, quoted in Meier and Rudwick, *CORE*, 56n41.

42. Meier and Rudwick, *CORE*, 65, 74.

43. Lang, *Grassroots at the Gateway*, 96.

44. Jeanne Theoharis and Brian Purnell have documented how northeastern political leaders crafted narratives about civil rights, and what did and did not constitute inequity in public institutions, as a way of protecting their own racial structures even as they outlawed explicit segregation. Brian Purnell and Jeanne Theoharis, "Introduction: Histories of Racism and Resistance, Seen and Unseen; How and Why to Think about the Jim Crow North," in Purnell and Theoharis, eds., *Strange Careers*, 2–5, 8–10.

45. Lang, *Grassroots at the Gateway*, 145–46. Lang attributes the failure of this campaign to class tensions within the movement.

46. Ibid., 143–44.

47. Ernest Patterson, *Black City Politics* (New York: Dodd, Mead, 1974), 92–93.

48. On the People's Art Center, see Martin G. Towey, "Design for Democracy: The People's Art Center in St. Louis," in *Art in Action: American Art Centers and The New Deal*, ed. John Franklin White (Metuchen, NJ: Scarecrow Press, 1987), 79–97.

49. Lang, *Grassroots at the Gateway*, 160. Lang mentions Curtis's presence at Fairgrounds. Further analysis of the incident can be found in Jolly, *Black Liberation in the Midwest*, 13–16.

50. Patterson, *Black City Politics*, 94.

51. Lang, *Grassroots at the Gateway*, 162–66; Patterson, *Black City Politics*, 103–9. Patterson, in *Black City Politics*, particularly highlights this event as a major misstep of the white power structure, one that ignited rather than quashed Black protest.

52. Patterson, *Black City Politics*, 120.

53. "Negroes State Demands, Assail Sentences in Contempt Charges," *St. Louis Post-Dispatch*, Nov. 22, 1963.

54. Lang, *Grassroots at the Gateway*, 183.

55. When writing his biographical study of Perry's life and activism, George Lipsitz looked into Perry's dishonorable discharge and his arrest record and concluded that much of it was the result of racism and corruption. Lipsitz, *A Life in the Struggle*, 4–6.

56. Ibid., 85; Robert J. Moore Jr., "Showdown under the Arch: The Construction Trades and the First 'Pattern or Practice' Equal Employment Opportunity Suit, 1966," *Gateway Heritage* 15, no. 3 (Winter 1994–1995): 34–36.

57. Thomas M. Spencer covers one of the other iconic moments in ACTION's campaign in Chapter 7 of this volume. Clarence Lang also follows the rise of Black Power organizations, which ACTION prefigured, in Chapter 4 of this volume.

58. Judge Nathan B. Young Jr., interview by Richard Resh, Jul. 15, 1970, Oral History T-020, Oral History Collection, S0829, State Historical Society of Missouri, available online at https://shsmo.org/sites/default/files/pdfs/oral-history/transcripts/s0829/t0020.pdf. Young began the interview with a statement: "I want to stress and emphasize that if you wanted the story of the history of civil rights in the U.S.A. and had to confine it to one city, you could write the entire story of civil rights by going back to the history of the city of St. Louis. I think the complete civil rights background and history could be taken and understood better by knowing the history of St. Louis, Missouri, completely."

59. The resulting "Clock Tower Accords" led to a set of promises by the university to address continued racial disparities both on and off campus. See Saint Louis University, "Clock Tower Accords," at https://web.archive.org/web/20220303082320/https://www.slu.edu/diversity/occupy-slu/clock-tower-accords.php.

60. Matt Pearce, "Ferguson October Rally Shows Divide over Civil Rights," *Detroit Free Press,* Oct. 13, 2014. Sometimes the charge was recorded as "This ain't your grandmother's civil rights movement."

61. The permutations of the refrain are fascinating. One version was made famous in a viral photo showing a young female activist whose T-shirt reads "This Ain't Yo' Mama's Civil Rights Movement." Peggy McGlone, "'This Ain't Yo' Mama's Civil Rights Movement' T-Shirt from Ferguson Donated to Smithsonian Museum," *Washington Post,* Mar. 1, 2016. Tef Poe himself used "This ain't your daddy's civil rights movement" as the chorus to "War Cry," a protest song about Missouri politics and racism.

62. Barbara Reynolds, "I Was a Civil Rights Activist in the 1960s: But It's Hard for Me to Get behind Black Lives Matter," *Washington Post,* Aug. 24, 2015.

63. See the Organization for Black Struggle website at https://web.archive.org/web/20220128144432/https://www.obs-stl.org.

2. The St. Louis Baby Tooth Survey and Women's Environmental Activism

Portions of this chapter originally appeared in Luke Ritter, "Mothers against the Bomb: The Baby Tooth Survey and the Nuclear Test Ban Movement in St. Louis, 1954–1969," *Missouri Historical Review* 112, no. 2 (Jan. 2018): 107–38. Research for the original article was funded by the Environment in Missouri History Fellowship at the State Historical Society of Missouri's Center for Missouri Studies.

1. David Stradling, ed., *The Environmental Moment, 1968–1972* (Seattle: University of Washington Press, 2012); Carolyn Merchant, ed., *Major Problems in American Environmental History,* 2nd ed. (Boston: Houghton Mifflin, 2005), 427–66. See Andrew Hurley, "Common Fields: An Introduction," in *Common Fields: An Environmental History of St. Louis,* ed. Andrew Hurley (St. Louis: Missouri Historical Society Press, 1997), 1–12.

2. High-profile test-ban supporters such as American chemist Linus Pauling, after all, faced extensive red-baiting and reprisals into the late 1950s and early 1960s—well past the peak of McCarthyist persecution. In 1961, anticommunists picketed Washington University demanding investigations of faculty who had signed Pauling's test-ban petition. See "Evangelist to Seek House Red Inquiry," *St. Louis Post-Dispatch*, Apr. 13, 1961.

3. Amy Swerdlow, *Women Strike for Peace: Traditional Motherhood and Radical Politics in the 1960s* (Chicago: University of Chicago Press, 1993), 21. For a more general account of global antinuclear activism, see Lawrence S. Wittner, *Resisting the Bomb: A History of the World Nuclear Disarmament Movement, 1954–1970* (Stanford, CA: Stanford University Press, 1997).

4. Adam Rome, *The Genius of Earth Day: How a 1970 Teach-In Unexpectedly Made the First Green Generation* (New York: Hill and Wang, 2013), 33.

5. See B. L. Larson and K. E. Ebner, "Significance of Strontium-90 in Milk: A Review," *Journal of Dairy Science* 41, no. 12 (Dec. 1958): 1647–62.

6. For an early popular article on nuclear fallout in the stratosphere's jet stream, see "Jet Stream Is Believed to Collect Fallout," *St. Louis Post-Dispatch*, Dec. 21, 1958. Barry Commoner, *The Closing Circle: Nature, Man, and Technology* (New York: A. A. Knopf, 1971), 49–65; Larson and Ebner, "Significance of Strontium-90," 1647–62.

7. St. Louis's preeminent newspaper, the *Post-Dispatch*, mentioned strontium-90 for the first time on January 27, 1954. "Strontium-90," *St. Louis Post-Dispatch*, Jan. 27, 1954; William K. Wyant Jr., "Strontium-90 in St. Louis: 50,000 Baby Teeth," *The Nation*, Jun. 13, 1959; "Strontium 90—Its Nature, Its Dangers," *St. Louis Post-Dispatch*, Dec. 21, 1958, 156. Wyant's wife, Carita, was the editor of the League of Women Voters of St. Louis's official newsletter, the *League Reporter*, at the time he wrote this article and others about St. Louis's nuclear women.

8. Results showed that between August 1957 and August 1958, a period of intense nuclear bomb tests in both the United States and the Soviet Union, "Milk supplies in the St. Louis area . . . had the highest concentration of radioactive strontium-90 of ten cities surveyed by the United States Public Health Service." In July 1958, Project Sunshine scientists measured a whopping 18.7 Sunshine Units in St. Louis's milk supply. A picocurie is a millionth of a millionth of a curie. A curie is the amount of radioactivity associated with one gram of radium. The Public Health Service later determined that the reported levels of Sr-90 in St. Louis's milk supply between 1957 and 1958 were based on false data. Harold L. Rosenthal et al., "Regional Variation of Strontium-90 Content in Human Deciduous Incisors," *Archives of Oral Biology* 11, no. 1 (Jan. 1966): 135–37; James Deakin, "Milk Here High in Strontium: Tops in 10 Cities," *St. Louis Post-Dispatch*, Nov. 30, 1958; Marguerite Shepard, "Tooth Survey Shows Area Not Fallout Hot Spot," *St. Louis Globe-Democrat*, Nov. 23, 1961. See the following issues of the *St. Louis Post-Dispatch*: Jan. 20, 1956, 26; Aug. 28, 1956, 16; Oct. 12, 1956, 8; Oct. 16, 1956, 5.

9. Larson and Ebner, "Significance of Strontium-90," 1647–62.

10. Barry Commoner suggested the AEC should have followed the recommendation of the International Commission on Radiological Protection that the MPC

460

be set to 30 picocuries per liter of milk. Commoner, *Science and Survival* (New York: Viking Press, 1963), 111. See "Fallout: Moment of Tooth," *Newsweek*, Apr. 25, 1960, 70; "A Statement by the Greater St. Louis Committee for Nuclear Information on the Strontium 90 Content of Milk, Prepared at the Request of the St. Louis Dairy Council," Jan. 26, 1959, Committee for Environmental Information Records, 1956–1977, S0069, State Historical Society of Missouri (hereinafter CEI, SHSMO), box 13, folder 193.

11. Charles L. Dunham, Congressional Hearings, 1959, quoted in "Fallout in Our Milk: A Follow-Up Report," *Consumer Reports*, Feb. 1960, 67; Statement by the Greater St. Louis Citizens' Committee for Nuclear Information, "How Radioactive Is St. Louis Milk? It Could Reach Danger Point in 1964 if Bomb Tests Continue; One Fourth of Way in July," *St. Louis Post-Dispatch*, Dec. 9, 1958; "Strontium in Milk at Top in November," *St. Louis Post-Dispatch*, Nov. 30, 1958.

12. See Katharine T. Corbett, *In Her Place: A Guide to St. Louis Women's History* (St. Louis: Missouri Historical Society Press, 1999); LeeAnn Whites, Mary C. Neth, and Gary R. Kremer, eds., *Women in Missouri History: In Search of Power and Influence* (Columbia: University of Missouri Press, 2004). Other founding nuclear women such as Elsie Langsdorf had been extremely active and influential in the realms of education and child development. Langsdorf organized St. Louis's first Parent Education Movement in 1922. "Partial Biography of Edna Gellhorn," Mar. 23, 1967, Gellhorn, Edna (1878–1970) Scrapbook, S0642, State Historical Society of Missouri; interview with Gertrude Faust, conducted by William Sullivan, Jan. 1982, tape 673, CEI, SHSMO; Elsie H. Langsdorf, "Report on the Parent Education Movement in St. Louis," 1962, Langsdorf Family Papers, Missouri Historical Society Library and Research Center, St. Louis.

13. Carolyn Merchant, "The Women of the Progressive Conservation Crusade, 1900–1915," in *Environmental History: Critical Issues in Comparative Perspective*, ed. Kendall E. Bailes (Lanham, MD: University Press of America, 1985), 162–63.

14. The Women's Organization for Smoke Abatement was the successor of a women's anti-smoke group, known as the Wednesday Club, which began protesting air pollution as early as 1907. See Mrs. Ernest Kroeger, "Smoke Abatement in St. Louis," *American City* 6 (Jun. 1912): 907, 909. See also Suellen Hoy, "Municipal Housekeeping: The Role of Women in Improving Urban Sanitation Practices, 1880–1917," in *Pollution and Reform in American Cities, 1870–1930*, ed. Martin V. Melosi (Austin: University of Texas Press, 1980), 173–98; and Joel A. Tarr and Carl Zimring, "The Struggle for Smoke Control in St. Louis: Achievement and Emulation," in *Common Fields*, ed. Hurley, 199–220.

15. Henry Obermeyer, *Stop that Smoke!* (New York: Harper, 1933), 37–45.

16. See Hurley, "Common Fields: An Introduction," 1–12; Craig E. Colten, "Environmental Justice in the American Bottom: The Legal Response to Pollution, 1900–1950," in Hurley, *Common Fields*, 163–75; and Tarr and Zimring, "The Struggle for Smoke Control in St. Louis," 199.

17. See, for example, St. Louis Office of Civil Defense, *Before Disaster Strikes What to Do Now: A Family Handbook* (St. Louis: Allied Printing, 1957), 5, Civilian

Defense Collection, Missouri Historical Society Library and Research Center, St. Louis (hereinafter CDC, MHS), box 1.

18. Commoner, *Science and Survival*, 111.

19. "Dr. Condon Urges Nations to Cut Atomic Arms," *St. Louis Globe-Democrat*, Nov. 24, 1958. For more on Condon's role and the role of his colleagues at Washington University, see Allen Smith, "Democracy and the Politics of Information: The St. Louis Committee for Nuclear Information," *Gateway Heritage* 17, no. 1 (Summer 1996): 2–6.

20. Gertrude Faust, "For Interested Consumers," *St. Louis Post-Dispatch*, Oct. 12, 1956.

21. Gertrude Faust, "After Dr. Teller," *St. Louis Post-Dispatch*, Mar. 10, 1958; "28 Women Urge Milk Be Tested for Strontium-90," *St. Louis Post-Dispatch*, Oct. 29, 1956. The women who signed the petition were: Mrs. Frederick (Gertrude) Faust, Mrs. Mark D. Eagleton, Mrs. G. L. Whetton, Mrs. M. E. Huether, Mrs. Roscoe Anderson, Mrs. Thomas S. Hall, Mrs. H. L. Johnson, Mrs. Jack O'Toole, Mrs. William L. Smiley, Mrs. Gertrude Gray, Mrs. Mary Ryder, Mrs. Christopher E. McEwen, Mrs. Rose Kerber, Mrs. Henry F. Chadeayne, Mrs. Olia Ellis Calloway, Mrs. Herman Maas, Mrs. George (Edna) Gellhorn, Mrs. W. Victor Weir, Mrs. W. W. Burke, Sonja Lawrence, Elizabeth J. Zentay, Marcelle Malamas, Dr. Helen E. Nash (pediatrician), Virginia Brodine, Julia Shanahan, Della J. Cox, Doris B. Wheeler, and D. Jean Younce. Virginia Warner Brodine, interview by D. Scott Peterson, May 12, 1972, Committee for Environmental Information, 1972–1973, Herman B. Wells Library, Indiana University, Bloomington, IN (hereinafter CEI, HBWL).

22. "Seek to Determine if 'Fall-Out' Affects Milk," *St. Louis Globe-Democrat*, Oct. 30, 1956. Edna Gellhorn testified at this 1956 hearing as well. Nancy McIlvaney, "The Tooth Fairy vs. the Atom Smashers: The Baby Tooth Survey Records in the Committee for Environmental Information Collection (1956–1977)," *Missouri Historical Review* 109, no. 2 (Jan. 2015): 129.

23. Mrs. Frederick Faust, St. Louis, to Admiral Lewis Strauss, Atomic Energy Commission, Washington, DC, Nov. 29, 1956, CEI, SHSMO, box 13, folder 199; Women's International League for Peace and Freedom—St. Louis Branch, memo, Sep. 1958, CEI, SHSMO, box 13, folder 193a; US Congress, "The Nature of Radioactive Fallout and Its Effects on Man," *Hearings before the Special Subcommittee on Radiation of the Joint Committee on Atomic Energy, Congress of the United States, Eighty-Fifth Congress*, 1st sess., part 2, Jun. 4–7, 1957 (Washington, DC: US Government Printing Office, 1957); Brodine, interview, May 12, 1972, CEI, HBWL; and James A. Deakin, "U.S. to Measure Radioactivity in Nation's Air, Food and Water: Public Health Service to Make Survey to Determine Danger from Nuclear Tests," *St. Louis Post-Dispatch*, Jan. 9, 1957.

24. Associated Press dispatch from Washington, DC, Oct. 24, 1956. Adlai Stevenson, Eisenhower's opponent in the 1956 election, campaigned against H-bomb testing and made a final plea to end it in a message published two days before Election Day; see "Humanity's Good Requires Ending of H-Bomb Tests," *St. Louis Post-Dispatch*, Nov. 4, 1956.

25. "Fallout in Our Milk: A Follow-Up Report," 64–69; Commoner, *Science and Survival*, 111; Swerdlow, *Women Strike for Peace*, 41.

26. St. Louis Consumer Federation, memo, ca. 1958, CEI, SHSMO, box 3, folder 193a; Wyant, "Strontium-90 in St. Louis"; Women's International League for Peace and Freedom—St. Louis Branch, memo, Sep. 1958, CEI, SHSMO, box 13, folder 193a; "Women Here Urge End to H-Tests," *St. Louis Globe-Democrat*, Sep. 12, 1957. The plan to send Mother's Day cards to Mamie Eisenhower was made in tandem with the National Committee for a Sane Nuclear Policy's campaign. The greeting was signed by Mrs. Walter (Louise) Baumgarten, Mrs. George (Dorothy) Roudebush, and Mrs. Thomas B. (Chloe) Sherman. "Bomb Test Foes Ask First Lady's Help," *St. Louis Globe-Democrat*, May 10, 1958. The Women's Committee to End Nuclear Tests sent another petition to President Eisenhower and other selected officials in February 1960 to immediately bar all atmospheric atomic tests as a step toward "general controlled disarmament." This petition was signed by Mrs. Roscoe (Frances) Anderson, Mrs. Robert J. (Margaret) Kline, Mrs. Carl Moe, Mrs. Thomas B. (Chloe) Sherman, and Mrs. Robert S. (Adele) Starbird. "Women's Group Urges U.S. to Declare Atom Test Bar," *St. Louis Globe-Democrat*, Feb. 18, 1960. Chloe Sherman and the Women's Committee to End Nuclear Tests sent another petition to President Eisenhower at the beginning of 1960 calling for a ban on all atmospheric tests. Also signing the petition were Frances Anderson, Mrs. Margaret Kline, Mrs. Carl Moe, and Adele Starbird.

27. League of Women Voters of St. Louis, "Notes for the New Year," *League Reporter*, ed. Mrs. Harry (Mary) Greensfelder, Jan. 1959, League of Women Voters of Kirkwood and South St. Louis County Records, 1937–1968, State Historical Society of Missouri (hereinafter LWV, SHSMO), box 24, folder 320; Avis Carlson, "Dame Edna of Saint Louis," *Saint Louis Magazine*, Nov. 1968, 21–22.

28. "A Great Lady of St. Louis Is 89," *St. Louis Post-Dispatch*, Dec. 18, 1967; League of Women Voters of St. Louis, "Mrs. George Gellhorn Urges Agreement to End H-Bomb Testing: Tells Disarmament Subcommittee Risk to Children from Fall-Out Is Too Great," *League Reporter*, ed. Mrs. W. K. (Carita) Wyant Jr., Jan. 1957, LWV, SHSMO, box 24, folder 320.

29. League of Women Voters of St. Louis, "Mrs. George Gellhorn Urges Agreement to End H-Bomb Testing," LWV, SHSMO.

30. For official literature on preparing for a nuclear attack on St. Louis, see St. Louis Office of Civil Defense, *Before Disaster Strikes*; St. Louis Office of Civil Defense, *Escape from the H-Bomb: St. Louis City and County Evacuation Plan* (St. Louis: Allied Printing, 1958); and Department of Defense, Office of Civil Defense, "Fallout Protection: What to Know and Do about Nuclear Attack," Dec. 1961, CDC, MHS, box 1. For commentary on the bomb survival kits recommended by the St. Louis Office of Civil Defense, see Beth A. Rubin, "The Sheltered Life of the 1950s," *Gateway Heritage* 16, no. 1 (Summer 1995): 48; Holly Thornton, daughter of Bonnie Hart, interview by Kenn Thomas, Jul. 16, 2002, transcript, Bonnie Hart Papers, 1948–1977, S0657, State Historical Society of Missouri (hereinafter Hart Papers, SHSMO), box 20, folder 224; Women's International League for Peace

and Freedom, St. Louis Branch, 1968, List of Membership, Women's International League for Peace and Freedom Records, S0214, State Historical Society of Missouri (hereinafter WILPF, SHSMO), box 2, folder 8.

31. Bonnie Hart, to an unknown congressman, ca. 1957, Hart Papers, SHSMO, box 1, folder 3.

32. St. Louis Office of Civil Defense, *Before Disaster Strikes*, 5; St. Louis Office of Civil Defense, *Escape from the H-Bomb*; Bonnie Hart, "This Is a Protest: Lies and Evasions on Fallout Shelter Program as Protection from Nuclear War," ca. 1963, box 1, folder 3, and Holly Thornton, interview by Kenn Thomas, Jul. 16, 2002, both in Hart Papers, SHSMO. If not for Hart, St. Louis citizens might have remained in the dark for much longer about the fact that from 1942 to 1957 the Mallinckrodt Chemical Company of St. Louis processed uranium for the production of the Manhattan Project's atomic weapons. The chemical company haphazardly disposed of radioactive waste in drums in several places, including a site near Lambert Airport. First Hart and later Kay Drey, another St. Louis nuclear woman who has since been hailed as "Missouri's leading opponent of nuclear power," uncovered many other secret nuclear waste sites around the metropolitan area. For detailed investigations into St. Louis's nuclear industrial cover-up, see the Bonnie Hart Papers; Kay Drey Mallinckrodt Collection, S0826; Kay Drey Toxic Chemicals and Nuclear Waste Collection, S0842; Kay Drey Callaway Nuclear Plant Collection, S1028; Kay Drey Callaway Nuclear Hazards Collection, S1029; Kay Drey Hematite Addenda, S1045; all located at State Historical Society of Missouri. See also Kenn Thomas, "From the Stacks: Kay Drey, Environmental Champion," *Missouri Historical Review* 106, no. 1 (Oct. 2011): 48–51.

33. "St. Louis Group Praised for Fight for H-test Ban," *St. Louis Globe-Democrat*, Aug. 24, 1958. The Soviet Union likewise agreed to stop weapons testing for about a year; their last test in 1958 occurred on November 3. Michael Egan, *Barry Commoner and the Science of Survival: The Remaking of American Environmentalism* (Cambridge, MA: M.I.T. Press, 2007), 48. In 1967 the CNI was renamed the Committee for Environmental Information (CEI) to reflect its broader ecological studies on environmental hazards like air and water pollution.

34. There was a similar science information group in New York known as the Scientists' Committee for Radiation Information, but at the time it did not include nonscientists. Commoner, *Science and Survival*, 120.

35. Wyant, "Strontium-90 in St. Louis"; Egan, *Barry Commoner and the Science of Survival*, 11; Brodine, interview, May 12, 1972, CEI, HBWL.

36. Greater St. Louis Citizens' Committee for Nuclear Information, Founding Resolution, Apr. 21, 1958, CDC, MHS, box 1. For more on the CNI, see Commoner's autobiographical account in *Science and Survival*, 110–20; Egan, *Barry Commoner and the Science of Survival*; William Cuyler Sullivan, *Nuclear Democracy: A History of the Greater St. Louis Citizen's Committee for Nuclear Information, 1957–1967* (St. Louis: Washington University, 1982); Smith, "Democracy and the Politics of Information," 2–13. Judy Baumgarten, the president of the CNI, issued a statement to the *Globe-Democrat* explaining that the group sought only to disseminate

the information, not to take positions regarding it. Edward W. O'Brien, "Group Here Used by Reds, Study Reports: Citizens Committee for Nuclear Information Cited," *St. Louis Globe-Democrat*, Oct. 16, 1960.

37. Doris Deakin, "Mothers Ask—What Should We Feed Our Kids?," *Nuclear Information* (Oct. 1959): 3; "A Statement by the Greater St. Louis Committee for Nuclear Information on the Strontium 90 Content of Milk"; "Fallout in Our Milk: A Follow-Up Report," 69; Greater St. Louis Citizens' Committee for Nuclear Information, "How Radioactive Is St. Louis Milk?"

38. Commoner also noted that the article appeared in the *Saturday Review*, *St. Louis Post-Dispatch*, *Houston Post*, *San Francisco News-Call Bulletin*, and a dozen or more periodicals in Canada, Denmark, France, Great Britain, and Sweden as well as in the United States. Commoner, *Science and Survival*, 115.

39. Florence Moog, "Nuclear War in St. Louis: One Year Later," *Nuclear Information* (Sep. 1959).

40. Ibid.; "Nature in Atomic War," *St. Louis Post-Dispatch*, Oct. 26, 1963.

41. Herman M. Kalckar, "An International Milk Teeth Radiation Census," *Nature* 182 (1958): 283–84; Greater St. Louis Citizens' Committee for Nuclear Information, "Information," newsletter, Dec. 24, 1958, CEI, SHSMO, box 14, folder 207.

42. The Consumer's Union kick-started the Baby Tooth Survey with a grant of approximately $3,000 to send its first batch of teeth to a laboratory in New Jersey called Isotopes, Inc. See CEI, SHSMO, box 14, folder 209; "Fallout in Our Milk: A Follow-Up Report," 64–69. The Baby Tooth Survey also received fetal teeth and fetal skeletons for comparative analysis. The Public Health Service eventually underwrote the Baby Tooth Survey directly. Baby Tooth Survey, St. Louis, to Clarissa Start, *St. Louis Post-Dispatch*, Dec. 3, 1964, CEI, SHSMO, box 13, folder 202.

43. The design for this unique equipment came out of Argonne National Laboratories. Office of Information, Washington University, "News for Release," Nov. 28, 1960, CEI, SHSMO, box 13, folder 193.

44. Louise Zibold Reiss, "Strontium-90 Absorption by Deciduous Teeth: Analysis of Teeth Provides a Practicable Method of Monitoring Strontium-90 Uptake by Human Populations," *Science* 134, no. 3491 (Nov. 24, 1961): 1673; Dennis Hevesi, "Dr. Louise Reiss, Who Helped Ban Atomic Testing, Dies at 90," *New York Times*, Jan. 10, 2011.

45. Greater St. Louis Citizens' Committee for Nuclear Information, minutes of first meeting of Baby Tooth Survey subcommittee, Dec. 15, 1958, CEI, SHSMO, box 13, folder 194. Reiss was succeeded in 1962 by E. S. Khalifah of Washington University's School of Dentistry and Donald E. Flieder of Saint Louis University's School of Dentistry. "Organization Plan," CEI, SHSMO, box 13, folder 193; Mrs. Sophia Goodman, Executive Secretary, Baby Tooth Survey, St. Louis, to Jane Clark, Editor, Women's Page, *St. Louis Globe-Democrat*, Feb. 18, 1963, CEI, SHSMO, box 13, folder 201.

46. Yvonne Logan is listed as a member in 1953 of the League of Women Voters of Kirkwood and South St. Louis County. League of Women Voters of Kirkwood, Membership, Mar. 1953, LWV, SHSMO, box 2, folder 25. While a member of

WILPF, Logan served on the national board as a delegate in overseas conferences in the early 1960s, acted as the Membership Committee chairman in 1966, temporarily helped edit the monthly bulletin of the St. Louis branch, and served as their lead chairman between 1969 and 1972. She remained a member for decades after. Women's International League for Peace and Freedom, St. Louis Branch, 1968, List of Membership, WILPF, SHSMO.

47. For example, the Baby Tooth Survey reached out to the WILPF and individual women's activists for support in gathering teeth from "hot spot" areas in North Dakota in 1965 and 1966. Mrs. Joseph P. (Yvonne) Logan, Executive Director, Baby Tooth Survey, St. Louis, to Mrs. John W. Anderson, Williston, North Dakota, Nov. 10, 1965, CEI, SHSMO, box 13, folder 203.

48. In March 1959, Monsignor Hoffley of St. Louis also gave his permission to allow the Baby Tooth Survey to send informational literature to all 250 parish offices in the St. Louis area. Louise Reiss worked closely with the educational director for the National Council of Jewish Women, Mrs. John E. (Anna Lee) Brown, and Mrs. Carl W. (Caesarina) Huenke of the Council of Catholic Women over the following years. Greater St. Louis Citizens' Committee for Nuclear Information, minutes of fifth meeting of Baby Tooth Survey subcommittee, Mar. 3, 1959, CEI, SHSMO, box 13, folder 195; Mrs. Sophia Goodman, Executive Secretary, Baby Tooth Survey, St. Louis, to Mrs. Carl W. (Caesarina) Huenke, Council of Catholic Women, St. Louis, Nov. 8, 1962, CEI, SHSMO, box 13, folder 200.

49. For more on the Baby Tooth Survey as an innovation in the history of science, see Eileen Catherine Neville, "The Tooth of the Matter: Science Meets Public through Operation Tooth" (MA thesis, Harvard University, 1998), CEI, SHSMO, box 30, folder 438.

50. Mrs. Joseph P. (Yvonne) Logan, Executive Director, Baby Tooth Survey, Public Service Announcement, Spring 1968, CEI, SHSMO, box 14, folder 221; "Baby Tooth Survey News," *Nuclear Information* 1 (May 1960): 1; Commoner, *Science and Survival*, 112; CNI members' newsletter, Oct. 1960, CEI, SHSMO, folder 392; Greater St. Louis Citizens' Committee for Nuclear Information, *Baby Tooth Survey News*, Apr. 1960, CEI, SHSMO, box 14, folder 207; "Fallout: Moment of Tooth," 70.

51. In June 1961, Louise Reiss estimated that only about 60 percent of the teeth mailed in to the Baby Tooth Survey actually derived from children born in the St. Louis area, which presented a logistical problem. According to the "Official Procedures" of the Baby Tooth Survey, samples had to generate from locations within 150 miles of St. Louis. Dr. Louise Reiss, Baby Tooth Survey, St. Louis, to Mrs. William (Ethel) Kesler, Montreal Baby Tooth Survey, Montreal, Quebec, Jun. 7, 1961, CEI, SHSMO, box 13, folder 199; "Office Procedures for Processing Incoming Teeth," CEI, SHSMO, box 13, folder 193; Mrs. Sophia Goodman, Executive Secretary, Baby Tooth Survey, to Ethel Kesler, Chairman, Montreal Baby Tooth Survey, Montreal, Quebec, Oct. 12, 1962, CEI, SHSMO, box 13, folder 200; Mrs. Sophia Goodman, Baby Tooth Survey, St. Louis, to Mrs. Ethel Kesler, Montreal, Quebec, Canada, Nov. 7, 1963, CEI, SHSMO, box 13, folder 201. Collections were frequently reported in St. Louis newspapers as well; see, for example, "7600 Baby Teeth Collected Here,"

St. Louis Globe-Democrat, Dec. 21, 1963. The Baby Tooth Survey informed the *St. Louis Post-Dispatch* and the *St. Louis Globe-Democrat* that the survey had collected 200,000 baby teeth by the end of 1965. Baby Tooth Survey, St. Louis, to Clarissa Start, *St. Louis Post-Dispatch*, Dec. 3, 1964, CEI, SHSMO, box 13, folder 202; "200,000 Baby Teeth Give Nuclear Data," *St. Louis Globe-Democrat*, Dec. 21, 1965; "Facts Concerning the Baby Tooth Survey," Jan. 1968, CEI, SHSMO, box 13, folder 206; Fred Commoner, "Baby Tooth Survey," 1959, CEI, SHSMO, box 13, folder 197; Kent D. Votaw, Pasco, WA, to Baby Tooth Survey, St. Louis, Apr. 5, 1967, CEI, SHSMO, box 13, folder 197.

52. Leslie Pierce, Lansing, MI, to Operation Tooth, St. Louis, undated, Baby Tooth Survey, box 13, folder 198; Gene Smith, Decatur, GA, to Office of the Mayor, St. Louis, May 12, 1960, box 13, folder 197; Raymond R. Tucker, St. Louis, to Gene Smith, Decatur, GA, May 17, 1960, box 13, folder 197; Mrs. W. D. Roberts, Staff Secretary, Baby Tooth Survey, St. Louis, to Mary Jane's Mother, Jan. 16, 1959, box 13, folder 199; Jill to Tooth Fairy, Operation Tooth, Baby Tooth Survey, box 13, folder 197; Don to Tooth Fairy, Operation Tooth, Baby Tooth Survey, box 13, folder 197; Amy to Operation Tooth, St. Louis, undated, Baby Tooth Survey, box 13, folder 198, all in CEI, SHSMO.

53. Patty Hamley to Operation Tooth, Jun. 9, 1961, Baby Tooth Survey; Peter Trapolino, Rochester, New York, to Operation Tooth, St. Louis, May 11, 1960, Baby Tooth Survey, both in CEI, SHSMO, box 13, folder 197.

54. James G. Terrill Jr., Assistant Chief, Division of Radiological Health, Public Health Service, Washington, DC, to Greater St. Louis Citizens' Committee for Nuclear Information, St. Louis, Mar. 27, 1961; H. V. Christiansen, Director, City of Beloit–Civil Defense, Beloit, WI, to Mrs. Donald Fagin, Circulation Manager, Committee for Nuclear Information, Apr. 23, 1965; Minnesota Senator Hubert H. Humphrey, US Senate, Committee on Foreign Relations, Washington, DC, to Mrs. Virginia Brodine, Editor, Committee for Nuclear Information, Apr. 4, 1963, all from CEI, SHSMO, box 14, folder 211.

55. Irene Hoglund, Chair, Women's International League for Peace and Freedom–Massachusetts Branch, Concord, MA, to Mrs. Sophia Goodman, Executive Secretary, Baby Tooth Survey, St. Louis, Mar. 2, 1963, CEI, SHSMO, box 14, folder 232.

56. See CEI, SHSMO, box 14, folder, 233.

57. Activists and scientists in New York City showed strong interest within a few months of the survey's founding in St. Louis. New York hosted a nuclear watch organization, the Scientists' Committee for Radiation Information, consisting solely of scientists. That group formed the New York Baby Tooth Survey as a near replica of the St. Louis model, with one major difference: neither nonscientists nor women played a central role. The New York initiative adopted the same logo of a smiling, toothless child and disseminated pamphlets written in St. Louis as well as issues of the CNI's *The Scientist and the Citizen* before they founded their own journal, *Radiation Information*. Eventually the organization followed the St. Louis model and permitted nonscientists to join. It became especially active when New York

City developers seriously considered constructing a nuclear reactor in the heart of Manhattan. Arthur Bushel, Director, Bureau of Dentistry, New York, to Dr. Louise Reiss, Director, Baby Tooth Survey, St. Louis, May 26, 1959, and Morton L. Shapiro, Chairman, Research Committee, Queens County Dental Society, NY, to Louise Reiss, Director, Baby Tooth Survey, St. Louis, Jun. 3, 1959, both in CEI, SHSMO, box 14, folder 236. For an article similar to Florence Moog's in the September issue of *Nuclear Information*, see New York Scientists' Committee for Radiation Information, "Effects of a 20-Megaton Thermonuclear Explosion on Columbus Circle," *Radiation Information* (Fall 1961), CEI, SHSMO, box 18, folder 277.

58. Mrs. William (Ethel) Kesler, Chairman, Baby Tooth Survey, Montreal, Quebec, to Dr. Louise Reiss, Director, Baby Tooth Survey, St. Louis, May 27, 1960, and Enquete Sur Les Dents des Jeunes Enfants de Montreal, Citoyens De Montreal pour le Desarmement Nucleaire, "Instruction Pour L'Envoi des Dents," ca. 1960, both in CEI, SHSMO, box 14, folder 227; Secretary, Baby Tooth Survey, to Mr. Henry F. Niedringhaus III, President, Al Wallenbrock and Associates, Inc., St. Louis, Mar. 28, 1961, and Dr. Louise Reiss, Baby Tooth Survey, St. Louis, to Mrs. William (Ethel) Kesler, Montreal Baby Tooth Survey, Montreal, Quebec, Jun. 7, 1961, both in CEI, SHSMO, box 13, folder 199.

59. "Baby Tooth Survey Is Started in Japan," *St. Louis Globe-Democrat*, Feb. 1, 1962, and Japan Baby Tooth Survey, Report, both in CEI, SHSMO, box 14, folder 231.

60. Greater St. Louis Citizens' Committee for Nuclear Information, *Baby Tooth Survey News*, Dec. 1964, CEI, SHSMO, box 14, folder, 207. See also the October 1964 issue of *Scientist and the Citizen*. Sylvia Raymond, Secretary to Dr. Harold L. Rosenthal, to Freda Ilana Guth, De Soto, Missouri, Jun. 27, 1967, CEI, SHSMO, box 13, folder 205; Mrs. Sophia Goodman, Executive Secretary, Baby Tooth Survey, St. Louis, to Jane Clark, Editor, Women's Page, *St. Louis Globe-Democrat*, Feb. 18, 1963, CEI, SHSMO, box 13, folder 201. To celebrate the tenth anniversary of the Baby Tooth Survey in 1968, St. Louis's mayor, Alfonso J. Cervantes, pinned a button reading "I Gave My Tooth to Science" on two children: "a black child from Hamilton School (public) and a white child from St. Roch's (Catholic) who have recently lost teeth." The week of January 13 was declared Baby Tooth Week. Mrs. William F. (Helen) Bueler, Executive Secretary, Baby Tooth Survey, St. Louis, to Alfonso J. Cervantes, Mayor, St. Louis, Dec. 19, 1968, CEI, SHSMO, box 13, folder 206.

61. Committee for Nuclear Information, *Baby Tooth Survey News*, Dec. 1964, CEI, SHSMO, box 14, folder 207.

62. For example, see Mrs. Kay Johnson, Women Strike for Peace, Washington, DC, to CNI, St. Louis, Sep. 26, 1963, CEI, SHSMO; Virginia Brodine, St. Louis, to Mrs. Jeanne Bagby, Washington, DC, May 13, 1963, both from CEI, SHSMO, box 26, folder 391.

63. Dr. Eric Reiss, CNI, St. Louis, to J. Earl Smith, Health Commissioner, St. Louis Health Division, St. Louis, Oct. 25, 1961, CEI, SHSMO, box 18, folder 278. For

a news story on the possible use of potassium iodide to protect against iodine-131 in nuclear fallout, see "Nuclear Test Milk Hazard Measures Urged," *St. Louis Globe-Democrat*, Aug. 8, 1962.

64. Vitaly I. Khalturin, Tatyana G. Rautian, Paul G. Richards, and William S. Leith, "A Review of Nuclear Testing by the Soviet Union at Novaya Zemlya, 1955–1990," *Science and Global Security* 13, no. 1–2 (2005): 1–42. A formerly top-secret CIA document described the yield of the Tsar Bomba as 58 megatons, but these numbers were later revised. See Director of Central Intelligence, "National Intelligence Estimate: The Soviet Atomic Energy Program," May 16, 1962, Top Secret, 23, Central Intelligence Agency website, accessed Oct. 23, 2017, http://www.foia.cia.gov/sites/default/files/document_conversions/89801/DOC_0000843187.pdf. Soviet Premier Nikita Khrushchev announced the Soviet Union's intention to resume H-bomb testing at Novaya Zemlya, the site of the Tsar Bomba test, and many smaller nuclear devices and three massive H-bombs were detonated at Novaya Zemlya. Two of them registered at around 20 megatons each, and the final test of 1962 yielded an explosion of 24.2 megatons. John F. Kennedy, "Statement on Atmospheric Nuclear Tests," *St. Louis Post-Dispatch*, Nov. 2, 1961.

65. See "Women March throughout US in a Mass Strike for Peace" and "Anti-Nuclear Protest," in *St. Louis Post-Dispatch*, Nov. 2, 1961.

66. Swerdlow, *Women Strike for Peace*, x, 8, 26, 41. See also Irene Diamond and Gloria Feman Orenstein, eds., *Reweaving the World* (San Francisco: Sierra Club Books, 1990).

67. Dorothy Steffens, National Legislative Chairman of the WILPF, "Women as a Resource for Change," Oct. 19, 1967, WILPF, SHSMO, box 1, folder 6. See Diamond and Orenstein, *Reweaving the World*; Rome, *The Genius of Earth Day*, 36–37.

68. Swerdlow, *Women Strike for Peace*, 8; "Women March throughout US in a Mass Strike for Peace," *St. Louis Post-Dispatch*; Jo Davis, "1964 Soviet-American Women's Conference," *Four Lights* 24, no. 5 (May 1964): 214, WILPF, SHSMO, box 1, folder 7; Women's International League for Peace and Freedom, *Four Lights* 23, no. 2 (Jul. 1963), WILPF, SHSMO, box 1, folder 7. WILPF sent twelve American women to a second round of peace talks in Moscow in May 1964 to discuss disarmament with the same Soviet women who had attended the original conference at Bryn Mawr in 1961.

69. John W. Finney, "Nevada Fallout Found a Hazard: Children Possibly Harmed, Congress Panel Is Told," *New York Times*, Aug. 22, 1963.

70. Jerry E. Bishop, "Debate over Fallout: Peril Seen in 'Ventings' of US Underground Nuclear Explosions," *Wall Street Journal*, Sep. 27, 1963.

71. Dorothy Hutchinson, *Four Lights* 23, no. 2 (Jul. 1963), WILPF, SHSMO, box 1, folder 7; "Nevada Fallout Called Menace to Children," *St. Louis Globe-Democrat*, Aug. 22, 1963; "St. Louis Group Challenges AEC Fallout Report," *St. Louis Globe-Democrat*, Nov. 8, 1963.

72. Women Strike for Peace, Committee on Radiation, "Statement for Fallout Hearings," Aug. 1963, CEI, SHSMO, box 26, folder 391.

73. Committee for Nuclear Information, *Baby Tooth Survey News*, Dec. 1964, CEI, SHSMO, box 14, folder 207. See also the October 1964 issue of *Scientist and the Citizen*. Commoner, *Science and Survival*, 118; Swerdlow, *Women Strike for Peace*, 12.

74. Brodine, interview, May 12, 1972, CEI, HBWL; for the end of the Baby Tooth Survey tests on Sr-90, see "Levels of Strontium 90 Are Said to Be Static Now," *St. Louis Post-Dispatch*, Jun. 8, 1969. The Committee for Environmental Information disbanded in 1977. Greater St. Louis Citizens' Committee for Nuclear Information, newsletter, ca. 1964, CEI, SHSMO, box 14, folder 207. Philip Lesser, "Air Pollution in Saint Louis" (Saint Louis: Committee for Environmental Information, 1973), CEI, SHSMO, box 18, folder 276. The US Public Health Service even awarded the CNI a $140,000 grant to provide objective information on "specific problems of air and water pollution and environmental contamination due to pesticides." "Group Gets Pollution Study Grant," *St. Louis Globe-Democrat*, Nov. 16, 1966. See also Sullivan, *Nuclear Democracy*.

75. Brodine, interview, May 12, 1972, CEI, HBWL.

76. Coalition for the Environment, "Pesticides and Herbicides Fact Sheet," n.d., Coalition for the Environment Records, 1968–1978, State Historical Society of Missouri (hereinafter CE, SHSMO), box 3, folder 59. Rachel Carson's *Silent Spring*, first published in 1962, was one of the first popular books raising awareness of the detrimental effects of a common post–World War II pesticide, DDT (dichlorodiphenyltrichloroethane), used by farmers until it was banned in 1972. Carson's writing focused on the beauty and harmony of natural ecology in juxtaposition to man-made technology, and she often appealed to women, who in her view "have a greater intuitive understanding" of beauty. "They want for their children not only physical health," she told one sorority, "but mental and spiritual health as well." Although Brodine claimed not to have been particularly influenced by Carson's *Silent Spring*, the two quickly found each other. Carson notified the CNI in November 1963, "I was much interested to read . . . that CNI is planning to extend the scope of its interests and activities to include environmental contaminants other than radioactive substances. I have long admired your organization and have repeatedly referred to it as a model when I am asked about setting up a similar organization for the study of pesticide problems." Carson was particularly fond of one of Brodine's issues in *The Scientist and the Citizen* (formerly *Nuclear Information*), titled "War and the Living Environment," and she hoped to collaborate with the organization—that was, before she became ill. Rachel Carson, *Silent Spring* (Boston: Houghton Mifflin, 1962); Rachel Carson, speech to Theta Sigma Phi, quoted in Rome, *The Genius of Earth Day*, 32. See Linda J. Lear, "Rachel Carson's *Silent Spring*," *Environmental History Review* 17, no. 2 (Summer 1993): 23–48; Sue V. Rosser, ed., *Women, Science, and Myth: Gender Beliefs from Antiquity to the Present* (Santa Barbara, CA: ABC-CLIO, 2008), 381–2; and *Reweaving the World*. Rachel Carson, Silver Spring, Maryland, to Dr. Walter C. Bauer, Committee for Nuclear Information, Letter, Nov. 12, 1963, CEI, SHSMO, box 14, folder 211; Brodine, interview, May 12, 1972, CEI, HBWL.

77. Swerdlow, *Women Strike for Peace*, 4.

78. See Women's International League for Peace and Freedom, "Many Demonstrations Decry Vietnam Slaughter," *Four Lights* 25, no. 3 (Mar. 1965); Milnor Alexander, "Anti-Communism as American Credo," *Four Lights* 25, no. 7 (Jul. 1965); Elizabeth Weideman, "Annual Meeting Seeks Change on All Fronts," *Four Lights* 28, no. 7 (Jul. 1968); Katherine Camp, "From the President's Desk," *Four Lights* 28, no. 10 (Dec. 1968); Katherine Camp, "Where There's a WILPF," *Four Lights* 29, no. 1 (Jan. 1969); and Women's International League for Peace and Freedom, "The Ecology Crusade," *Peace and Freedom* 30, no. 4 (Apr. 1970); all in WILPF, SHSMO, box 1, folder 7.

79. Women's International League for Peace and Freedom, St. Louis Branch, 1968, List of Membership. Joy Guze was the President of WILPF-St. Louis in 1958 during the early St. Louis protests against nuclear weapons testing. Women's International League for Peace and Freedom–St. Louis Branch, newsletter, ed. Enola Ledbetter, vol. 3, no. 2 (Feb. 1958). These women joined the organization as early as 1962: Mrs. Walter (Marcia) Bauer, Mrs. Barry (Gloria) Commoner, Kay Drey, Mrs. Mortimer (Sophia) Goodman, Mrs. Samuel (Joy) Guze, and Mrs. Joseph P. (Yvonne) Logan. Women's International League for Peace and Freedom, St. Louis Branch, 1962–1963, List of Membership, WILPF, SHSMO, box 2, folder 8. These women remained active members or on the bulletin mailing list of the organization all the way until 1980: Kay Drey, Joy Guze, Yvonne Logan, Marcia Bauer, Judy Baumgarten, Doris Bolef, Virginia Brodine, Bonnie Hart, and Edna Rosenthal. Women's International League for Peace and Freedom, St. Louis Branch, 1979, List of Membership, WILPF, SHSMO, box 2, folder 8.

80. The Coalition for the Environment was another St. Louis innovation. Its uniqueness rested in its determination to bring together all sorts of environmental activists under one umbrella on the grounds that each of their objectives was fundamentally connected. Affiliated organizations included various chapters of the American Association of University Women, the Eliot Chapel Women's Alliance, the Junior League of St. Louis, League of Women Voters, National Council of Jewish Women, Planned Parenthood Association of Greater St. Louis, and a host of other organizations. Joining in 1970 were WILPF, Housewives Elect Lower Prices (a consumer group), and the Committee for Environmental Information. See CE, SHSMO. The official newsletter of the coalition, *Alert*, kept all member organizations informed.

81. Doris Bolef, "Let Us Begin," *Peace and Freedom* 30, no. 6 (Jun. 1970), WILPF, SHSMO, box 1, folder 7; Katherine Camp, "Don't Agonize—Organize," *Four Lights* 29, no. 2 (Feb. 1969), WILPF, SHSMO, box 1, folder 7.

82. Donna Bocco, "Women's Lib Can Aid Other Movements," *Peace and Freedom* 30, 10 (Philadelphia: Women's International League for Peace and Freedom, Dec. 1970), WILPF, SHSMO, St. Louis Branch 214, box 1, folder 7; and Marion Edman, "What's in Our Name," *Peace and Freedom* 30, 10 (Philadelphia: Women's International League for Peace and Freedom, Dec. 1970), WILPF, SHSMO, St. Louis Branch 214, box 1, folder 7.

83. Women's International League for Peace and Freedom, "WILPF National Meeting 1971," *Peace and Freedom* 31, 5 (Philadelphia: Women's International League for Peace and Freedom, May 1971), WILPF, SHSMO, St. Louis Branch 214, box 1, folder 7. For more information on St. Louis's feminist organizations in the 1970s, see the National Organization for Women, Metro St. Louis Chapter Records, 1971–1989, and the Coalition of St. Louis Women Records, both at the State Historical Society of Missouri. The St. Louis branch of the National Organization for Women (NOW) was formed in February 1971 under the leadership of President Mary Ann Sedey.

84. Eleanor Fowler, "Board Discusses Priorities," and Pat Samuel, "ERA Testimony Submitted to Senate Judiciary Unit," both in *Peace and Freedom* 30, no. 8 (Philadelphia: Women's International League for Peace and Freedom, Nov. 1970), WILPF, SHSMO, box 1, folder 7; "What Can Women Who Want Peace Really Do?," Monthly Bulletin of the St. Louis Branch of the Women's International League for Peace and Freedom, May 1970, WILPF, SHSMO, box 2, folder 14; Diamond and Orenstein, *Reweaving the World*, xi.

85. Earth Day in 1970 was so successful that Congress and governors around the country, including Warren E. Hearnes in Missouri, declared the week of April 19 "Earth Week." The Coalition for the Environment planned to hold teach-ins all that week, and Richard B. Ogilvie, the governor of Illinois, even made April 22, 1971, an official "Environmental Teach-In Day." Various delegates of the coalition appeared on KETC-TV, Channel 9, and various radio stations to promote their causes. Environmental activists created one of the nation's first ecology centers in St. Louis at the end of 1970. A major meeting there resulted in the formation of the Ecology Center Communications Council (ECCC) in Washington, DC. "Earth Week," *Congressional Record: Proceedings and Debates of the 92nd Congress, First Session*, 117, no. 8 (Washington, DC, Feb. 1, 1971); Governor Warren E. Hearnes, Proclamation, State of Missouri, Mar. 1971, CE, SHSMO, box 2, folder 23; Governor Richard B. Ogilvie, Proclamation, State of Illinois, Mar. 10, 1971, CE, SHSMO, box 2, folder 23; "City Will Observe 'Earth Week' in April," *St. Louis Globe-Democrat*, Mar. 19, 1971; "Environmental 'Teach-ins' Scheduled Here," *St. Louis Globe-Democrat*, Dec. 31, 1969; Coalition for the Environment, "Teach-In," Olivette Grade School, Mar. 16, 1971, CE, SHSMO, box 3, folder 54; Mrs. J. K. Street, Coordinator for Earth Week, Coalition for the Environment, memo, Apr. 7, 1971, CEI, SHSMO, box 2, folder 23; Stradling, *The Environmental Moment, 1968–1972*; Merchant, *Major Problems in American Environmental History*, 427–66.

3. The Gospel of the Gay Ghetto

1. Laud Humphreys, *Out of the Closets: The Sociology of Homosexual Liberation* (Englewood Cliffs, NJ: Prentice Hall, 1972), 82; *Mandrake* 1, no. 4 (Jun. 1970): 1, Laud Humphreys Papers, ONE National Gay and Lesbian Archives, Los Angeles, California, (hereinafter Humphreys Papers, ONGLA).

2. *Mandrake* 1, no. 9 (Feb. 1971): 4, Humphreys Papers, ONGLA.

3. "Apathy Cited for Lack of Gay Churches Here," *St. Louis Post-Dispatch*, Apr. 23, 1971.

4. Elizabeth B. Platt, "History of Trinity Church, St. Louis, 1855–1955," 1955, Trinity Episcopal Church Parish Archives, St. Louis (hereinafter Trinity Archives); Charles F. Rehkopf, "Trinity Church, St. Louis: A Congregation That Loves," *The Living Church*, Jul. 18, 1965; Arthur E. Walmsley to Jennifer [M. Phillips], Oct. 18, 1999, Trinity Archives.

5. Rehkopf, "A Congregation That Loves."

6. Humphreys, *Out of the Closets*, 80–81.

7. Colin Gordon, *Mapping Decline: St. Louis and the Fate of the American City* (Philadelphia: University of Pennsylvania Press, 2008).

8. David Hollinger, "After Cloven Tongues of Fire: Ecumenical Protestantism and the Modern American Encounter with Diversity," *Journal of American History* 98, no. 1 (Jun. 2011): 48.

9. John D'Emilio, *Sexual Politics, Sexual Communities: The Making of a Homosexual Minority in the United States, 1940–1970* (Chicago: University of Chicago Press, 1983), 192–95, 199–200, 214–15.

10. Heather Rachelle White, *Reforming Sodom: Protestants and the Rise of Gay Rights* (Chapel Hill: University of North Carolina Press, 2015). Other notable works on queer religious history include John Howard, *Men Like That: A Southern Queer History* (Chicago: University of Chicago Press, 1999), ch. 6; Kevin J. Mumford, "The Trouble with Gay Rights: Race and the Politics of Sexual Orientation in Philadelphia, 1969–1982," *Journal of American History* 98, no. 1 (Jun. 2011): 49–72; Mark Oppenheimer, "'The Inherent Worth and Dignity': Gay Unitarians and the Birth of Sexual Tolerance in Liberal Religion," *Journal of the History of Sexuality* 7, no. 1 (Jul. 1996): 73–101; and Heather Rachelle White, "Proclaiming Liberation: The Historical Roots of LGBT Religious Organizing, 1946–1976," *Nova Religio: The Journal of Alternative and Emerging Religions* 11, no. 4 (May 2008): 102–19.

11. On religious opposition to LGBTQ rights, see, for example, Daniel K. Williams, *God's Own Party: The Making of the Christian Right* (Oxford: Oxford University Press, 2010).

12. G. Paul Musselman, *The Church on the Urban Frontier* (Greenwich, CT: Seabury Press, 1959), 1–2. See also Mark Wild, "Liberal Protestants and Urban Renewal," *Religion and American Culture: A Journal of Interpretation* 25, no. 1 (Winter 2015), 110–46; Mark Wild, *Renewal: Liberal Protestants and the American City after World War II* (Chicago: University of Chicago Press, 2019).

13. For a discussion of Episcopal and Presbyterian urban missions in nineteenth-century St. Louis, see Mary G. Bard, *A History of Second Presbyterian Church, St. Louis, Missouri, 1838–1938* (St. Louis: Second Presbyterian Church, 1987), 3, 6–7; and Platt, "History of Trinity Church," 5–6, 9.

14. Hollinger, "After Cloven Tongues of Fire," 26, 30–32. See also Gardiner H. Shattuck Jr., *Episcopalians and Race: From Civil War to Civil Rights* (Lexington: University Press of Kentucky, 2003); and William R. Hutchison, ed., *Between the Times:*

The Travail of the Protestant Establishment in America, 1900–1960 (New York: Cambridge University Press, 1989).

15. Musselman, *The Church on the Urban Frontier*, iii–iv, 1.

16. Rev. Joseph G. Moore, "St. Louis Parishes Advised to Evangelize," *Forth*, Nov. 1953, Missouri edition.

17. "Church's Work in the City . . . Everybody's Responsibility," *Forth*, Feb. 1955, Missouri edition.

18. *The World Within*, directed by Jack Alexander, National Council of the Protestant Episcopal Church, 1956, VHS at the Archives of the Episcopal Diocese of Missouri, St. Louis, Missouri. The film is also digitized and accessible via the Internet Archive. See also "Episcopal TV Series Starts Sun., September 9, on KSD-TV," *Now in the Episcopal Church, Diocese of Missouri* (hereinafter *Now*), Sep. 1956; and Mary Kimbrough, "St. Stephen's House Plans a Move," *St. Louis Post-Dispatch*, Feb. 17, 1956.

19. "St. Stephen's Chapel Brings Episcopal Church to Projects," *Now*, Feb. 1957.

20. Ibid.

21. "Street Corner Witness in South St. Louis," *Now*, May 1957.

22. *Now*, Dec. 1958.

23. "Inner City Homecoming," *Now*, Feb. 1961; "Parish Plans Fall Crash Program of Neighborhood Evangelism," *Now*, Jun. 1960.

24. "Eight Parishes Aid Door-to-Door Survey," *Now*, May 1963.

25. George L. Cadigan, "Our Goal: Reconciliation! What You May Do to Help," *Now*, Sep. 1963.

26. Platt, "History of Trinity Church," n.p.

27. On the history of the Central West End, see Suzanne Goell, ed., *The Days and Nights of the Central West End: An Affectionate Look at the Last Twenty Years in the City's Most Exciting Neighborhood* (St. Louis: Virginia Publishing, 1991); and Candace O'Connor, *Renaissance: A History of the Central West End* (St. Louis: Reedy Press, 2017).

28. Tim Fox, ed., *Where We Live: A Guide to St. Louis Communities* (St. Louis: Missouri Historical Society Press, 1995), 134. David T. Beito and Bruce Smith, "The Formation of Urban Infrastructure through Nongovernmental Planning: The Private Places of St. Louis, 1869–1920," *Journal of Urban History* 16, no. 3 (May 1990): 264–303.

29. James Neal Primm, *Lion of the Valley: St. Louis, Missouri, 1764–1980*, 3rd ed. (St. Louis: Missouri Historical Society Press, 1998), 347.

30. Ibid., 445.

31. Louis LaCoss, "Most Exclusive of Villages," *St. Louis Globe-Democrat*, Feb. 18, 1934. For the history of St. Louis's prototypical elite automobile suburb, see Charlene Bry, *Ladue Found: Celebrating 100 Years of the City's Rural-to-Regal Past* (St. Louis: Virginia Publishing, 2011).

32. Elizabeth Gentry Sayad, "Euclid and McPherson," *St. Louis Magazine*, Jun. 1963, 55; Walmsley to Phillips, Oct. 18, 1999, Trinity Archives.

33. Platt, "History of Trinity Church"; Rehkopf, "A Congregation That Loves," 8.

34. Walmsley to Phillips, Oct. 18, 1999, Trinity Archives.

35. Sayad, "Euclid and McPherson," 56.

36. Walmsley to Phillips, Oct. 18, 1999, Trinity Archives. Reports on the relative numbers of Black and white congregants at Trinity during these years vary slightly. In May 1960, *Now* said that 80 percent of the parish's communicants were white. According to Sayad, "Euclid and McPherson," 24 percent of the congregation was Black in 1963.

37. "One Block from the Altar . . . 70 Kids!," *Now*, May 1960.

38. Sayad, "Euclid and McPherson," 56; Rehkopf, "A Congregation That Loves," 9; Charlotte V. Brown, ed., "History of Trinity Church, St. Louis, 1955–1975," Trinity Archives.

39. "One Block from the Altar . . . 70 Kids!"

40. Brown, "History of Trinity Church"; "One Block from the Altar . . . 70 Kids!"; Sayad, "Euclid and McPherson," 56.

41. Rehkopf, "A Congregation That Loves," 8; "National Recognition for Trinity Church, St. Louis," *Now*, Sep. 1965.

42. Rehkopf, "A Congregation That Loves," 8–9, 12.

43. Humphreys, *Out of the Closets*, 80–81; Martin P. Levine, "Gay Ghetto," in *Gay Men: The Sociology of Male Homosexuality*, ed. Martin P. Levine (New York: HarperCollins, 1979), 182–204. On the historical trajectory of "gayborhoods" from the perspective of urban sociology, see Amin Ghaziani, *There Goes the Gayborhood?* (Princeton, NJ: Princeton University Press, 2014).

44. "Suit for Liquor License Taken under Advisement," *St. Louis Post-Dispatch*, Oct. 4, 1936; "Four Night Clubs and Taverns Cited for Sunday Sales," *St. Louis Star and Times*, Apr. 4, 1938.

45. For classic discussions of how similar neighborhoods contributed to the emergence of dissident sexual subcultures in other cities, see George Chauncey, *Gay New York: Gender, Urban Culture, and the Making of the Gay Male World, 1890–1940* (New York: Basic Books, 1994), esp. ch. 6; Joanne J. Meyerowitz, *Women Adrift: Independent Wage Earners in Chicago, 1880–1930* (Chicago: University of Chicago Press, 1988); Joanne Meyerowitz, "Sexual Geography and Gender Economy: The Furnished Room Districts of Chicago, 1890–1930," *Gender and History* 2, no. 3 (Autumn 1990): 274–96.

46. Humphreys, *Out of the Closets*, 80–81.

47. Police Report, Complaint No. 412758, Nov. 1, 1969, 4, Records Division, St. Louis Metropolitan Police Department, St. Louis, Missouri (hereinafter SLMPD).

48. On the implications of post–World War II urban change for the history of sexuality, see Clayton Howard, *The Closet and the Cul-de-Sac: The Politics of Sexual Privacy in Northern California* (Philadelphia: University of Pennsylvania Press, 2019); Josh Sides, *Erotic City: Sexual Revolutions and the Making of Modern San Francisco* (Oxford: Oxford University Press, 2009).

49. Walmsley to Phillips, Oct. 18, 1999, Trinity Archives.

50. "Modern Mission Jan. 25," *Now*, Jan. 1963.

51. Carol W. McDonald to Charles Rehkopf, Mar. 20, 1964, and Paul Pic, "THE EXIT Annual Report," n.d. [ca. April 1966], Metropolitan Church Federation Records, S0618, State Historical Society of Missouri, folder 281; "A Coffee House Gospel . . . Modern Expression of God's Love," *Now*, Dec. 1964. On similar Christian coffeehouses in other cities during this period, see John D. Perry Jr., *The Coffee House Ministry* (Richmond, VA: John Knox Press, 1966).

52. *The Phoenix* 1, no. 4 (Aug. 1966).

53. "A Coffee House Gospel."

54. Police Report, Complaint No. 412758, 1–2, 4, SLMPD; Humphreys, *Out of the Closets*, 85, 89.

55. Humphreys, *Out of the Closets*, 85, 87–88; "Presenting the Mandrake Society," n.d. [ca. 1969], St. Louis Lesbian, Gay, Bisexual, and Transgender History Project, S1038, State Historical Society of Missouri, box 1.

56. Humphreys, *Out of the Closets*, 84, 90; *Mandrake*, Mar. 1970, 1, Humphreys Papers, ONGLA.

57. Ellie Chapman, interview by author, St. Louis, Jul. 15, 2011.

58. Martha K. Baker and Etta Taylor, *A History of Trinity Church, St. Louis: 1975–2005* (St. Louis: Trinity Episcopal Church, 2005), 18, Trinity Archives.

59. "Apathy Cited for Lack of Gay Church Units Here"; *Mandrake*, May 1971, 2, Humphreys Papers, ONGLA.

60. Chapman, interview; Jim Pfaff, telephone interview by author, Mar. 25, 2014.

61. Baker and Taylor, *A History of Trinity Church*, 33–41; Ellie Chapman and Etta Taylor, interview by author, Jul. 15, 2011; Ellie Chapman, interview. The diary of Eda Houwink, a member of Trinity in the 1970s, offers telling glimpses of social interactions between straight and gay members of the parish. See Eda Houwink Papers, Missouri Historical Society Library and Research Center, St. Louis, especially box 1, folder 5.

62. *Mandrake*, Mar. 1971, 3; *Mandrake*, Feb. 1971, 14; both in Humphreys Papers, ONGLA.

63. *Mandrake*, Mar. 1971, 4, Humphreys Papers, ONGLA.

64. Jesse Todd, interviews by author, St. Louis, Aug. 16 and Sep. 19, 2011.

65. Todd, interview; Concerned Citizens Community Center, meeting minutes for Apr. 28, 1976 (copy in author's possession); Baker and Taylor, *History of Trinity Church*, 4.

66. "Lent—1976," n.d., Trinity Archives.

67. On racial segregation in local queer history, see the interactive online essay "The Impact of Segregation: Race in LGBTQ St. Louis, 1945–1992," *Mapping LGBTQ St. Louis*, http://library.wustl.edu/map-lgbtq-stl, 2017.

68. My description of the 1980 St. Louis Celebration of Lesbian and Gay Pride and the organizing that preceded it draws on contemporary press coverage and the articles, documents, and interviews compiled online by local historian Jym Andris, including Geof Dubson, "Fear, Pride in Step in Gay March Here," *St. Louis Post-Dispatch*, Apr. 21, 1980; and Jym Andris, "Even Alexander the Great," *No*

Bad News, Jul. 1980; found at Jym Andris, "The First Walk for Charity in St. Louis, Missouri, Sunday, April 20, 1980 and First Celebration of Lesbian and Gay Pride, April 12–20, 1980," *GLBT History in St. Louis* (website), n.d., https://web.archive.org/web/20220709165422/http://jandris.ipage.com/history/h80.2.html.

69. Lori Teresa Yearwood, "Gays Give Five Mayoral Candidates a Grilling," *St. Louis Post-Dispatch*, Feb. 8, 1993.

70. Judith VandeWater, "Gays Get a Voice on Panel," *St. Louis Post-Dispatch*, Jun. 28, 1993.

71. Doyle Murphy, "Higher Calling: Trinity Episcopal Church and the Fight for Gay Rights," *Riverfront Times* (St. Louis), Feb. 26, 2020.

72. "Missouri Episcopalians Ordain Openly Gay, Black Bishop," *St. Louis Post-Dispatch*, Jun. 14, 2020; Patrick Collins, "Matters of the Divine: Bishop Deon Johnson's Open Invitation to Dream Big," *Out in St. Louis*, Mar. 27, 2021.

4. Black Power on the Ground

This chapter originally appeared in the volume *Neighborhood Rebels: Black Power at the Local Level*, edited by Peniel E. Joseph (New York: Palgrave Macmillan, 2010). Accompanying images and captions, as well as the author's 2022 postscript, are new to this volume's version.

1. Clayborne Carson, "Civil Rights Reform and the Black Freedom Struggle," in *The Civil Rights Movement in America*, ed. Charles W. Eagles (Jackson: University Press of Mississippi, 1986), 19–37.

2. Jeanne F. Theoharis and Komozi Woodard, eds., *Freedom North: Black Freedom Struggles outside the South, 1940–1980* (New York: Palgrave Macmillan, 2003); Theoharis and Woodard, eds., *Groundwork: Local Black Freedom Movements in America* (New York: New York University Press, 2005); Robert O. Self, *American Babylon: Race and the Struggle for Postwar Oakland* (Princeton, NJ: Princeton University Press, 2003); Nikhil Pal Singh, *Black Is a Country: Race and the Unfinished Struggle for Democracy* (Cambridge, MA: Harvard University Press, 2004); Matthew J. Countryman, *Up South: Civil Rights and Black Power in Philadelphia* (Philadelphia: University of Pennsylvania Press, 2006); Jacquelyn Dowd Hall, "The Long Civil Rights Movement and the Political Uses of the Past," *Journal of American History* 91, no. 4 (Mar. 2005): 1233–63; Timothy B. Tyson, *Radio Free Dixie: Robert F. Williams and the Roots of Black Power* (Chapel Hill: University of North Carolina Press, 1999); Peniel E. Joseph, "Waiting *till the* Midnight Hour: Reconceptualizing the Heroic Period of the Civil Rights Movement, 1954–1965," *Souls* 2, no. 2 (2000): 6–17; Peniel E. Joseph, ed., *The Black Power Movement: Rethinking the Civil Rights–Black Power Era* (New York: Routledge, 2006); Charles E. Jones, ed., *The Black Panther Party Reconsidered* (Baltimore: Black Classic Press, 1998); Yohuru Williams, *Black Politics/White Power: Civil Rights, Black Power, and the Black Panthers in New Haven* (St. James, NY: Brandywine Press, 2000); Jama Lazerow and Yohuru Williams, eds., *In Search of the Black Panther Party: New Perspectives on a Revolutionary Movement* (Durham, NC: Duke University Press, 2006); Komozi Woodard, *A Nation within a Nation: Amiri Baraka (LeRoi Jones) and Black Power Politics* (Chapel

Hill: University of North Carolina Press, 1999); Scot Brown, *Fighting for US: Maulana Karenga, the US Organization, and Black Cultural Nationalism* (New York: New York University Press, 2003); Bettye Collier-Thomas and V. P. Franklin, eds., *Sisters in the Struggle: African American Women in the Civil Rights–Black Power Movement* (New York: New York University Press, 2001). See also Jeanne Theoharis, "Black Freedom Studies: Re-imagining and Redefining the Fundamentals," *History Compass* 4, no. 2 (2006): 348–67.

3. See, for example, Theoharis and Woodard, eds., *Freedom North*; Self, *American Babylon*; Hall, "The Long Civil Rights Movement and the Political Uses of the Past"; and Robert O. Self, "The Black Panther Party and the Long Civil Rights Era," in *In Search of the Black Panther Party*, ed. Lazerow and Williams, 15–55. See also Sundiata Keita Cha-Jua and Clarence Lang, "The 'Long Movement' as Vampire: Temporal and Spatial Fallacies in Recent Black Freedom Studies," *Journal of African American History* 92, no. 2 (2007): 265–88.

4. Scott H. Decker, Jeffrey J. Rojek, and Eric P. Baumer, "A Century—or More—of Homicide in St. Louis," in *St. Louis Metromorphosis: Past Trends and Future Directions*, ed. Brady Baybeck and E. Terrence Jones (St. Louis: Missouri Historical Society Press, 2004), 257.

5. V. O. Key Jr., *Southern Politics in State and Nation* (New York: A. A. Knopf, 1949); John H. Fenton, *Politics in the Border States: A Study of the Patterns of Political Organization, and Political Change, Common to the Border States—Maryland, West Virginia, Kentucky, and Missouri* (New Orleans: Hauser Press, 1957).

6. Clarence E. Lang, "Community and Resistance in the Gateway City: Black National Consciousness, Working-Class Formation, and Social Movements in St. Louis, Missouri, 1941–64" (PhD diss., University of Illinois at Urbana-Champaign, 2004), 50; Fenton, *Politics in the Borders States*, 7.

7. Segregation Scrapbook, Missouri Historical Society Library and Research Center, St. Louis (hereinafter MHS); Lawrence O. Christensen, "Black St. Louis: A Study in Race Relations, 1865–1916" (PhD dissertation, University of Missouri–Columbia, 1972); John E. Farley, "Racial Housing Segregation in the St. Louis Area: Past, Present, and Future," in *St. Louis Metromorphosis*, ed. Baybeck and Jones, 200; and Deborah Jane Henry, "Structures of Exclusion: Black Labor and the Building Trades in St. Louis, 1917–1966" (PhD diss., University of Minnesota, 2002).

8. Priscilla A. Dowden, "'Over This Point We Are Determined to Fight': African American Public Education and Health Care in St. Louis, Missouri, 1910–1949" (PhD diss., Indiana University, 1997); Paul Dennis Brunn, "Black Workers and Social Movements of the 1930s in St. Louis" (PhD diss., Washington University, 1975).

9. Brunn, "Black Workers and Social Movements."

10. David M. Grant Papers, S0552, State Historical Society of Missouri (hereinafter SHSMO).

11. Brotherhood of Sleeping Car Porters Records, St. Louis Division, Chicago Historical Society; Patricia L. Adams, "Fighting for Democracy in St. Louis: Civil Rights during World War II," *Missouri Historical Review* 80, no. 1 (1985): 58–75.

12. "'A Strong Seed Planted': The Civil Rights Movement in St. Louis, 1954–1968," Oral History Collection, MHS.

13. National Negro Labor Council, Vertical File, Archives of Labor and Urban Affairs, Wayne State University; Kenneth S. Jolly, *Black Liberation in the Midwest: The Struggle in St. Louis, Missouri, 1964–1970* (New York: Routledge, 2006), 150.

14. Joseph, "Waiting *till the* Midnight Hour."

15. Ernest Calloway Papers, S0011, SHSMO; Clarence Lang, "Civil Rights versus 'Civic Progress': The St. Louis NAACP and the City Charter Fight, 1956–1957," *Journal of Urban History* 34, no. 4 (2008): 609–38.

16. Ibid. See also Lon W. Smith, "An Experiment in Trade Union Democracy: Harold Gibbons and the Formation of Teamsters Local 688, 1937–1957" (PhD diss., Illinois State University, 1993).

17. Calloway Papers, SHSMO.

18. Negro Scrapbook, vol. 2, MHS.

19. William L. Clay, "Anatomy of an Economic Murder: A Statistical Review of the Negro in the Saint Louis Employment Field, 1963," pamphlet, MHS.

20. Negro Scrapbook, vol. 2, MHS; Lang, "Community and Resistance in the Gateway City." See also George Lipsitz, *A Life in the Struggle: Ivory Perry and the Culture of Opposition* (Philadelphia: Temple University Press, 1988); and Jolly, *Black Liberation in the Midwest*, 37–41.

21. Clarence Lang, "Between Civil Rights and Black Power in the Gateway City: The Action Committee to Improve Opportunities for Negroes (ACTION), 1964–75," *Journal of Social History* 37, no. 3 (2004): 725–754. See also Steve Estes, *I Am a Man! Race, Manhood, and the Civil Rights Movement* (Chapel Hill: University of North Carolina Press, 2005).

22. Ula Taylor, "Elijah Muhammad's Nation of Islam: Separatism, Regendering, and a Secular Approach to Black Power after Malcolm X (1965–1975)," in *Freedom North*, ed. Theoharis and Woodard, 177–98.

23. Sidney M. Willhelm, *Who Needs the Negro?* (Cambridge, MA: Schenkman Pub. Co., 1970).

24. Negro Scrapbook, vol. 2, MHS.

25. Buddy Lonesome, "Youth—Handcuffed—Shot to Death by a Policeman Here," and "A Shocking Incident" (news editorial), *St. Louis Argus*, Jun. 18, 1965; Lonesome, "Rights Groups Oppose Cop Slaying of Handcuffed Youth," *St. Louis Argus*, Jun. 25, 1965; Negro Scrapbook, vol. 2, MHS.

26. Negro Scrapbook, vol. 3, and "Strong Seed Planted," MHS.

27. Negro Scrapbook, vol. 2, MHS.

28. Jolly, *Black Liberation in the Midwest*, 42, 52–59.

29. "Strong Seed Planted"; and Benjamin Looker, *"Point from Which Creation Begins": The Black Artists' Group of St. Louis* (St. Louis: Missouri Historical Society Press, 2004), 26–27.

30. Jolly, *Black Liberation in the Midwest*, 120; Looker, *"Point from Which Creation Begins,"* 85–87.

31. Jolly, *Black Liberation in the Midwest*, 88–89, 95; Looker, *"Point from Which Creation Begins,"* 15, 42, 48, 96. See also James Edward Smethurst, *The Black Arts Movement: Literary Nationalism in the 1960s and 1970s* (Chapel Hill: University of North Carolina Press, 2005).

32. Looker, *"Point from Which Creation Begins,"* 42–43; and Jolly, *Black Liberation in the Midwest*, 68.

33. Negro Scrapbook, vol. 3, MHS; Jolly, *Black Liberation in the Midwest*, 63–64, 72; and Looker, *"Point from Which Creation Begins,"* 41–44.

34. Looker, *"Point from Which Creation Begins,"* 44.

35. Negro Scrapbook, vol. 3, MHS; Jolly, *Black Liberation in the Midwest*, 75, 163. See also William B. Helmreich, *The Black Crusaders: A Case Study of a Black Militant Organization* (New York: Harper and Row, 1973), 174; and Helmreich, "The Black Liberators: A Historical Perspective," in *Black Power in the Belly of the Beast*, ed. Judson L. Jeffries (Urbana: University of Illinois Press, 2006), 281–95.

36. Lang, "Between Civil Rights and Black Power in the Gateway City"; Jolly, *Black Liberation in the Midwest*, 77–84; and Helmreich, "The Black Liberators," 292.

37. See James Forman, *The Making of Black Revolutionaries* (1972; repr. University of Washington Press, 1985); Judson L. Jeffries, ed., *Comrades: A Local History of the Black Panther Party* (Bloomington: Indiana University Press, 2007); Yohuru Williams and Jama Lazerow, eds., *Liberated Territory: Untold Local Perspectives on the Black Panther Party* (Durham, NC: Duke University Press, 2008); and Hasan Kwame Jeffries, *Bloody Lowndes: Civil Rights and Black Power in Alabama's Black Belt* (New York University Press, 2009).

38. See Woodard, *A Nation within a Nation*; Brown, *Fighting for US*; and Looker, *"Point from Which Creation Begins,"* xxiii, 47, 82.

39. Negro Scrapbook, vol. 3, MHS; and Jolly, *Black Liberation in the Midwest*, 105.

40. Negro Scrapbook, vols. 2 and 3, MHS.

41. Negro Scrapbook, vol. 3, MHS.

42. Ibid. See also Lipsitz, *A Life in the Struggle*, 148; Looker, *"Point from Which Creation Begins,"* 82–84.

43. See Countryman, *Up South*; Williams, *Black Politics/White Power*; and Rhonda Y. Williams, *The Politics of Public Housing: Black Women's Struggles against Urban Inequality* (New York: Oxford University Press, 2004).

44. Negro Scrapbook, vol. 3, MHS.

45. Ibid. See also Jolly, *Black Liberation in the Midwest*, 163–69; Helmreich, "The Black Liberators," 283.

46. See Kenneth O'Reilly, *"Racial Matters": The FBI's Secret File on Black America, 1960–1972* (New York: The Free Press, 1989); Ward Churchill and Jim Vander Wall, *The COINTELPRO Papers: Documents from the FBI's Secret Wars against Domestic Dissent in the United States* (Boston: South End Press, 1990), n351.

47. Federal Bureau of Investigation, COINTELPRO, Black Nationalist-Hate Groups File, microfilm reels 1 and 2. By 1970, Koen had returned to his native Cairo, Illinois, where he resumed his organizational efforts amid white police and vigilante terror—and continued FBI subterfuge.

48. Federal Bureau of Investigation, COINTELPRO, Black Nationalist-Hate Groups File, microfilm reel 3.

49. Clarence Lang, *Grassroots at the Gateway: Class Politics and Black Freedom Struggle in St. Louis, 1936–75* (Ann Arbor: University of Michigan Press, 2009); David Lucander, *Winning the War for Democracy: The March on Washington Movement, 1941–1946* (Urbana: University of Illinois Press, 2014); Keona K. Ervin, *Gateway to Equality: Black Women and the Struggle for Economic Justice in St. Louis* (Lexington: University Press of Kentucky, 2017); Rhonda Y. Williams, *Concrete Demands: The Search for Black Power in the 20th Century* (New York: Routledge, 2015); Ashley D. Farmer, *Remaking Black Power: How Black Women Transformed an Era* (Chapel Hill: University of North Carolina Press, 2017); Walter Johnson, *The Broken Heart of America: St. Louis and the Violent History of the United States* (New York: Basic Books, 2020); *The Pruitt-Igoe Myth*, directed by Chad Freidrichs (Unicorn Stencil Documentary Films, 2011); and *Whose Streets?*, directed by Sabaah Folayan and Damon Davis (Magnolia Pictures, 2017).

50. *Annual Report of Missouri Vehicle Stops* (Jefferson City, MO: Office of the Missouri Attorney General, 2014).

5. Surveillance and Subversion of Student Activists, 1967–1970

1. I have written on the transformation of history as it enters popular media in Nina Gilden Seavey, "Film and Media Producers: Taking History off the Page and Putting It on the Screen," in *Public History: Essays from the Field*, rev. ed., ed. James B. Gardner and Peter S. LaPaglia (Malabar, FL: Krieger Publishing, 2006), 117–28.

2. Section 231 of the Civil Obedience Act concerning Civil Disorders states, "Whoever commits or attempts to commit any act to obstruct, impede, or interfere with any fireman or law enforcement officer lawfully engaged in the lawful performance of his official duties incident to and during the commission of a civil disorder which in any way or degree obstructs, delays, or adversely affects commerce or the movement of any article or commodity in commerce or the conduct or performance of any federally protected function . . . Shall be fined not more than $10,000 or imprisoned not more than five years, or both."

3. On September 5, 2000, *Dateline NBC* aired a one-hour special entitled "The Fugitive," in which Mechanic's co-defendant, Larry Kogan, admitted to having thrown the cherry bomb at the police officer.

4. Michael Linfield, *Freedom under Fire: US Civil Liberties in Time of War* (Boston: South End Press, 1990), 119.

5. In some of his sworn statements, Bird said that he had witnessed Mechanic using a slingshot to propel the firecracker. In a later statement, he omitted the reference to the slingshot and simply asserted that he had seen the cherry bomb "propelled from the person of Howard Mechanic."

6. Mechanic sold various of his possessions, wrote his family a note, and adopted a new identity in November 1971. The US Supreme Court denied certiorari on May 15, 1972, supporting the conviction upheld by the US Court of Appeals.

7. Seven students were tried and convicted on federal charges stemming from the May 4, 1970, riot on the Washington University campus. Four of the six served various sentences, ranging from ninety days in the psychiatric wing of the Federal Medical Facility in Springfield, Missouri, to seven years in federal prison. Charges against two of the students were ultimately dropped after multiple years of appeals.

8. Judge Gladys Kessler, Filing 59, Memorandum Opinion and Cross-Motion for Summary Judgment, May 16, 2017, *Seavey v. Department of Justice.*

9. FBI memo from Director, FBI, to SAC Albany, RE: Counterintelligence Program, Internal Security, Disruption of the New Left (hereinafter COINTELPRO New Left), May 10, 1968.

10. Ibid.

11. FBI Memo from Director, FBI, to SAC Albany, RE: COINTELPRO New Left, Oct. 9, 1968.

12. FBI Memo from Director, FBI, to SAC Albany, RE: COINTELPRO New Left, Jul. 5, 1968.

13. Ibid.

14. Ibid.

15. Ibid.

16. This overarching penetrative goal was articulated in an FBI memo from Philadelphia, PA, "Report on the New Left," Sep. 1970, and this characterization became the coined phrase for field offices nationally.

17. Memo from Director, FBI, to SAC Albany, Jul. 5, 1968.

18. A vivid testimonial outlining the methods and means of obtaining confidential informant (CI) cooperation through coercion related to criminal prosecutions appeared on the public broadcasting program *The Great American Dream Machine* in an investigative report by Paul Jacobs on Oct. 8, 1971.

19. Frequently, agents assigned to COINTELPRO activities were seated separately, behind closed doors and away from their peers. In the case of the COINTELPRO against Dr. Martin Luther King Jr., the activities were so expansive that its operations were moved off-site, away from the Atlanta Bureau office, so as to guarantee their continued secrecy.

20. An excellent discussion of the public revelation of COINTELPRO is found in Betty Medsger, *The Burglary: The Discovery of J. Edgar Hoover's Secret FBI* (New York: A. A. Knopf, 2014).

21. Deposition of William C. Sullivan, Nov. 1, 1975, in US Senate Select Committee to Study Governmental Operations with Respect to Intelligence Activities (also known as the Church Committee), *Intelligence Activities and the Rights of Americans, Book II* and *Supplementary Detailed Staff Reports on Intelligence Activities and the Rights of Americans, Book III,* Apr. 1976, 92–93, 97–98.

22. FBI memo from Director, FBI, to SAC Albany, RE: COINTELPRO New Left, May 10, 1968.

23. FBI memo from SAC New York to Director, FBI, RE: COINTELPRO New Left, May 28, 1968.

24. For example, special intelligence units such as Police Cruiser No. 217 of the St. Louis County Police Department provided detailed daily logs and summary

memoranda of their visits to organized meetings and informal conversations of student and civil rights activists throughout the metropolitan area.

25. *CBS Evening News*, Mar. 25, 1971, Vanderbilt Television News Archive (hereinafter VTNA).

26. Frank Donner, *The Age of Surveillance: The Aims and Methods of America's Political Intelligence System* (New York: A. A. Knopf, 1980), 270–71.

27. Loch K. Johnson, *A Season of Inquiry: The Senate Intelligence Investigation* (Lexington: University Press of Kentucky, 1985), 82.

28. Donner, *Age of Surveillance*, 272.

29. Paul J. Scheips, *The Role of Federal Military Forces in Domestic Disorders, 1945–1992* (Washington, DC: Center of Military History, US Army, 2005).

30. It is difficult to fix the number of confidential informants used by the FBI. In Donner's *Age of Surveillance*, 137, the author cites 7,893 informants in category 170 ("racial and extremist"), although he cautions that these are quite conservative estimates.

31. Donner, *Age of Surveillance*, 169.

32. Cartha DeLoach, *Hoover's FBI: The Inside Story by Hoover's Trusted Lieutenant* (Washington, DC: Regnery, 1995), 280–81.

33. Devereaux Kennedy, interview by author, St. Louis, MO, Oct. 23, 2017.

34. FBI Memo from SAC St. Louis to Director, FBI, RE: Devereaux Kennedy, Nov. 29, 1967.

35. FBI Memo from SAC St. Louis to Director, FBI, RE: Devereaux Joseph Kennedy, Feb. 7, 1968.

36. The Security Index included those "dangerous individuals who might commit acts inimical to the national defense and public safety of the United States in time of emergency." For a fuller history of the Security Index, see Athan G. Theoharis, ed., with Tony G. Poveda, Susan Rosenfeld, and Richard Gid Powers, *The FBI: A Comprehensive Reference Guide* (Phoenix: Oryx Press, 1999), 27–29. Kennedy's Main File number was 100-20324. The "100" classification series refers to files dealing with "Domestic Security."

37. Further memoranda articulating and codifying activities and expectations to be garnered from COINTELPRO New Left were issued from Hoover to SACs in the field on May 23, May 28, and Jul. 5, 1968.

38. C. D. Stelzer, "Howard's End," *Riverfront Times* (St. Louis), Feb. 16, 2000, quoted police estimates of the number of students in SDS on the Washington University campus at only twenty in 1969. Such a number is obviously difficult to verify and may refer to the number of "card-carrying members of SDS," and not the number of students who would attend rallies or protests on any given day, but it does attest to the lack of a large number of known activists at WU.

39. Kennedy, interview.

40. *Anatomy of a Revolutionary Movement: Students for a Democratic Society*, report by the Committee on Internal Security, House of Representatives, Ninety-first Congress, Second Session, Oct. 6, 1970, 1.

41. Walter Johnson, *The Broken Heart of America: St. Louis and the Violent History of the United States* (New York: Basic Books, 2020), 297.

42. Ibid., 282–87.

43. Pat Byrne, "Protest Prevents Dow from Recruiting Here," *Student Life* (Washington University), Feb. 16, 1968, 1.

44. Walter Johnson, oral history interview for the podcast *My Fugitive*.

45. The presence of ROTC on campus was not just an issue for the student body, but an ongoing, hotly debated topic for the administration and faculty. It wasn't until August 18, 1970, that Chancellor Thomas Eliot decided the ROTC program would be permanently moved off of the university campus.

46. The types of anti-ROTC activities in 1967–1968 reported on by the FBI included an SDS satirical play held on the ROTC drill field on October 15, 1968, in which a small number of children, aged ten to twelve, shot cap guns and then declared a truce while a loudspeaker played "The War Is Over." At that same demonstration, according to FBI reports, SDS members approached cadets, offered them bread, wine, and lollipops, and taunted them. According to the FBI memorandum, "Drill was not disrupted." LHM SAC St. Louis, "Students for a Democratic Society Activities, SLMO," Oct. 15, 1968.

47. FBI Memo from SA Spurgeon J. Peterson to SAC St. Louis, RE: [Redacted] Unknown Subject (hereinafter UNSUB) Attempted Firebombing ROTC Building, Washington University, St. Louis, Dec. 12, 1968.

48. FBI Memo from SAC St. Louis to Director, FBI, RE: [Redacted] Fugitive; UNSUB Firebombs ROTC Building, WUSTL Dec. 3, 1968–Bombing Matters–Sabotage–IS–SDS, Dec. 4, 1968.

49. Letter from J. Walter Yeagley, Assistant Attorney General, to Veryl Riddle, US Attorney for the Eastern District of Missouri, RE: United States v. [Redacted] No. 68 CR 283(1), U.S.D.C., E.D. MO, Jan. 31, 1969.

50. Ibid.

51. Ibid.

52. "Student Gets Five Years: Sentenced in Bombing," *St. Louis Post-Dispatch*, Feb. 20, 1969.

53. *CBS Evening News*, Feb. 10, 1969, VTNA.

54. FBI Memo from Director, FBI, to SAC St. Louis, RE: [Redacted] Unknown Subject; Sabotage, Feb. 13, 1969.

55. Ibid.

56. Journalist Tim Weiner, in his book *Enemies: A History of the FBI* (New York: Random House, 2012), 119–20, summarizes his exhaustive study of Hoover by saying, "Hoover hated ideologies more than individuals, pressure groups more than people; above all Hoover hated the threats to the stability of the American political system, and anyone who might personify that danger was an enemy for life."

57. FBI Memo from Director, FBI, to SAC St. Louis, RE: [Redacted] UNSUB; Sabotage, Feb. 13, 1969.

58. FBI Memo from SAC St. Louis to Director, FBI, RE: COINTELPRO New Left, May 28, 1968.

59. Ibid.

60. Ibid.

61. In a memorandum between William C. Sullivan, FBI Director of Domestic Intelligence, and his aide, Fred Baumgartner, dated Oct. 8, 1962, approval was given for the feeding of anti-MLK propaganda to five newspapers: the *Long Island Star-Journal*, the *Birmingham (AL) Chronicle*, the *Birmingham (AL) News*, the *New Orleans Times-Picayune*, and the *St. Louis Globe-Democrat*.

62. Patrick J. Buchanan, *Right from the Beginning* (Boston: Little, Brown, 1988), 283.

63. FBI Memo from SAC St. Louis to Director, FBI, RE: COINTELPRO New Left, May 28, 1968.

64. FBI regulations required regular reporting on all field-agent activities, but for COINTELPRO, where tangible results were closely monitored, Hoover issued directives establishing frequent reporting to qualify and quantify the progress of the program. J. Wallace LaPrade was appointed to take Joseph Gamble's place as Special Agent in Charge on May 14, 1969.

65. While the names of confidential informants are always redacted in FBI files due to the highly sensitive nature of their work, periodically in this research, I found that government agencies would simply neglect to redact these names prior to the release of documents. It should be noted that these are code names, as the true identity of the individuals would not be held in subject matter files.

66. Confidential informant reports garnered in this research date from Apr. 26, 1968, to May 12, 1976, with the bulk of the reporting gathered from 1968 to 1973.

67. Confidential informant reports dated Feb. 8, Mar. 9, and Mar. 14, 1969.

68. FBI Memo from Director, FBI, to SAC St. Louis, RE: UNSUB; Possible Arson Army ROTC Building, Washington University, St. Louis, Missouri, Feb. 23, 1970, in which Hoover expresses his frustration at the non-responsiveness of uncooperative witnesses and suggests that there may be fifteen who should be subpoenaed and questioned under oath by a federal grand jury, Mar. 19, 1970.

69. FBI Investigative Memorandum Feb. 23–Mar. 4, 1970, RE: UNSUB: Possible Arson Army ROTC Building, Washington University, St. Louis, Missouri, Feb. 23, 1970, St. Louis SA Richard Hradsky.

70. Ibid.

71. Ibid.

72. FBI Memo, SAC, Cleveland to SA [Redacted], Possible Arson Army ROTC Building, Washington University, St. Louis, Missouri, Feb. 23, 1970, Apr. 17, 1970.

73. "Criminals on Campus," *St. Louis Globe-Democrat*, May 4, 1970.

74. The full extent of the St. Louis office of the FBI's ties with the *St. Louis Globe-Democrat* finally came to light in a FOIA document release in November 1977 and was reported in a series of *St. Louis Post-Dispatch* articles, the first of which was Curt Matthews, "FBI Says It Used *Globe-Democrat* to Discredit 'New Left,'" Nov. 23, 1977.

75. *CBS Evening News*, May 5, 1970, VTNA.

76. A temporary restraining order was issued by St. Louis County Circuit Court Judge George E. Schaaf on March 24, 1970, in response to a series of protests that disrupted campus operations and resulted in increasingly violent encounters with

the police in which several officers were injured and a number of students were arrested.

77. US Attorney General John Mitchell described these provisions as potentially the most promising weapon against student unrest in a speech at the annual convention of the Tennessee Bar Association on June 12, 1969.

78. Memo from Assistant Attorney General for Civil Rights Jerris Leonard to Director, FBI, RE: UNSUB; U.S. Army, ROTC Unit at Washington University (WU)–Victim; Disruptions of Army ROTC Classes and Activities at WU; Conspiracy, CIVIL RIGHTS ACT OF 1968, Mar. 27, 1970, outlined the strategy to use St. Louis for levying charges for conspiracy to violate the 1968 Civil Rights Act and instructed the FBI to use additional investigative techniques for supporting these charges in investigations already underway.

79. To discourage further acts of violence against the on-campus military presence, Washington University and Saint Louis University combined their ROTC programs and began housing them at 4200 Forest Park Blvd. "Off-Campus ROTC Site Leased," *St. Louis Post-Dispatch*, Aug. 19, 1970.

80. "3 Bombs Damage U.S. Buildings Here," *St. Louis Post-Dispatch*, Mar. 9, 1971.

81. Interview Report of [redacted] source, Apr. 1, 1971.

82. FBI Memo from Director, FBI, to SAC Albany, Counterintelligence Program (COINTELPROs), Internal Security—Racial Matters, Apr. 28, 1971.

6. The Saga of Howard Mechanic

1. Nixon remarks from May 1, 1970, quoted in May 8, 1970, news-conference transcript, available at *The American Presidency Project*, https://www.presidency.ucsb.edu/documents/the-presidents-news-conference-144.

2. Revard quoted in Lisa Belkin, "Doesn't Anybody Know How to Be a Fugitive Anymore?," *New York Times Magazine*, Apr. 30, 2000.

3. H. Bruce Franklin, *Vietnam and Other American Fantasies* (Amherst: University of Massachusetts Press, 2000), 130.

7. "Whacking the Elephant Where It Hurts"

This chapter is a version, with minor revisions, of Chapter 5 from Thomas M. Spencer, *The St. Louis Veiled Prophet Celebration: Power on Parade, 1877–1995* (Columbia: University of Missouri Press, 2000). Accompanying images and captions are new to this volume's version.

1. Ed Bishop and William H. Leckie, "Unveiling the Prophet: The Mysterious Origins of the Kingdom of Khorassan," *Riverfront Times* (St. Louis), Jun. 17–23, 1987; Tommy Robertson, "Rope Trick by ACTION Unveils the Prophet," *St. Louis Post-Dispatch*, Dec. 23, 1972; Gary Ronberg, "How They Unveiled the Prophet," *St. Louis Post-Dispatch*, Dec. 31, 1972; "Veiled Prophet Unveiled by *Review*: *Post* and *Globe* Withhold Identity," *St. Louis Journalism Review*, Jan. 1973; Jane Sauer, member of ACTION, 1969–1974, interview by author, tape recording, St. Louis, Sep. 30, 1993; and Gena Scott, member of ACTION, 1970–1974, interview by author, tape recording, St. Louis, Oct. 7, 1993.

2. Tom K. Smith, 1972 Veiled Prophet, and Harry E. Wuertenbaecher Jr., executive director of the Veiled Prophet organization, interview by author, St. Louis, Oct. 12, 1993; Ronald Henges, VP Fair chairman, 1983–1987, interview by author, tape recording, St. Louis, Sep. 8, 1995.

3. Jack M. Bloom, *Class, Race, and the Civil Rights Movement* (Bloomington: Indiana University Press, 1987), 208–9; Herbert H. Haines, *Black Radicals and the Civil Rights Mainstream, 1954–1970* (Knoxville: University of Tennessee Press, 1988), 57–63; and Manning Marable, *Race, Reform, and Rebellion: The Second Reconstruction in Black America, 1945–1982* (Jackson: University Press of Mississippi, 1984), 106–8.

4. Walter B. Stevens, "Notes of Committee Meetings and Rules of the Veiled Prophet Organization, 1878–1899," 41, Veiled Prophet Papers, Missouri Historical Society Library and Research Center, St. Louis (hereinafter VPP, MHS).

5. Thomas Spencer, "Knights for Revenue Only: The Origins of the Veiled Prophet Organization in St. Louis, 1877–1880" (MA thesis, University of Missouri–Columbia, 1992), 5–24; Thomas Spencer, "Power on Parade: The Origins of the Veiled Prophet Celebration in St. Louis," *Gateway Heritage* 14, no. 2 (Fall 1993): 38–53; the parade themes come from Ted Satterfield's "Royfax copies of VP information," 1960–1993, VPP, MHS.

6. Spencer, "Knights for Revenue Only," 111–18.

7. Jeffrey Beckner, "Are the Rich Really Different from You and Me?," *St. Louis Magazine*, Dec. 1985, 62–66.

8. Karen McCoskey Goering, "Pageantry in St. Louis: The History of the Veiled Prophet Organization," *Gateway Heritage* 4, no. 4 (Spring 1984): 2–16.

9. James Ralph, *Northern Protest: Martin Luther King, Jr., Chicago, and the Civil Rights Movement* (Cambridge, MA: Harvard University Press, 1993), 185; it must be pointed out that King ultimately decided against this sort of economic target—the Chicago Freedom Movement centered on attacking discrimination in the Chicago housing market.

10. Percy Green, chairman of ACTION, 1965–1984, interview by author, tape recording, St. Louis, Sep. 14, 1993.

11. August Meier and Elliott Rudwick, *CORE: A Study in the Civil Rights Movement, 1942–1968* (New York: Oxford University Press, 1973), 312–13.

12. Gerald J. Meyer, "Percy Green's Tactic: Stir Public Outrage," *St. Louis Post-Dispatch*, Jul. 12, 1970.

13. Sauer, interview.

14. Green, interview; Sauer, interview.

15. Sauer, interview.

16. Jacqueline Bell, member of ACTION, 1975–1984, telephone interview by author, tape recording, St. Louis, Oct. 14, 1993; Green, interview.

17. Green, interview.

18. Margaret Phillips, member of ACTION, 1968–1971, interview by author, tape recording, St. Louis, Sep. 30, 1993.

19. ACTION, *Why You Must Raise Hell: A Seven-Year Public Document Featuring ACTION's Scientific-Struggle against St. Louis' Institutional Elitism and Racism (1970 thru 1976)* (St. Louis: ACTION, 1977), sections 1–2; Scott, interview; Phillips, interview. *Why You Must Raise Hell* is a compilation of newspaper clippings that chronicle ACTION protest activities from 1969 to 1976.

20. Sauer, interview.

21. Phillips, interview.

22. Alice Echols, *Daring to Be Bad: Radical Feminism in America, 1967–1975* (Minneapolis: University of Minnesota Press, 1989), 92; Phillips, interview.

23. Phillips, interview; Barbara Torrence, member of ACTION, 1965–1970, interview by author, tape recording, St. Louis, Sep. 21, 1993.

24. Torrence, interview.

25. Robert Tooley, VP Den superintendent, interview by author, St. Louis, Aug. 4, 6, and 11, 1995.

26. Judge (George) Johnson, co-chairman of ACTION, 1967–1975, interview by author, tape recording, St. Louis. Sep. 27, 1993; Sauer, interview.

27. Sauer, interview.

28. James C. Scott, *Domination and the Arts of Resistance: Hidden Transcripts* (New Haven, CT: Yale University Press, 1990), 17–20 and 202–27. See also Robin D. G. Kelley, *Race Rebels: Culture, Politics, and the Black Working Class* (New York: Free Press, 1994), 6–7.

29. Sauer, interview; Green, interview; Bell, interview.

30. Phillips, interview; Sauer, interview.

31. Green, interview; Bell, interview.

32. Phillips, interview; Scott interview.

33. Johnson, interview; "Two Found Guilty, Fined for VP Ball Disturbance," *St. Louis Globe-Democrat*, May 28, 1970.

34. ACTION, *Why You Must Raise Hell*, section 6; Green, interview.

35. Torrence, interview.

36. Ibid.

37. Tooley, interview; Rusty Hager, VP Fair chairman, and Molly Hager, VP queen, 1995, interview by author, tape recording, St. Louis, Aug. 18 and 23, 1995.

38. Tooley, interview.

39. Ibid.

40. "Royfax Copies," 1960–1993, VPP, MHS.

41. Tooley, interview.

42. Green, interview; Torrence, interview.

43. Scott, interview.

44. Ibid.; Sauer, interview.

45. Sauer, interview; Scott, interview.

46. Scott, interview.

47. Ibid.; Smith and Wuertenbaecher, interview; Sauer, interview.

48. "ACTION Files Suit to Prohibit Use of Kiel for Veiled Prophet Ball," *St. Louis Post-Dispatch*, Nov. 15, 1973; "Veiled Prophet Looking for New Home," *St. Louis*

Post-Dispatch, Dec. 7, 1973; and "Decision Announced in Court: ACTION Calls Exodus of Veiled Prophet Ball from Kiel a Victory," *St. Louis American*, Dec. 13, 1973.

49. Bishop and Leckie, "Unveiling the Prophet"; Tod Gest, "Ousted Professor Wins Pay, but Wants to Teach," *St. Louis Post-Dispatch*, Oct. 9, 1973; "Veiled Prophet Ball Disrupted," *St. Louis Globe-Democrat*, Dec. 24, 1975; and "VP Ball Charge Is Dismissed," *St. Louis Post-Dispatch*, Mar. 2, 1976.

50. Phillips, interview; Sauer, interview.

51. Bell, interview; Edward L. Cook, "VP Demonstrators Hired to Disrupt Ball, Police Say," *St. Louis Globe-Democrat*, Dec. 25–26, 1976; "Two Seized in Spraying of Gas at Veiled Prophet Ball," *St. Louis Post-Dispatch*, Dec. 24, 1976; "Convicted in Veiled Prophet Ball Incident," *St. Louis Post-Dispatch*, Jun. 1, 1978.

52. Smith and Wuertenbaecher, interview.

53. Henges, interview; Bell, interview.

54. Bell quoted in "Judge Webster Lists Assets of $898,296," *St. Louis Post-Dispatch*, Jan. 31, 1978.

55. Richard Dudman, "Webster to Watch His Clubs' Policies," *St. Louis Post-Dispatch*, Jan. 29, 1978; "Judge Webster Lists Assets of $898,296"; Sally Bixby Defty, "Prophet Lifting His Veil to Blacks after 101 Years," *St. Louis Post-Dispatch*, Sep. 7, 1979.

56. For example, see "Why Not Just a Night of Fun?," *St. Louis Globe-Democrat*, Sep. 17, 1968; "A Community Thrill," *St. Louis Globe-Democrat*, Oct. 7, 1972; and "VP Shows a White Feather," *St. Louis Globe-Democrat*, Dec. 8, 1973.

57. Evarts Graham, former managing editor of the *St. Louis Post-Dispatch*, telephone interview by author, tape recording, St. Louis, Oct. 14, 1993; Jake McCarthy, columnist for the *St. Louis Post-Dispatch*, 1971–1982, telephone interview by author, tape recording, St. Louis, Nov. 2, 1993.

58. Graham, interview; Smith and Wuertenbaecher, interview; "Veiled Prophet Unveiled by *Review*."

59. Green, interview; Sauer, interview; Scott, interview; Torrence, interview.

60. Green, interview; Carter Stith, "Judge Meredith Dismisses Suit by Percy Green," *St. Louis Post-Dispatch*, Feb. 27, 1975.

61. FBI, Memorandum, SAC, St. Louis to Director, FBI, Jun. 19, 1970. This memorandum is from the contents of Jane Sauer's FBI file.

62. Bishop and Leckie, "Unveiling the Prophet," 13a.

63. Curtis Wilson, "Aura of Veiled Prophet Fades, with an Assist from Percy Green," *St. Louis Post-Dispatch*, Mar. 8, 1972.

64. See Austin Huguelet, "Unveiled: How the Veiled Prophet Society Is Responding to the Ellie Kemper Fiasco," *St. Louis Post-Dispatch*, Jun. 14, 2021; Michael Ordona, "Why Twitter Is up in Arms about Ellie Kemper's 'Racist' Debutante Crown from 1999," *Los Angeles Times*, Jun. 1, 2021; Hannah Yasharoff, "Ellie Kemper's Co-stars, Celebs Show Support after Apology for Veiled Prophet Ball Controversy," *USA Today*, Jun. 1, 2021; and Kara Weisenstein, "Ellie Kemper and the Veiled Prophets Controversy, Explained," *Mic*, Jun. 2, 2021, https://web.archive.org/

web/20210602195226/https://www.mic.com/p/ellie-kemper-the-veiled-prophets
-controversy-explained-81047262.

65. Green, interview; Sauer, interview.

66. Phillips, interview.

67. Green, interview.

68. Ralph, *Northern Protest*, 229.

69. Ibid., 234; J. Mills Thornton III, "Commentary," 151, as quoted in Ralph, *Northern Protest*, 235.

8. "The Seed Time of Gay Rights"

This chapter is a reprint, with minor updates and expansions to the endnotes by the volume editors, of an article originally published in *Gateway Heritage* 15, no. 2 (Fall 1994): 34–47. That article was the first academic piece ever published focusing on LGBTQ+ history in St. Louis. Due to access and permission issues, some images and captions in this printing differ from those accompanying the original.

Author acknowledgments (from original printing): I want to thank Gerda W. Ray, Frances L. Hoffmann, and John Works of the University of Missouri–St. Louis, Gail Egleston and Harold Austin, colleagues at Mehlville High School, and Martha Kohl, editor of *Gateway Heritage*, for their support and criticisms of this paper. In addition, I want to express my thanks to the Western Historical Manuscript Collection at the University of Missouri–St. Louis [now the St. Louis Research Center of the State Historical Society of Missouri] and to those who took the time to answer my never-ending string of questions: Jim Thomas, Bill Cordes, Lisa Wagaman, Brad Wishon, Laura A. Moore, Wilbur Wegener, two anonymous informants, and, of course, Carol Cureton.

1. Judith VandeWater, "Gays Get a Voice on Panel," *St. Louis Post-Dispatch*, Jun. 28, 1993; Ruth Marner, "Lesbian Appointed by Bosley," *Lesbian and Gay News-Telegraph* (St. Louis), Jul. 1993, 1, Missouri Historical Society Library and Research Center, St. Louis. St. Louis police estimated that 2,500 people attended the festival; the *News-Telegraph* put the estimate at six thousand. The *News-Telegraph* is well known for attempting to get as accurate as possible an accounting of individuals at various events; its editor literally stands off to the side and counts.

2. Bill Cordes, interview by author, St. Louis, Sep. 22, 1993. Unless otherwise noted, all interviews were conducted by the author and cassettes from them remain in his possession.

3. Margaret Cruikshank, *The Gay and Lesbian Liberation Movement* (New York: Routledge, 1992), 30. See also Andrea Weiss and Greta Schiller, *Before Stonewall: The Making of a Gay and Lesbian Community* (Tallahassee, FL: Naiad Press, 1988).

4. Cruikshank, *Gay and Lesbian Liberation Movement*, 69, 149.

5. Laud Humphreys, *Out of the Closets: The Sociology of Homosexual Liberation* (Englewood Cliffs, NJ: Prentice Hall, 1972), 82–83; John D'Emilio, *Sexual Politics, Sexual Communities: The Making of a Homosexual Minority in the United States, 1940–1970* (Chicago: University of Chicago Press, 1983), 60.

6. Humphreys, *Out of the Closets*, 85–89; "Gay Organizations in St. Louis," *Gay St. Louis* 4 (Jul./Aug. 1978): 15, St. Louis Lesbian and Gay Archives Collection, S0545,

State Historical Society of Missouri (hereinafter SLLGA, SHSMO), series 6, box 9, folder 267.

7. Humphreys, *Out of the Closets*, 90.

8. Ibid., 90–94.

9. Ibid., 8, 93.

10. "Gay Organizations in St. Louis."

11. Laura A. Moore, interview by author, St. Louis, Aug. 26, 1994.

12. Art and Paul, interview by author, St. Louis, Nov. 16, 1993 (no last names are given because these individuals asked to retain their anonymity); Lisa Wagaman, interview by author, St. Louis, Oct. 21, 1993.

13. Art and Paul, interview.

14. Gary T. Marx, *Protest and Prejudice: A Study of Belief in the Black Community* (New York: Harper and Row, 1967), 94–95.

15. Humphreys, *Out of the Closets*, 152.

16. Wilbur Wegener, interview by author, St. Louis, May 26, 1994.

17. Carol Cureton, telephone interview by author, Nov. 13, 1993; James E. Adams, "Homosexual Focus for a Church," *St. Louis Post-Dispatch*, Feb. 28, 1974; Carol Cureton, remarks at Gay Pride Rally, MCC, St. Louis, recording, Jun. 9, 1977, in the private collection of Lisa Wagaman (hereinafter Wagaman Personal Collection).

18. Cureton, interview; Cureton at Gay Pride Rally, recording, 1977, Wagaman Personal Collection.

19. Cureton, interview; Carol Cureton, sermon at Berea Presbyterian Church, St. Louis, recording, Dec. 16, 1974, Wagaman Personal Collection.

20. Cureton, interview.

21. Ibid.; Adams, "Homosexual Focus."

22. "Rev. Carol Cureton Elected Elder," *In Unity* 5 (Oct. 15, 1975): 5, Lisa Wagaman Papers, 1974–1992, S0542, State Historical Society of Missouri (hereinafter LWP, SHSMO), series 4, box 2, folder 47.

23. Wagaman, interview.

24. Cureton quoted in Adams, "Homosexual Focus."

25. "Homosexuals Gather for Church Meeting," *St. Louis Post-Dispatch*, Mar. 12, 1974; Bill Bryan, "A Church for Those 'Neglected by Own,'" *St. Louis Globe-Democrat*, Mar. 12, 1974. Perry also admonished the crowd to "learn to love yourself."

26. "Homosexuals Gather for Church Meeting"; Bryan, "A Church for Those 'Neglected by Own.'"

27. Cureton, interview; Bruce Michael, "Interview," *GPU News*, Sep. 1974, 24, LWP, SHSMO, series 4, box 2, folder 45.

28. Sermon by Rev. Carol Cureton, MCC, St. Louis, recording, Mar. 20, 1975, Wagaman Personal Collection.

29. Wegener, interview.

30. Galen Moon, "Member Speaks Out!!!," *The New Light* 1 (Sep. 1974): 3–4, SLLGA, SHSMO, series 6, box 9, folder 285. Moon's letter to the editor was never printed by the *St. Louis Post-Dispatch*, but it did run in the church's newsletter, *The New Light*, as cited here.

31. Michael, "Interview."

32. Hard statistics on sex, class, and ethnic background are difficult to uncover. The demographic generalizations contained in this paragraph were compiled from information from the interviews I conducted. A *Globe-Democrat* story on the church suggests a slightly different demographic profile. It reported, "The congregation was of all ages, black and white, male and female." Bryan, "A Church for Those 'Neglected by Own.'"

33. Art and Paul, interview; Moore, interview.

34. "Homosexuals Plan Church Dedication," *St. Louis Post-Dispatch*, May 30, 1975. In addition to the need for a building to accommodate the growing congregation, protests arose among Berea members concerning the gay church in their midst when the press began to carry articles linking their church's name with MCC.

35. Troy Perry, sermon during dedication of Waterman building, MCC, St. Louis, recording, May 30, 1975, Wagaman Personal Collection.

36. Description provided in Wagaman, interview. The building on Waterman, currently a private residence, was also toured by the author on Mar. 12, 1994.

37. "Past, Present, and Future," *Prime Time* 1, no. 3 (Nov. 1, 1975): 1–3, SLLGA, SHSMO, series 6, box 12, folder 309.

38. "Gay Social Life in St. Louis," *Prime Time* 3, no. 7 (Jul. 1977): 25–31, SLLGA, SHSMO, series 6, box 13, folder 311.

39. "Past, Present, and Future," 3. According to "A Report to the People: Questions and Answers about MLSC," *Prime Time* 3, no. 1 (Jan. 1977): 3, SLLGA, SHSMO, series 6, box 13, folder 311, there were 232 calls that first Sunday. The hotline opened Wednesday, Oct. 15, 1975. That day, a two-line ad appeared in the personals column of the *Post-Dispatch*. The ad read: "MLSC Gay Hotline, 367-0084."

40. "Past, Present, and Future," 3; "Directory: Gay Organizations and Services," *Prime Time* 3, no. 1 (Jan. 1977): 30–31, SLLGA, SHSMO, series 6, box 13, folder 311.

41. List of programs recited by Carol Cureton at the dedication of the Waterman building, MCC, St. Louis, recording, May 31, 1975, Wagaman Personal Collection. Other programs mentioned were a twenty-four-hour crisis/referral line, handicapped ministries, and ongoing community relations and public education. Cordes, interview.

42. Wagaman, interview.

43. Anita Bryant, *The Anita Bryant Story: The Survival of Our Nation's Families and the Threat of Militant Homosexuality* (Old Tappan, NJ: Revell, 1977), 41–42.

44. Cordes, interview.

45. Rick Garcia, speech at Gay Pride Rally, MCC, St. Louis, recording, Jun. 9, 1977, Wagaman Personal Collection; Paul I., "Rick Garcia and the St. Louis Task Force for Human Rights," *Prime Time* 3, no. 6 (Jun. 1977): 9, SLLGA, SHSMO, series 6, box 13, folder 311. According to Garcia, in addition to the movie, the Task Force organized two beer blasts attended by 150 and 200 people.

46. Bryant, *Anita Bryant Story*, 125–27.

47. Cureton at Gay Pride Rally, recording, 1977, Wagaman Personal Collection.

48. Garcia at Gay Pride Rally, ibid.

49. Jim Alexander, remarks at Gay Pride Rally, ibid.

50. Galen Moon, remarks at Gay Pride Rally, ibid.

51. Troy Perry, remarks at Gay Pride Rally, ibid.; see also James E. Adams, "Gay Rights Drive Lives, Pastor Says," *St. Louis Post-Dispatch*, Jun. 10, 1977.

52. Cureton at Gay Pride Rally, 1977, Wagaman Personal Collection.

53. Paul Wagman, "Antihomosexual Campaign Challenges Area's Gays," *St. Louis Post-Dispatch*, Jun. 19, 1977.

54. Wagaman, interview.

55. Dan Shapiro, "Political Graffiti," *Gay Life Magazine* 1 (Fall 1978): 22, SLLGA, SHSMO, series 6, box 9, folder 265.

56. Ibid.; "Gay Organizations in St. Louis," 15, 30.

57. Jim Thomas, interview by author, St. Louis, Sep. 30, 1993.

58. Rev. Brad Wishon, interview by author, St. Louis, Nov. 10, 1993; Cordes, interview. Information about the church's relocation can be found in Pamela Schaeffer, "Homosexual Congregation Gets Church," *St. Louis Post-Dispatch*, Aug. 17, 1984.

59. Cordes, interview.

60. Thomas, interview; Cordes, interview. Other gay organizations created in the 1970s were Dignity–St. Louis (an organization for gay Catholics), Integrity–St. Louis (an organization for gay Episcopalians), Lutherans Concerned, and Gay Academic Union. Groups which had met or continued to meet at MCC in the early 1980s included Gay Alcoholics Anonymous, Washington University's Concerned Gay Students, Gateway Men's Chorus, Dignity, Parents of Gays, Women's Rap Group, Men's Rap Group, the Gay Hotline, MLSC, Growing American Youth, and Gay Overeaters Anonymous.

61. Thomas, interview.

9. The Limits of Middle-Class Activism

1. Harry C. Boyte, *The Backyard Revolution: Understanding the New Citizen Movement* (Philadelphia: Temple University Press, 1980), 69.

2. David Ley, *The New Middle Class and the Remaking of the Central City* (Oxford: Oxford University Press, 1996).

3. Boyte, *Backyard Revolution*, xiv, 179; Benjamin Looker, *A Nation of Neighborhoods: Imagining Cities, Communities, and Democracy in Postwar America* (Chicago: University of Chicago Press, 2015), 233.

4. Jo Ann Vatcha, Marj Weir, Kathleen M. Harleman, Georgiana B. Stuart, Susan K. Tepas, and The Times of Skinker-DeBaliviere, *Celebrating Skinker-DeBaliviere: History and Comeback* (St. Louis: Blurb, The Times of Skinker-DeBaliviere, 2009), 50.

5. "Soulard and Lafayette Square: A Tale of Two Neighborhoods," *St. Louis Post-Dispatch*, Sunday Pictures Magazine, Apr. 16, 1972, 24–39.

6. Andrew Hurley, *Beyond Preservation: Using Public History to Revitalize Inner Cities* (Philadelphia: Temple University Press, 2010), 11.

7. Suleiman Osman, "The Decade of the Neighborhood," in *Rightward Bound: Making America Conservative in the 1970s*, ed. Bruce J. Schulman and Julian E. Zelizer (Cambridge, MA: Harvard University Press, 2008), 110.

8. Kotler quoted in Boyte, *Backyard Revolution*, 69.

9. Lawrence Creighton Stone, letter to Richard L. Cole, Oct. 3, 1972, Alfonso J. Cervantes Mayoral Records, Department of Special Collections, Washington University in St. Louis (hereinafter Cervantes Records, WUSC), series 2, box 59, folder 7.

10. Clarence N. Stone and Robert P. Stoker, eds., *Urban Neighborhoods in a New Era: Revitalization Politics in the Postmodern City* (Chicago: University of Chicago Press, 2015), 6–9, 20.

11. Boyte, *Backyard Revolution*, 50–53.

12. Ibid., 46.

13. Lucius Cervantes, letter to Samuel Bernstein, Aug. 31, 1966, Cervantes Records, WUSC, series 1, box 40, folder 1.

14. Durwin Gerald Ursery, "The Skinker DeBaliviere Community of St. Louis" (MArch thesis, Washington University in St. Louis, 1973), 3.

15. Ibid., 2, 17.

16. US Census Data, 1970, St. Louis Districts 5A and 5B, 1970: Housing, Count of Owner Occupied Housing Units for Which Value is Determined, Count of Black Owner Occupied Housing Units for Which Value is Determined.

17. US Census Data, Census, 1970, Districts 1051 and 1052.

18. "Residential Service Formed to Attract New Residents," *The Paper*, May 1970, 3, accessed at http://sdtimes.org.

19. Ursery, "Skinker DeBaliviere Community," 11; Thomas J. Sugrue, *The Origins of the Urban Crisis: Race and Inequality in Postwar Detroit* (Princeton, NJ: Princeton University Press, 1996), xv.

20. US Census Data, 1960 and 1970, Districts 1051 and 1052.

21. Colin Gordon, *Mapping Decline: St. Louis and the Fate of the American City* (Philadelphia: University of Pennsylvania Press, 2008).

22. "The New Skinker DeBaliviere Community Council," *The Paper*, Oct. 1970, 1, accessed at http://sdtimes.org.

23. Vatcha et al., *Celebrating*, 67–72.

24. Harvey L. Molotch, *Managed Integration: Dilemmas of Doing Good in the City* (Berkeley: University of California Press, 1973); Carole Goodwin, *The Oak Park Strategy: Community Control of Racial Change* (Chicago: University of Chicago Press, 1979); Ingrid Gould Ellen, *Sharing America's Neighborhoods: The Prospects for Stable Racial Integration* (Cambridge, MA: Harvard University Press, 2000).

25. Abigail Perkiss, *Making Good Neighbors: Civil Rights, Liberalism, and Integration in Postwar Philadelphia* (Ithaca, NY: Cornell University Press, 2014), 57.

26. L'Ecuyer quoted in Vatcha et al., *Celebrating*, 72–76.

27. Vatcha et al., *Celebrating*, 50.

28. Molotch, *Managed Integration*, 166.

29. Vatcha et al., *Celebrating*, 61.

30. West End Townhouse, Inc., *Welcome to Our Neighborhood* (St. Louis: SDCC Inc., n.d.), 5, Frances Hurd Stadler Papers Relating to St. Louis Neighborhoods, Missouri Historical Society Library and Research Center, St. Louis, folder 1.

31. Roger W. Collins, letter to neighbors, Oct. 21, 1967, 1, Saint Louis Neighborhoods Collection, Missouri Historical Society Library and Research Center (hereinafter SLNC, MHS), folder: Washington Heights Neighbors, Assorted Flyers 1969–70.

32. Robert Blackburn, "Hereford Housing proposal in SD," Sep. 19, 1966, Office of the Chancellor: Thomas H. Eliot Records, Washington University Archives (hereinafter TE Records, WUA), series 5, box 5, folder: Skinker DeBaliviere Area 1967–1968.

33. "People Power," *The Paper*, Sep. 1970, 2, accessed at http://sdtimes.org.

34. Perkiss, *Making Good Neighbors*.

35. *Washington Heights Neighbors Newsletter*, Dec. 1966, 3, SLNC, MHS, folder: Washington Heights Neighbors Newsletter 1959–1966, 3B 2.1–2.2.

36. *Washington Heights Neighbors Newsletter*, Oct. 1963, 3, SLNC, MHS, folder: Washington Heights Neighbors Newsletter 1959–1966, 3B 2.1–2.2.

37. Ursery, "Skinker DeBaliviere Community," 24.

38. Vatcha et al., *Celebrating*, 72.

39. Ellen, *Sharing America's Neighborhoods*, 178.

40. *Washington Heights Neighbors Newsletter*, Dec. 1966, 3, SLNC, MHS, folder: Washington Heights Neighbors Newsletter 1959–1966, 3B 2.1–2.2.

41. Roger W. Collins, letter to neighbors, Oct. 21, 1967, SLNC, MHS, folder: Washington Heights Neighbors Assorted Flyers 1969–70.

42. "Draft letter to residents from Skinker DeBaliviere Community Council" and "Call scripts," TE Records, WUA, series 5, box 5, folder: Skinker DeBaliviere Area 1967–1968.

43. Bruce Hall, Consultant, "Recommendations for Funding of Staff Components of Council Programs for the Board of Directors, SDCC," Jan. 24, 1969, TE Records, WUA, series 5, box 5, folder: Skinker DeBaliviere Area 1967–1968.

44. Ellen, *Sharing America's Neighborhoods*, 2, 9, 178.

45. Ibid., 162.

46. Pat Kohn, "Residential Service Formed to Attract New Residents," *The Paper*, May 1970, 2; Jean Eberle, "Residents Confront Realtors, Landlords," *The Paper*, May 1970, 3; accessed at http://sdtimes.org.

47. "Residential Service," *The Paper*, Dec. 1972, 7, accessed at http://sdtimes.org.

48. "Residential Service," *The Paper*, May 1970, 2, accessed at http://sdtimes.org.

49. Ursery, "Skinker DeBaliviere Community," 16.

50. *Washington Heights Neighbors Newsletter*, May 21, 1967, SLNC, MHS, folder: Washington Heights Neighbors Newsletter 1959–1966, 3B 2.1–2.2.

51. Timothy Bleck, "Skinker-DeBaliviere Group Seeks to End Pockets of Blight," *St. Louis Post-Dispatch*, Jun. 29, 1967.

52. "White Influx," *The Paper*, Dec. 1972, 1, 3, accessed at http://sdtimes.org.

53. Molotch, *Managed Integration*, 120.

54. US Census Data, 1960, 1970, 1980, St. Louis Districts 1051 and 1052.

55. Vatcha et al., *Celebrating*, 62–72, 77–86.

56. Charles M. Brown, "Letter to the Editor," *The Paper*, Sep. 1970, 2, accessed at http://sdtimes.org.

57. Ursery, "Skinker DeBaliviere Community," 15.

58. Ibid., 62.

59. Ibid., 62.

60. Ibid., 15.

61. Ibid., 15.

62. Ibid., 62.

63. Ibid., 15.

64. Ibid., 62.

65. Ibid., 53.

66. Vatcha et al., *Celebrating*, 55.

67. Ibid., 57.

68. Ursery, "Skinker DeBaliviere Community," 14, 62.

69. Chuck Rowley, "Selling Soulard," *Soulard Restorationist*, Nov. 1977, 32.

70. Mark Abbott, "A Document That Changed America: The 1907 *A City Plan for St. Louis*," in *St. Louis Plans: The Ideal and the Real St. Louis*, ed. Mark Tranel (St. Louis: Missouri Historical Society Press, 2007), 36–39.

71. Lew Cohn, "Soulard Historic District: The New Must Exist with the Old," *Subject to Change*, Oct. 26, 1978, 15, Soulard News Clippings, St. Louis Public Library, folder 1.

72. Jay Corzine, Irene Dabrowski, Naureen Spitzer, Marcia Warren, and Jill Okyle, "Soulard," in *Ethnic Heritage Studies Colloquium* (St. Louis: Social Science Institute, Washington University, 1975), 36–37, 42.

73. Social Explorer, Housing Tract: Occupancy Status, St. Louis Census Tract 23D, 1940; Social Explorer, Housing Tract: Occupancy Status, Tract 1234, 1970.

74. Social Explorer, Housing Tract: Occupancy Status, St. Louis Census Tract 23D, 1940; Social Explorer, Housing Tract: Occupancy Status, Tract 1234, 1970.

75. Jay Corzine and Irene Dabrowski, *The Ethnic Factor and Neighborhood Stability in St. Louis: The Czechs in Soulard and South St. Louis* (St. Louis: Washington University, 1975), 5; City of St. Louis, *Program Area 16* (St. Louis: City of St. Louis, 1970).

76. Sandra Schoenberg, ed., *Urban Neighborhoods Colloquium* (St. Louis: Washington University, 1974), 9.

77. City of St. Louis, *Program Area 16*.

78. Janet G. Hurwitz, "Participatory Design Study: An Urban Neighborhood Process; The Politics of Participatory Planning in Soulard, St. Louis, Mo." (MArch and MSW thesis, Washington University in St. Louis, 1975), 18.

79. Schoenberg, *Urban Neighborhoods*, 9.

80. Florence Shinkle, "A Tale of Two City Neighborhoods," *St. Louis Post-Dispatch*, Sunday Pictures Magazine, Apr. 16, 1972, 39.

81. Schoenberg, *Urban Neighborhoods*, 9.

82. "Soulard and Lafayette Square," 25, 33.

83. Jake McCarthy, "View from the City: A Personal Opinion; Demolition On and Off," *St. Louis Post-Dispatch*, Dec. 17, 1971; "Soulard and Lafayette Square," 33.

84. Elaine Viets, "Home Repair Rescue Service," *St. Louis Post-Dispatch*, Nov. 23, 1973; "Soulard Benefit," *St. Louis Post-Dispatch*, Dec. 16, 1973.

85. McCarthy, "View from the City"; "Soulard and Lafayette Square," 33.

86. Virgil Tipton, "The Soul of Soulard," *St. Louis Post-Dispatch*, Sep. 24, 1992.

87. McCarthy, "View from the City."

88. Ibid.

89. "Soulard and Lafayette," 33.

90. Charlene Bry, "Senior Citizens Crochet Their Way to Soulard," *St. Louis Globe-Democrat*, Aug. 3, 1978.

91. Jake McCarthy, "A Personal Opinion: Taking a $12,000 Soaking," *St. Louis Post-Dispatch*, Oct. 18, 1972.

92. Tipton, "Soul of Soulard."

93. Bry, "Senior Citizens Crochet."

94. Carolyn Hewes Toft, ed., *Soulard: The Ethnic Heritage of an Urban Neighborhood* (St. Louis: Social Science Institute, Washington University, 1975).

95. *Soulard Restorationist*. The Missouri Historical Society Library and Research Center houses issues of *Soulard Restorationist* from 1976 to 1996.

96. "Soulard Group, Boys Club, Battle over 12-Foot Fence," *St. Louis Globe-Democrat*, Apr. 1, 1980; *Soulard Restorationist* 2, no. 7 (Sep. 1977).

97. *Soulard Restorationist* 1, no. 8 (Mar. 1977); *Soulard Restorationist* 3, no. 5 (Jun. 1978).

98. *Soulard Restorationist* 4, no. 1 (Jan. 1979).

99. *Soulard Restorationist* 4, no. 3 (Mar. 1979).

100. Robert Brandhorst and Joyce Sonn, "Tyranny of the Minority," *St. Louis Globe-Democrat*, Jun. 7, 1990; Fred Andres, "Guidelines Would Protect Historic Area," *St. Louis Globe-Democrat*, Jun. 7, 1990.

101. Phyllis Young, "Notes from the Brick House," *Soulard Restorationist*, Mar. 1979, 9–10.

102. Schoenberg, *Urban Neighborhoods*, 58.

103. Soulard Restoration Group, "Back to the City," *Soulard Restorationist* 2, no. 3 (May 1977): 9.

104. Hurwitz, "Participatory Design Study," 46–48, 284.

10. "We Were on a Mission"

1. One exception to this pattern is scholarship on the underground abortion support network in Chicago known as "Jane." See, for example, Laura Kaplan, *The Story of Jane: The Legendary Underground Feminist Abortion Service* (New York: Pantheon, 1995).

2. See, for example, Stephanie Gilmore, *Groundswell: Grassroots Feminist Activism in Postwar America* (New York: Routledge, 2013); Benita Roth, *Separate Roads to Feminism: Black, Chicana, and White Feminist Movements in America's Second Wave* (New York: Cambridge University Press, 2004); Finn Enke, *Finding the*

Movement: Sexuality, Contested Space, and Feminist Activism (Durham, NC: Duke University Press, 2007); and Annelise Orleck, *Rethinking American Women's Activism* (New York: Routledge, 2015).

3. This was the first year that the US Census released statistics on religious affiliation. The Church of the Nazarene Global Ministry Center, St. Louis City, 1980, *Data Planet Statistical Datasets: A SAGE Publishing Resource*, data set ID: 098-001-002, doi:https://doi.org/10.6068/DP17B8EE2F0A67.

4. Orleck, *Rethinking American Women's Activism*, x. See also Roth, *Separate Roads to Feminism*; Gilmore, *Groundswell*; and Enke, *Finding the Movement*.

5. Jo Freeman, *The Politics of Women's Liberation: A Case Study of an Emerging Social Movement and Its Relation to the Policy Process* (New York: McKay, 1975).

6. Keona K. Ervin, *Gateway to Equality: Black Women and the Struggle for Economic Justice in St. Louis* (Lexington: University Press of Kentucky, 2017).

7. Clarence Lang, *Grassroots at the Gateway: Class Politics and Black Freedom Struggle in St. Louis, 1936–75* (Ann Arbor: University of Michigan Press, 2009), 240.

8. Ibid., 103.

9. Gilmore, *Groundswell*. See also Stephanie Gilmore, ed., *Feminist Coalitions: Historical Perspectives on Second-Wave Feminism in the United States* (Urbana: University of Illinois Press, 2008).

10. Freeman, *Politics of Women's Liberation*.

11. Enke, *Finding the Movement*; Arlene Zarembka, video-conference interview by authors, Apr. 9, 2020.

12. Sondra Stein, video-conference interview by authors, Jul. 20, 2020.

13. Kayla Vaughan, video-conference interview by authors, Jun. 26, 2020.

14. Ibid.

15. Ibid.

16. Ibid. For more on the *St. Louis Outlaw*, see Devin Thomas O'Shea, "Remembering the *Outlaw*, STL's Premiere Counterculture Publication," *Riverfront Times* (St. Louis), Jan. 6, 2022, https://web.archive.org/web/20220217222010/https://www.riverfronttimes.com/stlouis/remembering-the-outlaw-stls-premiere-1970s-counterculture-publication/Content?oid=36910661.

17. Vaughan, interview.

18. Ibid.; Sister Mary Louise Denny, video-conference interview by authors, Mar. 19, 2021.

19. Stein, interview.

20. Benjamin Looker, *"Point from Which Creation Begins": The Black Artists' Group of St. Louis* (St. Louis: Missouri Historical Society Press, 2004).

21. Stein, interview.

22. Ibid.

23. Margaret Flowing Johnson, video-conference interview by authors, Jun. 29, 2020.

24. Zuleyma Tang-Martinez, video-conference interview by authors, Apr. 9, 2020.

25. Laura Cohen, video-conference interview by authors, Jul. 6, 2020.

26. Freeman, *Politics of Women's Liberation*.

27. Margo McNeil, video-conference interview by authors, Jul. 13, 2020.

28. Sally Barker, video-conference interview by authors, Jul. 1, 2020.

29. Ibid.

30. Ibid.

31. Ibid.

32. Ibid; Marcia Mellitz, interview by authors, Sep. 30, 2021.

33. McNeil, interview; Marcia Cline Morelan, interview by authors, Jul. 8, 2020; Lynn Liss, video-conference interview by authors, Jul. 28, 2020.

34. McNeil, interview.

35. Gilmore, *Groundswell*.

36. John C. Deken, "Women of the Heartland: Tradition and Evolution in the Missouri Women's Movement" (MA thesis, University of Missouri–Columbia, 2009), 13.

37. Winifred D. Wandersee, *On the Move: American Women in the 1970s* (Boston: Twayne, 1998).

38. Arlene Zarembka, video-conference interview by authors, Apr. 9, 2020.

39. Dave Roediger, "Central *Turnhalle*, May Day, and the Movement of Labor," in *The St. Louis Labor History Tour*, ed. Rose Feurer (St. Louis: Bread and Roses, 1994), 4, accessed at http://www.laborhistorylinks.org/PDF%20Files/SLLHT%20booklet.pdf.

40. Ibid.

41. Cline Morelan, interview.

42. Malone also held what came to be called "the revolutionary basement" in the basement of her house, and, according to Cline, "it was always a matter of some distinction if you were invited into her revolutionary basement." Cline Morelan, interview.

43. Joan Suarez, video-conference interview by authors, Aug. 7, 2020.

44. Cline Morelan, interview.

45. Ibid.

46. Ibid.

47. Ibid.

48. Ibid.

49. Suarez, interview.

50. Ibid.

51. Ibid.

52. Suarez, interview.

53. Roz Sherman Voellinger, video-conference interview by authors, May 10, 2021.

54. Jamala Rogers, video-conference interview by authors, Sep. 4, 2020.

55. Ibid.

56. Ibid.

57. Ibid.

58. Ibid.

59. Ibid.

60. Ibid.

61. Ibid.

62. Ibid.

63. Ibid. See also Ashley D. Farmer, "'Abolition of Every Possibility of Oppression': Black Women, Black Power, and the Black Women's United Front, 1970–1976," *Journal of Women's History* 32, no. 3 (Fall 2020): 89–114.

64. Rogers, interview.

65. Roth, *Separate Roads to Feminism*.

66. Rogers, interview.

67. Ibid.

68. Ora Lee Malone, interview by Bill Morrison, May 3, 1973, Oral History Collection, S0829, State Historical Society of Missouri, available online at https://shsmo.org/sites/default/files/pdfs/oral-history/transcripts/s0829/t0344.pdf.

69. Richard Rothstein, "The Making of Ferguson: Public Policies at the Root of Its Troubles," Economic Policy Institute, Oct. 15, 2014, https://www.epi.org/publication/making-ferguson/.

70. Rogers, interview.

71. McNeil, interview.

72. Ann Braude, "A Religious Feminist—Who Can Find Her? Historiographical Challenges from the National Organization for Women," *Journal of Religion* 84, no. 4 (Oct. 2004): 555–72.

73. Ibid., 560.

74. Ibid., 566.

75. Liss, interview.

76. Braude, "Religious Feminist."

77. Denny, interview.

78. Ibid.

79. Nathalie Pettus, personal correspondence with Ilene Ordower, Jul. 3, 2021.

80. Cynthia Gorney, *Articles of Faith: A Frontline History of the Abortion Wars* (New York: Simon and Schuster, 1998).

81. Ibid.; Sarah McCammon, "50 Years Ago, a Network of Clergy Helped Women Seeking Abortions," *All Things Considered*, National Public Radio, May 19, 2017.

82. Gorney, *Articles of Faith*.

83. Marian Faux, *Crusaders: Voices from the Abortion Front* (New York: Carol Publishing Group, 1990).

84. Vivian Zwick, video-conference interview by authors, Apr. 10, 2020.

85. Ibid.

86. Gorney, *Articles of Faith*.

87. Ibid.

88. Ibid.

89. Kayla Vaughan, email communication with authors, Nov. 7, 2021.

90. Sherman Voellinger, interview.

91. "Credit Union Task Force Report," *Centering In* (official newsletter of the Women's Self-Help Center), Jul. 1977, Metropolitan Community Church of Greater

St. Louis Records, S0543, State Historical Society of Missouri (hereinafter MCC Records, SHSMO), box 2.

92. Sherman Voellinger, interview.

93. Ibid.

94. Ibid.

95. "Party Aids Center, Hotline Introduced," *St. Louis Globe-Democrat*, n.d.

96. Sherman Voellinger, interview.

97. "Battered Women Task Force Report," *Centering In* (official newsletter of the Women's Self-Help Center), Jul. 1977, MCC Records, SHSMO, box 2.

98. Denny, interview by authors.

99. Ann B. Lever, "Domestic Violence Legislation for Missouri: A Proposal," *Saint Louis University Law Journal* 22, no. 1 (1978): 152n1.

100. Ibid., 151–96.

101. The St. Louis groups were Legal Services of Eastern Missouri, the Women's Self-Help Center, the Abused Women's Support Project, and the St. Louis Women's Political Caucus. See Legal Services of Eastern Missouri, "Press Release," Jul. 21, 1978, Adult Abuse Remedies Act Records, S0359, State Historical Society of Missouri, box 1.

102. "Our History," Missouri Coalition Against Domestic and Sexual Violence website, www.mocadsv.org/our-history, accessed Aug. 31, 2021.

103. Don Conway-Long, video-conference interview by authors, May 19, 2021.

104. Ibid.

105. Ibid.

106. Ibid.

107. Ibid.

108. Ibid.

109. Gilmore, *Groundswell*, 9.

11. Is Ivory Perry an Environmentalist (and Does It Matter)?

This chapter is a substantially revised version of Chapter 2 from Robert R. Gioielli, *Environmental Activism and the Urban Crisis: Baltimore, St. Louis, Chicago* (Philadelphia: Temple University Press, 2014). Accompanying images and captions are new to this volume's version.

1. Melvin Small, *Antiwarriors: The Vietnam War and the Battle for America's Hearts and Minds* (Wilmington, DE: Scholarly Resources, 2002); Jeanne Theoharis, *A More Beautiful and Terrible History: The Uses and Misuses of Civil Rights History* (Boston: Beacon Press, 2018).

2. David Naguib Pellow and Lisa Sun-Hee Park, *The Slums of Aspen: Immigrants vs. the Environment in America's Eden* (New York: New York University Press, 2011); Dorceta E. Taylor, *The Rise of the American Conservation Movement: Power, Privilege, and Environmental Protection* (Durham, NC: Duke University Press, 2016).

3. James Neal Primm, *Lion of the Valley: St. Louis, Missouri, 1764–1980*, 3rd ed. (St. Louis: Missouri Historical Society Press, 1998); Joseph Heathcott and Málre Agnes Murphy, "Corridors of Flight, Zones of Renewal: Industry, Planning, and

Policy in the Making of Metropolitan St. Louis, 1940–1980," *Journal of Urban History* 31, no. 2 (2005): 151–89.

4. David M. P. Freund, *Colored Property: State Policy and White Racial Politics in Suburban America* (Chicago: University of Chicago Press, 2007); Paige Glotzer, *How the Suburbs Were Segregated: Developers and the Business of Exclusionary Housing, 1890–1960* (New York: Columbia University Press, 2020); Colin Gordon, *Mapping Decline: St. Louis and the Fate of the American City* (Philadelphia: University of Pennsylvania Press, 2008); Beryl Satter, *Family Properties: Race, Real Estate, and the Exploitation of Black Urban America* (New York: Metropolitan Books, 2009).

5. Robert Eugene Quinn and Michael A. Mendelson, *The Decline of an Urban Housing Entrepreneur: Congratulations or Condolences?* (Edwardsville: Center for Urban and Environmental Research and Services, Southern Illinois University at Edwardsville, 1977); Charles A. Liebert, "The Role of the Middleman in the Housing Market," in *The Politics of Housing in Older Urban Areas*, ed. Robert Eugene Quinn and Michael A. Mendelson (New York: Praeger, 1976).

6. Clarence Lang, *Grassroots at the Gateway: Class Politics and Black Freedom Struggle in St. Louis, 1936–75* (Ann Arbor: University of Michigan Press, 2009).

7. Charles Kimball Cummings, "Rent Strike in St. Louis: The Making of Conflict in Modern Society" (PhD diss., Washington University in St. Louis, 1975).

8. Much of the biographical information comes from George Lipsitz, *A Life in the Struggle: Ivory Perry and the Culture of Opposition*, rev. ed. (Philadelphia: Temple University Press, 1995). Lipsitz conducted a number of interviews with Perry, but Perry died in 1989 and left no papers or records.

9. Florissant: Metropolitan Housing Characteristics, St. Louis, Mo.-Ill. Standard Metropolitan Statistical Area HC (2)-187, US Department of Commerce, Bureau of the Census.

10. "Ecology: The New Jeremiahs," *Time*, Aug. 15, 1969, 46; "Fight to Save the Earth from Man," *Time*, Feb. 2, 1970, 4–11; "Paul Revere of Ecology," *Time*, Feb. 2, 1970, 6.

11. Kelly Moore, *Disrupting Science: Social Movements, American Scientists, and the Politics of the Military, 1945–1975* (Princeton, NJ: Princeton University Press, 2008), ch. 4; Michael Egan, *Barry Commoner and the Science of Survival: The Remaking of American Environmentalism* (Cambridge, MA: M. I. T. Press, 2007).

12. Barry Commoner, *Science and Survival* (London: Gollancz, 1966).

13. Barry Commoner, "By Using Nature as a Lab," *SR*, May 7, 1966; Sheldon Novick to Senior Fellows, Aug. 16, 1968, Barry Commoner Papers, Library of Congress, Washington, DC (hereinafter Commoner Papers, LOC), box 422, folder: "Center: Senior Fellows"; Julian McCaull to Senior Fellows, Feb. 4, 1969, Commoner Papers, LOC, box 422, folder: "Center: Senior Fellows"; Wilbur Thomas, "Environmental Field Program: Second Annual Report to the W. K. Kellogg Foundation," Jan.–Dec. 1970, Commoner Papers, LOC, box 423, folder: "Research Proposals of Center Senior Fellows '71–72."

14. Glenda Webb, "A Study of Lead Poisoning," 1969, Commoner Papers, LOC, box 413, folder: "Lists of CBNS Publications."

15. The best overview on lead poisoning in twentieth-century America is Christian Warren, *Brush with Death: A Social History of Lead Poisoning* (Baltimore, MD: Johns Hopkins University Press, 2000). See also Elizabeth Fee, "Public Health in Practice: An Early Confrontation with the 'Silent Epidemic' of Childhood Lead Paint Poisoning," *Journal of the History of Medicine and Allied Sciences* 45, no. 4 (1990): 570–606; and Samuel P. Hays, "The Role of Values in Science and Policy: The Case of Lead" and Jane S. Lin-Fu, "Modern History of Lead Poisoning: A Century of Discovery and Rediscovery," both in *Human Lead Exposure*, ed. Herbert Needleman (Boca Raton, FL: CRC Press, 1992).

16. See especially Kriss Avery, *Ivory Perry: Pioneer in the Struggle against Lead Poisoning*, documentary film (St. Ann, MO: Rainbow Sound, 2006).

17. Lana Stein, *St. Louis Politics: The Triumph of Tradition* (St. Louis: Missouri Historical Society Press, 2002); Lipsitz, *A Life in the Struggle*, 174–75.

18. Albert Nerviani to A. J. Wilson, May 20, 1971, Alfonso J. Cervantes Mayoral Records, Department of Special Collections, Washington University in St. Louis (hereinafter Cervantes Records, WUSC), box 42, folder: "Lead Poisoning—April 1970"; Charles Copley, "Lead Poisoning Prevention in St. Louis," in *Childhood Lead Poisoning Prevention and Control: A Public Health Approach to an Environmental Disease*, ed. Flora Finch Cherry (New Orleans: Maternal and Child Health Section, Office of Health Services and Environmental Quality, Dept. of Health and Human Resources, 1981).

19. "Robert Knickmeyer," obituary, *St. Louis Post-Dispatch*, Sep. 3, 1996.

20. "Lead-Poison Foes Plan Strike," *St. Louis Post-Dispatch*, Dec. 22, 1970; "Rent Strike Being Organized in Wake of Lead Poisoning Cases," *St. Louis Globe-Democrat*, Dec. 22, 1970.

21. On rent strikes as an organizing tool, see Ronald Lawson, "The Rent Strike in New York City, 1904–1980: The Evolution of a Social Movement Strategy," *Journal of Urban History* 10, no. 3 (1984): 235–58.

22. "Sit-In against Lead Poisoning," *St. Louis Globe-Democrat*, Nov. 12, 1970.

23. William Preston to Block Brothers Portraits Manager, and Vatra Tanner to Kenneth Brown, both May 26, 1971, Cervantes Records, WUSC, box 42, folder: "Lead Poisoning—April 1970."

24. "Lack of Funds Reported in Fight on Poison Paint," *St. Louis Post-Dispatch*, May 3, 1971; "City of St. Louis Lead Poisoning Statistics and Projects," Lead Poisoning Control Service, City of St. Louis, 1971, Cervantes Records, WUSC, box 42, folder: "Lead Poisoning—April 1970"; "Tenant Groups Seek Funds to Fight Lead Poisoning," *St. Louis Post-Dispatch*, Mar. 21, 1971.

25. Charlie Staples, "City Officials Named in Lead Poisoning Suit," *St. Louis Globe-Democrat*, Feb. 4, 1971.

26. Heathcott and Murphy, "Corridors of Flight, Zones of Renewal"; George E. Curry, "Seeking Funds for Lead Fight," *St. Louis Post-Dispatch*, Jun. 25, 1975; "The Convention Center," editorial, *KMOX*, Nov. 1, 1972, Cervantes Records, WUSC, box 19, folder: "Convention Center"; Spencer Allen, "Reply to KMOX Editorial on the Convention Center," *KMOX*, Nov. 3, 1972, Cervantes Records, WUSC, box 19,

folder: "Convention Center"; Sally Thran, "Center Could Boost Revenues," *St. Louis Post-Dispatch*, Oct. 30, 1972.

27. Ad Hoc Committee on Lead Poisoning, "Statement of the Ad Hoc Committee on Lead Poisoning," Jan. 13, 1971, Cervantes Records, WUSC, box 42, folder: "Lead Poisoning—April 1970"; "Get the Lead Out," conference program, 1971, Freedom of Residence Committee Addenda, State Historical Society of Missouri, box 348, folder: "Lead Conference."

28. Wilbur Thomas, "Black Survival in Our Polluted Cities," *Proud*, Apr. 1970, Missouri Historical Society Library and Research Center, St. Louis, MO.

29. Ernie McMillan, "Proud's Platform," *Proud*, May 1970; Peniel E. Joseph, *Waiting 'Til the Midnight Hour: A Narrative History of Black Power in America* (New York: Henry Holt and Co., 2006); Lang, *Grassroots at the Gateway*.

30. Carolyn Burrow, "Environmental Racism," *Proud*, Dec. 1970.

31. Freddie Mae Brown and the St. Louis Metropolitan Black Survival Committee, "Black Survival: A Collage of Skits," in *Earth Day—The Beginning: A Guide for Survival*, comp. and ed. Environmental Action (New York: Bantam Books, 1970).

32. Sheila Bixby Defty, "Inaction Protested in Lead Poison Case," *St. Louis Post-Dispatch*, Nov. 9, 1972; People's Coalition Against Lead Poisoning, "Injunctions to Save the Children," Nov. 13, 1972, Committee for Environmental Information Records, S0069, State Historical Society of Missouri (hereinafter CEI, SHSMO), folder 288.

33. "City to Step up Fight against Lead Poisoning," *St. Louis Globe-Democrat*, Oct. 14–15, 1972.

34. Sheila Bixby Defty, "Inaction Protested in Lead Poison Case," *St. Louis Post-Dispatch*, Nov. 9, 1972; "City's Agreement to Enforce Anti-lead Law Ends Sit-In," *St. Louis Globe-Democrat*, Nov. 17, 1972; People's Coalition Against Lead Poisoning, "Injunctions to Save the Children"; People's Coalition Against Lead Poisoning to Helen Bruce, Nov. 16, 1972, Cervantes Records, WUSC, box 42, folder: "Lead Poisoning—April 1970."

35. "Landlords Blamed in Lead Poison Study," *St. Louis Post-Dispatch*, Mar. 16, 1972.

36. Walter Stradal to Charles Salisbury, Oct. 21, 1971, Cervantes Records, WUSC, box 42, folder: "Lead Poisoning—April 1970."

37. Ibid; Helen Bruce to Robert Karsh, Dec. 4, 1975, CEI, SHSMO, folder 288.

38. Copley remark from ARCH Environmental Health Planning Task Force, City of St. Louis, Jul. 1, 1975, CEI, SHSMO, folder 288. In the transcript of that meeting, the health-board member is identified only as "Mr. Grist." Michael A. Mendelson and Robert Eugene Quinn, *The Feasibility of Lead Paint Removal in St. Louis Rental Housing* (Edwardsville: Center for Urban and Environmental Research and Services, Southern Illinois University at Edwardsville, 1978), 13, 30–31.

39. George E. Curry, "Seeking Funds for Lead Fight," *St. Louis Post-Dispatch*, Jun. 25, 1975; Department of Community Medicine, "Let Them Eat Paint," *St. Louis Post-Dispatch*, Oct. 17, 1977.

40. "Get the Lead Out: Conference Report," May 22, 1971, Cervantes Records, WUSC, box 42, folder: "Lead Poisoning—April 1970"; "Robert Knickmeyer," *St. Louis Post-Dispatch*, Sep. 3, 1996; Lipsitz, *A Life in the Struggle*; Warren, *Brush with Death*, 224–43.

41. George Lipsitz, "Ivory Perry and the Fight against Lead Poisoning in St. Louis," *Synthesis/Regeneration* 41 (Fall 2006): 16–17.

42. Kevin Drum, "America's Real Criminal Element: Lead," *Mother Jones*, Jan./Feb. 2013, http://www.motherjones.com/environment/2013/01/lead-crime-link-gasoline; Stephen Janis, "Full of Lead," *Baltimore City Paper*, Mar. 9, 2005, http://www2.citypaper.com/news/story.asp?id=9738; Gerald E. Markowitz and David Rosner, *Lead Wars: The Politics of Science and the Fate of America's Children* (Berkeley: University of California Press, 2014).

43. Rob Nixon, *Slow Violence and the Environmentalism of the Poor* (Cambridge, MA: Harvard University Press, 2013).

12. "Save Homer G. Phillips and All Public Hospitals"

1. Barnes Hospital moved from downtown St. Louis to the Central West End to become Washington University's teaching hospital.

2. St. Louis's numerical hospital nomenclature was not unique. Kansas City, for example, also maintained public hospitals named City Hospital No. 1 for whites and No. 2 for African Americans. This naming system, though not unique, highlighted the subordinate position of African American health particularly in the Jim Crow era. While Starkloff (City Hospital No. 1) largely operated in the same building from 1907 to 1985, City Hospital No. 2 operated from 1919 to 1937 and was succeeded by Homer G. Phillips Hospital in 1937. Throughout this essay, I will not refer to St. Louis's public general hospitals by their numerical names (Nos. 1 and 2) so as not to perpetuate the subjugated status of Black people's health. Rather, I will refer to both hospitals by the historic figures for whom they were respectively named. This is anachronistic, given that City Hospital No. 1 was not renamed Max Starkloff Hospital until pioneering St. Louis Health Commissioner Max C. Starkloff, who successfully curtailed the spread of the 1918 Spanish influenza epidemic, died in 1942. Homer G. Phillips Hospital was named after a maverick anti-segregationist lawyer who was assassinated in 1931 while waiting on a streetcar.

3. Aaron Henkin, "Out of the Ville Part 1," *Out of the Blocks* podcast, WYPR-St. Louis, Dec. 5, 2017, https://www.wypr.org/show/out-of-the-blocks/2017-12-05/out-of-the-ville-part-1; Mary Tillman, oral history interview by author (2nd of 2), Apr. 25, 2017, Homer G. Phillips Hospital Oral History Collection, Department of Special Collections, Washington University in St. Louis, https://libguides.wustl.edu/WUA00479.

4. "Comptroller Raymond Persich to Robert McDuffie," Aug. 16, 1979, City of St. Louis, Office of the Mayor: James F. Conway Records, 1977–1981, Department of Special Collections, Washington University in St. Louis (hereinafter Conway Records, WUSC), series 2, box 23, folder 1; Tillman, interview (1st of 2), Apr. 19, 2017.

5. Tillman, interview (1st of 2).

6. Joyce Fitzpatrick and Brian Shackelford, dir., *The Color of Medicine: The Story of Homer G. Phillips Hospital*, documentary film (2018; Del Ray, CA: Flatcat Productions and Tunnel Vizion Films, 2020).

7. KSDK-TV footage from closing day was posted on the television station's website circa 2009, as a retrospective video titled "August 17, 1979: Homer G. Phillips Hospital Closes Its Doors." It has since been removed from the station website, but the posted video remains on file with the chapter author.

8. Veronica Banks, "Phillips Leaders Turn to Boycott," *St. Louis Argus*, Aug. 23, 1979.

9. "No Surprise," *St. Louis Argus*, Feb. 8, 1979.

10. This historical episode has been studied by other scholars, notably Jaclyn Kirouac-Fram in "'To Serve the Community Best': Reconsidering Black Politics in the Struggle to Save Homer G. Phillips Hospital in St. Louis, 1976–1984," *Journal of Urban History* 36, no. 5 (2010): 594–616. While Kirouac-Fram frames this episode from the urban studies perspective, this essay incorporates insights from the history of medicine. This essay also expands upon Kirouac-Fram's periodization, tracing these debates to the 1950s when St. Louis public hospitals were desegregated.

11. Robin D. G. Kelley, *Freedom Dreams: The Black Radical Imagination* (Boston: Beacon Press, 2003).

12. Ibid., ix.

13. For more on the linkage between federal reimbursement and hospital desegregation, see David Barton Smith, *The Power to Heal: Civil Rights, Medicare, and the Struggle to Transform America's Health Care System* (Nashville, TN: Vanderbilt University Press, 2016).

14. Tillman, interview (1st of 2).

15. Herbert Donke, "'Quick Review' on Phillips/Starkloff Consolidation Proposals Thru 1964," George D. Wendel Manuscript Collection, Saint Louis University Archives (hereinafter Wendel Collection, SLUA), series 003, box 35, folder: "Healthcare Reports Phillips/Starkloff Consolidation 1964."

16. "Famed St. Louis Phillips Hospital May Be Closed," *Cleveland Call and Post*, May 13, 1961.

17. Ibid.

18. "Carl V. Moore to Edward Dempsey about 'City Hospital Patients,'" Nov. 5, 1963, Central Administration, Washington University School of Medicine, Bernard Becker Medical Library, Washington University in St. Louis (hereinafter Central Administration WUSM, Becker Lib.), subgroup 1, series 10, box 38, folder 8.

19. "Statement to Joseph Clark for 'Ear on St. Louis,'" 1961, Central Administration WUSM, Becker Lib., subgroup 1, series 10, box 38, folder 8.

20. Donke, "'Quick Review' on Phillips/Starkloff Consolidation Proposals Thru 1964," Wendel Collection, SLUA.

21. Ibid.

22. Archaic spelling of "intern." The internship (apprenticeship) model of training originated in medicine, which used this form of the term in the early twentieth century.

23. "Closing of Phillips Hospital Discussed, City Official Says," *St. Louis Post-Dispatch*, Oct. 9, 1964.

24. Ibid.

25. "Mound City Doctors Oppose Hospital Plan," *St. Louis Post-Dispatch*, May 10, 1961.

26. Committee of the People of St. Louis of the Hills Chapel Church, "Closing Protest Letter," 1961, Raymond Tucker Collection, Department of Special Collections, Washington University in St. Louis (hereinafter Tucker Collection, WUSC), series 3, box 22, folder: "Homer G. Phillips Hospital—Letters of Protest Re: Closing."

27. Ibid.

28. The only cohort of people who are guaranteed the right to healthcare in the United States are incarcerated people. See Homer Venters, *Life and Death in Rikers Island* (Baltimore: Johns Hopkins University Press, 2019). On the St. Louis City charter and its mandate to provide indigent care, see Daniel R. Berg, "A History of Health Care for the Indigent in St. Louis: 1904–2001," *Saint Louis University Law Journal* 48, no. 1 (Sep. 2003): 191. For a case study of this emergent "health rights" language in Los Angeles, see Jenna M. Loyd, *Health Rights Are Civil Rights: Peace and Justice Activism in Los Angeles, 1963–1978* (Minneapolis: University of Minnesota Press, 2014).

29. Lana Stein, *St. Louis Politics: The Triumph of Tradition* (St. Louis: Missouri Historical Society Press, 2002); Tim O'Neil, "A Look Back: Clearing of the Mill Creek Valley Changed the Face of the City," *St. Louis Post-Dispatch*, Aug. 9, 2009, http://www.stltoday.com/news/local/a-look-back-clearing-of-mill-creek-valley-changed-the/article_04738cde-b0f8-5688-a20e-6fd86266d1ac.html.

30. Dick Gregory, with Robert Lipsyte, *Nigger: An Autobiography* (New York: Darnton, 1964).

31. Baptist Pastors Council of St. Louis to Mayor Raymond Tucker, May 11, 1961, Tucker Collection, WUSC, series 3, box 22, folder: "Homer G. Phillips Hospital—Letters of Protest Re: Closing."

32. Les Bonnes Amiee Study Club to Mayor Raymond Tucker, Mar. 15, 1961, Tucker Collection, WUSC, series 3, box 22, folder: "Homer G. Phillips Hospital—Letters of Protest Re: Closing."

33. John Dittmer, *The Good Doctors: The Medical Committee for Human Rights and the Struggle for Social Justice in Health Care* (New York: Bloomsbury Publishing, 2009).

34. George W. Harvey to Mayor Raymond Tucker, Mar. 15, 1961, Tucker Collection, WUSC, series 3, box 22, folder: "Homer G. Phillips Hospital—Letters of Protest Re: Closing."

35. Robert Osborne, Assistant to the Mayor, to Arthur D. Taylor, Jul. 7, 1961, Tucker Collection, WUSC, series 3, box 22, folder: "Homer G. Phillips Hospital—Letters of Protest Re: Closing."

36. "'Integration' Threatens to Close St. Louis Hospital," *Jet*, Oct. 26, 1961.

37. On the "urban crisis" generally, see Thomas J. Sugrue, *The Origins of the Urban Crisis: Race and Inequality in Postwar Detroit*, updated ed. (Princeton, NJ: Princeton University Press, 2014).

38. "Charges Are True Hospital Head Says," *St. Louis Globe-Democrat*, Oct. 18, 1972.

39. "Homer G. Phillips: A Historic Hospital Faces Closing," *Urban Health: The Journal of Healthcare in the City*, Oct. 1976, 22–23.

40. Ibid., 23–24.

41. On the history and legacy of St. Louis's "Team Four Plan" from an urban planning history perspective, see Patrick Cooper-McCann, "The Trap of Triage: Lessons from the 'Team Four Plan,'" *Journal of Planning History* 15, no. 2 (2016): 149–69.

42. Arnold R. Hirsch, *Making the Second Ghetto: Race and Housing in Chicago, 1940–1960* (Cambridge, UK: Cambridge University Press, 1983).

43. Stein, *St. Louis Politics*.

44. This downtown revitalization plan included the construction of Cervantes Convention Center, the revitalization of Union Station, and a restored waterfront warehouse district. See Kirouac-Fram, "'To Serve the Community Best.'"

45. Ruth Thaler, "Conway to Move on Phillips in Nine Days," *St. Louis Argus*, Mar. 15, 1979.

46. Ad Hoc Committee to Save Homer G. Phillips, "Ad Hoc Citizen's Committee to Save Homer G. Phillips and All Public Hospitals," ca. 1980, Zenobia Thompson Personal Collection.

47. Sheila Rule, "Inner Cities' Hospitals Vanishing in Wake of Sharply Rising Costs," *New York Times*, Sep. 2, 1979.

48. In a special *Hospitals* issue focused on the future of public hospitals, an article author noted, "The public hospital also can assume leadership in overcoming the segregation of healthcare by implementing the growing national consensus that healthcare is a right, and by acknowledging that segregation of care cannot ensure equal rights." Lester Breslow, "Role of the Public Hospitals," *Hospitals: The Journal of the American Hospital Association* 44, no. 13 (Jul. 1, 1970): 44–46.

49. Walter Johnson, *The Broken Heart of America: St. Louis and the Violent History of the United States* (New York: Basic Books, 2020). On the longer history of communism and African Americans, particularly in the US South, see Robin D. G. Kelley's classic study, *Hammer and Hoe: Alabama Communists during the Great Depression*, 2nd ed. (Chapel Hill: University of North Carolina Press, 2015).

50. "Christmas Shopping Boycott Campaign Is about to Be Launched by the Ad Hoc Committee," *St. Louis Argus*, Nov. 11, 1979.

51. Thaler, "Conway to Move on Phillips in Nine Days."

52. Martha Shirk and George B. Freeman, "Drive to Reopen Phillips Hospital Enters Fifth Year," *St. Louis Post-Dispatch*, Aug. 18, 1983.

53. "UNITY Flyer" (St. Louis, MO, 1979), Conway Records, WUSC, series 2, box 23, folder 1.

54. Ruth Thaler, "Citizens March to Save Homer Phillips Hospital," *St. Louis Argus*, Feb. 1, 1979.

55. "Bloody Protest on Hospital Close," *St. Louis Post-Dispatch*, Nov. 6, 1980.

56. Ruth Thaler, "Phillips Supporters Unite!," *St. Louis Argus*, Mar. 22, 1979.

57. Ibid.

58. Veronica Banks, "Bosley Calls for Boycott of City Hospital," *St. Louis Argus*, Aug. 9, 1979.

59. It is evident that Mayor Conway took note of Gregory's criticisms. Pages of *Nigger* with highlighted paragraphs concerning the hospital were found in the mayor's archival collections.

60. Dick Gregory, with Sheila P. Moses, *Callus on My Soul: A Memoir* (New York: Kensington Publishing Corporation, 2000), 36–37.

61. Stein, *St. Louis Politics*, 93.

62. J. B. Banks, "Senate Bill No. 788," Pub. L. No. 788 (1979).

63. J. Pulitzer, "Sen. Banks Preparing Bill for State Takeover of Phillips," *St. Louis Post-Dispatch*, Nov. 28, 1979.

64. US Representative Cardiss Collins to Colleagues, Jan. 8, 1980, Richard Gephardt Collection, Missouri Historical Society Library and Research Center, box 467, folder 14.

65. Frank Chapman, "Public Healthcare and Homer G. Phillips," n.d., p. 2, UMSL Black History Project (1980–1983) Collection, 1895–1983, S0201, State Historical Society of Missouri (hereinafter BH Collection, SHSMO), box 6, folder 201: "Ad Hoc Committee to Save Homer G. Phillips Hospital, 1980."

66. Ibid., 5.

67. Robert L. Joiner, "Alderman Calls NAACP Here Too Timid on Phillips Issue," *St. Louis Post-Dispatch*, Nov. 6, 1979.

68. D. D. Obika, "Clay Assails City Religious Leaders, Colleagues for Not Aiding Phillips," *St. Louis Post-Dispatch*, Sep. 11, 1979.

69. Task Force on Rights of Labor, National Alliance Against Racist and Political Repression, St. Louis Branch, "Justice for Zenobia Thompson & All Public Health Workers," 1980, BH Collection, SHSMO, box 6, folder 201: "Ad Hoc Committee to Save Homer G. Phillips Hospital, 1980."

70. "Phillips Shutdown Begins: Protest Grows," *St. Louis Argus*, Aug. 2, 1979.

71. "The Concerned People" to James F. DeClue, Aug. 13, 1979, Conway Records, WUSC, series 2, box 23, folder 1. This letter also ended up in the hands of Mayor Conway.

72. "Phillips Shutdown Begins: Protest Grows."

73. Ibid.

74. Ibid.

75. Rule, "Inner Cities' Hospitals Vanishing in Wake of Sharply Rising Costs."

76. "August 17, 1979: Homer G. Phillips Hospital Closes Its Doors."

77. Roger Wilkins, "Loss of Hospitals in Central Cities Said to Cause Array of Problems," *New York Times*, Sep. 17, 1979.

78. "Homer G. Phillips: A Historic Hospital Faces Closing," 22.

79. Untitled document, ca. 1980, Zenobia Thompson Personal Collection.

80. Charles Oswald, "Phillips Used as Doctor Substitute," *St. Louis Globe-Democrat*, Oct. 3, 1972.

81. "We Accuse," Jul. 1980, BH Collection, SHSMO, box 6, folder 201: "Ad Hoc Committee to Save Homer G. Phillips Hospital." On fears of racial genocide in the early twentieth century from a cultural history perspective, see Michele Mitchell, *Righteous Propagation: African Americans and the Politics of Racial Destiny after Reconstruction* (Chapel Hill: University of North Carolina Press, 2004).

82. Sharon L. Green and Edward Dubois, "Trial Begins Monday: Phillips Issue Refuses to Die," *St. Louis American*, Jan. 7, 1982.

83. Ibid.

84. "William Russell: Lawyer, Businessman," obituary, *St. Louis Post-Dispatch*, Jun. 2, 1996. Attorney Russell was best known for participating in *Liddell v. St. Louis Public Schools* (1972), which desegregated the St. Louis Public School system.

85. Edward Kohn, "Group Seeks Injunction," *St. Louis Post-Dispatch*, Mar. 16, 1980.

86. Debra L. Buck, "The Closing of Homer G. Phillips Hospital" (MA thesis, Claremont University, 1984).

87. Veronica Banks, "HEW to Investigate Phillips," *St. Louis Argus*, Mar. 28, 1979.

88. Smith, *Power to Heal*.

89. Ibid.

90. Veronica Banks, "Hospital Issue to Reconvene," *St. Louis Argus*, Dec. 24, 1981.

91. Danita C. Thomas to Mayor James Conway, n.d., Conway Records, WUSC, box 22, folder: "H&H—Homer G. Phillips Hospital Sep. 1979."

92. "Mayor Conway Wants Another Term," *St. Louis Post-Dispatch*, Nov. 25, 1980.

93. "Why Phillips Hospital Is a Big Emotional Issue," *St. Louis Globe-Democrat*, Nov. 28, 1981.

94. Rosemary L. Plitt, "Certification," 1981, Conway Records, WUSC, box 22, folder: "H&H—Homer G. Phillips Hospital Sep. 1979."

95. "HGP Issue Faces Candidates," *St. Louis Argus*, Nov. 15, 1981.

96. "Why Phillips Hospital Is a Big Emotional Issue."

97. Shannon L. Green, "Schoemehl Still Undecided on Phillips Re-Opening," *St. Louis American*, Feb. 4, 1982.

98. Ibid.

99. Phil Sutin and Gregory B. Freeman, "Schoemehl Details Plan on Phillips," *St. Louis Post-Dispatch*, Apr. 18, 1982.

100. Ibid.

101. Ibid.

102. Shirk and Freeman, "Drive to Reopen Phillips Hospital Enters Fifth Year."

103. Angela Y. Davis, *Women, Culture, and Politics* (New York: Random House, 1989), 59.

104. "A Plan to Maintain Phillips," *St. Louis Argus*, Apr. 26, 1979.

105. George Lipsitz, *The Sidewalks of St. Louis: Places, People, and Politics in an American City* (Columbia: University of Missouri Press, 1991), 52.

13. "Together We Can Make a Safe Home"

"Together we can make a safe home," the phrase used in the chapter title, is a lyric from Holly Near, "Fight Back," 1978, as printed in the Red Berets' song booklet, https://riseupfeministarchive.ca/wp-content/uploads/RedBerets-LyricsBooklet.pdf.

1. Margaret Flowing Johnson, "Living a Surprising Life," unpublished manuscript, 2020, provided electronically to the author.

2. Near, "Fight Back"; Johnson, "Living a Surprising Life."

3. Christina B. Hanhardt, *Safe Space: Gay Neighborhood History and the Politics of Violence* (Durham, NC: Duke University Press, 2013).

4. Finn Enke, *Finding the Movement: Sexuality, Contested Space, and Feminist Activism* (Durham, NC: Duke University Press, 2007).

5. Kristen Hogan, *The Feminist Bookstore Movement: Lesbian Antiracism and Feminist Accountability* (Durham, NC: Duke University Press, 2016).

6. Bonnie J. Morris, *The Disappearing L: Erasure of Lesbian Spaces and Culture* (Albany, NY: SUNY Press, 2016), 30–31.

7. Kris Kleindienst (queer femme activist), interview by author, Jan. 28, 2021; Diana Campbell, Laura Cohen, Janice Gutman, and Clare Kinberg (Lesbian Alliance members), group interview by author, Jan. 29, 2021.

8. Kris Kleindienst, interview by Monietta Slay, Aug. 3, 1994, Gay Liberation Movement in St. Louis, Communications Class Oral History Project, 1987–1995, S0512.93, State Historical Society of Missouri.

9. Barb Goedde (Lesbian Alliance member), interview by author, Jan. 6, 2021; Kinberg, interview.

10. Campbell, interview; Gutman, interview.

11. David K. Johnson, *The Lavender Scare: The Cold War Persecution of Gays and Lesbians in the Federal Government* (Chicago: University of Chicago Press, 2004).

12. Ibid., 10.

13. Josephine Donovan, *The Lexington Six: Lesbian and Gay Resistance in 1970s America* (Boston: University of Massachusetts Press, 2020), xii.

14. "Lesbian Alliance," *Moonstorm* 1, no. 5 (Nov./Dec. 1974): 8, emphasis added, University of Missouri–St. Louis Women's Studies Collection, S0489, State Historical Society of Missouri (hereinafter UMSLWSC, SHSMO), box 4, folder 128.

15. Kleindienst, interview by Slay.

16. Ibid.

17. "Lesbian Alliance," *Moonstorm* 1, no. 5 (Nov./Dec. 1974): 8, UMSLWSC, SHSMO.

18. Ibid., 8.

19. *Lesbian Alliance Newsletter* 2, no. 3 (Feb. 1975): 1, Lesbian Alliance of St. Louis Records, S0129, State Historical Society of Missouri (hereinafter Lesbian Alliance, SHSMO), folder 3.

20. "Womenergy in St. Louis," *Moonstorm* 2, no. 2 (1975): 53, Lesbian Alliance, SHSMO, folder 2.

21. *Moonstorm*, no. 17 (Aug. 1979): 2, Lesbian Alliance, SHSMO, folder 3.

22. Ibid., emphasis added.

23. Gutman, interview; Goedde, interview.

24. Francesca Polletta, *Freedom Is an Endless Meeting: Democracy in American Social Movements* (Chicago: University of Chicago Press, 2002), 2.

25. "Who We Are," *Moonstorm* 3, no. 1 (Spring 1976): 6, Lesbian Alliance, SHSMO, folder 2.

26. "Homer G. at Crisis Point," *Moonstorm,* no. 17 (Aug. 1979), Lesbian Alliance, SHSMO, folder 3.

27. "Lesbian Alliance," 8.

28. Kleindienst, interview.

29. Campbell, interview; Cohen, interview; Kinberg, interview.

30. Campbelll, interview.

31. *Moonstorm*, no. 17 (Aug. 1979): 5, Lesbian Alliance, SHSMO, folder 3. The location referenced here was at 905 South Yale Avenue.

32. Nanora Sweet, "Herstory: Finding the Lesbian Heritage," *Lesbian and Gay News-Telegraph*, Nov. 1988.

33. "Become a Member" [scanned advertisement], St. Louis LGBT History Project, n.d., https://www.pinterest.com/stlqueerhistory/projects-lesbian-archives/.

34. Ibid.

35. Hogan, *Feminist Bookstore Movement.*

36. Trysh Travis, "The Women in Print Movement: History and Implications," *Book History* 11 (2008): 276.

37. Kleindienst, interview.

38. Ibid.; Kleindienst, interview by Slay.

39. Sue Hyde, interview by Ellen Fitzgerald, transcript of video recording, Nov. 23, 2008, pp. 8–11, Sophia Smith Collection, Smith College, Northampton, MA, https://www.smith.edu/libraries/libs/ssc/activist/transcripts/Hyde.pdf.

40. *Lesbian Alliance Newsletter* 2, no. 1 (Jan. 1975): 1, Lesbian Alliance, SHSMO, folder 3.

41. "Back on the Streets Again," *Moonstorm* 1, no. 2 (Fall 1973): 8, Lesbian Alliance, SHSMO, folder 1.

42. "Dykes Find a New Home," *Moonstorm* 2, no. 2 (Sep. 1975): 10, Lesbian Alliance, SHSMO, folder 2.

43. Ibid.

44. *Lesbian Alliance Newsletter* 2, no. 3 (Feb. 1975), Lesbian Alliance, SHSMO, folder 3; Gutman, interview; Campbell, interview; Laura Ann Moore (Lesbian Alliance member), interview by Jeanette Sanchez, Sep. 25, 2011, transcript provided to the author by historian Jym Andris.

45. Johnson, "Living a Surprising Life"; Donovan, *Lexington Six.*

46. Campbell, interview.

47. "The F.B.I. and You," *Moonstorm* 2, no. 2 (Sep. 1975): 44–45.

48. *Moonstorm,* "Separatism" issue (n.d. 1975), Lesbian Alliance, SHSMO, folder 2.

49. *Lesbian Alliance Newsletter* 2, no. 3 (Feb. 1975): 1, Lesbian Alliance, SHSMO, folder 3.

50. *Lesbian Alliance Newsletter* 1, no. 3 (Dec. 16, 1974): 1, Lesbian Alliance, SHSMO, folder 3.

51. *Lesbian Alliance Newsletter* 2, no. 3 (Feb. 1975): 1, Lesbian Alliance, SHSMO, folder 3.

52. *Moonstorm,* "Separatism" issue (n.d. 1975): 6, Lesbian Alliance, SHSMO, folder 3.

53. Goedde, interview.

54. Nancy Fraser, "Rethinking the Public Sphere: A Contribution to the Critique of Actually Existing Democracy," *Social Text* 25/26 (1990): 56.

55. "Interview with Mac," *Moonstorm,* no. 14 (Sep. 1978): 2, Lesbian Alliance, SHSMO, folder 3.

56. Ibid., 1–7.

57. Ibid.

58. Marjorie Mandel, "Explosion, Fire Destroy Women's Bar," *St. Louis Post-Dispatch*, Sep. 11, 1979.

59. "Help! Mac's in Danger," *Moonstorm,* no. 17 (Aug. 1979): 1, Lesbian Alliance, SHSMO, folder 3; Mandel, "Explosion, Fire Destroy Women's Bar"; Victor Volland, "Manager Arrested in Fire at Women's Bar," *St. Louis Post-Dispatch*, Sep. 13, 1979.

60. Volland, "Manager Arrested."

61. Ibid.

62. "Interview with Mac," 4.

63. Judith Miller, "Firebombing Remains a Rubble," *Big Mama Rag* (Denver) 7, no. 10 (Nov. 1979): 4, Independent Voices collection, https://www.jstor.org/stable/community.28034040?seq=1.

64. Ibid.

65. "Bar," *St. Louis Post-Dispatch*, Sep. 9, 1979.

66. Joyce L. Armstrong, "Bar Conflict," letter to editor, *St. Louis Post-Dispatch*, Sep. 27, 1979.

67. A Reader, "Victims and Women," letter to editor, *St. Louis Post-Dispatch*, Sep. 24, 1979.

68. Ibid.

69. "We Are Present as a Group of Persons Responding to This Most Immediate Act of Violence against Women," *Sister Advocate* (Oklahoma City), Oct. 25, 1979, 5.

70. Miller, "Firebombing Remains a Rubble."

71. "About Take Back the Night Foundation," Take Back the Night Foundation (n.d.), https://takebackthenight.org/about-us/.

72. Johnson, "Living a Surprising Life."

73. Near, "Fight Back."

74. Ibid.

75. Johnson, "Living a Surprising Life."

76. "Women's Center Coordinator Resigns," *Current* (University of Missouri–St. Louis), Sep. 27, 1979, 2, https://irl.umsl.edu/cgi/viewcontent.cgi?article=1279&context=current1970s.

77. Margaret Flowing Johnson, interview by author, Jan. 14, 2021.

78. Johnson, "Living a Surprising Life."

79. Johnson, interview.

80. Johnson, "Living a Surprising Life."

81. Ibid., 5.

82. Johnson, interview.

83. Jo Mannies, "Several Men Heckle Anti-rape Marchers," *St. Louis Post-Dispatch*, Jun. 11, 1979.

84. Ibid.

85. Clare [Kinberg], "Take Back the Night," *Moonstorm*, no. 22 (Oct. 1980): 1–3, Lesbian Alliance, SHSMO, folder 3.

86. US Census Bureau and Social Explorer, "St. Louis City, MO: Race, 1980 Census," table prepared by Social Explorer, https://www.socialexplorer.com/data/C1980/metadata?ds=SE&table=T012.

87. Kinberg, "Take Back the Night."

88. Johnson, interview.

89. Johnson, "Living a Surprising Life."

90. "Women's Center Coordinator Resigns."

91. Campbell, interview.

92. Kleindienst, interview by Slay.

14. The Time Is Now

1. National Alliance Against Racist and Political Repression, NAARPR Conference, https://conference.naarpr.org.

2. Daniel Rosenberg, "The Free Angela Movement in the United States, 1969–1991," *American Communist History* 19, nos. 3–4 (2020): 191–261.

3. Third Annual Dr. Martin Luther King Jr. Human Rights Award Banquet, Jan. 15, 1979, St. Louis Branch, National Alliance Against Racist and Political Repression, Amalgamated Clothing and Textile Workers Union Records, S0741, State Historical Society of Missouri (hereinafter ACTWU Records, SHSMO), box 17, folder 603; Michael S. Sherry, *The Punitive Turn in American Life: How the United States Learned to Fight Crime Like War* (Chapel Hill: University of North Carolina Press, 2020); Julilly Kohler-Hausmann, *Getting Tough: Welfare and Imprisonment in 1970s America* (Princeton: Princeton University Press, 2017); Philip Jenkins, *Decade of Nightmares: The End of the Sixties and the Making of Eighties America* (New York: Oxford University Press, 2006); Daniel Robert McClure, *Winter in America: A Cultural History of Neoliberalism, from the Sixties to the Reagan Revolution* (Chapel Hill: University of North Carolina Press, 2021).

4. Frank Edgar Chapman Jr., *The Damned Don't Cry: Pages from the Life of a Black Prisoner and Organizer* (Pittsburgh: Changemaker Publications, 2019), 121.

5. Angela Davis, *Angela Davis: An Autobiography* (New York: International Publishers, 1974), 397.

6. Chapman, *The Damned Don't Cry*, 131.

7. Published abridged remarks from Charlene Mitchell's keynote address at the NAARPR Conference in Defense of Labor Rights, May 21, 1977; Charlene Mitchell, "Labor's Rights: First Line of Defense of Democracy," Third Annual Dr. Martin Luther King Jr. Human Rights Award Banquet, Jan. 15, 1979, 4, St. Louis Branch, National Alliance Against Racist and Political Repression, ACTWU Records, SHS-MO, box 17, folder 603.

8. Fifth Annual Dr. Martin Luther King Jr. Human Rights Award Banquet Program, Jan. 15, 1981, National Alliance Against Racist and Political Repression, St. Louis Branch Records, S0582, State Historical Society of Missouri (hereinafter NAARPR Records, SHSMO), folder 20.

9. Keona K. Ervin, "The National Alliance Against Racist and Political Repression," in *Remaking Radicalism: A Grassroots Documentary Reader of the United States, 1973–2001*, ed. Dan Berger and Emily K. Hobson (Athens: University of Georgia Press, 2020), 140–41.

10. Gerald Horne, *Communist Front? The Civil Rights Congress, 1946–1956* (Rutherford, NJ: Fairleigh Dickinson University Press, 1988). In 1948, Rosa Lee Ingram and two of her sons, Wallace Ingram and Sammie Lee Ingram, were charged with the murder of a white Georgia landowner and sentenced to death. The three were released on parole in 1959. World War II veteran Willie McGee was arrested for the alleged rape of Wiletta Hawkins, a white woman, and sentenced to death. McGee was executed by the state of Mississippi six years later. The Martinsville Seven were seven Black men—Francis DeSales Grayson, Frank Hairston Jr., James Luther Hairston, Howard Lee Hairston, Joe Henry Hampton, Booker T. Millner, and John Claybon Taylor—charged with the rape of Ruby Stroud Floyd, a white woman. The seven were executed by the state of Virginia in 1951.

11. Kenneth Robert Janken, *The Wilmington Ten: Violence, Injustice, and the Rise of Black Politics in the 1970s* (Chapel Hill: University of North Carolina Press, 2021); Danielle L. McGuire, *At the Dark End of the Street: Black Women, Rape, and Resistance—A New History of the Civil Rights Movement from Rosa Parks to the Rise of Black Power* (New York: A. A. Knopf, 2010), 246–78.

12. Chapman, *The Damned Don't Cry*, 131–35.

13. Mitchell, keynote address; Mitchell, "Labor's Rights," ACTWU Records, SHS-MO, box 17, folder 603.

14. Ibid., 4.

15. Ibid., 4–5.

16. Chapman, *The Damned Don't Cry*, 128.

17. Ibid., 138.

18. Ibid., 139.

19. David Lucander, *Winning the War for Democracy: The March on Washington Movement, 1941–1946* (Urbana: University of Illinois Press, 2014); Clarence Lang, *Grassroots at the Gateway: Class Politics and Black Freedom Struggle in St. Louis, 1936–75* (Ann Arbor: University of Michigan Press, 2009); Keona K. Ervin, *Gateway to Equality: Black Women and the Struggle for Economic Justice in St. Louis*

(Lexington: University Press of Kentucky, 2017); Robert Bussel, *Fighting for Total Person Unionism: Harold Gibbons, Ernest Calloway, and Working-Class Citizenship* (Urbana: University of Illinois Press, 2015); Walter Johnson, *The Broken Heart of America: St. Louis and the Violent History of the United States* (New York: Basic Books, 2020).

20. Dan Berger, *The Hidden 1970s: Histories of Radicalism* (New Brunswick, NJ: Rutgers University Press, 2010); Lane Windham, *Knocking on Labor's Door: Union Organizing in the 1970s and the Roots of a New Economic Divide* (Chapel Hill: University of North Carolina Press, 2017).

21. Dan Berger, *Captive Nation: Black Prison Organizing in the Civil Rights Era* (Chapel Hill: University of North Carolina Press, 2014).

22. Chapman, *The Damned Don't Cry*, iv–v, 28, 29–30 (quoted passage), 31, 75–76.

23. Ibid., 30, 41.

24. Dean Johnson to Bob Williams, Oct. 13, 1974, 1–3, NAARPR Records, SHS-MO, folder 15.

25. Chapman, *The Damned Don't Cry*, 30, 51–52.

26. Ibid., 52–58.

27. Heather Ann Thompson, *Blood in the Water: The Attica Prison Uprising of 1971 and Its Legacy* (New York: Vintage Books, 2017).

28. Chapman, *The Damned Don't Cry*, 56–59, 122–23.

29. Right On! Black Community News Service, Trial News, Nov.–Dec. 1972, 4, The Freedom Archives, Berkeley, CA.

30. "Kentucky Lawyer Is Jailed for Contempt of Court," *New York Times*, Oct. 31, 1971; Chapman, *The Damned Don't Cry*, 69.

31. Chapman, *The Damned Don't Cry*, 96.

32. Ibid.

33. In 1964, Percy Green scaled the Gateway Arch to protest the lack of hiring of Black workers for the massive construction project, and in December 1972, with ACTION, he staged a protest of the racist and sexist Veiled Prophet Parade and Ball hosted by white St. Louis business and political elites. Around the time that Green was at the Brodines' home, the US Supreme Court ruled in his favor in *McDonnell Douglas Corporation v. Green*, unanimously deciding that, under Title VII of the 1964 Civil Rights Act, the initial burden of proof rests with the complainant and then shifts to the employer. Lang, *Grassroots at the Gateway*, 184, 201, 241–42.

34. Chapman, *The Damned Don't Cry*, 109.

35. Ibid., 112.

36. Ibid., 115–16, 127.

37. Ibid., 120.

38. Ervin, "The National Alliance Against Racist and Political Repression." See also Janken, *The Wilmington Ten*.

39. Ben Chavis, quoted in "National Alliance, St. Louis, Mo. Branch: 1979 Priorities," Third Annual Dr. Martin Luther King Jr. Human Rights Award Banquet Program, Jan. 15, 1979, 7, ACTWU Records, SHSMO, box 17, folder 603.

40. "National Alliance, St. Louis, Mo. Branch: 1979 Priorities," Third Annual Dr. Martin Luther King Jr. Human Rights Award Banquet Program, Jan. 15, 1979, 7, ACTWU Records, SHSMO, box 17, folder 603.

41. Chapman, *The Damned Don't Cry*, 120.

42. Ibid., 121.

43. Ibid., 125.

44. Calvin Tyrone Burks to the Committee to Free the Missouri Nine, Mar. 14, 1975, NAARPR Records, SHSMO, folder 10; Memo re: Missouri Nine, Apr. 1, 1975, NAARPR Records, SHSMO, folder 10.

45. Memo re: Missouri Nine, Apr. 1, 1975, NAARPR Records, SHSMO, folder 10; "Committee for Defense of Missouri Nine Bar-b-cue Saturday," *St. Louis Argus*, May 8, 1975.

46. Walle Amusa, "Political Prisoners, Racist Frame-Ups and the Fight-Back," 3–4, NAARPR Records, SHSMO, folder 8.

47. "Newlon Sentenced to Die," *St. Louis Globe-Democrat*, Nov. 9, 1979.

48. Amusa, "Political Prisoners, Racist Frame-Ups and the Fight-Back," 1.

49. "Newlon Sentenced to Die."

50. "First Death Sentence under New State Law Pronounced," *St. Louis Post-Dispatch*, Nov. 9, 1979.

51. NAARPR Task Force on Police Crimes memo, "George Peach Threatens to Close Book on Dennis Benson Case," Sep. 30, 1980, NAARPR Records, SHSMO, folder 5.

52. "U.S. Inquiry in Death of N. Side Man Sought," n.p., Jul. 30, 1980, NAARPR Records, SHSMO, box 4.

53. NAARPR Task Force on Police Crimes memo, "George Peach Threatens to Close Book."

54. "Alleged Police Brutality in Death Protested by Group at Courthouse," *St. Louis Post-Dispatch*, Aug. 24, 1980.

55. Ibid.; Paul Wagman, "Suspect Handcuffed When Beaten, 14 Say," *St. Louis Post-Dispatch*, Aug. 10, 1980.

56. "Alleged Police Brutality in Death."

57. Thompson quoted in "Alliance Failed to Produce Witnesses, Says Peach," *St. Louis American*, Oct. 2, 1980.

58. "Conway Petitioned to Investigate Death," *St. Louis Post-Dispatch*, Sep. 3, 1980.

59. "Letter: 'Callous Disregard' for Citizens' Lives," *St. Louis Argus*, Jul. 24, 1980.

60. Mitchell, keynote address; Mitchell, "Labor's Rights," 5–6.

61. Mitchell, keynote address; Mitchell, "Labor's Rights," 4.

62. Mitchell, keynote address; Mitchell, "Labor's Rights," 4–6.

63. Windham, *Knocking on Labor's Door*.

64. Chapman, *The Damned Don't Cry*, 152–58, 161.

65. Ibid., 138, 152.

66. Ibid., 151–52.

67. Mitchell, keynote address; Mitchell, "Labor's Rights," 5.

68. Chapman, *The Damned Don't Cry*, 140.

69. Striking poultry workers at Sanderson Farmers in Laurel, MS, "Boycott Miss Goldy Chickens" flyer, n.d., NAARPR Records, SHSMO, box 1, folder 12.

70. Flyer on J. P. Stevens boycott/strike, Third Annual Dr. Martin Luther King Jr. Human Rights Award Banquet, Jan. 15, 1979, ACTWU Records, SHSMO, box 17, folder 603.

71. Mitchell, keynote address; Mitchell, "Labor's Rights," 5; Chapman, *The Damned Don't Cry*, 131–35.

72. Priscilla A. Dowden-White, *Groping toward Democracy: African American Social Welfare Reform in St. Louis, 1910–1949* (Columbia: University of Missouri Press, 2011), 167–81; Candace O'Connor, *Climbing the Ladder, Chasing the Dream: The History of Homer G. Phillips Hospital* (Columbia: University of Missouri Press, 2021), 243–71.

73. Chapman, *The Damned Don't Cry*, 142.

74. Ibid., 140–43.

75. Ibid., 152, 131–35.

76. "'Freedom Is a Constant Struggle': National Alliance Against Racist and Political Repression Position Statement on Closing of Homer G. Phillips Hospital," n.d. 1980, NAARPR Records, SHSMO, box 2, folder 55.

77. Ibid.

78. Berger, *The Hidden 1970s*; Jacquelyn Dowd Hall, "The Long Civil Rights Movement and the Political Uses of the Past," *Journal of American History* 91, no. 4 (Mar. 2005): 1233–63.

15. Where It Took Place

1. Katharine T. Corbett, *In Her Place: A Guide to St. Louis Women's History* (St. Louis: Missouri Historical Society Press, 1999), xiii.

2. Colin Gordon, *Mapping Decline: St. Louis and the Fate of the American City* (Philadelphia: University of Pennsylvania Press, 2008); Colin Gordon, *Citizen Brown: Race, Democracy, and Inequality in the St. Louis Suburbs* (Chicago: University of Chicago Press, 2019).

3. John A. Wright, *Discovering African American St. Louis: A Guide to Historic Sites*, 2nd ed. (St. Louis: Missouri Historical Society Press, 2002). The original edition was released in 1994.

4. Andrea Friedman and Miranda Rectenwald, project leads, *Mapping LGBTQ St. Louis*, http://library.wustl.edu/map-lgbtq-stl.

Index

Page numbers in italics refer to illustrations.

Index

Metropolitan Community Churches (UFMCC)
Metropolitan Life Services Corporation/ Mid-Continent Life Services Corporation (MLSC), 228–30, *230*, 231–32, 234, 430
Mid-City Community Congress, 15, 127, 132, 135, 430
Middle of the Road bar, 383, 388
Miller, Peggy, 376
Mill Creek Valley, 45; clearance of, 11, *12*, 17, 241; evictions, impact of, 125, 245, 311, 314, 344
Minneapolis (Minnesota), 144
Miss America protest (1968), 198, 202
Mississippi, 158–59, 515n10
Missouri, 30, 110, 125, 136, 155, 170, 232, 279–81, 286, 309; abortion laws, 22, 452n40; Adult Abuse law, 302, 304; as border state, 38, 114–15; political climate of, 105, 158–59, 164, 170, 270, 305–6; right-to-work referendum (1978), *24*, 417; State Penitentiary, 402, 405, 406–7, 408–9, 412–13. *See also individual place names*
Missouri Coalition Against Domestic Violence, 302, 306
Missouri Coalition to Abolish the Death Penalty, 410
Missouri National Education Association, 281, 305
Missouri Nine, 412–13, 415–16
Missouri Women's Network, 305, 306
Mitchell, Charlene, 402, 403, 416, 418
Mitchell, Eugene, 355, 362
Mitchell, John, 486n77
Mitchell, Luther, 128–29, *197*
Mitchell, Roscoe, *18*
Moberly Community College, 406, 409
Model Cities, 135, 321
Monsanto Company, 21, 160, 187, 191; Monsanto Fund, 300
Montgomery bus boycott, 25, 118–19
Moog, Florence, 71
Moon, Galen, 226–27, 232, 491n30
Moonstorm (magazine/newsletter), 365, 372–76, 378, *381*, 393, 396, 397;

on harassment of lesbian-feminist collectives, 384–87; on Muriel "Mac" McCann, 387–88, 389
Moore, Gwen, 32–33
Moore, Joseph G., 92
Moore, Laura Ann, 219, 227, *227*, 376, 379–80, 384
Morely, Anthony, 98–99, 102
Mor or Les bar, 383, 388, 426; arson of, 389–91, *390*
Mound City Medical Forum, 343
Moye, Lew, 405, 417
Muhammad, Clara, *120*
Muhammad, Elijah, 120, *120*, 124
Municipal Art Museum, 47
Murphy, Margaret, *177*
Myers, Vonderrit, Jr., 56

National Abortion Rights Action League, 281
National Alliance Against Racist and Political Repression (NAARPR), 27, 401–2, *407*, *414*; founding of and relationship to "Free Angela Davis" movement, 403–4; St. Louis chapter, anti-carceral activism of, 406–16, *412*, *415*; St. Louis chapter, founding and composition of, 404–5; St. Louis chapter, labor activism of, 416–18; St. Louis chapter, Homer G. Phillips Hospital activism of, 418–20
National Association for the Advancement of Colored People (NAACP), 13, 37, 41, 46, 48, 55, 105, 116, 117–18, 121, 124, 272, 406; and Homer G. Phillips Hospital activism, 346, 349, 354; in St. Louis city charter campaign (1957), 119
National Coalition Against Domestic Violence, 304
National Coalition Against Sexual Assault, 304
National Coalition of American Nuns, 294
National Committee for a Sane Nuclear Policy, 463n26
National Conference of Black Lawyers, 410, 419

531